Florida's Peace River Frontier

UNIVERSITY PRESS OF FLORIDA

Florida A&M University, Tallahassee
Florida Atlantic University, Boca Raton
Florida Gulf Coast University, Ft. Myers
Florida International University, Miami
Florida State University, Tallahassee
New College of Florida, Sarasota
University of Central Florida, Orlando
University of Florida, Gainesville
University of North Florida, Jacksonville
University of South Florida, Tampa
University of West Florida, Pensacola

Florida's Peace River Frontier

CANTER BROWN, JR.

University Press of Florida
Gainesville · Tallahassee · Tampa · Boca Raton
Pensacola · Orlando · Miami · Jacksonville · Ft. Myers · Sarasota

First cloth printing, 1991
First paperback printing, 2024

29 28 27 26 25 24   6 5 4 3 2 1

Library of Congress Cataloging-in-Publication Data
Brown, Canter.
Florida's Peace River Frontier / Canter Brown, Jr.
    p. cm.
Includes bibliographical references and index.
ISBN 978-0-8130-1037-3 (cloth)
ISBN 978-0-8130-8060-4 (pbk.)
1. Peace River Valley (Fla.)—History. I. Title.
F317.P37B76   1991   90-44257
975.9'57—dc20   CIP

The University Press of Florida is the scholarly publishing agency for the State University
System of Florida, comprising Florida A&M University, Florida Atlantic University,
Florida Gulf Coast University, Florida International University, Florida State University,
New College of Florida, University of Central Florida, University of Florida, University
of North Florida, University of South Florida, and University of West Florida.

University Press of Florida
2046 NE Waldo Road
Suite 2100
Gainesville, FL 32609
http://upress.ufl.edu

With deepest appreciation
to my friend,
Kenneth John Nemeth

Ben Hill Griffin, Jr., a native and lifetime resident of the Peace River Valley, was born on October 20, 1910, near Fort Meade in the community of Tiger Bay, a town that no longer exists. An alumnus of the University of Florida, Mr. Griffin was a citrus grower, cattleman, businessman, and philanthropist and served in the Florida House of Representatives (1956–64) and State Senate (1964–68). A defender of the Peace River, he spent much of his time on his beloved Peace River Ranch between Wauchula and Arcadia. He died on March 1, 1990, in Avon Park.

The publication of *Florida's Peace River Frontier* has been assisted by a grant in memory of Ben Hill Griffin, Jr., by Citrus and Chemical Bank of Polk County, where he was formerly chairman of the board and majority stockholder.

Contents

Preface   xi
Prologue   xvii

Part One: *"The brand of Osceola and his warriors"*
          (1800-1842)

1. Early Migrations   3
   "Tellaugue Chapcopopeau, a creek which enters the
   ocean . . . at a place called the Fishery"
2. Upheavals and Explorations   17
   "In this remote situation"
3. Beginning of the Second Seminole War   34
   "The water of the land is my blood"
4. Conclusion of the Second Seminole War   47
   "A perfect grave yard"

Part Two: *"The society of a frontier" (1842-1858)*

5. The Frontier Moves to South Florida   63
   "To play off a shabby trick"
6. The Army and the First Settlers   75
   "The crack of the rifle will be heard"
7. Permanent Settlement   91
   "The country was absolutely new"
8. The Third Seminole War   106
   "A veritable clap of thunder from a clear sky"

Part Three: *"Wild enthusiasm swept like vengeance over the whole country" (1858-1877)*

9. Between the Wars   123
   "They were simply pouring into South Florida"
10. Prelude to Fort Sumter   136
   "There is but little apprehension of danger"
11. Civil War in the River Valley   155
   "The times hear is vary squally"
12. Republicans in Power   176
   "The passions & prejudices of the people"
13. Cattle and Reconstruction Politics   195
   "As fair as any vote ever held in the world"
14. Communities on the Frontier   215
   "Peas Creek could be made navigable to Fort Meade"

Part Four: *"Progress that our people did not dream of" (1877-1899)*

15. The Problem of Violence   239
   "We have to kill men to recruit our graveyards"
16. Isolation and the Need for Transportation   255
   "We need something to cheer us up"
17. The Miracle of Railroads   272
   "Improvements have gone up and on like magic"
18. Politics of Redemption   292
   "A great deal of political strife among us"
19. Phosphate and Freezes   312
   "It is at best a serious disaster"
20. At the End of the Century   326
   "When can I expect you?"
21. The Legacy of the Nineteenth Century   343
   "A little better than it used to be"

Appendixes

1. Soldiers of the Patriot War   349
2. Selected Residents of Old Columbia, Hamilton, and
   Alachua Counties (c. 1830-1832)   351

3. Selected Members of the Columbia Volunteers
   (1835–1836)   353
4. Selected Members of Capt. William B. North's Company,
   Florida Volunteers (1838–1839)   354
5. Selected Residents of Columbia and Hamilton Counties
   (1842–1843)   355
6. Armed Occupation Act Claims   356
7. Sparkman's and Parker's Volunteer Companies (1849)   358
8. Selected Enlistments, Second Florida Cavalry (U.S.)
   (March–June 1864)   360
9. Partial Roster, F.A. Hendry's Independent Company,
   Munnerlyn's Battalion (1864)   362
10. Capt. W.H. Cobb's Company (Company C), U.S.
    Volunteers (1898)   363

Abbreviations   365
Notes   367
Bibliography   431
Index   453

Preface

THE HISTORY of the Peace River Valley of Florida in the nineteenth century is a tale of violence, passion, struggle, sacrifice, and determination. It was written with the lives and deaths of Creeks and Seminoles who refused to surrender their independence; of runaway slaves and fierce black warriors; of white frontiersmen struggling to build a better world for themselves and their families; of men and women who supported the Confederacy and their brothers and sisters who would not abandon the Union; of settlers from the defeated South and, later, from the North and Midwest; and of freedmen and -women who suffered to overcome the shackles of slavery, who farmed, who built the railroads, and who toiled in the broiling heat of open-pit phosphate mines. Some of those men and women bore famous names; many are unknown to us. All, however, came together to create a drama that had an impact upon generations of their descendants, upon the state of Florida, and, in instances, upon the history of the United States.

To understand what happened in the Peace River Valley and, by extension, South Florida in the nineteenth century, it is important to grasp that for most of that time the Peace River area was a frontier as wild and woolly as any in the West. Little has been written of Florida as a frontier, yet the legacy of those days remains important in Florida's social, economic, and political fabric. It is only reasonable to want to understand how the settlement of that frontier occurred and whether that settlement affected regional and national history, as well.

It is tempting to note, for example, the critical role of Peace River political leaders and voters in the election of Republican Rutherford B. Hayes to the presidency in 1876. But it is also true that sparsely populated South Florida and the Peace River Valley helped launch, in the nineteenth century, the careers of three men who became governors of Florida—Ossian Hart, Henry L. Mitchell, and Albert W. Gilchrist—and provided much of the margin by which Democrats were able to "redeem" Florida from Reconstruction Republicans and retain their control thereafter.

Pro-Union sentiments of many Civil War era residents of western North Carolina, eastern Tennessee, and adjacent areas are well documented. Less recognized is the sharp split among the residents of the Peace River frontier which led in 1864 and 1865 to bloody personal confrontation between Union and Confederate troops raised from the area, a confrontation that affected the Civil War by delaying and, for a time, stopping the flow of desperately needed beef to the Confederate Army of Tennessee.

Although the Peace River was a scene of war and terrible violence during the nineteenth century, it also served as a haven for Red Stick Creek, Seminole, and black warriors and their families fleeing from the wrath of Andrew Jackson in the wake of the First Seminole War. From those survivors came much of the leadership of the Second Seminole War, the river valley serving in particular as an early home for the two most famous of Florida's warriors, Osceola and Billy Bowlegs.

Important, too, in Peace River history was the role, largely ignored, of black slaves and freedmen in the taming of the frontier. Deserving of attention also were the efforts of Reconstruction era Regulators to drive freedmen from the area and the eventual settlements of large numbers of black men, women, and children with the coming of the railroad and phosphate mines late in the century.

These and numerous other facets of the history of the Peace River Valley in the nineteenth century paint a rich, interesting, and important story of life on America's southern frontier. This story never has been approached in a comprehensive manner, and its telling will provide clues to understanding not only today's Peace River but also significant events in the nineteenth-century history of the state of Florida and of the United States.

This book examines only nineteenth-century Peace River history. My decision to limit the scope to that century was made for a number of reasons. Foremost among them was that, as the nineteenth century dawned, the Peace River area and most of the rest of South Florida were uninhabited on any permanent basis. As discussed in Part One, certain Indian tribes from the north—particularly the "Alachua" Seminoles from North Florida and the "Upper Creeks" from northern Alabama—used the area for seasonal hunting, but the older South Florida inhabitants and tribes for the most part had succumbed to the white race's diseases and slave raids or else to their own internal and intertribal conflicts. Additionally, a number of historians, most recently Janet Snyder Matthews in her *Edge of Wilderness*, have explored the prehistory and Spanish exploration of southwest Florida, and I did not feel I could add to their work without further original research in Spanish language primary sources, a task for which I neither was prepared nor had sufficient time or resources.

Having decided upon the beginning of the nineteenth century as the jumping-off point for this story, I then was forced to come to grips with the question of where to end it. The history I wanted to discover and relate was of the settlement of the Peace River area, and the towns and institutions reflecting that process were in place by 1900. The 1800s, which witnessed the closing of the Florida frontier, seemed a logical and appropriate period for treatment; accordingly, I set the end of that century as my point of termination.

Some readers will notice that the text of this book contains far more detail—particularly the identification of individuals and families with events being described—than strictly is necessary for the telling of the story. The inclusion of this material was deliberate. Through four years of research and writing I came to believe that the stories of individuals and families—especially those families who became Peace River's first American pioneers—should not be submerged in painting a broad picture. I have attempted to minimize disruption of the narrative by the inclusion of much of this detail through the liberal use of appendixes and endnotes, and I hope that the detail remaining in the text will lend itself to a more personal and interesting story.

Two subjects that properly could have been explored in detail but are not are the day-to-day lives and the folklore of South Florida pioneers. Since several authors have written extensively on these fascinating topics, and in light of space limitations on this book, I decided not to attempt their treatment here.

The Peace River went by many names in the nineteenth century. To the Creek and Seminole Indians, the river was known as the Talakchopco hatchee or "river of the long peas." To the whites this Indian name translated as "Peas" or "Pease" Creek. For centuries before the Creeks and Seminoles named the river, however, it was designated in various languages on European maps as the River of Peace, perhaps suggesting an early role as boundary line or neutral zone—a role the river again briefly assumed in the nineteenth century. By the mid-to-late 1800s, the name Peace River had become commonplace and it remains so.

The question of the spelling of family names is fraught with difficulty. With one major exception, I have adopted the most common spellings used by individuals and families named. The exception is the Whidden family, whose names have been recorded in so many ways—even for the same individual—as to reduce to confusion any attempt to sort them out. Accordingly, unless used in a direct quotation, the name is spelled "Whidden." Incorrect spellings and usages in direct quotations, similarly, have been left as they appear in the original, and the use of [*sic*] has been avoided.

In good part the information appearing in this book is derived from original source materials, and it could never have been compiled without the encouragement and assistance of numerous individuals and institutions. Of paramount importance to me in this regard were the insights and hard work of Katharine Emerson Brown of Atlanta and John Eugene Brown of Fort Meade. I also am particularly indebted to Dr. Jerrell H. Shofner, chairman of the Department of History of the University of Central Florida, and to Dr. Samuel Proctor, professor of history at the University of Florida, both of whom provided me with their gracious support and encouragement.

Of the many individuals I have come to know in the process of preparing this book, I am no more indebted to any than to Kyle S.

VanLandingham. It is also appropriate to note the contributions of a number of persons who, over the decades of the past half century, have worked quietly and often without recognition to preserve and identify historical information related to the Peace River Valley. While asking pardon for names that should have been mentioned but inadvertently are not, I would extend thanks for the work of Edward T. Keenan, Albert DeVane, Park DeVane, Tom Brown, Elisabeth S. Brown, Walter Crutchfield, Louise K. Frisbie, Glenn Hooker, George Lane, Jr., Richard M. Livingston, Vernon Peeples, Spessard Stone, and Charles C. Rushing.

I owe a debt of gratitude to Dr. Dorothy Dodd for her friendship, the loan of her research notes, and her assistance in tracking down information which allowed me a greater insight into several pivotal events. Likewise, I am thankful for the friendship and assistance of LaCona Raines Padgett, Kathleen M. Greer, Hazel Bowman, and June Beadle of the Polk County Historical and Genealogical Library and Tissie Watson of the Manatee County Historical Records Library. I cannot fail to mention the contributions of my friends Stephen Prine, Kenneth J. Nemeth, Alexander F. Freeman, Pat Freeman, Douglas H. Morford, Cherry L. Emerson, and Arthur Wacaster, each of whom assisted in the research for this book or in the preparation and review of the manuscript.

Other persons who were of particular help to me were: Winnifred T. Brown; Vernice Williams; Lewis G. Schmidt; David J. Coles and Delbra McGriff of the Florida State Archives; Barbara Mattick, Beverly P. Byrd, and Mary Ann Cleveland of the Florida Collection of the State Library of Florida; Richard A. Shrader and John White of the Southern Historical Collection of the University of North Carolina at Chapel Hill; and Joe A. Akerman, Jr., of the North Florida Junior College. In addition, I am indebted to Krista K. Theiler and Ed Powell for their work in copying and enhancing many of the photographs used in this volume; to Ted Starr for the original maps he created, which add significantly to my narrative; and to the staffs of the Strozier Library of the Florida State University; the P.K. Yonge Library of Florida History of the University of Florida; the St. Augustine Historical Society Research Library; the Library of Congress; the National Archives; the Pennsylvania Historical Society; the U. S. Army Military History Institute at Carlisle Barracks; the United States

Military Academy Library; the Bowdoin College Library; the Oswego, New York, Public Library; the New York Public Library; the South Caroliniana Library of the University of South Carolina; the Georgia State Archives; the University of Georgia Library; the Thomas Gilcrease Institute of American History and Art; the Stetson University Library; the University of North Florida Library; the interlibrary loan office of the St. Johns County Public Library; and last, but certainly not least, the University Presses of Florida.

Each individual and institution I have named contributed to this book and assisted me greatly in telling the story of the history of the Peace River Valley in the nineteenth century. Responsibility for the interpretation of events and for errors of fact is mine alone.

Prologue

HE PEACE RIVER originates in Lake Hamilton, one of the many beautiful lakes that dot the heart of interior peninsular Florida in northern Polk County, although some of its waters can be traced as far to the north and northwest as the great reservoir of the Green Swamp—an area skirted by millions of vacationers driving along Interstate 4 between Tampa and Orlando. Just to the east of the river's source and paralleling its course through Polk County is Florida's natural spine, the chain of high sandy hills known as "The Ridge," which marked in ancient times all of peninsular Florida remaining above the sea.

From Lake Hamilton the narrow stream of Peace River today is channeled by drainage canals first to the south and then to the west where, just to the north of Polk's county seat of Bartow, it joins Saddle Creek, an outlet of Lake Hancock two miles to the north. From the junction, the river plunges southward again past Bartow and the town of Fort Meade. Three miles below Fort Meade the stream, continuing its southward course, is combined with the waters of Bowlegs Creek, which rises to the east on the Ridge, near Lake Buffum.

At Bowling Green, a little less than 40 miles along its course, the river enters Hardee County as well as the beginnings of the low South Florida prairie through which it will pass for most of its remaining journey to the sea. For half of the distance through Hardee's 21-mile width, the river continues its southward flow, edging in its progress the county seat of Wauchula. At Zolfo Springs, however, its course bows to the southwest, then turns to the south before bowing again, this time to the southeast and a junction with Charlie Apopka Creek at a point just to the north of the DeSoto County line. The enlarged river then carries its waters to the southwest and, on an ever more twisting and turning course, passes Arcadia and Fort Ogden, strengthened along the way by the discharges of Joshua and Horse creeks. Three miles below Fort Ogden the widening stream enters Charlotte County and begins a slow turn to the west, which carries it beyond Punta Gorda to its meeting with the sea at Charlotte Harbor on Florida's southwest Gulf of Mexico coast. On a straight line Peace River's length totals only about 110 miles, but its often serpentine course doubles that distance.

For much of its length, Peace River passes through a portion of Florida still rural, and even remote, late in the twentieth century. In its upper reaches the land is scarred by huge open pit phosphate mines, while farther to the south cattle still graze on the prairies through which it flows. No great metropolises line the river's banks and no commerce passes along its waters, but once, less than two centuries ago, the Peace River witnessed events that brought the dynamics of history into play in South Florida, and the Peace River bent and molded those events into this story.

Part One

*"The brand of Osceola
and his warriors"
(1800-1842)*

*"Tellaugue Chapcopopeau, a creek
which enters the ocean . . . at a
place called the Fishery"*

1

Early Migrations

APART FROM SMALL SETTLEMENTS east and north of the St.
Johns River, the outposts of Spain's colonial empire, peninsular Florida at the dawn of the nineteenth century
belonged to the Indians, most of them relative newcomers themselves. A combination of disease, war, slave raiding, and volun-
tary departures had eliminated almost entirely the indigenous
tribes of the peninsula, and into the vacuum had come several
thousand Creek Indians, great numbers of whom were becoming
known as Seminoles. These early Floridians were concentrated
around the Alachua Prairie or Alachua Plain in what would
become Alachua County. There, under a succession of powerful
rulers, the Alachua Seminoles prospered while their vast herds of
cattle fattened on the surrounding prairie grasses.[1]

South Florida, the site of extensive earlier Indian civilizations,
was virtually uninhabited in the early 1800s but for the seasonal
presence of Spanish fishermen at fishing *ranchos* at Tampa Bay
and Charlotte Harbor. The exception was a cluster of Indian settlements in or near the Big Hammock in what is today Hernando
County. Known after its principal town as Chocachatti, these settlements had been founded in 1767 by Creek Indians from the
town of Eufala. These immigrants were known as Upper Creek, a

3

collective label applied to Creeks whose homes lay along the Tallapoosa, Coosa, and Alabama rivers in the present state of Alabama. At Chocachatti and in small villages stretching southward to Tampa Bay, their numbers supplemented by later arrivals, these Upper Creeks thrived in the last three decades of the eighteenth century.[2]

Also in South Florida for part of each year were numerous parties of Creeks and Seminoles who, for decades and, possibly, generations prior to 1800, had journeyed to South Florida for the November to March hunting season. They followed the ancient trail from the north down to the falls of the Hillsborough River and from there to the crossing of the Alafia River south of today's Plant City, the scattering ground where hunting parties separated into smaller expeditions. Those headed for the Myakka range west of Peace River simply continued on their way. Those determined to hunt farther south, down to the Caloosahatchee River and below, turned to the east to the fords on Peace River or what they knew as the Talakchopco hatchee, the River of the Long Peas. Specifically, they forded the Peace River about fifteen miles south of the lake they believed to be at the head of the river where, by 1819, a permanent village was established. It took the name of the river, Talakchopco.[3]

Traditionally, the annual Creek and Seminole hunting expeditions centered around the hunt for deer, although bear, panther, and other animals figured as well. Using the game for food during the hunting season, the Indians would trade deerskins and other products of their hunt for guns, clothing, whiskey, and similar commodities. The hunts in South Florida were not always solely for deerskins, however. From as early as 1708 come reported incidents of slave raiding by Yemassee Indians of South Carolina deep into South Florida, a traffic which seems to have been continued by the Creeks well into the century.[4]

By the 1790s the Creeks in South Florida and their cousins from further north were so involved in the life and economy of the peninsula that they wanted to regularize their trading relationships with Spanish Cuba. Previously content with exchanging the rewards of their South Florida hunts through Charlotte Harbor's Cuban fishermen or St. Augustine middlemen, in 1793 the Creeks dispatched a delegation to Havana to petition for the erection of a store convenient to their hunting grounds. The request

Two Tallahassee Creek chiefs, allies of Peter McQueen, were arrested with Alexander Arbuthnot, an Englishman, at St. Marks just prior to the April 1818 battle at Bowlegs Town on the Suwannee River. In the aftermath of the battle, McQueen sought refuge at Peace River. Courtesy Florida Photographic Collection, Florida State Archives.

specified that the store should be located at Pea Creek, described as "down in the Point of Florida, where the Spaniards always fish, and where the Indians take vessels to cross over to Havana." Although the Creek request resulted in a Spanish exploratory mission to the Tampa Bay area, no store appears to have been built there or at Charlotte Harbor. The incident, however, clearly illustrates a substantial Creek presence and interest in South Florida from the 1790s. Since the Creeks understood the location and importance of Peace River, which the Spanish explorers mistook for Tampa Bay, it also suggests a knowledge of the area on their part far greater than that held by the officials of Spain and her agents.[5]

The hunting towns at Talakchopco

A marked difference existed between Seminoles and Creeks when it came to their pursuit of game on the South Florida hunting grounds; by custom Creeks left their wives and children at home, while Seminoles seemed to prefer having their families with them. The presence of these Seminole families on the hunt no doubt prompted the establishment of seasonal villages on high fertile land near the hunting grounds, since, for a good part of each year, much of South Florida's low, flat land was under an inch to a foot or more of water. Accordingly, when in 1799 Creek Indian agent Benjamin Hawkins noted the existence of seven "towns of the Simenolies," he noted among them "Tal-lau-gue chapco pop-cau" and "Cull-oo-saw-hat-che." These towns must have been located on the rivers which their names suggest, Talakchopco and Caloosahatchee, and most logically would have been sited near the great crossing places on each of them.[6]

The Peace River hunting towns occasionally served as refuges, as well. A letter from Hawkins, dated in mid-January 1813, mentions that the leader of the Alachua Seminoles, King Payne, recently had died, and his people were in turmoil as a result of their conflict with Georgia and North Florida frontiersmen in what has come to be known as the Patriot War [see appendix 1]. "I received from an Indian of note . . . the following information," wrote Hawkins. "Paine is dead of his wounds . . . [and] the warring Indians have quit this settlement [Alachua], and gone down to Tellaugue Chapcopopeau, a creek which enters the ocean south of Moscheto river, at a place called the Fishery. Such of their stock as they could command have been driven in that direction, and the negroes [Seminole slaves] were going the same way. The lands beyond the creek towards Florida point, were, for a considerable distance, open savannas, with ponds; and, still beyond the land, stony, to the point."[7]

Hawkins's letter preserves for us not only the name of the town or area to which the Seminoles fled in 1812 but also a description of where it lay. The Moscheto (or Mosquito) River is known to us as the Halifax, and by south of the Moscheto River Hawkins meant below or farther down the peninsula. The creek flowed into the place called the Fishery, which was Charlotte Harbor, where for at least fifty years Cuban fishing ranchos had been located. Tellaugue Chapcopopeau to the Seminoles meant "the place where long peas are eaten." It was Hawkins's spelling for Talakchopco River. The refugees had gone to Peace River and their seasonal hunting towns.[8]

Where exactly were these seasonal towns located? The great

ford of the Peace River lay at what is now Fort Meade. The banks of the river from just below the site of Fort Meade northward to the vicinity of Lake Hancock, with the banks of adjacent creeks, constituted an area of rich and high hammock land prized by the Indians for its agricultural potential and other natural resources. Behind the banks for several miles in each direction lay what was known as "2d rate pine land," land elevated above the adjacent country, healthy and high in productivity. It was in this band of country, about five or six miles in width and fifteen to twenty miles long, that the Seminoles had located their hunting towns and that other Indians and blacks before too many years passed were to attempt to establish more permanent lives.[9]

Black plantations at Sarasota Bay

The years from 1812 to 1818 were a time of almost constant turmoil for the Indians of Florida and their black slaves and allies. In East Florida the Patriot War flamed on and off from July 1812 until May 1814, sending many Seminoles in flight—with their slaves and cattle—to Peace River. During much of the same period of time war also raged within the Creek Nation in Georgia and Alabama, a conflict finding Upper Creeks, known as Red Sticks, on one side and southern frontiersmen and their "Lower Creek" Indian allies on the other. At the Battle of Horseshoe Bend, Alabama, in March 1814, Tennessee militia general Andrew Jackson, with the support of Lower Creeks and Cherokees under the command of Chief William McIntosh, crushed the Red Sticks and forced over a thousand of their number to seek refuge in Spanish Florida.[10]

While the Patriot and Creek wars flared, so also did the War of 1812. Anxious to find support for their cause among Florida Indians, two British agents, Col. Edward Nicolls and Capt. George Woodbine, successfully recruited 3,000 refugee Red Stick Creeks, blacks, and Seminoles. After a series of engagements, these native forces were defeated decisively at the Battle of New Orleans on January 8, 1815, and again forced to retreat into Florida. When Nicolls withdrew his British forces from the province the following June, some of his black allies, concerned for their own safety, sailed for Tampa Bay under the leadership of Captain

Woodbine. At Sarasota Bay they established a substantial farming community where for the time being they and their families could live in peace and safety.[11]

Why was the Tampa Bay area selected for the black planta- tions? Major advantages, certainly, were that the locale could be supplied easily by sea from the Bahamas and that the bay afforded ocean-going vessels a safe harbor. But perhaps most importantly, the area already enjoyed a reputation as a haven for blacks. At least as early as 1813, black refugees from the Alachua Seminole towns had sought protection in the area. There were several rich hammocks for farming near the bay, and access to trade was available through contacts with the Cuban fishermen at Charlotte Harbor and at Tampa Bay itself. In fact, by 1812 some of those fishermen were living at Sarasota Bay on the Oyster River near where Woodbine located the black settlement. Many of the black refugees, together with runaway slaves, no doubt remained in the area in 1815, and from them Woodbine could recruit laborers as well as supporters for future operations he had planned for Florida.[12]

The black plantations at Sarasota prospered for several years and in one form or another still were in operation as late as 1821. They proved a magnet for runaway blacks and the memory of their existence lingered. Pioneer Floridian John Lee Williams, confusing Captain Woodbine with two other famous Britons who became involved in the lives of Florida's Indians and blacks, wrote of the plantations as they appeared in 1833: "Oyster river at the south-east side of Tampa Bay, was explored by twenty miles. . . . A stream that enters the bay joining the entrance of Oyster River, on the S.W., was ascended about six miles. . . . The point between these two rivers is called Negro Point. The famous Arbuthnot and Ambrister had at one time a plantation here cultivated by two hundred blacks. The ruins of their cabins, and domestic utensils are still seen on the old fields."[13]

Over the years additional black settlers were drawn to the plantations at Sarasota. When, during the summer of 1816, American and Creek troops destroyed Florida's other principal settlement of runaway slaves, Negro Fort on the Apalachicola River, it was said that most of the survivors fled to the east and, by the end of the year, had located near Seminole settlements on the Suwannee and in small villages reaching southward to Tampa

Bay. Thus, after the settlement of Upper Creek Indians at Chocachatti and Cuban fishermen from Tampa Bay to Charlotte Harbor, black warriors, many of whom had served as British soldiers
during the War of 1812, became with their families the next year-
round residents of South Florida.[14]

The First Seminole War

The First Seminole War generally is considered to have begun
in November 1817, but for several years tensions along the
Florida-Georgia frontier had been heightened as parties of Georgians crossed the border to raid Indian towns in Florida with
consequent counterraids by Seminoles into U.S. territory. Complicating an already difficult situation, whites from the Georgia
frontier, many of whose descendants were to become pioneer
settlers of the Peace River Valley, also kidnapped free and other
blacks in Florida to sell in American territory.[15]

Once the First Seminole War did get under way, it did not take
Andrew Jackson long to conclude it. By April 6, 1818, the American general had forced the surrender of the Spanish garrison at
St. Marks. Jackson then turned his attention eastward toward
the Suwannee. On the way, a column of Creeks moving in support of the attack encountered an Indian encampment on the
Econfina River. Hearing the encampment to be that of the Red
Stick chief Peter McQueen and about two hundred of his warriors, Jackson's Creeks, again led by William McIntosh, attacked.
When the smoke had cleared, McIntosh discovered among his
captives a young boy of the Tallahassee tribe, Billy Powell, the
grandson of one of Peter McQueen's sisters. Peter McQueen
had escaped.[16]

Jackson's army reached the main Seminole encampment on the
Suwannee at sunset on April 16. The Indians, having received
warning of Jackson's approach, had disappeared into the woods to
the south and east along with Peter McQueen, his ally the Ockmulgee Creek chief Oponay, and their followers. Blacks from the
villages on the western bank of the river ferried their possessions
across the Suwannee while three hundred black warriors remained to protect them. Pausing only briefly after his arrival,
Jackson ordered his troops to attack. The black warriors bought
just enough time for all to escape. One veteran of the entire cam-

paign declared the fight "the severest brush that I was engaged in during that campaign." The following day Jackson ordered his Creek allies to cross the river in pursuit, but most Seminoles, Red Sticks, and blacks escaped.[17]

Old Hickory stayed but a short while on the Suwannee. He destroyed all the black and Indian towns on the river, in the process burning three hundred houses. When McIntosh and his Lower Creek warriors left for home, Jackson sent with them instructions to destroy Oponay's "town and all his warriors, and to take possession of all his property of every description, so as effectually to destroy him." That done, Jackson turned again to the west and, with his capture of Spanish Pensacola, brought the war to its conclusion.[18]

The Red Sticks and Seminoles, with their black allies, had fled into the Florida peninsula to escape the terror of Andrew Jackson. So profound was the confusion and disruption in the aftermath of the war that historian Kenneth W. Porter has described the situation as "a muddy pool stirred violently with a stick." Four years later one observer wrote that "many of the chiefs most prominent in their depradations, fled away, and traversing the Seminole nation, settled themselves about Tampa Bay, Charlotte Harbor and their waters." Jackson's aide, Lt. James Gadsden, writing the summer after the end of the war, noted of the Tampa Bay area, "It is the last rallying spot of the disaffected negroes and Indians and the only favorable point from whence a communication can be had with Spanish and European emissaries." He suggested that Col. Edward Nicolls might still be involved in Woodbine's plantation: "Nicholas it is reported has an establishment in that neighborhood and the negroes and Indians driven from Micosukey and Suwaney towns have directed their march to that quarter."[19]

Red Sticks at Talakchopco

Although the principal Seminole and black towns on the Suwannee River were destroyed by Jackson's forces in April 1818, their former inhabitants survived. Within only a year or two, many were settled from 100 to 150 miles to the southeast of the old Seminole town on that stream in the present-day counties of Marion, Lake, Sumter, Hernando, and Pasco. By 1821 the Big

Hammock area of Pasco and Hernando counties was described as "the most numerous of the Seminole settlements" and the neighborhood of Chocachatti, the nearest Indian town, as "the seat of the Seminole Nation." In the vicinity of these settlements Seminole slaves resided in their own communities where they specialized in farming while the Seminoles principally tended cattle. In the old Seminole heartland in Alachua, a band of Mikasuki Indians from villages north of Tallahassee settled under their chief, John Hicks. Others of the Mikasuki bands, and some Red Stick Creeks, already had resigned themselves to their defeat and were headed back to their destroyed homes and farms in the area between the Suwannee and the Apalachicola rivers.[20]

For many of Florida's other Indians and blacks, the situation was more desperate. Presumably without possessions or substantial quantities of supplies, more than a thousand of these refugees faced starvation. Only deep in the peninsula could they find the two essentials to their survival: game on the great South Florida hunting grounds and relief by sea from their Spanish and British allies. On the way to both of these objectives lay Tampa Bay and the black plantations at Sarasota. So, as James Gadsden reported to Andrew Jackson, the Indians and blacks "directed their march to that quarter."

The first bands to start out down the peninsula would have been those with the most reason for concern: the blacks facing reenslavement and the personal followings of the two great fugitive Creek chiefs still at large, Peter McQueen and Oponay. Their immediate goal, just as James Gadsden had suggested, was Tampa Bay and the black plantations, and there in October 1818 they finally found relief in the form of an English trading vessel. Within the next several weeks additional help arrived from the Spanish at St. Augustine so that by the end of November they could be described as "well supplied with ammunition and provisions." Fed and armed, they could take the time to begin rebuilding their homes and their lives.[21]

With the Seminoles occupying the best lands immediately to the north and northeast of Tampa Bay, the refugees looked for promising locations closer at hand. For the independent blacks the most desirable areas were around Tampa Bay itself, particularly near the magnet of the black plantations at Sarasota Bay. For the fugitive Creeks, the matter was complicated by their

The Peace River bridge at Fort Meade in the 1890s. This site was a historic crossing point. To the north until 1836 lay the Indian town of Talakchopco. Courtesy Florida Photographic Collection, Florida State Archives.

greater numbers. Some had remained at or returned to the vicinity of the Suwannee River. One group of Red Sticks moved to the west of Tampa Bay on the coast and founded Watermelon Town. About thirty warriors with their women and children moved twenty or so miles to the east of the bay and settled at Itchepuckesassa (the place of tobacco fields) near where Plant City stands today. Many of the remainder, under Oponay and Peter McQueen, moved with their black slaves to those abandoned Seminole hunting towns on Peace River.[22]

Prior to the battle on the Suwannee Oponay had been known as Chief of the Ockmulgee Towns of the Creek Nation. As early as 1797 his tribe was located in southwest Georgia. Twenty years later they remained in the same general location, well within the boundaries of the territory ceded by the Creeks in 1814 in the aftermath of the Battle of Horseshoe Bend. In the late winter of 1817 Oponay, who also was named Ochacona Tustenatty, was sent into Florida as a representative to the Seminoles on behalf of the Creek chiefs remaining loyal to the United States. On that visit, apparently, he was won over to the Red Stick cause. Late the same year he again was serving as an intermediary but soon was caught up in the aftermath of the First Seminole War. The only available description of him as an individual was written about three years after his arrival at Peace River and shortly before his death. He was said by a U.S. official at St. Augustine to be "a very intelligent and interesting and perhaps honest Indian chief."[23]

Oponay selected for his settlement at Peace River a location near Lake Hancock, north of present-day Bartow. Florida frontiersman and Indian trader Horatio Dexter visited the chief's plantations there in July of 1823, as apparently also did James Gadsden in the following year. Dexter wrote that Oponay built his home on a hill to the west and about sixty or seventy feet above the level of the lake, "a comfortable two story house built of plank & hewed timber" which resembled in all respects "the residence of a substantial planter." Nearby, Dexter found "a dairy house, Corn house, Stables, Sheds, etc. etc.," as well as "an extensive peach orchard, & a considerable crop of Corn, Potatoes, etc. etc." Oponay's slaves lived about two miles from the residence, on the other side of the lake and to the east of Saddle Creek, amidst their master's corn and rice fields. Dexter felt the plantation contained "more conveniences than that of any Indian in the Nation."[24]

Peter McQueen not only was a Red Stick chief, he also was the son of a Scotsman who had come to Georgia as a soldier with James Oglethorpe in 1733 and who, by 1797, was the oldest white man in the Creek Nation. Peter McQueen's mother was an Upper Creek of the Tallahassee tribe. During the American Revolution the Tallahassees had been very friendly with the future United States, but experiences after the war so embittered them that, by 1799, the tribe constituted a center of opposition to American interests within the Creek Nation. Peter McQueen, known to the Creeks as Talmuches Hadjo and already a chief in 1799, enjoyed a reputation as a sharp trader and a wealthy man, possessing valuable properties in stock and black slaves. Defeats in the wars of the decade of the 1810s had stripped him of all or most of that wealth, however, and his establishment at Peace River, as presumably also was the case with Oponay, depended on English and Spanish generosity.[25]

The memory of the descendants of the Tallahassees remaining in Florida in the early twentieth century, as preserved through the efforts of the late Albert DeVane and others, was that after their defeat by Jackson in 1818, Peter McQueen and his band "moved south to Peas River in the vicinity of Bartow and Homeland." For confirmation, we need look only to Billy Powell, captured by William McIntosh on the Econfina River before the battle on the Suwannee.[26]

Billy Powell, described as a "lad" at the time, was luckier than many of the other ninety-six Indian women and children captured from Peter McQueen's party on April 12, 1818. The quick thinking of his grandmother, who was McQueen's sister, apparently won release for Billy and others of the family by Andrew Jackson on a promise to secure McQueen's surrender. The Indians headed at once for the Okefenokee Swamp where they eventually learned that McQueen was at "Peas Creek," and they departed to meet him there. Billy was to live with his Tallahassee relatives, first at Peace River and then at other locations in Florida, until he emerged by another name as the most famous of Florida Indians, Osceola.[27]

Among the Seminole hunting towns on Peace River, which lay in a five- or six-mile-wide belt of land centered on and running down the river from Lake Hancock to below present-day Fort Meade, Oponay occupied the land adjacent to Lake Hancock and Saddle Creek. Necessarily, and just as the Tallahassees informed Albert DeVane, Peter McQueen and his party occupied the area to the south of Bartow. Quite likely their settlement included the remains of Seminole lodges and other facilities located on the west bank near the great ford of the river at Fort Meade. This important strategic position would have allowed the Red Sticks to control not only access to the hunting grounds to the south, but communication and trade with the Cuban fishermen at Charlotte Harbor, and the passage of representatives of Spain and England through the harbor.[28]

And so, with the arrival of Oponay, Peter McQueen, and their followers late in 1818 or early in 1819, the Peace River Valley witnessed the beginnings of permanent and continuous settlement in the nineteenth century.

As was the case with most of South Florida, the Peace River Valley was devoid of a permanent population at the dawn of the nineteenth century. The fords of the river, particularly the one at modern Fort Meade, were utilized extensively by hunting parties

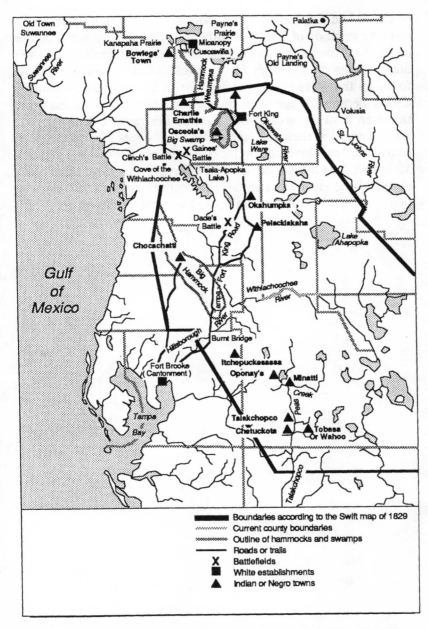

Boundaries of the Indian reservation, about 1829. Drawn by Ted Starr, adapted from Mark F. Boyd, "The Seminole War: Its Background and Onset," *Florida Historical Quarterly* 30 (July 1951).

of Creek and Seminole Indians bound for or returning from the hunting grounds of South Florida and, by 1800, seasonal camps or hunting towns had been established by Seminoles and their black slaves on the high fertile banks of the river near those fords. In the wake of the Patriot War of 1812–14, those hunting towns became refuges for Seminoles driven by Georgia frontiersmen from the area of the Alachua Prairie and, half a decade later, hosted the remnants of the Red Stick Creek alliance defeated time after time by Andrew Jackson and his Creek ally, William McIntosh. The arrival of those Red Stick Creeks and their black slaves at the river represented the beginnings of permanent settlement of the Peace River Valley in the nineteenth century.

2

Upheavals and Explorations

W HILE THE second decade of the nineteenth century saw the beginnings of permanent settlement in the Peace River Valley, the nature of that settlement radically altered in the 1820s. The black and Red Stick Creek haven proved far less safe than they had supposed it to be, and by the end of the decade others would come to dominate the river's fording places and fields and white men would have begun to expose its secrets.

The destruction of the black plantations

On February 22, 1819, almost coincidental with the arrival of Oponay and Peter McQueen at Peace River, the Kingdom of Spain agreed to transfer Florida to the United States pursuant to the Adams-Onís Treaty. Although transfer of possession did not occur for more than two years, what had been a relatively safe Spanish refuge for the fugitive blacks and Creeks overnight became a potential U.S. stalking ground. News of the treaty would have reached the Tampa, Sarasota, and Peace River areas quickly, given the opportunity for communication with the Spanish through Charlotte Harbor and the British through the black plantations at Sarasota Bay.[1]

It appears that, once word of the Adams-Onís Treaty reached South Florida, the Creeks wasted little time in appealing to the Spanish government at Havana. During 1819 five parties of South Florida Indians, including at least seventy-eight Indians from the area of Tampa, visited Havana. If the Indians were in Havana on what might be termed diplomatic missions, it seems they found little satisfaction there because, by late September, a delegation of fugitive Red Sticks was in Nassau. Displaying documents of support issued to them by the British in 1815 and pleading for supplies, they told of being "driven from their homes, and hunted as Wild Deer." Stating their own numbers as about two thousand, the Red Sticks spoke of the Cowetas, the Lower Creek tribe of which William McIntosh was chief, as their greatest enemies, "who having made terms with the Americans are set on by them to harrass and annihilate [them]." Their pleas, as well as a request to appeal to higher authorities, fell on deaf ears. The Indians continued their efforts. In the following year, 1820, four more groups of South Florida Indians were in Havana, this time consisting of at least six chiefs and 120 Indians from "Tampa." Although the trips provided a fine opportunity for trade, there is no indication of other positive results from them, and time was running out.[2]

Two years to the day after the original agreement for the transfer of Florida was reached, the United States and Spain exchanged ratifications of the treaty, although actual transfer of possession was delayed for five months, until July 1821. Events in the interim would destroy the black presence in South Florida and dramatically affect life and settlement in the Peace River area.[3]

On the face of things the blacks and Indians of Florida should have been delighted with the Adams-Onís Treaty because one of its provisions specifically guaranteed their protection: "The inhabitants [of Florida] . . . shall be . . . admitted to the enjoyment of all privileges, rights and immunities of the citizens of the United States." "You have nothing to fear," Spanish officials in Havana must have told the Indian delegations of 1819 and 1820. "You will be American citizens!" Those would-be American citizens knew better from their own experiences with Britain's half-hearted attempts to protect them after the War of 1812. Any remaining doubt must have been dispelled when they learned that their most bitter American enemy had been appointed to rule over them. On January 24, 1821, Secretary of State John Quincy Adams offered the governorship of Florida to Andrew Jackson.[4]

Because South Florida's Indians and blacks had reason to doubt the guarantees of the Adams-Onís Treaty did not mean that others would be able to ignore them. While Andrew Jackson had been able to stymie implementation of a similar guarantee after the War of 1812, the situation then had been quite different from that of Florida in 1821. In 1815 Jackson had been a great national hero following the Battle of New Orleans and, to a large degree, was operating in an area remote from public attention. In 1821 public attention was focused on the Florida cession and Jackson's personal star shone less brightly. Consequently, anyone desiring to pursue action against the blacks and Indians of South Florida—at least anyone desiring to do so without the endorsement of the U.S. Government—was well advised to take action during the period of inevitable confusion after the ratifications were exchanged and before Florida actually came under the U.S. flag.

As early as October 1818, David Mitchell, Benjamin Hawkins's successor as Creek Indian agent, had intrigued with loyal Creek chiefs to send William McIntosh and his Cowetas to capture and bring away all the fugitive blacks in Florida. Two years later the idea still was alive. Late in December 1820, commissioners negotiating with the Creeks insisted that the blacks be taken and returned from Florida. The resulting treaty, that of Indian Springs, contained specific provisions guaranteeing a payment by the federal government to any Creek returning a runaway black to Georgia.[5]

By April 1821 Andrew Jackson had begun to ready himself to assume the governorship and, right from the beginning, his thoughts were of Peter McQueen, the fugitive Red Stick Creeks, and the blacks at Tampa Bay. On April 2 he wrote the secretary of state strongly intimating that removal of the fugitives from Florida was essential. On May 1 Jackson's letter was answered by Secretary of War John C. Calhoun, who ordered the soon-to-be governor to take no immediate steps against the Indians or the blacks.[6]

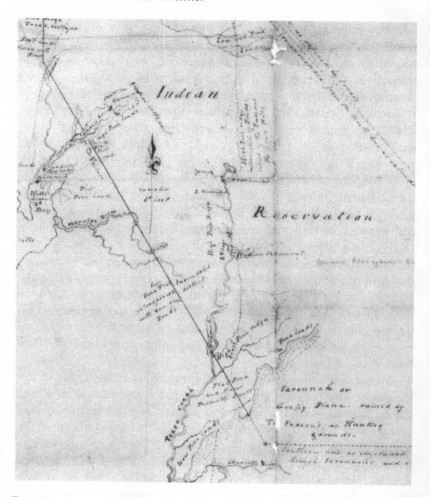

Detail from an official Army map of the Seminole Indian Reservation showing the Peace River and Tampa Bay areas, about 1827. Courtesy National Archives.

In Florida the Indians were desperate for information on American intentions—and Jackson's. While the future governor was seeking authority for the removal of Red Sticks and blacks, a delegation of Seminole and, possibly, Creek chiefs was escorted to St. Augustine by Horatio Dexter to confer with the Spanish governor. On May 24, fifty-four "principal Indians" of Florida met in council with Dexter and his partner, Edward M. Wanton, and were advised to assert their rights with the president. Meanwhile, to the north, others were preparing to assert themselves in a far different manner.[7]

As Andrew Jackson awaited a reply from Washington to his request for instruction, "some men of influence and fortune" decided to take the matter of South Florida's blacks into their own hands. In late April they hired Charles Miller, a half-blood Creek chief associated with William McIntosh, and William Weatherford, a former Red Stick leader befriended by Andrew Jackson after the Battle of Horseshoe Bend, to put an end to the black colonies in Florida and return their inhabitants to slavery. Miller, Weatherford, and other chiefs organized a regiment of two hundred Coweta warriors, and, about the time Jackson was told not to take action against the refugee Creeks and blacks, the Cowetas descended into still-Spanish Florida. As the raiding party advanced down the old route from the north into the South Florida hunting grounds, the Seminoles and Creeks living in its path, particularly those north of Tampa near Chocachatti and the Big Hammock, fled in terror.[8]

Arriving at Tampa Bay early in June 1821, the Cowetas proceeded to destroy all black settlements they could find and to kidnap their former residents. Not even vessels in the bay were safe; one ship believed by the Cowetas to be owned by the Red Sticks' old friend, Col. Edward Nicolls, was boarded and a black taken from it. At the black plantations on Sarasota Bay the raiders "surprised and captured about 300 of them, plundered their plantations, [and] set on fire all their houses." With blacks and Indians fleeing from them "in great consternation," the Cowetas on June 17 plundered the Cuban fishing ranchos at Charlotte Harbor. Then, herding their hundreds of captive blacks, as well as cattle stolen from the Creeks and Seminoles, the raiders finally returned to Coweta in early August.[9]

The charred remains of the homes and fields of the settlements at Tampa and Sarasota bays were still smoldering when, on June 14, 1821, Andrew Jackson entered Florida peacefully for the first time. While the Cowetas slowly made their way back into Georgia and Alabama, the future president awaited the formal transfer of the territory at Pensacola. The ceremonies ultimately were performed in that town on July 17 and, on the same day, four hundred miles to the east at St. Augustine, word was dispatched to the U.S. government and the country about the savage slave raid deep into South Florida. Receiving the news from a small group of Seminoles whom he described as "a wretched, miserable Set," one official added in a letter to Secretary of War Calhoun, "the commander of the party [of Cowetas] had sent them information that in a short time he should return and drive all the Indians off."[10]

Word of the slave raid touched off a round of fervid denials of involvement in official Washington, resulting in orders from the secretary of war to Creek agent John Crowell forbidding any repeat of the incident. "It is understood from information from Florida," wrote John Calhoun, "that another expedition of the kind is contemplated. Should that be the fact, you will inform the chiefs that as the Country [Florida] belongs to the United States, the President will view any attempt of the sort with the most marked disapprobation, and will hold the Creek nation responsible for the consequences." While the controversy swirled, Governor Jackson spent his time at Pensacola organizing a government, arguing with the former Spanish governor over the question of public records, and denouncing Peter McQueen while demanding the removal of the Red Stick Creeks from Florida.[11]

Aftermath of the Coweta raid

"The terror thus spread along the Western Coast of East Florida," an observer of the Coweta raid wrote several months after the event, "broke all the establishments of both blacks and whites, who fled in great consternation." He added that "the blacks principally, thought they could not save their lives but by abandoning the country."[12]

The disruptions of the Coweta raid and of the subsequent transfer of Florida to the United States by no means were limited to the blacks of South Florida.[13] To the north of Tampa Bay, communities of Seminoles and Red Sticks from the Suwannee down to the Big Hammock had been displaced out of fear of the raiders' return. Feeding on those fears, unscrupulous whites spread rumors among the Indians that the United States intended to take their slaves and other property at ridiculously low prices. The Seminole settlements in the Big Hammock, including Chocachatti, particularly were affected. What had been "the seat of the Seminole Nation" in early 1821 contained only twenty inhabited houses two years later. Seminole blacks were described as being "in the greatest poverty" and the Seminoles themselves as "now dispersed in small squads and single families over the country: a few still inhabit the small villages between the Alachua and Tampa bay."[14]

The possible return of the Cowetas and the arrival of the Americans posed a particularly severe dilemma for the Red Stick Creeks in South Florida. Under the impression that they would be allowed for a time to live in peace if they returned to their old homes west of the Suwannee many, including members of Peter McQueen's Peace River band, returned to the Panhandle. Others "dispersed themselves in the woods or retired to remote situations." These Indians, no doubt, soon were engaged in raids for food up into South Georgia. As early as July 1821 they stole a quantity of hogs and cattle near the St. Marys River and were themselves attacked on their return by Seminoles anxious for peace with the whites. Possibly the same group again visited the St. Marys area the following spring when Israel Barber, William Gibbons, and Joseph Tillis—all the fathers of future South Florida pioneers—reported substantial losses of cattle to the Indians.[15]

The Peace River settlements of Oponay and Peter McQueen, as well as the Red Stick village at Itchepuckesassa (today, Plant City), appear to have escaped entirely the destruction of the Cowetas.[16] Shortly afterwards, however, Itchepuckesassa fell on hard times due to problems, possibly from flooding, with raising cattle in the Alafia River country. By the summer of 1823 the village was deserted, although its houses still were standing and beautiful peach and "Pride of India" trees were flourishing. The residents moved to Chocachatti, Lake Tohopekaliga, and an "extensive settlement" fifteen miles to the north named after its chief, Tomakitchky.[17]

On Peace River the situation was quite different. Bolstered by an increased work force of refugees from the Tampa Bay settlements and possibly by aid from the British, the Peace River towns—at least Oponay's plantation—flourished. Just as at Itchepuckesassa, cattle were being raised at Peace River, perhaps on Hooker's Prairie to the west of Talakchopco or on the Kissimmee range to the east. The prosperity of the settlements, however, depended as much or more on agriculture supported by black slave labor. On Oponay's fields around the southern borders of

Lake Hancock the blacks worked an extensive peach orchard and produced crops of corn, potatoes, rice, and other products. By early 1822 Oponay was visiting St. Augustine to sell one hundred head of cattle and to arrange for the purchase of seed corn. Later the same year the Ockmulgee chief dispatched his rice crop to the

James Gadsden (1788–1858) was a protégé of Andrew Jackson. In 1824, six years after this portrait was done, he surveyed the bounds of Florida's Indian nation, exploring, in the process, much of the Peace River valley. Courtesy Florida Photographic Collection, Florida State Archives.

East Florida capital by pack horses.[18] When Oponay died in May 1823, his home and personal buildings were destroyed according to Creek custom. Despite that loss, when Oponay's son left for his new home west of the Suwannee, he drove off "300 head of cattle, about 100 head of horses, principally packed with rice, merchandise & specie, the latter to the amount of 7000 dollars."[19]

Peter McQueen, in his late fifties or early sixties, was reported still alive in the fall of 1821 by his old friend, the chief Neamathla. The Red Stick leader may even have been one of the chiefs who made a return visit to Nassau in the wake of the Coweta raid; if so, he must have returned more brokenhearted than when he left as the chiefs were imprisoned for a time by British authorities and then sent back into Florida exile. The shipmasters providing their involuntary transportation were ordered never to bring them to the Bahamas again.[20]

A man who knew Peter McQueen well reported that he died "on a little barren island on the Atlantic side of Cape Florida." This could well have occurred on that return trip from Nassau in 1821 when McQueen, heavily burdened with the loss of his fortune and the pain of his defeats, knew that his allies had abandoned him forever. It is possible that he lived a few years longer. In September 1823 Neamathla mentioned that a "Tullis Hajo" (which may have been another spelling of McQueen's Creek name, Talmuches Hadjo) had a town on the "west side of Cape Florida, on the seacoast." In either case, Peter McQueen's life and presence in the Peace River Valley ceased not long after the Coweta raid and, upon his death, even his widow left their South Florida exile and returned to home and remarriage in the Creek Nation. McQueen's legacy, that of a great warrior who never would surrender, would be honored by many of Florida's surviving Tallahassees throughout their lifetimes. It would help prolong the Seminole wars until 1858, and it would result in a Tallahassee presence in the Peace River Valley until almost the beginning of the twentieth century.[21]

The return of the Seminoles

Peter McQueen's settlement at Talakchopco may have begun to lose population even before the transfer of Florida to American ownership. Andrew Jackson believed members of McQueen's band were making settlements at Miccosukee and on the Suwannee as early as April 1821. Although some evidence suggests members of McQueen's Tallahassee following remained at Peace River until 1832, many appear to have moved further to the north shortly after McQueen's death or, as the memory of the Tallahassees had it, "after 1823." By 1827 the Red Sticks occupied the Big Hammock area of Hernando and Pasco counties, more or less abandoned by the Seminoles in the wake of the Coweta raid, as well as the old Upper Creek town of Chocachatti. In the meantime, just as the Tallahassees replaced Seminoles in the Big Hammock, some very important Seminoles replaced the Tallahassees at Talakchopco. One of them was the young Billy Bowlegs.[22]

The name of Billy Bowlegs's father is uncertain. By Seminole and Creek custom inheritance descended through the mother, and Bowlegs's mother, Buckra Woman, was a member of the most powerful of Seminole families. Not only was she a member of the important snake clan; she also was a descendant of Cowkeeper, the Oconee Creek chief recognized as "Founder of the Seminole Nation." Clarifying the situation somewhat, one military officer who knew Bowlegs well explained, "His mother was the sister of King Payne and old [King] Bowlegs," both of whom were head chiefs of the Seminoles during the 1810s.[23]

In early 1822, Indian Agent Bell noted the presence near Long Swamp, east of the Seminole concentrations at the Big Hammock, of a town called Bucker Woman's Town. When Horatio Dexter visited Oponay's settlement near Lake Hancock in July 1823, he encountered to his surprise "a part of the late Payne's family" who recently had left "their fields & settlements near the sea coast in consequence of the rise of the Water."[24] With the additional aim of avoiding "the frequent incursions of the Cowetas," the party had determined to settle at Peace River "in this remote situation," as Dexter put it.[25]

Given Dexter's comments, it is clear that a group of King Payne's relatives moved to Peace River at about the time of Oponay's death. If this party was the Buckra Woman's it would have been particularly sensitive to the Coweta threat because she was involved heavily in the cattle business and, like other members of the Cowkeeper line, must have owned considerable numbers of black slaves. The "remote situation" of Peace River offered her protection for both and was well known to the Seminoles from their hunting trips prior to 1813. Additionally, the grazing lands to the east and west of the river, which had helped make Oponay wealthy and which were to become famous later in the century, were ideal for the Seminoles' cattle interests.[26]

Within only a few years after their arrival at Peace River, at least a portion of the Seminole party at Oponay's, including the young Billy Bowlegs, moved to a new village on Hatchee Thlokko or Big Creek, which enters Peace River from the east three miles south of present-day Fort Meade and which, since at least the early 1850s, has been known as "Bowlegs Creek."[27] The exact date of the move is unknown, but a map dating to early 1825 is the first to show a village on the site. The reason for the move also is unclear. A partial answer might lie in the proximity of the new village to the cattle ranges of the Kissimmee River Valley and to the market for beef at Charlotte Harbor's Cuban fishing ranchos. Not later than 1833 an active cattle trade was carried on at the site, and at least one herd was driven down the east side of the river to the falls of the Caloosahatchee and on to Punta Rassa.[28]

After the arrival of the Seminoles, it may be that the Indians and blacks living at Peace River, having cattle to herd and fields to tend, were among the most fortunate of Florida's natives in the 1820s, for almost everywhere in the territory dislocation and starvation were facts of life. At Peace River, life appears to have been lived quietly. From a population high of around 500 in July 1823, the total number of residents seems to have dropped to around 100 to 150 within the next year, possibly as a result of the removal of many of the Tallahassees to the Big Hammock area. Until the early 1830s there is little evidence that the population at the river settlements varied significantly from that of 1824. Except for the occasional mention of a patrol sent from Fort Brooke at Tampa Bay, usually in connection with runaway slaves, the inhabitants of the river valley barely received notice in the official records. Exceptions primarily concerned exploration.[29]

Early explorations

Although by 1821 many Creeks, Seminoles, and blacks had detailed knowledge of South Florida and its hunting grounds, Florida's new owners, the Americans, knew little of the new land but rumor. As one South Florida historian put it, "interior Southwestern Florida was an unexplored wilderness." During the first four years of American exploration, expeditions were led primarily by government agents to accomplish particular goals. The first such expedition was the exception.[30]

Anxious to take advantage of the vast tracts of land available in Florida, a group of Philadelphia investors organized themselves in 1821 as the East Florida Coffee Land Association. To coordinate their efforts and to select appropriate lands in Florida, the association employed a Frenchman and former West Indian coffee grower named Peter Stephen Chazotte. Charged with exploring South Florida, Chazotte was directed to set out immediately "accompanied by six labouring men and five volunteers, including a surveyor and doctor."[31]

Employing the sloop *Hunter*, Chazotte's expedition arrived at St. Augustine by July 19, 1821. Within a month of their arrival, the members of the party were at Cape Florida where they encountered black and Indian refugees from the Coweta raid at Tampa Bay. Rounding the cape, the expedition explored the Florida Keys and then followed the Gulf Coast north to Charlotte Harbor. They went up the Caloosahatchee River for forty-five miles, at which point Indians told the party of the great lake to the east named Mayaco. Charlotte Harbor and its keys and fishing ranchos, including at least the mouth of Peace River, were mapped. Moving further up the coast the party explored and charted the ruined black plantations at Sarasota Bay as well as the Manatee River.[32]

By September the Chazotte party had explored Tampa Bay, noted its four rivers, and mapped its waters and keys. Turning back at Tampa Bay, the expedition retraced its steps down the Gulf coast, along the keys, and up the Atlantic seaboard, arriving at Philadelphia in mid-November. Based upon Chazotte's explorations, the East Florida Coffee Land Association petitioned Congress for the purchase at a nominal price of the island of Key Largo. The request was denied in relatively short order, and the brief life of the East Florida Coffee Land Association came to an end.[33]

Within two years after Chazotte's departure from South Florida, another American explorer, Horatio Dexter, entered the area in July 1823. In the two years following the raising of the American flag over Spanish Florida, the government determined that all Florida Indians must be concentrated in the peninsula. To facilitate that policy, a council of Indian chiefs was called for early September 1823 at Moultrie Creek near St. Augustine. Horatio Dexter was designated to notify the Seminoles and Creeks already living in the peninsula of the council and to explore the area with an eye as to where a reservation sufficient to support the Indians might be located.[34]

Setting out in late June, Dexter proceeded into the peninsula from his home at Volusia on the St. Johns River and toured Indian and black settlements from there to the Gulf coast. Faced with flooding upon his arrival at the Alafia River, however, he turned to the east and Oponay's plantation where, he understood, a boat was kept. Dexter found no boat at Oponay's, but he did find about five hundred Indians and blacks as well as the ruins of Oponay's plantation house.[35] Stymied in his attempts to penetrate farther to the south, Dexter skirted the lower shore of Lake Hancock (which he attempted to name Lake Simmons after his friend Dr. William H. Simmons) and returned homeward to the east of the lake. Once home, he wrote a detailed report of his trip which is the only source for many of the facts available on Peace River in the early 1820s. He also left a map, the first detailed, though highly inaccurate, map of interior central Florida and the headwaters of Peace River [see p. 30].[36]

As planned, the Indian council was held near St. Augustine in early September 1823 and resulted in the adoption of a Treaty of Moultrie Creek which established, based in part on Dexter's report, an Indian reservation in interior central and southern Florida. The Indians' refusal to accept land south of Charlotte Harbor and the Americans' desire to cut off all communications and trade between the Indians and Cuba through the fishing ranchos at the bay placed the entire reservation north of Charlotte Harbor, encompassing most of the Peace River Valley.[37]

In early December 1823 James Gadsden, Andrew Jackson's former aide, set out overland from St. Augustine to mark and map the limits of the new reservation. By January 18, 1824, he had arrived at Tampa Bay where he was joined four days later by a detachment of troops from Pensacola under the command of Lt. Col. George M. Brooke. There, he established a site for a fort on the Hillsborough and named it Fort Brooke. During the ensuing

The earliest known map of the Peace River area, drawn in 1823 by explorer and trader Horatio S. Dexter. While it contains many inaccuracies, it is an important document in the history of peninsular Florida. Courtesy National Archives.

months Gadsden plunged into the interior of the country, surveying the western line of the reserve and visiting the Indian towns at the headwaters of Peace River. By February 20, at Charlotte Harbor, he entered the land of prairies to the east of Peace

River and attempted to mark the eastern boundary of the reserve as he returned to the north.[38]

Commissioner Gadsden issued a report of his survey and findings in mid-June 1824 and described the new reservation: "The Hammocks of best character, and of greatest extent are to be found at Okahumky—Negro settlements at Withlacouchy Creek & Pelacklekaha—Checuchatty—near the sources of Hillsborough river—and on Peace Creek & its tributaries—In addition to these hammocks, the banks of Pear [Peace] Creek, from its source in a large pond for 15 miles south, furnishes a body of 2nd rate pine land elevated and productive—There are two Indian villages in this district of pines, the condition of which are favorable evidences of the productiveness of the soil and healthiness of the country—The settlements will necessarily be confined to the above districts." Accompanying Gadsden's report was a map of the Indian reservation and adjacent areas. The location of Oponay's former plantation house at Lake Hancock, Indian towns near present-day Bartow and Fort Meade, and Bowlegs, Charlie Apopka, and Joshua creeks, though unnamed, are shown in somewhat simplified form. With the exception of those mentioned, Gadsden found no other Indian settlements on the river in 1824.[39]

James Gadsden's failure to provide U.S. officials at Tampa or the Indian agency with much significant information concerning the Indian settlements near Tampa Bay resulted in a second 1824 visit to the Peace River towns. Indian agent Gad Humphreys and a small military patrol under Lt. Jeremiah Yancey in June made a circuit of all the settlements within a fifty-mile radius of Fort Brooke, including the "Tolok-Chupco or Pease Creek Settlements." At Peace River, the party found the two Indian settlements noted by Gadsden, containing about fifteen families. Thirty blacks still were living at the site of Oponay's old plantation. Most of the Indians and blacks were sick with fevers, and Lt. Yancey was critical of the area. "In our whole route which we were ten days performing, I can safely say that I did not see Two hundred acres of good land." Agent Humphreys disagreed, however, and several years later wrote, "I cannot but consider the region extending along the gulf from Tampa Bay eastward and southward, superior in many respects to any other part of our country with which I am acquainted."[40]

While the upper reaches of Peace River were becoming familiar to the officials at Fort Brooke, the lower reaches of the river and surrounding countryside were still only vaguely known. This problem was alleviated somewhat in February 1825 when Maj. Isaac Clark was ordered to chain and mark a road from Fort Brooke to Charlotte Harbor. Moving to the southeast, Clark arrived at Charlotte Harbor near the mouth of Peace River. Finding that his party could not cross the river, Clark traveled upstream some "sixty miles" where he found a ford "about three miles below the junction of the two branches." There he crossed and returned to Charlotte Harbor after failing, due to swamps and high waters, to penetrate the country more than twelve miles to the east of the river. Clark's final report recommended a route for the road which included a ferry across Peace River thirty-four miles above Charlotte Harbor. The difficulties of the route were too great given the resources at hand, however, and the project was abandoned.[41]

Information collected from these early explorers and from patrols sent out from Fort Brooke permitted the compilation of a more detailed map of the Peace River area. One example, apparently dating from early 1825, shows an established path or roadway from Fort Brooke to Oponay's where it intersected a north-south route from the Oklawaha River to the Indian town at present-day Fort Meade. At that point the route crossed Peace River at the ancient ford and ran down the east side of the river to Charlotte Harbor and beyond. For the first time, an Indian village is shown on Bowlegs Creek. This map was refined further over the next year or two until the creation, probably in 1827, of a more detailed map of the reservation. The later map clearly illustrates the routes shown previously and pinpoints the locations of the settlements connected with Oponay, the Indian town just south of Bartow, the villages at and just north of Fort Meade, and the village on Bowlegs Creek. At that date and for the remainder of the decade, Peace River retained a permanent population, but the limits of settlement remained in the area from Lake Hancock to Bowlegs Creek.[42]

The 1820s began for Peace River's Indian and black residents on a note of alarm. Their safe haven in Spanish territory was snatched away by the cession of Florida to the United States, and the nearby black plantations at Sarasota Bay were destroyed in a savage raid by the Red Sticks' old enemies, the Coweta Creeks. In the wake of the Coweta raid and the deaths of Oponay and Peter McQueen, the Red Sticks drifted to new homes farther north. In their places Seminoles, displaced by fears of the Cowetas, returned to their old Peace River hunting towns to farm and graze their cattle in safety on the vast ranges to the east and west.

3

Beginning of the
Second Seminole War

WHILE THE INDIAN AND BLACK population of the Peace River
Valley stabilized in the early and mid-1820s, American
settlers poured into the frontier areas of North Florida
and began seeping down the southern peninsula. As their numbers grew, they pressured the U.S. government for a final resolution of the problem of Florida's natives, their demands aggravated
by incidents between whites and starving Indians brought on by
the theft of cattle. As tensions heightened, war became a more
distinct possibility.

The beginnings of American settlement

The flow of American settlers, many of them known as Crackers, into the Florida peninsula in the 1820s and early 1830s was
most dramatically evidenced in the large area bordered on the
east by the St. Johns River and on the south by the Indian reservation; that is, in the areas of present-day Baker, Columbia, Hamilton, Suwannee, Union, Bradford, and Alachua counties [see appendix 2].[1] Closer to the Peace River settlements, however, white
newcomers also began to make their presence felt. Levi Collar, a
soldier of the Patriot War, arrived with his family at Tampa Bay

as early as 1824 and, within five years, had moved further inland to Six Mile Creek. In 1829 the Reverend Daniel Simmons, a Baptist missionary, settled fifteen miles east of Tampa at what became known as Simmons Hammock. The previous year saw the opening of Tampa's first civilian store with the arrival of William Saunders, who became the village's first postmaster in 1831. Of many of the earliest settlers in the area Col. George M. Brooke had feelings none too charitable. In the fall of 1828 he noted, "The chief and may be said, the only object of those settlers is to dispose of whisky to the troops and Indians which they have and continue to do, to the great annoyance of the command and injury to the Soldiers & Indians." Whatever Colonel Brooke's concerns and whatever problems for the future were posed by the settlers, one fact was certain—white settlement of South Florida had begun.[2]

The very first white American settler at Tampa was neither a Cracker veteran of the Patriot War nor a whisky trader. Robert Hackley was the son of a New York lawyer, Richard Hackley, who had purchased in 1822 a grant made by the king of Spain about the time the treaty ceding Florida to the United States was signed. Although the Alagon Grant ultimately was found invalid by the U.S. Supreme Court, Hackley was convinced he owned most of central and southern Florida including Tampa Bay, Charlotte Harbor, and the Peace River Valley.[3]

In the summer of 1832, Hackley, in association with George W. Murray and associates of New York, sponsored an expedition to further explore the Charlotte Harbor area. On September 10 they entered the mouth of Peace River which they mistakenly called the Macaco. After five days the party reached a point most likely in present-day Hardee County. Indians they encountered told them that the head springs of the river were "distant three days journey" and that around those springs were "some hundreds of Indians."[4]

Among the Hackley-Murray party was P.B. Prior, who in March of the following year travelled overland from Tampa Bay to buy cattle at Peace River from an Indian named Seweky. After a three-day journey with Seweky as guide, Prior reached the river at present-day Fort Meade. Crossing the stream at the ancient ford, the cattle buyer proceeded to Seweky's town, named Tobasa or Wahoo, two miles up Bowlegs Creek from its junction with the river. The following day Seweky and Prior, aided by Indian and black cowmen, hunted the cattle which the American had sought to buy. Shortly thereafter, Prior left Seweky's with eight steers and two cows with calves and began the first recorded cattle drive down the east side of the river. For more than ten days the cattle were led to the southeast, then around the headwaters of and over Fisheating Creek. They were swum across the Caloosahatchee near the future site of Fort Thompson and finally reached their goal at Punta Rassa by paralleling the Caloosahatchee to the south. Because of Prior's connections with Hackley and Murray and the direction of his drive, it seems likely the cattle he purchased were destined for the use of a small colony the men had established on Sanibel Island.[5]

The Pease Creek Tallahassees

As P.B. Prior recorded in his journal, new Indian settlements were appearing south of Bowlegs Creek. The first, he noted, was eight miles south-southeast of the town on Bowlegs Creek and, being "just built," was without a name. Eighteen miles farther down was "a small Indian settlement" where Prior was able to purchase a "sorrel horse" for his Indian drovers. About eleven miles to the north of the crossing of Fisheating Creek another "small Indian town" was noted, and three miles further on the party encountered the camp of two runaway blacks. The Hackley-Murray expedition of the previous year also had noticed isolated Indian settlements on Peace River and had received reports of "some hundreds of Indians" on the river's headwaters. Those Indians and others located near the headwaters of the Caloosahatchee reportedly were raising two or three crops of corn each year.[6]

The Hackley-Murray and Prior reports clearly indicate the presence on Peace River and further to the south of substantially increased numbers of Indians during the early 1830s. Who were these Indians and how did they come to settle in the Peace River Valley?

By the early 1830s, pressure from white settlers had prompted the U.S. government to renew its efforts for the final removal of Indians and blacks from Florida. Andrew Jackson again turned to his old protégé and Florida hand, James Gadsden, who in very

Osceola in January 1838, shortly before his death. Painted from life by George Catlin at Fort Moultrie, S.C. Original in the National Portrait Gallery, Smithsonian Institution. Courtesy Florida Photographic Collection, Florida State Archives.

questionable circumstances arranged for the conclusion of the treaties of Paynes Landing and Fort Gibson calling for removal of the Creeks, Seminoles, Mikasukis, and blacks to the west. The treaties were promptly disavowed by many of the most prominent Indian and black leaders.

Faced with a United States determined to force their removal, some Indian leaders must have looked for an opportunity to slip

away from the attention of the whites to prepare for whatever
the future held. To some extent that opportunity was provided
when U.S. troops were withdrawn from Fort Brooke at Tampa
Bay in the summer of 1832 and when, shortly thereafter, the Indian agent left the territory.[7]

One who opted to slip away in those early years of the 1830s
was Holata Micco, chief of one of the larger Tallahassee bands.[8]
He first comes to attention, at least under that title or name, in
September 1823, when he was described as chief of the town of
Wachitokha, east of the Suwannee River toward the Santa Fe.
Less than a month later an article in the St. Augustine newspaper included him in a group of important chiefs who had made
"considerable advances in civilization." In May 1826 he was one
of seven chiefs who visited Washington and New York City to
urge the secretary of war and the president to extend the boundaries of the Indian reservation. Their talk to the secretary of war
suggested that Holata Micco and his band then were living in
or near the Big Swamp just to the east of the Indian Agency at
Fort King (Ocala).[9]

Holata Micco was visited near the Big Swamp in the summer
of 1829 by a young circuit-riding Methodist preacher. The Reverend Isaac Boring, seeking permission to preach to the Tallahassees, spoke with Holata Micco (whose name he spelled Olacklim-
ica) on July 22. Of the Tallahassee chief Boring recorded: "He said
that he had nothing against my preaching to his people, and that
he would like to hear preaching himself. He said that he could not
do any thing toward giving me liberty to preach to the Indians;
until the chiefs were assembled together; this he said would take
place on next Friday. He also said that he would then name my
request and do his best to get the chiefs willing to grant it. I am
much pleased with this chief and think that if all the chiefs of the
Nation were like him, it would not be long before these savages
would hear the Gospel of Christ." As was the case with so many
of Holata Micco's actions expressing a peaceful or accommodating
intention toward whites, his promise to the circuit rider came to
nothing. The young Methodist never preached to the Tallahassees.[10]

Shortly after his encounter with the Reverend Boring, Holata
Micco and his band may have moved a few miles farther south to
the neighborhood of the Withlacoochee River. Certainly by the

summer of 1832 the population of the Peace River Valley was increasing with reports of "some hundreds of Indians" near the river's headwaters, and settlements, however isolated, beginning to grow south of Bowlegs Creek. By 1836 it could be noted that the main river settlement of Talakchopco (Fort Meade), located at and to the north of the ancient ford of the river, had grown into an "extensive town" containing, with a nearby village, perhaps as many as three hundred log houses. The Indians fueling this growth were the Pease Creek Tallahassees, and their chief was Holata Micco.[11]

Little is known about the Pease Creek Tallahassees apart from the names of several of the towns in which they lived and of several of the warriors who lived in them. By the early 1830s, Minatti, the village at or just to the south of present-day Bartow, may have included the blacks settled near Lake Hancock since Oponay's time. Living there or just to the north on Lake Hancock was Eneha Micco, while the subchief at Minatti was Emathloche (Emathla chee). Perhaps also at Minatti or the colony at Lake

"An Indian Town, Residence of a Chief" drawn by J.F. Gray in 1836 may depict the Peace River town of Talakchopco as it looked prior to its destruction. Gray was a South Carolina volunteer in the Second Seminole War. Courtesy Library of Congress.

Hancock lived the great black chief, Harry, who was to play a major role in events only a few years in the future.[12]

South of Minatti was the town of Tolopchopco (Talakchopco), stretching from the ancient ford at Fort Meade for several miles to the north. Presumably that town was the seat of the Pease Creek Tallahassees, and there Holata Micco would have been headquartered. Possibly there also lived his subchiefs, Mad Lizzard and Hac-to Hal-chee, as well as Holata Micco's brother, Hath-la-po Ha-jo (the All-Conquering Warrior). Just a few miles to the south, opposite Bowlegs Creek, was a third village, Chetuckota, with its subchiefs, Ta Cosa Fiscico and Yaha Fiscico. In addition, Seweky's personal village on Bowlegs Creek was known as Tobasa or Wahoo.[13] To close out the list, the soon-to-be-famous black chief, Gopher John, likewise was connected with the river and was known to some as Pease Creek John.[14]

It was a former resident of the Peace River Valley, however, who was about to focus attention again on the settlements there. That man would ignite a firestorm which, very shortly, would destroy those settlements completely.

The rise of Osceola

It is not known exactly when Osceola, who joined Peter McQueen at Peace River in the aftermath of the First Seminole War, first left the settlement at Talakchopco. It appears, though, that by about 1832 he was living in or near the Big Swamp in the neighborhood of Fort King. He in fact may have lived in the village of Holata Micco because not long after his arrival he recognized the Tallahassee leader as his chief. When Holata Micco left the Big Swamp area, Osceola remained behind and may have begun to represent the chief's interests to authorities at Fort King and the Indian agency.[15]

Osceola first comes to official attention in October 1833 when, in the apparent absence of Holata Micco, he appeared as one of a number of chiefs requesting permission to visit Washington and discuss with the president the whole matter of Seminole emigration. Meanwhile Holata Micco at Peace River pursued a dual policy. While professing support for emigration, he established himself in a location remote from the prying eyes of government officers but close to sources of food and items for trade on the

South Florida hunting grounds, in the line of communication of Seminoles and Creeks coming south for the winter hunt, and near arms, ammunition and other trade goods available through the Cuban fishing ranchos at Charlotte Harbor.[16]

Throughout 1834 pressure increased for the removal of the Indians from Florida. In the Tampa Bay area this desire became particularly acute among settlers who had experienced a growing number of cattle thefts since the Army had withdrawn from Fort Brooke in the summer of 1832. By November 1834, twenty-six Hillsborough County citizens, "aware of the dangerous and very treacherous character of the Indians and the numerous threats held out by them should the Government insist upon their removal," petitioned for the return of the troops to Tampa. The request was granted before the end of the year.[17]

Meanwhile, toward the end of October 1834 at a private council of Indians, a "bold and dashing" Osceola, as yet only a sub-chief, urged resistance to emigration. Meeting shortly thereafter with Indian agent Wiley Thompson, Holata Micco, Osceola's chief, flatly refused to go west, and other chiefs joined him in denouncing the emigration treaties. Six months later another council was held. During that meeting Osceola worked quietly in the background urging resistance to any emigration. As one observer put it, "His presence was felt without being seen." When called upon publicly to explain his opposition to the treaties, Osceola merely stated that his chief, Holata Micco, disapproved of them. Another chief expressed his disapproval more eloquently, stating that "the trees were his body; their branches as his limbs; and the water of the land as his blood." Because of the opposition, U.S. officials decided to delay any attempts at Indian removal until January 1836 at the earliest.[18]

The start of the Second Seminole War

For several months after the April 1835 council, relations between Indians and whites simmered. The heat of summer and several incidents, including the murder of an express mail rider near Fort Brooke on August 11, brought them to a boil. By the end of summer Holata Micco, Osceola, and other Creeks, Seminoles, and blacks were actively preparing for war. One of their first requirements was arms and ammunition. Either fortuitously or through the active collusion of Cubans at the fishing ranchos, the government inspector at Charlotte Harbor was suspended in late July. This paved the way for Spanish traders to enter the bay, and by late in the year they were reported to be landing arms and ammunition for the Indians. A second concern was protection for Indian women and children, as well as for black slaves responsible for growing their food. As soon as the 1835 crops were gathered, many Indians moved their families, cattle, and supplies deep into the peninsula. When Osceola murdered one chief outspoken in favor of emigration, Charley Emathla, on November 26, many of the Indians and blacks remaining in the north rendezvoused at the Big Swamp and Long Swamp and then disappeared. Agent Thompson believed they had retreated "to the wild region on the peninsula of Florida, in the neighborhood of what is called the Everglades." Osceola's family was reported to be at Peace River where others shortly would be concentrated as well.[19]

News of the murder of Charley Emathla stirred white Americans, as well as Indians, to action. At Tampa settlers took refuge at Fort Brooke from the depredations of a band of one hundred Pease Creek warriors under the black war chief, Harry, who had begun a campaign of plunder and arson in the vicinity. For their own protection, about thirty of the refugees at Fort Brooke formed a ranger company to patrol roads near the post, an action reflecting accurately the weakness of the garrison.[20]

In the meantime, militia companies were being formed to the north of the Indian reservation. On December 17, 1835, a battalion of volunteers under the command of Col. John Warren, raised principally in the area of Duval, Columbia, Hamilton, and Alachua counties and including many men who would pioneer the settlement of the Peace River Valley, was ordered to scour the country southeast from Paynes Prairie. The following day the battalion's baggage train, which had been detached from the main force, was crossing to the south of the Alachua prairie near Black Point when it was attacked and captured by Osceola. Those members of the small guard party not killed in the attack retreated until they encountered Maj. John McLemore, who attempted to reengage the hostiles with the remainder of his company [see appendix 3]. Only a few of McLemore's men advanced with him, however, and they were forced to retreat. Two days later when the Indians were again discovered, Warren's entire command attacked, and the fighting continued for almost an hour. Eventually the Indians fled, and the militiamen were able to recover some of their papers and cooking utensils. The ammunition and stores remained the prize of Osceola.[21]

Thus passed the first two engagements of the Second Seminole War. In both instances, citizen soldiers from the frontier areas to the north of the Indian reservation clashed with Indian and black warriors under the command of Osceola. Many of those white settlers, or members of their families, had fought the Seminoles more than twenty years earlier during the Patriot War and in only a few more years would become pioneers of South Florida and the Peace River Valley. On both sides this personal struggle, begun so long ago, would become over the next twenty years even more bitter and personal, and its scene would be the Peace River Valley.

The destruction of Talakchopco

Over the four months following the Battle of Black Point the Seminole War accelerated. On December 28, Osceola and his party attacked the Indian agency at Fort King and murdered agent Wiley Thompson and others. Little more than fifty miles to the south, the Seminole chiefs Micanopy and Alligator with 180 followers massacred a relief column under Maj. Francis L. Dade on its way to Fort King. Three days thereafter the Indians struck again. At a crossing of the Withlacoochee River, Osceola, wearing a U.S. Army coat, led 220 Indians and 30 black warriors against Gen. Duncan L. Clinch and about 750 men, 500 of whom were Florida volunteers including those serving under Col. John Warren. After fighting for more than an hour Clinch was forced to withdraw, and the Indians again were victorious.[22]

War and destruction raged throughout Florida for the next two months, although no major engagement was fought. Then, on February 27, 1836, the Indians and their black allies again attacked on the Withlacoochee, their prey this time a column under the command of Gen. Edmund P. Gaines. For over a week the Indians besieged Gaines's hastily fortified position. After Gaines had begun negotiating with the Indians, relief arrived and the Indians and blacks retired into the woods.[23]

While the hostiles parleyed with General Gaines, the remainder of their women, children, and slaves moved to join the others who had sought haven below Peace River and Lake Tohopekaliga. In early April this information reached Gen. Winfield Scott, then commanding in Florida, from a half-blood Spaniard captured near Charlotte Harbor who confessed to having traded supplies to the Indians. The Spaniard told Scott that the Indian women, children, blacks, and plunder were concentrated at the head of Peace River. On the condition that his life be spared, he offered to lead the army there. He also may have suggested that Osceola was at the river, prepared to make a desperate stand.[24]

Present when this news was received was James Gadsden who proposed to General Scott that an expedition be sent to Peace River to capture the Indian families and slaves and to destroy their settlements. As the plan developed, five hundred mounted South Carolina volunteers under Col. Robert H. Goodwyn were to travel directly to the main Indian settlements on Peace River. Simultaneously, Louisiana volunteers under Col. Persifor F. Smith would ascend the river from Charlotte Harbor, destroy all settlements found, and, ultimately, make a juncture with the South Carolinians.[25]

As fine a plan as it was, Scott's scheme had certain major flaws. Both the South Carolinians and the Louisianians were nearing the end of their enlistments and were very tired. They had been marching and, to some extent, fighting for several months and were beset with food, forage, and medical problems. Additionally, they were being asked to coordinate a simultaneous movement of two columns over several hundred miles of untracked wilderness, a task requiring close support of the U.S. Navy as well as the army. It was too much to ask.[26]

Colonel Goodwyn immediately grasped the problems inherent in his mission and approached General Scott with a request that he and his men be excused. When that request was refused, the South Carolinian attempted to execute his orders, but trouble plagued him from the start. On the morning of April 14 Goodwyn and his men left Fort Brooke for Peace River. Only a few miles along the way Goodwyn's men mistook some campfire smoke for Indians and poured a volley of fire into fellow South Carolina volunteers. Compounding this disastrous start, the battalion's horses, suffering from lack of forage, were unable to carry their riders, and the mounted volunteers, leading the animals, were required to walk to Peace River carrying on their backs haversacks loaded with eight days' provisions. By the time the column arrived at Talakchopco (present-day Fort Meade) on April 16 the Indians, blacks, and supplies were long gone. A frustrated and impatient Goodwyn, surveying the site that had meant so much in the past decades to Seminole and Red Stick refugees, ordered Talakchopco burned. He then crossed the river where his men discovered in the river swamp an Indian fort made of brush. The South Carolinians quickly destroyed the fort and another "town of considerable size" they chanced upon nearby. Without hesitation, the exhausted troops then turned back to the west to rejoin fellow South Carolinians at Fort Alabama on the Hillsborough River. They arrived there after dark on April 18, four months after the Battle of Black Point.[27]

On the same day, Persifor Smith and the Louisianians began their ascent of Peace River. Setting out with half their force marching by land and half traveling by water, the column made only twelve miles before Smith decided it was impractical to proceed as planned. Offering anyone who wanted to turn back the opportunity, Smith was left with 152 men. This remaining force proceeded for two days, mainly using canoes, until it arrived at a lovely spot that the volunteers named Live Oak Camp and where they found the remains of a deserted village. Along the route, a detachment under Capt. Hezekiah Thistle explored Horse Creek for about eight miles into the interior. After a night's rest at Live Oak Camp, the Louisianians left their boats and began a march up the south side of the river. For two more days the troops marched, occasionally seeing signs of former Indian settlements. On April 21 they forded the river to the north bank and continued their march. The following day, at a point that Smith figured was fifty-two miles above Charlotte Harbor, the expedition ran out of food and turned back to the south.[28]

By April 25, 1836, Colonel Smith and the Louisiana volunteers were back at Tampa Bay awaiting transport home.[29] At Peace River they had fought no desperate Indians, destroyed no Indian towns, and captured no black slaves. The one positive thing Persifor Smith could claim was the discovery which many other white Americans would make in the years to come. "The country," Smith reported, "seems favorable for the pasturage of cattle."[30]

Almost as an anticlimax, one final effect of the opening of the Second Seminole War was realized in South Florida by the end of April 1836—all troops were withdrawn from Charlotte Harbor and about one hundred individuals connected with the fishing ranchos were transported to Tampa Bay to begin their lives and work anew. The great Cuban fishing ranchos, which had played so prominent a role in the history of South Florida for the past eighty years, were left deserted.[31]

During the first six years of the 1830s, the Peace River Valley experienced a radical swing from substantial growth due to Indian immigration to the destruction of her oldest settlements by U.S. military might. The growth during the early 1830s centered around the return of the Tallahassee creeks, principally under the chief Holata Micco, to the place that had offered them haven after the First Seminole War. The destruction came in the early days of a war brought about in great part by the actions and leadership of the Red Stick, Billy Powell, who had been one of those early refugees and who, by the 1830s, had grown to manhood as Osceola. The first serious encounters of that war pitted Indian and black allies under leaders nurtured at Peace River against white frontiersmen, many of whom had direct ties to the violent Indian struggles of the Patriot War of 1812–1814. These foes were to meet again and again in conflicts that would result in the permanent settlement of the Peace River Valley. In April 1836, however, six years of war remained before the first steps toward that settlement could be undertaken.

4

Conclusion of the
Second Seminole War

T HE SECOND SEMINOLE WAR began in December 1835 in great
part through the leadership of a Tallahassee warrior,
Osceola, who had found in his youth a home and haven on
Peace River. Within only a few months, however, Osceola's war
had visited fire and destruction upon the very Peace River town
that had welcomed him. In the end, the presence at Peace River of
Seminole, Tallahassee, and black warriors was obliterated, and in
their place appeared the roads and encampments of the U.S.
Army.

General Jesup's Fort Dade Treaty

After the campaigns of April and May 1836, which included
the army descent upon Peace River and the burning of Talakchopco, the Second Seminole War settled for the rest of the year
into a series of relatively small engagements. Many of them
involved North Florida militiamen who themselves or through
their descendants were to pioneer the Peace River area. An
unusual instance took place beginning April 12 when a group of
fifty Florida volunteers from the command of Maj. John McLemore, head of the Columbia Volunteers, was besieged by approx-

imately five hundred Indians near the mouth of the Withlacoochee River for more than forty-eight days. Although most of the volunteers were rescued, the survivors declared that the regular army had abandoned them, a portent of ill feelings to come.[1]

By early December 1836 the Florida war had a new commander, Gen. Thomas Sidney Jesup. Upon taking command, Jesup analyzed the disposition of the hostiles arrayed against him. Osceola and bands of Tallahassees, Mikasukies, and blacks reportedly were secreted near the Withlacoochee River, while the Pease Creek Tallahassees and their leader Holata Micco had returned to Peace River where they easily could monitor any movement of troops to the east out of Fort Brooke and where their black slaves could continue to grow and harvest desperately needed food. Large concentrations of Seminoles and captured blacks were said to be near Lake Tohopekaliga, however, and it was in that direction that Jesup decided to make his move, destroying in the opening months of 1837 numerous Indian settlements and capturing hundreds of cattle, horses, and mules.[2] Jesup's action brought the Seminole chiefs to the peace table. At Fort Dade (Dade City) on March 6, 1837, several principal chiefs, though not including Osceola or other Tallahassee chiefs, agreed to cease hostilities and emigrate from Florida. By April 10 the Indians were to withdraw south of the Hillsborough River where they would be furnished provisions until transport could be arranged for them.[3]

For three months after the Fort Dade agreement was signed, Indians and blacks gathered for emigration, principally at two large camps near Tampa. Not all Indians came quickly, however, nor did they all gather at Tampa. Before Micanopy, the leading Seminole chief, decided to come in, for instance, he held a council at Peace River on April 2. The meeting must have been punctuated with argument because, although Micanopy shortly moved to one of the camps at Tampa, Holata Micco boldly entered Fort Brooke on April 5 and announced to General Jesup's face that, although he was for peace, he would not emigrate.[4] A number of Holata Micco's band had second thoughts, though, for on May 23 several of them appeared at Tampa with seventeen of their slaves. Osceola and others, opting for a middle road, came in at Fort Mellon (Sanford), explaining their appearance so far from the port of emigration as being required by the need to sell their cattle.[5]

The euphoria surrounding General Jesup's peace came crashing down on June 2, 1837. Eighty warriors, led by Coacoochee and Alligator, swooped down on the camps at Tampa and led away with them Micanopy and many of the others awaiting emigration. The entire party traveled almost due east across Peace River to the Kissimmee, where the Indians concentrated in two large camps, one of Mikasukies on the west side of the St. Johns River two days march south from Fort Mellon, and one centered on Micanopy and the Seminoles east of the Kissimmee. One band of Tallahassees encamped northeast of Micanopy's men, and Micanopy sent for Holata Micco and the other Pease Creek Tallahassees to join him on the Kissimmee.[6]

At this effrontery Jesup and most Floridians were enraged. "Our southeastern frontier is again to be desolated," the St. Augustine *Herald* declared. "Many of the planters and small farmers in Madison, Hamilton, Columbia, Alachua, and Mosqueto," it concluded, "had returned to their homes, which they must now, for the third time, abandon to the brand of Osceola and his warriors." Although military action on the general's part would have to wait until the end of summer, immediately he took one step which was to have long-term repercussions. On June 11 he handed the Florida Cracker volunteers a license to steal. "There is no obligation to spare the property of the Indians, they have not spared that of the citizens," Jesup wrote. "Their negroes, cattle and horses, as well as other property they possess, will belong to the corps by which they are captured." For the first time, the U.S. Army had turned Florida volunteers loose on the Indians and blacks.[7]

Fort Fraser and the Battle of Okeechobee

Over the summer of 1837 General Jesup prepared to take his revenge on the Indians for the escape of June 2, and by early August he had pinpointed the Indian concentrations on the St. Johns and Kissimmee rivers, as well as the presence of captured and runaway blacks between the St. Johns and Kissimmee rivers and of Indian blacks on the Kissimmee, Caloosahatchee, and

Peace rivers. In addition, Jesup had learned that the settlements on Peace River, Indian and black, had come to encompass the entire river valley as far north as the present Polk-Hardee county line. With this information, Jesup developed a comprehensive plan for attack which relied, in great part, on the actions of two columns: Col. Zachary Taylor would be sent from Tampa to the Kissimmee River to seek out and destroy the hostiles there; and Col. Persifor Smith, back again in Florida, would ascend the Caloosahatchee to the falls and attack the Indians and blacks in that quarter.[8]

One problem for Jesup and Taylor lay in locating the most desirable route from Tampa to the Kissimmee. For this information they turned to three captives held at the garrison at Fort Brooke: the black chiefs Abraham and Murray and the Seminole Billy Bowlegs.[9] Before the information obtained from them could be put to use, however, other and far more important prisoners were taken. On October 20 in the vicinity of Six Mile Creek near Fort Brooke a returning patrol stumbled across and captured Holata Micco, one of his subchiefs, and a third warrior. The chief of the Pease Creek Tallahassees was placed in irons pending transportation to the west. The following day near St. Augustine an ill and suffering Osceola, with seventy of his warriors, was seized under a white flag of truce. Neither Osceola nor his chief, Holata Micco, would fight another day in Florida.[10]

Flushed with the success of these captures, Jesup put his campaign plans into effect. By mid-November Lt. Col. William S. Foster was on the old path from Fort Brooke to Oponay's former plantation with orders to construct a stockade and supply depot on Peace River and a substantial bridge over the river itself. Foster selected as the site for his stockade a slight elevation dotted with live oaks just to the west of Saddle Creek at the point where the creek flowed out of Lake Hancock. Over the creek he constructed a bridge and causeway some three hundred feet long. By the time Colonel Taylor and eighty wagonloads of supplies reached the river on November 29, Foster's men had completed their task and the new fort had been named in honor of Capt. Upton S. Fraser, a victim of the Dade massacre.[11]

Pausing at Fort Fraser only long enough to deposit his supplies and reorganize his men and equipment, Taylor pushed on to the east with the bulk of his army. At Buffalo Ford, near present-day

Waverly, he constructed a four-hundred-foot bridge. From there he proceeded to the Kissimmee where he arrived on December 3.[12] Over the next several weeks Taylor's troops established their camp on the Kissimmee, named Fort Gardner, and reconnoitered the area to the south and southwest. By December 18 the colonel had issued orders to move his force against the Indians and blacks on Peace River. At the last minute, however, Taylor changed his mind and ordered his men down the Kissimmee. On Christmas Day, the soldiers met the Florida Indians in combat near Lake Okeechobee. Twenty-six soldiers were killed and 112 wounded. The Indian allies lost 11 killed and 14 wounded. Because the Indians left the field after fighting ceased, the Battle of Okeechobee has been called a U.S. victory. It was the last large pitched battle of the Second Seminole War.[13]

Although Zachary Taylor had turned away from Peace River on December 19, his campaign continued to have an impact there. Late in December the colonel dispatched Maj. George W. Allen and several mounted companies to rendezvous with Colonel Smith on the Caloosahatchee River. Once that mission was accomplished, Allen turned north and, carefully investigating the area, made his way by January 8, 1838, to Fort Fraser.[14]

That outpost was garrisoned, in part, by 140 Pennsylvania volunteers commanded by Capt. Hezekiah L. Thistle, the same Captain Thistle who had explored Horse Creek for Persifor Smith in April 1836. Since their arrival at the river just before the Battle of Okeechobee, Thistle's men had been engaged in road and bridge building to the east and had scouted to within ten or twelve miles of Alligator's camp near Lake Istokpoga. Among their accomplishments was the construction of a bridge about eight miles east of Fort Fraser. Permitting north-south travel down the eastern side of the stream, this first bridge over Peace River was known for decades as Thistle's Bridge.[15]

From late December 1837 to late May 1838 Fort Fraser saw a steady stream of wounded and sick soldiers and captured Indians, horses, and cattle. By May 4, 1838, Zachary Taylor had returned to the post and established about four miles to the west a headquarters which he designated Camp Walker. There and at Fort Fraser were 325 Indians and 30 blacks awaiting emigration. After a stay of about three weeks spent collecting the last of his captives, Taylor abandoned Camp Walker and returned to Fort

The Seminole chief Alligator, who lived for a time before 1835 on the Peace River, was believed by Army officials to be the brother of Billy Bowlegs. Portrait by George Catlin is in the Smithsonian Institution. Courtesy Florida Photographic Collection, Florida State Archives.

Brooke. Shortly thereafter Fort Fraser was closed, an action which Taylor had recommended two months earlier with the rationale that "Peas Creek in the opinion of the Medical Gentlemen would be a perfect grave yard & that not ten men in a hundred would survive in summer there."[16]

A cordon of forts

On May 15, 1838, Thomas S. Jesup surrendered command of the U.S. forces in Florida to Zachary Taylor. Jesup's contribution to the war effort, through the use of aggressive military operations and seizures in defiance of flags of truce, had netted about 2,900 captives and an additional 100 Indians killed. When Taylor brought in Alligator late in April, the two commanders had made an almost clean sweep of the Seminole leadership. The Mikasukies and Tallahassees fiercely continued to resist emigration, however, and with the remaining Seminoles and a few renegade Creeks they constituted a continuing menace to the white settlers in Florida.[17]

Zachary Taylor was cut from a different bolt of cloth than his predecessor in command. Having personally disapproved of the policy of forcible removal, he adopted a much more pacific course after Jesup's departure. Taylor felt the Indians should be driven south of a line running from St. Augustine to Garey's Ferry on the Oklawaha River and from there along the road from Fort King (Ocala) to Tampa Bay. North of that line settlement was to be encouraged by the placement of numerous centrally located garrisons.[18]

While Colonel Taylor awaited approval of his plans, isolated Indian attacks aroused alarm and calls for protection from white settlers, especially those in Alachua and Columbia counties. Frontier settlers came more and more to believe that their protection lay with local militia companies, rather than with the regular army [see appendix 4]. Taylor, barely concealing his contempt for the volunteers, refused to place any reliance upon them. The Indians, to round out the equation, increasingly avoided contact with the regular army and began to concentrate their assaults on Cracker settlers and militia units.[19]

Taylor reacted to this situation by deciding to further separate frontiersmen and Indians. Specifically, he determined that his new line of demarcation across the peninsula should run from New Smyrna to Fort Brooke, a considerable distance south of the old. To anchor this line he ordered the creation of a road and line of posts linking the two points. On January 7, 1839, Col. Alexander Cummings, with three companies of artillery and two of infantry, marched out of Fort Brooke toward the old Indian town of Itchepuckesassa (Plant City). There he constructed a fort 110 feet square with two blockhouses and two storehouses, which he christened Fort Sullivan on January 23. A few days earlier Cummings had instructed Maj. DeLafayette Wilcox to proceed in the direction of Fort Maitland (Maitland) and to establish posts every twenty or thirty miles along the way. Wilcox complied by establishing Fort Cummings (Lake Alfred) twenty miles to the east on January 22 and Fort Davenport (Davenport) twenty miles farther along shortly thereafter. The road to connect Fort Brooke with Fort Davenport required the construction of five bridges and numerous causeways.[20]

The road from Fort Brooke to Fort Davenport was not the only one blazed early in 1839. On February 9 Col. William Davenport was ordered to transfer his command by overland march from Fort Davenport to the Caloosahatchee. The following day he left for Fort Cummings to replenish his supplies. On the morning of February 12 he set out on the thirteen-mile march south to Peace River where he built a new bridge over Saddle Creek and rebuilt Thistle's Bridge to the east. From February 14 to 19 the colonel led his column south from Thistle's Bridge to the Caloosahatchee. His route paralleled that of Captain Allen one year earlier to a point near Lake Istokpoga, where he veered to the east around the headwaters of Fisheating Creek, following the same Indian trail used by P.B. Prior on his 1833 cattle drive. From Fisheating Creek the column turned southwest until it arrived at Fort T.B. Adams near the falls of the Caloosahatchee. The road that Davenport followed from Thistle's Bridge to the Caloosahatchee, together with the more direct route of Captain Allen, was the main north-south route down the east side of Peace River for the remainder of the nineteenth century. For twenty years it bore the name Davenport's Road.[21]

Just as Zachary Taylor's plans were falling into place a new variable, Gen. Alexander Macomb, entered the picture. Macomb was the highest ranking general in the army and, on March 18, 1839, was ordered by the secretary of war to Florida with broad discretion to do whatever was necessary to end the war. Sensing the war was a no-win situation, Macomb called a peace conference. The main Indian representative to the conference was a Seminole, Chitto Tustenuggee, whom the army held out to be the recently elected principal chief of the Seminoles and Mikasukies and whom Indian agent John Casey later would describe as the close relative or brother of Billy Bowlegs. By May 22 Macomb had won an agreement from the Indians present to withdraw south of Peace River within the next two months. At some time in the fall, so the agreement stated, a great council was to be held on the river at which time further arrangements were to be made. In the meantime, Chitto Tustenuggee asked that a store be established for the Indians on Peace River.[22]

The peace promised by General Macomb's treaty did not endure for long. In July a detachment of twenty-six men under Lt. Col. William S. Harney was dispatched to the Caloosahatchee River to open the promised trading store.[23] Some 15 or 20 miles upstream, Harney and his men were attacked on the night of July 23, 1839, by a Seminole war party under the command of Micanopy's half-brother, Chakaika, and including Chitto Tustenuggee's brother, Billy Bowlegs. In the resulting carnage only fourteen men, including Colonel Harney, escaped. The meaning of the attack was clear —the remnants of the Cowkeeper dynasty, the most powerful of Seminole families, had rejected peace bought at the price of emigration.[24]

Armistead and Worth in the Peace River Valley

For the remaining months of Zachary Taylor's command in Florida, war dragged on in a stalemate punctuated by frequent atrocities. As public opinion outside the territory turned against the war, members of the regular army became disenchanted and Florida volunteers refused to serve away from their homes. Only a month before Taylor received permission on April 21, 1840, to leave his Florida command, future Confederate general Joseph E. Johnston described the situation: "The state of military affairs in that territory is disgusting in the extreme."[25]

To remedy the Florida debacle Gen. Walker Keith Armistead was named by the secretary of war to replace Zachary Taylor. Armistead's plan was to divide the Florida peninsula by an east-west line running through Fort King (Ocala). In a reversal of Taylor's opposition to the use of citizen volunteers, Armistead decided to turn over the defense of the area north of his line to the Floridians and to concentrate his own forces to the south. By late 1840 his plan had been approved and transformed into action.[26]

At the resumption of operations in mid-November 1840 Armistead authorized the establishment of a post, afterwards named Fort Armistead, on Sarasota Bay. The location was chosen to facilitate operations against Seminoles and Mikasukies believed to be living from Peace River south through the Big Cypress Swamp to the Everglades. From Indians found near Charlotte Harbor it was learned that several Peace River bands had fled inland at the sight of the troops, including that of Hospetarke.[27] A delegation of Indians brought from the west attempted to open negotiations, as did Armistead himself on a visit to Peace River and Charlotte Harbor early in January 1841. Slowly a few Indians did come in at Fort Armistead and, on March 20, Billy Bowlegs arrived for a twelve-day chat. All the while, however, Hospetarke refused to come in from his camp at Peace River.[28]

While these efforts continued at Sarasota and on the southern reaches of Peace River, other events were taking place at the northern end. Late in January 1841 Armistead dispatched Col. William Jenkins Worth into the interior from Fort Brooke to make contact with bands under Coacoochee and the Mikasuki chief Arpeika (Sam Jones). Although Worth's efforts were frustrated by high water, he established a supply depot a mile west of Fort Fraser, which he named Fort Carroll, and ordered the reestablishment of Fort Cummings.[29] At the newly reopened Fort Cummings, one-half mile west of its former location, Worth met in private conference with Coacoochee on March 5, 1841. In return for a secret bribe of $4,000 and other considerations, Coacoochee agreed to emigrate with his people. By early April Fort Cummings again was abandoned, although it served temporarily that summer as a point for collecting the members of Coacoochee's band. At Tampa early in August, Worth (by then commander in Florida) reported possession of all the Indians "West of Pease Creek, Ochechobee &c." East of Peace River was another matter entirely. Many Indians still found refuge there, Hospetarke prominent among them.[30]

On July 11, 1841, a detachment was posted on the southern bank of Peace River about twenty miles from its mouth.[31] The post, Camp Ogden, was named for Edmund Augustus Ogden, the assistant quartermaster at Fort Brooke. It was located near Hospetarke's village and was intended to serve both as an advance position facing the Indians to the east and south and as a convenient spot for obtaining materials for canoes to be used in future operations. Only six days after the camp was established a party of Indians arrived there claiming protection. On their heels was a war party from the south that fired on a wood-cutting detail near the camp and killed one soldier. The Indians seeking protection were saved and, later, taken to Tampa for emigration.[32]

In pursuit of Hospetarke, Colonel Worth arrived at Camp Ogden on August 25. With the colonel was his new ally, Coacoochee, who had already arranged to meet Hospetarke at his village near the camp. Before sunset that day Coacoochee had returned with Hospetarke, and an indecisive council was held. Worth's patience at that point appears to have been exhausted, and on the following afternoon he lured the chief and his warriors on board the government vessel anchored in the river and seized them. On October 12, 1841, Coacoochee and Hospetarke, with their warriors, women, and children, were emigrated from Tampa. The camp on Peace River already had been broken up.[33]

The end of the war

During the year following the seizure of Hospetarke at Camp Ogden, the final act of the Second Seminole War was played out in small incidents and engagements all over the territory of Florida. Bit by bit the strength of the Indians was reduced as their numbers grew smaller and their homes and fields were destroyed. By February 1842 Colonel Worth estimated that only 301 Indians remained.[34]

Of Colonel Worth's 301 Indians, 60 Seminoles were believed to be living along the Kissimmee River under the chief Assinwa. Early in 1842 a force commanded by Maj. William G. Belknap, guided by the now-friendly Alligator, was ordered to march north from the Everglades to Lake Istokpoga to induce those holdouts to emigrate. By February 18 Belknap was headquartered at Fort Cummings, having repaired Thistle's Bridge where he established a base camp designated Camp McCall in honor of his fellow soldier and friend, George A. McCall. Early in March Belknap finally arranged an interview with one of the chiefs of Assinwa's band, Tustenuggee Chopco, who agreed to surrender with 41 of his people on March 15. On that date, when the Indians did not arrive at the prescribed point on Davenport's

Road fifteen miles below Thistle's Bridge, Belknap pursued and captured 27 of them. By March 22 the major, his men, and his captives had withdrawn to Fort Brooke and, for the Peace River Valley, the Second Seminole War was over.[35]

On August 5, 1842, Billy Bowlegs, the recognized chief of the Florida Seminoles by that time, met in conference at Tampa with Colonel Worth. At that meeting Bowlegs accepted Worth's offer of peace and his condition that the Indians withdraw to the reservation south of the Peace River, first agreed to by General Macomb in 1839. Although Bowlegs at first objected to the inclusion of the few remaining Creeks and Tallahassees within the limits of the reservation, their representatives approved the agreement at Cedar Key on August 12. Two days later, August 14, 1842, William Jenkins Worth declared the Second Seminole War at an end.[36]

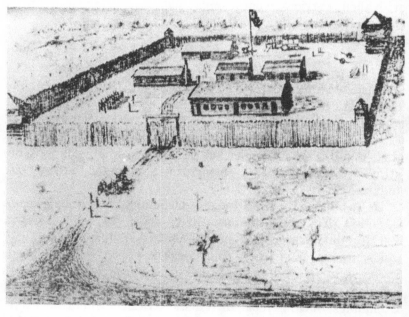

This drawing by James C. Buchanan is reported to be Fort Fraser, erected just north of Bartow in 1837. From *DeVane's Early Florida History*, 2:163.

The return of the Tallahassees

Fifteen months later the final band of hostiles gave themselves up. In the best traditions of their fathers, the Red Stick Creeks, this tiny band of Creeks and Tallahassees had held out until November 1843. Numbering only about twenty warriors, they slowly made their way south into the reservation. Their chief was Halpatter Tustenuggee, and among the band were two brothers, Cotsa Fixico Chopco and Echo Emathla Chopco, whose father had died fighting Andrew Jackson in 1818. As boys, they had moved with Peter McQueen to the refuge at Talakchopco,[37] and in years to come they again would live at Peace River with the other members of their band. Many of them would fight and die there.

The Second Seminole War ended the first long chapter of life on the River of Peace in the nineteenth century. The great Indian cattle herds on the South Florida ranges had been decimated and the few Indians allowed to remain pressed into the Everglades. No longer a symbol of life and freedom in 1842, the river represented the line that separated white frontiersmen and surviving Indians, nursing the pains and grudges of generations of conflict.

Part Two

"The society of a frontier"
(1842–1858)

5

The Frontier Moves
to South Florida

WHEN GEN. WILLIAM J. WORTH declared the end of the Second
Seminole War on August 14, 1842, the Peace River Valley
lay deserted. Particularly on the high fertile lands which
ran on both sides of the river from below present-day Fort Meade
to the vicinity of Oponay's old plantation north of abandoned Fort
Fraser, the Indian and black settlements that had dotted its
landscape lay in ruin, their former inhabitants killed, transported
to the west, or establishing more secure refuges further down the
peninsula. Over the next decade the vacuum created by the
forced departure of the Indians and their black allies attracted to
South Florida hundreds of families from the old North Florida
counties of Alachua, Columbia, and Hamilton. The influx of these
families into the area eventually resulted in pressures for the
final removal of the Seminoles, Tallahassees, and Mikasukies
from Florida, which culminated in the outbreak and prosecution
of the Third Seminole or Billy Bowlegs war.

Along the Suwannee after the Seminole War

In April 1842, Alachua, Columbia, and Hamilton counties, the
home of scores of future Peace River settlers, lay in desolation

from the Seminole War. Since December 1835 the lives of these settlers had been disrupted and in many cases filled with terror and tragedy. The experiences of those years left many frontiersmen and their families unprepared to reassume their former lives after peace was declared.

The seed of the frontiersmen's problem lay in an emergency measure taken six years before in the opening days of the Second Seminole War. In early 1836 the Congress had authorized the issuance of rations from public stores to Florida inhabitants driven from their homes by Indian depredations. The assistance thus provided desperately was needed by many but, within nineteen months, abuses had forced the War Department to place substantial restrictions on the program. Of particular importance to the future, the new regulations barred assistance to the family of any able-bodied man who refused to enter militia service or do such other work as assigned to him.[1]

As might be imagined, the requirement of militia service for rations spurred a widespread desire for soldiering, even when unnecessary, on the part of Florida frontiersmen. That service had its downside as well. "If mustered into service, each man inevitably leaves his home unprotected," wrote one Seminole War veteran. "While absent, solicitous for the safety of others, his own dwelling may be fired and his family murdered," he added, "[and] his farm, from which he draws his daily food, becomes a barren waste, and the habits of industry, which have grown with his growth, become enervated by pernicious example. Indolence is as well rewarded as patient toil, his daily pay is as much when spent in vice and slothfulness as when usefully engaged, and that zeal which should stimulate him in his new vocation is weakened by a consciousness, that, when executing his duty, he is liable to the fate of a soldier, and knows, and feels too, that when snugly in camp, participating in the revels of a militia force, he is free from all danger." The disenchanted veteran concluded with the sad comment, "The society of a frontier once thrown from its axis, revolves in disorder until it is lost in ignorance, slothfulness, and vice."[2]

By mid-1841, after the families of North Florida militiamen had enjoyed the benefits of army provisions for a great part of the previous five years, the army adopted a new policy. Its purpose was to minimize costs and to stablilize the frontier area by encouraging settlers to return to their farms or, in the case of persons without farms or from outside Florida, to settle at new locations on the frontier. Arms and ammunition were issued to the settlers, along with monthly rations until such time as the farms were reestablished and self-sufficient. For the duration of the program, thirty-two groupings of settlements were supported, including one on the Manatee River.[3]

The army did not intend to continue supplying rations indefinitely and early in 1842 notified settlers that provisions would not be issued after crops were harvested that summer. Six years of dependence on the government for subsistence had turned many settlers away from the idea of farm work, however, and few North Floridians prepared for planting. An army officer writing from the Columbia and Hamilton county area that spring reported: "Many of these people are too idle and indolent to labor for the means of subsistence; many live by hunting and fishing; and hence the distress of these inhabitants, and their desire to get into service for a maintenance. They are but little improved beyond the Indians themselves."[4]

Faced with the threatened loss of government subsistence, some Suwannee River area settlers did try to get back into government service. Throughout the late winter and early spring reports were circulated of terrible Indian atrocities in Columbia County, along with demands for the formation of new militia companies. When these reports proved false, on June 6, 1842, orders were issued specifying that no further subsistence would be issued after August 31 [see appendix 5].[5]

At the same time North Florida settlers were being notified that rations no longer would be available, a bill was introduced in the Congress to authorize the grant of 160-acre parcels of Florida land to settlers willing to live on and protect their homesteads. This Armed Occupation Act, which was approved in final form on August 4, 1842, permitted settlements from present-day Gainesville south to Peace River and the Seminole reservation. A claimant had to be eighteen and able to bear arms. The law required him to make an actual settlement by August 4, 1843, to "erect thereon a house fit for the habitation of man," to clear and cultivate at least five acres, and to reside on the land for five years.

The act excluded persons owning 160 acres or more of land and prohibited settlements within two miles of a fort or on any coastal island.[6]

For many serious farmers and planters the provisions of the Armed Occupation Act offered little incentive.[7] The lands subject to settlement in most cases were remote from markets for farm products, and the 160-acre limitation on land ownership excluded many large planters. For North Florida frontiersmen who had turned away from farming and toward cattle for a livelihood, however, the act offered possibilities.

Cattle had been an interest of North Floridians since the first American settlements in the area. Before 1835, the broad uninhabited expanses of Columbia, Hamilton, and Alachua counties, in particular, offered a hospitable environment for cattle ranging. The Second Seminole War tended to turn settlers away from farming and to provide a substantial incentive for turning toward cattle. Particularly important was Gen. Thomas S. Jesup's order of June 11, 1837, which granted a license to Florida militiamen to take from the Seminoles their "negroes, cattle and horses, as well as other property they possess." Statistics are not available as to the numbers of Indian cattle seized, but it may be assumed that any number of Florida cattle holdings were begun or supplemented in that manner.[8]

By 1842, then, Florida frontiersmen increasingly were attracted to cattle raising. At the same time, possibilities for that industry in the Suwannee River area were declining as new settlers pushed into the area determined to make a life based upon producing cotton with slave labor. With this new population came a different economic, social, and political life and a corresponding drop in opportunity and influence on the part of many earlier settlers. Many frontiersmen saw the Armed Occupation Act as a godsend and moved south where lay immense open range lands and storied herds of wild cattle. As the changes in North Florida's economy and social life intensified in the 1840s, many of their relatives, friends, and neighbors decided to join them.[9]

About thirteen hundred permits for settlement under the Armed Occupation Act were issued during the one-year period beginning August 4, 1842. While most of these settlements were substantially north of the Peace River area, a considerable number were just west of the river's headwaters, particularly in the area stretching from Lake Thonotosassa to the site of the former Indian town of Itchepuckesassa and nearby Fort Sullivan (Plant City), then south to the Alafia River and west toward that river's mouth [see appendix 6]. For settlers planning a life in the cattle business, these sites were located ideally in relation to the Alafia and Myakka ranges to the south and east.[10]

Two Armed Occupation Act settlers would play major roles in the settlement of the Peace River Valley. Rigdon Brown, born about 1790, had moved by the mid-1820s from Camden County, Georgia, to Nassau County, Florida, where in March 1826 he was appointed a justice of the peace. Before leaving Georgia he married Joseph Howell's sister, Esther, and by 1824 the couple had two sons: William, born about 1820 in Georgia; and Rigdon H., born in Florida about 1824. In 1830 the family was living in that portion of Alachua County soon to become Columbia County, and there during the next five years Rigdon Brown plunged into politics. In October 1835 he was elected to a seat on the Florida Territorial Council. In his home precinct, where he lost only two votes, Brown was supported by friends and neighbors including Jesse Pennington, Burris Brewer, William Wiggins, William Pennington, Maxfield Whidden, Willoughby Whidden, and Joseph Howell. Choosing not to run for re-election in 1836 and 1837, Brown unsuccessfully sought election in 1838 as a delegate to the Florida Constitutional Convention and in 1839 attempted, also unsuccessfully, to regain his seat on the council. In the latter effort he enjoyed the support, in addition to that of the men mentioned above, of John Green, Rabun Raulerson, Charles Scott, Charles Whittemore, Jacob J. Blount, and others, all of whom soon were to play active roles in the settlement of South Florida.[11]

Politically frustrated at the close of the Seminole War and faced with changing economic and political dynamics in Columbia County, by December 1842 Rigdon Brown and his family had moved their home and cattle to Itchepuckesassa where he had selected an Armed Occupation Act homestead. Once in Hillsborough County, increasingly surrounded by his friends and former supporters, Brown's political star again began to rise. By the summer of 1848 he would become chairman of the combined Democratic senatorial convention for Hillsborough, Hernando, and Levy counties and, shortly thereafter, a true pioneer of the Peace River Valley.[12]

William Brinton Hooker (1800–1871), a man of public and business affairs, was South Florida's ":cattle king" before the Civil War. Courtesy Kyle S. VanLandingham.

A contemporary of Rigdon Brown's, James W. Whidden was born in 1790, and, like Brown, grew to maturity in Camden County, Georgia. He married Mary Altman in 1818 and moved in December 1830 to Hamilton County, Florida. Thereafter, while his brothers Maxfield and Willoughby continued their friendship in Columbia County with Rigdon Brown, James appears to have become associated with cattleman William B. Hooker. By late 1838 James was elected second lieutenant of North's company, Florida Mounted Volunteers, a command which included Reading, Riley, and Jacob J. Blount, as well as numerous other soon-to-be South Florida pioneers. In February 1839 Whidden's daughter, Tempie, married Noel Rabun Raulerson on the Suwannee River, and four years later another daughter, Mary Ann, married William L. Campbell in Hamilton County. Shortly thereafter Whidden moved his family to his Armed Occupation Act claim north of the Alafia River. After five years Whidden would become along with Rigdon Brown one of the first two white American pioneers to establish homes in the Peace River Valley.[13]

Growth on the Hillsborough County frontier

Because of its strategic location near the Peace River boundary of the Seminole Nation, settlement in the area of Thonotosassa, Itchepuckesassa, Fort Sullivan, and Alafia was deemed of particular importance to military leaders in Florida. Accordingly the army, under the command of William J. Worth, offered incentives to prospective settlers, including a guarantee of military protection. This guarantee resulted in almost fifty Armed Occupation Act claims in the area. Once those settlements were established, additional settlers began arriving in a slow, steady stream.[14]

Among the first of the new settlers was James W. Whidden's son-in-law, Noel Rabun Raulerson, who, along with his brother John B. Raulerson and in-laws John Thomas and William Wiggins, drove their cattle down from Columbia County to the Alafia range in 1844. By May 1845 the families of these men were established near Itchepuckesassa and were joined in that area by Whidden's other son-in-law, William L. Campbell; Whidden's brothers Maxfield and Willoughby, as well as Noah Whidden; Maxfield Whidden's soon-to-be son-in-law, David J.W. Boney; Rigdon Brown's son, William; William Wiggins's brother-in-law, John Futch; and former Columbia countian Israel Green.[15]

During the next eleven months the families of Jesse Knight, Joel Knight, Jacob Summerlin, Silas McClelland, Andrew McClelland, and Isaac Waters arrived, further enlarging the settlements around Itchepuckesassa and south to the Alafia. Later in 1846 they were joined by the family of Henry M. Frier, perhaps moving to be closer to his in-law John B. Raulerson. About the same time, other new settlements included those of William Brewer, William Hancock, Moses A. McClelland, John McClelland, Peter Platt, Isham Deas, Richard D. Prine, William Weeks, William Brown's brother-in-law, Charles H. Scott, Joseph and David Summerall, and Thomas Summeralls.[16]

By 1848 the area available for settlement north of the Alafia River in present-day eastern Hillsborough County was becoming crowded by pioneer standards. This situation was further intensified by a twenty-mile-wide strip of land immediately west of Peace River and at least as far north as Charlie Apopka Creek that since May 1845 had been reserved from settlement as a buffer between white settlers and the Seminole Nation. While no Americans had settled in this neutral zone as late as 1847, pressures for movement to the east continued to grow as more settlers and more cattle moved into Hillsborough County. By October 1848 these newcomers included Benjamin Guy, Frederick Varn, Daniel Gillett, John Underhill, William McCullough, John

Green, Louis Lanier, William H. Willingham, Joseph Howell, Aaron Whittemore, Rigdon H. Brown, and B.J. Newsome. All these men, as well as the settlers already in place, had an interest in cattle. To pursue that interest, they needed the vast expanses of range land east of Peace River in the Seminole Nation.[17]

Growing tensions on the frontier

As Armed Occupation Act settlers combed Hillsborough County in late 1842 and 1843 for suitable homesteads, the remaining Florida Indians were attempting to reestablish their lives to the east and south beyond Peace River. In late 1843 it was estimated that only 300 remained in Florida and, of that number, perhaps 120 or 130 were Seminoles living near Lake Okeechobee and the Caloosahatchee River under the chief Billy Bowlegs, who in the late 1830s had assumed the title Holata Micco. Of the remaining Indians perhaps 100 were Mikasukies under the chief Sam Jones (Arpeika) living somewhat to the north in the vicinity of Lake Istokpoga. A few Creeks and Tallahassees rounded out the total, many of whom constituted the last party of Indians to enter the reservation in the final days of 1843. This last group, under the leadership of Halpatter Tustenuggee, also settled near Lake Istokpoga.[18]

Even Gen. William J. Worth, Army commander in Florida, felt called upon to compliment the Florida Indians on their behavior following the peace. "These people have observed perfect faith," he reported in November 1843, "and strictly fulfilled their engagements." He added, "Not an instance of rudeness towards the whites has yet occurred." The Indians' peaceful disposition, however, did not prevent Worth two months later from secretly ordering his commander at Tampa to attempt to seize Halpatter Tustenuggee and his people and "at once dispatch them" to the west. Nor had it prevented him in July 1843 from refusing the Indians permission to shoot any of the "large numbers of wild cattle" in their vicinity, an action which may suggest another of the incentives General Worth held out to white settlers in Hillsborough County.[19]

Throughout this period the Indians had freely visited Tampa to trade and, in the process, engaged in frequent peaceful encounters with settlers. During the summer of 1843 General Worth had appointed an official "Indian Trader" to reside at Tampa. The trader, Thomas P. Kennedy, took over the Indian store from the military disbursing agent at Fort Brooke on August 10. His special qualification for the job was that he had served in St. Augustine as "confidential clerk" to Gen. William J. Worth.[20]

However peaceful the Indians might be, General Worth never lost sight of his real mission. As early as July 1843 he had stated, "It is the desire of the Government, as soon as it can be done without the risk of renewing difficulties, to remove them [the Indians] West." This position was reenforced by the secretary of war on January 20, 1844, and again the following October 18. In the meantime, Worth began formulating a secret plan to effect this goal, a plan which he "verbally" communicated to the secretary of war in February 1844.[21]

The general's plan involved as a first step moving the Indian store to the more remote (at least from prying eyes) location of Charlotte Harbor, a move to which Billy Bowlegs assented in March 1845. The following month Worth confided to one of his subordinates that "besides the propriety of the thing itself a convenient and natural occasion will be afforded for slipping some troops into that quarter." He intended, he went on, "if it be possible between this and Decr to play off a shabby trick upon these Indians."[22]

The shabby trick Worth proposed was the kidnapping of Bowlegs and other Indian leaders in an unguarded moment at the new store. The plan progressed through the summer of 1845 and by mid-September Thomas P. Kennedy had opened his Charlotte Harbor establishment on the mainland just east and slightly north of the northern tip of Pine Island. A rival and unlicensed trader, William McCrea, soon alerted the Indians to Worth's plan, however, and the plot collapsed.[23]

Just as his careful plot began unraveling, General Worth was transferred from Florida to Texas in anticipation of the outbreak of a war with Mexico. As late as December, though, some circles in official Washington seemed to hold out hope that the plan might be resurrected as suggested by the adjutant general's December 1 comment to Fort Brooke's new commander. "Make yourself acquainted with the train of affairs as left by General Worth," he wrote, "and follow it out to the best of your ability." When Worth's aide, John T. Sprague, finally was able to meet with the chiefs at Kennedy's Trading Store on January 8, 1846, Billy Bowlegs and Sam Jones proved they had learned their lesson well. They bluntly informed Sprague that, thereafter, they would meet with officials only inside the Indian reservation and only when accompanied by not more than six soldiers with three tents. There would be no opportunity to kidnap the leaders of Florida's Indians.[24]

At the time of General Worth's transfer, forces began to build on the frontier to force the removal of Indians from what was by then the state of Florida. As early as September 1845 unfounded rumors of Indian depredations were reported and circulated. Similar rumors recurred throughout the next several years and, at times, tensions ran high. John T. Sprague commented on the Indian situation early in 1847: "Their ears are open to every idle tale insidiously told them by vagrant whites infesting the coast and frontier, who without any thing to lose, hope to create a conflict in which they can become participants in the gain resulting from an influx of public money."[25]

In June 1846 Thomas P. Kennedy unsuccessfully sought permission to abandon the trading store at Charlotte Harbor due to Indian attitudes that he described as "anything but friendly."[26] After an unpleasant incident at William Hancock's farm near Tampa in the summer of 1847, the highly suspicious Indians even had the Indian messenger sent to them by the commander at Fort Brooke put to death. Three months later Kennedy again wanted to withdraw from Charlotte Harbor, sensing an outbreak on the horizon. A later examination revealed that the cook at the Indian store had "outraged the feelings of the Indians" with his conduct toward an Indian woman. When the store clerk, Mr. Tyson, fled in terror with most of the trading goods, the Indians protected the store until Kennedy's return. Tyson was less fortunate. During his flight his boat capsized in Charlotte Harbor, the trade goods were lost, and his feet were lacerated on an oyster bar.[27]

Throughout most of the period from 1845 to 1848 Indians continued to visit Tampa in small groups. There on August 27, 1848, one of the saddest episodes of the failure of law and justice for the Florida Indian occurred. Two Mikasukies, one of them a nephew of Sam Jones, were "wantonly" beaten by a citizen named McCord. Military authorities filed complaints on behalf of the Indians, whose conduct was described as "soberly and orderly," with the

Noel Rabun Raulerson (1820–1910) lived near modern Bartow in 1850. His family was among the first three American families to settle in the Peace River Valley. Courtesy Charles C. Rushing.

local justice of the peace, Simon Turman. In Turman's court the next day McCord appeared and "grossly insulted the court and the parties in attendance." For contempt of court McCord was fined three dollars. For assault and battery on the Indians he was assessed no penalty at all.[28]

The close of the Second Seminole War in 1842 found many Florida frontier settlers, particularly in the area of Alachua, Columbia, and Hamilton counties, unable or unwilling to return to the life of a North Florida farmer. More and more of these men were attracted to the cattle industry, but economic and social changes in North Florida posed problems for them in pursuing that livelihood. Many saw the Armed Occupation Act, passed in August 1842, as a possible solution and moved farther south. Almost fifty of these men and their families settled in the area between Tampa and the headwaters of Peace River. Over the next six years they, and their relations, friends, and neighbors who followed, built a new life based upon cattle. By 1848 their grazing lands had been pushed east almost to Peace River and the Seminole reservation, and their areas of settlement had begun to grow crowded.

As these settlers were pioneering in Hillsborough County, Gen.

William J. Worth secretly plotted to end Florida's Indian question by kidnapping the leaders of the Seminole and Mikasuki nations. This plan called for the establishment of a trading store at Charlotte Harbor where the Indians would be entrapped. Although the store was built, the general's plan collapsed when word of it was passed to the Indians by a rival trader. Thereafter, relations with the Florida Indians tended to be difficult, the Indians now wary of white intentions. The desire of some Floridians to force Indian removal increased tensions, by late 1848, incidents were occurring which easily could have led to hostilities. These forces finally would clash in 1849, and the history of South Florida and the Peace River Valley would be altered forever.

6

The Army and the
First Settlers

A S WOULD BE THE CASE time and again for the remainder of the nineteenth century, in September 1848 natural forces changed the Peace River Valley. A devastating hurricane along the South Florida frontier caused frontier settlers to consider the advantages of new homes and range lands near or in the Seminole Nation and prompted the removal of the Indian store from Charlotte Harbor to a site near modern Bowling Green. A fatal encounter between renegade Indians and white traders at that store resulted in a near-war and, shortly thereafter, in the construction of roads, bridges, and military posts in the Peace River area and the withdrawal of most Indians far to the south.

The hurricane of 1848

On Saturday and Sunday nights, September 23 and 24, 1848, the Gulf horizon from Tampa Bay to Charlotte Harbor pulsed with a deep phosphorescent glow. On Sunday a "sultry" atmosphere gave way to heavy rain and winds of increasing strength. Early the next morning the winds shifted, first to the south and then to the southwest, and built to an almost unbelievable intensity. Amidst a torrential downpour and whipped by hurricane winds, monstrous waves crashed ashore through most of the day. By noon water levels had risen by fifteen feet, and there they stayed for hours. When the waves and waters finally receded late in the afternoon, grim survivors pondered the aftermath of "the most terrible gale ever known."[1]

The hurricane of 1848 sowed a path of destruction through central and southern Florida. At Manatee (Bradenton) homes were flattened, fields inundated, and citizens drowned. From as far east as the settlement of Tallahassees near Lake Istokpoga came reports of "the hurrycane . . . sweeping everything before it." At Thomas P. Kennedy's isolated trading post at Charlotte Harbor "the buildings were badly damaged," and the sloop, *Virginia*, with nine passengers was crashed upon the shore, the only trace of her passengers the lifeless body of a young woman and a mutilated arm. At Tampa, with its concentration of people and property, destruction was evident at every hand. Fort Brooke, in particular, was a shambles. Officers' quarters were swept away by the waves, as were the wharves along the Hillsborough River. On the post most of the public buildings were a total loss.[2]

Immediately upon receiving reports of the destruction of Fort Brooke, the War Department ordered a board of officers to proceed to Charlotte Harbor "and there make a careful examination . . . for the site of a new post within the limits assigned for the temporary residence of the Seminoles, in place of Fort Brooke." Some citizens of Tampa, having a direct financial stake in the army's presence and the economic vitality of the town, were aghast. By the first week of November these men, led by Thomas P. Kennedy and his partner John Darling, had conceived a plan by which the fort would be saved for Tampa and its business saved for themselves. This goal was to be achieved by moving the damaged Indian store from Charlotte Harbor to a site on Peace River to the east of Tampa. The Indian agency would be moved from Tampa to the site of the new store, and Fort Brooke would continue to serve as a supply depot and garrison point. Their first choice as a site for the new store was at "Peas Creek old field," the remains of the Indian town of Talakchopco at and to the north of present-day Fort Meade.[3]

Kennedy and Darling faced problems with their plans. In addition to the opposition of Indian agent John C. Casey, their proposed location for the Indian store and agency was far to the north and west of the Indian settlements, particularly those of the friendlier Seminoles under Billy Bowlegs who lived on the Caloosahatchee River about thirty-five miles from the old store at Charlotte Harbor. Closer to the proposed site were the less numerous and more hostile Mikasukies and Tallahassees near Lake Istokpoga. Relations between these more hostile Indians and the Seminoles were so poor that in the summer of 1848 the Indians divided their territory, Bowlegs and the Seminoles thereafter controlling the area south of the old trading store and Sam Jones and the Mikasukies controlling the area to the north.[4]

During November and December 1848 the board of officers appointed to select a site for the new post toured Charlotte Harbor and Peace River up to the site of old Camp Ogden. They concluded that the new post should be established on Useppa Island, a decision in which Billy Bowlegs and Sam Jones concurred. Recognizing the continuing pressures for removal of the Indians from Florida, the board also recommended the reservation of land for a future military post on Peace River due east of Tampa. In doing so they stated that "a strong post will be required there whenever the removal of the Indians shall be determined on, whether by peaceable means or by force."[5]

In fact, pressures for just such a removal were building to a fever pitch. Responding to frontier settlers anxious for expanded range and farm lands and to business and land interests generally, the Florida legislature in January 1849 made it a state crime for Indians to leave the reservation for any purpose. At the same time the Congress was requested to mandate the "speedy removal of the Indians of Florida." Sensing the trend of events the clerk at Kennedy's Charlotte Harbor, George Payne, wrote, "That they have to go before long by fair or foul means is certain but I almost think that the crack of the rifle will be heard before that desirable event takes place." Attempting to reassure a friend, Payne added, "I do not consider myself in any immediate danger though."[6]

A decision about removing Fort Brooke to Useppa Island was not long in coming. On February 8, 1849, Gen. George Mercer Brooke, founder of Fort Brooke in 1824 and commander of the Fifth Military Department at New Orleans in 1849, handed Kennedy, Darling, and their associates a major victory. "It appears to me," concluded Brooke, "that the new fort should be somewhere on Pease Creek & some distance from its mouth." Concerning the

The State of Florida,

TO THE SHERIFF OF *Hillsborough*   COUNTY :—GREETING.

You are hereby commanded to take

Oskstunce Tustenecoche (alias Jim) Yoho Sacha, and take to war

if *they* be found within your County, so that you have *their* bod*ies* before the Judge of our Circuit Court for *Hillsborough* county *Southern* Circuit, at the Court House at

Tampa   on *the 7 th day (first Monday) of April*

next

to answer the State of Florida, of an Indictment for *Murder*

and have you then and there this writ.

Witness, Martin Cunningham Clerk of our said Court, this *27th*
day of *April*   A. D. 18*52*, and *76th* year of American Independence.

(Signed) Martin Cunningham Clerk

Oscen Tustenuggee, known among early Peace River settlers as the
fiercest and most determined of South Florida's Indian leaders. As indicated by this warrant, he was suspected of the murders at Chokonikla in
1849. He was killed in the aftermath of the attack on the Tillis place near
Fort Meade in June 1856. Courtesy Florida Photographic Collection,
Florida State Archives.

fort named in his honor Brooke added that "the Depot for the
new work if established, as suggested, might still remain at Fort
Brooke." Two days later Brooke's decision was approved by Maj.
Gen. Edmund P. Gaines who added as a postscript, "Let us make
an effort to prepare these miserable Indians for their removal to
the west, the sooner the better."[7]

The beginnings of settlement

Word of General Brooke's decision appears to have been expected at Tampa for, by the first week of February, Indian agent
Casey already had made arrangements to accompany John Darling
on a visit to Peace River to select an appropriate location for the
new store and Indian agency. Illness prevented Casey from making
the trip, however, and Darling proceeded without him. Within
two weeks Darling had returned to Tampa and urged that per-

mission be granted to build the store and agency at Hatse Lotka, a creek flowing into Peace River some eight or ten miles south of the ruins of the town of Talakchopco. On March 2 Maj. W.W. Morris, commanding at Fort Brooke, granted that permission to Kennedy and Darling.[8]

News of Kennedy and Darling's victory and the promise of a store on Peace River was taken in Hillsborough County as a sign that the Peace River frontier was about to be opened up, in spite of the president's twenty-mile-wide neutral zone west of the river that continued to bar the presence of American settlers. By April 1849 this attitude officially was recognized when the Hillsborough County Commission approved the construction of two public roads to the river.[9] William B. Hooker, Joseph Howell, and John Parker were appointed as commissioners to lay out a road from Tampa to the site of Fort Carroll near Fort Fraser. William B. Hooker, Louis Lanier, and James W. Whidden were to lay out a second road from Lanier's home on the Alafia River directly to the new Indian store on Peace River. These two roads ran straight to the new homes of the first two American settlers in the Peace River Valley.[10]

Both James W. Whidden and Rigdon Brown probably were settled in the valley by April 1849 when roads to their homes were authorized, but historical sources do not confirm Brown's presence until November 27, 1849, when Lieutenant George G. Meade visited his settlement three miles northwest of present-day Bartow. More than eight months earlier, however, John Casey had visited "Jimmy Whidden's" settlement on Whidden Creek six miles north of the new Indian store and had commented in his diary about the "pretty girl," Whidden's daughter Leacy, and "healthy looking boys & children" he found there.[11]

As in the case of Rigdon Brown, James W. Whidden's move to the Peace River Valley resulted from a number of factors. Population growth in frontier Hillsborough County and the ever increasing need for expanded grazing lands were creating substantial pressures for movement eastward by late 1848. In August of that same year the period of residency required of Armed Occupation Act settlers had expired, allowing claimants such as Brown and Whidden to obtain title to their lands while permitting them to move away from their claims without penalty. Less than two months later, the hurricane decimated the settlements along the

Hillsborough frontier, a further reason to relocate. Kennedy and Darling's efforts to locate on Peace River proved the final incentive. Whidden probably moved shortly after January 1, 1849, when he is recorded as having sold his cattle, "50 Head More or Less," to Jacob Summerlin.[12]

Whidden and Brown were accompanied by their families and, in the case of Brown, by at least two slaves.[13] Of these first black settlers of the river valley during this era the name of only one, 18-year-old Harriet, is known with certainty. It is likely, though, that the 18-year-old male slave who accompanied her was the same William Brown who remained as a freedman for several years in Polk County following the close of the Civil War. These black pioneers gave birth to two children, apparently one each in 1849 and 1850, who almost certainly were the first children born in the Peace River Valley in this era. Rounding out the list of these first settlers, Rigdon Brown also may have been accompanied by his son, William Brown, his daughter-in-law, Sabra Scott Brown, and their two children, Jane and William. They were living next door to Rigdon by November 1850 at the latest.[14]

Murder at the Indian store

As the settlements of Whidden and Brown began to take form, Kennedy and Darling's clerk, George Payne, busied himself with preparations for moving the Indian store. By April 1849 he had "broke up" the Charlotte Harbor store and loaded its goods into boats for the trip north. On that slow voyage up Peace River, Payne was fascinated by the game and fish he encountered, not to mention the skeleton of a mastodon he discovered exposed on the river bank about half way into the trip. Charmed by the river, he arrived at the new store before April 15, although he remained only briefly before walking to Tampa and a meeting there with Indian agent Casey.[15]

Awaiting Payne on the south side of the creek soon to bear his name was the beginning of "a fine large log building" which, he thought, "when furnished will be very convenient." The new store had two floors, each about twenty-two feet square, and was built of "pit-saw" lumber. It was furnished with a fireplace and chimney as well as a detached kitchen connected to the main building by a "floor." The store was supplemented with several outbuildings for storage. A wharf was constructed along the creek and a narrow, wooden bridge was built to span it.[16]

In late May 1849 Indian agent Casey, urgently hoping to meet with Billy Bowlegs to discuss emigration, paid a visit to the new Indian store, his second visit to the site.[17] By that time Indians regularly were visiting the store and, during Casey's five-day stay, brought in three hundred deerskins and forty pounds of wax to trade. Casey noted in his diary for May 25, "Every Indian coming in receives a present of a quart of whisky = issued across the river." The following day he wrote that "Nelkup Hajo with his brother Fuso Hajo chee Indian boy a young man—rifle shooting—whisky & Indians—bad—yelling all night." Frustrated when Bowlegs failed to arrive, Casey held an interview with the Tallahassee chief, Cotsa Fixico Chopco, and then, leaving a sick George Payne at the store, departed for Tampa.[18]

George Payne had recovered from his "rhumatism" sufficiently by late June to make another trip to Tampa. His ability to leave the store suggests that Dempsey Whidden, James W. Whidden's twenty-one-year-old son, already had been employed there as an assistant. On July 3 the staff was increased when William McCullough, an Alafia farmer, was employed as an assistant, and his

William McCullough (1821–90) and Nancy Whidden McCullough (1830–1908) were both wounded in the renegade attack at Chokonikla in 1849. William fought in the Second and Third Seminole wars and was a lieutenant in the 2d Florida Cavalry (Union). Courtesy Colleen Uhl.

wife, Nancy, Dempsey Whidden's sister, was taken on as cook and cleaning woman. The McCulloughs brought to the store with them their infant daughter, Elisabeth.[19]

As this staff was being assembled Indian agent Casey continued to seek an interview with Billy Bowlegs. Having failed to accomplish the meeting at the new store in late May, he set out by boat from Tampa on June 30 for the mouth of Peace River. There on July 6 he encountered a small party of Indians who agreed to take a message to the Seminole chief. The next morning he left Peace River for the Caloosahatchee and the hoped-for interview but, again, Bowlegs declined to appear. It was July 21 before Casey returned to Tampa, and awaiting him was shocking news from the Indian store.[20]

On the morning of Tuesday, July 17, four Indians, who four days previously had participated in a rogue attack upon a settlement four miles north of Fort Pierce, chanced upon the Tallahassee chief Echo Emathla Chopco, known to history as Chipco, on his way with a small party to trade at the Indian store.[21] At that time of year, the approximately one hundred miles west of Fort Pierce consisted mostly of flooded prairies and swamps, and the presence of the four Indians so near Peace River would be difficult to understand save for one fact. At the Indian store they could obtain the whiskey that Florida law prohibited them from obtaining anywhere else—whiskey for celebration and, perhaps, whiskey to brace them for the inevitable aftermath of their attack at Fort Pierce. The encounter with Chipco offered the renegades an opportunity to safely scout the area of the store, and they enlisted the Tallahassee chief to accomplish that for them.[22]

Chipco and the three women of his party arrived at the Indian store about noon, bringing for trade melons, venison, sweet potatoes, deerskins, and beeswax. They remained for almost four hours and, as William McCullough later stated, "they appeared more friendly than usual." Chipco certainly reported the presence of "a large quantity" of whiskey, with only three men to guard it, to the four fugitive Indians, who proceeded to the store, expecting to be offered a quart of whiskey each, as was the custom. They encountered a different situation.[23]

George Payne hated whiskey with a vengeance and had accepted his job with Kennedy and Darling only after a promising partnership broke up in disagreement over its sale. "No pecuniary inducement," stated Payne after the break-up, "will lead me to embark in any business which is directly against the best interests of mankind." At first Payne had little say about policy at the Indian store but, by June 8, he could boast, "I am now in charge." In line with his new authority, and possibly after receiving permission during his visit to Tampa in late June, Payne stopped giving whiskey to the Indians.[24]

The four fugitive Indians were shocked when Payne did not offer them whiskey and asked Payne to accompany them across the river where, they knew, the whiskey usually was dispensed. Payne refused that request, at least for the time being, and then refused a second request that the Indians be allowed to remain at the store. The confused Indians left and soon were joined outside by Payne and Dempsey Whidden. There the Indians demanded the whiskey they felt was their due and were refused point-blank by Payne. The discussion ended abruptly when Nancy McCullough called Payne and Whidden to dinner. The furious Indians resolved on immediate action.[25]

William McCullough later recalled, "We had scarcely got seated at the supper-table when they fired in at the door from the outside, one Indian standing on either side of the door and two in front, one behind the other. By this shot Captain Payne and Dempsey Whidden were killed dead, and I received a bullet in my left shoulder. I was shocked for an instant, but saw Payne spring up and fall back on the floor. Whidden fell forward, his face and hands resting on his plate. I sprang to the door and shouted, when the Indians gave back reloading their rifles. My wife was closing the shutters of the windows, but I told her our only chance was to leave the building. My wife then took her child and started for the bridge, which was about a quarter of a mile from the store. . . . I followed my wife with the rifle."[26]

On Nancy and William McCullough's heels followed two of the fugitive Indians and Echo Emathla Chopco. Firing at the fleeing family, the Indians were able to wound both William and Nancy, but were unable to keep them from reaching the bridge. Once there the McCulloughs, using the darkness as an ally, were able to hide until the Indians had passed. They made their way to the home of William J. ("Jockey") Whidden at Alafia about twenty five miles east three days after the murders. Meanwhile at the Indian store, all day Wednesday was taken up with celebration and plunder climaxed that night when the store and its outbuildings were put to the torch. The following morning four Indians fired into James W. Whidden's homestead six miles to the north and wounded one of Whidden's sons. The terrified family also fled to Jockey Whidden's Alafia home where they were resting on Friday when Nancy and William McCullough "staggered up bareheaded and barefooted." The Indians left Whidden's homestead untouched, but retreating to the south they ripped the planks from the bridge and threw them into the creek before disappearing into the interior.[27]

The Indians left a mocking and ironic message for those who would come after them. Found a few days later near the ruins of the Indian store and the charred remains of George Payne and Dempsey Whidden was one "untouched" barrel of whiskey. For his sacrifice, George Payne soon was memorialized when the creek upon which he died came to be called Paynes Creek. The site, itself, soon was known as Chokonikla, the Creek and Seminole word for "burnt house."[28]

Rumors of war

"The inhabitants of Hillsborough County have abandoned their homes," militia commander Jesse Carter reported from Tampa as news of the murders at Peace River spread along the frontier. Frontiersmen, he noted, "have assembled at points most convenient to their crops and stocks and are erecting Block houses and Pickets for the safety of their families." The vulnerability of those families, in the event of genuine Indian war, was extreme. The only army garrison in the vicinity, at Fort Brooke, was small and the frontier could be overrun by the time reinforcements could arrive from New Orleans. The frontiersmen established several volunteer militia companies to protect their families.[29] Many of the men "had not a gun or serviceable arm in their cabins," however, and their activities remained purely defensive [see appendix 7].[30]

As frightened settlers gathered, others were intent on spreading alarm and, if possible, bringing about a real war. One week after the attack John Casey noted, "I think K.D. & B. are all anxious for war." In the shorthand he used, Casey was referring to Thomas P. Kennedy and his business partners, John Darling and

Micajah C. Brown. Brown at the time was serving as state senator for Hillsborough County. Outrageous rumors and reports initiated at Tampa circulated throughout the state, including an early report that one hundred warriors had confronted an army patrol at the burned store. Within a month terrified settlers had abandoned their homes as far north as Fort King (Ocala). Accounts so inaccurate were published in Florida newspapers that, when asked by an editor for information on Indian depredations, one South Florida resident responded, "Your paper is so full of lies, there is not room for a single fact in it." Shortly after his arrival on the scene, Gen. David E. Twiggs expressed his own disgust: "It is astonishing to find how many persons, in & out of Florida, are whetting their appetites, expecting to share in the plunder of another 'Florida affair.' I will make every effort to disappoint them."[31]

Before General Twiggs's arrival at Tampa on August 25 the settlers' only real protection consisted of several state volunteer companies called into service after Hillsborough assemblyman James T. Magbee made a hurried trip to Tallahassee and a personal appeal to officials there. Capt. James G. Dell's company from Alachua County was first to arrive. The next day, August 11, Captain William Fisher's mounted company from Leon County appeared. Over the next two months, at first without assistance and then while regular army forces arrived and were deployed, these volunteer companies constantly scouted between the settlements and Peace River, camping at times by the river itself. Accomplishing this task despite widespread flooding from rains, the volunteers reported "no signs of Indians." Seeing first hand the plight of local settlers, Captain Fisher remarked, "I should hate to be the Indian seen by a white man this side of Peas Creek."[32]

On August 25, 1849, Gen. Twiggs assumed command of the army in Florida.[33] Within days he began sending small detachments to the outlying settlements, as one officer's wife put it, "more to gratify the people than for any other purpose." In spite of the constant rains, terrible supply problems, and shipping accidents, Twiggs built his army by the end of September to 1,700 men.[34]

While the army was being assembled, Twiggs and John C. Casey's efforts to contact Billy Bowlegs culminated in a meeting

near the old Charlotte Harbor store on September 18 and 19.
Bowlegs agreed to deliver the murderers to Twiggs by October 19,
and both Twiggs and Casey came away from the meeting convinced that the murders were an isolated incident and that the
Indians wanted peace. Acting upon that impression, possibly
with the concurrence of Twiggs, Casey then went over the heads
of his superiors in the army and the War Department, as well as
of influential Florida politicians, and privately wrote his old
friend Zachary Taylor, by then president of the United States. On
October 16 William W.S. Bliss, another old friend of Casey's as
well as Taylor's son-in-law and private secretary, responded to
Casey on the president's behalf. "The President seems very
clear," wrote Bliss, "that if the Indians comply with their obligations by surrendering the murderers, the question of removal is
not to be forced upon their decision." Continuing, Bliss stated, "I
am afraid that the Govt. is somewhat committed in regard to
making a peaceable effort, through a delegation, to induce the
Indians to go West & it is to be regretted that such a step has
been taken." Bliss went on to convey the president's endorsement
of a line of posts across the state to separate Indians from settlers
and noted that Taylor personally had conveyed his feelings on the
subject to the secretary of war.[35]

General Twiggs's line of posts

The events of subsequent months flowed directly from President Zachary Taylor's decisions of October 1849. In spite of continuing pressure for forced removal of the Indians, General Twiggs
pursued a steady course. Upon the satisfactory compliance by the
Indians with their promise to turn over the murderers, the general attempted by peaceful means to induce them to emigrate.[36]
After many misunderstandings and disappointments, Twiggs actually obtained at Chokonikla on January 21, 1850, a commitment
by Bowlegs and other chiefs to move west. Although Bowlegs
renewed the promise to John Casey in February, fewer than one
hundred Indians actually came in, and of that number a substantial portion demanded military protection from the vengeance of
Echo Emathla Chopco.[37] On April 11 at Fort Myers Bowlegs dispelled any doubt as to his intentions by telling Casey to his face
that "he would not go west, nor could he induce his people to go."

Casey accepted Bowlegs's decision, but insisted that the Seminoles be concentrated further south. The chief suggested "a line from the mouth of Pea river to the south end of Istokpoga lake in lieu of the former northern boundary," and it was so agreed.[38]

As Twiggs and Casey pursued their contacts with the Indians, Twiggs also began implementation of the policy calling for a line of posts across the state to serve as a buffer between settlers and Indians. On October 12, 1849, he chose a site "near the head of steamboat navigation" on the Manatee River for a "grand depot for his future operations." Twiggs named the depot Fort Hamer, after General Thomas L. Hamer, and let it be known that he intended to place there the entire garrison of Fort Brooke.[39]

To anchor the proposed line of posts on Peace River, General Twiggs in mid-November ordered Maj. William W. Morris to erect and garrison a post in the vicinity of Chokonikla. At the same time, John Casey was instructed to establish there an Indian

Traditional "double pen" log house of the John Wesley Hill family at Homeland. *Left to right*: Horace, James, Ned, Holly (Bowen), and Roxie Hill. From *DeVane's Early Florida History*, 1:294.

agency to be housed in "a comfortable domicile." Beating Morris and Casey to the site, however, was a detachment under the command of Maj. Gabriel Rains which, in cooperation with Lt. George G. Meade, had been scouting a new road from Tampa to the river. When Morris and Casey arrived on October 25, Rains's troops already had repaired the bridge over Paynes Creek. It took Morris and Casey only a short while to select "a pine bluff" in the forks of Paynes Creek and Peace River as the site for Fort Chokonikla.[40]

To complete the line of posts between Forts Hamer and Chokonikla, as well as to construct a road between them, troops were ordered about ten miles east of Fort Hamer on October 20. In a driving rain they arrived at the selected site about dark on October 21 and there established Fort Crawford, named in honor of Secretary of War George W. Crawford.[41] A final post, Fort Myakka, was established November 16 at the crossing of the Myakka River.[42]

Even as those posts were being opened, problems developed with General Twiggs's plans.[43] After an extensive survey of the proposed route from Manatee to Chokonikla, Lieutenant Meade reported October 31 that the entire route was "bad road." On the heels of that news came more unwelcome information. Previous reports to General Twiggs that the Indian reservation lay only as far north as Charlie Apopka Creek had been in error. Under General Macomb's agreement of 1839, the reservation extended to Bowlegs Creek, which meant that any line of posts extended eastward from Chokonikla would run through it, clearly a violation of the terms of the peace.[44]

Twiggs considered reactivating Fort Fraser, located almost twenty-five miles to the north, and completing the line of posts eastward from that point. He sent Lt. Col. Edward J. Steptoe on a scout of the area, but on November 22 Steptoe reported the route between Fort Fraser and the Kissimmee River to be impassable. Wanting additional information the general dispatched George G. Meade to the same area, but Meade's report of eight days later confirmed the difficulties of the river crossing at Fort Fraser. Meade also mentioned to the general that he had examined and been impressed by the "old Indian ford" near the ruins of the Indian town of Talakchopco, a spot called to his attention by volunteer Capt. James G. Dell. Less than two weeks later, on

December 13, 1849, General Twiggs returned with Meade to the site of that "old Indian ford" and, pleased with what he found there, directed that the main river crossing and depot be constructed at that point. The fort he named Fort Meade.[45]

During the week following the siting of Fort Meade, Twiggs ordered Lt. Col. Henry Bainbridge and his troops there from an encampment near Fort Fraser. Bainbridge was directed to erect "light frame houses" covered with clapboards for the storage of supplies, to improve the river crossing and build a "flat" for ferrying wagons, and to construct from the river crossing to the west a road to intersect the military wagon road from Tampa to Chokonikla. While these efforts were underway, Lieutenant Meade surveyed to the east of his namesake fort to find suitable locations for Forts Clinch and Arbuckle which were established, respectively, on January 13 and 23, 1850. By mid-January Twiggs informed the secretary of war that the line of posts from Tampa to Fort Meade to the Atlantic was established and that his wagon road ran "through a country where good roads are practicable and have been made, all the streams bridged, and communications secured."[46]

Twiggs's cordon of posts across the Florida peninsula survived for only a few months. Just four days after Billy Bowlegs finally refused on April 11, 1850, to emigrate to the west, the general recommended most of the posts be closed. Of those retained he suggested that two companies be stationed at Charlotte Harbor (Fort Casey), one or two at Indian River, and one each at Forts Hamer, Chokonikla, and Meade. Fort Myakka already had been broken up on March 22, and Fort Crawford followed on April 26. The line to the east of Fort Meade was ruptured on May 15 when troops were withdrawn from Fort Arbuckle. Fort Clinch followed on June 8. Although Fort Chokonikla initially had been promised a longer life, widespread sickness at the post forced its closure on July 18. When Chokonikla's troops arrived at Fort Meade on that day, Lieutenant Meade's namesake post on the site of the former town of Talakchopco represented the only military presence in the Peace River Valley.[47]

After a last and unsuccessful attempt in May 1850 to convince Billy Bowlegs to emigrate, General Twiggs left Florida for a visit to the national capital. There he met with Zachary Taylor and discovered what a friend indeed Bowlegs had in the president.

"Genl. Twiggs," Taylor told him, "tell Bowlegs whenever you see him, from me, that if his people remain within their limits—& behave themselves, they shall never be distured while I remain in office." As Twiggs left the White House neither he nor anyone else could know that within one week the president would be dead.[48]

In late September 1848 a hurricane devastated Indian and white settlements in central and southern Florida. It set in motion forces which brought about the removal of the Indian trading store at Charlotte Harbor to a site on Peace River near present-day Bowling Green and prompted the first white American settlers to seek homesteads in the Peace River Valley. Only a few months after the new Indian store was built, its clerk and an assistant were murdered by a band of renegade Indians. In the aftermath of the murders federal troops poured into Florida. While military conflict was avoided, the military stamped its presence on the land through the establishment of a line of posts intended to serve as a buffer between frontiersmen and Indians. When the Indians purchased the right to remain in Florida by agreeing to remove the northern limits of their settlements from Bowlegs Creek south to the mouth of Peace River, most of the posts were abandoned. By July 1850 the military remained on the river only at Fort Meade and, with the security that post provided, circumstances became favorable for the continuation and expansion of settlement in the upper Peace River Valley.

7

Permanent Settlement

I N THE AFTERMATH OF the murders at Chokonikla in 1849 the
northern limits of Indian settlement were pushed a considerable distance to the south. Hillsborough County cattlemen
then drove their herds to the vast cattle ranges east of Peace
River and permanent settlers brought social, religious, and civic
institutions to the upper river valley. Despite the withdrawal of
most Indians to the south, however, pressures continued to build
for their complete expulsion from the state, a situation which at
mid-decade again led to open war.

The slow growth of settlement

"In October, 1851," recalled Benjamin F. Blount in his later
years, "my grandfather, Readding Blount, and four sons, viz:
Riley R., wife, and four children; Owen R., wife and two children;
Nathan S., unmarried; Jehu J., not grown; Streaty Parker (his
son-in-law), wife and two children; John Davidson, wife and one
child (later Mrs. Solomon Page); making 21 white persons and
about a dozen negro slaves, constituted our colony that came
from near Alligator, now Lake City, in this State, and located
about one mile west of the present Court House in Bartow." Con-

tinuing, Blount noted, "The country was absolutely new as there were not more than a dozen families in what is now Polk County. Silas McClelland and Mr. Hill lived near the present site of Medulla. Rigdon Brown and his son, William, lived three miles northwest; Jack Raulerson lived one and one-half miles northwest, and N.R. Raulerson (Uncle Rabe) three and one-half miles northeast of Bartow. . . . Two or three families lived in that section of the country, now known as Socrum, and a few in the neighborhood of Fort Meade."[1]

The murders at Chokonikla in July 1849 resulted in the abandonment of the first pioneer settlements on Peace River. James W. Whidden, William McCullough, and their families fled to Alafia where they remained for several years. Rigdon Brown's settlement near Bartow temporarily was abandoned, as was Noel Rabun Raulerson's if, in fact, it existed by that time. By March 1850, however, Brown had returned to the river, and both he and Raulerson established permanent homesteads. Not later than November of that year Brown had been joined by his thirty-year-old son, William; William's wife, Sabra Scott Brown; and their children, Jane and William. At William's homestead also were Mary Bryant, possibly a housekeeper, and a forty-eight-year-old Irish laborer, Patrick Scoot. Father Rigdon also had brought back with him, in addition to his four black slaves, an English helper named James White.[2]

Other settlements followed slowly. As Ben Blount explained, by October 1851 the only additions to the river community were Noel Rabun Raulerson's relation Jack Raulerson and his family. Some miles to the northwest, at Medulla, Silas McClelland's lonely homestead had been buttressed by the arrival, probably in late 1850, of Marion County farmer Chesley D. Hill and his family. Hill's settlement did not prove permanent, however, and by 1855 the family had moved away.[3]

Still, the promise of future growth near Peace River was evident in the work of government surveyors who, in February and March 1850, sectioned the area surrounding Lake Hancock and by January 1852 had extended their work south and west to within a few miles of the future site of Homeland. In the wake of these surveyors one prospective settler, James D. Green, built in 1850 a small cabin near the present Polk County courthouse and cleared four of the 160 acres of his claim. By the time the Blount family arrived in October 1851 Green had been elected along with Jacob Summerlin a justice of the peace for the area of Itchepucke-sassa (Plant City) and chose to remain there. He sold his claim, the site of the future town of Bartow, to Riley R. Blount for forty dollars.[4]

Why were settlers not flocking to the Peace River Valley? Poised to make the move were cattlemen in the areas of Itche-puckesassa and Alafia attracted by the vast open rangelands available east and south of the river. The cattlemen were convinced, though, that before their herds ever could be safe on those ranges the Indians must be removed once and for all from the state.

Just prior to his death President Zachary Taylor had guaranteed the Seminoles that their good behavior earned them homes in Florida. With Taylor's sudden death in July 1850, however, came a quick reversal in policy. On September 12 the secretary of war instructed Indian agent John Casey, "It is the settled policy of the government to effect the removal of these people." Pressure for such a policy was encouraged not only by cattlemen, but also by slaveowners anxious to exploit South Florida lands for cultivating sugarcane. By January 1851 the pressure from these groups had resulted in action on two fronts. To make large tracts of land available for purchase from the state, the Congress approved in 1850 the Swamp and Overflowed Lands Act. The following January the state reacted by creating a board of internal improvement to oversee the sale of those lands. Appointed to the board to represent South Florida was John Darling. In a related action the Florida legislature also approved "An Act to provide for the final removal of the Indians now remaining in Florida, beyond the limits of the State." Besides calling on the federal government to take action, the new law authorized the governor to raise up to two regiments of mounted volunteers to act, at the governor's discretion, "as an independent force for the removal of the Indians."[5]

Behind these actions lay a highly charged incident triggered August 6, 1850, by the disappearance of eight-year-old Daniel Hubbard in Marion County. Despite sweeping searches by Jacob Summerlin, Simeon L. Sparkman, and others from Marion County to the headwaters of Peace River, no trace of the boy was found, although suspicion focused on Echo Emathla Chopco's

Tallahassee band then living illegally outside the reservation near Fort Gardner on the Kissimmee River. After months of frustration, Casey learned through the help of Billy Bowlegs that the boy had been murdered by members of Chipco's band in retaliation for the theft of three ponies by Jacob Summerlin the previous April. With Bowlegs's further assistance three members of Chipco's band were arrested for the murders at Fort Myers on May 17, 1851. Interviewed by Casey, all three agreed that Chipco and three others actually had killed the boy, but, before the matter could be pursued, the three captives were found hanging in their jail cell in Tampa. At the time of their deaths the Indians were in the custody of justice of the peace Simon Turman. Their jailers were William L. Campbell and James L. Whidden, respectively the son-in-law and son of James W. Whidden whose son, Dempsey, had been murdered by Indians at Chokonikla two years previously.[6]

Throughout 1851 and into 1852, while regular army patrols from Fort Meade attempted to keep Indians within the reservation and settlers out of it, Hillsborough County residents clamored for action. At meetings held at Tampa, Alafia, and Itchepuckesassa in December 1851, demands were made for immediate removal of the Indians. Instrumental in calling the meetings were John Darling, Thomas P. Kennedy, and Micajah C. Brown.[7]

Darling, Kennedy, and Brown had a lot on their minds toward the end of 1851. Their business interests were tied to the town of Tampa, and once again the possibility of the army's removal from Fort Brooke had been raised. In January 1852 Col. John H. Winder, commanding troops in Florida from his headquarters at Fort Myers, actually ordered that Fort Brooke be dismantled and that a new post and supply depot be established about fifteen miles up Peace River from its mouth. By the end of January construction had begun at the river site and two log buildings, each about twenty by forty feet, had soon been erected. Toward the end of February, however, enough influence had been brought to bear that Winder's superior, Gen. David E. Twiggs, prohibited the further dismantling of Fort Brooke. Shortly thereafter the new post, remembered at Fort Winder, was abandoned. Darling, Kennedy, and Brown had won a stay, but they saw the writing on the wall: their future economic prospects lay not in the peaceful army presence at Tampa, but either in armed conflict with the

James Dopson Green (1823–86) and Eliza Whidden Green (1827–1903), two of the earliest American pioneers of the Peace River Valley. Jim Green served as a county officer in the 1850s, a captain in the Union Army, and the area's principal Republican leader during Reconstruction. Courtesy Mrs. Billie Herndon.

Indians or in the commercial exploitation of South Florida after the Indians' removal.[8]

While the dismantling of Fort Brooke was still under way, frontier tensions intensified when Aaron Jernigan, pioneer settler of the Orlando area, accompanied by Jacob Summerlin, Simeon L. Sparkman, and William H. Kendrick, came across and fired upon a small party of Indians near Lake Tohopekaliga. Although most of the party escaped, the frontiersmen captured an old woman and a small child. Only a short time after being confined at Jernigan's home, the Indian woman was discovered "hanging by the neck Dead."[9]

Soon afterward Aaron Jernigan made his way to Tampa where he held a conference with General (an honorary title) Luther Blake, who had been appointed by the federal government to attempt to induce the Indians to emigrate.[10] Jernigan appears to have agreed to continue to stir up the frontier by attempting to capture Indians or, as John Darling put it to Gov. Thomas Brown, "If there is any understanding between Blake and Jernigan, it probably is one about live Indians and money. . . . If it were so, it will answer our purpose just as well."[11]

John Darling's purpose was to get rid of the Indians any way he could, and he was happy to make use of Aaron Jernigan in that cause. "The Indians finding the country up against them in their favorite and most fortunate hunting grounds will be more disposed to listen to the proposals of Genl. Blake," Darling informed the governor. He continued with a recommendation. "I think about three companies of Mounted Volunteers dispatched along the frontier would materially aid the operation of peaceable removal."[12]

Gov. Brown, anxious himself for Indian removal, complied with John Darling's suggestion and ordered state troops into the field under the command of Gen. Benjamin Hopkins. Hopkins left Jacksonville for Lake Monroe by steamer on March 5, 1852, and on his arrival three days later found Aaron Jernigan awaiting him. In the conversation that followed, Jernigan convinced Hopkins to accompany him deep into the Lake Tohopekaliga and Kissimmee River country. Two weeks later Hopkins, Jernigan, and the state troops discovered an Indian camp ninety miles south of Fort

Cattleman, politician, and Confederate "cow cavalry" captain Francis Asbury Hendry (1833–1917) and Ardeline Ross (Lanier) Hendry (1835–1917). Courtesy Spessard Stone.

Gatlin (Orlando) on the St. Johns River. During the encounter that followed nineteen Indians were taken captive.[13]

By the summer of 1852 General Hopkins was cooperating directly with Luther Blake, maintaining mounted patrols as late as November of that year. John Darling doubted Blake's ultimate success, however, and pushed for more state action. "We want the country," Darling wrote the governor in June, "and I think the state cannot do less than take possession of the whole district north of the Caloosahatchee River early in the fall. . . . An armed occupation of this district will facilitate the ultimate removal of the Indians."[14]

Before that armed occupation could come about, Billy Bowlegs agreed to negotiate with Luther Blake. In September Bowlegs accompanied Blake to Washington where, on September 20, 1852, he and several other leaders agreed to go west. Several months after the Indians' return to Florida, frontiersmen, jubilant over the Indians' surrender, learned it had all been a sham; Billy Bowlegs had never intended to emigrate.[15]

Cattle east of the river

In October 1851 the family of Readding Blount, including sons-in-law Streaty Parker and John Davidson, moved to the vicinity of Bartow. With the family caravan came "about a dozen" black slaves, including six who were the property of Readding Blount, the family patriarch. Two of these black pioneers were men of about forty-five to fifty years of age, and two were women, Ann and Rachel, of about the same age. Two children, boys aged about ten and twelve, completed the group. Riley R. Blount, one of Readding's sons, owned five slaves at the time of the family move. Among the group was long-time Peace River resident Stepney Dixon, whose post–Civil War household, including Sarah Washington and family members Charles and Jackson Dixon, appears also to have been included in the original 1851 caravan. Rounding out the list, the household of Streaty Parker included a black woman of about seventeen years of age.[16]

Ben Blount mentioned that, upon his family's arrival, "a few" families were living "in the neighborhood of Fort Meade." The families to which he referred were the Durrances, particularly the families of Francis M., William Hutto, Joseph Lemuel, and

John Rufus Durrance. When exactly the various Durrance families arrived near modern Homeland is uncertain, although in January 1852 a young boy of one of the families became lost in the woods and was found "nearly dead" by the Seminoles after an eight-day search. By the end of April 1852 Francis M. Durrance was serving as a road commissioner for the area of the Peace River settlements and, six months later, he and his brother, John Rufus, were recorded as having voted at the Peas Creek precinct. With Francis M. Durrance came three black slaves, including two men aged about forty and fifteen and a woman of about sixteen.[17]

By April 1852 the settlements on Peace River had grown sufficiently to justify both a road district and a voting precinct for the area.[18] Two months later the first preacher, Jeremiah M. Hayman, appeared at "Peace Creek." On an occasional basis over the next two years the Reverend Hayman offered the comfort of his ministry to the families of isolated Baptist settlers, leading in September 1854 to the creation of the river valley's first church.[19]

Only three months after the Reverend Hayman's appointment at Peace River and while Billy Bowlegs and Luther Blake were making their way to Washington, another monstrous hurricane descended upon Tampa and the countryside to the east. In its aftermath a nineteen-year-old cattleman, Francis Asbury ("Berry") Hendry, left his family's homestead on the Alafia River and moved into the garrison at Fort Meade. Along with Berry Hendry came his seventeen-year-old wife of only a few months, Ardeline Ross Lanier. During the following weeks in late 1852 Hendry established a homestead about two miles northeast of Fort Meade and, more importantly, became along with his father-in-law, Louis Lanier, the first white cattleman to drive his herd to the ranges east of Peace River. By 1860, Hendry owned eight slaves and Lanier owned seven. It seems likely that at least some of these slaves had accompanied the men to Fort Meade.[20]

In Hendry's wake other cattlemen made the move to Peace River. By March 1853 James W. Whidden's son, James Lawrence Whidden, had built a house two miles west of Fort Meade. Five months later Louis Lanier, who held the contract to supply beef at Fort Myers and Fort Meade, built a dwelling near the river about eight hundred yards east of the fort. Along with Lanier came Berry Hendry's younger brother, 14-year-old George Washington Hendry. A little further north Frederick Varn and his family moved to join his son-in-law, Riley R. Blount. Varn brought with him to the Bartow area ten slaves, the names of four being Harriet, Charlotte, Steven, and Manirva. Perhaps as early as the fall of 1852 David J.W. Boney and Thomas Summeralls were in the same vicinity, where they were joined early in 1853 by William Brown's brother-in-law, Charles H. Scott.[21]

By June of 1853 it was estimated that Peace River settlers and other cattlemen already had four to five thousand head ranging east of Peace River and south to the Caloosahatchee. By that time the Peace River settlements had conducted two elections, and the beginnings of law enforcement were in place with the selection of Rigdon Brown and Francis M. Durrance as justices of the peace.[22] Along with these advances in civilization came land prospectors eager to make a killing on the newly opened frontier. One such man, W.W. Tanner, would write his father in April 1853: "I am getting more and more pleased with the country. The part I last visited on Peace creek is the best I have yet seen." Tanner went on to say, "The settlers are constantly trying to scare me off with the name of Bowlegs, but I do not fear him."[23]

Moving the Indians south

W.W. Tanner was wrong not to fear Billy Bowlegs. In the four months since Bowlegs had renounced his agreement to emigrate, a firestorm of demands for forced removal of the Indians had swept the state. In a letter to Hillsborough County's state representative, James T. Magbee, John Darling sounded a common theme when he demanded immediate state action. "I think the first operation should be to secure the frontier settlements, then to clear the country north of the Caloosahatchee," Darling wrote on December 22, 1852, admitting the possibility of "some panic on the frontier." In response to this public clamor the Florida legislature in January 1853 prohibited Indians from living or trading anywhere in the state. By May the pressure had reached Washington where on May 18 President Franklin Pierce turned the matter over to Secretary of War Jefferson Davis with orders to use "pacific & persuasive or forcible measures as he may deem proper" to remove the Indians.[24]

For most of the year following President Pierce's order Indian agent John Casey resisted plans for forcible removal of the

Indians while attempting to bring about the same result through
negotiation. By the end of 1853, however, Bowlegs had communicated that he hoped never to hear the matter mentioned again,
and in the early months of 1854 Casey recommended to the secretary of war that the Indian boundary formally be shifted farther
to the south, which would open to settlement the lands along

Author, cattleman, and political leader George Washington Hendry (1838–
1914). From Jacksonville *Florida Times-Union*, April 2, 1899.

Peace River in present-day Hardee County. On March 24 Jefferson Davis agreed to permit the settlements and endorsed a Casey proposal to use federal troops to enforce the prohibition on trading with the Indians. Davis ordered in April that government surveys be extended to the newly opened area and, one month later, directed Casey to hold no more talks with the Indians. As one officer at Fort Brooke put it, "The object of having troops here is not to restrain the Indians (who are perfectly quiet) from committing hostilities, but to keep them within their limits and by exploring the country, and keeping troops in motion through it, to impress them if possible with the necessity of emigrating."[25]

As the rainy season ended late in the summer of 1854 armed patrols reexamined the ancient Indians trails throughout South Florida and began constructing improvements to make them usable. In particular, Lts. Henry Benson and George Hartsuff, with assistance from local guides such as Francis A. Hendry and Louis Lanier, traced routes from Fort Meade to the headwaters of the Caloosahatchee River where the troops from Fort Meade would be sent to garrison the old Seminole War post, Fort Thompson. As these routes were mapped, surveyors extended their lines south and east of the Bartow area. In August 1854 they had mapped the area of Lake Buffum, named for the survey crew's axman, R.V. Buffum. By May of the following year all of the land adjacent to Peace River as far south as present-day Wauchula had been sectioned and platted.[26]

Throughout 1854 and 1855 survey crews and government troops pushed farther south, pressing hard upon the Seminoles and other Florida Indians. Naturally these actions created serious concerns among the Indians, concerns which grew deeper throughout 1855 as troops scoured South Florida including the areas of Lake Okeechobee and the Big Cypress Swamp.[27]

An onrush of settlement

In early December 1854 the army garrison at Fort Meade withdrew from the five-year-old post and began its slow march down the ancient Indian trail to the crossing of the Caloosahatchee River and Fort Thompson. Already on hand at Fort Meade was William B. Hooker's thirty-two-year-old brother, John I. Hooker, who had the contract to supply beef to Fort Myers beginning

December 7. Hooker bought all the buildings at Fort Meade from the army for two hundred dollars. Moving into the abandoned fort with the Hooker family were five black slaves, including Charlotte, Augustus, and Henry.[28]

John I. Hooker was only one of many settlers to benefit from the government's new policy of encouraging settlement. Early in 1854 the community near Fort Fraser had been enlarged by the arrival from Mississippi of Zachariah G. Seward, Henry S. Seward, and their families. Along with the Sewards came as many as twelve slaves, including Charity, Jim, Sarah, Frank, and Matilda.[29] Following the Sewards by August of that year was the family of William P. Rodgers, son-in-law of Stephen Hollingsworth. On September 3, 1854, these families organized the first Christian congregation in the Peace River Valley, the Baptist Church of Christ at Peas Creek, which numbered among its first eight members the slave Jim Seward.[30]

During the next nine months numerous families settled between Fort Fraser and Fort Meade, including those of Almond Johnson, Thomas Ellis, John Altman, John C. Oats, Eli English, Sherrard B. Maguire, William W. Hall, Wyley Baxter, William Parker, John Green, Joseph Underhill, William Underhill, and Alderman Carlton. James W. Whidden had relocated about seven miles west of Fort Meade. Just south of the fort were Francis C.M. Boggess, William McCullough, David Russell, and William P. Brooker. In the vicinity of Homeland within a short time also were John L. Skipper and Julius C. Rockner.[31]

These new arrivals pumped lifeblood into the society of the Peace River Valley. Seven months before the formation of the first church in September 1854, a board of trustees had been appointed by the Hillsborough County Commission for "Peas Creek School house," the valley's first school. Its board consisted of Riley R. Blount, Francis M. Durrance, and Frederick Varn. In January 1855 a new district was added at "Fort Meade School house." Albert Carlton, Francis M. Durrance, and James L. Whidden were appointed trustees for the new school, and Henry S. Seward, Joseph Lemuel Durrance, and Riley R. Blount were designated the same for "Peas Creek." Tuition fees of forty dollars were granted to each of the districts.[32]

During the same period the government road from Tampa to Fort Meade and Fort Fraser was declared a public highway and maintenance was undertaken. A new road was ordered to be laid out to run from Joseph Howell's farm "thence by the nearest and best ground to a Point where the Line dividing Townships 30 and 31 crosses Peas Creek." The road would give direct access from the settlements at Itchepuckesassa to the new homesteads in the vicinity of modern Homeland.[33]

Elections continued in 1855 and the precinct at William Brown's was supplemented by one at Fort Meade. At mid-year four justices of the peace were elected for the river area, Rigdon Brown and John Davidson for the upper settlements and Francis M. Durrance and John C. Oats for Fort Meade. In October Francis M. Durrance won election to the Hillsborough County Commission as a Democrat, replacing Louis Lanier who had been elected as a resident of Fort Meade two years earlier.[34]

As the population expanded in the area between Fort Fraser and Fort Meade, the government's policy of encouraging settlements opened the door to the south as well. Beginning in the fall of 1854 pioneer families pressed down the military roads into present-day Hardee County with members of the Whidden family in the vanguard. By April 1855 the frontier was defined by the homestead of Willoughby Whidden, located just north of modern Wauchula. About ten miles to the northwest, on the military road from Tampa to Chokonikla, lay the settlement of Whidden's son-in-law, James D. Green. Jesse Alderman lived nearby, and three miles to the northeast on the north side of Paynes Creek was the home of Richard Pelham. A little farther north on Little Paynes Creek, just inside the present Polk County line, were the homes of Pelham's brothers-in-law, Thomas Summeralls, and William Simmons. Three miles northeast of Pelham, on another military road to Chokonikla, was the home of Thomas Underhill. Farther south and to the west of these settlements, by late 1855, lay the settlement of cattleman John Parker on Troublesome Creek near Ona. Farther still was the isolated homestead of John Platt on Horse Creek near Lily.[35]

The pioneer families migrating south down Peace River in 1854 and early 1855 moved into the middle of a major political storm. In December 1854, at the urging of planters and merchants living on the Manatee River and at Sarasota Bay, Hillsborough County's state representative Jesse Carter with the assistance of Sarasota resident and Florida Senate President

Hamlin V. Snell procured the passage of legislation to split Hills-borough County. Approved January 9, 1855, the legislation created a new county of Manatee encompassing more than half of greater Hillsborough and including all of the Peace River Valley south of the present Polk-Hardee county line. Although the creation of Manatee County imparted great power over local affairs to those living at Sarasota and on the Manatee, it effectively isolated the Peace River settlers from their family ties and political loyalties farther to the north on Peace River and at Alafia and Itche-puckesassa.[36]

As more families moved into the Peace River settlement in Manatee County during 1855 the political influence of their com-munity in the sparsely populated county increased proportion-ately. In May, James D. Green, son-in-law of Willoughby Whidden, was elected justice of the peace for the eastern half of the county and, at the first election for other county officers on October 1, Maxfield Whidden, brother of Willoughby and James W., received the highest number of votes, forty-one, for county commissioner.[37] Sensing their increased political power the residents of the river settlements then demanded that the eastern area of the new county, including all of the Peace River Valley, be returned to Hillsborough County. A petition was circulated through the river settlements and in Hillsborough County to that effect and for-warded to the legislature at Tallahassee.[38] There, however, the settlers ran into a stone wall. Although newly elected representa-tive John Darling presented the petition to the legislature on November 30, he in fact was allied with Manatee River planters against the proposal. Arranging to have the petition referred to a special committee consisting of himself and two others, Darling sat on it for ten days before reporting back to the house that no action should be taken. The political reunification of the Peace River Valley had been forestalled.[39]

The permanent settlement of the Peace River Valley began in the aftermath of the murders of Payne and Whidden at Choko-nikla in July 1849. For several years the pace of this settlement was extremely slow, although several large family groups, includ-ing a number of black slaves, did move to the areas that would become known as Homeland and Bartow. Substantial numbers of settlers did not arrive, though, until cattlemen began to drive their herds to the east of the river in late 1852 and, particularly, after Secretary of War Jefferson Davis adopted a policy in mid-1854 of encouraging the expansion of settlement into what is now southern Polk and Hardee counties.

By late 1855 the settlement of southern Polk and Hardee was signified by the emergence of churches and schools. The river had been divided politically, however, by the creation of Manatee County and thereafter personal and political frictions began to develop between Peace River settlers, Manatee River planters, and Tampa politicians. Before those frictions could be assuaged, the government's policy of surveying and patrolling South Florida in order to encourage the remaining Florida Indians to emigrate to the west erupted in violence.

8

The Third Seminole War

B Y THE MID-1850S THE U.S. government, prompted· by the
Florida legislature, land speculators, sugarcane growers,
and frontier settlers, had undertaken a series of efforts
directed at pressuring Florida's remaining Indians to emigrate to
the west. Instead of succumbing to the pressures, the Indians,
under Billy Bowlegs, reacted by opening warfare on the frontier.
For over two years the hostilities continued until in the spring of
1858 Bowlegs accepted inducements proffered him by the government and agreed to leave Florida with most of his followers. With
their departure, it appeared finally that the entire length of the
Peace River Valley could be opened to an increased and prosperous settlement.

The Billy Bowlegs War

Beginning in the spring of 1854 the U.S. government initiated
a series of policies aimed at intimidating the Indians remaining in
Florida to emigrate to what then was known as Arkansas. As a
first step a complete ban on trade was imposed. This action soon
was followed by others encouraging settlers to move closer to the
Indian home grounds, extending government surveys deep into

the heart of Indian country, and garrisoning frontier posts close to the borders of the Seminole Nation. As army patrols and surveyors penetrated the areas of Lake Okeechobee and the Big Cypress Swamp in 1855, Seminole leaders complained directly to Indian agent John Casey that these provocations made hostilities inevitable. The protests were ignored, however, as the patrols and surveys continued.[1]

By the fall of 1855 Indian concerns and resentments had reached such an intense state that a general council of all Florida Indians was held near the site of the 1837 Battle of Okeechobee. Sentiment for hostilities ran high at that meeting with only the Tallahassee chief, Echo Emathla Chopco ("Chipco"), opposing the war. Chipco and his band had been living south of the Caloosahatchee River since July 1853, and his relations with Billy Bowlegs were described as "exceedingly bitter." The Tallahassee chief's opposition to war only widened that rift and resulted in Chipco's banishment from the Indian nation.[2]

The spark that ignited an Indian war was struck by Lt. George L. Hartsuff and his men in December 1855. Leading a survey party in the Big Cypress Swamp, Hartsuff came across a field belonging to Bowlegs which contained a grove of banana plants prized by the Seminole chief. Both Seminole and army sources agree that Hartsuff's troopers destroyed Bowlegs's grove. When the chief appeared on the scene a short while later, he demanded redress from the lieutenant for this action. Hartsuff, outraged at what he considered Bowlegs's insolence, kicked the chief to the ground and refused his demands. At about 5:00 A.M. on December 20 Bowlegs and thirty warriors blanketed Hartsuff's camp with rifle fire, killing four soldiers and wounding four, including Hartsuff.[3]

Army reaction was restrained and confident. "The Seminoles finding no alternative left but Emigration or hostilities have chosen the latter," John Casey informed Gov. James E. Broome on December 23. "Although a different result was strongly hoped for," Casey continued, "yet, in anticipation of this decision, the government has had, and has, a large force in the Indian country." Casey mentioned almost as an afterthought, "I would respectfully suggest the propriety of promptly placing, say, two companies of volunteers in position on *Pea River*, to give confidence & protection to the extreme frontier settlers."[4]

Initial reaction on the Peace River frontier to the Indian outbreak was recalled by Francis A. Hendry some fifty years later.
"On Christmas Day, 1855, a courier was dispatched from Tampa,
informing us, and all frontier people, that an Indian war was
upon us and to care for ourselves the best we could. . . . This was
a veritable clap of thunder from a clear sky." He added, "The
people were excited and quickly congregated for self-protection."
Those settlers living on the river in Manatee County "forted-up"
their families at James D. Green's homestead. The site, soon
called Fort Green, offered plenty of fresh water from nearby
springs and lay directly on the military road to Tampa. John I.
Hooker, "with his great, large, generous heart," opened the
numerous buildings at Fort Meade to residents of the vicinity,
and further to the north families sought refuge at Fort Fraser
and at the Riley Blount homestead (Fort Blount) in what is now
downtown Bartow.[5]

With their families concentrated and secure, the Peace River
frontiersmen turned to more militant measures of defense. By
December 29, 1855, Francis M. Durrance had organized a company of volunteers at Fort Meade. In recognition of his efforts
Durrance was elected captain, with Edward T. Kendrick and
Alderman Carlton first and second lieutenants. Durrance immediately stationed his company at Fort Meade and initiated scouting patrols all along the frontier. He reported to the governor that
the residents at Peace River "have determined to stand."[6]

Unknown to Captain Durrance, on December 24 the residents
of Tampa had met and elected William B. Hooker as commander
of militia forces in the area. Hooker occupied four days making
preparations and on December 28 set out from Tampa with forty
men for Fort Meade where he incorporated into his company
forces raised by Leroy G. Lesley and Henry A. Crane as well as
Captain Durrance's company.[7]

Captain Hooker then dispatched troops to garrison posts "at
such points as to give the greatest protection to the settlers in
this vicinity." Twenty men were stationed at Fort Meade, sixteen
were sent to protect Fort Green, and an additional twenty-four
were directed to Fort Hooker, which Hooker described as being
sixteen miles north of Fort Meade. To protect his southern flank
on Peace River, the captain decided to create a new position at a
point on the western side of the river just northwest of present-

day Zolfo Springs. A squad of twenty-five men under the command of Marvin M. Edwards was dispatched to the spot, which Hooker named Fort Hartsuff in honor of the wounded and thought-to-be-dying lieutenant. Four of the families gathered at Fort Green accompanied Evans and his men to the new location. The balance of Hooker's command was ordered to patrol the river from Fort Meade to Charlotte Harbor.[8]

The Battle of Peace River

And there matters stood for two months. While regular army troops patrolled and prepared for action near the Seminole heartland south of the Caloosahatchee River, undersupplied volunteer units protected the settlements on, and patrolled up and down, Peace River. The volunteers—their families huddled together at the isolated and underprotected frontier forts—found no Indians, but did meet with undisguised resentment on the part of regular army officers. "The Volunteers are called Crackers and as a general thing they are a very corrupt set of men," commented Lt. Oliver O. Howard in a statement echoed by numerous others. "They drink, gamble, & swear and do all manner of discreditable things," he continued, "and are not withal very good soldiers." In response, Cracker resentment of the U.S. Army, a sentiment

Seminole War veteran Willoughby Tillis (1808–1895). From *Polk County Historical Quarterly*, June 1983. Photograph in possession of Tillis's great-grandson Doyle Tillis of Mooresville, NC.

having its roots in the Second Seminole War, grew and intensified.[9]

As tensions heightened between regular army and volunteer troops, the initial panic on the Peace River frontier faded and fear of Indian attack became desperation for food and other supplies. A volunteer officer reported, "I dont know what will become of some of them if there should be a protracted war—they are generally very poor and some of them have not been living on their places long enough to make bread for their families, and must quit the country or starve without speedy relief (or at least suffer for bread, meat they have)." Concerning the possibility of Indian attack Jacob Summerlin expressed the reality of the time, "We are not yet affraid of a large body of Indians as long as there is a regular scout kept up on the frontier but we are affraid (in our situation) of a sculking party." He added a thought which must have been common to the frontier. "Some of us has got danger by heart from experience in [the] las war."[10]

Summerlin's "danger by heart" was felt nowhere more intensely than at the most exposed of the Peace River gathering places, Fort Green. Although a detachment of Captain Hooker's volunteers was stationed at the site, they often were without fodder for their horses or ammunition for their guns. On February 28, 1856, Matthew P. Lyons appealed to the army commander at Tampa for protection for his "exposed fellow citizens at this place," but received no response. In a series of letters to the Tampa newspaper Lyons pleaded the case of the twenty families at Fort Green. When a supply train finally arrived on April 30 it was not a day too soon, for an officer reported "the supplies there being exhausted to day." Initially the fears and resentments at Fort Green focused on the army command, but with time that focus shifted to the command and supply offices of the state volunteers, particularly to Capt. William B. Hooker whose priorities were rumored to lie with protecting his own and his friends' private interests. "The people have asked, begged, demanded," James D. Green proclaimed as late as December 1856, "in fact, they have done everything that has suggested itself to their minds, to get protection for their women and children, and all to no effect." He added, however, "We are still at Ft. Green, and hope to be able to hold our position."[11]

The military situation during the first several months of 1856 generally was quiet, although on January 18 an Indian party under the leadership of Oscen Tustenuggee, a subchief of Echo Emathla Chopco's band and a close lieutenant of Bowlegs, attacked a small army detachment near Fort Denaud on the Caloosahatchee River and killed all but one of the soldiers. The army's activities were hampered by drenching rains which began late in January. By the first week of March one officer would write a friend, "The whole country is nearly covered with water, and this at what is called the dry season, thirteen inches of rain has fallen in five weeks." Four months later the area still was suffering from what had begun to be called "the flood of '56."[12]

The Indians were busy with their preparations in spite of the rain, and by mid-March they had scouted and camped within two miles of the enclosure at Fort Hartsuff. Two weeks earlier a raiding party had struck the settlement of Hamlin V. Snell at Sarasota Bay and, in response, volunteer troops under Capt. Leroy G. Lesley were ordered to protect the southern reaches of Peace River by garrisoning the site of Fort Winder.[13] Arriving at his new post on March 23, one of Lesley's men noted "bee trees cut in every direction by the Indians, yet no sign of them."[14]

On Monday, March 31, the Indians attacked the elegant plantation home of Dr. Joseph W. Braden in the heart of the Manatee River settlements. Led by Oscen Tustenuggee, the seven-man raiding party fired on the occupants of the house, took a number of slaves, and retreated toward the east. Alerted to the raid at Fort Meade on Wednesday morning, a detachment of Captain Hooker's company immediately was dispatched to Manatee where, with seven volunteers under the command of Capt. John Addison and with John W. Whidden as guide, they took to the Indians' trail. By mid-afternoon on Friday the volunteers had reached Peace River at a point opposite the Indians' camp.[15]

With provisions low, Bennett Whidden was sent to Fort Hartsuff for supplies and reinforcements and two other men were directed back to Manatee in the hope they might encounter troops of Captain Lesley's company. The following morning when Addison returned to camp after surveying the river for a crossing, the volunteers had been joined by a detachment of Lesley's company under the command of Lt. Henry A. Crane. Discovering the Indians had left their camp on the east bank, this combined force crossed Peace River in pursuit. At about 1:00 that afternoon, eight miles east, the Indians were found camped on the south bank of Big Charlie Apopka Creek. Addison promptly ordered a charge across the creek, and a thirty-minute gun battle erupted. When the smoke had cleared at least two of the seven Indians had been mortally wounded, although the volunteers reported others as killed and carried away. Before withdrawing, the volunteers scalped the two Indians remaining, one of whom lived long enough to ask in English for a doctor and to tell the story of the raid on Braden's plantation. When the scalped and wounded Indian was unable to march to Manatee, he was shot by a volunteer.[16]

Raids and murders west of Peace River continued in April and May as the Indians desperately attempted to draw the army's attention away from Seminole women, children, and property hidden to the south. The army failed to be swayed, however, and in April most of the volunteers stationed in the Peace River Valley were ordered south to join the regulars. At mid-month one hundred of these troops marched from Fort Meade followed within a few days by one hundred and forty more including many from the companies of Captains Hooker, Durrance, and Sparkman. Of the few volunteers remaining, those under Captain Durrance were headquartered at Fort Fraser and those under Captain Hooker at Fort Meade. They were to be assisted in scouting east and west of the river by militia troops under Capt. Leroy G. Lesley and Lt. Henry A. Crane.[17]

Early in June, twenty of Captain Durrance's men were detached to examine the swamps at the head of the Hillsborough River. A few days later Captain Lesley with twenty-five of his men, as well as twenty men from Hooker's and Sparkman's companies, was withdrawn from Peace River to look into reports of Indians in Hernando County.[18] On June 10, William B. Hooker further reduced the garrison at Fort Meade by taking a detachment ostensibly to scout the Alafia River but possibly, according to charges made by Matthew P. Lyons, to gather his cattle and drive them to sale.[19]

At sunrise on June 14, 1856, Celia Tillis, daughter of Joseph Durrance and wife of Willoughby Tillis, with her sons Dallas and Calhoun and her black slave Aunt Line, set about milking the family cows at a farm the family shared with Thomas Underhill about one and a half miles from Fort Meade. Mrs. Tillis sensed something bothering the cattle and saw the copper-colored faces of Indians in the direction the cows were gazing. Crying out, "Indians! Run for the house!" Mrs. Tillis bolted with the others from the field as the Indians opened fire. The four made it safely to their house, although as Willoughby Tillis slammed the door behind them a bullet splintered its planks and wounded Aunt Line in the forehead. Tillis and Underhill began a desperate defensive fire, hoping for the quick arrival of help from Fort Meade.[20]

At Fort Meade the sound of gunfire at the Tillis place was heard by the young sons of Daniel Carlton. Carlton's father, Lt. Alderman Carlton, rushed to the scene with six men: Daniel Carlton, John C. Oats, William Parker, William McCullough, John H. Hollingsworth, and Lott Whidden. As Carlton and his men approached the Tillis home the Indians withdrew to a nearby hammock where Carlton's small force charged them at once. Within minutes Alderman Carlton, Whidden, and Parker were dead; Daniel Carlton, Hollingsworth, and Oats were wounded.[21] Daniel Carlton, his ammunition exhausted, slashed the throat of an Indian struggling with William McCullough. Although the soldiers felt they had killed three Indians, his was the only body that remained on the field.[22]

John C. Oats and William McCullough dragged the wounded John H. Hollingsworth to the safety of the Tillis house. Daniel Carlton grabbed a horse and sped away through a hail of bullets toward Fort Fraser. Again he was wounded but arrived safely at Fort Fraser within hours. Nevertheless, little help would be forthcoming that night for the beleaguered defenders at the Tillis place. Capt. Francis M. Durrance, with few men at his disposal and anxious for the safety of the many women and children at Fort Fraser, allowed only a few men to make their way to Fort Meade. The following morning, June 15, an additional fifteen men under the command of Sgt. Francis C.M. Boggess and Celia Tillis's brother, Joseph L. Durrance, were allowed to depart and arrived at the battle site about noon.[23]

On the scene were Lt. Streaty Parker of Captain Lesley's company and several additional volunteers from the neighborhood. Parker took command of his total force of about twenty-five men and with William P. Brooker and James L. Whidden as guides, trailed the Indians south down Peace River. Parker's force camped

Holata Micco, or Billy Bowlegs, resided early in the nineteenth century in a village on Bowlegs Creek, southeast of Fort Meade. Courtesy Florida Photographic Collection, Florida State Archives.

on the river the night of the fifteenth and early the next morning left a five-man guard for the horses and again took up the trail. By 10:00 A.M. the nineteen-man force had encountered and fired upon an Indian sentinel and, shortly thereafter, discovered that the hostiles had taken up a position "under a bluff in the bend of the river."[24] Parker ordered his men to charge the position and a bloody battle ensued. Robert F. Prine and George Howell were killed, and Brooker, Whidden, and John L. Skipper were wounded. Estimates of Indian casualties ranged from four to seventeen dead. One of those casualties was the chief, Oscen Tustenuggee.[25]

Reduced to a force of only fourteen effective men, the volunteers broke off the engagement at Peace River and slowly retreated with the wounded to William P. Brooker's homestead south of Fort Meade. A short time after their arrival Capt. Hooker arrived with twenty-three men of his own company and additional volunteers from several others. After Hooker had conveyed the dead and wounded to Fort Meade, his force set out in search of the surviving Indians. Over the next three days the search extended for miles down the river, but on June 19 Hooker returned to Fort Meade without finding the hostiles. The Battle of Peace River was over.[26]

The end of the Third Seminole War

Recoiling from the attack at the Tillis place and the subsequent Battle of Peace River, frontier settlers gathered at Fort Meade on July 8, 1856, to demand that five thousand volunteers be called into service and that the frontier inhabitants be issued government rations. The apprehensions of these men and their families were heightened late in July by raids on homesteads in the vicinity of Fort Hartsuff and the destruction of stock and crops at all nearby farms except those of Willoughby Whidden and Mathew Driggers. A month later Willoughby Tillis discovered that Indians had revisited his deserted home.[27]

Military operations and patrols continued for the next year and a half to be a fact of life on Peace River.[28] In January 1857 a new post, Camp Whipple, was located on the south bank of the river near its mouth, while Fort Kissimmee, on the river of the same name, was reopened and garrisoned with regular army troops. By March Fort Meade's volunteer defenders were supplemented by a regular federal garrison which remained until early September. Scouting parties, drawn from local volunteer units and numerous companies from throughout the state, constantly combed the banks of Peace River during this time and extended their careful searches far to the east and west.[29] The river itself came under scrutiny by numerous water-borne expeditions. Typical of these reconnaissances was one made by regular army troops from Camp Whipple in February 1857 that penetrated at least thirty-five miles upstream. The officer in charge reported, "I could see no indications of Indians having been in the country for a long time," and added that "for all practicable purposes navigation ceases at 25 miles from the mouth."[30]

The frontier settlers who met at Fort Meade in July 1856 got most of what they had asked for. Numerous volunteer companies were called into service throughout 1856 and 1857, and their duties continued well into 1858. "All or nearly all the inhabitants here are mustered as volunteers," wrote an army officer in March 1857. "They perform very little duty but are paid and provisioned by government for retaining their homes in the interior." He concluded that "without this assistance from the government the war is over and [when] the troops [are] withdrawn the people will almost starve."[31]

All was not drudgery, however, for the frontier families "forted-up" at Forts Hartsuff, Green, Meade, Blount, and Fraser. Families were often concentrated with their relatives which helped relieve the routine and boredom of camp life.[32] Romances blossomed, marriages were performed, and babies were brought into the world. Francis A. Hendry's little sister, Oregon, later Mrs. Benjamin F. Blount, remembered life at Fort Meade as "lots of fun" and in 1931 could still recall playing there with her companions and experiencing the thrill of a life that was "exciting and new." A feeling of real community developed at Fort Green as well and, as early as March 1856, it was reported that the twenty families there had prepared for themselves "snug log cabins" and were instituting "an interesting school." Out of these enforced communities would emerge by 1858 the beginnings of the first true towns in the Peace River Valley since the destruction of the Indian town of Talakchopko in April 1836.[33]

By the summer of 1857 Peace River settlers both in Hillsborough and Manatee counties again found the freedom to devote time to politics. On July 18 a Democratic convention was held at Alafia at which Francis A. Hendry was nominated for the Hillsborough County Commission and Louis Lanier for county surveyor.[34] On October 5 both were elected. The same day, James D. Green was chosen by a vote of twenty-one to twelve over William H. Whitaker as the sheriff of Manatee County, and Peace River area settlers John Platt and Henry Langford were elected to the county commission. All the victors were Democrats.[35]

Meanwhile a full-scale program sending military patrols deep into South Florida had forced the Indians to seek refuge in small encampments in the vast expanses and hidden places of the Everglades and the Big Cypress Swamp. Increasingly, responsibility for these patrols was delegated to volunteer companies as regular army units first were withdrawn from the frontier and then from Florida. In July 1857 ten new companies were added to the volunteer army, and citizen soldiers began swarming around the Indians' formerly inaccessible havens. The Indian warriors attempted to hold back the tide of these troops with sniper fire and ambushes, but it simply was too late.[36]

Billy Bowlegs agreed with Indian agent Elias Rector in February 1858 to negotiate emigration.[37] By late March he and other Seminole leaders had come to terms. Out of fear that the Seminoles otherwise would not come in by the agreed time, the

Pioneer Homeland settler Alderman Carlton (1803–56), killed in the Indian attack on the Tillis place near Fort Meade on June 14, 1856. Courtesy Barbara Welles Probasco.

volunteer troops were withdrawn to the vicinity of Tampa and concentrated there. On May 7, after formal ceremonies and iced champagne at Egmont Key in Tampa Bay, Billy Bowlegs, dressed "in his red leggings, silver crown, and feathers," left Florida forever. With him were 164 Seminoles, Mikasukis, and Talla-hassees. The following day Col. Gustavus Loomis declared the Florida war closed with the assurance that "the people can now return to their homes and usual avocations without fear of further molestation."[38]

Echo Emathla Chopco

Not all the Florida Indians left with Billy Bowlegs on May 7, 1858. Early in 1859 Colonel Rector, the Indian agent, returned to Florida and induced seventy additional men, women, and children to leave with him. One Indian with whom he spoke, Echo Emathla Chopco, "came in peace and friendship" but refused to emigrate. "The Great Spirit," the Tallahassee chief informed the Indian agent, "told me to die here in the land I love."[39]

At the outbreak of the Third Seminole War, Chipco had been expelled from the Seminole Nation and had moved his small band to an island in Lake Marion, east of present-day Haines City. He lived there quietly until April 1857 when Captain Simeon L. Sparkman came across the fortified settlement and forced the Tallahassees to move a few miles southwest to an island in Lake Hamilton, where they remained for the duration of the war. In the summer of 1858 a detachment under Capt. John McNeill was sent to encourage the Indians to emigrate. McNeill eventually secured a meeting with Chipco, who suggested that he would emigrate if it were up to him but insisted on "time to see his people." Chipco failed to appear at a second meeting arranged for five days later.[40]

Before meeting with Indian agent Rector in February 1859, Chipco traveled throughout the South Florida Indian settlements to gain information on the true state of affairs. Apparently reas-sured, the Tallahassee chief met with Rector at Fort Myers and informed him of his resolve not to leave Florida. Described at the time by Henry A. Crane as "a sad relic of former greatness," Chipco then "left on his lonely march for his home on the head waters of Peas Creek."[41]

Chipco and his band remained on the lakes at the headwaters of Peace River for the rest of his life. Occcasionally the chief and other members of his band would visit the nearby settlements of Fort Meade, Bartow, and Tampa. In April 1881, "bound with the weight of years," he traveled to Orlando to seek medical advice and treatment. Six months later, on October 16, 1881, he died at his village on the headwaters of the river where he, along with Peter McQueen and his fellow Tallahassee, Osceola, first had sought refuge sixty-three years before. Echo Emathla Chopco was the last of the surviving Red Stick warriors whose lives had so influenced the Peace River Valley.[42]

Chipco's band, under the leadership of his nephew, Tallahassee, remained on Peace River until the spring of 1888 when they removed to near Lake Okeechobee. The descendants of those Tallahassee warriors remain in Florida today.[43]

The Third Seminole War erupted in December 1855 as a result of pressures designed to intimidate the Indians remaining in Florida to emigrate to the west. These pressures stemmed from demands of cattlemen for the expansion of their range lands east of Peace River and from the growth of settlements in the upper river valley. During the first seven months of the war many of these settlements were abandoned as their inhabitants sought refuge by "forting-up" at strategic locations and a series of bloody engagements was fought on or near the river as high as Fort Meade.

The war created divisions that significantly affected the history of the Peace River Valley in years to come. Existing tensions and resentments between U.S. Army regulars and Cracker frontiersmen increased and deepened. Settlers in present-day Hardee County came to believe that influential political and military leaders had jeopardized their survival for private motives. River settlers in Hillsborough and Manatee counties had begun to reassert political influence in opposition to population centers in coastal areas.

Hundreds, perhaps thousands, of volunteer soldiers from throughout Florida patrolled Peace River and its adjacent lands in 1856 and 1857, and many became enchanted with its beauties and the possibilities it offered. Growing out of the enforced concentration of settlers in forts during the same period there began to emerge in 1858 the beginnings of the first true towns of the frontier era in the river valley. Although many families had suffered from poverty and hunger through the war, the population of the river valley in 1858, with the Indian threat resolved, stood on the brink of an era of dynamic growth and prosperity. Before these forces of change could be felt, however, a wave of private violence and death would wash over the Peace River Valley.

Part Three

*"Wild enthusiasm
swept like vengeance
over the whole country"
(1858-1877)*

9

Between the Wars

T HE DEPARTURE OF BILLY BOWLEGS and his followers from
Florida in the spring of 1858 signaled the opening of the
Peace River frontier to settlement. The line of homesteads
soon reached as far south as old Camp Ogden and by the beginning of the 1860s newcomers had staked their claims throughout
the area. Growth came at a price, though. As the Third Seminole
War wound to its conclusion frontier violence flared into the Regulator movement and, by the end of the decade, political turmoil
engulfed the river settlements of both Hillsborough and Manatee
counties.

An influx of settlers

As Billy Bowlegs prepared in 1858 for his final departure from
Florida, spring came to the Peace River Valley. On April 30 an
exhausted Louis Lanier, contemplating his post-war world at Fort
Meade, wrote a sister in Georgia, "The weather is extremely dry
and the nights quite cold, [and] our cattle dont look as fine this
spring as they generally do. . . . Times in this Country with
regard to money matters is very hard. Government has not paid
the Volunteers off for the last 12 months consequently money

123

matters is scarce. Our country has a very bad appearance from
the fact that people has been broken up nearly three years, and
their places gone to rack besides some of our best citizens have
been killed by the Savage Indians. The Settlers have just commenced moving to their respective homes to commence anew." In
spite of this gloomy report he added, "If you want to move to this
Country I don't think you need be afraid of Indians and I should
certainly be glad that you should make up your minds and move
here[;] if you do the Sooner the better on account of selecting good
places."[1]

Between the close of the Third Seminole War and the firing on
Fort Sumter, a pause of only three years, new families were
drawn to the Peace River area. "Polk County had never known
such an influx of settlers as it did between 1858 and 1861,"
recalled Benjamin F. Blount. "They were simply pouring into all
of South Florida for that matter." Newspapers trumpeted the
potential of the area. "To our citizens, and all others who are desirous of cultivating the soil," proclaimed the *Florida Peninsular*,
"now is the time to brush up your plantations or seek new ones.
Strike while the iron is hot, on Peas Creek are large bodies of
good land, and throughout South Florida are lands that cannot be
exceeded anywhere."[2]

Scores of families relocated in the Peace River area from Lake
Hancock to the southern portion of what is now DeSoto County.[3]
As early as 1858 the old line of frontier settlement near Fort
Hartsuff in present-day Hardee County was extended by the families of Rowland Williams and James Washington Mathis into
what soon was to be known as the Brownville area. Not long
thereafter, Enoch Daniels, captain of a volunteer company during
the Bowlegs War, moved his family even further to the south,
settling in the vicinity of the old Second Seminole War post Camp
Ogden, rechristened Fort Ogden as it became a focal point for the
cattle industry.[4]

Among the advantages these newcomers found in the Peace
River Valley were well-built roads and bridges courtesy of the
U.S. Army. In fact, a number of volunteer companies spent the
last months of the Bowlegs War doing nothing but reopening and
improving a road from Tampa to the east side of Peace River at
Fort Meade and from there south down the river to the vicinity of
Fort Ogden. This military road came complete not only with

bridges over the various creeks, but also with the first bridge erected at the old Indian ford at Fort Meade.[5]

Complementing this system of roads and bridges was the first real town or village on Peace River in the frontier era. During the Bowlegs War families from the Alafia and Peace River areas had "forted up" for mutual protection at Forts Hartsuff, Green, Meade, Blount, and Fraser. At Fort Meade particularly, strategically located at the main crossing point on Peace River, a sense of community emerged that by the end of the war led to a small, permanent settlement stretching along the mile of military road between the fort and the new bridge. An army commissary store finished in the last month of the war and taken over by Louis Lanier offered settlers access to goods and supplies until then available only at Alafia. By January 1860 Lanier had supplemented his store with "one of the most complete saw-mills I ever saw," allowing residents of Fort Meade the luxury of plank board homes rather than log cabins, and just to the north near modern Homeland Levi Pearce had erected on the river a grist mill for grinding corn into flour. A month after Lanier's sawmill began operating, the U.S. government authorized the establishment

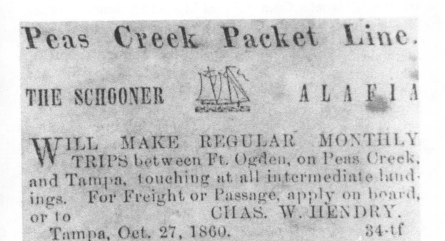

The spread of population south into the Peace River Valley following the Billy Bowlegs War led to the establishment of regular shipping connections between Fort Ogden and Tampa. This advertisement appeared in Tampa's *Florida Peninsular* in October 1860. Courtesy Gary Mormino.

there of the first post office in the river area and named Louis Lanier postmaster.[6]

The early promise of town life also was present in the Fort Blount area. Just after the war's end Riley R. Blount moved his family to a spot about one mile south of the present Polk County courthouse and there by August 1858 had opened a store and "carriage manufactory." His son, Ben, later recalled that his father carried "everything suitable to life in this country as we lived it then." Close to this store Blount also constructed a small log cabin for use as a school and a church. That fall, thirty-four boys and girls attended classes there under teacher Daniel Waldron.[7] Nearby, the Peas Creek Baptist Church, where services had been suspended on account of the war, was reorganized and continued while, in 1860 just to the south near Homeland, the predominantly Methodist settlers of the area established a campground which served for decades as a center for religious and social life.[8]

Support for schools existed throughout the settled areas of the Peace River Valley. In April 1859 the Manatee County Commission created three school districts in present-day Hardee County. John Parker, Daniel Carlton, and Enoch Daniels were appointed trustees of Manatee County School District #3, Henry Langford, Maxfield Whidden, and Willoughby Whidden, of district #4, and John Parker, David J.W. Boney, and John Pierce, of district #5. Eight months later the Hillsborough County Commission created school districts at Fort Meade (Edward T. Kendrick, Rufus Durrance, and F.C.M. Boggess, trustees), Levi Pearce's mill near Homeland (Levi Pearce, John L. Skipper, and John McAuley, trustees), and Peas Creek (Henry Seward, James Hamilton, and Riley R. Blount, trustees). Francis C.M. Boggess served as the first teacher at the Fort Meade school, and Alexander Watson acted in the same capacity at Homeland.[9]

The Regulators

For Peace River residents, the settlement of the frontier exacted costs beyond the lives of settlers and the loss of homes and possessions. One survivor of the time remembered, "The demoralizing influences of war swept like a cyclone, which operated disastrously on the young men."[10] Another, George W. Hendry, recalled that "at the close of the Indian war thousands of men were mustered out of service—a class of men no country would welcome or invite. Immediately, hordes of horse jockies, gamblers, swindlers and cut-throats ran roughshod over the whole country from Fort Meade to Tampa." Fort Meade "was run over and dominated by a class of men destitute of all moral restraint or conscientious impulses. The place was cursed with a grogshop in those days that brought about the murders, shootings, knockdowns and dragouts. So bad were existing conditions that no self-respecting lady could venture on the streets unless some male friend accompanied her." At Tampa similar conditions prevailed resulting in night after night of robberies and burglaries. As the Tampa newspaper put it, "Vice was triumphant, riotous villainy was rampant—aye, stalked forth boldly in broad day."[11]

In the face of these conditions and the absence of effective law enforcement, private action was undertaken by "the better class" of citizens. At Fort Meade a band of men, known after frontier custom as Regulators, was formed to rid the area of those "who were painting the country red." The organization soon spread to Tampa, and action commenced through the region aimed at a return to law and order. At first, Regulator efforts were relatively low keyed. For a first offense a hickory switch might be placed as a warning in the night at a man's cabin door; for a second, the switch would be used on the offender's back. Quickly, however, the violence escalated and, at Tampa, evolved into almost public lynchings.[12]

The political aspect of this Regulator violence had immediate and long-term impacts on Peace River settlers. The vigilante organization at Tampa centered upon a group of men who controlled town, as distinguished from Hillsborough County, politics (Hillsborough County at the time including the greater part of modern Polk County). Leading this group was the mayor of Tampa, Madison Post. Among other members were Bowlegs War veteran Henry A. Crane, temporary editor of the *Florida Peninsular*, physician Franklin Branch, and a young lawyer, John A. Henderson. Most of these men, particularly Post and Crane, were newcomers to Hillsborough County Democratic party ranks, having belonged during the period 1854–1857 to the American or Know-Nothing party.[13] After a series of bitter elections, by 1858 the Know-Nothings had been eliminated as an organized political force in Hillsborough County, and many of its former members had gravitated to a Democratic party wary of their intentions.[14]

Recalling in old age events of the spring of 1858, one pioneer explained "Like everywhere else where unrestrained and unlimited power is enthroned, many wrongs were perpetrated and involved many of the best meaning people into unpleasant relations which for years rankled into the hearts. . . . It seemed at the time to be the only measure adequate to the emergency." Some of those wrongs were perpetrated against James T. Magbee, a leading figure in the Hillsborough County Democratic party who by 1853 had represented the county for three terms as state representative and who in April 1858 held a powerful federal appointment as the collector of revenues at the Port of Tampa.[15]

When Magbee opposed the increasing Regulator violence, Regulator leadership began focusing blame for the breakdown of law and order on juries misled by defense attorneys such as Magbee. Just as the Regulators condemned and lynched individuals they found guilty of serious transgressions, they formulated and made public charges against Magbee, primarily based on the lawyer's drinking habits, aimed at replacing him as collector of revenues with their associate, Hamlin V. Snell. Getting wind of these plans, Magbee undertook a public defense of himself on June 5 in a four-column letter to the Tampa newspaper in which he exposed the workings of the "secret sworn band" and laid blame at the feet of Post and *Florida Peninsular* editor Henry A. Crane. One week later Crane called Magbee a "blackguard" in the columns of his newspaper, and, purporting to speak for the Democratic party, declared, "We have done with Col. Magbee,—so has the party!!" On June 15 the situation intensified when Magbee for a second time in as many months was hauled before Tampa's mayor's court, with the temporary mayor William B. Hooker presiding, and again was convicted and fined upon a petty charge.[16]

Four days later Crane reported to his readers the news of Magbee's replacement by Hamlin Snell. However, within a few weeks of Magbee's downfall, Crane was relieved of the editorship of the Tampa paper and by early August had moved with a small party to the deserted remains of Fort Myers. For a while Post prospered and even received an important federal appointment as receiver of the Tampa District Land Office. Within two years, however, the *Florida Peninsular* reported of him, "Post has been a rank Democrat, and has brought upon the party the well-merited charge of corruption." Magbee, free from his responsibilities as collector of the port, concentrated on a busy law practice until in 1860 he stepped again into the political arena and, after a fierce struggle, turned the tables on his political foes.[17]

Politics and the Peace River Valley

A bitter political legacy lay behind ensuing events in Magbee's political career. In both Hillsborough and Manatee counties, settlements in the river area containing a substantial portion of each county's population lay fifty miles from the centers of county government at, respectively, Tampa and Manatee (Bradenton). This distance, over dirt roads often flooded, made access to government and, specifically, the courts extremely difficult and at times impossible. Ocean access at Tampa and Manatee, coupled with the impracticality of navigation on Peace River above Fort Ogden, also gave merchants and politicians on the coast control of commerce to and from the interior, a situation which caused further resentment of the coastal areas by frontier settlers.

Before the Bowlegs War and only one year after the creation of

Early Hardee County settlers Daniel Wilson Carlton (1823-91) and his wife, Sallie Ann (Murphy) Carlton (1823-1905). From *DeVane's Early Florida History*, vol. 2.

Manatee County, residents of modern-day Hardee County attempted without success to secede from the new county and reunite with other areas of the Peace River Valley in Hillsborough County. During the war, the frustrations and resentments of those settlers were heightened as they came to feel abandoned at Forts Green and Hartsuff by military and civil authorities from coastal areas. Even before the war's end, those emotions led to efforts aimed at gaining influence for the river areas in Manatee County government and, ultimately, to the October 1857 election of James D. Green as sheriff and John Platt and Henry Langford as county commissioners. A year later these political efforts suffered a setback when Green narrowly failed to defeat Manatee resident Archibald McNeill in a race for state representative, a powerful position having control over local laws affecting the county.[18]

Soon after the 1858 house election, on January 10, 1859, two members of the Manatee County Commission from the western part of the county, N.P. Hunter and J.G. Williams, met with Probate Judge Ezekiel Glazier, who by law served as president of the board. They granted Glazier a contract for a thousand dollars to build a courthouse and jail at Manatee. Taken in the absence of the Peace River area commissioners and in the face of a competing proposal for a more elaborate building at the same cost, their action goaded residents of the eastern half of the county to bring about change at the next opportunity.[19]

Elections for Manatee County offices were held in the fall of 1859 and the results, at first blush, appeared to be a triumph for residents of the eastern portion of the county. Fabricus Reynolds was elected probate judge; Willoughby Whidden's son, John W. Whidden, was elected sheriff; and, for the office of commissioner, William H. Addison, James D. Green, William C. Hair, and David J.W. Boney received the highest number of votes. The election was not so easily decided, however, nor would the power brokers at Manatee so easily surrender control of county affairs.[20]

William H. Addison was a cattleman who resided in the Myakka area far from Peace River and much closer in proximity and interest to Manatee. William C. Hair, the brother-in-law of wealthy cattleman John Parker, had business and personal ties far removed from the relatively less well-to-do majority of settlers on Peace River. These two men, in tandem with Ezekiel Glazier as probate judge, acted to perpetuate Glazier in office by refusing to grant the necessary bond to Fabricus Reynolds "until the Commissioners can be satisfied he is a resident of Manatee County." In the case of sheriff-elect John W. Whidden the commission declined to swear him into office on the grounds that he "was not of age," an action which left the county without a sheriff for over a year until William H. Addison's brother, Joel, was appointed to the position in February 1861. Since the sheriff also served as tax assessor and collector, the commission's action resulted in a failure to assess taxes for 1860—a major boon for sugar planters at Manatee and the owners of large cattle herds throughout the county. And then there was the question of James D. Green.[21]

Under a provision of the Florida Constitution, no public official having control over public funds was eligible for any other office until he had accounted for, and paid over, all the public funds in his possession. A county official accounted for such funds and paid them over to the board of county commissioners. Approval was usually routine. Taking advantage of this provision, however, the majority of the Manatee board of commissioners arbitrarily refused to accept Green's final accounts as sheriff and tax collector—the total amount in contention being $11.35. The effect was immediate: Green was barred from taking his seat on the board of commissioners and the vacancy was filled by the next highest vote getter, William J. Hooker, twenty-three-year-old son of the man blamed for not protecting Fort Green during the Bowlegs War, William B. Hooker of Tampa. As Green himself stated, "never has been a Tax Collector so rigidly dealt with in Florida." The Manatee-based sugar and business interests were not done yet with Jim Green, however. On April 17, 1860, a Manatee County grand jury dominated by Manatee planters and businessmen, including Ezekiel Glazier, and with Green's election foe Archibald McNeill as foreman, indicted Green for refusing to pay over monies into the state treasury. Prosecution was not pursued, but the charge was left pending.[22]

The frustration of Peace River residents was increased that fall by the failure of their petition to the Florida legislature calling for the creation of a new county out of eastern Manatee. This new entity, to be called Ranshaw County, was to be bounded by the Kissimmee River on the east, the Caloosahatchee River on the south and the present western boundaries of Hardee and DeSoto counties on the west. Under the watchful eye of Representative Archibald McNeill, however, the petition quickly was referred to a select committee from which it never emerged.[23]

Many residents of the Peace River area again in late 1860 supported Jim Green for the state legislature, this time on a platform demanding that the county seat be moved and that state aid be granted for clearing and straightening the channel of Peace River. Against Green, Manatee interests supported cattleman John Parker and again Green narrowly was defeated. There, for the time being, matters stood.[24]

River settlers to the north in Hillsborough County felt similarly distanced from their county government. Lack of easy access to the courts was a problem and, although residents of eastern Hillsborough had not felt themselves abandoned during the Bowlegs War, numerous instances of petty irritations with Tampa officialdom had increased sentiment for a county government centered on the Peace River settlements. Typical of these irritations was the arrest and transportation under guard to Tampa in April 1858 of James L. Whidden, Louis Lanier, and John I. Hooker on charges of non-attendance as witnesses during times they were serving as volunteers in the Seminole war. Although the three were discharged without penalty, bitter feelings remained.[25]

While Manatee countians were requesting the creation of Ranshaw County, petitions were circulated in the Peace River areas of Hillsborough calling for the creation of Perry County, named presumably for Florida Governor Madison S. Perry whose support for the effort was essential. Tampa-based State Representative James Gettis introduced legislation authorizing the new county on December 6 and three days later it passed by a 34-5 vote. Arriving in the senate on December 12, the bill quickly fell victim to politics and eventually was referred to the judiciary committee. In the apparent absence of support from either Governor Perry or State Senator John Eubanks of Brooksville, whose district included Hillsborough County, the Perry County bill died on December 21 when the judiciary committee recommended it "Do Not Pass."[26]

Residents of the Peace River settlements in Hillsborough County were shocked and then furious over the failure of the Perry

THE FIRST SCHOOL HOUSE IN BARTOW FLA. 1858
Dr Daniel Waldron Teacher.

Bartow's first schoolhouse as it appeared in 1858. Courtesy Florida Photographic Collection, Florida State Archives.

County bill and what was considered the duplicity of Senator Eubanks. As one frustrated pioneer put it, "Our people feel that they have either been treated with the utmost contempt, or that their interests have been shamefully neglected." The sudden death of Senator Eubanks on May 30, 1860, ignited a political firestorm which resulted in a battle for control of Hillsborough County politics. In both the regular biennial contest for state representative and the special election for state senator the key issue became the creation of a new county out of eastern Hillsborough.[27]

James T. Magbee, a supporter of county division, was the first candidate to announce in the senate race. Furious at the thought of a Magbee victory, the lawyer's old nemesis, Madison Post, attempted to pull together and manipulate against Magbee the Hillsborough County Democratic party. The result of Post's efforts was the convening of a county Democratic convention to determine a nominee for the house seat and to appoint delegates to a senatorial convention of Hillsborough, Manatee, Hernando, and Levy counties for the purpose of selecting a nominee in the senate race. At that county meeting, held at Alafia on July 7, 1860, Post's attempts to control the convention became so evident that the delegations from Itchepuckesassa, Fort Blount, Fort Meade, and Alafia walked out. Nonplussed, Post and his associates, including Hamlin V. Snell, then mayor of Tampa, proceeded to Brooksville where the senatorial convention was held on August 10. Although attended only by the Hernando delegation, representatives of Tampa precinct in Hillsborough County, and, possibly, a lone representative from Manatee, the convention, upon Snell's motion, nominated William B. Hooker's son-in-law, Samuel E. Hope of Brooksville, to oppose Magbee.[28]

While Magbee and Hope canvased the huge senatorial district for support, the house race in Hillsborough also became quite heated. In the wake of the aborted county Democratic convention four candidates announced for the house seat: William I. Turner, Joseph Howell, Benjamin Moody, and Dr. S.B. Todd. After sampling potential support, both Moody and Todd withdrew, leaving the race a head-to-head contest between Howell, who supported county division, and Turner, who opposed it.[29]

Although Election Day was October 1, returns from the sprawling senatorial district were slow in being reported. Within a week or two, however, it became clear that Magbee had defeated Hope in every county in the district. Manatee supported the new senator by a vote of 53 to 39 and in Hillsborough the vote was 212 to 171. The Peace River precincts of Hillsborough reported lopsided votes for Magbee of 34 to 22 at Fort Meade and 32 to 1 at Fort Blount. With the election of a pro-county division senator assured, attention quickly shifted to the house race in Hillsborough, and there was found a great surprise—out of 357 votes cast, William I. Turner and Joseph Howell each had received 178 votes, with one additional vote going to S.B. Todd. The election was a tie.[30]

A new election was called for the Hillsborough house seat to be held October 19. Joseph Howell, William I. Turner, S.B. Todd, and Louis Lanier quickly jumped into the race. The only real issue was county division, and supporters of the split generally rallied around Howell while opponents campaigned for Turner. After a short, furious campaign, county division prevailed as

Howell edged out Turner by a vote of 183 to 152, with 23 votes split among others. By that 31-vote margin, the creation of the new county was assured.[31]

On January 17, 1861, State Representative Joseph Howell of Hillsborough County introduced legislation to create a new political subdivision out of portions of eastern Hillsborough and western Brevard counties. The new county was to be named, at the suggestion of Reading Blount, in honor of President James K. Polk with whom Blount had a personal acquaintance. The bill passed the house on January 30 and five days later, at the urging of State Senator James T. Magbee, was approved by the senate. On February 8, 1861, Polk County came into being with a stroke of Governor Madison S. Perry's pen. Twenty-one days earlier the State of Florida had seceded from the Union.[32]

The conclusion of the Third Seminole War found Peace River settlers wearied but hopeful as they returned to homesteads abandoned for more than two years. Not only had the Indian threat been removed, but the army had left in place a system of roads and bridges allowing relatively easy movement into the Peace River Valley. Down these roads in the three years prior to the Civil War poured scores of families intent upon beginning life anew. With these newcomers in the vanguard, the line of frontier settlement was pushed in 1858 into present-day DeSoto County and not long thereafter as far south as Fort Ogden.

Greeting new settlers in the Peace River area were institutions reflecting the growth of society on the frontier, including the first village, at Fort Meade, together with the first stores, mills, and post office. Schools and churches having their origins in the years immediately preceding the war were revived and expanded. With this growth and progress came increased demands for political and economic independence by residents along the river. In Manatee County these demands were frustrated by a coalition of prominent cattlemen with business and sugar interests at Manatee, but in Hillsborough County victory was achieved after a fierce battle with Tampa area politicians.

10

Prelude to Fort Sumter

A S CIVIL WAR LOOMED ON the horizon, Peace River settlers busied themselves with building new homes, establishing local governments and attempting to find a dependable market for their cattle. The war's opening rounds had little effect on the river settlements, although Confederate conscription agents and the ravages of nature brought tragedy to the area. By mid-1863, however, the residents of the river valley were poised for the onset of a war most of them did not want.

Slavery

"Just as the country became settled and everyone inspired with new life," recalled one Peace River pioneer, "the convulsions of 1860 demoralized everything." Memories of the Civil War still vivid in his mind, the old settler continued, "For years, no sign of thrift or prosperity was visible around the cottage home of the pioneer. That wild enthusiasm, which is the concomitant to war, swept like vengeance over the whole country. . . . Without a dollar to begin with, that eventful period opened upon Polk, as elsewhere; nothing to sell, nothing to buy with. Other sections had the advantage of boat or railroad facilities—could garden and sell, but not so with Polk. It was 'root hog or die,' and it seemed that it was 'die hog if you do root.' But our climate was mild, our soil productive, and the inhabitants healthy; being a range country, too, afforded us beef; raised the 'tater, pease, rice, corn, vegetables, sugar-cane; grazed our horses, hunted our scattering beeves, and we lived."[1]

The interrelated issues of slavery and state sovereignty had dominated national politics for more than a decade prior to 1860. In frontier South Florida, however, where settlers for the most part struggled without the assistance of slave labor to protect and feed their families, these issues generally simmered on the back burner. When the possibility of a dismemberment of the nation did arise early in the 1850s, most settlers opposed the idea, as evidenced by the election in 1850 and 1852 of strongly pro-Union Democrat James T. Magbee as Hillsborough County's state representative.[2]

During the 1850s, though, economic and political power in Manatee and Hillsborough counties increasingly was concentrated in the hands of merchants, planters, and cattlemen who either had substantial slave holdings or were dependent for their livelihoods on those who did. This trend was particularly evident in Manatee County where, out of a total 1860 slave population of 253, Manatee sugar planter John C. Cofield held title to 190 bondsmen, and Dempsey D. Crews, Josiah Gates, John Parker, William B. Hooker, and William H. Whitaker each owned five or more. Just to the north in Hillsborough, planter Edmund Jones led the list of slaveowners with 26. Among those residing at Alafia and Tampa and owning five or more slaves were William I. Turner, William B. Hooker, James T. Magbee, Ossian B. Hart, Leroy G. Lesley, C.L. Frebele, James McKay, William Cooley, Franklin Branch, John Darling, and William S. Mobley. Of Manatee's total 1860 population of 854, 30 percent were slaves. In Hillsborough (including future Polk County) the respective figures were 2,979 and 19 percent. Total numbers of slaveowners ran only about 120 in Hillsborough and, in Manatee, just 20.[3]

After the withdrawal of Indians and their black allies from the Peace River area during the Second Seminole War, slavery had been reintroduced to the river valley in 1849 by Rigdon Brown. Brown's slaves were supplemented in 1851 by approximately 12 slaves who accompanied the Blount families, and the number of bondsmen grew slowly thereafter so that, by 1861, 31 families in Polk County possessed 143 slaves. Eight men—Readding Blount, James Hamilton, George Hamilton, Francis A. Hendry, Louis Lanier, John C. Oats, Henry S. Seward, and Frederick Varn—held 55 percent of that number. The 15 owners of five or more slaves controlled 83 percent of the total.[4] It was estimated that the slaves, for the most part concentrated in the areas of Forts Blount and Fraser, had a combined 1861 monetary value of $81,450. By way of comparison, the value of cattle ranging in the county was placed at $128,367.[5]

As a general rule, the farther south one traveled down Peace River from Fort Blount, the fewer slaves one encountered. Below the Polk County line, only Dempsey D. Crews possessed more than five blacks, and Maxfield Whidden's holdings were limited to two young women. Slaves owned by William B. Hooker and his son, William J. Hooker, may have worked the cattle ranges to the east of the river, but more than likely their activities were confined to the Manatee River area. John Parker, living near Ona, did control five slaves in the estate of his brother, William, but it is uncertain where they were located.[6]

It is far easier to deterimine the numbers and locations of black slaves than it is to understand the nature of their lives. Few accounts of slavery in the area, particularly from the perspective of a slave, have come to light. Except in the case of blacks owned by Manatee County sugar planters, however, it does not seem likely that life for the average slave in the Peace River area fit the classic picture of southern plantation slavery. "Slavery here is a very mild form," reported future Union hero Oliver O. Howard from Tampa in 1857, hinting at a curious insensitivity to the plight of bondsmen on the part of the man who, within less than a decade, would be appointed to head the Freedmen's Bureau. Howard then continued, "You wouldn't know the negroes were slaves unless you were told. White men work with the negroes particularly at any trade. . . . The Quartermaster hires a good many as teamsters."[7] Despite Howard's comments, the blacks held in bondage certainly felt every day of their lives that they were slaves, but local practice may have allowed a few to live and work apart from their masters. A correspondent writing from Key West in 1862 noted a custom "long in vogue here" which allowed some bondsmen "to hire their own time and make what they could, paying the master a portion of their earnings."[8]

Most slaveowners in the Peace River area owned only a single slave or, at most, a slave couple with one or more small children. As Oliver O. Howard suggested, it would have been common practice for these masters and slaves to work alongside each other on the owner's farm or to tend the owner's cattle on the Myakka, Peace River, and Kissimmee ranges. In most instances, though, the heaviest manual labor and the least desirable chores were performed for white masters by black men and women. In light of that difficult and continuing labor and rigid slave codes prohibiting them from learning even to read and write, few slaves were able to improve their lives or the lives of their loved ones.[9]

$50 REWARD!

My Boy, NIMROD, formerly owned by Dr. E. Branch, having run away from my plantation on the Hillsborough River, I offer the above reward of FIFTY DOLLARS to any person who will return him to me, or safely lodge him in jail and inform me of the fact, so that I may get him into my possession.

Nimrod is stout built, of low stature, having a downcast countenance, and a muttering way of speaking. He has a very large foot and hand for a person of his age, being about fifteen or sixteen years old. His color is that of a dark mulatto.

EDMUND JONES.

Tampa, Nov. 17, 1860.   37-tf

Slaves in South Florida may have escaped the harshness that characterized the Cotton Belt states, but many understandably sought any opportunity to gain their freedom. The slaveowner advertising here moved his slaves during the Civil War to a plantation near Bartow. From the Tampa *Florida Peninsular*, November 17, 1860. Courtesy Gary Mormino.

The patterns of slavery in South Florida permitted some familiarity across racial bounds. For example, many slaves—barred from attending churches not under white supervision—joined and participated fully in churches to which their owners belonged. In the case of slave women the relationship between master and slave, always under the absolute control of the master, offered opportunity for familiarity to be debased by sexual domination and exploitation. No account survives to tell the personal story of a black woman from the area, but the letter of an Army officer written from Fort Meade in 1857 hints at the tragic reality of her situation, as well as that of the wives of some slaveowners. "What must be the . . . desolate heart of [the slaveholder's] wife," wrote soon-to-be Union general Thomas Williams, "who, perhaps childless herself, sees around her, in the pale black & yellow faces of the slave children, in glaring contrast with the ebony of the mothers, the features of the husband repeated."[10]

Secession

Ownership of one or many slaves was not necessarily the same thing as supporting the breakup of the Union. As the national crisis broadened during 1860, a number of prominent slaveowners stood against succession. At Tampa these individuals included James T. Magbee and Ossian B. Hart, while on Peace River Readding Blount, Jacob Summerlin, Francis A. Hendry, John L. Skipper, and Francis C.M. Boggess all were known to support continuation of the Union.[11]

Abraham Lincoln was not on the 1860 presidential ballot in Florida, nor was the regular Democratic nominee, Stephen A. Douglas. Instead, Floridians were allowed to choose between conservative Southern Democratic nominee John C. Breckenridge of Kentucky and Constitutional Union party candidate John Bell of Tennessee. Neither voiced support for secession, and Bell's party, described as "a coalition of old-line Whigs, ex-'Know-Nothings,' proslavery Unionists, and moderate southern rights men," was founded upon a promise to stand by the Constitution and the Union.[12]

On Election Day, November 6, 1860, residents of Hillsborough selected the most conservative candidate, Breckenridge, by a vote of 303 to 60, while Manatee residents supported the same man by a vote of 50 to 0. Those results failed to reflect the wishes of residents of the Peace River Valley. At Fort Fraser precinct, which had cast 33 votes in the state senate election one month previously, only 13 votes were cast—all for Breckenridge. At Fort Meade 52 votes were cast, 4 fewer than one month previously, and 14 of them were cast for the more moderate Bell. Precinct returns are not available for Manatee County but, compared to 92 votes cast in the October state elections, only 50 votes were tallied in November. Based on the concentration of slave interests in the western part of the county, it may be assumed that many—if not most—of those who declined to support Breckenridge or Bell were residents of the Peace River settlements. The election had exposed no overwhelming enthusiasm on Peace River for constitutional crisis and disunion.[13]

Such enthusiasm was present west of Peace River at Alafia and Tampa, where in late November a series of political rallies was held to express disgust at the election of Abraham Lincoln and to issue demands for a state convention to discuss secession. Taking the lead at those sessions were William I. Turner and others who constituted a roll call of the top slaveowners in the county, as well as politicians including Madison Post and Hamlin V. Snell. Noticeably absent, with the exception of Francis M. Durrance, were slaveholders and other residents at Peace River.[14]

Responding to Lincoln's election, the Florida legislature called a state convention to discuss secession. Ezekiel Glazier, Massachusetts-born foe of James D. Green, was chosen as delegate from Manatee County, and twenty-four-year-old Hillsborough County probate judge, Tampa newspaper editor, and Indiana native Simon Turman, Jr., represented Hillsborough. When on January 10, 1861, the convention voted in favor of secession, both Glazier and Turman cast their votes with the majority. No public referendum on the question ever was held.[15]

Once Florida was out of the Union it began to give some thought to the idea of raising an armed force to defend itself. In Hillsborough and Manatee counties, a state militia had been organizing only since the early months of 1860. One of Hillsborough's four military beats encompassed the Fort Meade-Fort Blount-Fort Fraser area, and one of Manatee's two beats was focused on Fort Hartsuff. Elections for officers of the local regiment and companies were held May 7, 1860. William I. Turner, soon to be a prominent secessionist, was elected colonel of the twentieth Regiment, and John Parker was selected as his lieutenant colonel. At Peace River, William B. Varn defeated John R. Durrance by a single vote for election as captain, and Thomas C. Pearce and George W. Hendry were elected lieutenants. No election was held at Fort Hartsuff.[16]

Organizational progress was slow. Commissions for the officers were not available until late July, and the first full-scale muster of the Peace River company does not appear to have taken place until April 27, 1861, seven weeks after President Lincoln's inauguration. Thereafter, for almost a year, the company met "at stated times" at the county seat "to practice mustering." On March 10, 1862, it and all other Florida militia companies were abolished by the Florida legislature.[17]

Perhaps out of frustration with the leadership and progress of the militia, a separate company of mounted volunteers was organized at Fort Meade the week of the Lincoln inauguration. Nicknamed the "Hickory Boys," this company elected Streaty Parker as its captain and John R. Durrance and Zachariah Seward as its lieutenants. A detachment of the company under the command of John R. Durrance took up station at Fort Meade from July 14 to August 27, 1861.[18]

Polk County organizes

Until the spring of 1862 the Civil War had little impact on the Peace River Valley. As late as June Tampa minister W.L. Murphy could assert, "There is but very little excitement or apprehension of danger . . . and God has blessed . . . the country with abundance of the necessaries of life." During the same month in nearby Brooksville, the Reverend Samuel W. Carson, soon to become a respected clergyman and resident of the Peace River area, would echo Murphy's claim, stating, "We are less affected here except taking almost all our men away, than any other portion of the Southern Confederacy."[19]

At Peace River life passed quietly after the war erupted at Fort Sumter April 12, 1861, although a little excitement was felt in March 1862 when militia captain William B. Varn received orders to forward forty volunteers to the Confederate army. At a muster near Fort Blount the required number "promptly volunteered" and, after "a great dinner" had been held in their honor, the volunteers marched off to the north.[20] Otherwise, the routine of life was interrupted only by attempts to organize and maintain local government and to collect, drive, and sell cattle.[21]

The legislation which created Polk County in February 1861 required that an election for county officers be held immediately and that, at the same time, voters be permitted to select a county seat. Accordingly, on April 13, 136 men appeared at Fort Meade, Fort Fraser, and Socrum to elect Levi W. Cornelius as probate judge and de facto president of the board of county commissioners, George W. Hendry as clerk of the circuit court, William H. Durrance as sheriff, Silas McClelland as coroner, William B. Varn as county surveyor, and William S. Harris, James Hamilton, Isaac Waters, and Joseph Mizell as county commissioners. The first option for a county seat was a tract of land about four miles south of Fort Blount near what would soon be known as Kissengen Springs. On the tract James Hamilton and Zachariah Seward, Jr., had erected a log cabin stocked with goods, which they hoped would serve as a focal point for a new settlement. The second possibility was "a beautiful parcel of land" on the west side of Mud Lake, northwest of present-day Highlands City and convenient to the settlements at Fort Fraser, Medulla, and Socrum.[22] Prompted by a public "jealousy" of Hamilton and Seward's real estate scheme, voters overwhelmingly opted for the Mud Lake site.[23]

The new board of commissioners held its first meeting at Mud Lake on June 18, 1861, with all members present. In regular order they divided the county into election precincts and road districts, appointed road commissioners, declared public roads, and approved the county's first expenses, including the purchase of a county seal. Before the commission could proceed further, however, fall elections on October 7, 1861, produced a new slate of officials.[24] L. W. Cornelius was returned to office as probate judge; Edward T. Kendrick defeated incumbent sheriff William H. Durrance; Jehu J. Blount was elected as clerk of the circuit court; Eli English became coroner; and a new county commission consisting of Joseph Mizell, Francis A. Hendry, Readding Blount, and Isaac Waters was chosen.[25]

Three days later Polk countians returned to the polls to select the county's first state representative. Of 135 votes cast, Henry

Lewis Hicks, former slave of
Fort Green settler Robert Hen-
dry. Courtesy Mrs. Jean B.
Burton.

S. Seward was elected over William S. Harris by a majority of 27
votes. On November 8 voters again cast their ballots, this time for
members of the electoral college in the first presidential election
of the Confederate States of America. Strongly pro-Confederate
candidates James Gettis and Jesse Carter, both of Tampa, were
shunned in Polk as well as in Manatee County, perhaps reflecting
a continuing lack of enthusiasm in the area for the secessionist
cause.[26]

The burning issue of the October 10, 1861, election was continuing controversy over the location of the Polk County seat at
Mud Lake, some residents considering the site to be "impractical." Apparently the election of Henry S. Seward insured a
reconsideration of the matter for by December 13 the new representative had secured the enactment of legislation requiring Polk
countians again to vote on the question. Within a short time that
election was held and, although Mud Lake again was offered to
the voters as a possible county seat, the electors opted for a site
about a mile south of Fort Blount which, when surveyed by William B. Varn, was given the name of Jefferson. The county com-

mission soon ordered lots sold in its new seat, and plans were begun for the erection of a courthouse from the proceeds. The county proved unable to obtain title to the land, however, and with the onset of the Civil War all plans were shelved for the duration of the conflict.[27]

One more matter of government remained to be settled. After ties with the United States had been severed, the post office at Fort Meade, the only such office in the Peace River Valley, remained in operation. Early in 1862, however, the Confederate States postal service decided to move the office closer to the settlements near the county seat—clearly a more central location—and finally settled upon Fort Blount. When local residents were asked by what name the post office should be known, the Reverend Robert N. Pylant proposed that Col. Francis Stebbins Bartow, Confederate hero killed the previous summer at the First Battle of Bull Run, be honored. Thereafter, the settlement was known as Bartow. W.P. Brown served as its first postmaster.[28]

Meanwhile in Manatee County, which had been "perfectly lawless for over a year" in the absence of a sheriff, residents struggled to continue its government. On October 7, 1861, elections were held for county officers, and the total vote of 121 more than doubled that of the presidential election of the previous November. The powerlessness and disaffection felt by Peace River settlers, perhaps magnified by the death on May 27 of patriarch Willoughby Whidden, was reflected by few river residents standing for office. For the first time since the birth of Manatee County the name of James D. Green—still under indictment—did not appear on the ballot, and Manatee area residents tightened their grasp on county government. Resentments of those Manatee residents by citizens of the eastern half of the county continued to simmer, though. By November 1861 the intensity of feeling had increased enough to prompt state representative John Parker to introduce legislation requiring the transfer of the county seat from Manatee to "a place at or near Hagan's Bluff, on Peas Creek," a location in the vicinity of the Joshua Creek settlements. Parker's bill was enacted and approved December 5, but was ignored for the duration of the Civil War.[29]

As residents of Polk and Manatee counties grappled with their political and governmental problems, the population of the area was increasing as families were driven by threat of war to the relative security of interior southern Florida. In today's DeSoto County this trend was evidenced by the arrival of George Camp Tippens and his family near Fort Ogden and of the Francis B. Hagan and Enoch E. Mizell families in the Horse Creek–Pine Level area. A few miles to the north in present-day Hardee County, Robert Hendry settled near Fort Green and Wade Hampton Whidden at Fort Hartsuff. Perhaps the trend was best evidenced in Polk County where, among others, Robert N. Pylant, Jeremiah M. Hayman, George W. Gandy, James Hansford Johnson, Alderman Wilson, James T. Wilson, and George W. Williams all settled during the period.[30]

Some individuals moved to Polk County in the early years of the war to protect more than their families. In 1862 Hillsborough County's largest slaveholder, Edmund Jones, moved to Bartow with 26 slaves. At about the same time his father-in-law, Dr. Daniel Stanford, physician and Baptist minister, made the same move with nine slaves. From as far away as Charlotte County, Virginia, came affluent planter William Joel Watkins with his wife, five children and 16 slaves. Some who did not make the move sent their slaves instead, a case in point being that of Hillsborough countian George Wells who, by 1863, kept 16 slaves in Polk. Between 1861 and 1863 the total number of slaves in Polk County rose from 143 to 237, an increase of 60 percent.[31]

Cattle for sale

Upon the close of the Third Seminole War, South Florida cattlemen had more beef than they knew what to do with, many of the beeves driven to the area by new settlers and countless thousands found wild on the South Florida ranges. It must have seemed an answer to a prayer for them when Capt. James McKay of Tampa purchased a brig, *Huntress*, and, in association with Jacob Summerlin, William B. Hooker, and other cattlemen, opened up a cattle trade with Cuba. In 1859, 679 beeves made the voyage from Ballast Point on Tampa Bay to Havana, and the following year the number jumped to over 4,000. The trade was not without its problems, however, and during the long summer drought of 1860 it experienced a major disaster when McKay's new steamer, *Salvor*, failed to arrive at Tampa on time and hundreds, if not thousands, of cattle died of thirst. [32]

Faced with this calamity, James McKay and his cattle suppliers decided to shift their operations from Tampa Bay to Peace River. The Fort Ogden area already had become a meeting place for cowhunters and just south near Punta Gorda McKay and Summerlin erected "a wharf of unpeeled pine saplings, which extended eight hundred feet into the water to a deep channel."[33] Cattle shipping from the new wharf commenced in November 1860.[34]

The Republican presidential victory and the ensuing clamor for secession prompted McKay and Summerlin to step up their operations. In February 1861, Francis C.M. Boggess moved his family from Fort Meade to Fort Ogden to assist in the cattle business. Shortly thereafter Summerlin, too, in the words of his son, "moved his family and only necessary supplies in a small sailboat from Tampa to the location of Fort Ogden." McKay later would state that from November 1860 until June 1861 he did not spend ten days away from his ship and wharf. He not only carried his shipments to Cuba, he also sold beef to U.S. troops garrisoning Key West and the Dry Tortugas. And that soon landed him in trouble.[35]

On June 6, 1861, McKay's cattle boat, *Salvor*, was detained by the U.S. Navy at Key West. Subsequently the Navy leased the vessel from McKay and permitted him to return to Tampa in a fishing smack. Tampa proved no welcoming home port, however, for soon after his arrival McKay was arrested for treason and brought before a tribunal of two justices of the peace. Accusing McKay of supplying beef to the Union enemy, prosecutor James T. Magbee, caught up in the fervor of the times and now describing himself as an "undoubted secessionist," demanded the accused be hanged. After a long and acrimonious trial and a spirited defense by lawyers James Gettis and Ossian B. Hart, McKay was bound over for further proceedings in the circuit court. At that point, Tampa's military commander, Gen. Joseph M. Taylor, stepped in and allowed McKay to post a $10,000 bond and to return to Key West.[36]

At Key West McKay was able to reclaim the *Salvor* and immediately took the boat to Havana for repairs. On October 14, while making for the Florida coast, the *Salvor* was stopped 20 miles south of Tortuga by the U.S. Navy steamer, *Keystone State*. Ordered to Key West, the *Salvor* was found upon arrival to contain 600 pistols and 500,000 percussion caps, as well as hats, shoes, cigars, coffee, and other dry goods. The ship automatically was confiscated, and McKay and his son Donald were seized as prisoners of war. McKay's crew of slaves was freed and released.[37]

For the next five months James McKay was held as a Union prisoner of war, first in military custody at Key West and after February 1, 1862, in the custody of the state department in Washington, D.C. After personal interest in his case was expressed by President Lincoln, McKay was allowed to take an oath of allegiance to the United States, then paroled. On April 21 he returned to Key West and there informed the commanding officer, "You may rest assured of everything in my power being done for the restoration of the Union." Shortly afterwards, McKay returned to Tampa.[38]

In McKay's absence, Jacob Summerlin agreed to supply cattle to a new market, the Confederate States army. Allowed a detail of twenty-four men from the Fourth and Seventh Florida Infantry Regiments, recruited in great part from the Tampa–Peace River area, Summerlin, Francis A. Hendry, Francis C.M. Boggess, and others drove cattle from as far south as the Caloosahatchee River to the railhead at Baldwin, Florida. Beginning in 1862 and continuing in 1863, Summerlin and other cattlemen were credited with driving up to six hundred head per week during the April to August season. In Confederate currency, the contractors received for their efforts, including expenses of the drive, almost thirty dollars per head. During the period of June to September 1862, Francis A. Hendry alone received in excess of fifty thousand dollars.[39]

James McKay returned to Florida about midway through the 1862 cattle driving season, and he and Summerlin made plans to revive their Cuban cattle trade. Summerlin had some personal business to take care of first, however. Blessed with an abundance of Confederate money and concerned for its future value, the cattle king looked around for more secure financial alternatives. Unable to exchange his Confederate bills for gold, Summerlin journeyed to Charleston, South Carolina, where finally he was able to obtain Confederate bonds ultimately redeemable in gold. Closer to home, Summerlin looked for an investment whose value was not dependent upon the war's outcome. Sensing possibilities for growth in the Peace River area and anxious in the short term to provide a safer home for his family, he hit upon the idea of investing in a site with potential for development as a town. Since title to most land in the Peace River Valley still was held by the government and impossible to obtain, Summerlin's possibilities were limited. By summer, though, he had found just the thing and, on June 25, he purchased for three thousand dollars in Confederate bills the 160-acre Riley R. Blount homestead where only months before the Bartow post office had been opened.[40]

Beginning in the summer of 1862 and ending in October 1863, James McKay made six runs in his steamer, *Scottish Chief*, through the Union naval blockade to Havana. At first he carried primarily Summerlin's cattle, but as time went on he shifted to cotton, a commodity at once more profitable than cattle and more easily handled. On return trips McKay brought back commodities

The Jacob Summerlin family at Bartow in 1887. Summerlin (1821–93) is the man standing in the center. His wife, Frances (1824–96), is to his immediate right. On the far right is their son, Jasper, and on the far left their son-in-law, John Fewell. Courtesy Florida Photographic Collection, Florida State Archives.

and supplies needed by local civilians, much of which was sold through Summerlin's house at Fort Ogden. McKay's blockade running ended the morning of October 17, 1863, when a Union raiding party, guided by Tampan Henry A. Crane, discovered and burned the *Scottish Chief* while it was moored in the Hillsborough River.[41]

The realities of war

James McKay was not the only blockade runner to operate out of Peace River, nor did the destruction of the *Scottish Chief* signal the end of attempts to pierce the Union blockade. As early as July 6, 1863, activities of blockade runners had drawn U.S. Navy warships into Peace River. Acting on a tip from refugees James Henry Thompson and Milledge Brannen, the Navy sloop, *Rosalie*, encountered two ships at anchor just inside the river's mouth. Over the next two days the *Rosalie* and the U.S. bark, *Restless*, played hide and seek with the blockade runners until they cornered their prey about five miles up Horse Creek. The boats had been abandoned, but their loads of cotton remained to be seized. As the two naval vessels with their prizes made their way back to Charlotte Harbor, they were shadowed—but not attacked—by Rebel forces on the banks of Peace River.[42]

Perhaps the most notorious blockade runner to use Peace River as a base was Robert Johnson, "a regular daredevil of a fellow, who feared neither God or man." Early in the war Johnson was running his "old superannuated schooner" out of Cedar Key. There, towards the end of 1862, he struck a deal with several cotton growers anxious to have their crops run through the blockade to Havana. While "a long wagon train of mules and oxen" bore the cotton overland to Charlotte Harbor, Johnson crept along the coast to a safe anchorage below Punta Rassa near Mound Key and the Estero River.[43]

For two weeks "lighters and craft of every kind" were used to transfer the 175 bales of cotton from the mouth of Peace River to the schooner secreted below Punta Rassa. After the job was completed in December 1862 and while surveying the Estero Bay channel prior to sailing, Captain Johnson happened upon a "beautiful little sail boat, flying the Union flag." In fact, the boat was the schooner *Laura*, a U.S. naval mail carrier. Rather than risk being sighted and reported by the Union ship, Johnson seized the *Laura*, imprisoned her crew, and forwarded the captured mail to the Confederate government at Richmond. Even Francis A. Hendry later acknowledged that Johnson's action placed him "in the attitude of pirates on the high seas, a crime punishable with death by all nations of the earth."[44]

Johnson sailed hurriedly from Estero Bay after the capture of the *Laura*, narrowly escaped from a Union gunboat, and reached Havana with his ship and cargo intact. For the return trip the blockade runner stocked his ship with medicines, hospital stores, surgical instruments, coffee, tea, liquors, and other goods in demand, and made a dash for the mouth of Peace River, where "runners were despatched for teams of any and every description and the cargo conveyed far into the interior, passing the counties of Manatee and Hillsborough." The Union blockade already was beginning to be felt, however, for, as F.A. Hendry commented, "Johnson's was one of the very few successful adventures of blockade running."[45]

Johnson was not intimidated by the blockade and, to further his efforts in that regard, decided to set up shop in the vicinity of Fort Ogden. There in January 1863 he married a local girl and took up trade between Peace River and Nassau. While Johnson was absent on a run early in September of that year, Union naval forces—memories of Johnson's piracy fresh in their minds— descended upon his Peace River settlement, burned his dwelling and storehouse, and destroyed four boats discovered nearby. Johnson's turn came a few weeks later when his schooner, *Director*, was intercepted running the blockade at Punta Rassa. The "notorious villain" was arrested, shipped to the north, and there imprisoned. He never returned to the Peace River Valley.[46]

U.S. warships may have first entered Peace River in July 1863, but the realities of war had intruded on the river settlements since the spring of the previous year. News received from along the coast early in 1862 had all been bad. Union troops had landed at Cedar Key in January and early in February had engaged in a confrontation at Manatee. Food was scarce at Tampa, and Union sympathizers were being forced to flee. A tremendous blow to already sagging morale had been struck with news of the fall of

Fort Donelson, Tennessee, to Gen. Ulysses S. Grant. At Tampa, worried Confederates proclaimed "death to all Union men who dare express their sentiments," and soldiers began to plunder gardens in areas outside the town. The flow of pro-Union refugees out of Tampa had resulted by the first week of March in the Union occupation of Egmont Key in Tampa Bay and the establishment there of a place of refuge.[47]

As serious as these developments were, they did not directly affect Peace River. Only a week or so after the forty volunteers of the "South Florida Bulldogs" proudly marched out of Bartow in early April, however, the Confederate States Congress took a step which would be felt there. Faced with a shortage of volunteers for the war effort, the Confederacy enacted its first Conscription Act on April 16, 1862. All nonexempt white males of the ages of eighteen to thirty-five were drafted for three years or until the war was over. Five months later, in even more desperate straits, the Confederacy raised the upper limit to forty-five years of age. In response to the mandates of this law Confederate forces in South Florida began "scouring the woods, looking after deserters and conscripts." For those who refused Confederate service, the penalty could be immediate. As a Union officer reported, "Union men they threaten to hang, and do shoot, as we have lamentable proof." By late October "every man between the ages of 18 and 45 in that section of rebeldom [was] being remorselessly pressed into the rebel army, and if any objections are made they are handcuffed and tied, and then marched off, no matter what the condition of their families."[48]

In the Peace River Valley many men were caught by the conscription agents but others, taking advantage of the isolated nature of the surrounding country, "layed out" while the agents prowled. And, as luck would have it for some, the Confederate Congress came to their rescue. Reflecting the increased dependence of Confederate armies on beef, the Congress on October 11, 1862, granted one exemption from the draft for each five hundred head of cattle. In Polk and Manatee counties, reporting in excess of sixty thousand head of cattle, the new law protected a considerable number of cattlemen and their helpers. Nonetheless, the Conscription Act and "laying out" had taken a toll. In elections held in October 1862 the number of voters in Polk County had dropped to 40 from a previous total of 135. In Manatee County, which had reported 121 voters in October 1861, only 43 voters appeared one year later.[49]

The violence and disruption caused by conscription agents was not the only tragic note sounded at Peace River late in 1862. Sometime before the end of the year came an outbreak of small-pox so violent at its height that the congregation of the Peas Creek Baptist Church at Bartow was afraid even to meet for prayer. In that climate of fear and despair, word arrived in early 1863 that Robert Johnson's blockade runner had brought a cargo of medicines to Fort Ogden, but even with those medicines life after life was lost. Among the victims were: Piety Collier Crews, wife of Dempsey D. Crews, at Zolfo; Thomas Summeralls at Horse Creek; Solomon Godwin's wife, Mariah Tyner Godwin, at Fort Meade; Francis B. Oats, wife of John Oats, at Homeland; John Green at Fort Meade; Robert and Zilla Ann Moody Hendry at Fort Green; Willoughby Whidden's daughter, Lavina (Mrs. William H. Williams), and her grandfather, Jesse Pennington, at Fort Hartsuff; and Perlina Hollingsworth, wife of Stephen, near Fort Meade.[50]

The election of President Lincoln and the subsequent move-ment towards secession and Civil War had little immediate impact in the Peace River Valley. Although the area surrounding Bartow contained a substantial concentration of slaves, less than thirty families in the river settlements owned even one. Reflecting this fact, attention in 1860 had been centered far more on local than on national issues, and when secession became a reality little enthusiasm was expressed for war.

Throughout 1861 energy along Peace River was expended in organizing local government and in building up a lucrative cattle trade with Cuba. In coastal areas such as Manatee and Tampa, however, war fervor began to take on a far more serious and per-sonal tone, with increasingly forceful and even violent action taken against those not supportive of the war effort. By 1862 these coast-based sentiments exploded upon the Peace River area as Confederate conscription agents scoured the country for mil-itary draftees, forcing men to choose between service in an unwanted war or a life of "laying out" in the hiding places of

South Florida. When late in the year the Confederate Congress exempted from the draft many of those in the cattle business, no time was allowed for respite before a deadly outbreak of smallpox ravaged the river population. Hard on the heels of this deadly pestilence came the first military operations in the area as Union naval forces began action against blockade runners, effecting destruction as high up the river as Fort Ogden.

11

Civil War in the
River Valley

IN THE PEACE RIVER VALLEY, for the most part the Civil War was fought among neighbors and even within families. Fissures which earlier had appeared in the social and political foundations of the area widened. From Fort Meade south, settlements were devastated.

Beef for the Confederate Army

"To be situated as a Union man in the South," Confederate veteran Francis C.M. Boggess recorded, "it was anything but pleasant. . . . If a man's sympathies were with the Union, he could not forsake his family and all he possessed. Captain Boggess let everything shape its own course and abided by chance. He remained out of the army until he was driven into it by the force of circumstances. . . . He did little fighting and, in fact, it was a war distinct from the real war. They [the Unionists] had been neighbors [before] fighting with the Confederates. It was a war [by Confederate sympathizers] against [Union] refugees and for the possession of this country."[1]

The final chapters of the history of the Civil War in southwest Florida began during the first four days of July 1863. For the first three of those days Robert E. Lee's Confederate Army of Northern Virginia fought on the fields and ridges surrounding Gettysburg, Pennsylvania, against Union general and Peace River veteran George G. Meade and his larger Army of the Potomac. After the slaughter that followed Pickett's charge on the afternoon of July 3, the war became one of defense and containment for the southern states. The following day at Vicksburg on the Mississippi River George G. Meade's boyhood friend and fellow Peace River veteran, Confederate general John C. Pemberton, surrendered his twenty thousand men to Ulysses S. Grant. Even more than the defeat at Gettysburg, the fall of Vicksburg directly affected the Peace River Valley, for Vicksburg was the last point at which Confederate armies were able to obtain beef from beyond the Mississippi. With Vicksburg in Union hands, all Confederate beef supplies had to come from the east, and the greatest remaining concentration of cattle was in interior South Florida.[2]

During the April to August cattle driving season of 1862, and beginning again in April 1863, Jacob Summerlin and other South Florida cattlemen supplied beef on a contract basis to the Confederate government. Although their efforts resulted in up to twenty-four hundred head of cattle furnished per month, that supply became woefully inadequate after the fall of Vicksburg. Fortunately for the Confederate army, steps already had been taken to regularize and expand the Florida beef supply operation through the appointment of a chief commissary officer for Florida, Pleasant W. White. White, who believed four thousand beeves a month could be obtained in South Florida, divided the state into commissary districts, and for the district encompassing all the cattle-producing counties of South Florida he designated former Union prisoner of war and blockade runner James McKay as the officer in charge.[3]

When in August 1863 James McKay accepted appointment as commissary officer, he already had overcome the bitter feelings surrounding his trial for treason in the summer of 1861 and had reestablished his popularity through successful blockade running adventures in partnership with Jacob Summerlin. In fact, McKay still was in business as a blockade runner. When his steamer, *Scottish Chief*, was discovered and burned by a Union naval force on the Hillsborough River on October 17, 1863, the boat was loaded with cotton and prepared for a run to Havana. Perhaps in part because McKay's attention was diverted by these personal affairs, he was slow to begin shipments of cattle to the north. Pleading the problems of heavy rains and flooding, together with the scattering of cattle at the end of the driving season, the commissary officer was unable to report the departure of any beeves until September 24, when Francis A. Hendry set out from Fort Meade with 344 head.[4]

Although in the several months that followed that initial cattle drive James McKay enlisted the assistance of F.A. Hendry, Jacob Summerlin, Louis Lanier, and others to send off several herds, he encountered a succession of problems. The first was a reluctance on the part of cattlemen and their hired cowhunters to drive the herds north. Even when drovers could be found, further complications arose. "Our emergency at present really requires a go ahead man with every five men," a frustrated McKay complained on October 10. "It is really bad the lack of energy of some." So desperate did the problem become that 160 men, mostly from South Florida, finally were detailed from the Army of Tennessee to assist with the drives; their commander, at the request of commissary agent McKay, was James McKay, Jr. With drovers on hand, McKay faced an even more serious dilemma when many cattlemen refused "to sell for Confederate and when they do, they insist upon my Agents for an enormous price." Meetings were being held, McKay noted, aimed at requiring the Confederate government to pay for beef only with silver and gold coin. Pointing out that inflation had raised the price of beef to almost sixty dollars per head, he recommended confiscation at a lower price because the higher amount "places our funds at little value amongst those cool to our cause." In spite of these problems, by November McKay's hands were gathering cattle east of Peace River, and Jacob Summerlin was assisting with herding as far south as Charlotte Harbor. On December 9, P.W. White acknowledged that three-fourths of the cattle being furnished from Florida were coming from the southern cattle counties.[5]

Refugees and the Second Florida Cavalry

Meanwhile, the situation became more tense for anyone in South Florida who withheld his support from the Confederacy. Conscription agents continued to prowl for nonexempted men of draft age, and a number of Peace River residents—along with others—sought refuge and protection with Union naval forces at Charlotte Harbor. One of these men, Enoch Daniels, approached Union officials early in December with a suggestion that a volunteer force be formed to occupy and conquer the territory between Tampa Bay and Charlotte Harbor. Gen. Daniel P. Woodbury, commanding at Key West, so liked Daniels's suggestion, with its potential for disrupting the Confederate cattle supply operation, that he organized nineteen of the refugees as the Florida Rangers, appointed Daniels as their captain, and authorized them to establish a post at Charlotte Harbor.[6]

On December 17, 1863, the Florida Rangers, their number increased to twenty-four, embarked from Key West for Useppa Island along with six privates and a sergeant of the Forty-seventh Pennsylvania Volunteers under the command of Lt. James F. Meyers. Although returning to the mainland with high hopes, the new Union recruits carried with them additional uniforms for only nineteen new enlistees. Within a week a camp had been erected on Useppa Island, and Daniels had set out with fifteen men on a recruiting expedition and reconnaissance to Peace River. The small force landed at the mouth of the Myakka River on Christmas Day and began to make its way inland. By December 27, four men had been dispatched to Fort Hartsuff to obtain current information, and the remainder of the detachment was encamped on Horse Creek with an eye to the capture of a small group of cowhunters in the vicinity. The next night, however, six of Daniels's men, all from areas other than South Florida, deserted while on guard duty, and the volunteer force, faced with betrayal and possible attack, was required to retreat to the Myakka. Before the rangers could rendezvous with their naval escort, thirty to forty Confederate troops led by the deserters attacked the Union naval force waiting at the Myakka and, in a brisk gunfight, drove the sailors from their camp to a ship anchored nearby. Hearing the gunfire, Daniels's men hid out until they were picked up by the naval escort on December 31. The four men sent to Fort Hartsuff returned a few days later to find no ships awaiting them. General Woodbury later reported their subsequent adventures: "Unable to find any boats or any means of return, [they] traveled up the country along the north bank of Pease Creek, until they came across a small schooner loaded with

4½ bales of cotton. Of this they boldly took possession and succeeded in delivering their capture and 2 prisoners [to Charlotte Harbor]."[7]

In Daniels's absence, General Woodbury had had second thoughts about the command of the Florida Rangers and had decided to replace Captain Daniels with Third Seminole War veteran Henry A. Crane, then serving in the U.S. Navy. Woodbury also determined to establish a more permanent base on the mainland. Accordingly, a company of the Forty-seventh Pennsylvania Volunteers was disembarked at Punta Rassa on the evening of January 7, 1864, with instructions to occupy Fort Myers. Upon the arrival of the detachment from Useppa Island, the Union troops moved to Fort Myers on January 10. The new Union outpost came under the command of Captain Richard A. Graeffe of the Forty-seventh Pennsylvania, while the Florida Rangers, renamed the Second Florida Cavalry, were placed under the command of Captain Crane.[8]

Less than a week after the arrival of Union troops at Fort Myers, a detachment of twenty-five men was detailed to scout up the Caloosahatchee River as far as Fort Thompson. After exchanging shots with a Confederate picket discovered there, the patrol returned to Fort Myers but numerous other armed detachments were sent out to search both sides of the Caloosahat-

John Henry Hollingsworth (1822–93) was wounded in June 1856 in the fight at the Tillis place near Fort Meade. He served during the Civil War as a member of Manatee County's Board of Commissioners. Courtesy Kyle S. VanLandingham.

chee for cattle and rebels. On January 31 Captain Graeffe decided on a more permanent presence in the interior and ordered a four-man detachment of the Second Florida Cavalry under Captain Crane to post a picket at Fort Denaud. On February 3 that small force was attacked by forty to forty-five mounted Confederate cowhunters while at a cattle pen near Twelve Mile Swamp. Fortunately for Crane's men, a patrol of the Forty-seventh Pennsylvania heard the shooting, drove the Confederates from the field, and pursued them through the night. The following morning the Union troops drew up in a line of battle against the Confederates and, in the words of the Union commander. "We dare[d] them to incite them to action but without avail." Both sides withdrew. Only one casualty, a slightly wounded private of the Second Florida Cavalry, was noted for the official record.[9]

The Union attacks

The presence of Union troops in South Florida was news which traveled quickly around the Confederacy. By January 7 James McKay had reported the fact to his superior, stating, "It is the intention of the enemy to destroy the Cattle business with the assistance of the traitors from us who have joined them." A frustrated McKay, whose cattle supply efforts had yet to meet expectations, also was forced to suspend operations on account of "the poor condition of the Cattle, as also the poor pasture on the way." Shortly thereafter the Gainesville *Cotton States* noted, "It is reported that a number of the citizens and deserters from the Confederate army have gone over to the Yankees and have taken the oath of allegiance to Lincoln. It is also said that some have agreed to furnish large numbers of cattle to the enemy, but arrangements are being made to take care of them . . . and we hope to be able to record a brilliant affair before long."[10]

That "brilliant affair" was a planned Confederate attack upon Fort Myers. The 160 men of Captain McKay's Confederate cowhunter detachment, idle since suspension of cattle driving the previous month, were ordered to meet at Fort Meade on February 10 with 60 cavalrymen under the command of Florida's Confederate hero, J.J. Dickison. Like so many best laid plans, however, this one went awry when Union troops marched out of Jacksonville headed for the state capital of Tallahassee. Among troops who answered the call for all Confederate forces to concentrate in the path of the Union army were Captain Dickison's cavalrymen and Captain McKay's cowhunters. A day before the two armies clashed on February 20 at Olustee near Lake City, Union general Woodbury at Key West already had received word "that the soldiers have all left Tampa, and that none remained in Western Florida south of Tampa."[11]

Although the Confederate army won the Battle of Olustee, the withdrawal of Confederate troops presaged disaster in South Florida. Not only was the influence, protection, and intimidating presence of these regular soldiers removed but, in a coincidental action, the underpinnings of wartime South Florida and the Peace River Valley were ripped away. On February 17, 1864, the Confederate States Congress again drastically revised its conscription law and repealed draft exemptions for cattlemen. By the middle of March the impact of that change was already apparent in South Florida. Commissary officer P.W. White reported to Richmond that the South Florida cattlemen "live in a wilderness country, inhabited by but few persons, and take interest, as a general thing, *only in the stock business.*" He explained that "many of these men alarmed by reports that they would be conscripted have gone to the enemy & others have left their homes and taken refuge in the remote southern portion of the Peninsula, and in many instances large stocks of cattle have been left unattended by the men employed by the owners to look after them." White concluded, "I do not believe there are men enough left in South Florida to provide good for the women and children left at home by the men in service."[12]

For the first two months of the Union army's presence in South Florida, recruitment by the Second Florida Cavalry had proceeded slowly, as Henry Crane reported on February 24. He assigned as the cause rebel harassment of his position and the forcible removal by Confederate troops of all Peace River inhabitants to the north side of the river. With fewer than 50 men, Crane could hardly conduct any action against the Confederates, even after the withdrawl of rebel troops toward Olustee, and his situation had been further damaged when the Forty-seventh Pennsylvania Volunteers were withdrawn in mid-February.[13]

With the repeal of the conscription exemption for cattlemen, however, Crane's recruiting success increased. When Fort Meade resident and Indian war veteran William McCullough arrived at Fort Myers on February 22, Crane recognized the esteem in which McCullough was held and arranged for him to be commissioned a first lieutenant. A greater coup came sixteen days later on March 10, when there appeared at Fort Myers Polk Countian William McClenithan, together with the most influential political leader of the Peace River area of Manatee County, James D. Green.[14]

Like so many residents of the Peace River Valley, Jim Green, then in his early forties, had attempted to live out the Civil War without joining either army. His pro-Union sentiments had brought him early in the war into a correspondence and friendship with loyal residents of Tampa, particularly James T. Magbee. Otherwise, his energies had been spent mainly in providing for his family and attempting to clear his name from the politically motivated indictment issued against him in 1860 for withholding public monies from the Manatee County Board of Commissioners. By November 1863 his popularity had recovered to the extent that he, along with Francis C.M. Boggess and George C. Tippins, was elected a justice of the peace for eastern Manatee County.[15] Perhaps in response to Green's political rejuvenation, Representative William T. Duval, who narrowly had defeated Green for his seat in the state house of representatives, felt compelled to introduce a bill to relieve Green of the obligations upon which the indictment against him had been based.[16] As late as February 1, 1864, Green still intended to remain at home and fulfill his duties as justice of the peace, but it soon became clear that Duval had no intention of passing the bill for Green's relief, and on the heels of that disclosure came word that the draft exemption had been repealed. On March 7, 1864, Green set out for Fort Myers.[17]

Green and McClenithan brought with them to Fort Myers exciting news for Henry A. Crane. "They informed me," Crane related to his superiors, "that since the arrival of Troops to this Post, no cattle had been driven, but small scouting parties had been watching us, fearing an attack on Ft. Meade. That since the battle near Lake City, & great loss of provisions the Confederates were compelled to have cattle, and had stored supplies for that purpose at that point. (Ft. Meade) That the forces or most of them had been ordered to Gainesville." Almost unable to contain his glee, Crane added, "I felt an irresistable desire to destroy their supplies & Capt. Green offered to accompany any command I might detach for that service."[18]

On March 13, thirty men were dispatched from Fort Myers for service under James D. Green. Their orders were to attempt to seize the Confederate supplies held at Fort Meade and to gather recruits from the Peace River area. By March 21 new recruits had swelled Green's detachment to about fifty and, divided into two parties, the Union force descended upon the Willoughby Tillis homestead south of Fort Meade where many of the supplies were stored [see appendix 8]. As Tillis's son, James, later recalled, the troops "came on to our place and my father was away. They took all his horses and wagons—took the Negro men and all firearms." Passing from the Tillis place, Green's force moved on to the neighboring homestead of Confederate Thomas Underhill. Unlike Tillis, Underhill was at home when the attackers arrived and in the ensuing encounter was shot twice and killed. With confiscated supplies, the Tillis slaves, twelve captured horses, two mules, and twenty-six new recruits, Green then withdrew from Fort Meade and made his way directly to Fort Myers.[19]

No sooner had Green and his men returned to Fort Myers than Captain Crane settled on a more ambitious plan. Receiving word that Capt. James McKay, Jr., had been sent to Fort Meade with forty men under orders to organize Confederate sympathizers for an attack on Fort Myers, Crane instructed Green, whom he had appointed a lieutenant, to take a force of almost a hundred men back to Fort Meade in an attempt to occupy the fort and "Capture (or kill if necessary)" leading Confederates including Willoughby Tillis, Streaty Parker, Louis Lanier, Francis A. Hendry, Jacob Summerlin, Francis M. Durrance, Francis C.M. Boggess, and Dr. Gilbert L. Key. Co-commanded by William McCullough, Green's force passed quickly up the east side of Peace River until it was spotted by Confederate pickets within fifteen miles of Fort Meade. Given this warning, James McKay, Jr., massed his forces, including local Confederate sympathizers, astride the road as it passed over Bowlegs Creek. There, on April 7, 1864, the Union and the Confederacy met in brief but determined battle. When the firing ceased the Confederates had withdrawn closer to Fort Meade, and the Union force's advance had been stopped. Pausing only long enough to cross Peace River and burn the Willoughby Tillis homestead where additional supplies were seized, the soldiers of

THE ESCAPED SLAVE IN THE UNION ARMY.—[SEE PAGE 422.]

Artist's representation of a black infantryman during the Civil War. The uniform and equipment shown are similar to those of black soldiers who fought in South Florida. Courtesy Library of Congress.

the Second Florida Cavalry returned to Fort Myers [see appendix 8]. The battle produced two casualties, both Confederate. Henry A. Prine had been wounded, and James Lanier, a "leading Guerilla," was killed.[20]

Choosing up sides

The repeal of the Confederate draft exemption for cattlemen had served to crystallize political, economic, and personal divisions that had been evolving along the Peace River Valley for almost a decade. To the Union army flowed principally the less well-to-do nonslaveholding men of families living near and below Fort Meade, particularly those living in present-day Hardee County. Opting for the Confederacy were the sons and fathers of families living at and above Fort Meade, including members of the slaveholding families clustered around Bartow and Fort Fraser, as well as the leading cattle kings of the region. In great part these men knew each other well, and in many cases they and their families had lived, worked, and served together for generations. When the rupture between them finally was forced, the resulting struggle became bitter and personal.

One Union officer had an opportunity to examine closely the men of the Second Florida Cavalry. Of them he wrote: "This was a regiment not to be lumped. Each man had a history of his own, sometimes more startling than fiction. In some the burning cottage, the destruction of home and household goods, the exposure of wife and children to cold, penury, and starvation, if not a worse fate, filled the background of a picture not colored by imagination. Nearly all had been hunted, many by dogs. It's not a pleasant thing for a man to be hunted as though human life was of no more value than that of a fox or a wolf, and it leaves bitter thoughts behind. Finally, through many perils, after lying for weeks in swamps and woods, they had straggled one by one into the Union lines." To those whose loyalty lay with the Confederacy, however, these men were nothing but "Traitors, Deserters &c" who had turned their backs on their homes and country.[21]

In the aftermath of the raids on Fort Meade, both sides in the conflict were desperate for reinforcements. On April 13, Henry A. Crane had requested the transfer to Fort Myers of at least fifty black troopers. That request was quickly granted, and within a few days three companies of the Second Regiment, U.S. Colored Troops, were dispatched to the Florida mainland. Raised at Washington, D.C., the Second USCT was described as "the very beau ideal of black soldiery." As was the case with all black units, however, its officers were white. Among them were a new commander for Fort Myers, Capt. J.W. Childs, and a man who would choose to remain in the Peace River area, Capt. John F. Bartholf.[22]

On the Confederate side, James McKay was outraged over the Union activities at Peace River. On March 25, 1864, along with news of the first attack at Fort Meade, the commissary agent bluntly informed his superior, "No cattle may be expected from this District untill the enemy is got Rid off, hopeing you will urge the necessity of immediate action by those whose duty it is to do so." Confederate authorities waited until April 24 to order elements of the Sixty-fourth Regiment, Georgia Volunteers, to "proceed to Fort Meade, and commence a vigorous campaign against the deserters and others, who have been depredating in that section." Having proceeded only "a little over 100 miles" from Gainesville, however, the force was recalled. Again on May 11 Confederate troops were directed south to "drive the deserters and tories before you, and strike the enemy every time an opportunity presents." They again were diverted. It was the last heard from the regular Confederate army in South Florida.[23]

As an alternative to regular army help and as a solution to the draft problem now faced by James McKay's cattleman associates, the commissary agent suggested in late March the creation of a special military unit within the commissary department to gather and protect the cattle herds and perform such other functions as necessary. By early July the concept of a cow cavalry had been approved and Col. Charles J. Munnerlyn, a former Confederate congressman from Georgia, had been designated to command the battalion. As executive officer Munnerlyn quickly appointed a Florida cavalry officer, Capt. William Footman.[24]

Anticipating approval of the cow cavalry and anxious to avoid Confederate conscription agents, South Florida residents from Tampa to Fort Meade, at least those who refused to join the Union forces, began in the spring of 1864 to form volunteer companies. Perhaps the first of these companies was formed at Tampa under the command of Capt. John T. Lesley. Known as the Sandpipers and based at Itchepuckesassa (Plant City), the company was composed primarily of men from Hillsborough County, although numerous Polk countians also were in its ranks. Within a few months other companies were formed in the vicinity of Peace River. At Fort Meade, Francis A. Hendry organized a company which eventually totaled 133 men [see appendix 9]. Just to the north of Brooksville John T. Lesley's father, Methodist minister Leroy G. Lesley, based yet another company.[25]

The burning of Fort Meade

The organization of the cow cavalry came a little too late, for an explosion of Union activity followed right on the heels of the April raid on Fort Meade. Taking only a few weeks to drill new recruits and to scout cattle herds in the vicinity of Fort Thompson, black and white Union troops were embarked on Union naval vessels and transported to Tampa Bay. At daylight on Friday, May 6, the troops were landed three miles from Tampa and advanced upon the town. With small parties under the command of James D. Green and William McCullough in the advance, the Union men occupied Tampa without incident. During their thirty-six-hour stay, they arrested a number of leading citizens, spiked the artillery at Fort Brooke, and seized the Confederate mails.[26]

At two o'clock on that Friday afternoon, Captain McKay received word of the occupation of Tampa while working at Fort Meade, where he and fifty-five men were assembling the first cattle drive of the year. He immediately set out with thirty-five men and arrived at Tampa's outskirts about eleven o'clock that night. Because he needed reinforcements before taking action, McKay waited until Saturday afternoon before sending Gideon Zipprer into town with notice of his intention to attack within twenty-four hours. The Union troops continued loading confiscated property and prisoners, then withdrew. Not all the Union men returned to Fort Myers by ship, however. Jim Green and four of his men, sent by land with "ten good horses," passed through McKay's pickets at night without challenge.[27]

The men of the Second Florida Cavalry and the Second USCT had no sooner reached Fort Myers than word was received that enemy troops had been systematically destroying the homes and property of those suspected of Union sympathies, as well as rounding up the families of Union volunteers and concentrating them in the vicinity of Fort Meade. Those families were reported to be "destitute of subsistence and subjected to most cruel treatment from the enemy."[28] Captain Childs, after consultations with Crane and Green, "determined to attack the enemy at Fort Mead, relieve the distressed families and secure as many Beef Cattle as posable." On the morning of May 14, 100 men of the Second Florida Cavalry and 107 black troopers of the Second USCT, a total including officers of 212 men, set out from Fort Myers on the long march to the north. After four days' progress and within twenty-five miles of their goal, the advancing column was discovered by Confederate pickets who raced to spread the news.[29]

At Fort Meade a cannon was fired to sound the alarm and settlers rushed for protection to the Methodist campground at Homeland. The local home guard assembled at the nearby schoolhouse and took up a defensive position in front of the settlers' refuge. As these measures were taken, Confederate forces under the command of Willoughby Tillis and Francis C.M. Boggess hurriedly were assembled and prepared an ambush in the hammock lying along the road from Bowlegs Creek to the bridge at Fort Meade. The Union column escaped the trap, however, when two pickets were captured only a few miles down the road and induced to divulge the Confederate plans.[30]

Camping six miles from Fort Meade on the night of May 18, the Union force the following morning crossed the river below Bowlegs Creek and advanced on the town without resistance. Arriving at the fort with a detachment of fifty men, Crane and Green encountered but a single sentry. About an hour later, though, a party of mounted Confederate troops showed themselves in the vicinity, and a Union skirmish line was prepared to meet them. After a short but tense interval, the Confederates withdrew without attack, and for the next eleven hours the Union force loaded confiscated forage and provisions and searched the area for Union family members, Confederate sympathizers, and slaves. Their mission accomplished, the Union men then put the fort's buildings to the torch and the entire force, with captives, slaves, and family members, turned south down the road to Fort Thompson. Despite constant shadowing by a thirty-man Confederate detachment under Francis C.M. Boggess, the entire column arrived safely at Fort Myers on May 27 with sixteen new recruits, seven prisoners of war, seventy women and children, twenty-two horses and a thousand head of cattle [see appendix 8].[31]

Triumph of the Union

The sack and destruction of Fort Meade brought the war to a new level of intensity throughout southwest Florida. "In consequence of the operation of the enemy," reported Hernando County tax assessor J.L. Peterson on May 28, "every man who could use a musket was placed in Servis." Peterson added, "A good deal of time has been lost in scouting after the enemy and in running Negroes from their reach." Closer to Peace River a Bartow man wrote a friend, "The times hear is vary squally . . . [and] there is only one hundred soldiers to compet with all the yanky raiders that may cum in our Country." Even those one hundred soldiers were no longer nearby. By mid-June Francis A. Hendry's cow cavalry force had been withdrawn from Fort Meade and stationed twenty-five miles away at the Alafia River, leaving, as one Union officer put it, "all south of the River to our paternal care & affection." On July 5, Manatee County sheriff J.J. Addison confirmed that statement when he reported, "There is over half the Taxpayers of this County gone to the Yankees. . . . One [of] our County Commissioners has gone to the Yankees, two of the outhers taken and Priseners and disqualified from doing any business."[32]

The revulsion felt by many South Floridians at the zeal displayed by Confederate agents against individuals suspected of disloyalty may be credited as a contribution to Union successes in May and June 1864. One illustration was the case of Daniel W. Carlton who, early in the war, "drove his sons in the Rebel Army, with shouts of exultation." Notwithstanding his former actions, Confederate agents seized Carlton in May 1864 and shipped him northward "in Irons." Carlton's son, Reubin, at home on furlough from the 7th Florida Infantry (CSA), was furious at seeing his father so humiliated and promptly made his way to Fort Myers where he enlisted in the Union army. Shortly thereafter his brother, Albert, joined as well.[33]

Even so wealthy and influential a man as Jacob Summerlin was subject to the violent passions which raged in the aftermath of the destruction of Fort Meade. In early June a squad of Confederate volunteers singled him out "for their special malediction," threatened his family, and drove the Summerlins from their home north of Bartow. Until the end of the war Summerlin's family was forced to remain at a house just south of Fort Meade.[34]

As May and June passed into July and August, the fever of war began to ease. While the cow cavalry slowly evolved, Union troops at Fort Myers refocused their sights further north. In early July they staged a major raid in the area of Brooksville and destroyed plantations of a number of the more prominent Confederates, including those of Leroy Lesley, David Hope, and Thomas B. Ellis. Off and on over the next six weeks, elements of the Second Florida Cavalry engaged in a number of actions from a base at Cedar Key, and on August 3 black troops landed at Manatee (Bradenton) and for several weeks occupied the town. Before withdrawing, the troops destroyed the sugar refining facilities at the former Gamble plantation, as well as a grist mill owned by Josiah Gates, John Curry, and Ezekiel Glazier.[35]

While Union forces were counting those victories, problems were brewing back at Fort Myers. By late August, the Union stronghold contained 416 refugee men, women, and children. Exposed to the summer heat and primitive sanitation, the refugees fell victim to fever and dysentery. Having been forced in most cases to leave their valuables behind, they also were close to destitution. An officer of the 110th New York Infantry, an element of which had joined the forces at Fort Myers, wrote his hometown newspaper pleading for aid to support these families. "The houses of these families," he wrote, "have been pillaged and burned, their fields laid waste, and their stock driven off to feed the armies of our foe," he wrote. "These soldiers have never received any of the high bounties that enables the northern soldier to place his family in circumstances of comfort and security from want before leaving home. Many of them, as yet, have not received one dollar. The $13 per month of most of them is exhausted at the commissary for the plainest of soldiers' fare, and does not suffice to feed those dependent on them. . . . The sufferings of these people cannot be understood unless seen."[36]

In the absence of the men of the Second Florida Cavalry and amidst sickness and destitution, friction began to develop between black troopers and the white families. By August 20 Captain

Crane was reporting: "It has become really necessary to separate the Cold. Troops from the Refugee families. During our last months absence they have become greatly demoralized, and to such an extent has it been carried, that a long continuance can only tend to open irruption, & all this from a laxity of discipline that is truly unpardonable." Two weeks later Crane added of the black and white groups, "The ignorance of the one and the sensitiveness of the other tends to make every duty unpleasant."[37]

When James D. Green and William McCullough returned to Fort Myers from Cedar Key in late October, they had little trouble assigning blame for the entire state of affairs. Green later wrote, "At Fort Myers during the command of Capt. J.W. Childes . . . gross corruption and immorality . . . prevailed. Mock marriages were celebrated, gambling encouraged, beef cattle driven in and sold for the benefit of the officers. The refugees deprived of their rations and supplied with unwholesome flour." Their feud with Childs became so public and so personal that towards the end of the year Childs had both Green and McCullough detained. He kept them under house arrest until February 1865.[38]

Resurgence of the Confederacy

As the level of Union activity decreased and problems at Fort Myers increased in the later summer and fall of 1864, Confederate cow cavalry companies began to establish their authority in the Peace River Valley and on the cattle ranges stretching from the Kissimmee to the Caloosahatchee rivers. By early August fears of imminent attack had diminished to the extent that William J. Watkins at Bartow could assert that his family was "as safe as any where in the Confederacy." Two months later the Confederate commissary-general reported that the cow cavalry "has checked desertions and restored the confidence of the people." The same month Captain Childs at Fort Myers acknowledged the Confederates to be actively engaged in driving cattle and noted that "to facilitate their purpose [they] have established small picket guards from Pease Creek through to Fort Thompson." In early January 1865 the cow cavalry commander himself, Col. Charles Munnerlyn, reported that Captain Hendry's company "had caused federal troops to virtually cease cattle confiscating in the area."[39]

Ohio-born Confederate veteran James Manley (1837–1905) photographed at Fort Meade prior to 1880, probably about 1877. Manley lost his left arm at the Battle of Fredericksburg in December 1862. Courtesy Tom and Meredith Albritton Manley.

The resurgence of Confederate strength had not eliminated all fears of another Union strike. When war-weary residents of Polk and Hillsborough counties met for the annual camp meeting at Homeland in early October, the mood of the first two days was described as "uneasy, because we felt ourselves exposed to the raiders." The meeting was saved, however, when, as one witness explained, "On Thursday evening, the vigilant Capt. Hendry, with his command, arrived—pitched their tents, and put out a strong picket guard around the encampment; and from that time the meeting went on harmoniously."[40]

As Confederate strength increased, more thought was given to the idea of a direct attack on Fort Myers. A preliminary approach had been made on August 27 when a party of sixty-five Confederate cow cavalrymen seized a refugee slave of Dempsey D. Crews and used him to lure a party of Union soldiers across the Caloosahatchee River in response to a distress signal. In the ensuing ambush Union refugee James H. Thompson, a young man named Griner, and a trooper of the Second USCT were killed. The Union troops and families were furious at what they considered the "premeditated barbarity" of the action and carefully noted the names of several of the participating Confederates: Francis A. Hendry, John E. Fewell, John M. Pearce, John Blount, Moses A. McClelland, David Hughes, Zora J. Curry, John Prine, George Albritton, William A. Williams, William Allen, William Carney, W.R. Hollingsworth, William B. Varn, and William Raulerson.[41]

On January 9, 1865, when the cow cavalry battalion ceased its cattle gathering and herding operations, preparations were undertaken, under the command of cow cavalry executive officer Maj. William Footman, for a concerted attack on Fort Myers. In early February, Footman drew together near Jacob Summerlin's house at Fort Meade between 150 and 275 Confederate troops of the companies of F.A. Hendry, John T. Lesley, Leroy G. Lesley, and others. Just after mid-month the eager force set off down the Fort Thompson road with "all the supplies we could pack on our horses, one piece of artillery and one wagon with a large skiff and this skiff was loaded with corn."[42]

On February 19, Footman stopped his column short of the Caloosahatchee River and delivered a brief pep talk. The Confederates then launched their skiff, which promptly capsized, ruining most of the artillery ammunition. After eight hours the Confederate force and its supplies finally were gotten across the rain-swollen river. Then, a veteran recalled, "It began to rain and rained all night and that being a low country, the water rose up about a foot deep all over the face of the earth. We could not tell where the road was, much less travel." A planned night attack was canceled, and the troops spent a sleepless night in the downpour.[43]

The following morning the Confederate column advanced as far as Billy's Creek, about a mile from Fort Myers. Lt. William M. Hendry, with Frank Saxon, Gideon Zipprer, Benjamin F. Blount, and others, attacked a Union picket post and captured Edward Ashley, James F. Barnes, Charles C. Whidden, and William Bush. A short while later Francis M. Williams and John Williams were taken at a nearby pond while on laundry detail, and William McClenithan, Jr., and James Whidden were chased down and seized while tending cattle. Black sergeant Henry Sanders, who refused to surrender at the washing pond, was shot and killed.[44]

Not only had they lost the element of surprise by the gunfire, but Major Footman learned that almost all the ammunition carried by his troops had been ruined by the rain. He chose to demand the fort's surrender rather than attack. Capt. John F. Bartholf was given the honor of refusing Footman's demand on behalf of Fort Myers's commander Capt. James Doyle of the 110th

New York Infantry. Thereupon, at 1:10 in the afternoon Footman opened fire against the garrison. A Union skirmish line composed of members of the Second Florida Cavalry under the command of Lt. William McCullough, released from arrest only a few days previously, returned the Confederate fire. Upon his request, James D. Green was released from confinement, "took his rifle, and went into the ranks" to join the fight.[45]

"After firing at the fort, and the fort returning their fire," F.C.M. Boggess recalled: "it was seen that nothing was accomplished. The Confederates drew off to where the cattle were and killed some of them as they were short of anything to eat. After supper they resumed their march homeward." Another veteran, E.J. Hilliard, remembered, "That night we took up our line of march back to Fort Meade and our wagon train never came to us, making it just one week without one mouthful of bread." James McKay, Jr., echoed Hilliard's words. "We returned to Fort Meade the most worn out and delapidated looking set of soldiers you ever saw," he recalled, "horses jaded and men half starved." Where a few days before they had dreamed of victory, the bedraggled Confederates had only a few cattle and eleven Union prisoners for their efforts. The prisoners were taken to Bartow where Wiley D.K. Pollard, a blacksmith, fashioned handcuffs for them, after which they were sent north to prison camp. The way Boggess summed up the experience could have applied to the entire Civil War in southwest Florida: "The whole thing had been a failure and . . . the whole command was demoralized."[46]

Gen. Robert E. Lee surrendered his Army of Northern Virginia to Gen. Ulysses S. Grant at Appomattox, Virginia, on April 12, 1865, ending the Civil War. In the Peace River Valley the war had ended upon the Confederate withdrawal from the walls of Fort Myers on February 20. Less than a month later, on March 18, the last Union troops withdrew from Fort Myers, joining their comrades who had left earlier in the month to participate in the ill-fated Union attempt to capture Tallahassee which resulted in a Confederate victory at the Battle of Natural Bridge. About the same time, most of the Confederate troops in South Florida were ordered to Brooksville where they remained until the end of the war. No more cattle were driven to the Union or to the Confederacy, nor did any neighbor again attempt to strike down his uniformed former friend because of a conflict neither of them

Streaty Parker (1823–84) in his Confederate military uniform during the Civil War. Courtesy Kyle S. VanLandingham.

wanted to begin with. The war's epitaph was delivered by Francis A. Hendry at Fort Meade, when he learned that the war had indeed come to an end. "Thank God it is over with one way or the other."[47]

For the first three years of the Civil War an uneasy truce prevailed in much of the Peace River Valley which allowed settlers to continue their lucrative cattle operations and to avoid committing to either side's army. By the end of 1863 the strains of that truce were beginning to tell as refugees began making their way to the protection of Union naval forces at Charlotte Harbor. That trickle became a stream when in February 1864 the Confederate draft exemption for cattlemen was repealed, and the threat of Confederate conscription agents drove virtually every draftable man either to the Union army or the Confederate cow cavalry. At that point the war exploded upon the Peace River Valley, leading to the widespread destruction of homes, livestock, and farms. Relationships with roots in decades and generations past were torn asunder, and seeds of bitterness and pain were planted which would bear fruit for decades to come. At the war's end, except for thousands of cattle left upon the ranges, life in the Peace River Valley was in a shambles.

12

Republicans in Power

T HE SURRENDER of Confederate forces brought an end to the
Civil War, but it did not bring peace to South Florida. The
divisions between former Confederates and former Unionists ran deep, however reluctantly they had come to occupy those
roles and, in the two years immediately following the Union victory, were heightened as Union men and their families were
denied access to the courts to compel return of their confiscated
property. In 1867 the tables were turned as Unionist Republicans
came to power, but the bitterness and divisions remained un-
resolved.

Surrender and emancipation

Company A of the Second Florida Cavalry occupied Tampa on
May 27, 1865. On June 5 at Bayport and three days later at
Tampa, the officers and men of Munnerlyn's battalion, the Con-
federate cow cavalry, were required to muster for a final time as
U.S. commissioners accepted their surrender. While defeated
Confederates headed back to their homes, Union loyalists were
jubilant. Tampa lawyer Ossian B. Hart witnessed the arrival at
Tampa of "a large delegation of country people" and "On catching

sight of the old flag once more, which was 'floating in the breeze,' each man with one accord reverently lifted his hat, and greeted the return of the starry emblem of their country's greatness and honor with every token of respect and delight."[1]

Shortly after the surrender black troops were dispatched into the interior to free all former slaves. "The first experience I remember of the Union army," recalled Margaret Watkins Gibbs, daughter of Bartow planter William Joel Watkins, of her life at ten years old, "was when one white officer appeared with some negro soldiers." Gibbs explained that "they didn't come to the house, they went to the [slave] cabins and I remember their behavior was perfect in every way."[2]

By the time black troopers arrived at Peace River, many freedmen already had taken their liberty. "We advised them all to make the very best arrangements they could with their former owners to secure for themselves and families permanent homes, with those who had in many instances raised and taken care of themselves and children," explained Baptist minister Jeremiah M. Hayman, "but our advice was treated with contempt, and not a single one, that we know of, could be induced to enter into any arrangments to remain at their 'old homes.' " Some plantation owners merely transported their former slaves to Tampa and, as Emma Bryant the daughter of slave parents in that town termed it, "dumped" them.[3]

Some freedmen did remain in the Peace River Valley following the Civil War. From a total of 237 slaves reported on the Polk County tax list for 1863, 128 blacks remained four years later, most of them children. Only 22 men and 31 women were twenty-one or older in 1867. In Manatee County, from an 1860 slave population of 253, only 55 blacks remained in the huge county in 1867, including 23 men and 8 women twenty-one and over.[4]

The 1866 Polk County tax roll lists the names of twenty adult freedmen: William Brown, Caesar Cook, Solomon Carrington, Stepney Dixon, Young Houston, Patrick Henry [Jones], Prince Johnson, Buck Jones, Simon Jackson, Albert Lewis, Andy Moore, Sam Manuel, Charles Phillips, Royal Read, Nathaniel Read [or Redd], Joseph Sterling, Joseph Sexton, Alexander Stillings [or Stallings], Jacob Williamson, and Neptune Willingham. By the following year, Patrick Henry [Jones], Manuel, Phillips, Sterling, Williamson, and Willingham had left the county. At the same time, Andrew Denson, William Johns, Richard A. Lark, James Powell [or Pernell], and Nathaniel Trammell either reached adulthood or established homes in Polk. By 1870, the family of A.C. Robinson of Sneads, Florida, also arrived and settled in the county.[5]

Thanks to an 1867 voter registration list, it is possible to locate in a general way the areas of Polk County in which each freedman and his family lived. Two of the county's four precincts covered the entire length of the Peace River and its adjacent areas in Polk. Precinct #2 constituted Fort Meade and areas north towards Homeland, and no freedmen are recorded as residing in that community. Bartow, Fort Fraser, and the territory down to about Homeland made up Precinct #3, and there were found twelve black men of voting age: Solomon Carrington, Andrew Denson, Young Houston, Simon Jackson, William Johns, Prince A. Johnson, Buck Jones, Richard A. Lark, Andy Moore, James Powell [or Pernell], Royal Read, and Nathaniel Trammell. Independent evidence suggests that Stepney Dixon, Albert Lewis, and William Brown also lived in the Bartow area.[6]

At best, sketchy information exists on these black pioneers. William Brown is thought to be the male slave of Rigdon Brown, brought to the river in 1849; he does not appear in the 1870 census.[7] Stepney Dixon was the slave of Riley R. Blount and accompanied the Blount family caravan to Bartow in 1851. He appears to have been about forty at the end of the war, and he and Sarah Washington already had at least two children, Sally and John. In 1870 their family also included Charles Dixon, nineteen, and Jackson Dixon, seventeen, whose relationship to Stepney and Sarah is uncertain. Another Dixon, Ann, likely the former slave of Readding Blount, married in Polk County in January 1867 to Young Houston, James Hamilton's former bondsman.[8]

Prince A. Johnson was the slave of Jacob Summerlin. The cattle king purchased Johnson in 1863 from William I. Turner of Hillsborough County. After the Civil War Johnson, then about 30, continued to work for Summerlin until the latter moved from Bartow in 1867-68. Johnson then settled on the eastern outskirts of Bartow where he lived until his death in 1896. The freedman was a farmer and grove owner and also was widely known as an expert at digging and cleaning wells.[9]

Andy Moore and Royal Read were the slaves of Virginian Wil-

The family of John Wesley Whidden (1839–1910) and Ellen Hendry Whidden (1842–1929) about 1875. Whidden, a prominent cattleman, businessman, and Confederate officer, was also one of Southwest Florida's most influential political leaders in the final quarter of the nineteenth century. Courtesy Barbara Welles Probasco.

liam J. Watkins who moved to just north of Bartow in 1862. Margaret Watkins Gibbs, remembering Moore, explained, "Among our negroes was Andy the fiddler. The slaves had dancing and plenty singing. Andy had five children, and I remember when word came that Lincoln had freed the slaves my father dolefully shook his head as he said, 'Poor Andy with five children to feed.' " Moore, who was about forty in 1865, was married to Tanner Reid, about thirty-five, who seems to have been related to Royal Read. At the end of the war their children included Jack, 17, Samuel, 13, James, 9, Henry, 7, Ellen, 6, and Sarah, 4.[10]

Royal Read was approximately twenty-seven when the Watkins family moved to Polk in 1862. At the war's end he married the freed slave of Frederick Varn, Harriet, and established himself as a farmer. It is possible that the Nathaniel Read (or Redd) listed in Polk in 1866 was Royal's brother or, at least, a fellow Watkins slave. The Nathaniel Trammell listed on the 1867 voter list was Virginia born and may have been the same man as Nathaniel Read. Three years later Laurena Read was living next door to Royal at Bartow and he may have been the same man as Nathaniel. Two additional Polk County freedmen were Virginia born and may have been among Watkins's slaves. Solomon Carrington was about thirty at the war's end and shortly thereafter formally married Tennessee-born Jane Williams. In 1865 the couple were parents of at least three children: Eliza, 6, Alex, 4, and Martha, 1. Twenty-three-year-old Buck Jones, a Virginian by birth, was residing in the county immediately after the war.[11]

Of Andrew Denson and William Johns nothing is known except that they were born in Georgia, had resided in Polk County for at least a year before registering to vote on August 30, 1867, and disappeared from Polk County records in 1870. Georgia-born Albert Lewis, who failed to register to vote, also lived in Polk only a few years. He may have been a bondsman either of the Varn family or of a family residing near the Varns for his wife, Ceily, appears to have been the slave of Josiah Varn. James Powell (Pernell), a North Carolinian, married Minerva Bishop who also may have been owned by the Varn family. The final two freedmen residing in the Peace River area of Polk at the end of the war were both Florida born, twenty-five-year-old Simon Jackson and twenty-year-old Richard A. Lark. Both these men remained in

South Florida and founded substantial families whose descendants live in the area today.[12]

The Peace River area of Manatee County held few slaves prior to the Civil War and few freedmen immediately thereafter. Only eleven black men were listed on the 1866 county tax list, although their names echoed those of slaveholding families of the recent past: John Waldron, Samuel Prine, Joe Prine, Joseph Crews, Richmond (or Richard) Crews, Henry Smith, George Hooker, Thomas Summerlin, Jeffrey Bolden, Albert Clark, and Primus Gates [Smith]. Of these eleven men, two represented the largest slaveholding in the Manatee County area of Peace River prior to the war—Richmond and Joseph Crews were brothers and had come to the river just after the end of the Third Seminole War with the family of Dempsey D. Crews. Within two years after 1866, both Prines, Henry Smith, Summerlin, Bolden, and Clark had left the county.[13]

Early in 1866, Nathan H. DeCoster, a Maine-born officer of the Second Regiment, U.S. Colored Troops, moved to the vicinity of the modern community of Charlotte Harbor where he homesteaded, farmed, and, at nearby Fort Winder, operated a store. Arriving with DeCoster were four black hired hands: Joseph Chapman, 40; Richard Hambleton (Hamilton), 30; Mitchell Harrison, 20; and District of Columbia native John Lomans, 25. Within the next two years other freedmen who would live and work in the Peace River Valley also would arrive in Manatee. Among them were Frank Griffin and Julius Caesar.[14]

Elections and a new beginning

It is commonly assumed that the end of the Civil War also brought the end of native white government in Florida until "redemption" in 1876. Tales are told of sly Yankee carpetbaggers corruptly influencing the votes of tens of thousands of ignorant freedmen all to the detriment and oppression of war-ravaged poverty-stricken white settlers. Although Florida did have its share of Reconstruction scandals, this folk memory, particularly as it relates to Polk and Manatee counties, could not be further from the truth.

Reconstruction in Florida began with a military occupation,

but as early as October 1865 statewide elections were held for delegates to a constitutional convention designed to serve as a vehicle for bringing Florida back into the Union. Freedmen were not allowed to vote in that election, and the only new qualification for most white voters was the acceptance of an "amnesty oath" or a pardon from the president. By election day, ninety-one Polk County voters had taken the oath, and in Manatee County, where many Union volunteers still were in active service, the number was eighty-three. On October 8 at the annual camp meeting at Homeland the Reverend Leroy G. Lesley, a former Confederate officer, lambasted Union Capt. James D. Green as having "committed a Heinous Sin in destroying Rebel property" and suggested that all Union officers required Lesley's "Special Prayer for there Redemption." Two days later seventy-four Polk County voters selected Green's wartime opponent, cattleman Francis A. Hendry, as their delegate. In neighboring Hillsborough and Hernando counties, voters also turned to secessionists and former Confederate officers by electing, respectively, Tampa lawyer James Gettis and planter Samuel E. Hope. Manatee County was a far different story, however, for when seventy-four voters had cast their ballots on election day, the victor was Union officer James D. Green.[15]

The constitutional convention met on October 25, 1865, and quickly repealed the ordinance of secession, abolished slavery, and limited the vote, political office, and jury duty to white men. The convention also urged the acting governor, William Marvin, to restore to office all civil officials serving before May 1865 and called for elections for state officials and a congressman on November 29. A few days later, on November 10, Marvin did restore authority to local and civil officials. His action had the effect of restoring Polk and Manatee County governments to the hands of officials with Confederate sympathies. In Polk County, John Davidson served as probate judge, while Readding Blount, Jordan Hancock, James B. Crum, and E.E. Mizell acted as county commissioners.[16] In Manatee, Henry R. McLeod served as president of the board of commissioners, and W.H. Vanderipe, D.L. Hawkins, and J.W. Curry completed the panel.[17]

At the state election held on November 29, voters were asked to select state representatives for each county and a state senator for each of twenty-nine senatorial districts. Polk elected as its representative Dr. Daniel Stanford—a Bartow physician, Baptist minister, former slaveholder, and father-in-law of the county's greatest slaveowner. The choice in Hillsborough was secessionist John A. Henderson, and in the senate contest Confederate William I. Turner received the most votes in that county while his colleague Francis A. Hendry won in a senatorial district including Polk. James D. Green secured a seat as Manatee's representative in the Florida house. Also of significance, secessionist James Gettis was selected as judge for the judicial circuit covering all of Polk, Manatee, and Hillsborough counties.[18]

Perhaps in response to the still-smoldering Confederate sympathies evidenced in the fall elections, the Peace River area received its first and, as it proved, only resident Union occupation forces. Late in October a company of the Ninety-ninth United States Colored Troops was ordered to Manatee County, half at the village of Manatee and half at McKay's Wharf ten miles up Peace River. An additional ten-man detachment was ordered to Fort Meade but located its camp instead near the county seat of Jefferson just south of Bartow.[19]

Neither remained in place for long. At McKay's Wharf, the Union troops arrived late in December and remained for six miserable weeks with no particular duties or assignments, living the entire time "in some old tents, without a board or nail for any additional comforts or conveniences." At the recommendation of the first ranking officer to visit the camp, the detachment on February 12, 1866, was ordered to Tallahassee. Jacob Summerlin's son, Sam, remembered the Union stay at Jefferson as having been of "a few months" duration, but that was plenty of time for the black soldiers to run afoul of Frederick Varn. As told by Summerlin, events proceeded as follows: "An old man by the name of Varn had a large sweet potato patch, which yielded abundantly. When dug they were placed in the jams of the rail fence. He sold some of his crop to the camp and one morning he noticed that one of the banks had been broken into and a bushel or two had been stolen, and he saw the soldiers' tracks. When he reported the affair to the officers they paid no attention to his story so when night came he took his gun and sat in the jam of the fence and awaited their arrival. They came and opened up a bank and when they began filling their sacks he filled them full of birdshot. They dropped their sacks and ran for camp. The next

New York-born John Francis Bartholf (1837–92), a Union officer in
South Florida during the Civil War, remained in the area after the surrender of Confederate forces and became a key leader in old Manatee
County's Republican party. He is justly remembered as the father of
public education in much of the Peace River Valley. From Vernon Peeples, *Punta Gorda and the Charlotte Harbor Area* (Norfolk, VA: The Don-
ning Company Publishers).

morning Varn sent for the officers and invited them into the house and told them all about the happening and he was not troubled with them again."[20]

Conflict in the courthouses

The new Florida legislature met on December 18, 1865, and, over the next month or so, the Confederate-dominated assembly enacted a harsh and defiant black code regulating black life and labor, while taking only those progressive steps absolutely necessary to permit Florida's reentry into the Union. The legislature's actions set the tone for Florida politics for the next fifteen months, a tone which would be reflected in the actions of local officials throughout South Florida.[21]

Manatee and Polk County boards of county commissioners did little to affect the political climate. Both boards spent most of their time simply attempting to organize themselves and their counties. Of particular concern in both was the location of the county seat.

Carrying out a promise made in 1860, Manatee representative James D. Green procured the enactment in January 1866 of a law requiring a referendum on removing the county seat from the village of Manatee. When in April a majority of the voters approved removal, the county commission, controlled by Manatee-area residents, was forced by the terms of Green's law to appoint a board to decide on a new location for the courthouse.[22] By April 29 a location was agreed to on Horse Creek, almost forty miles southeast of Manatee and within ten miles of Peace River, and at the board's suggestion named Pine Level. Within a short time at the new county seat "a rough log house 20 x 30—clapboard roof & puncheon floor—with seats of similar material were constructed in which to hold the Courts of the County."[23]

Polk County had been struggling to get title to the land on which its county seat, Jefferson, was located since 1861. After the war attempts were renewed, but on March 5, 1866, the minutes of the state's Internal Improvement Trust Fund Board recorded: "A letter was received on behalf of Polk County asking what arrangments could be made by the Board to secure for the county site of said County certain lands selected for Internal Improvement purposes but not yet confirmed, which was read and laid upon the table." Into the vacuum formed by the state's inability to act stepped Jacob Summerlin. Having purchased for its development potential in 1863 the 160-acre Riley R. Blount homestead at Bartow, Summerlin offered in October 1866 "to give of my lands at Fort Blount—Forty (40) acres for County purposes, Forty (40) acres for school purposes, and Forty (40) acres for the purposes of building a Methodist and a Baptist Church." A petition recommending acceptance of the offer was circulated by Summerlin and received the signatures of sixty-seven Polk countians, after which the county commission on October 29 formally approved the relocation. Within a month Representative Daniel Stanford had introduced an appropriate bill in the Florida house and, with the cooperation of Senator Francis A. Hendry, had secured its enactment and approval by December 1. Seven months later, on June 15, 1867, the commission contracted with John McAuley to construct a thirty-by-forty-foot, two-story courthouse on Summerlin's donated land. For his work, McAuley received the sum of thirty-eight hundred dollars.[24]

The courts were the focus in 1866 and 1867 of mounting bitterness and frustration in Polk and Manatee between Union and Confederate loyalists. Many Union families had returned to the Peace River Valley to find their homes destroyed, their fields burned, and their livestock and other moveable property confiscated.[25] Arriving too late in the year to plant and harvest crops, they faced hunger as well as exposure, a condition that prompted the Union army to issue them rations during the winter of 1865–66. As the courts began to organize following the election of November 29, 1865, these former Union refugees attempted to assert their rights either to have their property returned or to receive compensation for it. By June 1866, however, Manatee's agent of the Freedmen's Bureau, James D. Green, would express his frustration with the process: "I have entertained a hope until recently that the Refugees would be able to get there just dues by a corse of Civil Law but I am now of opinion that it will be time and money spent in vain to bring Civil action against any of the partys—from the fact that the Court the Bar and the Jury have been concerned in the Trafic of confiscated property."[26]

Within three months of Green's statement the situation had grown so bad that three men, James A. Jones, John W. Platt, and James W. Jackson, were unable even to secure a lawyer to handle their cases. The court in which redress for their claims was sought was that of circuit judge James Gettis. In mid-1867 United States officials still were reporting of the judge and his court: "The Civil Courts will not entertain suits for damages for the taking of property during the war. A case was recently brought up before the Circuit Court of Polk Co. and was thrown out by the Judge. Other cases were to be brought before the Circuit Court in Manatee County, But for some cause the Court did not meet, notwithstanding that the Law Requires the Judge to hold Court on the fourth monday in April."[27]

Late in 1866 an attempt was made to circumvent Judge Gettis by the establishment of a special Freedmen's Bureau court at Tampa. By the end of the year thirty cases for Civil War claims were pending before the court, but the effort proved futile after President Andrew Johnson refused his permission for the court to render judgments. To some extent fate intervened to help resolve the impasse when Judge Gettis unexpectedly died on December 14, 1867. However, another judge was not appointed to fill the vacancy until August of the following year.[28]

Military reconstruction

On March 2, 1867, a revolution in Florida political life occurred when the Congress enacted the First Reconstruction Act. That law declared that no legal governments existed in ten southern states, including Florida, and divided them into five military districts. The act also mandated that the right to vote be extended to freedmen and called elections for delegates for new constitutional conventions in each of the states. Three weeks later the Congress supplemented this law with the Second Reconstruction Act, which placed responsibility for voter registration upon the commanding generals of each military district and specified that, at the election for constitutional convention delegates in each state, voters be given a choice as to whether a convention should be held at all. If the vote was yes, the convention would be held within sixty days.[29]

On April 8, Maj. Gen. John Pope, commanding the military district that included Florida, divided the state into nineteen election districts and directed Col. John T. Sprague, the military commander in the state, to submit the names of three individuals in each district to become voter registrars, one of whom was required to be a freedman. Responsibility for overall supervision of the registration process was placed in the hands of Republican leader and former Tampa lawyer Ossian B. Hart. The appointments of registrars for Polk and Manatee were delayed somewhat by the difficulty involved in finding and appointing qualified blacks. "There is only one man in Manatee County who can read & write & none in Polk County," reported a military official on July 13. "I can get good intelligent & practical men," he added, "But they have no education whatever." Polk countian Henry Keen already had recommended "a good man," however, in the person of Stepney Dixon, and the appointment process was able to move forward. Ultimately, Enoch E. Mizell, former Union officer John F. Bartholf, and John Lomans, the board's black member, served as registrars in Manatee County. James M. Keen, James M. Hendry, and Stepney Dixon exercised the same responsibilities in Polk.[30]

As the mechanisms for voter registration were established, Union men in South Florida were described as "jubilant" and "industriously at work perfecting their organization as a political party." At the beginning of June a "union political meeting" was held in Manatee County. Its participants, mostly whites, expressed satisfaction at the results. Seven weeks later a similar meeting attended by whites and blacks was held in Polk "in the most orderly manner." Meanwhile, other citizens also had begun to act. Initial reports on the impact of the reconstruction acts in South Florida revealed "an honest and earnest disposition on the part of the people to accommodate themselves to the new order of things." Within several months, though, that spirit of cooperation was damaged, if not destroyed, when, on August 17, voter registration notices were ripped down at Bartow and registrar James M. Hendry was "abused." The four men responsible, Julius C. Rockner, William M. Bowen, John M. Pearce, and Nathan S. Blount, temporarily fled the county, but the seed of resistance to Reconstruction had been planted.[31]

Despite growing hostility to Reconstruction, voter registration proceeded smoothly throughout the Peace River area. By the time registration books were closed on September 20, 155 voters had qualified in Manatee and 176 in Polk. Sixteen of the Manatee total were freedmen, while Polk County registered seventeen.

When the rolls were reopened for five days on October 31, an additional thirty-five names were added in Manatee, and forty-seven in Polk.[32]

The election for delegates to the constitutional convention was held November 14–16, 1867. In Polk and Manatee a single election precinct was available for voters at the county seats of Bartow and Pine Level. Under the watchful eyes of small detachments of troops, the elections proceeded "in a quiet and orderly manner." Voters in both counties overwhelmingly favored a new convention, although only eighty-three of Manatee's voters and one hundred twenty-four of Polk's cast their ballots. As to the election of a delegate, the two counties had been lumped with Hillsborough in the Seventeenth Election District, and the choice came down to either Hillsborough Freedmen's Bureau agent C.R. Mobley or former Confederate officer William Marion Hendry of Polk County. Although Hendry easily outdistanced Mobley 100 to 23 in Polk, Mobley, a Republican, triumphed in Hillsborough and Manatee by totals of 115 to 72 and 77 to 6.[33]

The constitutional convention convened on January 20, 1868, and, after weeks of political maneuvering and tumultuous debate, the Republican-controlled body produced a constitution that called for a strong governor with the power to appoint all county officials except constables, state representatives, and state senators. Polk and Manatee each were authorized a state representative, although Polk was to be joined in a senatorial district with Sumter County and Manatee was to be linked with Monroe. First elections under the new charter were to be held May 4–6.[34]

As the election campaign was launched, some conservative politicians, including Tampa's John A. Henderson, urged defeat of the proposed constitution. Referring to the Republicans, Henderson counseled, "It is best to fight them on every line." Given such rhetoric, feelings soon began to harden. "The late Rebels show more hatred toward the Govt. at the present time than I have noticed at any time during the past two years," wrote an army officer at Tampa on April 30. "The political campaign now in progress in this part of the State has brought up to the surface some of the worst men of both parties, who deem it their province to stir up the passions & prejudices of the people."[35]

In spite of fears of violence, the election went quietly and routinely at Bartow and Pine Level. Statewide, the constitution was approved by a vote of 14,520 to 9,491, and Republican Harrison Reed was elected governor. Polk County sailed against the tide and unanimously elected Democrat John McAuley to the house of representatives and former Confederate William H. Kendrick of Sumter County to the senate. William M. Bowen, one of the four men who had attempted to disrupt voter registration at Bartow the previous summer, was elected constable. In Manatee County, Democrat John E. Fewell of Fort Ogden lost the race for state representative to James D. Green, and Republican Homer V. Plantz, although losing to Daniel Davis of Monroe, led in Manatee by a vote of forty-seven to fifteen. With this election, the lines were drawn. Polk had become a center of overwhelming conservative Democratic strength, while Manatee was under the control of the Republicans.[36]

James D. Green and the return of James T. Magbee

With the election of May 1868 James D. Green stood at the pinnacle of political power in Polk and Manatee counties. As a result of his support for Republican Governor Reed's agenda during a legislative session beginning June 8, Green was able to name those "loyal Citizens" who would assume command of both county governments under the new constitution.

In a first round of recommendations to Reed in early July, Green suggested James T. Wilson as Polk County judge, Daniel Waldron as tax assessor and clerk, Archibald Hendry as tax collector and sheriff, and John W. Hendry and Albert J. Hendry as county commissioners. Reed immediately appointed Wilson and Archibald Hendry, but not until January 29, 1869, did he appoint—presumably with Green's concurrence—a county commission consisting of J.C.A. Polk, John C. Benton, N.S. Blount, and Robert Wilkison. Reed also designated William B. Varn as superintendent of schools, Felix Seward as county treasurer, and John Davidson as Daniel Waldron's successor as clerk of the circuit court and tax assessor.[37]

For Manatee County, James Green designated Enoch E. Mizell as county judge, John F. Bartholf as clerk of the circuit court, Andrew W. Garner as sheriff, and James M. Youmans as tax collector. All these appointments promptly were made by the governor, but when several of the Manatee appointees declined to serve, Green came back in late September to nominate Bartholf for a second office as collector of revenues and to suggest a board of commissioners consisting of Asbury Sellers, Lewis B. Platt, James A. Youmans, Henry Messer, and Robert Waterston. So ascendant was Republican power at the time that many of Manatee's former Confederates revived the idea of splitting the county, leaving control of the eastern half in the hands of Peace River Republicans while ensuring Manatee River Democrats control in the west. A petition signed by over a hundred residents of the Manatee River area urging the split was forwarded to the legislature but was buried by Representative James D. Green.[38]

Late in the year Green's star rose even higher. The Florida legislature in special session in November decided to cancel the presidential election in the state, where thousands of newly enfranchised black voters were certain to vote Republican, and to award Florida's three electoral votes to Ulysses S. Grant. In line with this plan the legislature chose three presidential electors, including James D. Green. Of the three, Green was appointed to the prestigious position of messenger to present the ballots in the nation's capital. On the heels of this achievement, he scored another political triumph at home. The death of Daniel Davis had left vacant the office of state senator for Manatee and Monroe counties. Manatee Democrats rallied around Green's old nemesis, Archibald McNeill, and there were reports that prominent Republicans were abandoning the party to support the Democrat. Undeterred, Green backed his fellow Republican, Key West resident and former Union army commander Henry A. Crane. By election day, December 29, Green's strength had forced McNeill from the field, and Crane was elected to the senate by Manatee's unanimous vote. That only 30 voters bothered to cast their ballots portended trouble.[39]

At the height of Jim Green's rise in 1868 came an event which led to the destruction of his power and contributed greatly to a split in the Republican Party. Under the new constitution adopted in May the power to appoint circuit judges lay with Governor Reed, who in August appointed his friend, former Tampa lawyer James T. Magbee, to the position left vacant at the death of circuit judge James Gettis on December 14, 1867.[40]

James T. Magbee had become Harrison Reed's friend by a cir-

Francis Asbury Hendry, posing in the late 1860s with representatives of Florida's remaining Seminole and native black populations. Courtesy Florida Photographic Collection, Florida State Archives.

cuitous route. Following the expiration of his term as Hillsborough County state senator in early 1862, a term during which Magbee was instrumental in the creation of Polk County, he had returned to Tampa, sold his considerable properties, and moved to Wakulla County. Until the end of the war he busied himself with life as a planter, assisted by seven slaves. Magbee's political career was revived after the war when he was elected as Wakulla's delegate to the 1865 constitutional convention, an assembly also attended by James Gettis, F.A. Hendry, and James D. Green. That experience led him to establish a law practice at Tallahassee early in 1866 where he met all the state's leading Republicans, including Reed. By April 1868, former Democrat Magbee stood firmly in the Republican camp as an advocate of the new constitution and of Harrison Reed for governor.[41]

Initial reaction to Magbee's appointment as circuit judge was favorable, even among some former Confederates. "We would have preferred many others to Magbee," the very conservative *Florida Peninsular* reported, "yet under the circumstances we are satisfied and have some cause to rejoice." That satisfaction quickly turned to fury, however, when on October 21 Magbee stood at a racially mixed Republican rally at the Tampa courthouse and damned the Democratic party as "responsible for the late war." The new judge thundered at the former Confederates that "their hands are dyed in the blood of more than half a million loyal men." Soon, the anger felt by highly partisan former Confederates spread to many others, including some Union men, when Magbee compelled reluctant white men to serve on juries with blacks.[42]

Early in the Civil War, James Magbee and Jim Green, both Union men, had been friends and correspondents. However, the combination of Magbee's appointment in lieu of Green's friend and political ally, C.R. Mobley of Tampa, and Magbee's aggressive political stance, made them political rivals. Less than two weeks after Magbee's speech Green struck a blow against Magbee's friend and patron, Governor Reed. Joining with political opponents of the governor, Green actively sought Reed's impeachment and ouster from office, paralyzing state government for several months and setting the stage for political battles which would not be played out until 1875.[43]

Within months after the surrender at Appomattox, defeated Confederates again were in control of local government in Polk and Manatee counties. As post-war tensions grew between former Union and Confederate loyalists, that control was exercised to deny Union families the opportunity to recover through the courts their properties confiscated during the war. Bitterness and frustration came to surround these attempts and helped set a pattern for post-war relations throughout South Florida.

The enactment of the first and second Reconstruction acts in March 1867 altered the political landscape of the South. Although Polk County, with few freedmen and white Republicans, consistently voted for conservative Democrats, its local officials were to be appointed by a Republican governor upon the recommendation of South Florida's leading Unionist, James D. Green. Green exercised control, too, in Manatee County where he easily had been elected to the legislature in 1865 and again in 1868, principally by white Republicans and former Union soldiers living in the Peace River Valley. Already in 1868, however, there were clouds on the horizon for the political establishments of both Polk and Manatee counties. Complicating this situation was the re-emergence of James T. Magbee as a political power and Republican rival to Green.

13

Cattle and Reconstruction Politics

ITHIN THREE YEARS AFTER the end of the Civil War, Republicans led by South Florida pioneer and former Union officer James D. Green were in the ascendant in Manatee County while Democrats, then known as Conservatives, held a lock on politics in Polk County. The tide of immigration quickly redrew that picture as refugees from other southern states surpassed the numbers of Manatee's Republicans and, in Polk County, grappled with long-time settlers for political control. Despite the increase of Conservative voters in both counties, the power of appointment of most local officers was vested by the state constitution in the governor, until 1877 a Republican. That fact led in 1876 to a scheme by which many Peace River voters were to be denied their franchise in order fraudulently to elect a president of the United States.

Immigration and cattle

On June 25, 1868, the Congress authorized the readmission of Florida to the Union and, with a minimum of flourish, on July 4 federal authorities relinquished control of the state to its Republican governor, Harrison Reed. For over a year the protective arm of federal troops, although only a token force, remained in South Florida. On August 15, 1869, even those few soldiers were withdrawn from Tampa, setting in motion or accelerating forces that led to violence, death, and the transfer of political power throughout the Peace River Valley. To understand those events, it first is necessary to return to South Florida in the dying days of the Confederacy.[1]

Amelia Ellis was an unlikely person to symbolize the beginnings of a large movement of people, but when her husband, Aaron, died as a Confederate soldier, she felt she had no option but to move south from her Marion County farm to find a new life for herself and her family. "Just before Lee's surrender," her obituary later explained, "she moved her little family to near Keysville and later on to her home at Tiger Bay, and spent the remainder of her life in this section." Hundreds of families were to follow within a few years.[2]

At first the stream of immigration was only a trickle, as evidenced by the arrival in the Bartow area in December 1865 of the Jefferson County, Florida, families of William T. Carpenter and Joseph F. Granger. Beginning in the spring of 1866 the trickle became a steadily increasing flow which, in February 1867, was described as a "tide of emigration." "Every few days," a Thomasville, Georgia, newspaper reported, "trains of carts, wagons and other vehicles, pass through Thomasville on their way to 'Flurdys,' in search of new homes." That September the *Tallahassee Sentinel* described how "A large industrious white emigration have already wended their way to the lands of Peas Creek, and will be followed this fall by many more from the old southern states."[3]

One factor distinguished many of these Peace River settlers from those who arrived prior to the Civil War. While most earlier settlers were involved to a greater or lesser extent in the cattle business, the newcomers were mostly farmers, many of them poor. Although the war had reduced most of the earlier settlers to modest economic circumstances, that was not true of the cattlemen. Those men were growing wealthy, and their interests were clear and distinct from those of the newcomers.

There is a common misimpression that the effects of the Civil War destituted the entire population of South Florida. While many families, particularly those of Union men and of wounded and killed Confederate soldiers, were impoverished, many who were well off before the war continued to be so thereafter. The exceptions were planters such as Edmund Jones, Frederick N. Varn, Readding Blount, William J. Watkins, and Rigdon Brown who were heavily invested in slaves and who, after the war, were unable to obtain labor to help them work their farms. By 1867 these men no longer stood among the top taxpayers in the Peace River Valley; in their places stood cattlemen.[4]

Immediately following the Civil War, cattlemen in Polk and Manatee counties reported for taxation in excess of one hundred thousand head of cattle, a figure which may be presumed to be an underestimate. Of these, fully fifteen thousand were owned by Jacob Summerlin, over six thousand by William H. Willingham, four thousand by the estate of John I. Hooker, and three thousand each by Francis A. Hendry and W. H. Addison.[5] While many of the cattlemen had suffered substantial losses when their Confederate currency and bonds had become worthless, their remaining cattle represented a fortune in Spanish gold if only the cattle could be gotten to the Cuban market. And, just as he had provided the key to that market in 1858 and 1859, so again did James McKay, Sr., offer a way to Cuba after the Civil War.[6]

Writing of his father's activities in the months following the end of the Civil War, James McKay, Jr., recalled, "My father succeeded in getting to Havana by a fishing smack and from his friends in Cuba got sufficient funds to take him to New York landing there with only a few dollars in his pocket." Once there, according to the younger McKay, his father contacted merchants he had dealt with prior to the war and "they assisted him in buying the Steamer Honduras, which he named the Governor Marvin, costing $72,000. He also bought a stock of goods valued at $24,000. He left New York in October, 1865, with his vessel loaded and 165 passengers."[7]

By the end of December 1865 McKay had arrived at McKay's Wharf ten miles up Peace River and was loading cattle in cooperation with Jacob Summerlin. Paying stock raisers "10 to 15 dollars (in gold) per head," McKay and Summerlin expected to clear on each beef up to twenty-seven dollars in Cuban gold.[8]

Assisting in the cattle operation at McKay's Wharf were "ten or twelve men" who represented those pre-War settlers who were not fortunate enough to own substantial cattle herds of their own. A visiting Union army officer, unused to the ways of the

Florida frontier, described them for his journal. "They are as a class," he wrote, "entirely destitute, ignorant, and generally ambitious only for enough to eat regardless of quality to satisfy their hunger. They are governed almost exclusively by the cattle proprietors." In particular, the visitor recorded, "The poor look up to [Jacob Summerlin] as their superior and receive his orders as law." The sophisticated eye of the Union officer missed an important facet of the character of those cowhunters, as well as of the owners; their feelings for their occupation and way of life could be described only in terms of love. A correspondent writing from Pine Level in the late 1870s tried to capture that emotion when he wrote, "The older people are utterly wrapped up in the cattle business, and can conceive of no greater happiness to a dying mortal than to take the last expiring breath, holding a cow-whip in one hand and a cow's tail in the other."[9]

In 1865, 722 head of cattle were shipped from Florida to Cuba, with large numbers reportedly also shipped to Savannah and Charleston, South Carolina. The following year 1,627 made the trip and 7,089 in 1867. In the summer of 1868, however, the Cuban government imposed a seven dollar per head import duty on cattle, and the trade dropped off to less than 3,000.

Despite the Cuban import duty, cattlemen had high hopes for the 1869 shipping season. By May, Summerlin, David Hughes, and Julius C. Rockner had shifted some of their operations from Peace River to Punta Rassa and were reportedly shipping "a cargo weekly." Some owners, also including Summerlin, continued to ship from Peace River, and by August two schooners were engaged in the trade between Fort Ogden and Havana. Louis Lanier, looking ahead to the potential of the Cuban market, visited New Orleans about the same time in an attempt to purchase an additional schooner to add to the run. Acknowledged to be "uncertain and fluctuating," the Cuban market failed to sustain a demand for the beef, however, and total shipments for the year amounted only to 2,933 head. Francis A. Hendry already had turned his sights to New York City as a market for his beef, and, by late September, Jacob Summerlin was in Georgia where he announced that "for the future, he will drive all his beef cattle to Savannah."[11]

Although shaky from 1865 to 1869, the Florida cattle kingdom firmed up in 1870, for in that year Cuban demand for beef exploded when the effects of an insurrection began to be felt in Cuba's cattle producing regions. Beginning with shipments amounting to 7,285 head in 1870 and increasing to 15,177 in 1871, the market boomed for the rest of the decade. With this greatly expanded trade came a shift of shipping operations from Peace River to the old military wharf at Punta Rassa where, by 1872, 18,000 of the 21,165 cattle sent to Cuba from Florida were onloaded. Within five years Francis A. Hendry controlled all shipping at Punta Rassa through his own newly constructed wharf, purchased the following year by Jacob Summerlin.[12]

As the cattle industry began to revive after the Civil War, many cattlemen decided to move their homes and families closer to their cattle and to the shipping points of Fort Ogden and Punta Rassa. To an extent this decision was made in response to immigration into the upper Peace River Valley, a circumstance that many cattlemen felt encroached upon and endangered the ranges and that, not incidentally, threatened to eclipse their political control in Polk County.

Archibald Hendry (1820–97), Polk County's sheriff during the era of Reconstruction. Courtesy Kyle S. VanLandingham.

Leading off with such a move was Louis Lanier who had relocated from Fort Meade to Fort Ogden by early 1866, quite possibly in connection with the cattle interests of his late son-in-law John I. Hooker and his sons-in-law Francis A. Hendry and Julius C. Rockner. Two years later Lewis Henry Parker, son of John Parker, made a similar move from Homeland to Joshua Creek where he acted as agent for the Summerlin interests and became in his own right one of South Florida's leading cattlemen. By the mid-1870s Parker was joined at Joshua Creek by his brothers, Jasper Newton Parker and Thomas Owen Parker. Also to Fort Ogden, in 1869, came merchant Ziba King, a man who over the next three decades was to build a cattle empire in South Florida.[13]

The single most important of these moves was made by Francis A. Hendry in 1870.[14] For several years prior to his relocation, Hendry had been driving his cattle farther and farther south, looking for better range. In 1869 his need for good range lands increased dramatically when he purchased for fifty thousand dollars the cattle of his brother-in-law, Julius C. Rockner, as well as those of David Hughes. When the Cuban market opened so explosively in 1870, he determined to move all his operations closer to the shipping dock at Punta Rassa and drove twelve thousand head of cattle across the Caloosahatchee River to the prairie at Fort Thompson. By then the largest cattle owner in Florida, Hendry relocated his family from Fort Meade to Fort Myers where they made a new home in one of the abandoned officer's quarters. Within three years they were joined by others from Polk County including Hendry's brother, William Marion Hendry; his brother-in-law, Jehu J. Blount; his nephew, Frank J. Wilson, son of James T. Wilson; and his cousin, Charles W. Hendry and his wife, Jane, the granddaughter of Rigdon Brown. By 1875 Francis A. Hendry reportedly owned twenty-five thousand head of cattle and was on his way to becoming the cattle king of South Florida.[15]

Redemption in Manatee County

The decade of the 1870s opened in the Peace River Valley with James D. Green still seeking revenge against his former friend, James T. Magbee, and Magbee's mentor, Republican governor Harrison Reed. Shortly after the Florida legislature convened in

January 1870, Representative Green's resolution calling for an investigation of numerous charges against Reed was approved by the house, and Green was appointed chairman of the committee to conduct the investigation. On February 4 he issued a majority report calling for the governor's impeachment. After "a lively debate" and complex political maneuvering, Green's resolution was defeated.[16]

A Republican senator whose motives are open to question claimed that, once Green's impeachment committee was authorized, the Manatee representative approached the governor with an offer: if Magbee were replaced as circuit judge with C.R. Mobley, the Green committee would issue a report absolving the governor. Another rumor passed on by the same source suggested that Jim Green simply demanded a bribe. On his part, Green stated that "he stood firm and made the majority report in favor of impeachment." After the fight was over, however, the representative and the governor made up, and Green publicly pledged his future support to Reed. "I feel like the little boy," Green said, "who got besmeared twenty miles from water."[17]

Whatever the terms of an agreement, if any, both Reed and Green benefitted from the impeachment fight. Reed, of course, was relieved of the threat of removal from office. Within days Green received two rewards with the acquiescence, if not the assistance, of the governor. On February 9, Governor Reed approved as law "An Act to Incorporate the Peas Creek Immigrant and Agricultural Company." This innocuous sounding bill gave seven incorporators the right to "improve the navigation of the Peas Creek in this State as far as Fort Meade." What this meant was that, if the company could clear Peace River sufficiently to make it navigable most of the year for shallow-draft vessels, it would not only control the river's commerce, it also would receive "the alternate sections of lands contiguous to said stream for a distance of three miles on each side thereof" from Charlotte Harbor to Bartow. Along with others active in Florida politics in both Republican and Democratic parties, two incorporators who were to share this potential bonanza were the Democratic Polk and Sumter county senator, William H. Kendrick, and James D. Green.[18] Nine days, later, Jim Green received his second reward. Based primarily upon the testimony of Green and his friends and political allies C.R. Mobley and Matthew P. Lyons, Judge James

Cattle baron Ziba King (1838–1901). Courtesy Florida Photographic Collection, Florida State Archives.

T. Magbee was impeached by the house of representatives and suspended from office.[19]

A victorious Jim Green returned to Manatee County planning the further enhancement of his political career. On July 11, in a move that the Tampa newspaper insisted "surprises everybody," Green was nominated at Pine Level as an Independent candidate for state senator to succeed Henry A. Crane who was running for the Monroe County house seat. Green was depending upon support from voters still resentful of Magbee's integrated juries and from new voters recently immigrated from Georgia and Alabama. He added to his ticket respected Democrat Edgar M. Graham as a candidate for the Manatee house seat. Furious at Green's move, former Confederate Democrats met at Fort Ogden at the end of the month to name an opposition ticket. Under the leadership of George C. Tippins, F.H. Warren, Louis Lanier, and John E. Fewell, a Key West conservative, W.C. Maloney, Jr., was nominated for the senate and Francis C.M. Boggess for the house.[20]

Jim Green's political masterstroke turned to dust at the Republican State Convention at Gainesville on August 17, 1870. At that meeting Green worked in support of the candidacy for Congress (from a district encompassing the entire state) of black state senator Josiah Walls of Alachua County. The nomination of Walls was too much even for Union men in Manatee County, much less for former Confederates. To make matters worse, Walls's Democratic opponent was Silas Niblack of Columbia County, well known and even related to many of the former Columbia and Hamilton County families living in the Peace River Valley.[21]

The furor which greeted Jim Green's return from Gainesville must have been overwhelming. Green attempted to repair the damage by declaring even he could not vote for Walls, but it was a case of far too little, far too late. Edgar M. Graham disassociated himself from Green and aroused "the people in every part of the county to register and vote." Judge Enoch E. Mizell led many Republican voters into the conservative camp. When the votes were cast on November 8, Silas Niblack received every single vote of Manatee County. Against the Democratic landslide Green received only thirty-five votes, while his former ticketmate, E.M. Graham, easily was elected to the house.[22] Only when returns from Fort Ogden and Fort Hartsuff, both with very heavy conservative majorities, were thrown out on technicalities by the Republican canvassers was Key West Republican J.W. Locke able to edge out Democrat Maloney in the senate race. The *Florida Peninsular* summed up the election in its edition of November 23: "Manatee has shaken off Radical rule and stands to-day as fully redeemed as any county in the State."[23]

The controversy over the 1870 Manatee County elections did not end with the defeat of James D. Green. Although election day was November 8, it was weeks before either Polk or Manatee County reported its results. With the outcome of the congressional race riding upon a razor-thin margin, the Republican state attorney general, Sherman Conant, employed an Ocala man,

Harry E. Russell, to ascertain first-hand the reasons for the delay. When Russell departed from Tampa for Bartow and Pine Level, "he was met by a party of armed men, who told him they knew his business, and that he must leave that section of the State at once if he valued his life." When Manatee's returns were completed on December 1, they were sent by courier to Bartow telegraph operator W.H. Pearce in an envelope addressed to "S.L. Niblack, Lake City, Florida" rather than directly to the state elections officials. At about the same time, Pearce received a telegram from Lake City requesting him to open the envelope and telegraph its contents to Lake City. Pearce complied and then personally delivered the returns to the board of state canvassers. Despite these and other irregularities affecting both candidates, Walls was awarded the congressional seat only to be turned out of office after having served almost the entire term.[24]

Regulators and the freedmen

The racial discord surrounding the Florida congressional campaign of 1870 was reflected in tragic violence in the Peace River Valley. As early as December 1865 Union occupation officials had reported the formation of Regulator organizations in central Florida. By the following summer it was stated that in Manatee County "there is a secret order the object is to oppress the Refugees and all who manifest Union sentiment. One of the obligations is to not assist and to discountenance all Refugees and Union people." Former Confederates saw the issue as one of law and order. "From many parts of the South," George W. Hendry recorded, "men who were fleeing from justice sought seclusion from the main thoroughfares of public travel and to escape identity came to South Florida. Most of these people came to Polk County." "One, Dr. Harris from Jaxtown," Hendry continued, "said that when a man got so mean that someone had to kill him, [the man] would get on his horse and come 500 miles to Polk County to get the job done. . . . And he usually got it done in no uncertain way."[25]

Little specific documentation remains of Regulator activity in the Peace River area just after the Civil War, although one veteran of the Second Florida Cavalry, Samuel L. Green, was run out of Manatee for his "rascality." The existence and activities of the Regulators by no means were universally popular, however, and George W. Hendry even mentioned the presence of "anti-regulators." In any event, the activities of the Regulators do not appear to have been directed at freedmen so long as federal troops remained nearby at Tampa. That situation changed on July 25, 1869, after the troops had received orders to leave South Florida. On that day at Fort Ogden, a black man, John Lomans, one of Manatee County's voter registrars, was cow-whipped and shot at by Gus, Alonzo, and John Johnson. For several months a quiet peace was maintained between the races, and then on February 7, 1870, again at Fort Ogden, another black, Frank Griffin, was set upon and pursued by Joseph Brooker, F.C.M. Boggess, John L. Whidden, and David Whidden, who threatened to kill him. Eighteen days later James Cooper was shotgunned to death at Manatee by George T. Patten, and within a month thereafter William Fouis [Lewis?] also was the victim of homicide.[26]

When black state senator Josiah Walls received the Republican congressional nomination in mid-August 1870, the South Florida racial violence turned even more deadly. Although the name of the victim is unknown, the Tampa newspaper reported on October 5, "A negro man was killed in the eastern part of Manatee county about ten days since, by unknown parties." Five months later the Regulators reached up into Polk County where, in early February 1871, Nathaniel Redd, "a notorious thief," was lynched at Bartow, again "by parties unknown." The citizens of Bartow were characterized as "indignant at this outrage" and protested that "they had no hand" in the murder.[27]

After the lynching of Nathaniel Redd the racial violence built in pace and intensity. In March, John Lomans again was the Regulator target. William H. Hollingsworth later swore that he had seen Lomans "with a Rope around his neck, and William Allen had holt of the other end of it, that he saw four other men with him, says their names were Louis Lanier, Noah Browning, and Frank Griffin."[28] Lomans somehow survived the incident, but on April 22, near Bartow, Jim Pernell was shot dead in the dark "by some unknown party."[29]

On April 24 a mass meeting was held at Bartow where the participants resolved: "That we view with most indignant feelings the hanging of Nathaniel Red and the shooting of Jim Pernell, and believe it to be the duty of every good and honest citizen to assist the civil authorities in ferreting out and bringing before the courts of the country the perpetrators of such violence and unlawful acts." Judge Magbee, who had been reinstated when impeachment charges against him were dropped in January 1871, attempted to force a grand jury investigation. While regretting that "a number of crimes of a high grade have been committed in our county," the jury declined to act because "few of those crimes have been committed by *bona fide* citizens of the county."[30]

Regulator violence against freedmen in the Peace River Valley climaxed with the murder of Jim Pernell—for the very good reason that most freedmen left the Peace River area. In 1870 and 1871, Charles Brown, William Brown, Andrew Denson, Albert Lewis, and Alexander Stillings left Polk County. They were followed in 1873 by Buck Jones and Royal Read, in 1874 by Stepney Dixon, and in 1875 by Solomon Carrington and Simon Jackson. During the same period of time, Frank Griffin, Joseph Chapman, Richmond Crews, and Joseph Crews left Manatee. By October 1874, John Bartholf in Manatee County would note that "there are but few negroes here, making labor scarce and wages very high." In all of Polk County at the same time it was estimated that, of a total population of 3,500, only "about 100 are colored people."[31]

It is interesting to note that many of these freedmen and their families moved to and prospered in, the neighborhood of Simmons

Teacher, author, Confederate cow cavalryman Francis C.M. Boggess (1833–1902). Courtesy Bernice J. McLenon.

Hammock and Thonotosassa in Hillsborough County. Of the early Polk County freedmen there in 1880 were Caesar Cook, Buck Jones, Stepney Dixon, Alexander Stillings, Simon Jackson, Royal Read, Charles Brown, and Solomon Carrington. Initially encouraged, perhaps by a political climate in which a majority of the Hillsborough board of commissioners were blacks, the freedmen remained and over the next fifteen years built a community described by a correspondent in 1886. "They have their own school and meeting houses. They teach in the one and worship in the other. They hold camp meetings, and debating clubs, read essays and sing hymns and songs. They send their children to colored academies, and dress in store clothes. But above all they are the best farmers in the county, and are excelling their white neighbors in the quantity and quality of their products."[32]

The road to final redemption

In the aftermath of the elections of 1870, politics settled into a predictable pattern in Polk and Manatee counties. In general elections for state representative, state senator, constable, and other state and federal positions, Democrats, or, as they more commonly were known at the time, conservatives, piled up huge majorities with regularity. However, as long as the state had a Republican governor, until January 1877, local officials were appointed by the head of the opposition party. Given those facts, the situation in each of the two counties differed to some extent.

Polk County voters in the post-Civil War era had voted overwhelmingly and even unanimously time and again for conservatives and against Republicans. Beginning with the election of 1870, though, a split developed in county politics between those who lived in the Peace River areas of the county—Fort Meade, Homeland, Bartow, and Fort Fraser—and those living farther north and west in the vicinity of what soon was to be known as Lakeland. The former represented in great part the pre-Civil War residents of the county and were oriented toward the cattle business, while the latter tended to be more recent settlers and farmers. The newcomers scored their first major victories in 1872 when Mitchell G. Fortner defeated William H. Kendrick for the Polk-Sumter senate seat, and John W. Bryant edged out John McAuley and Robert N. Pylant in the Polk house election. For the remainder of the Reconstruction era, the balance of power swung back and forth as evidenced by Bryant's defeat in 1874 at the hands of Fort Meade merchant and cattleman Sherod E. Roberts, himself a relative newcomer from South Georgia. With Bryant and Roberts both declining to run in 1876, E.E. Mizell defeated old guard cattleman George W. Hendry of Fort Meade by almost a two-to-one margin.[33]

Concerning Polk's local officials, Jim Green had begun Republican rule in 1868 by attempting to secure the appointment of "loyal Citizens" to all Polk County offices. The shifting tides and turbulence of Reconstruction politics, coupled with the paucity of Republicans in Polk County, early had led Governor Reed to curry support from Polk's conservative legislators through the appointment of ex-Confederates and secessionists to county office. In January 1869 John Davidson was appointed to replace Daniel Waldron as clerk of the circuit court; ex-Confederate Nathan S. Blount was serving on the board of commissioners; and William B. Varn was appointed superintendent of schools. By mid-1872, with the appointment of a series of new county commissioners, conservative control of county affairs was confirmed, although Archibald Hendry remained for a time as sheriff and tax commissioner and James T. Wilson continued to hold office as a newly appointed county commissioner.[34] Time was running out on Hendry, however. On July 9, 1872, the governor appointed Felix J. Seward to succeed him in both the offices he held, and on October 28 of the following year Hendry was indicted in Polk County on a charge of embezzlement. The fact that the indictment was never prosecuted suggests that politics may have lain behind it, but Hendry took the hint and soon moved to Fort Pierce where his wife and children had lived since January 1872.[35]

Manatee County followed the lead of Polk in electing conservatives to office, but the Republican party continued to field candidates in all elections. Thanks to the organizational efforts of John F. Bartholf, who as clerk had controlled day-to-day county affairs since 1868, the Republicans rebounded somewhat in 1872 from the disaster of two years previously. In the 1872 contest, the Reverend John W. Hendry was able to tally 84 votes against Conservative F.B. Hagan's 199 for the Manatee house seat, and after no Manatee County votes in 1870, black Congressman Josiah Walls received 60 votes in his reelection bid. Manatee even contributed 81 votes to Republican Ossian Hart's successful campaign for governor.[36]

Republican strength remained at about eighty votes in 1874 in Manatee County elections that saw Conservative F.B. Hagan returned to the house and Francis A. Hendry, then a resident of Fort Myers, elected as senator from Manatee and Monroe. The following two years, however, saw the collapse of the Republican party as a viable political organization in Manatee. Edgar M. Graham in December 1876 explained that since 1874 "prominent men have changed, and changed with them a large number of persons who were then republicans." The Republicans failed even to offer a candidate for the house in 1876.[37]

Unlike Polk County, during the period of 1871–1876 Manatee's local government continued to be dominated by Republican appointees. After Jim Green's 1870 defeat, appointments rested upon the recommendation of county clerk John F. Bartholf with the concurrence of Judge Magbee. Although Bartholf was careful to keep county government under Republican control, he also sponsored the appointment of Democrats E.M. Graham as county judge, Ziba King as justice of the peace, Archibald McNeill and William Smith as county commissioners, and William I. Turner and F.B. Hagan as members of the board of public instruction. Bartholf later wrote, "I did not hesitate to call to my aid members of the opposite party, whom I thought competent and willing to aid me." Among Republicans Bartholf felt "competent and willing to aid" him were Jim Green, who served at various times as sheriff and member of the board of county commissioners, Nathan H. DeCoster, county judge and member of the board of commissioners, James M. Hendry, Daniel D. Garner, James M. Youmans, P.T. Tucker, Jesse H. Tucker, Daniel W. Carlton, Enoch E. Mizell, Jesse B. Mizell, John M. Bates, Dempsey D. Crews, Jr., Lewis B. Platt, James A. Jones, and Dennis Driggers.[38]

The election of November 5, 1874, signaled the beginning of the end of the political careers of the two most prominent Manatee County Republicans. On a statewide and on a local level Democrats were emboldened by their success in taking control of both houses of the Florida legislature. In Manatee County this new confidence led to the indictment in Judge Magbee's circuit court of James D. Green, sheriff of Manatee County, on a charge of false imprisonment. A grand jury dominated by conservatives and led by former Confederate officer William I. Turner claimed that Green, acting as a federal deputy marshal in December 1872, improperly had arrested Ziba King and carried him off to the U.S. attorney in Jacksonville after King had spurned Green's purported demand for a bribe. Under indictment, Green was forced to resign as sheriff on February 20, 1875, and to wait an entire year for trial. At the fall term of the Manatee circuit court in 1875, he was found innocent of all charges.[39]

Although there is no evidence of a direct linkage between the two events, two months after the indictment of Jim Green in Judge Magbee's court, Key West Democratic representative William Watkins Hicks revived the five-year-old impeachment charges against Magbee. Faced with certain defeat in the Democrat-controlled House, Magbee resigned his office on February 17, 1875, and, on the same day, Representative Hicks dropped the impeachment proceedings.[40] Within a few days Republican governor Marcellus L. Stearns, who had assumed office upon the death of Ossian B. Hart on March 18, 1874, had appointed Hicks as Florida's superintendent of public instruction. Stearns was an old friend of Green's and had been the speaker of the Florida house of representatives who appointed Green in 1870 to chair the impeachment committee in the case of Magbee's patron, Governor Reed.[41]

By the summer of 1876 it was obvious to all observers, given the shambles in which the county Republican party lay, that Manatee as well as Polk would vote overwhelmingly Democratic in the fall in elections that afforded Democrats their first real opportunity since the Civil War to regain control over state and national government. In the midst of this situation, Manatee court clerk John F. Bartholf, the man responsible for maintaining voter registration lists and running elections, fell seriously ill. By August 24, an alarmed and despairing Bartholf submitted his resignation to Governor Stearns along with a recommendation that the office be given to the county surveyor, G.H. Johnson. Bartholf's letter was received by the governor on September 20 and three days later he accepted it to take effect "on the qualification of his [Bartholf's] successor." Having taken that action, however, Stearns heard from his old friend and political ally Jim Green, who had a very interesting plan.[42]

"Stearns received the resignation and the name of the man

recommended," remembered a state senator, John Wallace, "but now the opportunity to silence a whole Democratic county, for to have no clerk made it impossible to have an election." Jim Green understood the implications of the situation, and upon his suggestion Stearns recovered Bartholf's resignation letter and struck through the words "to take effect on the qualification of his successor," which immediately removed Bartholf from office. Stearns then initiated some fancy political sleight-of-hand by appointing as Bartholf's replacement Andrew Green, the 24-year-old son of James D. Green. A number of weeks later, with November 7, election day, drawing near, Andrew Green received his appointment and took the oath of office, but delayed execution of the bond necessary for issuance of his commission. By this action, Green insured there would be no lawful clerk to hold elections in Manatee County.[43]

As Stearns and his allies played out their charade, state Democratic leaders alerted Manatee County Democratic officials Dr. J.C. Pelot, Josiah Gates, John W. Harllee, and Edgar M. Graham to the Republican plans, and provided for their use some printed election blanks. About two weeks before election day, Graham rode to Pine Level and demanded the voter registration lists from Andrew Green who declined to provide them, as he asserted, because "Mr. Bartholf . . . had instructed him not to let a paper go out of the clerk's office which he had possession of at the time." Rather than conferring with Bartholf, the Democrats sent messengers to all areas of the county alerting their supporters that they would hold an election on November 7. Graham, acting under authority he claimed as county judge, drew up what he considered the appropriate elections documents and distributed them to his political friends who were to serve as inspectors. Responding to these efforts, Jim Green began circulating around the county to urge Republicans not to participate in the rump election "on the ground that he did not consider the election legal."[44]

On election day, November 7, 1876, 305 Manatee County voters cast their ballots in the highly unorthodox election. After 16 Fort Ogden votes were thrown out on a technicality, 289 ballots were counted for Democratic gubernatorial candidate George T. Drew, 288 for Democratic presidential candidate Samuel J. Tilden. The Republican candidate for governor, Marcellus L.

Cattleman John Parker (1818–81), sheriff of old Hillsborough County by 1845, was a prominent figure among the pioneer settlers of the Peace River area for the next thirty-five years. Courtesy Kyle S. VanLandingham.

Stearns, and electors pledged to the Republican presidential hopeful, Rutherford B. Hayes, each received only 26 votes.[45] A single Republican voted at Fort Ogden. The remaining 25 Republican ballots were cast at Pine Level, but only after Edgar M. Graham took the stump that morning and, in his words, "I convinced them it was legal, and they voted." Graham later testified, "I believe, before God that the vote in Manatee County was as fair as any vote ever held in the world, because every man had as free an opportunity as he had anywhere in the United States to go the ballot-box and vote if he desired."[46]

Graham waited at Pine Level for six days for the ballot boxes to come in from all precincts, and then he, justice of the peace Ziba King, and sheriff J.B. Mizell counted the votes and prepared the county return. When that return, along with Polk's, was received at Tallahassee, Republican officials were furious and immediately dispatched two men, W.T. Webster and Samuel Hamblen, to investigate the validity of the election. Having traveled as far as Sumterville north of Polk County, the two men were confronted by a crowd which informed them, "We have given large majorities here, and we do not propose to have them investigated." The two men turned back, concluding "our lives were not safe to go on."[47]

For months the results of the election of 1876 were too close to call on both the state and national level. In early December the state election canvassing board, controlled by Republicans, attempted to exclude entirely the Manatee returns. After a month of bitter political infighting and litigation, the Florida Supreme Court ordered the inclusion of the Manatee votes, and in the resulting recount, George Drew was elected governor over Marcellus Stearns by only 195 votes. Florida was thus "redeemed" by the Democrats and Stearns was left to ponder his scheme of canceling the Manatee vote; had it succeeded, he, not Drew, would have been the winner.[48]

In the contest for president, Florida Republicans submitted electoral ballots for Rutherford B. Hayes based upon an electoral count which excluded the Manatee returns. Democrats did the same for Samuel J. Tilden claiming as their authority a vote count which included the Manatee ballots. In an election in which Florida's four electoral votes, had they gone for Tilden, would have elected the Democrat, the Congress was forced to establish a national commission to decide the outcome. Not until February 9, 1877, did the panel, with a slight Republican majority, decide to award Florida's vote to Republican Hayes based upon the principle that it had no authority to question the certificate of the state governor—Republican Marcellus L. Stearns. And so, while Stearns was counted out in Florida by the margin of Manatee's vote, he and James D. Green helped elect President Rutherford B. Hayes by causing the exclusion of the same votes.[49]

The era of Reconstruction saw the population of the Peace River Valley increase substantially, for the most part due to immigration of Confederate veterans and their families from the states of Georgia and Alabama. These new settlers caused an upheaval in the politics of both Polk and Manatee counties. In Polk, which had few Republicans, the newcomers found themselves in political and economic opposition to many earlier settlers whose interests lay with the cattle industry. As that industry grew through the 1870s and cattle owners became more affluent, many of the owners moved with their families farther south into Manatee and Monroe counties. Others who remained in Polk began to suffer a loss of influence as the newcomers began to fill elective and appointive office in the county. In Manatee County, where Republicans reigned as late as 1870, the Democratic new-comers swamped the polls and quickly took away any chance of elective office for their opposition. Republicans harmed themselves through intraparty squabbles, particularly involving James D. Green and James T. Magbee, and by 1876 found themselves politically isolated and impotent. An attempt by some Republicans to cancel the 1876 elections in Manatee resulted in the calling of a rump election by Democrats and contributed to the narrow redemption of the state by Democrat George T. Drew. The political turmoil of the Reconstruction era also led a band of Regulators to use intimidation and murder to drive many of the freedmen remaining in Polk and Manatee from their homes in the Peace River area. By January 1877, after almost twenty years of turmoil and bloodshed, the struggles of Indian and Civil War, as well as Reconstruction, lay in the past, and the Peace River Valley again stood a chance for peace and growth.

14

Communities on the Frontier

IMMIGRATION IN THE YEARS following the Civil War provided the Peace River area with a broad base upon which could be erected the institutional foundations of a more civilized life including towns, schools, and churches. What the area lacked and the river could not afford, however, was an inexpensive and reliable form of transportation for immigrants, residents, crops, and livestock.

Rebuilding after the Civil War

Beginning in May 1865, the survivors of the Civil War in the Peace River Valley, as elsewhere, began to pick up the pieces of their lives. In Manatee County, farms and homesteads along the river systematically had been burned and looted by Confederate troops and for the last year of the war the area had been depopulated. The military buildings at Fort Meade, the heart of the only true village on the river, lay in ashes, as did the nearby homestead of Willoughby Tillis, all burned by Union men who had so recently been friends and neighbors. The war's flames had not reached the rich farming country that stretched northward from Fort Meade through Bartow and Fort Fraser, but its impact nonetheless had been felt there through the loss of slave labor on farms and the pain of the death or injury of loved ones.

Nevertheless, a commitment to permanent and increasingly sophisticated settlement remained. Throughout the conflict, churches such as the Peas Creek Baptist Church near Bartow had continued to meet and in many cases had prospered. Early in 1863, Peas Creek Baptist even had constructed a "New Meeting House," the first in the Peace River Valley. The annual October church meetings at the Methodist campground at Homeland likewise continued without interruption throughout the war and, by 1865, had become a forum for political as well as religious and social concerns.[1]

At least in Polk County, some schools continued in operation through the fall of 1863, if not longer. At the war's end at least one school was open at Bartow under the tutelage of lawyer and Baptist minister Samuel C. Craft. At Bartow also in June 1865 the first Masonic chapter in the river valley was organized. Known as Bartow Lodge No. 9, the chapter's first officers included R.N. Pylant, Robert Wilkison, Samuel C. Craft, Jasper Summerlin, J.M. Hayman, A.P. Hampton, W.R. Hollingsworth, James T. Wilson, T.J. Kinney, and Louis Lanier.[2]

Wartime shortages had forced the closing in 1861 or 1862 of the Riley Blount store at Bartow and the Louis Lanier store at Fort Meade, but at Bartow "after the close of the war" Blount attempted to revive his business. When William T. Carpenter moved there in December 1865, he purchased from Jacob Summerlin the buildings of old Fort Blount, which may have included Blount's store, and himself went into the mercantile business. In an area where the government was slow to reestablish postal service, Carpenter's store served as an informal and unofficial post office until 1869.[3]

By 1867, town life had begun to emerge at Bartow, the previous year designated Polk County's new seat. In that year a two-story courthouse and a jail were constructed for the county and, about the same time, Jacob Summerlin built a frame, two-story, twenty-five-by-forty-foot building known thereafter as the Summerlin Institute. The first floor for years was used as a school and church, while the upper floor served as a masonic hall. On the west side of the courthouse, W.T. Carpenter erected a new building for his general store, and, nearby, Jacob Summerlin's stepson, Aaron G. Zipprer, and others built several fine frame houses. The wood for all this construction came from a steam sawmill Summerlin had purchased in St. Augustine, shipped to Tampa, and hauled with oxen to Bartow where it was set up on Carpenter's Pond. Another building erected at Bartow in 1867, a telegraph station, had a history of its own.[4]

Since 1854 great interest had been expressed in the idea of linking the American mainland with the Caribbean by an underwater telegraph cable, but work did not commence on such a line until January 1860 and the Civil War stopped all construction before any submarine cable was laid. A few months after Lee's surrender, however, a group of New Yorkers applied to the Florida legislature and to the Congress for charters for the cable. On January 2, 1866, Florida granted their International Ocean Telegraph Company an exclusive right for twenty years to connect the Florida coast with Cuba by cable and also the right to construct land lines "through the State of Florida and across the islands, keys, sand banks and reefs belonging to said State." Four months later the Congress added its approval.[5]

To supervise design and construction of the telegraph line, the IOTC employed engineer W.H. Heiss. After an initial false start in planning the cable's route down Florida's Atlantic coast, Heiss turned his attention to the Gulf coast. After months spent investigating possible routes, he determined that the line's terminus was to be the old U.S. Army facilities at Punta Rassa, and the cable's route from that spot to Lake City was to run straight through the Peace River Valley.[6]

Construction of the IOTC line proceeded quickly. On April 20, 1867, work commenced from a headquarters at Gainesville, with work gangs erecting poles and line north toward Baldwin and south toward Ocala. IOTC crews descended into "the wilds of Florida and traversed sawgrass glades, hammock land, pine barrens and cypress swamps, wading waist deep and cutting a swatch through over 250 miles" of the sparsely populated peninsula. In May the line wound its way into northern Polk County, skirted Lake Wire (incidentally giving its name to that body of water) and within a few days arrived at Bartow. "We learn that the office at Bartow upon the Telegraph line from Gainesville to Punta Rosso is in full and successful operation," the Tampa newspaper reported, "and that an association of gentlemen there, have perhaps, already consummated an arrangement by which they may be kept posted, in all the affairs transpiring in this outward world of ours." W.H. Pearce may already have set to work as Bartow's telegrapher, a position he held for eighteen years.[7]

From Bartow the work crews extended their efforts to the south, passing near the school house at modern Homeland and reaching Fort Meade a little over a mile due west of the Peace River bridge. From that point the line turned to the east, crossed Peace River, and then again veered to the south running down the old Indian and military road to Popash, Fort Ogden, and on to the Caloosahatchee River and Punta Rassa. Along the way, at intervals of thirty miles or less, testing stations for repairs were established, and at each of these men and horses were placed to maintain the line. In the Peace River area these stations were sited at Bartow, Fort Meade, Branchboro (eighteen miles south of Fort Meade), Joshua Creek, Spike Pens (twenty miles south of Joshua Creek), Fort Myers, and Punta Rassa. The road which connected them and which ran along the wire became known as the Wire Road and, later, the Old Wire Road.[8]

The telegraph line reached Punta Rassa May 29, 1867. By

The landing of the International Ocean Telegraph Company cable at Key West in 1867. *Harper's Magazine*, September 1867. Courtesy Florida Photographic Collection, Florida State Archives.

August 21 a submarine cable was laid and in operation between Key West and Havana. On September 10, the Punta Rassa to Key West link finally was placed into service, putting New York financiers, Peace River cattlemen, and countless others in almost instantaneous contact with their counterparts in Havana.[9]

Six weeks before the official opening of the IOTC line, Bartow businessmen, including William J. Watkins, began extracting national and world news from the telegraph line and forwarding it by courier to Tampa, which had no such facility. The cost of utilizing the wire for news soon proved prohibitive, however, and in 1877 Francis A. Hendry noted, "For several years the I.O.T.Co. line has been established, passing by our doors, without even dropping a word of news from the outstide world." Tampa went without any telegraphic services for eleven years until, on May 15, 1878, the Tampa and Fort Meade Telegraph Company opened a line connecting the two towns. Built under the superintendency of Fort Meade businessman Sherod E. Roberts, the new line was credited with imparting "new life and vigor to the facility of business in the two places."[10]

The growth of communities

The year 1867 had been a good one for Bartow, but its energetic growth could not be sustained after its patron, Jacob Summerlin, moved his family from the town late in 1867 or early in 1868. The encouragement for growth that might have been expected from county government and the courts failed to materialize for, as one writer put it in 1874, "The business of the courts is meagre, so much so that the county cannot afford business for two lawyers (not a single case, either civil or criminal, on the docket); one has to *cow-drive* and the other is an *accountant* in a merchantile house to make a genteel livelihood." In spite of the community's slow development, on February 23, 1869, the Bartow post office reopened with Robert Wilkison as its postmaster.[11] In 1870 David Hughes erected a general merchandise store and merchant Julius C. Rockner opened a branch of his Fort Meade store at the county seat. Having traveled to New York for his goods, Rockner boasted at the new store's opening, "Our stock is extensive and we flatter ourselves that the selection can not be beaten in this part of Florida."[12]

A Fort Meade merchant expanding his services to Bartow illustrates the reemergence and vitality that Fort Meade had experienced and enjoyed by 1870. Despite the death in 1862 of its principal founder and landowner, John I. Hooker, and the departures of cattlemen Louis Lanier and Francis A. Hendry, the town had rebuilt and grown as "the centre of the cattle trade." Writing of Fort Meade in 1877 Alafia resident George Wells explained the economic realities of South Florida. "Most of the trading is with the stock men and the stock raisers," he stated, "who handle more money, as a general thing, than any other class in South Florida."[13]

Among the first merchants of the post–Civil War era to take advantage of the stockmen's trade at Fort Meade were Dupont, Georgia, natives Cornelius B. Lightsey and Sherod E. Roberts. Their general merchandise business, opened in 1869, was followed by that of Julius Rockner in 1870. In the following year a post office was established with Rockner as postmaster. At the same time, the town was described as "a flourishing and growing little village" that already was "doing three-fourths of the whole business in a radius of 70 miles, north, east, and south."[14] An important part of that business was conducted by Frederick N. Varn who in 1870 had settled at Sink Branch just east of Fort Meade and opened a tannery and shoe-and-leather business. Of Varn's work it was said that "people came from as far as Gainesville, Tampa, and Sanford to have shoes, bridles, and saddle bags made. 'The Tannery,' as it was called, provided work for a large number of people." Within four years Varn was turning out four hundred pairs of shoes and boots a week, "with an equal proportion of harness and saddlery and other work, besides shipping a large amount of leather."[15]

By 1874 and despite the national economic collapse known as the Panic of 1873, William B. Varn had surveyed Fort Meade for a town plat, and it was reported that over half a million dollars in business was done in the community annually. "Fort Meade is a flourishing, busy, and bustling little town," one commentator remarked. "The health and water is fine, and society refined and orderly." At the end of Reconstruction, the town, then "quite a lively place," contained "five or six" stores, and the town fathers seriously were considering incorporation. Fort Meade reigned as the principal town of the Peace River Valley with "advantages possessed by few others."[16]

While Fort Meade enjoyed its commercial supremacy, immigration into the lower Peace River area, coupled with the growth of the cattle industry, brought the beginnings of other villages and communities. In 1866, former Union officer Nathan DeCoster opened a store at Fort Winder. At the same time, near the river's mouth, two wharves were under construction, one on the north bank erected by William Alderman and one on the south by Jacob Summerlin. A little farther upriver David Hughes was erecting a sawmill, and of the entire area it was said, "There are many good settlements on both sides of the river, near the wharves, and at no distant day there will be a town at both places." The town that emerged was on the south bank, and its name was Fort Ogden.[17]

"A few settlers were scattered over the country when in December, 1866, a store was opened by John E. Fewell," wrote a Fort Ogden resident in later years. "But few settlers located, however, for a number of years." One person who did locate at Fort Ogden in the summer of 1869 was Ziba King. For about a year prior to his move to Peace River, King had been a merchant at Tampa. In July 1869 he loaded his goods on a schooner, shipped them to Fort Ogden, and reopened his store for business. Soon he had superseded or bought out Fewell, who as Jacob Summerlin's son-in-law had succeeded to the cattlemen's retail interests in the area, and had added a barroom to his establishment.[18]

Within months after King's move to Fort Ogden, the young community was described, due to increased activity in the cattle business, as "becoming a place of importance." By 1870 the area's population had grown enough so that forty-nine men would vote at the Fort Ogden precinct, and, until its loss in a storm on October 17, 1875, the village was served regularly by at least one schooner, the *Laura*, which sailed between that point and Key West supplying early settlers with goods and provisions. By 1876 it was "attracting considerable attention" for being "as good a locality for the raising of oranges as there is in the State." A post office was established in 1876, with Francis C.M. Boggess as postmaster.[19]

The Manatee County seat at Pine Level received its first permanent residents, the family of John F. Bartholf, in 1869. It was graced with a post office two years later, but could report by the summer of 1876 a population increase of only "four families— three white & one colored." In addition to the log courthouse, the community contained only a few residences, two storehouses, and a "jail & Jury house"—all constructed of logs. That fall its appearance was enhanced by the erection of a "handsome, commodious framed Court House" and jail, but two years remained before the town even would be surveyed and platted. Throughout the era of Reconstruction, conditions at Pine Level never were far removed from the accommodations described by a January 1870 visitor on court day. "Every man had his blanket and at night all gathered around large lightwood fires, wrapped themselves in their blankets, and slept as comfortably as if they had been in a first class hotel."[20]

Apart from Fort Ogden and Pine Level, the eastern portion of Manatee County remained in 1876 "almost a barren wilderness, save here and there, at intervals of three or four miles apart, a squatter on the public lands, cultivating a potato patch and tending his cattle." North of Fort Ogden a store was established in 1874 about one mile south of present-day Wauchula, but the storekeeper, Eli English of Fort Meade, found only six families in the immediate vicinity.[21] The neighborhood soon took on the name of English and joined the ranks of similar small isolated communities of settlers at Chokonikla, Fort Green, Crewsville, Sulphur Springs (Zolfo Springs), Castalia (Lily), Brownville, Joshua Creek, Fort Winder, and Hickory Bluff.[22] These communities may have been few and settlers far between, but by the 1870s in every corner of the river valley could be found a tiny schoolhouse and a Methodist or Baptist congregation.[23]

Schools

Although Samuel C. Craft was a lawyer and Baptist minister, not a teacher, at the end of the Civil War he was conducting at Bartow the only school operating in the Peace River Valley. Craft's school had no blackboards, and, because of his vocation as a sometime preacher at the Peas Creek Baptist Church, it may have been conducted in that church's meeting house just south of the future town of Bartow. There, Craft drilled his students day

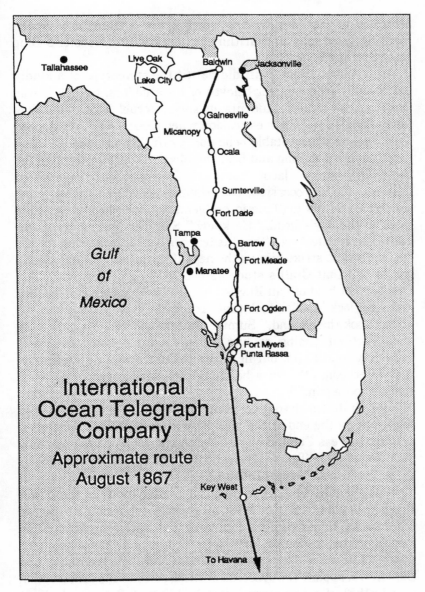

International Ocean Telegraph Company route. Drawn by Ted Starr.

after day in "reading, writing, spelling and arithmetic," supplementing geography and arithmetic texts with "Webster's Blue Back Spelling Book."[24]

An Irishman, Sam Craft did not fit the stereotype of a kindly old country schoolmaster beloved of his students. In fact, it was said that he treated students in such a cruel way that "they fairly hated him." On one occasion when Craft's own son stepped over the line of acceptable behavior, Craft "got a hickory switch three or four feet long and beat the blood out of him through his bed-ticking shirt." Jacob Summerlin's son, Sam, remembered that, on another occasion, the Irishman encouraged the young scholar to do his arithmetic problems by holding a large knife close to the boy's head. "He knew," Sam Summerlin was later quoted as recollecting, "that his teacher was only waiting for the opportunity to strike him on the head if he failed." Things finally got so bad that Craft's students decided to get even with him. One boy got hold of "an English horse pistol" which had "a flint and steel lock" and a stock that "reached the end of the barrel." "They took their stand," Summerlin remembered, "behind a log and practiced aiming at him when he came down the road, intending to kill him, but he happened to travel a different road that afternoon, otherwise he would not have appeared to teach their school again."[25]

Sam Craft survived two terms as Bartow's schoolmaster in 1865, but by the end of the year he withdrew from his membership in the Peas Creek Baptist Church and returned to preaching and lawyering in Tampa. His school the next year was taught by W. H. Pearce and George Tebault.[26]

Jacob Summerlin's generosity gave education in the Peace River Valley its first real boost after the Civil War. As a part of his proposal to move Polk's county seat to Bartow in 1866, Summerlin offered to donate forty acres of his land "for school purposes." The school lands were surveyed and some were sold, and Summerlin applied the proceeds of those sales to the construction in mid-1867 of a two-story frame building at Bartow, the first floor dedicated for use as a school. To manage the Summerlin Institute, Summerlin appointed a board of trustees composed of himself, Henry Frier, and Francis A. Hendry. The board, in turn, employed as principal Adam Hille and hired as his assistant young Stephen M. Sparkman to teach two five-month terms a year. For one term students were charged ten dollars for "Spelling, Reading, and Writing," with an additional two dollar fee for "Arithmetic, Geography, English Grammar, Composition, Philosophy, Chemistry, Botany, Geometry and Geology."[27]

By January 1870, perhaps in part due to a three hundred dollar grant from the Peabody Fund, "a flourishing school" had been established at Summerlin Institute under the superintendence of J.L. Mitchell, and potential patrons were advised that "competent and experienced assistants will be employed as necessity requires." Three years later the institute could boast eighty-three students and two teachers, Benjamin F. Blount and Miss S.J. Hayman (later Mrs. J.C. Blount). "There were sixty-six days taught," Ben Blount remembered of his year of teaching in 1873, "and the county paid $2.00 per scholar for the term; the patrons made up the balance, which amounted in all to $6.00 a scholar."[28]

No doubt, by 1869 schools other than Summerlin Institute were operating in the Peace River area. In that year, however, public education received a tremendous push when the Florida legislature responded to a mandate in the 1868 state constitution, by enacting a law providing for tax-supported, free public schools. Under the law, schools were required to be kept open at least three months a year and be free to all. Further, a superintendent and a board of public instruction were to be appointed for each county by the governor. Each board was to select trustees for each school, and teachers were to be appointed subject to the trustees' approval.[29]

By late spring of 1869, John F. Bartholf had been appointed superintendent of public instruction for Manatee County, a position he held until succeeded by Adam A. Robinson in July 1876.[30] Bartholf immediately set to work finding suitable teachers and opening schools. Some schools for whites were in operation by September 27, 1869, including one taught by John E. Savage at New Hope Church near Fort Hartsuff. Within only about a year, boards of trustees and teachers had been found for white schools at Sweet Water (near present-day Wauchula), Charlie Apopka ("near William Smith's"), Fort Hartsuff, "between Horse and Peace Creek," Fort Green, Joshua Creek, Fort Ogden, and Pine Level. Fort Winder and Hickory Bluff were added by 1875.[31]

Until 1873 all the Peace River area schoolhouses under John Bartholf's jurisdiction were built of logs. "The School-house is uncomfortable, and inconvenient and will need rebuilding," typically complained Joseph A. Patten, a teacher at Pine Level in November 1870. "There is great need of a privy." The Pine Level school, as many others, continued to experience problems. On November 1, 1872, Bartholf noted in the county records, "Owing to serious and continued sickness in the neighborhood, the attendance at Pine Level, became so much reduced, that the teacher kindly consented to annul his contract."[32]

Five frame schoolhouses were built in 1873 in Manatee County to replace log ones. The same year two hundred white pupils attended nine free schools, while Bartholf pursued funding from a northern benevolence society for an additional school, never built, for black children. By Reconstruction's last year, 1876, Manatee had seventeen schools and 300 students. Bartholf took great pride in Manatee's educational achievements and his part in them. "Free schools [were] established, and by my individual efforts, a liberal appropriation [was] secured to aid us in their maintenance." He wrote on another occasion, "The people generally are very much interested in the cause of education, through the influence of the many free schools that are established every winter, and I believe that if some good teachers would come and locate here, they could get schools the best part of the year."[33]

In Polk County a board of public instruction had been appointed on May 26, 1869, consisting of Dr. Daniel Stanford as chairman, F.A. Hendry, Mitchell G. Fortner, and Robert A. McAuley.[34] William B. Varn of Bartow at the same time was designated superintendent, a position he occupied until succeeded on November 28, 1874, by Stephen M. Sparkman. Those men by 1870 had levied and collected in excess of six hundred dollars in school taxes, a considerable sum for the time. Perhaps a lack of qualified teachers or a desire not to compete with Summerlin Institute and similar independent schools at Fort Meade and other locations led to the board's reluctance to commit those funds for expenditure. The state superintendent of public instruction included in a draft of his annual report the warning that "unless measures shall be soon taken by a county Board the funds will be expended under the direction of the Superintendent of Public Instruction, in the county as the law provides." In April 1871 it nonetheless would be reported from Fort Meade, "We have no public school in the county at the present time. The county has several independent schools in operation."[35]

By 1873, however, Polk County would report four public schools enrolling 100 pupils, all of whom presumably were white. The board complained of a "want of a corps of teachers" and the necessity of "a uniform series of text-books." Still skittish about free public education, the board recommended that tuition be charged each student in his first year in the system with the proceeds to be spent for "maps, globes, books, etc." Without charging the tuition, the board spent $515.65 on schools that year and retained on hand $839.79. Three years later fifteen schools were operated in the county with a total expenditure of $1,507.66. Although 277 pupils attended class, they represented only 38 percent of the county's school age children.[36]

Churches

Church life in the Peace River Valley during the Reconstruction era was limited to Methodist and Baptist congregations. Except in the case of Peas Creek Baptist Church, these congregations until 1866 worshipped in borrowed structures such as schoolhouses, open-air sanctuaries such as the Methodist campground near Bethel Church (at present-day Homeland), or in "arbor churches," such as that described by Charles B. Pendleton in 1877. "We steered our course northward for Josh Creek, where the Baptist Association was in session," he wrote. "The citizens had built an extensive arbor and when gathered beneath its shade, there were at least nine hundred souls listening to the words of eternal life as they fell from the preacher's lips."[37]

Those preachers were circuit riders, who traveled regularly on a circuit of country churches rather than taking up duties at a single church. The Methodists had two organized circuits in the Peace River area during the decade or so following the Civil War—the Bartow circuit encompassing the Fort Meade–Bethel–Bartow area and the Pease Creek circuit including Methodist communities along the river south of Fort Meade. These circuits were in the charge during the late 1860s and 1870s of the Reverends W.C. Jordan, William Davies, S.W. Carson, and William P. McEwen. The Reverends Levi Pearce, Enoch H. Giles, Robert A.

Carson, John W. Carlton, and Jared W. Brandon were among those who assisted in the work of the Methodist church.[38]

Baptist congregations were organized by associations rather than circuits. Beginning in 1871 five Primitive Baptist churches, including Peace Creek, were organized into the Absolute Mt. Enon Association. Until 1867, Missionary Baptists were organized under the umbrella of the Alachua Association. In that year, under the leadership of the Peas Creek Baptist Church at Bartow, a new association was formed, the South Florida Baptist Association. Peace River area churches included within the association soon after its formation were Bethel Church at Socrum, Maple Branch Church, and New Hope Church (the latter two in present-day Hardee County). In 1876 six Manatee County churches—New Zion (formerly Maple Branch), Mount Moriah (Joshua Creek), Friendship, Alafia, and Benevolence—withdrew from the South Florida Association and reconstituted themselves as the Manatee Association. Preachers active in these Peace River churches included Alderman Wilson, Jeremiah M. Hayman, Robert N. Pylant, Daniel Stanford, John Wright Hendry, and James M. Hendry.[39]

The circuit riders commanded enormous respect from many residents of the Peace River Valley. In a memorial written after the death of the Reverend Alderman Wilson, John Wright Hendry praised his fellow circuit rider. "He was a constant, humble and efficient worker," Hendry reflected, "never ceasing, everlasting, always ready with a willing heart to labor in his Master's vineyard, casting his lot with the people of South Florida when the country was sparsely settled, and when society in many places was almost in an unorganized condition. Many were the long rides, hardships, privations and exposures he endured in endeavoring to disseminate religious knowledge, and establish churches in the broad field of labor which he took upon himself. But amid all the disadvantages under which he labored, he evinced that Christian fortitude, patience and cheerfulness so characteristic of the true and earnest believer in Christ."[40]

Among the most beloved of the Peace River circuit preachers were a Baptist, John Wright Hendry, and a Methodist, W.C. Jordan. "The speaker—John W. Hendry—seemed to hold the minds of his hearers spellbound and members crowded the mourner's bench," one appreciative listener reported in 1877. "It was truly a great sermon and it did not take a great stretch of the imagination to carry one back to the early apostolic days and the sacred occasions around the 'Holy City.' " Upon Jordan's death in 1898, a Bartow newspaper noted, "No death which has occurred in a long time will cause more universal sorrow in this community than this one. For many years Mr. Jordan has lived and labored for the Master, suffering the privations and hardships incident upon the work of a pioneer minister, and yet he worked on unceasingly and successfully for the conversion of the sinners around him, until the very last week of his life, being enroute to a meeting of the District Conference at Lakeland when stricken down."[41]

At the close of the Civil War, Peas Creek Baptist Church at Bartow and, possibly, a Primitive Baptist congregation, Pease Creek, at the same place, together with the Methodist congregation at Bethel (Homeland), constituted the only organized churches in the Peace River Valley.[42] Returning soldiers and refugees combined with an increasing tide of immigration, however, led to new congregations. The first was a Baptist church at Maple Branch on the South Prong of the Alafia in modern-day Hardee County founded on September 29–30, 1866, with the Reverend S.L. Cross as minister and John W. Whidden as church clerk. The following year, the Reverend John Wright Hendry succeeded Cross as pastor and, in 1873, the church was moved several miles to the west of Ona, closer to Hendry's residence. Beginning April 23, 1873, the church, now the New Zion Baptist Church, met in a schoolhouse until an arbor was constructed as a place of worship. By the summer of 1882 a log church was erected on the site of old Fort Myakka, and the congregation once again had a roof over its head.[43]

The construction of Summerlin Institute in Bartow during the summer of 1867 offered local Baptists and Methodists a secure place to conduct services. Before the end of the decade, however, Peas Creek Baptist Church "became disorganized and went down," and not until September 1, 1875, was the Concord Church of Christ organized as its replacement.[44] Although Peas Creek Baptist had its problems, other Baptist congregations were springing up throughout the Peace River area. By 1868, a Baptist church met at Fort Hartsuff and the Mount Pleasant Baptist Church had been organized in modern-day DeSoto County. In the following year New Hope Church, less than five miles east and south of Fort Hartsuff, was admitted to the South Florida Baptist Association. In 1870 the Paynes Creek Primitive Baptist Church was established five miles west of modern-day Bowling Green, and Baptists and Methodists at Joshua Creek united to build the Davidson Union Church, used by both congregations until 1874 when the Baptists purchased land upon which Mount Moriah Baptist Church ultimately was built. As this land purchase was consummated, a small group of Baptists under pastor L.J. Simmons began meeting in Fort Meade with the active support of Solomon Godwin and Robert N. Pylant, but the church could not survive the death in July 1880 of its benefactor, Godwin. More fortunate was the Fort Hartsuff Baptist Church, organized in 1876 with seven charter members. The church survives today as the First Baptist Church of Wauchula.[45]

The Methodist campground at Homeland, at which annual camp meetings were begun in 1860, has been called the "Mother of Methodism in South Florida." Before the Civil War, a congregation known as Bethel Church was active there, and members of that congregation joined with Bartow's few Methodist families to hold meetings at Summerlin Institute beginning in 1867. The southern branch of the Methodist Episcopal church had been hurt seriously by the effects of the Civil War, however, and those losses were felt deeply in Florida where an 1862 membership of 19,000, 40 percent of whom were blacks, had dropped by 1867 to only 6,266, nearly all of whom were white. This drop in membership was reflected in the Peace River Valley where the establishment of new Methodist congregations after the war came slowly. A few hardy frontier Methodists did begin meetings at Pine Level in 1868, leading to the creation of what is now the Pine Level United Methodist Church. About the same time a congregation was meeting at Pleasant Grove just east of Fort Meade. The following year "a few faithful Methodists met to worship in a store building" in Fort Meade, the beginnings of the First United Methodist Church of Fort Meade.[46]

The year 1869 also saw the scheduling of an October camp meeting at Fort Ogden in addition to the customary festivities at Homeland. A year later Joshua Creek Methodists built the Davidson Union Church and, in 1873, Trinity Methodist Church was established in the thatched-roof schoolhouse at Charlotte Harbor. The Methodist church at Homeland by 1874 appears to have constituted one of the few racially integrated churches in Florida, and in the fall of 1875, under the stewardship of W.T. Carpenter, James T. Wilson, and James B. Crum, erected "a crude wooden structure having no glass windows and no lights except candles." Bethel Church, the mother church of Methodism in South Florida, thus for the first time had a permanent home. Another Methodist church, Mount Pisgah, was organized in a tiny log schoolhouse in 1876 a short distance north of the modern Polk-Hardee county line and just east of Peace River. Within a few years the congregation had its own building two hundred feet north of its original meeting site.[47]

Access to markets

"We presume it is well known by those who know much about Polk at all, that she occupies a central position in the peninsula of

Fort Meade residents enjoyed the luxury of planed board houses as early as 1860. Pictured here are the homes of Samuel Henry Robeson (1822-84) and his son, John Evans Robeson (1847-98). These buildings were erected in the early 1870s. Courtesy Joan Wilson Balega.

Florida with not a railroad Depot nearer than 150 miles, not a wharf nearer than 35 miles, and not a stream in whose waters floats a common scow." Written in September 1877, this Fort Meade man's words described settlement in the Peace River Valley since 1849. "Shut out, or rather shut in from the ordinary scenes of busy life, we here hump and heave, curse and swear, and encounter more ills and inconveniences than are incidental to human life ordinarily. In this discouraging situation the overplus of produce made in this prolific year is such in many cases as the 'cow will not eat,' and is left to lie and rot by the tons, and return to its mother earth on the very spot that gave it life."[48]

Peace River residents during Reconstruction desperately needed easy and inexpensive transportation. Robert LaMartin, writing from Fort Meade in April 1871, put the situation succinctly: "The *desideratum* that our section sadly feels the necessity of is accessibility to market, and transporting facilities with the outer world—Tampa being our chief market, and nearest, being 46 miles distant. Also the principal port of admission and transit to all produce shipped to or from this section, with this exception, that beef cattle, when bound for the Cuban market, find, en rout via Punta Rossa, an excellent port on the coast of Monroe County, 108 miles distant, which renders it very inconvenient and unpleasant. All transportation between Tampa and our section is carried on with ox teams, a very dilatory process indeed." Three years later John Bartholf at the lower end of the river reported, "Farming is not carried on to any greater extent than what is necessary for home consumption, as there is no market convenient."[49]

This dilemma had been addressed at least ten years before Robert LaMartin commented in 1871 that "Peas Creek, a very respectable stream, running in a serpentine course through the center of the county . . . could be made navigable for small steamers up to Fort Mead." In fact, that was just what the Florida legislature had in mind when in February 1861 it approved "An Act to Improve the Navigation of Peas Creek and to Drain the Swamps and Overflowed Lands thereon." Enacted too late to be effective before the Civil War intervened, the law authorized the board of trustees of the internal improvement trust fund "to pledge the alternate sections of land contiguous to said stream for a distance of three miles on each side thereof" in return for "the cleaning out" of the river's channel.[50]

After the war Jacob Summerlin approached the legislature and in December 1866 was granted authority "to clear out obstructions in Peas Creek, beginning at a place known as Fort Ogden, in Manatee county, and terminating at a place known as Brooker's Ford in Polk county, with the privilege of continuing as far as Hendry's Bridge, near Fort Meade." The law also granted Summerlin the right to collect tolls and fees on all river commerce, but required him to commence removal of obstructions by September 1, 1867, a deadline he failed to meet.[51]

In February 1870 a charter was granted for the Peas Creek Immigrant & Agricultural Company to "improve the navigation of the Peas Creek in this State as far as Fort Meade." The charter directed the trustees of the internal improvement fund to contract with the company for transfer to it of all the land embraced within the 1861 act. On February 13, 1870, the company executed a contract with the trustees for all "odd numbered sections up to the County site of Polk County," conditioned upon its improving the river "so as to permit a Steam-boat drawing two (2) feet of water to ascend and navigate said channel of said Peas Creek" from Charlotte Harbor to Fort Meade.[52]

The Peas Creek Immigrant & Agricultural Company also contracted with A.C. Mattoon of Oswego, New York, for assistance in clearing the river. At Oswego Mattoon converted the SS *Ellsworth* to a screw steamboat, placed on board "a large stock of provisions, groceries, etc., two portable saw-mills and two immense shingle machines, with all necessary appliances for working them," and in mid-November 1871 set off with fourteen men through the Erie Canal on a voyage to Peace River. By January 5, 1872, the ship and crew had docked in Savannah and only weeks thereafter reached Key West and disappointment.[53]

Just three months after receiving its charter, the Peas Creek Immigrant & Agricultural Company ran into problems. The minutes of the board of trustees of the internal improvement trust fund for May 21, 1870, explain it all: "A communication was presented from D.P. Holland setting forth that not more than thirty-five thousand acres of land could under the contract made with the company be conveyed to the Company by the

Sherod E. Roberts (1837–1906) and Eliza O'Kane Roberts (1848–1912). Courtesy Mrs. Enoch Walker and Mrs. Margaret Durrance.

Board, as some of the lands designated had never been surveyed, and some had been reserved for naval and military purposes by the U.S. Government and requesting the Board, in lieu thereof to convey to said Company 200,000 acres of land elsewhere. . . . The Board could not accede to the proposition [and the] Surveyor General [was] instructed to withhold delivery of titles." Those problems could have been solved had not the federal courts put a hold on everything in December 1871. Acting upon a suit filed by a holder of Florida bonds named Francis Vose, the court issued an injunction forbidding the internal improvement trust fund board from disposing of land for internal improvement purposes, including those of the Peas Creek Immigrant & Agricultural Company, until all Vose's claims against the state were satisfied.[54]

With its reward snatched away from its grasp, all the officers of the Peas Creek company could do was send A.C. Mattoon back home and bide their time.[55] As late as November 14, 1874, the company petitioned the internal improvement trust fund board for a two-year extension of the deadline for completion of its contract, but shifting political currents had snatched away its clout as well as its lands, for the board's minutes simply noted that the communication "was read and further consideration postponed." The postponement was forever.[56]

In November 1874 the same political currents were running in favor of Democratic conservatives. A group of those conservatives based on Peace River was encouraged the following month to incorporate at Fort Meade the Peace Creek Navigation Company to "clear out and navigate Peace River to Fort Meade with steamboats carrying freight and passengers.[57] Hoping to place their own claim on the 200,000-acre land grant authorized by the 1861 Peace River navigation act, the new company arranged for the construction at Fort Meade of a forty-foot steamboat with a fourteen-foot beam and about a one-foot draft. Built by John E. Robeson and Julius C. Rockner, the boat was given a test run of three hundred to four hundred yards down the river from Fort Meade bridge. In that short space the boat's machinery failed, never to operate again. Eventually the boat was poled down the river, but her failure to operate under steam collapsed hopes in the Reconstruction era of making Peace River a navigable artery of commerce.[58]

Peace River by January 1877 had weathered Indian wars, civil war, and the disturbances and dislocations of Reconstruction. The area's population increased markedly, and with that growth came town life and social institutions such as churches and schools. River settlers continued to be frustrated by lack of easy and inexpensive access to markets for their crops and a legacy of violence from war and its aftermath. How to overcome those problems remained a question desperately in need of an answer.

Part Four

"Progress that our people
did not dream of"
(1877–1899)

*"We have to kill men
to recruit our graveyards"*

15

The Problem of Violence

T HE END OF RECONSTRUCTION found most residents of the
Peace River Valley anxious to see the region develop opportunities beyond those arising from the cattle industry.
They were handicapped, however, by the lack of reliable, efficient, and inexpensive transportation, difficulties in securing
valid titles to their land, and a heritage of frontier violence. By
the mid-1880s the solution of the first two problems paved the
way for the area's first great boom, launched upon a foundation
of phosphate. Well before the end of the century the boom turned
to bust and nature again ravaged the area. Through boom and
bust, its violent heritage continued to plague Peace River, and
that problem proved the most elusive of all to overcome.

Violence on the frontier

"Fort Ogden has its school and church and saw mill, and is
rapidly building up with a class of citizens that reflect credit
upon any community," John F. Bartholf and F.C.M. Boggess
explained in 1881. "In connection with this matter, we would
wish to correct an opinion that has become too prevalent concerning the moral status of Fort Ogden. Owing to the fact that, in

239

days gone by, this place became the headquarters of a gang of cut-throats, it acquired a by-no-means enviable reputation but, by the vigorous enforcement of the law they have been forced to seek a more congenial locality, and since then there has been 'quiet on the Potomac,' with the exception of an occasional personal differ-ence, which has, unfortunately, in one or two instances in the last half dozen years, resulted fatally. Suffice it, however, for us to say, that such violations of the law meet the disapproval of the great mass of people, and the perpetrators are held strictly accountable for the laws they violate."[1]

The unifying theme of the history of the Peace River throughout the nineteenth century was violence. From the bitterness and pain of the Seminole and Civil wars to the tragic excesses of the Regulators, the legacy of violence in South Florida was a constant and continuing element of life on that raw frontier, and frontier it remained for the most part until well after the turn of the cen-tury. In 1890 the only state east of the Mississippi that had a sizeable area of land where there were less than two people per square mile was Florida. At that time, large sections of Texas and other western states had a greater density of population than the Florida peninsula south of Orlando.[2]

In the post–Civil War era this frontier violence first was mani-fested by the reemergence of the Regulators whose activities had resulted by the early 1870s in a brutal and deadly campaign aimed at freedmen. The presence of outlaws and other trouble-makers sometimes required individual efforts at law enforce-ment, however. Such appears to have been the case in the early 1870s when long-time river resident Readding B. Parker killed "a drunken desperado" by the name of William T. Branch on the streets of Bartow. Ten miles to the south at Fort Meade a similar incident in August 1871 resulted in the death of Will Johnson, "the man who shot J.D. Colding and young McGraw in Brevard County not long since." As the Tampa newspaper reported, "Steve Weeks and a man called 'Friday' were in company riding by Lightsey and Roberts' store, when Johnson who was at the store hailed Weeks and asked him to stop; but Friday said to Weeks, 'come on let's go.' Johnson answered and said 'go to hell, you [d--d] s-----b.' —Whereupon 'Friday' turned, went to Rockner's store and tried to get a gun, but James Jones, clerking for Rockner, refused to let him have it. 'Friday' then went off to a house, about a quarter of a mile distant, procured his own double-barreled shot gun, walked deliberately back to Rockner's store, where Johnson was standing with his pistol in his hands and when in thirty paces fired one barrel at Johnson and missed him, then he advanced to within but a few paces fired the other barrel and Johnson fell, the whole load of buck-shot having taken effect in the left side which produced death almost instantly. After Johnson had fallen, Friday walked up to him and said 'my name is "Friday," you called me a d--- s-----b,' looked on the dying man but an instant then mounted his horse and made his escape."[3]

The violence of the 1870s and later years was not all aimed at ridding the country of desperadoes. Much of the killing was random, provoked by personal grudge or affront and often fueled by whiskey, its impact often felt by the entire community and devastating to families and friends. A case in point was the family of Dr. Gilbert L. Key.

Key was a physician who came to Fort Meade during the Bowlegs War and decided to cast his lot with the Peace River area. In September 1878, after the Key family had been living at Fort Ogden for six years, the doctor's eldest son, John, died from exposure on shipboard during the great hurricane of 1878. Three months later his son Billy was shotgunned to death at Fort Ogden after James Driver "suddenly became offended" while the two were joking with one another. Three years later at a Fort Ogden Christmas party, Key's boy Oliver rushed to defend his sister Ann from David Youmans, "who had had a little too much to drink" and had asked Ann to dance. Youmans and Key agreed to meet the following morning to resolve their differences, and Oliver was stabbed to death. A sick and disheartened Gilbert Key left Fort Ogden and the Peace River Valley forever.[4]

In those instances where perpetrators of violence were apprehended, the primitive jail facilities in the Peace River Valley almost encouraged escape. One man, F.M. Allen, even escaped from custody in December 1873 while on his way to the penitentiary, having been convicted at Pine Level of murdering Fred McCarthy at Fort Ogden. For six years Allen's whereabouts were unknown to Manatee County authorities until Allen wrote Judge Henry L. Mitchell a letter explaining that he was about to be hanged for murder in Waynesboro, Mississippi.[5]

Allen's case shows that even a conviction held no assurance of punishment, and getting a conviction was no easy matter either. Throughout the nineteenth century Peace River area juries were extremely reluctant to convict anyone of first degree murder. From 1861 to 1884, for example, every one of Polk County's sixteen murder trials resulted in an acquittal. After six men had been killed in six years one county resident, reflecting the feelings of many, in 1877 defended the killings. "What will you say when we tell you that *not one* of the killed in Polk county was even a moral character." He added, "Some would say jocularly, when the unparalleled health of our country is spoken of, and the very few who die naturally; 'We have to kill men to recruit our grave yards.' " Exasperated at the lack of public support for convictions one Polk sheriff, C.C. Gresham, resigned in 1883 declaring, "Don't bang the sheriff when he has the opposition sometimes manifested in this county." As late as 1893 Polk County still had not seen its first legal execution, an event again postponed when convicted murderer William Woodruff's sentence was commuted by the governor to life imprisonment.[6] An almost identical scenario was played out two years later when John Henry ("Big Six") Johnson received the governor's clemency.[7]

In spite of the claim by John F. Bartholf and F.C.M. Boggess that in 1881 "vigorous enforcement of the law" and "the disapproval of the great mass of people" was helping to end killings in South Florida, waves of violence flowed up and down the Peace River Valley for the remainder of the century. Helping to launch and legitimize this course of events was the murder of cattleman Nelson Locklear near Popash in December 1884. The murderer was a Mississippi-born teacher known as S.W. Durfey, whose proper name was found to be Walker Cassidy. Durfey fled about fifteen or twenty miles southeast to Guano Hammock, where he was apprehended by a four-man posse and returned to Popash. After a preliminary examination by the justice of the peace, according to a witness, "The bailiff about sundown chained [Durfey] to a large pine tree near the scene of the slaughter. About 8 o'clock in the evening the mob drove away the guard and shot him down with more than a dozen bullets. His body lay there till 10 o'clock next day before it was buried."[8]

Soon after came the politically tinged assassination at Sarasota of Charles Elliott Abbe, which revealed the existence in Manatee County of a secret society known as SaraSota Vigilance

The International Ocean Telegraph Company station at Punta Rassa, about 1890, housed the renowned "Tarpon House" hostelry. Courtesy Florida Photographic Collection, Florida State Archives.

Committee composed of a number of prominent citizens. The trial at Pine Level of the committee's members and the startling details revealed about the SaraSota Vigilance Committee made statewide and national news. The climate of danger became so pronounced in the Peace River area that by the late summer of 1885 the Bartow *Informant* was demanding that lawmen who would not suppress lawlessness "ought to be called on to resign and let others be selected who will." Less than a year later, though, Marshal W.S. Campbell was gunned down and killed on Bartow's main street and a policeman, Jack McCormick, was wounded. That night their assailants, Dan and Lon Mann, were taken by a mob from the county jail and lynched from a nearby oak tree.[9]

While random violence ran the length of the river valley in the last decade and a half of the century, the town of Arcadia particularly began to develop a reputation for being "as rough and tough as any town in the Old West of the 1890s." "There were as many as fifty fights a day," reported one historian. "Four men were killed in one fight alone."

During the same period the cattle industry became the focus of thieves intent on quick profits through rustling. An outbreak of that frontier crime in 1888 led "a body of the principal stock owners" to surprise "the Corbett Brothers at their home, just before day-break," a newspaper related. "With stout ropes around their necks, the Corbetts confessed that they had just . . . disposed of thirty-three head of stolen cattle." Given the alternatives of leaving South Florida or hanging, the Corbetts took to the road. Two years later four rustlers were reported to have gotten as far as Titusville with two hundred head before they were overtaken by pursuing cattlemen. Two rustlers were killed in the resulting shootout and two were hanged. Despite those measures, the century ended with cattlemen still attempting "to devise ways and means for protecting themselves against cattle thieves, from whose depredations they have been great sufferers."[10]

The Johnson brothers

A closer look at some of the major characters may give a more complete picture of the violence on the South Florida frontier during the final three decades of the nineteenth century. Among them were those men whom Bartholf and Boggess suggested at the beginning of this chapter made Fort Ogden in the early 1870s "the headquarters of a gang of cut-throats," the Johnson brothers.

Isham Johnson was about fifty years old when the threat of Civil War compelled him to move his family south from Georgia into Hernando County. Opting to serve the Union, Johnson acted as a scout and guide for Union raiding parties, a decision that infuriated some of his Hernando County neighbors who in turn forced his wife to seek safety within Union lines. After the war, the Johnsons returned to their Hernando County farm only to discover their livestock and other property stolen. In 1866, his family facing starvation, Johnson became embroiled in a bitter dispute with a cattleman sympathetic to the Confederacy over a cow killed by Johnson for food, for which Johnson offered payment. Although given legal support by Union military authorities, a disgusted Johnson soon decided to try for a new life farther south, and probably in 1867 moved his family to the vicinity of Fort Ogden in Manatee County. With Isham Johnson came his sons: Alonzo, Augustus ("Gus"), John, and Raymond.[11]

Isham Johnson's support of the Union by no means implied a sympathy for freedmen, a reality brought home when three of his sons attacked black leader John Lomans at Fort Ogden on July 25, 1869. According to Lomans, he "was quietly passing in the vicinity of the residence of Gus Johnson [when] he was set upon by the said Gus Johnson, aided by Alonzo Johnson and John Johnson, beaten with a cow whip, and shot at with a revolver." The beating, stated Lomans, "was accomplished by the Gus Johnson aforesaid by holding a revolver in one hand pointed towards him, and the whip in the other, accompanied by threats to this effect— 'that if I made another step, he the said Gus Johnson would shoot my damned heart out'."[12]

Over the next several years Isham and his sons developed a reputation as "a very dangerous set of robbers." In late 1872 Isham was indicted for forgery and, at the same time, Alonzo was indicted along with Ziba King for selling liquor without a license. The following year the family's crime graduated to a more serious level when several of its members not only were suspected of killing, curing, and selling the hogs and cattle of others, but were apprehended for robbing houses—a crime which included drugging, beating, and robbing W.K. Barnwell who was keeping bar for Ziba King at Fort Ogden.[13]

Despite the family reputation for crime and several of its members having been caught in the act, a slow and imperfect Manatee court system permitted the Johnson brothers—Alonzo, Gus, and Raymond—to roam at large. In the spring of 1874, taking advantage of that freedom, the brothers seized 110 head of cattle "on the northeastern margin of the Forty Mile Prairie, in the vicinity of Guano Hammock" and turned them for a hurried drive north to the market at Live Oak. A man named Williams spotted the Johnsons and their rustled cattle and spread the alarm. In short order a posse was formed, and the chase was on.[14]

Thanks to a bad suggestion from "a man who advised them to go in the direction of Fort Bassinger," the posse lost several days in finding the Johnsons' trail. Near the headwaters of Charlie Apopka Creek, Solomon Godwin put them back on the right track. Returning home for provisions, the posse then reunited at Godwin's and finally caught up with the Johnsons about eight miles south of Ocala, drawing within "a few rods of the party (who were engaged with the cattle) before they discovered them."[15]

The Johnsons reacted first. Raymond jumped on his horse "and applied the spur furiously, but was soon overtaken and captured." Gus bolted over a fence and started to run, but "a charge from a double barrel gun brought him to a sudden halt." Shocked at the gun blast, "Alonzo stood as if spell-bound." Quickly, Raymond and Alonzo were secured "with ropes around their necks," and Gus, in a "helpless and paralyzed condition," was left to die in the care of a woman who was given ten dollars and a horse for her trouble.[16]

The saga of Raymond and Alonzo Johnson was only beginning with their capture. Brought back to Pine Level for trial, they soon escaped, stole some horses in Hillsborough County, and made it as far as Georgia before being recaptured. Once they had returned to Manatee County, their case was continued until April 1876 when they were granted a change of venue to Polk County with instructions that they be held in the Hillsborough County jail until trial. On the way to Tampa the brothers escaped a final time and disappeared from the record. Only in November 1879 was their case transferred to Manatee County's absentee docket and, effectively, dropped forever.[17]

Florida's Robin Hood

Undoubtedly the most legendary, poetic, and good-humored desperado in the history of South Florida was John W. ("Hub") Williams, who called himself Florida's Robin Hood. Hub's origins are obscure, but legend has it that tragedy entered his life when he was ten or twelve and his father was gunned down on the doorstep in the presence of his wife and children. What is certain about Hub Williams is that he loved to drink, frolic, and dance, he enjoyed many friendships among both blacks and whites, and he has been remembered for well over a hundred years for robbing the rich to help the poor.[18]

Hub Williams first came to official attention in 1873 when he was tried in Judge James T. Magbee's court in Tampa on a charge of horse stealing. Reflecting Hub's popularity, a large crowd turned out for the trial, but in spite of what one witness called "the preponderance of sentiment" in his favor Hub was found guilty and sentenced to five years' imprisonment. Not one to give up hope, Williams bided his time until the sheriff had him on a train headed for the state prison. As a newspaper reported, "Williams, it is said, leaped head foremost out of the car window in the night time, while the train was in motion, making his escape in a dense swamp where pursuit was impossible. Williams was hobbled with a chain but managed to free himself, whereupon he disappeared without saying good-by. In the jump his head plowed the ground like a spent cannon ball."[19]

Despite his narrow and dangerous escape, Hub maintained a sense of humor about his Tampa ordeal and in the years that followed composed a twenty-verse song to celebrate it. A few of his verses have survived:

> Bob Johnston came around about nine in the night,
> And in his right hand he held a small light,
> He tapped on the door and gave me a hail,
> To see if I was safe in the Tampa Bay jail!
>
> When breakfast came around it was a hunk of cornbread,
> As hard as a rock and as heavy as lead,
> And a cup of cold water from a dirty wooden pail,
> And I dam near starved in that Tampa Bay jail!
>
> Now, dear ladies, I've sung you my song.
> I know dam well I have sung nothing wrong.
> I was always fighting, and I never was afraid,
> But I'll never enter another jail gate![20]

For five years after his escape, Hub went "at large without any fixed habitation," leading "a daring and reckless life" in the counties of South Florida. In October 1878 he descended upon Philip Dzialynski's store at Fort Meade "with a drawn pistol" and demanded two hundred dollars in cash. When Dzialynski managed to elude him, Hub went to the nearby home of Morgan Snow where Snow shot him twice. Wounds and embarrassment notwithstanding, Hub made his getaway only to be captured one month later in Volusia County. Sent to "Col. Wise's convict-camp," Hub escaped and took with him a double-barreled shotgun and two of Colonel Wise's hound dogs.[21]

Early in 1879 Florida's Robin Hood was back in the Peace River Valley. Just north of Fort Ogden he encountered young George Mansfield and his friend Jim Bates who, not realizing the stranger to be Hub Williams, decided to have a little fun by pretending that one of them was the outlaw. Acting on impulse, Mansfield drew his gun, announced that he was Hub Williams, and demanded that the stranger dance. After "about 30 minutes,"

Mansfield let the stranger rest whereupon the real Hub Williams drew out "a pistol a foot long" and told the two, "Boys you are now looking at the real Hub Williams. . . . Step right over where I have been dancing and I mean pick-um up and lay-um down." Fort Ogden's townspeople took the event in stride and one citizen even remarked that "Fort Ogden owes Hub Williams a goodly gift and if he ever chances among us, we will treat him to the best; at last our practical joker has been matched."[22]

While Hub Williams's sense of humor remained strong, his luck had begun to run out. Late in 1879 he again was captured and imprisoned. A petition was circulated in Hernando County requesting that the governor pardon him on the grounds that the horse he was convicted in Tampa of stealing was Hub's own. The pardoning board complied with the request and by February 1880 Hub was free and in Brooksville, where a band of Regulators decided to put an end once and for all to the problem of Hub Williams. On the night of February 24 they called him out of a saloon and gunned him down. Florida's Robin Hood died the following morning at 10:00 A.M. from "a mortal wound in the head."[23]

Bill Ham Willingham

If Hub Williams was the most romantic of South Florida's desperadoes, William W. Willingham was the wealthiest. During the Civil War and for several years thereafter Willingham's father, William H. Willingham, was Polk County's largest taxpayer, basing his fortune on thousands of head of cattle roaming the ranges along the Kissimmee River. In the late 1860s, the father decided upon a more settled life, and moved to Fort Meade after transferring his Kissimmee Island land and cattle to his son. For fifteen years William W. ("Bill Ham") Willingham lived the life of a South Florida cattle baron, prominently noted as late as 1882 as one of Florida's "Cattle Kings." But Bill Ham's fiery temper and love for whiskey began to catch up with him in the late 1870s.[24]

In mid-May of 1877, an unknown assassin shot and killed Sam Lippencott one night while Lippencott was sitting quietly in his house about twelve miles below Fort Meade. Lippencott, a small-time cowhand, had just been indicted in Manatee County for "fraudulently altering marks and brands," and given his somewhat seamy reputation little was made of the killing. That situa-

Aaron Elijah Godwin (1846–1914) standing by his team of oxen on Main Street in old Fort Meade. The stores shown were destroyed by fire in July 1894. Courtesy Ben and Karla Speight.

tion changed dramatically on July 23, when cattle baron and Fort Meade merchant Julius C. Rockner was shotgunned to death from ambush three miles south of Fort Meade on the Wire Road. As Rockner lay dying in the arms of his friend Frederick Varn, the assassin bolted from his hiding place, but witnesses were "unable to give any definite description of him."[25]

Within hours of Rockner's death, rumors began circulating that "a deadly feud" had existed "between Rockner and another party for several months." Others suggested that Rockner and Bill Willingham had been involved in a dispute over stealing cattle. These rumors and the suspicions they aroused led Polk County sheriff R.H. Peeples to arrest Willingham and his in-law John Montes De Oca for murder. Within a few days Montes De Oca was released from custody. Ordered held without bail in the Tampa jail, Willingham "took leg bail and escaped to the country" where he vowed to remain "until he was promised a trial or to give bail."[26]

In his absence, Willingham was indicted in Polk County for the murder of J.C. Rockner in April 1878 and finally was offered a trial in July 1880.[27] After "the most indiscriminating trial on the part of the state attorney and very careful charge of the judge,"

Willingham was acquitted, and the courtroom spectators erupted "in a perfect roar of cheers for the jury for their verdict." It was reported to be "no uncommon thing to hear some of the citizens of [the] county say they believed Willingham killed Rockner, but as Rockner had at some time killed a man, and was a little dangerous if tampered with too much, Willingham did a good thing and must not be convicted."[28]

For two months after his acquittal, Bill Willingham stayed out of trouble, but his love for the bottle was too great. On September 12, 1880, he went on a drunken spree in Fort Meade. After partying awhile he decided to cross Peace River, possibly to go to his father's house just to the east. Arriving at the Fort Meade ferry, owned by his father and operated by his brother-in-law William McLaughlin, Bill was incensed to find McLaughlin away. In his anger and impatience, Willingham launched a boat into the rain-swollen river and soon capsized. McLaughlin and his black assistant, Bob Williams, quickly came to Willingham's rescue, but Bill in his drunken anger seized the ferryman by the collar and fired a pistol at him. In self-defense McLaughlin grabbed Willingham by the feet and upended him into the river. As Willingham clung to the ferry, McLaughlin picked up a pole and Willingham shot and killed him. Dazed by the series of events, Bill wandered for a while in the river swamp and then returned to town where he mingled among the crowd and tried to justify his actions. Soon, however, he left for the safety of Kissimmee Island.[29]

No one was in a hurry to go into the remote Kissimmee Island to arrest the deadly Bill Ham Willingham. Sheriff C.C. Gresham declined the honor, although ultimately he deputized William Bowen, who "knew the country much better than I did," to make an attempt. Bowen might just as well have stayed at home. Not until September 1883 was a reward, eventually five hundred dollars, offered to anyone daring to make the arrest. That someone turned out to be John Pearce who nabbed Willingham in April 1884 while the fugitive was aboard Pearce's steamboat on the Kissimmee River. The story reported at the time was that Bill came aboard to accuse Pearce of stealing cattle and that in the ensuing confrontation Willingham was knocked down and tied up. A later report suggested less heroic circumstances, however, by alleging that Pearce and his engineer, Charlie Dudley, lured Bill on board, then "got him drunk and tied him up like a hog."[30]

Bill Willingham's trial in Bartow in July 1884 marked many firsts. Bill was the first prisoner housed in Polk's new jail, and his trial was the first in Polk's new, unfinished courthouse. The trial was the first in Polk County history to utilize the testimony of blacks against a white man accused of a capital crime and, eventually, it marked the first time in the history of the county that anyone had been convicted of first degree murder.[31] The conviction also helped launch the political careers of judge and future governor Henry L. Mitchell, state's attorney and future congressman Stephen M. Sparkman, and assistant state's attorney, Bartow newspaper editor, and future judge G.A. Hanson. "Popular feeling" was reportedly so great against Willingham that the jury certainly would have sentenced him to hang had not a single juror, Dan Mann, held out for mercy. Bill was sentenced to life imprisonment.[32]

Willingham did not take well to prison and attempted several escapes, culminating in February 1889 in an incident at a turpentine work camp near Live Oak when he was shot and his arm shattered. Over the years his mother and friends circulated petitions for his release, but not until the spring of 1898 were they successful. When Bill returned home he found that his wife had sold off his cattle to Ziba King and divorced him. Starting over at Kissimmee Island, he grew guavas and hauled them to Bartow to be made into jelly. Eventually, a few friends gave him some cattle and he began to rebuild his herds. When he died in June 1910, his obituary read: "With his life closed a career as interesting as that of Jesse James. . . . It was a curious fate that he who had dared death so often with bullets should be the victim of disease at last."[33]

A cycle of death in DeSoto County

The final decade of the nineteenth century proved the DeSoto County area of the Peace River Valley to be as wild and dangerous as any part of the Wild West. Midway through the decade gunfights continued to break out on Arcadia's main street, and three years earlier the town had witnessed its first lynching when a black man, Walter Austin, was strung up by a mob for killing the deputy sheriff, Bert Hard.[34]

One chain of events that illustrates this continuing cycle of

DeSoto County's first courthouse and jail. From Jacksonville *Florida Times-Union*, October 18, 1896.

violence began on the night of April 13, 1891, when two despera-does named C. Quinn Bass and Belford Branch murdered a black man, Enoch Payne, near Arcadia. Although the circum-stances are murky, this murder may have been connected with a counterfeiting ring exposed during the spring of 1892. In any event, both culprits were arrested and subsequently released on bond. Fearful of conviction, Bass and Branch set out to eliminate the only witness, Hardy Johnson, by providing evidence against him on a counterfeiting charge and obtaining a warrant for his arrest. In March 1893 on Fisheating Creek about thirty-five miles east of Arcadia, Bass and Branch approached Johnson on the pretext of serving the warrant, and when within range shot him down.[35]

At about the same time, Jim North, "the best known outlaw of the Big 90" Prairie (a cattle range east of Arcadia), shotgunned and killed political leader and merchant S.A. Sauls on the steps of Sauls's store at Zolfo Springs. Although the motive for the killing was unclear, one report suggested that North's trial would "bring out some other terrible crimes of some years ago."[36]

North's trial, as well as those of Bass and Branch, was held in Arcadia in November 1893. The evidence against North seemed clear, and he was convicted of first degree murder and sentenced to be hanged. Bass and Branch were acquitted of the murder of

Payne because, as one reporter explained, "while everybody was satisfied that they killed the negro, the evidence was not sufficient to convict them." The two were less fortunate when it came to Hardy Johnson's murder and were found guilty and sentenced to life imprisonment.[37]

Like the Johnson brothers, Hub Williams, and Bill Ham Willingham, Jim North and Quinn Bass were not ones to sit around waiting for justice to run its course. On the night of December 27, 1893, they broke out of the Arcadia jail and for some time thereafter "remained at large." Bass became the first of the two to have his day of reckoning when Sheriff Foster C. Bethea and a posse composed of Will Bethea, Seph Granger, Joe Horne, and W.H. Sharp, acting on a tip, intercepted the outlaw in May 1894 on his way to a romantic rendezvous just outside Arcadia. When Bass discovered the trap, "he began firing" and in turn was "riddled with bullets and buckshot." The report of his demise concluded: "Thus was brought to an end the life of a deep-dyed criminal."[38]

Jim North continued to elude capture for almost two years. Sometime after November 1895, however, the reward offered for his capture proved too great a temptation for John Lucas, a man who himself had just been released for the "justifiable homicide" of Dempsey Crews, Jr., at Crewsville on June 10, 1895. Securing the assistance of one of North's friends, Jim Daniels, Lucas lured North on "a hog hunt." Hiding in the grass along a road North was to pass, Lucas waited until North was opposite him, then shot the outlaw point blank. Lucas and Daniels then loaded North's body onto a wagon and drove it to Arcadia to collect the reward.[39]

DeSoto County's cycle of violence was not quite ended. In November 1897 at a ranch on the Caloosahatchee River about thirty-five miles above Fort Myers, John Lucas fell into arguing with Dennis Sheridan, who had killed F.Q. Crawford "some years before." Sheridan drew his knife and stabbed Lucas "all to pieces." Lucas survived. Less than a year later, on June 6, 1898, he was riding beside his friend, Dan Byrd, near Fort Thompson "when some one emptied a load of buckshot into Byrd dropping him instantly." It was not known "whether Byrd or Lucas or both were the objects of the bushwackers aim." The event was just one more that made Lucas's experience, like that of South

Florida's other desperadoes, fit the 1897 description of his fight with Dennis Sheridan: "The whole story would read like a 'blood and thunder story' of the wild and wooly west variety."[40]

After the Civil War, the final thirty-five years of the nineteenth century saw a steady growth of population in the Peace River Valley, and with that population came towns, churches, schools, and other amenities of civilized life. Despite that growth, South Florida remained a rugged frontier area beset with violence. At times the violence was orchestrated, as in the case of the Regulators, but more often it was random, based on the passions of the moment. The stories the river valley's desperadoes during the era differed but the impact of their actions was the same: lives lost, families torn apart, and communities unsettled and anxious. Throughout the period government failed to quell this violence while politicians would seek to turn it to their own ends.

16
Isolation and the
Need for Transportation

THE PERVASIVENESS OF FRONTIER VIOLENCE in the Peace River
Valley was a concern not alleviated in the post-Reconstruction era, but in the early and mid-1880s the twin problems
of land titles and of reliable and efficient transportation were
solved. With those accomplishments, the Peace River area finally
stood on the brink of prosperity.

Poor transportation and bad weather

A Bartow man wrote in April 1877, "I take occasion to say a few
words on . . . South Florida and the subject of immigration.
Persons who live at a distance from South Florida in reading its
description find the common terms 'good land,' 'good range,'
'abundance of stock,' 'plenty of game,' 'good water,' 'excellent
health,' etc., which is all correct, but can all these advantages be
found to exist in the same locality? Certainly not." He noted
further that "many complain because they do not find as many
saw mills, cotton gins and manufactories, railroad facilities, together with elegant churches, academies and society in full blast,
without taking into consideration the fact that until within a few
years the most of South Florida was under the dominion of the

Red man, who was sole 'monarch of all he surveyed.' " In his conclusion, he pinpointed the problem. "It is true our people are at present struggling under many disadvantages for the lack of railroad facilities in our commercial interest by which the general prosperity is retarded, and of course our educational and social prosperity is dependent upon our pecuniary success. Railroad accommodation is all the country lacks to make it the garden of America. All honorable means have been employed to accomplish this important end. Our Legislatures have often enacted laws granting charters for this purpose, and they have as often been vetoed by our worthy chief State Executives, which is certainly a great misfortune to this entire country as well as to the whole of the State of Florida."[1]

The desire for a railroad in South Florida was not a product of the 1870s or 1880s. At least as early as the mid-1850s the need for such a line had been recognized but, prior to the Civil War, no rails were laid closer to Peace River than at Cedar Key. Following the war, businessmen promoted a line to Charlotte Harbor, and in 1867 newspapers trumpeted that the choice of a terminus for a line down the Gulf coast had been narrowed to either Tampa or Charlotte Harbor. Military reconstruction halted those plans, but two years later Republican governor Harrison Reed revived them by promising his cooperation to achieve rail connections to Tampa Bay, Charlotte Harbor, "and finally Key West." Reed made good on his promise by petitioning the Congress for aid in building the line as far as Charlotte Harbor.[2]

Governor Reed's action spurred an enthusiasm which led the Florida legislature in 1870 to authorize several rail lines to be run into South Florida. The Great Southern Railway Company was granted large tracts of land to build from Millen, Georgia, to Key West, while the Florida Railroad Company was to receive similar incentives for constructing a line to Charlotte Harbor. A number of state business and political leaders, including Francis A. Hendry of Polk County, also organized the South Florida Railroad Company to build a line from Waldo to Tampa. Throughout 1870 and early 1871 railroad fever ran high, even to the extent of encouraging additional lines. At Bartow on June 24, 1871, "a large assembly" convened under the leadership of W.T. Carpenter, Dr. Daniel Stanford, William B. Varn, and Dr. Alexander S. Johnston to encourage stock subscriptions for the proposed "Upper St. John's, Mellonville, Tampa & South Florida Rail Road."[3]

The railroad bubble burst later in 1871 when frustrated Florida bondholder Francis Vose obtained a federal court injunction forbidding the state's internal improvement trust fund from disposing of land for internal improvement purposes, such as railroads, until all Vose's claims against the state were satisfied. As in the case of the Peas Creek Immigrant & Agricultural Company, created to open Peace River to steamboat navigation in return for huge tracts of state land, railroad projects dependent for their financing on similar grants of land were doomed by the Vose injunction. Since the state remained subject to the injunction throughout the 1870s, no railroads were built during the decade in the Peace River Valley or anywhere else in South Florida.[4]

Without access to markets and transportation facilities, the Peace River Valley grew slowly during the 1870s. Occasionally, however, the rumor of a coming railroad spurred a new wave of immigration. One such report led Charles B. Pendleton of Fort Ogden to tell the state land commissioner in December of 1876 that "strangers are beginning to crowd us, the expected R.R. seems to be the great attraction." The railroad did not come, and things were going to get worse before they got better.[5]

Early in 1878 it began to rain in South Florida, and by mid-April Polk County's grand jury reported, "Our public roads are in wretched condition . . . by the protracted rains which for some time have, and still continue indeed to flood our country." Five months later the rains struck again. About noon on September 7, as related by George W. Hendry, "Showers of rain came thick and rapid, the clouds lowering and musky, while their somber glory brought with them no omen of good for us. . . . All night long the wind came steady and direct from a little N. of E. the clouds emptying a deluge of rain in torrents. Day light brought with it no abatement, the 8th being the holy Sabbath was sacredly kept indoors by the wiley pioneers of Polk. For about sixty hours the clouds, the rain and wind were an unchangeable feature and possessed an unabating firmness. Not until the afternoon of the 10th were signs favorable for its cessation."[6]

In the four-day deluge of September 7–10, 1878, "the various

streams of South Florida rose higher than was ever known before
in the recollection of the oldest inhabitants." Peace River rose so
high that its waters lapped the insulators on telegraph poles
strung alongside the bridge at Fort Meade. The bridge itself was
swept away when the flood waters "rose even above the railing
on it." Throughout the river area crops were submerged and
ruined, wells collapsed, roads and fences washed away, and thousands of cattle drowned. A pioneer proclaimed that "1878 has
been one of the most disastrous years in South Florida than any
known to the oldest settlers." Fort Green's residents, faced with
"a complete failure" of their crops, pleaded for "the sympathy of
every warmhearted citizen of the adjoining districts." The ruin
was so great in Manatee County that cattleman Ziba King of Fort
Ogden doubled the amount paid by the county to paupers and
offered "to pay the entire tax of the county and wait six months,
so as to give the people that much extension of time."[7]

Only days into the new year South Florida was visited by "a
terrible cyclone" which overturned houses and wrought havoc on
farms, causing particular suffering in Polk County. In February
the flood turned to drought and for months there was no rain
"worthy of mention." Crops remained unplanted or refused to
grow, and orange trees wilted and failed to bloom. On April 6,
1879, a "heavy frost" descended upon the area and destroyed
what few crops remained. By the fall farmers were "crying," and
the only money available was in the hands of stockmen. A Fort
Ogden resident summed it up in December. "Crops are short of
all kinds," he noted. "We need something to cheer us up, as we
have looked so long for the proposed railroad, that we have come
to the conclusion that there never will be one."[8]

Owning land

The fury of nature had lashed and scarred the Peace River
Valley in 1878 and 1879, but an underlying tragedy had an even
greater impact on settlers and settlement in the area. Most Peace
River residents did not and could not own the land upon which
they lived and from which they attempted to earn their livelihoods. In theory there were many methods by which a settler
might gain title to land in the 1870s, including homesteading it
and "entering" it with subsequent payment to the state. The

Right, John Evans "Jack" Robeson (1847-98) and an unidentified man believed to be Dr. Charles L. Mitchell (1848-1900). Courtesy Joan Wilson Balega.

issuance of the Vose injunction in 1871, however, prohibited the state from transferring its lands except for cash which, even at seventy-five cents or a dollar an acre, posed a considerable problem for many poor and recently arrived South Floridians.

A resident of the Peace River area who wanted to buy his land from the state soon discovered that the task was next to impossible. The problem became clear to settlers near the river from Homeland to the Polk-Manatee county line when in 1871 a naval officer visited the area, thickly settled with farms and homesteads, and posted most of the land within a quarter mile of the river as U. S. Navy property. Outraged residents learned that in October 1855 representatives of the navy had quietly reserved from sale or transfer to the state almost ten thousand acres of the river land as a naval live oak reservation, helping to guarantee the availability of precious oak so necessary for the navy's wooden ships. Not until October 1881 was most of this land made available for purchase.[9]

Complicating land purchasing in the rest of the Peace River area were two factors of great significance. The earlier was the impact of Civil War and Reconstruction in halting the transfer to the state of immense tracts of land selected by the state under the terms of the 1850 Swamp and Overflowed Lands Act. That law authorized the transfer of millions of acres of supposedly low-lying lands for "drainage and reclamation" and prompted the creation in 1851 of the state's internal improvement trust fund board to oversee their management. The later factor stemmed from that board's action of February 13, 1870, which guaranteed to the Peas Creek Immigrant & Agricultural Company all "odd numbered sections up to the County site of Polk County" to a breadth of three miles along both sides of the river. Although the board's contract was conditioned upon the company making the river navigable for shallow-draft steamboats, a condition which never came close to satisfaction, all of the guaranteed lands, whether already in state ownership or scheduled to be transferred to the state under the Swamp and Overflowed Lands Act, were reserved from sale to the public.[10]

The uncertainty and confusion caused by the failure of the Peas Creek Immigrant & Agricultural Company to meet the terms of its contract were reflected in a letter from Nathan H. DeCoster at Hickory Bluff to the state lands commissioner in September 1873. "Has the Pease Creek Co. yet got titles to their lands, and if not are they likely to," queried DeCoster. "Many settlers are at a loss to know how to proceed [—] they do not know whether their improvements are on the Co's or state land. What sections does the Co. take [—] odd or even No's." The company also faced a dilemma. It could not raise the capital to commence its work until the state transferred title to the lands it claimed, an act which the state could not perform until the federal government first transferred the lands to the state. Not until September 1876 was the internal improvement trust fund in a position to make good on its commitment to the company or to offer for cash sale the other lands it had been scheduled to receive. By that time shifting political power had killed the Peas Creek Immigrant & Agricultural Company, but not until it was abolished by law in February 1881 was the company's claim extinguished and its lands released for sale.[11]

When internal improvement trust fund lands along Peace River, other than those reserved for the Peas Creek Immigrant & Agricultural Company, were finally put on the market on September 1, 1876, settlers breathed a collective sigh of relief and many began applying for title to the lands. At the same time immigration was stimulated, and in November 1877 a Fort Ogden resident could note, "This country is rapidly settling up." That optimistic note soon turned flat, however, for along with the natural disasters of 1878–1879 came widespread confusion and rancor as overlapping and conflicting land claims at times reduced the situation to chaos. "Every one thinks his claim is the best," one observer recorded as the decade came to a close. "In fact the lands are in [a] great . . . muddle."[12]

Peace River's land muddle began to clear a bit in 1881 when the naval live oak lands and the Peas Creek Immigrant & Agricultural Company lands were released. Then wearied claimants learned that all the rules of the game had been changed.

By 1881 the state of Florida was desperate to clear up its financial problems and rid itself of the burden of the Vose injunction. As a last resort, Governor William D. Bloxham turned to Philadelphia businessman Hamilton Disston, and in June 1881 the two concluded an agreement by which Disston purchased from the state a total of four million acres of land for the sum of one million dollars, an amount sufficient to satisfy the Vose claim. Although Disston's subsequent development and drainage projects concentrated along the chain of the Kissimmee River, Lake Okeechobee, and the Caloosahatchee River, his company, the Florida Land and Improvement Company, ended up owning 102,000 acres in Polk and 370,000 acres in Manatee County. As the company advertised in 1885, their lands were selected only "after thorough inspection during a period of three years" and "were in general the best tracts owned by the State."[13]

Florida law gave squatters on Hamilton Disston's lands two years to purchase their claims for $1.25 per acre. Otherwise Disston and those who obtained titles from him or with his consent became the main sources of land for Peace River settlers. To market his lands in Polk and Manatee counties, Disston selected Peace River businessman and physician Charles L. Mitchell who established his main sales office at Fort Meade, then a subsidiary agency staffed by John Cross at Fort Ogden. A measure of Mitchell's success and Disston's influence was reflected in Mitchell's appointment in 1885 by the newly elected governor, Edward A. Perry, as state land commissioner.[14]

Settlement in 1880

By the early 1880s settlers in the Peace River Valley at last found themselves able to purchase clear title to their homes and farms, even though in many cases those purchases had to be made from private developers. Manatee County in 1880 included today's Hardee, DeSoto, Charlotte, Highlands, Glades, Sarasota, and Manatee counties. Despite its immense size, the county contained only 3,505 residents, up from 1,931 ten years previously. Almost two-thirds lived in the Peace River Valley area.[15] Included in Manatee's population were about one hundred blacks, a small increase over the eighty-eight of 1870. In the aftermath of Regulator activities in the early 1870s, few blacks chose to remain in the Peace River area, and in 1878 one Fort Green correspondent noted of an election day turnout, "Not a colored man was seen on the ground; in fact we have been informed that there is none living in the district." In the county thirty black men were registered in 1880 as voters.[16]

By far the largest Peace River town in Manatee County was Fort Ogden, with about one hundred residents. In 1880 the town boasted "two good stores which are well kept up by Messrs. T.C. Carr, Simmons & Baker; [and] 3 drug stores kept by Drs. E. Roch [Otto Roesch], W.C. Baker, & A. Smoot Johnson." A steam sawmill supervised by Charles B. Pendleton added to the town's industry. "A spirit of improvement" about Fort Ogden was evidenced by the construction of a combined office building and post office for Dr. Roesch and fine residences for T.C. Carr and W.H. Simmons, all the work of the town's carpenter, Sam Mauck. A school and church added a civilizing touch to the frontier community. One report added, "nearly every one has or is now planting a young grove, which seem to do fine down here."[17]

About ten miles below Fort Ogden on the river's north bank was the tiny hamlet of Hickory Bluff, with about a dozen families and a store, post office, church, and schoolhouse. Several "new and handsome private residences" adorned the town, as well as "an extensive cattle wharf, from which load after load of fine beef cattle is annually shipped to Cuba."[18]

Rounding out the Peace River area towns in Manatee County was the county seat, Pine Level. Containing about fifty inhabitants, the town had been surveyed and platted in January 1878 and held "six stores, one bar-room, two hotels, two churches—Baptist and Methodist," and a courthouse and jail. The "little village" also benefited from two nearby sawmills. Unlike Fort

Photograph of a railroad maintenance crew, probably taken somewhere on the line between Lakeland and Bartow in the mid-1880s. The presence of black workers illustrates the importance of their work in building South Florida's railroads. James W. Rushing, section foreman, fifth from left. Courtesy Charles C. Rushing.

Ogden, the town had no physician and admitted "a lucrative practice could be established."[19]

The remainder of Manatee's Peace River population was thinly spread over the farmlands and cattle ranges on each side of the river, with small clusters of settlement at Joshua Creek, Tater Hill Bluff, Brownville, Crewsville, Castalia, Popash, English, Fort Hartsuff, and Fort Green. Save for a scattered store, church, or school, those centers held little evidence of town life. As yet unbuilt were the towns of Bowling Green, Wauchula, Zolfo Springs, Arcadia, Nocatee, Liverpool, Cleveland, and Punta Gorda.

Polk County's 1880 population of 3,155 was slightly smaller than Manatee's. Of the county's eight precincts, two—Fort Meade and Bartow—contained over half the population. Polk's black population was small, only 122 men, women, and children, which represented a substantial decline from the 1870 total, primarily as a result of Regulator intimidation. Not all blacks left Polk's Peace River lands, however, and a few of the county's original freedmen remained fifteen years after their emancipation, including Prince Johnson and Andy Moore. Both were well respected in the county and of Moore it was said in 1881, "One of the best places within a mile of Bartow is that owned by a negro named Andy Moore. He has some 30 bearing trees, makes some 400 or 500 bushels of corn, raises his own meat, and is independent generally." More recent arrivals included: Dairey Arnold (1870); Charles McLeod, Abraham Tucker, and Toney Tucker (1873); Lewis Arnold (1875); Jack Vaughn (1877); Charles Glover (1878); and Moses Allen, Charles Harden, Lewis Honors, and Squire Newman (1880). Most of these men and their families, together with Polk's other black citizens, clustered in the vicinity of Bartow and Homeland.[20]

Bartow, Polk's county seat, in 1877 was "yet a small village, containing a court-house, two or three stores, and a telegraph office." The disasters of 1878–1879 did nothing to enhance that description, and 1880 found the town continuing its modest existence "in a quiet humdrum way, the people being virtually isolated from the outside world." Two years later, after a period of excited growth, the village still could count only twenty-eight legal voters.[21]

Six miles south of Bartow, just west of Peace River, lay the farming community centered around Bethel Methodist Church, still several years away from being known as Homeland. A remarkable community by frontier standards, Homeland was respected as an educational and teacher training center thanks to its Bethel Academy. For decades the area also had been a focal point for religious and social gatherings at its Methodist campground and, typical of the friendly and cooperative relations existing between white and black families in the area, its Methodist church may have remained one of the few integrated Methodist churches in the state. One resident in 1880, gazing upon the "twenty or more" nearby orange groves, remarked, "The improvements that have been made in the last five years can but please the most sanguine."[22]

Fort Meade in 1880 was the largest town in Polk County and in the Peace River Valley. Since the 1870s it had been a center for trade with cattlemen and had grown along with the cattle trade. The town had about two hundred inhabitants, although the population of nearby farms swelled that total to about five hundred. A veteran, traveling to the town in 1881 for the first time in seven years, was greatly surprised at the changes he encountered. "I had been familiar with Fort Meade and its surroundings, but could not recognize one familiar object. The trees planted by Capt. Louis Lanier looked like stately oaks, hanging full of oranges. In the business part of the village fine houses and orange groves were all that could be seen, having in a few years replaced oaks and pine thickets." Serving Fort Meade's inhabitants were "two religious organizations (Baptist and Methodist), with good memberships, a school of 40 scholars, three stores, a drug store, a tan yard, one saddlery and shoe shop, one doctor (who makes up the deficiency in his practice by planting orange groves and raising babies), a dentist, post-office, telegraph office and four operators, [and] two boarding houses." The town's Tampa and Fort Meade Telegraph Company provided Tampa and Hillsborough County with communications access to the outside world and, given the presence of R.C. Langford's "bar-room," the community easily lived up to its reputation as "quite a lively place."[23]

The Peace River Valley in 1880 had a unique mail delivery system. "If you wear a number twelve boot," noted a Polk County man in April of that year, "come along, we can match you, and the man at the end of which leg said foot is suspended, carries the

United States mail from Fort Mead to Fort Ogden, a distance of
sixty-five miles on foot, and is always reported on time." That
number twelve boot belonged to James Mitchell ("Acrefoot")
Johnson who was said to carry 250 pounds on his 6'7½" frame.
Fifteen-year-old Acrefoot had come to the river valley with his
family shortly after the Civil War. In January 1877 he married a
local girl and subcontracted to carry the mail from Fort Meade to
Fort Ogden for twenty-six dollars per month. Until his father's
death in 1884, Acrefoot walked the Wire Road between the two
towns round-trip at first once a week, then twice a week. Tradition has it that Johnson finally gave up the job only when the
government refused to allow him to carry passengers.[24]

The coming of the railroads

During November in the optimistic year of 1877, a group of
prominent Hillsborough and Polk county men gathered at Tampa
to discuss the possibility of "constructing a Railroad from Tampa
to the interior."[25] When a drive for subscriptions in the two counties proved "quite encouraging," the Tampa, Peace Creek and St.
John's Railroad was incorporated on January 4, 1878, and among
the incorporators were Peace River residents Alexander S. Johnston, George W. Hendry, and William B. Varn. Within months
surveys were undertaken of possible routes between Tampa,
Peace River, and the St. Johns River and in mid-May a report
stated that "the first preliminary line run terminates about four
miles south of Bartow . . . ; the second one mile north of Bartow,
and the third just north of what is known as Parker's lake in
Polk." The civil engineer, H.P. Hepburn, stated, "If the object of
the company is to extend the road to the St. Johns river, the
northern route by Parker's lake would be the cheapest." Complications arising from the possibility that the Great Southern
Railway might extend to Tampa caused the company "to postpone
any immediate steps toward initiating the construction" of the
line.[26]

The Tampa, Peace Creek, and St. John's Railroad received a
state charter in 1879 (amended in 1881) to build "its road or
branches, or extensions of such road, from the city of Tampa to
the city of Jacksonville, and through the counties of Hernando,
Sumter, Marion, Putnam, Clay, Duval and Manatee." In return

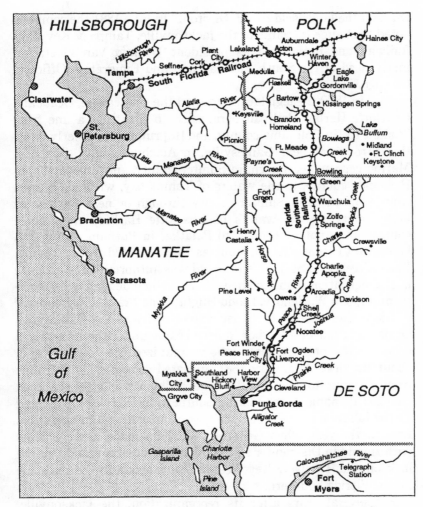

Peace River and Tampa Bay areas in the 1890s. Drawn by Ted Starr.

for its efforts, the company was granted, at its election, "the odd or even numbered sections" of land to a depth of six miles on each side of the line's survey, conditioned upon time limits for initiating and completing construction. After the Disston land purchase, Governor Bloxham was able to secure for the line "the alternate sections of land for six-miles on each side of said road through the lands sold to Mr. Disston." In June 1881 the company voted to change its name to the Jacksonville, Tampa & Key West Railway and designated as president William Van Fleet, formerly head of the South Florida Land and Emigration Office in Chicago.[27]

Also in 1879 the legislature granted the Gainesville, Ocala and Charlotte Harbor Railroad permission to construct a line from "Lake City, in Columbia county, and [to] run in a southerly direction through or near Gainesville, in Alachua county, Ocala, in Marion county, Leesburgh, in Sumter county, and Brooksville, in Hernando county, to the waters of Tampa bay, with one branch from some point in Sumter county through or near Bartow, in Polk county, to the waters of Charlotte Harbor, in Manatee county, and another branch to Palatka, in Putnam county." A land grant essentially the same as that awarded to the Tampa, Peace Creek, and St. John's Railroad was authorized, and a clause in the legislation required the railroad to include among its incorporators John W. Hendry, David Hughes, and Francis A. Hendry.[28]

Soon after receiving its legislative charter, the Gainesville, Ocala and Charlotte Harbor Railroad came under the control of a group of Boston capitalists who reorganized the company and, about the first of January 1881, initiated construction on a line from Palatka to Gainesville. The following month the road changed its name to the Florida Southern Railway Company and by the fall its line to Gainesville was completed and in operation. Late in the year when Governor Bloxham made arrangements with Hamilton Disston for right-of-way and adjacent lands for the Jacksonville, Tampa & Key West Railway, he kindly did the same for the Florida Southern.[29]

For several years after its reorganization, the Jacksonville, Tampa, and Key West Railway unsuccessfully sought funding for the construction of its Jacksonville to Tampa line. In October 1882 it appeared that funds sufficient to permit construction from Jacksonville to Palatka and from Tampa to Medora, Bartow, and Fort Meade had been secured from New York investors, but enough money was available for only the Jacksonville-Palatka line. Construction on that link began in March 1883, but the company faced a terrible crisis in that its franchise for a line between Kissimmee and Tampa would expire unless construction was completed prior to January 25, 1884.[30]

Into the picture in June 1883 stepped Florida railroad entrepreneur Henry B. Plant who was convinced that, expert advice to the contrary, he could complete the Kissimmee to Tampa line in the six or so months remaining under the franchise. Adopting the most northerly route proposed in 1878 by H.P. Hepburn, Plant set his South Florida Railroad crews to work clearing, grading, and laying track on both ends of the seventy-four-mile survey. On the Tampa end of the line trains were run by December 10, 1883, twenty miles to the new town of Plant City. On January 23, 1884, two days before his deadline, Plant saw his two segments joined at the trestle near Carter's Mill, five miles east of the present city of Lakeland. Two days later, regular service over the line was established.[31]

In the excitement over completion of the Kissimmee to Tampa line, Henry Plant's South Florida Railroad did not forget the original intent of its predecessor, the Tampa, Peace Creek & St. John's Railroad, to forge a link with Peace River. In November 1883 the company announced its intention to "speedily" build a spur line from Bartow Junction (Lake Alfred) to the town of Bartow. By the following spring work crews had completed grading on the 16.7-mile run and had bridged Saddle Creek, leaving only a bridge at McKinney's Branch to be completed before the road was ready for "the iron and ties." Progress thereafter was slow, and not until January 8, 1885, did the first passenger train arrive at Polk County's seat, "the grandest holiday ever known in Bartow."[32]

Over a year earlier, before Plant had begun construction of his Bartow branch or completed his link to Tampa, he had sought to eliminate competition by striking a bargain with the Florida Southern Railway which at the time had completed its line to near Leesburg. By the terms of that agreement the Florida Southern bound itself not to build into Tampa or on certain other routes. In return, Plant agreed not to build a line down the peninsula to Charlotte Harbor. The Florida Southern, agreement in hand, began cutting right-of-way at Pemberton Ferry on the Withlacoochee River in May 1884, but problems between the Florida Southern and the Plant system slowed progress. Not until late August 1885 was rail laid as far south as Lakeland, and then only after the two railroads had agreed that the Lakeland-Bartow link would be built by the South Florida Railroad and that the line south of Bartow would be "operated jointly." The South Florida Railroad met the terms of this accord by completing the line from Lakeland to Bartow on September 23, 1885.[33]

Despite delays and problems on the Pemberton Ferry–Bartow link, the Florida Southern went ahead with construction southward from Bartow on July 17, 1885, along a route surveyed that summer by a black crew working under the supervision of Albert W. Gilchrist.[34] It ran roughly two miles to the west of Peace River from Bartow to just south of Fort Hartsuff where it crossed the river about a mile north of Zolfo Springs. The remainder of the route paralleled the river to its mouth and Charlotte Harbor. By mid-August 1885, fifteen hundred primarily black hands were hard at work cutting and grading on that route, toward the promised completion date of February 1, 1886.[35] A month later, on September 19, the roadbed was certified as complete all the way to Fort Ogden.[36]

In November, rails were being laid on the Florida Southern south of Bartow, and by Christmas Fort Meade was preparing to celebrate the arrival of its first train. At the same time, company crews were working around the clock, using electric lights at night, laying one mile of track a day. By late January the rails stretched for forty-two miles below Bartow, and an "excursion" was being planned over the line "down nearly to Ogden." The Bartow *Informant* asked, "Is it not about time for our people to begin to prepare for a celebration of the completion of this line to the farthermost southern point reached by a railroad on our coast? It is an event of great magnitude, and in Florida's future history will mark an era of progress that our people did not dream of."[37]

"The 4th of March," reported a *Florida Times-Union* correspondent from Arcadia, "saw the Florida Southern railway in operation from Bartow to this place, forty-five miles, with the road bed graded, trestles and bridges built and ties laid over the thirty additional miles to its terminus at Charlotte Harbor." At that point construction activities ceased for almost two months, causing one Fort Ogden man to complain, "There is a dead dog under the house as regards the railroad movements." During this interval, in mid-March railroad officers and directors, with other dignitaries including Governor Edward A. Perry, were conducted on a "trial trip" to the end of the line. Particularly delightful for the excursion party was a stop on Peace River bridge for dinner. "The elegant narrow-gauge Pullman car that was our home, seemed perched like a bird on the topmost twig of a tree; twenty feet or more below flowed the dark waters of the river; around was the forest of sombre pine and cypress; stretching away from either end of the train were the slender lines of steel track, apparently touching each other in the dim distance, while to the whispering winds among the pines were added the liquid trills of a saucy mocking bird which swayed and sang in a tree-top close by. Everybody enjoyed the scene fully as well as the cold turkey and the sparkling Mumm."[38]

Track laying was resumed south of Arcadia in early May 1886. Trains were in operation to Fort Ogden by June 7, and soon connections for Fort Myers were being made at Cleveland with the steamer *Alice Howard*. On July 24, the first passenger train arrived over the Florida Southern line at its terminus of Punta Gorda. As historian Vernon Peeples has noted: "There were no large, cheering crowds and no city or state officials delivering speeches; in fact there was neither a mayor of Punta Gorda nor even a town yet. There was only a dream of settlement, growth, and prosperity."[39]

The Peace River Valley had waited for thirty years for some form of dependable transportation for people and crops when its first passenger train reached Punta Gorda in 1886. Time and again hopes for a solution had been crushed by civil war, Reconstruction politics, the state's near-bankruptcy, or just plain bad luck. In the meantime, settlement had grown only slowly, and for the most part the river area remained a raw frontier. With the coming of the railroad, little would remain the same.

17

The Miracle of Railroads

T HE FLORIDA SOUTHERN RAILROAD ran the length of the Peace
River Valley in 1885–1886, the only railroad in southwest
Florida below Tampa. Older river settlements along its
line enjoyed newfound prosperity while new towns and villages
blossomed. Away from the railroad, however, formerly vital communities began to wither as their residents were attracted to the
opportunities and convenience the iron rails promised.

Before the whistles blew

Construction had barely begun on the Florida Southern Railway line south of Bartow when in August 1885 a newspaper
editor prophesied, "This extension will open up a region that has
heretofore been but little known to the outside world, and whose
fertile soil and fine climate will soon win for itself an enviable
name." He concluded, "The lonely forests of Manatee and the
hills of Polk will bristle with new habitations, and land will
advance 500 per cent, or more. Young men who went far away
into the backwoods two or three years ago and took homesteads,
will suddenly find themselves in the midst of a civilization as
genuine and progressive as the world ever saw."[1]

Speculators had been crawling over Manatee and, more particularly, Polk County for more than four years attempting to take advantage of the possibility that rails finally would be laid. "Talk of the railroads was rife," noted one reporter, "and . . . prospective settlers and the agents of capitalists swarmed over Polk County, and many thousands of acres of land were purchased of the General Government and of the State."[2]

At the center of this flurry of land speculation was the Fort Meade office of Hamilton Disston's Florida Land and Improvement Company and his agent, Dr. Charles L. Mitchell. Mitchell was so prepared for speculators and prospective settlers that he not only would sell the land for farms and citrus groves but, from his Sunnyside Nursery, also would provide the "trees, plants, and seeds" to go with it. Venturing as well into the real estate game at an early date was Fort Meade's John E. Robeson who, by mid-1882, had established his Garden of Eden Land Office in the same building as Mitchell's agency. Following soon thereafter were Bartow's J.H. Tatum and Fort Meade's George W. Hendry.[3]

"No village or county in the United States had enjoyed the rapid prosperity and progress that has attended the county of Polk and the villages of Bartow, Ft. Meade, Medulla and Medora, in the past twelve months," newspapers were reporting by mid-1883. "Lands in many places have increased nearly five hundred fold in value—new houses, new improvements of every kind have gone up and on like magic." Along with speculators came new settlers, nearly all of whom were "starting small groves of oranges, lemons, limes, guavas, alligator pears, sugar apples, sour sop, sapodilla, pine-apples, bananas, etc." Reacting to this surge of population and attendant problems, the residents of Bartow on July 1, 1882, voted to incorporate their town, the first community in the Peace River Valley to take that step.[4]

The Polk County tax digest exceeded one million dollars in 1883, an increase of four hundred thousand dollars in a single year. At Bartow, Methodist and Baptist churches were built, the Blount House hotel was enlarged by thirty rooms, and "four neat, new stores, two livery stables, and a large furniture house" were opened. Energized community leaders, anxious to improve the appearance of their town, began demanding a new courthouse and jail to replace the "rickety old rookery" constructed in 1867. The town's first newspaper, the *Informant*, began publication under D.W.D. Boully on June 9, 1881.[5] By early 1884 it was said that Bartow "is a larger place than Ft. Meade." Four miles south a settlement had sprung up around the farm of John W. Brandon, on February 14, 1882, honored with its own post office and named Brandon.[6]

In October 1882, it was estimated that Fort Meade's population had grown 50 percent since 1880. In 1882 the community had built a tall-spired Methodist church considered "one of the finest churches in South Florida," and by the close of the following year had seen the opening of three new hotels—the Benedict House, the Dzialynski House, and the French House. A suburb known as Fairview began to emerge east of town, stretching for several miles across the farmlands of "the deadening" and ending atop the Ridge. Before the end of 1884, the new community had its own school. "Sixteen miles due east of Fort Meade, and situated between two beautiful lakes, named on the maps respectively Clinch and Istapogayoxee or Reedy lakes," a new development, Keystone City, remained in "an embryo" condition, but promised a happy future centered around A.R. Anthony's "60 horse power, water sawmill." Not for well over a decade would this fledgling community receive its permanent name of Frostproof.[7]

Polk County's assessed property values took another tremendous jump in 1884, to $1,686,373. In great part, however, this jump of well over one-half million dollars represented growth in the northern, rather than Peace River, area of the county, and reflected the completion through the area of the South Florida Railroad line from Kissimmee to Tampa. A center for this growth was the new town of Lakeland, which had seen its beginning when L.M. Ballard moved his store and sawmill about five miles from Medulla to the new railroad near Wire Lake. In February 1884, Abraham G. Munn and his associates Samuel A. Hartwell and Charles E. Hillman, acting as the Lakeland Improvement Company, surveyed and platted the future town and began clearing lots, building a market, opening the Tremont Hotel, and encouraging sales. On January 1, 1885, Lakeland's residents voted to incorporate, and four months later the population was said to stand at six hundred to seven hundred persons. By the end of the year it was remarked, "No place within the county . . . has made such rapid growth as Lakeland."[8]

Other communities also emerged along the rail line in northern

Polk County. Acton lay one mile east of Lakeland, between Parker and Bonnie lakes, and under the leadership of British navy veteran Piers Elliot Warburton, manager of the Florida Mortgage and Investment Company, and his fellow countryman Cecil H. Alleyne, sought to attract English settlers to the area. Farther along the rail line to the east came the new towns of Auburndale, Bartow Junction (Lake Alfred), Haines City, and Davenport. On the South Florida Railroad spur from Bartow Junction to Bartow, Harris Corner began to grow up around the store and post office of F.A.K. Harris. When time came to post the town's name at the depot, public relations conscious citizens adopted the new name of Winter Haven.[9]

Population and prosperity in the Peace River Valley area of Manatee lagged far behind Polk County. Although in mid-1884 one old-timer was "agreeably surprised" at the number of new settlements, groves, and farms between Fort Meade and Fort Ogden, the fact was that Mr. Plant's railroad was far to the north and the Florida Southern still noncommittal as to when and where it would build down the river. To add to the problems caused by this uncertainty came economic disaster caused by drought.

The year 1883 was long remembered in the Peace River area as a "phenominal dry year." The dearth of rain continued into 1884 and spread northward into Polk. By June wells were running low, crops and stock were suffering, and it was feared "that the public health is endangered by such long continued dry weather." While farmers watched their crops die in the fields, the area's principal economic mainstay, the cattle industry, came in for a series of tremendous shocks.[10]

During the summer of 1884 the Cuban government abruptly halted South Florida cattle shipments to that island. The impact on Peace River was immediate. "The financial condition of Manatee county, as well as the whole of South Florida, is at present alarming," reported an observer. The "cessation or stoppage in the annual shipments," the writer went on, "has brought a scarcity of money to an extent never before witnessed in these ends of the earth." Cattle which could not be sold remained on the ranges where they competed for forage, in extremely short supply due to the drought. By December, cattleman James E. Hendry was finding few cattle suitable for market and rightly predicting that "many cattle will perish . . . between this and spring."[11]

As cattle on the South Florida ranges weakened from starvation, a disease believed to be pneumonia broke out in the herds and played "wholesale havoc." W.B. Henderson reported in April 1885 that "more cattle have died this winter than in any previous year." Henderson believed Ziba King, alone, had lost two thousand head and stated that "in many sections of Manatee County the stench became so great that the people had to burn the carcasses." Even with those losses huge herds remained alive, and cattlemen spent their time that summer and fall, while the Florida Southern built its line down the river, urgently searching for new markets for beef in Key West, New Orleans, and the northern states. With no operational railroad by which to ship cattle north from Peace River, the herds which were sold to the north were driven overland to the railhead at Orlando.[12]

Despite Manatee County's economic doldrums, the promise of a railroad prompted the beginnings of a number of new communities. To the vicinity of old Fort Chokonikla and the farms of A.M. Chester and N.M. Bryan came a number of families from Kentucky and other northern states who named their new home Utica. A few miles south, close to Fort Hartsuff, a "new town of Stanely" was founded in December 1883 at "the head of deep water navigation" on Peace River.[13]

When T.J. Herndon moved in 1881 to Tater Hill Bluff a few miles above Joshua Creek, only two other families lived in the immediate area, those of Jim Waldron and Thomas Williams. In the summer of 1883 the Reverend James M. Hendry determined to move there and operate a sawmill. He decided to name his new community Arcadia, after the daughter of his friend, Thomas H. Albritton.[14] The following year Hendry's brother-in-law, John W. Whidden, and his son, Robert E. Whidden, opened in the town a general merchandise store.

Below Arcadia, several new towns were launched in 1884. Early in the year, Disston land agent John Cross laid out the town of Liverpool, erected a wharf, and began selling lots. The same year Cross sold to Isaac H. Trabue a tract of land across the river from Hickory Bluff, earlier the homestead of James Madison Lanier. Trabue employed Kelly B. Harvey to survey and plat a town that Trabue decided to call Trabue. Within three years

Trabue's new town began to be called, against his wishes, by the ancient name of its location, Punta Gorda. A.T. Halleyman, "working in the interest of a party of Northern gentlemen who have capital to make a success of the enterprise and expect to have a thriving city in a short time," laid off another town a few miles northeast of Trabue called Cleveland, in honor of the president of the United States.[15]

As the trains arrived

When the Florida Southern Railway began building its line south of Bartow in July 1885, the company had been playing for three years a cat and mouse game as to whether the line would run down the eastern or western side of Peace River. The decision, once made public, struck a death knell for the Manatee County seat of Pine Level, through which the rails were not to pass, and ensured the survival and growth of the towns of Bartow and Fort Meade, towns on the same side of the river as Pine Level. While the determination of its route was the single most important decision made by the railroad in terms of its impact on the settlement of the river valley area, the Florida Southern retained another power having a direct and immediate impact on the communities along its line, the power to decide whether to locate a depot in a community and to determine exactly where that depot would be placed. For the exercise of that power in favor of a community, the railroad demanded a price.

The circumstances surrounding the Florida Southern's dealings with each community over location of its depot are unknown, but it appears that in every case affecting established communities or communities with financially sound backing, the railroad demanded land or cash or both. At Homeland the deal was simple; the alternate blocks within the entire town were given outright to the railroad in return for a depot. Isaac Trabue made a similar arrangement by agreeing to deed one-half his holdings at Trabue to the railroad in return for which the company agreed to construct its line through the town. At Bartow, the city fathers settled the matter "according to the railroad company's proposition." Fort Meade first thought it had solved the matter by donating right-of-way and promising ten thousand dollars in cash, but after J.N. Hooker, E.E. Skipper, and F.A. Whitehead laid out a new "town of Fort Meade" about two miles south in January 1886, Fort Meade's residents found they had been outbid. Railroad workmen arrived one morning, tore up the town's side track, and announced the depot would be located in the new town. Aghast at the railroad's surprise move, the town offered to up the ante by one thousand dollars in cash and four hundred acres of land, but the railroad's counteroffer of twenty-five thousand dollars in cash proved too much for Fort Meade to take. Launching a counterattack, the town's leading citizens organized their own railway company and, by January 1887, had built a street railway running from the depot into downtown Fort Meade. Although the depot was moved closer to town in 1891, the Fort Meade Street Railroad Company operated its mule-drawn railway into the twentieth century.[16]

In less established communities, the railroad was even less subtle. In the vicinity of old Fort Hartsuff a community centered around Eli English's store, known as English, and the "new town of Stanley" was being developed. Settlers were informed that a depot would be built "across from the English home," but in May 1886 the Florida Southern's chief engineer, W.P. Couper, surveyed and platted a town half a mile to the north, and there the railroad placed its depot. When that facility was completed, the railroad posted the town's new name, Wauchula.[17]

In addition to its power of placing depots, the railroad could favor or harm a community by its timing. The impact of timing is easily seen by the advantage gained by Bartow's access to rail transportation a year prior to Fort Meade's. A similar example illustrates the arbitrary use of this power by the Florida Southern Railway to the advantage of a new town and its backers and to the detriment of an older and much larger one.

On March 4, 1886, the Florida Southern Railway was placed in operation between Bartow and Arcadia, and, even though the roadbed had been graded, trestles and bridges built, and ties laid for thirty additional miles to the south, construction abruptly and without explanation was suspended for two months. The town arbitrarily denied service during those two months was the largest town in Manatee County, Fort Ogden, at that time estimated to contain five hundred residents.[18]

When the railroad arrived at Arcadia, only sixteen families lived within a mile of that community. The town consisted of

J.W. Bailey's general store, which he had purchased from J.W. Whidden & Son, a post office run by T.J. Herndon, and a school with thirty-five pupils taught by D.S. Williams. What the town did have, however, was powerful friends in John W. Whidden and James M. Hendry.[19]

John Wesley Whidden in 1886 was easily the most powerful politician in Manatee County. A son of pioneer patriarch Willoughby Whidden, John W. had served as a Confederate officer and was considered a war hero. A staunch Democrat after the war, Whidden served at various times as sheriff, clerk of the circuit court, and representative of Manatee County. He had amassed a fortune in the cattle trade and in 1885 was serving as state senator for Polk and Manatee counties.[20]

James Madison ("Boss") Hendry was his brother-in-law. Hendry served in both Confederate and Union armies during the Civil War and afterwards became a Baptist preacher, farmer, cattleman, sawmill owner, and merchant. His brother, Baptist circuit rider John Wright Hendry, was the most popular preacher on the Peace River circuits and an incorporator, along with his cousin, cattle baron Francis A. Hendry, of the Gainesville, Ocala and Charlotte Harbor Railroad—the Florida Southern Railway.[21]

Punta Gorda's first city council, December 1887. *Left to right*: Tom Hector, J.O. Swisher, John Fishback, W.H. Burland, Kelly B. Harvey, Neil Dahl, and James Sandlin. Courtesy Vernon Peeples.

Whidden and Hendry had in common wealth, family connections, business ties, political influence, and investments at Arcadia. Although the written record is scanty, appearances suggest
these facts did not escape the attention of the Florida Southern
which, obligingly, pushed its railroad to Arcadia and then halted
construction long enough for a town to be "commenced," an
action which occurred on June 10, 1886. Only three days before,
the first train had finally arrived at the much larger and established town of Fort Ogden where a depot would be erected five
months later, to the rage of "indignant" citizens, one-half mile
from town.[22]

Those three months of being "the end of the line" worked like
a charm for Arcadia. Prospective settlers going as far as the
nation's southernmost railroad could take them poured into the
area, and by October the town had "about forty dwelling houses,
mostly two-stories, and about ten more being erected . . . four
stores, general merchandise, all doing a rushing business; three
boarding houses, all doing a good business, and still many a
campfire can be seen in town." Additionally, the "F. S. railroad
has a good depot and two section houses; there are two saw mills
and one plaining machine, all kept busy until ten o'clock at night
and still can't supply the demand for lumber; two drug stores
with a good supply of drugs, medicines, &c . . . [and a] hotel,
two-stories high." Local businessman W.S. Clay bragged that he
was "making money enough to burn a wet hog."[23]

Arcadia was incorporated on December 6, 1886.[24] In mid-
January 1887 the community was "still booming" and was poised
to make its bid to become the principal town in the soon-to-be-
created county of DeSoto. As a fitting mark of Arcadia's birth and
future prospects, it was announced that Capt. John W. Whidden
was constructing there "a large, two-story house" which would
be "a great improvement to the town" and one of her "finest
dwellings."[25]

After the trains came

The year 1887 in many ways was pivotal in the history of the
Peace River Valley. The railroad, after years of anxious anticipation, had arrived, but the phosphate boom and its attendant
effects were still a year or two in the future. The basis of town

life and development for the next century had been established through the location of the railroad's tracks and depots, coupled with the tide of immigration which flowed in its wake. This pivotal year is an appropriate point at which to take a closer look at the development of the river valley's communities and of the individuals who were building them.

Bartow

"At Bartow a complete transformation is apparent," noted a discerning visitor in January 1887. "The hamlet of former days has become a busy bustling beautiful city with the evidences of progress and prosperity greeting you at every corner." From a tiny village incorporated in 1882 with twenty-eight legal voters, Bartow and its adjacent areas had grown enough by the spring of 1887 to claim two thousand residents. Well over half that number had arrived in the previous two years.[26]

The town's appearance was dominated by "beautiful oaks and other delightful shade trees scattered throughout the corporation," orange groves, and "wide streets crossing each other at right angles." The focal point of its downtown was the county's two-story courthouse finished late in 1884 and described as "a gem of an ornament . . . to our town." In place at about the same time, in anticipation of the railroad's arrival in January 1885, were four hotels—the St. Mark's, Grove, Mansion House, and Semi-Tropical—as well as the town's new opera house. Completing its civilizing touches, the city gained a baseball team in 1884 and, for the railroad's opening ceremonies, the Bartow Cornet Band debuted.[27]

The business life of Bartow centered on the streets surrounding the courthouse. Until his retirement in early 1886, the principal retail establishment on those streets was the general merchandise store of Captain David Hughes, although George W. Smith, the Lang Brothers, the Reed Brothers, John C. Wright, and J.N. Hooker & Co. provided stiff competition. A fire in the business district on September 23, 1886, destroyed B.F. Johnson's three stores, Johnson, Daniels & Co.'s barroom, Baeumel & Oppenheimer's drugstore, Tigner & Tatum's real estate office, and numerous other buildings including the Florida Southern Railway offices. Another fire on November 27 destroyed "the Gresham House, the Bazar, Blount's store and the Cool Drink House," although by "dint of hard work the postoffice, pool hall, St. Mark's and Mr. Blount's residence were saved."[28]

From the ashes arose the Peace River Valley's first brick buildings, beginning in the spring of 1887 with the construction of the "handsome Lemoyne brick business block" on the southwest corner of the courthouse square. Later that summer the Jackson building was finished, "by far the handsomest building block in the city" and in which "all of the rooms on the second floor are arranged in suites and were engaged for offices before the building really commenced. The building has iron window cornices, an iron and glass front and heavy iron shutters with hard pressed brick trimmings and a tin roof, giving it a very ornamental, as well as substantial appearance." Complimenting these brick business buildings was a new brick Summerlin Institute, the cornerstone for which was laid May 12, 1887, as well as a twenty thousand dollar brick and steel jail completed early in the fall. A number of families during the year constructed "good substantial two story brick houses."[29]

Bartow also completed in 1887 its first firehouse, with a city hall located on the second floor. In late December 1885 or early January 1886, F.W. Page & Co., of Rochester, New York, opened the Polk County Bank with a capital of twenty-five thousand dollars. The bank's president was W.J. Emerson, also of Rochester, who soon was joined by Warren Tyler as cashier and J.W. Boyd and R.C. Beecher as assistants. In the summer of 1887 the bank was located in "newly furnished rooms on the corner of Main street and Central avenue," formerly the Lang Brothers' store, and in January 1888 it was reorganized into the First National Bank of Bartow. In 1886 the Crystal Ice Works also opened, operated by E.W. Codington, and the area's first local business association, the Bartow Board of Trade, elected G.A. Hanson president and George H. Thomas secretary.[30]

The South Florida and Florida Southern railroads were built primarily with black labor and, once the lines were completed, many of these men and their families elected to remain in the Peace River Valley, some continuing to work for the railroads as maintenance crewmen. These newcomers joined the few black families already living in the area, together with others who had come with the tide of settlers drawn by the railroads, all seeking better opportunities in the booming economy of the river valley.

Among the black population was the area's first black tradesman, Bartow barber John Henry Clay. The first known black church in the area, Saint James African Methodist Episcopal Church, was organized at Bartow in March 1885, largely through the work of Charles Henry Macon, Sr., C.C. Johnson, F. Hall, H. Burkett, L. Sims, R. Smith, J.C. Longworth, W.M. Wiley, and J.M. Perry. For the first decade of its existence the church met in members' homes or at Bartow's Negro Hall, which stood at least as early as September 1887. During 1886 and early 1887, the church was presided over by the Reverend G.B. Hill, who was succeeded by the Reverend J. Thomas. Mainstays of the congregation included S. Robinson, G. McCantt, Mrs. J.A. Wiley and Mrs. Jane Sadler.[31]

For relaxation, Bartow citizens went to Kissengen Springs, about four miles south of town near Peace River. Originally known as DeLeon Mineral Springs, the site was purchased in the mid-1880s by Dr. R.H. Huddleston who renamed it Kissengen Springs because "the water of this spring is almost identical with that of the famous German spring." Those waters were "in great repute as a curative for all diseases of the blood, and of indigestion, dyspeptics finding the use of its waters very beneficial." By the summer of 1887 Huddleston had erected bathhouses, cottages, and a small hotel at the springs, and it was deemed "a popular resort for both young and old." The young, particularly, it was said, loved not only the springs but also "boating down the creek leading from the spring to Peace River." Kissengen Springs retained that reputation and popularity well into the twentieth century.[32]

Homeland

Local memory suggests that the Bethel community received the name Homeland from "a weary Irish peddler who said it seemed more like his beautiful Ireland than any section in which he had exhibited his wares." The name first was given official notice on August 24, 1885, when James T. Hancock, Jr., signed an application for establishment there of a post office and entered on a blank after the words, "The proposed office to be called" the single word "Homeland." The name became official two weeks later when the post office was approved.[33]

Along with Bartow and Fort Meade, Homeland experienced substantial growth beginning about 1883. Adding to individuals and families who had arrived during the previous decade, including those of James A. Wilson and W.T. Denham, were such new-comers as James Stuart Wade of Phelps City, Missouri. Of importance to the community's growth was the arrival by wagon of a group of families brought to the area in early 1884 by T.W. Anderson from his native Newnan, Georgia. Among them were Martin B. Swearingen, L.W. Scroggins, Andrew McKillop, M.C. Puckett, Frank Clark, and two black men who likely were Early Mitchell and Jeff Marchman.[34]

With increased population, the farming community of Homeland began to look more like a town. In addition to the Bethel Methodist Church, which traced its roots to the 1850s, came the establishment in 1882 of the Homeland Baptist Church, for which a sanctuary was erected in 1886. In September 1887, Homeland's Methodist families began construction of a new and much larger sanctuary, while the community's black Baptists organized their first church, the Mount Bunyan Baptist Church, under the leadership of the Reverend G.W. McClendon. The growth of churches in Homeland and the rest of the upper Peace River Valley led in October 1883 to the announcement that no more camp meetings would be held at the historic Bethel campground. As stated at the time, "One by one the landmarks of older times are passing away; so with camp-meetings. Having served their purpose in a sparsely settled country, they are replaced by churches when the country becomes more populous."[35]

The town of Homeland was laid out in April 1886 by T.W. Anderson, and, shortly thereafter, a depot was constructed for which Anderson became agent. He also had opened a store that in the summer of 1887 received some competition when James B. Crum opened nearby "a first class store." James Wade operated a drug and "fancy goods" store, J.D. Crum owned a carriage and blacksmith shop, W.B. Lassiter managed the Polk County Nursery and Improvement Company, Mrs. T.W. Anderson served as postmistress, Mrs. Katie McKillop was proprietress of the Homeland Hotel, and Sam Lee and Wiley Scroggins worked as the town's builders and contractors.[36]

Fort Meade

The railroad provided Bartow easy access to the outside world on January 8, 1885, but not for another six to eight months was

Fort Meade even certain the route of the Florida Southern line would pass the town. This advantage increased the population of the tiny county seat well beyond that of the region's former largest town and trading center. As late as November of 1884 a Fort Meade resident would note, "no boom has struck us yet," although "several new buildings have just been completed."[37]

The year 1885 saw Fort Meade finally beginning to emerge from its transportation problems, as indicated by the town's incorporation on January 10.[38] The town already had completed a bridge "over 600 feet long" spanning Peace River, to replace the one washed away in 1878, and during the year it benefitted from the construction by Philip Dzialynski, Cornelius B. Lightsey, and R.C. Langford of a "fine academy" building. In the same year the first local newspaper, the *Pioneer*, was established by Frank Q. Crawford, assisted by J.F. Marsh. Ernest B. Simmons from Connecticut and Dr. William L. Weems and his nephews, Arthur B. and Sterling Canter, from Missouri arrived with their families. By the end of the year the town was described as "a lively place" where "everyone is in the land business that has money enough to buy forty acres of land."[39]

The railroad arrived at Fort Meade in the last week of 1885, and for most of the next year the town was occupied first battling with the railroad over location of its depot and then constructing a street railway connecting its downtown, located within half a mile of Peace River, with the depot over two miles south.[40] In the meantime the town continued to grow, although not at the pace of Bartow, and by the beginning of 1887 it could be said that "quite a change in travel and boom is evident. . . . Fifteen dwelling houses have been erected within the past twelve months with a proportionate increase probable for the present year; besides there are four or five dry goods stores by which groceries are sold, two standing hotels with many private boarding places, two drug stores, jewelry and watch and clock repairing establishments, millinery store, and a good meat market open at all hours of the day; law offices and real estate firms, surveyors and draughtsmen, artists and dentists, two organized churches, Methodist and Congregationalist [as the Episcopal church was sometimes called], Sabbath schools and a well organized temperance society doing much good by its efforts."[41]

In 1885 it was said that at Fort Meade "the attention is

arrested by the number, the vigor, and the beauty, of the orange groves." Two years later the town's appearance remained much the same. "Wagons can be seen in every direction laden with nursery trees on their way to clearings for permanent groves." The town's center was Main or Broad Street (the old Wire Road) running west from Peace River bridge, and there or nearby were all the town's leading businesses. Among them, in addition to a saloon, billiard room, restaurant, and carriage shop were: W.M. Ball & Co., J.N. Hooker & Co., Reif Brothers, S.N. Weeks & Co., and Hendry & Carter, all general merchandise stores; M. Ottinger and W.T. Sauls, grocers; Lightsey & Co., beef market; J.A. Hart, livery stables; Mrs. Edna Hayman, millinery; W.L. Weems and C.F. Marsh, doctors; S.G. Hayman, dentist; Dzialynski & Co., druggists; Whitehead & Alleyne, A.H. Thompson, J.F. Black, and J.A. Edwards, real estate; C.C. Wilson, attorney; F.F. ("Tobe") Hendry, postmaster; and J.C. Munroe, barber.[42]

Bowling Green

For the little community of Utica, 1886 was a very good year. The railroad arrived and built a depot there and, on May 26, it received a post office. The name Utica, however, did not sit well with many of the area's recent settlers, a great number of whom were from Kentucky, and with the leadership of the postmaster, William I. Mason, formerly of Bowling Green, Kentucky, they petitioned the Post Office Department for a change—a request approved on September 23, 1886. Thereafter the community was known as Bowling Green. The town's founders included A.M. Chester, I.A. Mason, William I. Mason, David McLean, James McLean, J.K. Freeman, Ira Powell, James Ott, George Rudisill, Howard Rudisill, Harvey Powell, John Powell, Jason Cook, Dudley Buck, Dell Buck, and Irving Keck.[43]

Wauchula

"Wauchula is a beautiful little village," it was reported in April 1887. "The place deserves special mention from the fact of its magic-like growth." A year away from incorporation, Wauchula already was home to numerous businesses and professional men.[44] Where two years before the only retail business was Eli English's store, Wauchula held six grocery, dry goods, and general merchandise businesses, including those of Simmons & Sparkman, M.A. McConnell (who also operated the livery stable), G.H. Gill, J.E. Tison, J.R. Barron and M.A. Cochran. The Southerland Brothers provided "drugs, fancy and toilet articles, etc."; the town's health was attended to by Dr. T.J. Maddox; visitors stayed at the "nicely kept" Seward House, F.J. Seward, proprietor; real estate needs were met by Dr. L. Roberts and A.A. Constantine; and the depot and telegraph office were under the management of A.G. Smith. A.A. Constantine had promised to donate four acres for a Baptist church and four acres for a town park. On January 18, 1888, the town's first fraternal lodge, Masonic Order No. 99, was organized. Serving as its officers were Peter Brown, H.E. Carlton, and E.F. Durrance. As one correspondent put it, "Much has been done . . . towards the upbuilding of the place by its industrious and hardworking inhabitants."[45]

Zolfo Springs

The name Zolfo, according to tradition, stems from a corruption of the words, "sulphur water," referring to the odor emanating from the springs located there and known as the Sulphur Spring since the 1850s. In 1860 one expedition reported the water as "very fine" and noted "it smelt and tasted as strong as any water we have tasted in South Florida." Prior to the Civil War, the families of Dempsey D. Crews and others had settled in the area. When the railroad located a depot at Zolfo Springs in 1886, a town was spoken of and a post office opened under William J. Carroll. The town grew only slowly, however, and was noted for several years only "as a center of trade for the surrounding area."[46]

Arcadia

The town of Arcadia was booming at the beginning of 1887, and two years later was still being described as "a city of abundant promise, a world of sunshine." In March 1887 the community's first newspaper, the *Arcadian*, was established by D.W.D. Boully; four months later it was taken over by a syndicate consisting of John W. Whidden, B.F. Baldwin, T.J. Herndon, and C.G. Johanson that installed Thomas J. Pepper as editor. The town's first bridge over Peace River was constructed that spring, and new businesses continued to open. The bustling community even organized a temperance society, the Arcadia Abstainers, and a literary club, the Shakespeare Society.[47]

Among Arcadia's leading business and professional men in 1887 were: Edwin Green, doctor; R.J. Boring, depot manager; Reed & Williams and J.G.S. Kabrich, builders; T.J. Pepper, real estate agent; Johanson & Isgren (A.H. Williams, business manager) and J.R. Boyd & Co., saw mill operators; T.J. Herndon, postmaster; C.H. Bonard, livery; the Misses Hurd and Williams, ladies' goods and millinery; Mrs. C.G. Johanson, proprietress of the Arcadia Hotel; B.F. Baldwin, hay, grain, and feed; and T. Gaskins, W.E. Daniel, J.W. Bailey, L.R. Restall (with G.H. Altree), T.J. Herndon, C.T. Tooke, B.F. Richards & Co., and Simmons, Carlton & Co., groceries, dry goods, and general merchandise.[48]

Fort Ogden

The railroad may have snubbed Fort Ogden for months in the spring of 1886, but when it finally arrived residents were on top of the world. "We have water and rail transportation," one resident reported, "our situation is excellent, the health of the town is good, and our merchants enjoy the confidence of the people for miles around us." At the time, Fort Ogden contained "about 500" residents, as well as "thirty residences, five general merchandise stores, two drug stores, three boarding houses, a harness shop, a blacksmith and wheelwright shop, a wood worker's shop, a saw mill, a Baptist church, a public hall, a public school, with from eighty to ninety pupils, a money order postoffice, two physicians, a jeweler, a notary public, a justice of the peace, two lawyers, one dentist, two photographers in tents, a skating rink and several teamsters."[49]

The Fort Ogden resident went on to list the town's leading citizens: "The leading merchants are Judge Z. King, J.O. Carr and Simmons & Carlton. W.H. Simmons is notary public, Carlton & Crawford are the popular and efficient attorneys. They are connected with the Orange Grove Land Agency and do a large amount of real estate business. Dr. O.H. Davenport is the skillful dentist, and J.O. Carr the postmaster. The physicians are Dr. O.E. Rush [Roesch] and Dr. J.S. Gibson. They also have drug stores. J.J. Vandiver has a fancy grocery store. Williams, Hoeffer & Pepper are the enterprising real estate agents. W.G. Gay keeps a hotel and runs a hack line, and W.J. Williams is hotel keeper and real estate agent. L.O. Gold, contractor for building the Florida Southern Railway, has a supply depot in charge of Geo. S. Willis. Ed. Carney does a general purchase and sale business."[50]

Despite Fort Ogden's fury at the railroad depot being located one-half mile out of town, at the end of 1886 the overall tone of the community remained optimistic. One correspondent suggested at that time that the only things Fort Ogden really needed were "a good restaurant and laundry." Things continued to look bright for the town into 1887, and by February it was being said, "Fort Ogden has started a boom. The Carleton House is nearly finished. The Central House is full all the time, and still they come." In August the residents of Fort Ogden agreed to incorporate. The first officers were J.O. Carr, mayor; J. Madison Williams, marshal; Stephen J. Carlton, president of the council; C.Y. Crawford, F.C. Bethea, W.A. Johnson and Elam B. Carlton, members of the council; and W.H.G. Smart, clerk and treasurer.[51]

Luke Bredin Flood (1851–99) and Alicia Whitney Flood (1852–1940) of County Wexford, Ireland. The Flood family came to Fort Meade in March 1886 on the first regularly scheduled passenger train to enter the town. Their arrival underscored not only the importance of the railroad in bringing new residents to the Peace River Valley but also the beginning tide of English and Irish settlement in the area. Courtesy Alice Flood.

Arcadia House in 1896. From the Jacksonville *Florida Times-Union*, October 18, 1896.

Nocatee, Liverpool, and Cleveland

Nocatee, with its depot about five miles south of Arcadia, was a creature of the railroad. The community's founders, including Florida Southern Railway surveyor Albert W. Gilchrist, attempted to capitalize on railroad access and proximity to the Joshua Creek settlements. In 1887 the tiny community had potential for growth, as had Liverpool and Cleveland. In February 1887 it was reported, "Liverpool is building up. Mr. Cross has completed one house of seven rooms, and his hotel of twenty rooms is nearly completed. There is some talk of a factory being started there." Cleveland was somewhat more successful, having the benefit by 1887 of the sixty-room Cleveland or National Hotel. "The prospect certainly looks bright," one resident reported, "[and] all anticipate a lively season."[52]

Punta Gorda

The coming of the railroad provided a tremendous boost for Trabue in 1886. The first trains brought construction materials for the railroad's planned 150-room Hotel Punta Gorda, and in August work began on a 4,200-foot dock designed to permit ocean-going vessels to meet the railroad. Tracks were laid to the end of the dock, a commercial complex was established, a 1,200-foot pier was added in front of the Hotel Punta Gorda, and the railroad began advertising the resort throughout the country. By March

1887 a depot had been built, and tourists were flocking to the area.[53]

On December 7, 1887, thirty-four men, four of whom were blacks, met in a poolroom above a store and voted to incorporate the town under the name of Punta Gorda. In the town's first election, W.H. Simmons defeated Albert W. Gilchrist for mayor, and other officers elected were: Thomas R. Hector, clerk; John Stansfield, marshal; and J.O. Swisher, J.L. Sandlin, W.H. Burland, K.B. Harvey, and Neil Dahl, members of the council. The year 1887 also saw the opening of the town's first newspaper, the *Charlotte Harbor Beacon*, edited and published by R.S. Hanna and J.F. Marsh.[54]

By mid-1888 it was said of Punta Gorda: "Here will be found improvements aggregating up into the hundreds of thousands of dollars. . . . There are a number of large business houses, the largest being the wholesale grain and heavy grocery house of S.P. Hinckley, formerly of Hinckley & Fuller of Tampa. . . . The Southland Hotel, of which Mr. T.M. Weir is proprietor, is a commodious and well-kept house and is becoming very popular." Punta Gorda was soon to become the largest town in the Peace River Valley south of Bartow.[55]

Where the railroad laid its tracks in the Peace River Valley in 1885 and 1886, towns grew and began to prosper. Many of these communities were new, among them Bowling Green, Wauchula, Zolfo Springs, Arcadia, Nocatee, Liverpool, Cleveland, and Punta Gorda, although older towns on the line, including Bartow, Homeland, Fort Meade, and Fort Ogden, prospered as well. Not so fortunate were communities the railroad did not reach, such as Pine Level, Fort Green, Popash, and Hickory Bluff. These settlements began to decline and for the rest of the century saw settlers always going somewhere else.

*"A great deal of political strife
among us"*

18

Politics of Redemption

RECONSTRUCTION ENDED IN THE Peace River Valley with Democrats in electoral control of both Polk and Manatee counties. Within each county, however, factions contended for control of political office in spirited and, at times, bitter fashion. The temperance movement soon added fuel to those political fires upon which, in the 1890s, also was heaped the cause of Populism. Along the way, a new county, DeSoto, was born out of old Manatee, and a county government for the southern reaches of the river valley was established at Arcadia. When the century ended, regular Democrats remained in as firm control of the area as at the beginning of the era of redemption.

Redemption and revenge

A Democratic governor, George F. Drew, was inaugurated on January 2, 1877, ushering in the political redemption of Florida from the Republicans. Within one week he had replaced all of Manatee County's officers with Democrats, many of whom were ex-Confederates.[1] A Tallahassee newspaper reported these removals under the headlines "The Guillotine" and "Republicans Requested to Scoot, while Democrats Waltz Joyfully up to Serve and Save the Country." On January 31 came Polk County's turn, although a number of Republican appointees, including N.S. Blount, W.B. Varn, Stephen M. Sparkman, John Davidson, and James A. Fortner, soon were given new jobs or reappointed to their old ones.[2] Similarly, Democratic leader Edgar M. Graham was reappointed Manatee county judge even though he previously had held a Republican appointment.[3]

It did not take long for South Florida's new officeholders to seek revenge for the long years of Republican rule. On April 13, 1877, a Polk County grand jury indicted former circuit judge James T. Magbee for "maliciously threatening an injury to the person of another with intent thereby to extort pecuniary advantages." Magbee, who was practicing law on the South Florida circuit as well as editing the *Tampa Guardian*, was held until John Davidson and Noel R. Raulerson helped him post bond. After a year's wait, the former judge was tried at Bartow and convicted on April 10, 1878. So improper were the proceedings, however, that on the following day the verdict was set aside and Magbee was granted a new trial. On May 19, 1879, the charges were dismissed.[4]

As James Magbee was struggling with his legal problems, James D. Green was attempting to revive his political career in Manatee County. "Jim Green, who is a self-resurrected specimen of the defunct Radical party, of this county," one report declared, "has again surfaced, and declares himself a candidate for the Legislature." Although Green lost the election, his campaign scared some Manatee Democrats who set out to silence him once and for all.[5] Ziba King filed criminal charges against him for "maliciously threatening to accuse another of a crime with intent of extorting money," a charge resembling that made against James T. Magbee. State's attorney Stephen M. Sparkman then took the case to a grand jury selected from a list of Green's enemies and improperly drawn by clerk John G. Spottswood, and on May 10, 1879, achieved an indictment. The bar set up a clamor for immediate trial in Judge Henry L. Mitchell's court but Magbee stepped in and saved his old friend (and sometime nemesis) by arranging for a continuance.[6]

In June the circumstances of Jim Green's indictment were made public in a letter to the Key West *Key of the Gulf*, and the ensuing criticism directed at Manatee officials became so intense that they looked around for a scapegoat and found one in Spotts-wood.[7] In early November the Manatee board of commissioners suspended Spottswood after he acknowledged "that the jury list had been changed," and two weeks later Mitchell, Sparkman, A.J. Knight, and Hillsborough sheriff D. Isaac Craft reached an understanding with the clerk that, if he would resign, no criminal charges would be brought against him. The matter of *State* v. *James D. Green*, although not dismissed, was allowed to fade quietly until forgotten.[8]

Bolstered by the failed effort to silence him, James D. Green acted in 1880 to reorganize the Manatee County Republican party. The attempt failed when his candidate for the state house of representatives, John F. Bartholf, withdrew in disgust at state-level Republican squabbles and announced that he had become a Democrat, ensuring the election of Green's brother-in-law, Democrat and cattleman John W. Whidden.[9] For the next few years Green continued to speak out, primarily through letters to Florida newspapers, while supporting himself and family with a successful farm and citrus grove. He died April 8, 1886, and was buried at Pine Level.[10]

While Democrats were consolidating their rule over Republicans in Manatee County, they were squabbling among themselves in Polk. Beginning in the early 1870s, Polk County politics had reflected a division between residents of the Peace River area, who tended to have been in the area longer and to be involved in the cattle business, and settlers in the county's northern half, who generally had lived in Polk a shorter time and who earned their living through farming. Because Polk County had never had a significant Republican vote, redemption on the local level simply meant a continuation of the old divisions within the Democratic party.

In the first election for member of the state house of representatives from Polk in the post-Reconstruction era, that split clearly was evident when on November 8, 1878, John Wesley Bryant, who lived north of modern-day Lakeland, defeated Fort Meade merchant and cattleman Sherod E. Roberts by a narrow majority. The opposite results, with the same two men, had come out of the 1874 election. In each of the next three such elections Bryant was challenged by a Peace River resident from an older family and each time he won, narrowly defeating Streaty Parker in 1880 and widening his majorities over Benjamin F. Blount in 1882 and S.I. Pearce in 1884.[11]

A county's state representative in the 1870s and early 1880s had a great deal of power because, under the state's constitution, almost all local officials were appointed by the governor, and recommendations for appointments made by a state representative of the same party carried a great deal of influence with the governor. While recognizing this power, John Wesley Bryant also realized that for every appointment he caused to be made, he would be alienating those who either did not get the job or who did not like the man who did. To escape the dilemma, he announced after his election in 1878 that Polk's voters could "meet at each Precinct in the county and elect our officers, and . . . that if the people would elect their officers, he would do all in his power to have them appointed." Residents held a Democratic convention that almost immediately "split all asunder" those from the northern and those from the Peace River areas of the county. As one local man put it, "We are all Democrats but there seems to be a great deal of political strife existing among us in regard to County Officers."[12]

Elections were held in Polk after the convention and Bryant did recommend the winners for appointment, but over the next eight years the continuing friction often caused long delays in filling vacancies. A description of the situation appeared in 1880 when John Davidson resigned as county treasurer. Signed by "Observer," the comments read: "Since Judge Davidson resigned there has been several efforts made by both parties, rather both rings, for we are not blessed with two parties, but are cursed with two rings. They watch each other, and when a motion is put on foot by one, the other will then set to work to thwart their designs. This is the reason that we are without a Treasurer, and for this reason there is a chance for us to continue without one for some time."[13]

The split in Polk County politics also affected the election of a state senator. In 1878 this had not been much of a problem. On September 4, 1878, representatives of Polk and Manatee counties— united in Senate District 27—had met at Fort Green and, after a series of votes, had nominated Manatee's F.B. Hagan for the senate, with the understanding that, at the next election in 1880, "Polk should have the choice of the nominations." Two months

Cornelius B. Lightsey (1831–90) (*standing*) and his son, Ulysses A. "Doc" Lightsey (1860–1928) about 1880–85. Courtesy Elizabeth Alexander.

later Hagan was elected unopposed. When it came time to elect Hagan's successor two years later, however, it was quite a different matter.[14]

The election of 1878 had shown Peace River area political leaders that Polk County's electoral balance of power was tipped slightly in favor of those living in the county's northern half. Anxious to preserve their own influence, the Peace River men decided upon a plan by which a candidate selected by them would be elected to the state senate. On the evening of July 27, 1880, which had been court day at Bartow, the Peace River men, under the leadership of David Hughes and Benjamin F. Blount, held "a meeting of the citizens of Polk County" pursuant to which a "Democratic Executive Committee" was organized to send delegates to a "Senatorial Convention" of Polk and Manatee counties. No prior notice of the meeting had been given north county men. The senatorial convention met at Fort Meade on August 13, and of the Polk County precincts only Fort Meade, Bartow, and Negro Ridge (near modern Mulberry) were represented. After a brief attempt to secure the nomination for George W. Hendry of Fort Meade, the convention chose the Reverend Adam A. Robinson of Manatee County. Robinson's selection, in light of the prior commitment that "Polk should have the choice of the nomination," was justified by pointing out that Robinson had been nominated by a Polk delegate, Solomon Page.[15]

The political leaders of northern Polk, among them former state senator Mitchell G. Fortner, were furious. Fortner announced his own intention to seek the senate seat, and the contest was joined. Campaigning against the respected A.A. Robinson, a well-liked Methodist minister and former superintendent of schools in Manatee, Fortner's supporters were reduced to spreading rumors that Robinson "favored the teaching of a negro school in his community," to which Robinson's backers responded by attacking Fortner for having supported a watered-down civil rights bill during his term in the senate. On November 2 Robinson beat Fortner by a combined vote of 654 to 446. Robinson's Polk County majority, however, was but 9 out of 417 votes. At the same election Polk's representative, John Wesley Bryant, defeated Peace River cattleman Streaty Parker by 27 out of 493 votes cast.[16]

Adam Robinson served in the senate only a single year before resigning to become Florida's commissioner of immigration. To fill his vacant seat it was necessary to call an election in 1882, an action that revived the political battle in Polk County. This time Fortner and his allies were ready. In late September Edgar M. Graham announced his candidacy with the support of Manatee's Democratic establishment. Poised for a run against Fortner, Graham also received the backing of Polk's Peace River leaders and of the county's only newspaper, the Bartow *Informant*. Many voters still harbored resentments at the manner of Robinson's nomination, and on election day Fortner carried Polk by a better than three to one margin, with a substantial majority in Manatee.[17]

County division

The principle of rotation by which Polk had claimed a right to the District 27 senate seat in 1880 and 1882 operated to guarantee the seat to a Manatee County man in 1884. For the purpose of selecting a Democratic candidate a convention was held at Fort Meade on September 2 and in "a political lovefeast" John W. Whidden was nominated by a unanimous vote. Two months later Whidden was elected to a four-year term without opposition.[18] On the same day Grover Cleveland was elected president of the United States, the first Democrat so honored since the Civil War. In celebration of that historic event a "grand demonstration" was held at Bartow during which "Captain Dave Hughes, mounted on a charger enveloped in a great flag on which were painted the names of Cleveland and [Governor] Perry, paraded, armed with a new broom, around the public square at the head of at least two hundred men."[19]

Between 1884 and 1886 the railroads came to Polk County and the Peace River Valley, and with them came more people and new towns. By the time for electioneering in 1886, however, the Peace River towns appeared to have a slight edge in population. Meanwhile, the state's constitution was being rewritten to provide, among other things, for local election of most county officers.[20]

To pave the way for local election of Polk's officers, a county Democratic convention was held at Bartow on October 2, 1886, its organization firmly in the hands of men from the northern part of the county. At their suggestion John W. Bryant was nominated by acclamation for reelection to the house and an entire slate for county offices was approved. The Bartow and Fort Meade delegates bolted and staged a rump convention at which Ulysses A. Lightsey of Fort Meade was nominated to oppose Bryant. After a short, fierce campaign, Lightsey edged Bryant out of office by 6 votes out of 1,312 cast.[21]

The Polk election of 1886 was an even more bitter struggle than usual between the county's northern and southern halves. The emergence of towns along the railroad and their subsequent growth had resulted by the summer of 1886 in a movement to transfer the county seat from Bartow to Lakeland, an effort strongly resisted by Bartow and Fort Meade that left "a great deal of hard feeling among the people of the different sections of the county." When Bryant lost to a Fort Meade man in November, north countians mounted a full-scale effort to divide the county. Representative Lightsey and Senator Whidden eventually were able to bar passage of any such legislation. Although feelings continued to run strong, subsequent political events overshadowed the issue and leaders of both sides agreed "that the discussion of county division be discouraged for the present."[22]

While Senator Whidden was working to stop a division of Polk County, he was doing his best to bring one about in Manatee. Since the county's creation in 1855, Peace River settlers had resented and at times tried to sever their county ties with coastal areas and residents. The coming of the Florida Southern Railway in 1886 gave the Peace River area easy access to transportation and markets, and along with the railroad had come new settlers to build and expand the area's towns. No longer was the coast needed for its markets, its ports, or its people.

On February 5, 1887, a citizens' meeting was held at Pine Level to discuss dividing the county. When some Peace River men indicated they would be satisfied with moving the county seat to somewhere on the railroad, they were opposed by Bradenton and Sarasota residents who for twenty-one years had been making the long overland trek to Pine Level to conduct legal and county business. At a second Pine Level meeting on March 15 it was agreed to divide the county. With appropriate enabling legislation processed through the legislature by Representative John Pelot and Senator Whidden, in April the more populous eastern portion of Manatee became the county of DeSoto. Named in honor of the

Spanish explorer Hernando de Soto, the new county contained within its bounds all of the present counties of Hardee, Highlands, DeSoto, Glades, and Charlotte.[23]

Governor Perry was prompt in appointing DeSoto County's first commissioners, who were, according to one resident, "a very efficient board" and "above suspicion or reproach . . . better fitted for the task of organizing, than any other five men in the county." These men were S.T. Langford, Marion G. Carlton, T.O. Parker, B.F. Richards, and Peter Brown. Also appointed for DeSoto were: T.J. Sparkman, superintendent of schools; Oscar T. Stanford, county judge; Bryant G. Granger, tax assessor; F.B. Hagan, treasurer; Bud P. Clark, surveyor; Charles W. Carlton, clerk of the circuit court; O.H. Dishong, sheriff; W.C. Hayman, superintendent of registration; and H.E. Carlton, tax collector.[24]

When DeSoto's board of county commissioners held its first meeting in early July 1887, it was a foregone conclusion that the county seat would be moved from Pine Level. The question was, to where? Albert W. Gilchrist had offered to donate lots at Nocatee for the public buildings and W.H. Pearce had offered more than eighty acres at a town he proposed to build at Mare's Branch, five miles north of Arcadia, but most people felt the choice would come down to Arcadia or Fort Ogden. A public meeting was held at Wauchula on July 23 to nominate places to be voted on and an election was scheduled for November 3.[25]

Prior to the election every community made its pitch. Isaac Trabue, for example, offered the county a city block at Punta Gorda and promised "to erect thereon a courthouse and jail, to cost not less than $10,000." Nocatee opted for a public relations spectacle and in late August held a "mass meeting" at Pine Level during which "Nocatee was declared the unanimous choice of the meeting."[26]

The November election proved so inconclusive that it prompted Isaac Trabue to demand an election on dividing the new county in two. That question, as well as the location of the county seat, was put on the ballot in late December. Although county division was voted down, in the poll for a county seat "ten different towns were voted for and the settlement of the question is as far off as it was when the county was divided." The 506 votes cast were divided by: Nocatee, 224; Arcadia, 159; Zolfo, 60; Trabue, 29;

DeSoto City, 16; Charlie Apopka, 7; Fort Ogden, 6; Punta Gorda, 2; Charlotte Harbor, 2; and Hickory Bluff, 1.[27]

Tired of the controversy, the county commission waited eight months before again placing the issue of the county seat before the voters. During the interim, Arcadia's backers lobbied hard to sell their offer to erect a courthouse costing not less than three thousand dollars, while Nocatee made "strong preparations to defeat Arcadia." Even Pine Level entered the contest, arguing that it "was the old county seat, and has a very substantial court-house, now occupied by the county." When the ballots were counted on August 4, no town received a majority: Arcadia, 295; Fort Ogden, 186; Nocatee, 110; and Pine Level, 59.[28]

When on November 6, 1888, 875 men cast ballots, Arcadia won by a majority of 21 votes. Where nothing resembling a town had stood less than four years before, John W. Whidden and others had created a city and made it the seat of a new county. Arcadia's offer of three thousand dollars for a courthouse was satisfied by a donation of that amount by Whidden, Lewis H. Parker, and Jasper N. Parker. The county appropriated a like sum and con-tracted with Peyton R. Read to erect the structure. By February 1889 it was reported, "The old court-house and jail at Pine Level was sold at public auction by Sheriff Dishong . . . to J.M. Bour-land of Pine Level, for $202, he being the highest bidder. The iron cage in the jail will be removed and hauled to Arcadia where it will probably be used in the new jail when it is built." As Arca-dia's success had doomed Pine Level, during this period the older and much larger town of Fort Ogden reported "a general moving to Arcadia."[29]

Prohibition

The cause of temperance was launched in the Peace River Valley on July 8, 1871, when the Reverend E.S. Tyner of Tampa made the long overland journey to Bartow "and succeeded in organizing a division of the Sons of Temperance." Although the Reverend Tyner's anti-liquor crusade did not result in immediate reform, it took firm hold on the Peace River frontier and built in intensity throughout the 1870s. By 1880 the cause had become so strong that the Polk-Manatee Democratic senatorial convention formally endorsed "what is known as 'The Local Option Law,' firmly believing that such legislation tends to the elevation of our people and the improvement of their morals." Local option laws would give local voters the opportunity to ban liquor sales. The convention's nominee, the Reverend Adam A. Robinson, was known widely as "an able exponent and advocate" of the "local option movement."[30] Some local option supporters urged more immediate action. As early as 1881 it was said that Fort Ogden and Pine Level would refuse to issue new liquor licenses, "yet we have the evil to contend with at Ogden and Pine Level till the present license expires." More direct action was taken at Fort Meade where merchant Philip Dzialynski succeeded in getting most citizens to sign a pledge "that not a foot of ground should be leased, sold or given away whereon might be built a drinking saloon of any kind where intoxicating beverages are sold." When R.C. Langford proceeded to construct a saloon in March 1881, arsonists destroyed his "bar-room and fixtures." A year and a half later, the Fort Meade post office was broken into and money "being sent off for the liquors to start a bar-room" was stolen.[31]

In April 1885 Polk County had not a single liquor license in effect, and it was reported, "The board of commissioners are inflexibly opposed to liquor saloons, as are also the majority of the better class of Polk county, even those who conscientiously take their toddy or their bitters." The flood of new settlers from northern states where the cause of temperance was less popular was about to change that established opposition, and the following month a majority of the registered voters of Bartow, Fort Meade, and Lakeland had signed petitions authorizing seven saloons. One such petition drive provided the backdrop for one of the most violent episodes in the history of the Peace River Valley in the post-Reconstruction era.[32]

One of the saloons opened in Bartow in 1885 was that of Johnson, Daniels & Co., owned by Churchill Johnson and H.B. Daniels. To get up enough signatures on their petitions, the proprietors had employed two brothers, Dan and Lony Mann, promising them a share in the profits of the saloon if the drive was successful. Dan, in particular, was well known in the county and had incurred the wrath of some Polk leaders when in July 1884 he had been the single juror who held out for mercy in the murder trial of William W. Willingham. Specifically, Dan had incurred the wrath of G.A. Hanson, editor of the Bartow *Informant*, ardent prohibitionist, and a prosecutor in the Willingham case. Dan also was well known for his love of a drink and his quick temper, a combination which had gotten him into trouble in the fall of 1885 when in "a little affair of honor" he nearly "whittled unto death" his brother-in-law. Subsequent to the knife fight, Dan had "skipped until his kinsman recovered," and not until May 1886 could he get back to claim his share of the saloon's proceeds of which he suspected he had been "frozen out."[33]

It was said that Dan and Lony Mann had been drinking when on May 15, 1886, they journeyed from their Winter Haven home to Bartow. Their tempers exploded when the saloon's proprietors refused to pay them. Dan yelled at the saloon keeper, "You get the money up, because I'll be back," and the two brothers rushed from the saloon to a nearby store where they purchased a box of .32-calibre cartridges. Loading their guns, the men set out again for the saloon, Dan in a buggy and Lony on foot.[34]

Alarmed at Dan Mann's threat, Johnson and Daniels hastily summoned the town marshal, W.S. Campbell, who intercepted the angry brothers on the street. Attempting to make an arrest, Campbell fell to loudly "remonstrating" with Dan when up rushed the town night watchman, Jack McCormick, who had a reputation as a "real tough character." Spotting McCormick, Campbell yelled to him for help, and the night watchman lunged at the mule drawing Dan's buggy and grabbed for its reins. In the excitement, Lony drew his pistol and jumped to his brother's defense, his shot grazing McCormick's left temple and ear. In the resulting "melee," both Manns apparently were wounded, and Dan shot Marshal Campbell through the heart and killed him.[35]

As Marshal Campbell fell, Lony Mann jumped into Dan's buggy and the two brothers fled from town. Sheriff R.P. Kilpatrick, who "happened to be on the spot," summoned a posse of fifteen from "the fifty men on the street" and sped off in pursuit. Half a mile out of town the Manns' buggy hit a stump and overturned, injuring one of the brothers badly. Dan and Lony made it only about another half a mile on foot before they were spotted by T.S. Hull, who held them "at bay" until the posse arrived. The brothers were returned to Bartow through crowds yelling, "Lynch them," "Hang them," "Kill them," and "Shoot them." It was about 6:00 P.M. when they were lodged in the county jail.[36]

As the Manns were being locked up, the crowd outside the jail grew violent when Marshal Campbell's wife and young children were brought out to view "the dead corpse lying in the street." Heads were cool enough, however, to notify the sheriff quietly that the Manns would be lynched, and at 8:00 P.M. a crowd estimated at two hundred descended upon the jail. After token resistance, the sheriff surrendered his keys and the prisoners were hauled to a nearby oak tree. While Dan was being strung up, Lony made a break for it and took about thirty steps before being shotgunned, then hanged as well.[37]

The deaths of W.S. Campbell and the Mann brothers did not end the saga of the Johnson, Daniels & Co. saloon, nor that of night watchman Jack McCormick. Through the summer of 1886 the proprietors of the saloon struggled unsuccessfully to obtain enough signatures on petitions to renew their license. At two o'clock on the morning of September 22, 1886, eight days before its license was due to expire, the saloon burst into flames and a great deal of Bartow's business district was destroyed in the resulting blaze. Six days later Churchill Johnson, H.B. Daniels, and Bartow night watchman Jack McCormick were arrested for arson. The disposition of the charges is unknown, although McCormick was allowed to remain in the city's employ as marshal until January 1888 when he was "impeached and removed" by the town council.[38]

A long held dream of prohibition supporters came true in 1885 when an amendment to the state constitution was proposed giving each county the local option whether to prohibit the sale of liquor. The first Polk County election under the new law was held on September 1, 1887, preceded by an intense campaign between Prohibitionists and Anti-Prohibitionists. Supporting the cause of temperance was G.A. Hanson, Bartow lawyer Frank Clark, county school superintendent John Snoddy, and long-time resident Benjamin F. Blount. Clark's law partner, James W. Brady, led the wets, assisted by county judge J.A. Fortner. So bitter did the atmosphere become in the closing weeks before the election that "a mob" threatened Homeland's black residents over their votes, an action which prompted white citizens to arm the blacks as well as to reserve for themselves "a few Winchesters for private purposes."[39]

Despite intense excitement generated over the election, only

1,180 of Polk's almost 2,000 registered voters turned out, and it appeared that prohibition had won by 839 votes—making Polk the first county in South Florida to go dry. While drys celebrated, however, the wets went to court and before long the election was adjudged "void for irregularities." While the election may have been void, its benefits to its backers were not. In 1888, lawyer Frank Clark was elected to the state house of representatives as a result of the notoriety gained through his prohibition work. Once in office, Clark helped secure G.A. Hanson an appointment to succeed Henry L. Mitchell as circuit judge.[40]

The Polk election of 1888 was wild by anyone's standards. Wets and drys faced off; north countians still harbored resentments against south countians; new settlers were pouring in; and a yellow fever scare erupted for the second year in a row. Polarization became so pronounced that the county Democratic convention was unable to agree on any nominations. The resulting race was dubbed a "free-for-all," and out of it emerged not only Frank Clark but also John W. Bryant who resurrected his career by achieving election to the state senate.[41]

A second wet and dry election for Polk County was held on December 30, 1891, and this time the drys prevailed by a vote of 524 to 125. After two years of prohibition a third election was held April 5, 1894. Wets argued that all the liquor anyone could want to drink was available from unlicensed outlets known as "blind tigers," while drys demanded tougher enforcement. When the ballots were counted a narrow victory was proclaimed for prohibition. The county remained dry while the "blind tigers" stayed open. Toward the end of the century a Law and Order League at Bartow, still trying to stamp out drinking, was "said to be contemplating the employment of professional detectives to assist in the suppression of gambling and whisky selling."[42]

From 1887 to 1895 DeSoto County also held a series of local option elections. The elections themselves did not cause much of a stir, and the results, wet or dry, did not seem to change much of anything. As one Fort Ogden man put it on October 1, 1890: "From the first day of October this county is legally dry but practically wet as before. The jug trade will now be in order and there will be no scarcity of patrons, and kerosene cans will be brought into use again to manufacture the large cane crop into stimulants. There is not an old cracker in the county that is not an expert in distilling with a kerosene can, and the county going dry makes this rum more plentiful and cheaper."[43]

On May 30, 1895, a number of DeSoto's leading citizens decided to organize to put an end to the liquor business once and for all. The result was the creation of a DeSoto County temperance association with S.B. Carson, president; C.J. Carlton, secretary; W.C. Hayman, treasurer; and T.J. Sparkman, chairman of the executive committee. After several months of effort, the association's work paid off when, on August 27, the county voted overwhelmingly dry, the wets tallying only 10 votes. One local observer asserted even before the election, "It requires no prophet to tell the result, which will be dry by a large majority, though all of those who vote 'dry' are not temperate. Saloons are an impediment to those who wish to make rum. The crop of sugar cane is large and good, and the sale of liquor will not be confined to Arcadia and Punta Gorda."[44]

Populism

For almost two decades preceding the 1888 elections, Polk County politics revolved around factions within the Democratic party. DeSoto County's first attempt at elections in 1888 revealed a similar split, as control of the party organization was seized by individuals closely associated with Arcadia and with the new county's agricultural community. To an extent these men found a leader and spokesman in Thomas J. Pepper, editor of the *Arcadian*. Furious at their exclusion from party affairs, the county's cattle interests shifted their support from the regular Democratic nominees to an independent ticket headed by the county's wealthiest cattleman, Ziba King, as a candidate for the state senate seat shared by DeSoto and Manatee. King won, but the regular Democratic nominee, the Reverend John W. Hendry, defeated King's choice for the DeSoto house seat by a narrow majority. No Republican organization existed at the time, and the Republican voters, numbering about two hundred, supported Hendry, himself a former Republican.[45]

Following the turbulent Polk and DeSoto elections of 1888, politics in both counties were dominated for the remainder of the century by the effects of the Populist movement. Growing out of poor economic conditions for farmers in the 1880s, populism generally is considered to have had its origins in the Farmers Alliance, which was introduced into Florida in 1887. Originally an economic rather than a political organization, the Farmers Alliance strove to improve the lives of its members through cooperative action. In 1890, however, the organization entered politics, basing its platform on the Ocala Demands, which included the abolition of national banks, the prohibition of dealing in farm futures, a graduated income tax, the recovery of land from railroads, direct election of U.S. senators, and the free and unlimited coinage of silver at the ratio of sixteen to one of gold. Most supporters of the Ocala Demands sought at first to work within the Democratic party, but by May 1891 activists had launched a national third party, the Peoples or Populist party.[46]

In 1890 Farmers Alliance members brought their influence to bear on the Democratic parties of both DeSoto and Polk counties. The main issue separating them from regular Democrats was the reelection of U.S. Senator Wilkinson Call, whom alliance members opposed over his support for national banks. In DeSoto, Call men, including John W. Whidden, Jasper N. Parker, Albert W. Gilchrist, Ziba King, F.B. Hagan, and S.A. Sauls captured control of the county organization, while anti-Call Democrats, irate at being excluded from county nominations, joined with Republicans in opposition. Regular Democrats handily won, but the impact of the victory was somewhat skewed because cattleman Thomas O. Parker, the regular Democratic nominee for the state house of representatives, also served as president of the Arcadia Farmers Alliance Exchange.[47]

Similar confusion occurred in Polk, where the state representative, Frank Clark, a strong supporter of the alliance, was a personal friend of Call's. Clark proved to be one of Call's strongest allies, and the senator's supporters, mostly regulars, easily won election. W.H. Pearce, who launched an independent candidacy for the legislature as an alliance man, was repudiated by the alliance leadership which honored an agreement to support the Democratic nominee. Frank Clark and John W. Trammell were returned to the house of representatives.[48]

The Democratic parties of both DeSoto and Polk "split wide open" in 1892. One regular Democrat, in comments applicable to both counties, observed, "Polk county has never had such a shaking up on a political question as it has had during the cam-

Left, William H. Reynolds (1843–1901) was first elected as state senator from Polk County in 1892. His election reflected the increasing political power of the new communities in the northern half of the county built along the line of the South Florida Railroad. Reynolds served as president of the Florida Senate and in 1896 was elected state comptroller. He died while serving in that office. From the Jacksonville *Florida Times-Union,* December 27, 1896. *Right,* John Wesley Bryant (1845–1926), Polk County's state senator in 1891. Jacksonville *Florida Times-Union,* May 27, 1891.

paign just closed. From the very start it was warm and the further it went the hotter it got. It was not the old contest between the democratic and republican parties, but it was a contest growing out of local ambition and in which third party people of the county, and our old enemy the republicans, took a hand."[49]

Just as the reelection of Senator Call had provided a focal point for the 1890 election, the candidacy for governor of Democrat Henry L. Mitchell, former circuit judge for Polk and DeSoto, proved to be divisive in 1892. Regular Democrats supported Mitchell, while many alliance members and Populists refused to accept him. In Polk the split came in mid-April when alliance members led by Frank Clark and Senator John W. Bryant, former president of the county alliance, walked out of the Democratic convention and established their own party, the Independent Jeffersonian Democrats. They nominated Bryant for reelection to his senate seat and Thomas J. Altman and John W. Durrance for the house. To oppose Bryant regular Democrats turned to William H. Reynolds of Lakeland, clerk of the house of representatives from 1885 to 1889, and tapped W. Jordan Durrance and Hardy F. Fortner for the lower house. In the end, the regulars eked out a narrow win with majorities of between twenty and sixty votes out of more than 1,300 cast.[50]

In DeSoto County sixteen delegates led by alliance president John W. Hendry walked out of the county Democratic convention when party regulars refused to adopt the Ocala Demands. Organizing themselves as the People's party, the bolters nominated a complete slate for county offices, including Charles A. Turner for the senate and Henry H. Norris for the house.[51] The regulars turned to John W. Whidden to succeed fellow cattleman Ziba King in the senate and to Albert W. Gilchrist to oppose Norris for the house. Whidden and Gilchrist outdistanced their opponents by respectable majorities, and all Democratic nominees were elected. One Democrat reported: "There is a grand jubilation in Arcadia tonight. The eyes of the whole state have been on this county."[52]

The results of the election of 1894 in DeSoto County proved a repeat of 1892. Henry H. Norris again served as the Populist nominee to oppose Albert Gilchrist, and again Gilchrist defeated him. Although Democrats once more carried all county offices the reappearance of two factions within the party was troubling. One was headed by Thomas J. Pepper, who had been elected mayor of Arcadia in December of 1893, and the other by John W. Whidden and Ziba King. Polk County Democrats likewise emerged victorious. The Independent Jeffersonian Democrats had become Populists under the leadership of James T. Hancock, Jr., and waged an energetic campaign, but all their candidates went down to defeat. In the legislative races, James W. Brady, former law partner of Frank Clark, and Dr. James S. Wade of Homeland defeated Populists J.W. Durrance and former county alliance president H.P. Walker, as well as Republican J.W. Powell. The race was closer than many Democrats expected, however, and Walker only narrowly failed to be elected.[53]

The high water mark of populism in the Peace River Valley came in 1896. As early as April of that year it was known that the race would be "a lively and close one" in DeSoto, but not until the summer did the Democratic party's two factions split over the question of remaining on the gold standard or authorizing the free coinage of silver as advocated by Democratic presidential candidate William Jennings Bryan. The party's old guard supported the gold standard. Thomas J. Pepper, *Punta Gorda Herald* editor H.B. Seward, and their followers supported Dr. Oscar T. Stanford against Gilchrist, running as an Independent, and M.S. Stevens against Democratic senatorial candidate Henry W. Fuller of Manatee County. The Populists immediately endorsed Stanford and Stevens and entered nominees for other county offices. Adding to the excitement, DeSoto's Republicans entered the fray, tapping former Democrat Francis C.M. Boggess as a candidate for the senate and William N. Hall to oppose Gilchrist for the house. Shifting coalitions and changing tickets caused one resident to state, "I'll be darned if I hardly know what I am these days. I've always voted the democratic ticket, but now I don't hear anything but free silver and gold standard; so if there's anything to be had free, I guess I'll drop in the swim." Enough DeSoto voters dropped in the swim to propel Stanford into the house and to elect Populists to county offices. Only in the senate race did the coalition falter when H.W. Fuller received a large enough majority in Manatee to elect him over M.S. Stevens.[54]

Polk County's Populists were not so fortunate. No split developed in the Democratic ranks, and the Democratic ticket was a strong one with James N. Hooker for the senate and J.A. Cox and F.A. Wolff for the house. To successfully oppose the Democrats, Populists needed Republican support, but the Republicans on August 11 nominated R.J. Hodgson of Fort Meade as their candidate in the senate race and William Oren and E.E. Mizell for the house. In the end, the Democrats swept everything. Two years later the county's Populists and Republicans offered a fusion ticket, naming Republican George Craig of Fort Meade and Populist H.P. Walker as their candidates for the legislature. Democrats George W. Hendry and D.H. Sloan easily took the field, and the regular Democratic party maintained the grip it had had on Polk County politics since the end of the Civil war.[55]

Ziba King and his DeSoto County allies were determined to prevent a recurrence in 1898 of the Populist sweep of 1896. In June 1897 editor H.B. Seward of the *Punta Gorda Herald* retired, leaving the paper in the hands of R.E. Watkins. The following month the board of county commissioners stripped Thomas J. Pepper and the *Arcadian* of its county printing contract, handing the lucrative county business to the *Herald*. Pepper was forced to suspend publication. King, together with J.H. Treadwell and J.L. Jones, then bought the *Arcadian's* plant from Pepper's creditors, opened a new paper known as the *DeSoto County News*, and hired *Herald* editor R.E. Watkins to run it for them. Watkins then surrendered the *Herald's* county printing contract, and the board of commissioners reawarded it to the *DeSoto County News*, thus eliminating the most visible symbols of the Democratic party split and at the same time guaranteeing a voice for the regular Democratic establishment. It worked like a charm.[56]

The reunited Democratic Party in 1898 fielded a full slate of candidates headed by Ziba King who ran for O.T. Stanford's house seat. The Populists selected M.G. Carlton to oppose King and named a full ticket to support him, but it was not nearly enough. The Republicans stayed out of the race, refusing to run their own candidates or to support the Populists, and soon it was assumed throughout the county that the Populists "cannot elect a single officer." On election day that forecast came true and the Democrats forced their way back into power. Through years of Republican rule and Populist revolt, the Democrats triumphed in the end.[57]

The post-Reconstruction era saw a radical change in the nature Peace River politics. Democrats used to fighting among themselves were confronted with new issues and new personalities as they strove to maintain their grip on elective office. Prohibition and populism were the key forces behind these confrontations, and for a time the pressures of those issues would tear the party apart. By the end of the nineteenth century, however, the regular Democratic party, even in the face of a reborn Republican party, reemerged in firm control of both DeSoto and Polk counties. The leadership of the two counties turned, in the final election of the century, to Ziba King and George W. Hendry, who numbered among the true pioneers of the Peace River Valley.

19
Phosphate and Freezes

T HE ARRIVAL OF THE RAILROAD in the mid-1880s brought thousands of new settlers, higher land values, and the promise of permanent prosperity to the Peace River Valley. Within a few years tremendous deposits of phosphates were discovered and, in a boom-time atmosphere, exploited. That economic boom ended in the 1890s, however, with economic depression, crippling freezes, and lost fortunes.

Pebble phosphate

In 1890 Florida caught a phosphate fever which a major state newspaper described as "apparently epidemic." While reviewing mining prospects throughout the state the paper noted "large and valuable deposits in Polk and DeSoto counties, . . . extensive plants already erected at Zolfo and Arcadia, and . . . the daily mining and shipping of phosphate from those places." At Peace River the phosphate craze had just begun to strike "in real earnest," and as early as January 2, 1890, it was reported that "spades and augers are in good demand."[1]

The history of the Peace River Valley phosphate boom dates to

1881, when Capt. J. Francis LeBaron, an engineer with the U.S. Army Corps of Engineers, was detailed to make a survey of the Peace River area to determine the feasibility of opening a navigable waterway for steamboats from the St. Johns River to Charlotte Harbor. LeBaron made two discoveries on his survey which still affect the life of the Peace River Valley. The first finding was that, in the absence of an expensive canal and lock system, the proposed waterway was impractical, and the second was his discovery "in the bed of the river certain bars or deposits of sand and gravel and pebble, which later he readily recognized as bone phosphate."[2]

For several years after his discovery of bone phosphate or, as it would be called, river pebble phosphate, LeBaron attempted without success to interest investors in its economic potential, specifically in the possible profits to be derived from the use of phosphates in the production of fertilizer. Word of LeBaron's finds had begun to leak out, and one of his associate engineers with the army, T.S. Morehead, capitalized on the news by purchasing in May 1887 a tract of two hundred acres of Arcadia which included "a fine bar or deposit in the river at that point." Morehead departed the area hurriedly, however, when yellow fever broke out in Havana and Key West, and rumors began circulating of a possible quarantine of northbound traffic out of South Florida.[3]

Morehead was not the only person to whom news of the phosphate discoveries was of interest. A few months before Morehead's purchase, John C. Jones of Orlando and W.J. McKee of Palatka went on a hunt down the river and concluded from their finds that immediate steps should be taken to initiate a more thorough survey and to prepare to purchase huge tracts of land. Among the persons to whom they turned was George W. Scott, president of the Scott Manufacturing Company, a "large fertilizer concern at Atlanta," who organized an expedition to test and evaluate the discoveries. In spite of the yellow fever threat, the Atlanta businessman departed down river from Fort Meade in late June 1887 along with his company's chemist, Dr. N.P. Pratt; W.J. McKee; Orlando engineer and geologist M.T. Singleton, who represented other investors; and their guide, British engineer M.G. Darbishire, a resident of Fort Meade.[4] Although the party attempted to disguise its purpose as a camp hunt, one resident of Fort Meade noted as it set off, "It is surmised that they are out for something else beside pleasure and will combine it with business, judging from the instruments they carried."[5]

The expedition had no trouble locating phosphate deposits, and within only a few days an Arcadia man reported "several parties in town lately who seem to be greatly interested in the extensive bone beds near the town. They don't give much information, but ask a thousand and one questions and spend most of their time digging and getting the [survey] numbers of the river land." To minimize suspicion, Scott and McKee put out the story that they were opening a plant to extract tannic acid from saw palmetto bushes and were easily able to purchase 5,500 acres of river lands near Arcadia. The increasing threat of yellow fever coupled with disagreements among investors hampered further activities for the rest of the year, and not until November 1, 1889, was the company revived, reorganized, and named the Peace River Phosphate Company. Under the supervision of M.T. Singleton, it began "erecting works, dry kilns, steam dredgeboats and barges" near Arcadia and projected the commencement of shipments for June 1, 1890.[6]

In the meantime, T.S. Morehead had been busy. In the year following his initial purchase of the sand bars at Arcadia, Morehead bought an additional four hundred acres and concluded an agreement by which George W. Scott would purchase his entire output of phosphate. In May 1888, Morehead's Arcadia Phosphate Company had begun mining, drying, and shipping phosphate to Atlanta. Scott also had been busy. In addition to his agreement with Morehead and his connection with McKee, the Atlanta businessman on his own purchased seven hundred acres of Peace River land and in May 1889 organized the DeSoto Phosphate Mining Company. Within six months the firm had purchased thirty-six miles of Peace River between Fort Meade and the mouth of Big Charlie Apopka Creek and had erected "a very complete plant on the river bank where the Florida Southern railroad crosses about a mile north of Zolfo." On November 25, 1889, the company placed in operation "a steam dredge boat and a centrifugal dredge for removing the gravel from the river" and seven barges, towed by mules "over about three miles of tow-path graded or built along the river banks," to carry the gravel to the company's plant.[7]

From its small beginnings at Arcadia and Zolfo, the phosphate craze spread the length of the Peace River Valley. Production in the year 1890 jumped to over 56,000 tons, compared to 2,813 tons marketed two years earlier. The 1890 production tripled in 1891, and in 1892 reached 354,000 tons. Creating this output were at least eighteen phosphate companies whose operations stretched from Bartow to Hickory Bluff and Cleveland. Most were owned by northern or English investors, but a few were wholly or partially controlled by Peace River residents, including the Moore & Tatum Phosphate Company near Homeland; the Homeland Pebble Phosphate Company, Judge T.W. Anderson, treasurer; the Whitaker Phosphate and Fertilizer Company, Isaac Whitaker of Homeland, president; and the Fort Meade Phosphate, Fertilizer, Land and Improvement Company, of which J.E. Robeson of Fort Meade was an officer.[8]

With the phosphate boom came another industry to Peace River. In January 1890 word arrived that a fertilizer factory would be built at Fort Meade. Fort Meade's *South Florida Progress* declared: "The importance of this simple announcement on the progress of the town and district can scarcely be appreciated at the present time. The business of the town will receive an impetus compared to which a boom, in the general acceptance of the term, will be a very trifling thing." One year later the Whitaker Phosphate and Fertilizer Company announced plans for a similar facility, while only a mile to the north the Homeland Phosphate Company launched its fifteen by fifty-foot Great Ark barge on the river, which meant that "the immense Heald & Cisco pump will soon be throwing Peace river pebbles, water, sand, etc., on the top of the barge at the rate of fifteen hundred gallons a minute, and it may be reasonably supposed a large portion of the result will be valuable phosphate."[9]

The proximity of "valuable phosphate" caused land prices to soar. Acreage that could be had for $1.25 to $1.50 an acre prior to 1888 jumped within a few years to twenty, fifty, and in some cases three hundred dollars. Everybody wanted to cash in on the bonanza, and wildcatters and speculators descended upon the area. New phosphate towns sprang up—Pebbledale, west of Bartow, Phosphoria, west of Homeland, and Acme, four miles south of Fort Meade. The flavor of the times was captured by the *Arcadian* in March of 1890. "The Peace river phosphate beds excite the wonder of all who see them, and fertilizer men pronounce them the finest in the world. The day is not far off when phosphate works will line the banks of Peace river from Bowling Green south. Thousands of hands will be employed and much capital will be invested. DeSoto County is destined to be the richest county in the state."[10]

After 1890, prices for phosphate dropped when low cotton prices lowered demand for fertilizers and when problems arose with the English export market. Many small mining companies were driven out of business, although more well established firms survived. A savage storm causing extensive damage to South Carolina's phosphate industry helped bolster Florida's phosphate mining companies in 1893, but thereafter river production of pebble phosphate declined in the face of increasing production costs, the effects of the great Panic of 1893, and competition from hard rock and land pebble mines. In December 1894, the four remaining phosphate companies on Peace River merged to form the Peace River Phosphate Mining Company. Five years later that firm was bought out by a land pebble company, the American Agricultural Chemical Company, and by 1908 production of pebble phosphate from Peace River had ceased.[11]

The cessation of pebble phosphate production in Peace River by no means meant the end of production in the Peace River area. Particularly in Polk County, land pebble deposits were discovered and exploited. As of 1892, such deposits already were being mined by the Pharr Phosphate Company two miles south of Bartow, the Florida Phosphate Company (Limited) at Phosphoria, the Virginia-Florida Phosphate Company three miles south of Homeland, and the Fort Meade Phosphate, Fertilizer, Land and Improvement Company at Fort Meade. As the 1890s passed, more plants began operation in the area west of Bartow and Homeland. Eventually, rail lines were constructed to serve those mines, and it became customary to unload freight destined for them at a spot near an old mulberry tree. Within a short while freight began to be labeled, "Put off at the Mulberry Tree," and in 1900 when a post office was established for the town that had grown up around that tree, it received the name Mulberry.[12]

The phosphate mines still operate in the Peace River area, but the boom had ended by 1900, a victim of national recession, new competition, spiraling costs, and the reduced demand for phosphate after the great freezes of 1894-1895. Of the four hundred

Christ Church, Fort Meade, erected in 1889. Courtesy Florida Photographic Collection, Florida State Archives.

companies in operation in Florida in 1895, only fifty remained five years later. As companies went out of business, many of their investors suffered and, in some cases, were bankrupted. Many Peace River residents were caught in the industry's bust, and for great numbers all that remained to them was their devalued land and their citrus groves.[13]

A force of black laborers

Phosphate mining was a labor-intensive business in the 1880s and 1890s requiring strong men with the stamina to perform back-breaking work under Florida's burning sun. In the industry's formative stages almost everything was done by hand. As one phosphate industry historian put it, "Workers waded into the rivers at shallow places or at low tide and pried lumps of rock loose with crowbars, picks, and oyster tongs. These lumps were loaded, largely by hand, upon barges for transport to the washer. In many instances, miners worked in deeper water and recovered lumps of phosphate rock by diving." In the 1890s, barges equipped with huge pumps took over some of the work, but, particularly in land pebble operations, the pick-and-shovel method remained in use until some companies began experimenting with steam shovels after the turn of the century.[14]

Like the railroads, phosphate companies turned to black men to perform much of the hardest physical labor connected with the mines.[15] They were paid a dollar a day like all phosphate laborers. One Fort Meade man described a typical operation in the spring of 1890: "On the brow of the hill, some fifty feet apart, are two pits, or rather large ditches, where a score of [blacks] are mining the phosphate rock and piling it up on the banks. Another gang of hands conveys this rock in wheelbarrows to a building thirty feet wide and one hundred feet long. Here two hands feed the rock to a Wilson crusher." And on the process went, from dawn to dusk.[16]

Employment in the phosphate and related industries drew hundreds of black laborers and their families to the Peace River Valley beginning in 1888, and they settled not only in Bartow and Homeland where substantial black communities already existed, but also throughout the river valley in DeSoto County where few blacks had lived sinced the early 1870s. By 1892, for example, both Arcadia and Punta Gorda contained large black settlements, and both were experiencing racial frictions and problems. At Arcadia in February 1892 Walter Austin, described as a black man "whose reputation was a notorious one," was lynched by an angry white mob after he reportedly killed Arcadia Phosphate Company assistant superintendent Bert Hard. Hard had been made a special deputy to help handle crowds on a circus night and had burst in on "a gang of negro gamblers." He had attempted to arrest Austin, upon which the Austin "emptied the contents of a Winchester rifle into the officer's abdomen."[17]

The story of black settlement in the Peace River Valley in the 1890s properly should be told in terms of individual accomplishments and the development of community institutions and not of isolated acts of criminality or violence. Documentary evidence is scanty about the lives of early black settlers, but sources record the contributions of such individuals as the young entrepreneur, Brown, who opened Fort Meade's first ice cream parlor in 1890. Paul Young in 1895 was supplying Fort Meade with fresh fish imported from Punta Gorda, while Charles Martin at the same time was operating a popular restaurant near Bartow's train station. Robert Meacham, former Reconstruction state senator from Jefferson County, during the early years of the decade served as Punta Gorda's postmaster.[18]

Before the Arcadia Phosphate Company opened its first mine in May of 1888, at least two black churches, St. James African Methodist Episcopal (A.M.E.) Church of Bartow and Mount Bunyan Baptist Church of Homeland, had been organized in the Peace River Valley.[19] The arrival of new families thereafter prompted the establishment of numerous additional congregations beginning at Arcadia in 1891 when Irvin Tillis, a Methodist, and Randall James, a Baptist, convened a Christian Society for common worship. Soon the Methodists had organized as the Mount Zion A.M.E. Church and were conducting services under the leadership of the Reverend John Tillman. By 1893 the Baptists had achieved a separate organization as Elizabeth Baptist Church with their own pastor, the Reverend E.D. McDonald. For the remainder of the decade both congregations met in the blacks' school building at Arcadia, each holding service two Sundays a month. Also in old DeSoto County, black Methodists at Punta

Black cattleman and citrus grower Corrie Davis (1873–1956) of Homeland. Courtesy Vernice Williams.

Gorda established Bethel A.M.E. Church and erected a house of worship. In early 1894, the congregation invited the newly organized St. Mark Progressive Baptist Church and its pastor, the Reverend G.W. Jones, to share the church building until the Baptists could erect one of their own.[20]

In Polk County, 1892 saw the organization at Fort Meade of the Galilee Baptist Church by the Reverends D.H. Brown and G.W. McClendon. The congregation's first meeting was attended by just six persons, including Mr. and Mrs. William Miles and Mr. and Mrs. Paul Young. A revival that year doubled the membership, however, and by 1895 the congregation had grown sufficiently to justify the erection of a small frame structure for church services. Fort Meade's black Methodists waited eight more years before their St. Paul A.M.E. Church was constituted in 1903 under Pastor C.H. Wright.[21]

Just to the north at Homeland and not later than 1893, black Methodists had established an A.M.E. congregation, quite likely the forerunner of the church known early in the twentieth century as Old Jones Chapel. During the same year, it appears that a Colored Methodist Episcopal Church (C.M.E.) was organized at Bartow. More certain was the founding in the same town on February 17, 1893, of the Mount Gilbert (Gilboa) Baptist Church, which was served by the Reverend A. Boone and which in 1896 constructed its own frame church. Primitive Baptists followed the lead of the Missionary Baptists and in 1894 constituted at Bartow the Burket Chapel Primitive Baptist Church with the Reverend B.J. Jones. The new building of the area's first black congregation, St. James A.M.E. Church, complete with bell tower, bell, and pipe organ, was dedicated in an "imposing and appropriate ceremony" in late January 1895 by the Right Reverend Bishop A. Grant, who preached the dedication sermon to a "large congregation" of both blacks and whites.[22]

The origins of schools for blacks in the Peace River Valley are obscure, although census reports suggest children of Andy Moore and Prince Johnson were attending school at Bartow as early as 1879. By 1885, it is certain that Polk had two schools established for black children, most probably at Bartow and Homeland. Increases in population attributable to the coming of the railroad raised that number to four in 1886, with sixty-seven boys and sixty-five girls in attendance. Black education was well enough established in Polk by the end of 1887 to warrant the first black teachers' institute, an event held in December at Mrs. J.A. Wiley's Bartow school. Four of the county's five black teachers attended, including Mr. R. Frederick of Alafia and Miss Ellen Dixon of Homeland.[23]

A school census in 1888 found 288 black children of school age in Polk County. As new families arrived with the phosphate boom that figure increased, although another census in 1892 reported only 314; almost 60 percent of black children of school age were enrolled in classes. The seven black schools in 1891 and 1892 dropped to four by the end of the century, at Bartow, Homeland, Lakeland, and Mulberry.[24] A new Bartow school opened on September 15, 1897, under the supervision of principal A.N. Ritchie.[25] One of the school's teachers, Lula Marion Simmons, was a graduate of Gainesville's Union Academy, a school established during Reconstruction by the Freedmen's Bureau. At Simmons's recommendation, the Bartow school, which provided primary and secondary education for thousands of Polk County students well into the twentieth century, was named the Union Academy.[26]

The educational record for old DeSoto County is quite spare. In 1896 only two schools served black students in the county, one at Arcadia and the other at Punta Gorda. At these two schools, however, fifty-four of the county's sixty-one black children of school age were attending at least some classes. The number of DeSoto County schools for black students does not appear to have changed until the twentieth century.[27]

The Great Freeze

On December 29, 1894, a cold wave descended upon the peninsula of Florida. Temperatures dropped to eighteen degrees at Tampa, vegetable crops were destroyed, and young citrus groves were damaged. Despite the losses, old-timers shrugged off the effects of the freeze as something to which they had become accustomed. Even not-so-old old-timers could remember the freezes of December 1885 and January 1886 when the temperature dropped to twenty-four degrees, ice covered ponds, snow fell in Manatee County, and tropical trees, shrubs, and vegetable crops were destroyed. In January 1891, the mercury dropped to twenty-five degrees at Fort Meade and in January 1892 to twenty-two degrees, a freeze of which one observer noted, "Very few oranges are injured, but all vegetables are ruined. Young orange trees are badly hurt and old ones severely scorched in some locations." On January 6, 1893, frost had reached as far south as Fort Ogden, causing major damage to the tomato crop. Certainly, freezing conditions were no stranger to the Peace River Valley.[28]

Following the freeze of December 1894, a six-week period of warm, balmy weather bathed South Florida, followed on February 7, 1895, by a hard freeze for four consecutive days. At Fort Meade the temperature dropped on succeeding nights to twenty-five, twenty-six, and thirty degrees, and at Bowling Green to twenty, seventeen, eighteen, and twenty-six degrees. Throughout most of the state citrus trees were killed to the roots and roughly $75 million in damages were sustained.[29]

In the Peace River area damages were varied. Everywhere, vegetable crops were injured or destroyed, the orange crop was lost, and many young orange trees were killed. At Bartow, "considerable damage" was reported in all groves, while at Arcadia "the old sweet seedling trees were but little damaged." So great was the damage at Avon Park that the community reportedly became "a ghost town." Bowling Green's Irving Keck summed up the general state of affairs. "It is well to look things squarely in the face. It is at best a serious disaster, to many it means ruin; to all it means a time of care, anxiety and doubt as to the future."[30]

Doubt as to the future confronted most Peace River settlers on the morning of Sunday, February 10, 1895, when the cold finally lifted. For two years they had been suffering from the effects of the great national depression known as the Panic of 1893, as well as from declining prospects for the phosphate industry. Their land values had plummeted, and their vegetable crops had been injured or destroyed by cold weather in every year since 1891. Now, overextended and unprotected, they had lost their orange crop and, quite possibly, their trees. A Bartow man said he'd be "dinged if the three f's—freezes, flour bins [a recent sales fraud], and fosfates—hadn't just about racked Polk county." Fort Meade's George W. Hendry put it more bluntly. "The (1894–95) freezes did the work for us all," he wrote, "sweeping away a lifetime's labor and savings, leaving us poor, which seems to be the inevitable doom of all pioneers in all countries."[31]

Some Peace River residents simply packed up and left, hoping to begin life anew somewhere else. Their places in many cases were taken by newcomers moving away from devastation farther north, who, together with the remaining survivors of the freeze, began picking up the pieces, replanting groves, and repairing damage. Meanwhile, some residents turned to a new crop and a new industry.[32]

At least by 1888 tobacco had been grown at Fort Meade and Arcadia with such satisfactory results that reports surfaced of a cigar factory to be located in the latter town.[33] In the phosphate craze, the tobacco crop soon was all but forgotten. The devastation of the Great Freeze of 1895 forced a reexamination in the Peace River area of tobacco's potential as a cash crop. At just the same time an influx of refugees arrived in Florida from a revolution-torn Cuba. E. Alonzo Cordery of Fort Meade was among those who sensed the time was ripe for full-scale production in Florida of Cuban tobacco and established the Cuban Tobacco Growers Company in cooperation with several Cuban planters anxious to relocate.[34]

Cuban tobacco workers began arriving at Fort Meade in December 1895. The following month fields were cleared and planted, and a cigar factory was erected. "A visitor to Fort Meade a year ago would scarcely know the place now. Everybody is infused with the tobacco-growing spirit," it was reported by the summer of 1896. "With the decline of phosphate, prospects seemed blighted, but tobacco culture holds out a better promise than ever did the rock or the pebble phosphate."[35]

Fort Meade's first tobacco crop proved a huge success, and in May 1897 the *Tampa Tribune* declared, "There is no longer any doubt of the success of this industry, and all Polk county are going into it with a rush." A few months later the paper reported, "The people in and near Bartow have planted heavily in tobacco this year, and the prospects for a large and profitable yield are truly flattering."[36]

The reputation of Peace River–grown tobacco had expanded so greatly by February 1898 as to command a visit of inspection by U.S. Secretary of Agriculture James Wilson. After touring tobacco fields from Bartow to Fort Meade, the secretary declared, "There seems to be no reason why Florida should not supply all the fine tobacco used in America." At the plantation of W.A. Evans and A.F. Gartner three miles north of Fort Meade in the area becoming

One of the Peace River area's favorite recreation spots, Kissingen Springs, in an engraving of about 1890. From the author's collection.

known as Pembroke, the secretary was given "two boxes of elegant cigars, made from and labelled 'from tobacco grown in Polk county, Florida, on La Cosmospolita plantation' " for presentation to the president and cabinet. Secretary Wilson "pronounced the cigars very good indeed, and was exceedingly glad to get hold of some which were genuine Florida's and labeled as such."[37]

One year after Secretary Wilson's visit, in 1899, "La Cosmopolita" plantation alone was shipping one thousand to three thousand cigars daily and expected to increase its crop "tenfold" in the next growing season. That increase would never be harvested. During 1898, the Spanish-American War had been declared after the sinking of the battleship *Maine* in Havana harbor with the loss of more than 260 American lives. As early as May 1896 many of the Cuban tobacco workers at Fort Meade had been "anxious to go back and fight for *Cuba libre* [see appendix 10]." Although they were not called upon to do that fighting, the Cubans had no thought but to return home when the war was over. With their departure, the Peace River tobacco industry collapsed. "Promptly upon the freeing of Cuba," remembered one river resident, "the Cuban population departed for their own *Patria* (Country) and Fort Meade was left in what seemed then to be in about as bad condition as possible. Times were certainly hard and just about all the work to be had then was with the road overseers working our country roads; but they were not 'good roads.' "[38]

As the tobacco industry prospered after the Great Freeze of 1895, the citrus industry slowly had begun its recovery. By August 1897 groves at Fort Meade were said to be "rapidly recovering from the damage." At Bartow, it was "almost impossible to detect the damage done to the old trees," and at Arcadia "it would now require an expert to detect that any damage at all had been done, even to the young budded groves." The confidence expressed in those reports proved premature. Late in 1897 cold weather again visited South Florida, resulting in a "slight freeze . . . which did small damage to the orange trees." In February 1899, frigid temperatures returned and snow blanketed the ground as far south as Fort Meade. Many settlers gave up the citrus industry, while others followed those who had departed after the Great Freeze. The century closed with the remaining Peace River farmers and grove owners once again struggling to pick up the pieces.[39]

The coming of the railroad and the discovery of phosphate had promised, after decades of frustration and disappointment, an era of unprecedented prosperity in the Peace River Valley. For a few years land values rose, new farms and groves were planted, and phosphate mines tapped an apparently inexhaustible source of wealth. Then with the Panic of 1893, the phosphate industry sagged and land values collapsed. In December 1894 and February 1895 at Peace River, "The freezes did the work for us all, sweeping away a lifetime's labor and savings, leaving us poor, which seems to be the inevitable doom of all pioneers in all countries."

20

At the End of the Century

I N 1885 AND 1886 THE POSSIBILITIES of the future of the Peace River area had seemed unlimited. Riding a wave of immigration and financed by a phosphate boom, river villages grew into towns and small cities while new communities were conceived to provide homes for settlers lured to the area by its mild climate and the rails of the Florida Southern Railway. With growth came a more sophisticated social structure, a deeper commitment to public education and also the introduction into the river area of new faiths and religions. By the end of the century the towns and many of the people remained, but confidence in the future had been shattered by economic reverses and the effects of punishing forces of nature, and the river residents looked to the future more with concern than with prospect.

Population growth and the need for schools

The close of the nineteenth century found the residents of the Peace River area struggling through hard times after a fifteen-year roller coaster ride from boom to bust. The families of the river valley had experienced hard times before, though, and most were determined to persevere in their chosen home until good times should come again. The bust did not destroy Peace River and its settlements, and the boom had left a legacy that would set a pattern for Peace River life lasting to the present day.

The overriding factor in the history of the final two decades of the nineteenth century at Peace River had been the arrival of new settlers. From a population of only 3,155 in 1880, Polk County had more than doubled its citizenry ten years later and by the end of the century contained 12,472 residents, four times the 1880 figure. All of old Manatee County held but 3,544 settlers in 1880, while the new and smaller county of DeSoto contained 4,944 at the end of the decade and 8,000 in 1900.[1]

Education at the turn of the century

"Great interest is being manifested in the cause of education," reported a former Manatee County school superintendent in 1881. "Every neighborhood that can make up ten or more pupils has the benefit of its proportion of free school funds which are derived from the State." He added that "Unfortunately, however, the amount thus realized is not sufficient to maintain the schools but three months during the year, but it is expected that by a slight increase in the school tax—or great economy on the part of the school authorities—the schools can be maintained free to all for five months in the year. At present, we cannot claim a strictly free school system, as the teachers are employed by the County Board of Instruction, through its superintendent, on the recommendation of the patrons, who make the best bargain they- can with the teacher. The county allows him one dollar per month per pupil, according to his returns, and the patrons make up the balance." Bemoaning the fact that "teachers employed are too often indifferent and lack experience and ability," the man also noted that "in addition to the free schools (so-called) private schools, well attended, are maintained in the more thickly settled sections the greater part of the year."[2]

In 1880, old Manatee County's school system served 811 pupils in forty-three schools, an increase of over 500 pupils and twenty-six schools from four years previously. By 1883, the numbers had jumped to 1,360 and forty-eight, with expenditures of $5,359.96, a six-fold increase since 1876. In all but five schools, the county had increased the school term to five months, but the statistics presumably reflect the availability of educational opportunities only for whites. In the final school year before the creation of DeSoto County, the system boasted 1,809 scholars attending sixty-eight schools, ten of which had a term of less than three months. Of the six largest schools in the county, four were located in the Peace River Valley: Joshua Creek, 60 pupils; Fort Ogden, 59; and Arcadia and Wauchula, 52 each.[3]

DeSoto County's first decade of existence saw the county school system under the stewardship of school superintendent T.J. Sparkman grow to fifty-eight public schools attended by over two thousand pupils. The basic school year remained at five months, however, except in school sub-districts at Arcadia, Punta Gorda, and Avon Park where local citizens had approved taxes to extend the term to as much as eight months. Most schools continued to be conducted in primitive structures in isolated rural communities, although Arcadia's school was described as "a hand-some two-story building, well equipped and arranged for convenience and comfort." Wauchula had just built a new schoolhouse, Punta Gorda's school reportedly was "first class," and Avon Park was building a new school to replace one destroyed by fire. One Arcadia resident ventured the opinion, "The schools and teachers generally all over the county are good and compare favorably in grade with those of any county in the state."[4]

Until the fall of 1897, DeSoto County still was without a high school. In that year, after an acrimonious debate throughout the county, the school board decided to erect and open one such school for whites, to be located at Arcadia. Accordingly, a solid two-story school was built and opened with appropriate ceremony on October 11, 1897. Professor E.T. Wilson, "formerly principal of the Peabody School, Lake City," was placed in charge, assisted by Mrs. Emma Alderman and *DeSoto County News* editor R.E. Watkins.[5]

DeSoto's school system was by no means immune to the economic ills facing the county's residents in the late 1890s. In January 1898 the county was forced to close a number of schools and to scale back the school year at others to a four-month term. Improving conditions in the fall of 1899, however, permitted a Fort Ogden resident to report, "The school board is having good, comfortable school houses built throughout the county, and furnishing them with good desks, stoves, blackboards, etc." Also facing the school board were problems with a modern ring. "Some of the teachers," an Arcadia man wrote in 1897, "think the readjustment of salaries in this county is out of proportion. In some instances teachers of several years' experience, and who have prepared themselves for this profession, and who hold first grade certificates, get very little more salary than young teachers with no experience, and low grade certificates. With no premium on experience and ability in teaching, the educational interest will no doubt decline." The subject of qualified teachers was also a theme in a September 1899 report: "All of the schools here commenced except those for which there are no teachers. Several more schools have been granted and there are no teachers for them."[6]

Until well into the 1880s, Polk County had lagged behind Manatee in its commitment to public education, relying in great part upon the private Summerlin Institute at Bartow and other private academies at Homeland and Fort Meade to educate its white children.[7] In 1883, the Polk County system served only 622 children in twenty schools, an actual decline in student population from the 1880 total. In the face of population growth in antic-

The Hotel Punta Gorda, opened in January 1888. Courtesy Vernon Peeples.

ipation of the coming of the railroad, the Polk system in 1884 grew to forty-three schools serving 938 pupils, and six years to eighty schools and 2,276 pupils, with a school budget of more than $16,000. The economic dislocations of the later 1890s reduced these numbers somewhat, but the public school system as a whole remained intact at the end of the century with more than seventy schools, including those in such Peace River locations as Bartow, Homeland, Fort Meade, Mt. Pisgah, Fairview, Whidden's, Lake Buffum, and McAuley's.[8]

Although in 1885 Fort Meade and Lakeland had constructed substantial wooden schoolhouses and two years later Bartow was claiming "one of the best public school buildings in the state," most Polk County schools at the end of the nineteenth century remained, as in DeSoto County, fairly primitive and located in isolated areas. A Polk County man described the country school he attended at Midland in the late 1880s. "On the homestead was a shingle cabin erected by a neighbor to furnish shelter for his children during the school term," he wrote. "One quarter mile away was the old log school house with desks built around the walls and backless benches. The house had a puncheon floor and a hand-planed blackboard, which had been stained with black-jack juice. There were two small openings in the walls at the sides. There was no provision for heat, and on cold days we went outside and warmed by a fire outdoors."[9]

However crude many of its school buildings may have been, Polk by August 1886 had extended its regular school term to six months. Within a few years some town schools had further lengthened the term, resulting, for example, in an eight-month term at Fort Meade by the fall of 1893. Fort Meade went a step further in May 1896 when it voted itself an independent school district and guaranteed its children a nine-month school year. The town of Bartow by then had taken over the operation of Summerlin Institute in a complex chain of financial events.[10]

By the mid-1880s the old Summerlin Institute, constructed in 1867, had begun to show its age. In 1884 it was "a rickety old frame building, containing only the rudest furniture and a promiscuous lot of pupils, ranging from infancy to manhood, whose course of study consisted of 'the three r's—readin', ritin' and rithmatick'—all taught in one room by one teacher." In 1886 a reporter described the same building as "a disgrace to the town."[11]

Fortunately, the coming of the railroad stimulated interest in the town of Bartow, and the institute's trustees, Jacob Summerlin, David Hughes, and G.A. Hanson, in February 1885 had been able to begin disposing of the remainder of the town lots from Summerlin's original donation to erect "a handsome school building." A sufficient amount had been raised by March 1887 to permit the trustees to enter into a $17,277 contract with Joseph Thompson for the erection of a brick school building to be "one of the finest of its kind in the State." On the following May 12, at elaborate ceremonies attended by dignitaries and other guests from all parts of Florida, Jacob Summerlin laid the cornerstone for his new institute.[12]

Despite minor delays, the roof and walls were completed by October 1, 1887, and carpenters were busy on the framework. The school's trustees were said to be "desirous of having it completed in time to open school this winter." No studies would be undertaken at the new Summerlin Institute in 1887 or in 1888, however, for it was discovered that "with such additions as were made to the contract that there was some five or six thousand dollars lacking in being able to complete and pay off the indebtedness." On behalf of the board, G.A. Hanson sued the contractor, Thompson. Thompson countersued the board and, after bitter litigation, was awarded $8,000.[13]

In the meantime, the old wooden Summerlin Institute had been sold and the trustees "had to rent rooms and buildings dividing up the school in different sections of the town." Finally, on January 2, 1889, two hundred students enrolled and, within two months, that number had increased to three hundred. Principal W.F. Yocum was required to employ an additional two teachers to aid the five already working at the school.[14]

Still the Summerlin Institute's money problems would not go away, including paying off Thompson's judgment. By the spring of 1892 Bartow newspapers and school officials were demanding that institute treasurer G.A. Hanson publicly disclose the school's finances. Hanson not only refused to accommodate the demands, he filed suit for libel against the *Courier-Informant* and Bartow school trustees Mayor E.W. Codington and B.F. Jackson. When the school board voted to pay the expenses of defending against the libel actions, Hanson attempted to publish in Fort Meade's *South Florida Progress* an account of the finances which, in the words of one observer, were "so vague as to leave the public almost as uninformed of the financial condition of the institute funds as before."[15]

Ben Blount, chairman of the Bartow City Council, reported that Summerlin was so "disheartened that he offered the Summerlin School lands, including the building and all the interests connected with it, to some Church or ecclesiastical organization that would start a college and build it and assume all responsibilities." His offer rejected by the Presbyterian and Methodist churches, Summerlin announced at a public meeting that "he could take that house and cut it up into rooms and make a hotel out of it and do something with it." Alarmed at this possibility, Bartow civic leaders prevailed upon Summerlin to give them some time to work out arrangements. In the end, Summerlin agreed to sell the school for the amount of its indebtedness, at the time about three thousand dollars, the payment to be borne in equal shares by the city council, board of county commissioners, and school board. Unable to come up with the cash, these officials

Laying the cornerstone for the Summerlin Institute at Bartow on May 12, 1887. School patron Jacob Summerlin stands immediately to the right of the cornerstone. Courtesy Florida Photographic Collection, Florida State Archives.

turned to George Hamilton and William B. Varn who agreed to loan the amount in question. Thus, Summerlin Institute in 1893 became the public school system of Bartow. The institute's founder, Jacob Summerlin, died shortly thereafter on November 4, 1893.[16]

The year 1893 also saw the genesis of another educational institution which was to help give Bartow a reputation as one of Florida's educational capitals. A former Confederate major general, E.M. Law, had decided to open a military school and was casting about for a suitable location. An old friend of Law's, Dr. J.M. Perry of Lakeland, heard of the general's plans and wrote requesting that he consider Polk County. Law was so pleased with Florida and the pledges of support he received, he returned with his family the following year and on September 3, 1894, opened in Bartow's old National Hotel the South Florida Military Institute.[17]

Law patterned his institute on the curriculum and discipline of the U.S. Military Academy, the Citadel, and the Virginia Military Academy. Its cadets, sixty in the original class, wore appropriate uniforms, while the general supervised all activities arrayed in his Confederate army uniform. When the school's first term came to an end on May 1, 1895, it was said that the institute had "flourished in a most flattering manner."[18]

Among the results of the great freeze, however, was the almost certain demise of the South Florida Military Institute. Bartow sponsored a delegation of J.H. Tatum, W.H. Johnson, and J.W. Boyd to lobby the state legislature for support. With the sympathetic Henry L. Mitchell in the governor's chair and soon-to-be state comptroller William H. Reynolds representing Polk in the senate, the lobbyists returned with a $6,400 appropriation and a state assumption of responsibility for what thereafter would be known as the South Florida Military and Educational Institution. General Law was left in day-to-day command while the state's power was vested in a local board of trustees composed of Tatum, Johnson, Boyd, Charles C. Wilson, and H.L. Davis of Bartow; William H. Reynolds of Lakeland; and E.A. Cordery of Fort Meade.[19]

The South Florida Military and Educational Institution never grew to match its founders' hopes. Although a commodious two-story building was constructed for the school in 1895 on a large tract of land about a mile south of Bartow's courthouse, enrollments seldom exceeded sixty cadets, thirty-one of whom were on state scholarships. After a series of clashes with members of the board of trustees, General Law resigned on January 1, 1903, to become editor of the *Courier-Informant.* Two years later, the legislature merged the institution into the University of Florida, and its buildings and property were sold.[20]

Greater diversity of religion

As vital a role as organized religion played in the lives of many pioneers, by no means all settlers belonged to the early churches. One pioneer attempted in 1881 to explain the situation. "Membership of these churches is small compared to the population," he wrote. "Were it not for the fact that the rules or 'discipline' of these churches are so extremely orthodox and puritanical in their character, amounting to positive prohibition of the most innocent means of recreation, there is no doubt but that the membership would be greatly increased." As it was, many settlers practiced their religion privately, and many frontier churches remained small and highly restrictive.[21]

The growth of population and town life early in the 1880s altered this situation. The organization of black Baptist and Methodist churches, reflecting the beginnings of substantial black communities in the river valley area, has been discussed in previous chapters. Many of the new white settlers were from northern and midwestern states where less orthodox philosophies prevailed, and their influence on local affairs was felt in a more flexible discipline on the part of some churches. Also, new settlers introduced new religions into the Peace River Valley, beginning with the establishment at Bartow in 1882 of the First Presbyterian Church. Holding their meetings at first in the Hughes Opera House, the Presbyterians struggled for membership under the Reverend W.G.F. Wallace, and by the fall of 1886 had constructed its own sanctuary, "the handsomest building of its character in the city." In 1898, Arcadia also had a Presbyterian church.[22]

The Episcopal church was introduced into the Peace River Valley on September 26, 1886, when the Reverend C.S. Williams of Palatka held services and celebrated communion at the home of Mr. A.J. Bulloch at Fort Meade. Present were the families of Bulloch and of Mr. and Mrs. George W. Black. An influx of English colonists at Fort Meade boosted the church's membership in 1887, and services began to be held at the Methodist church. Late that year, Bishop Edwin G. Weed placed the Reverend George S. Fitzhugh in charge of the Fort Meade mission, and Fitzhugh launched into missionary work which by 1891 not only had resulted in the erection of Christ Church at Fort Meade, but also had "stirred the ground and planted the seed" at numerous other South Florida communities including Bartow and Punta Gorda. Episcopal services began to be held at Arcadia in March 1894 by the Reverend C.E. Butler of Fort Meade, and by the summer of 1897 it was reported that "the Episcopalians have a small but devout congregation, but have no resident rector, though services are regularly held once a month."[23]

The Roman Catholic faith had been practiced at Fort Meade at least as early as the summer of 1853 when Father James H. O'Neill of Key West made the long overland trek from Tampa to celebrate mass and hear confessions of Catholic soldiers stationed at the garrison. A regular Catholic presence came to Peace River when the Reverend O.M. Widman of the Society of Jesus began celebrating mass at Fort Meade on April 14, 1891, for a congregation composed in great part of Italian phosphate workers. Soon thereafter, the Angola Catholic Church was organized at Bartow and in 1892 erected the river valley's first Catholic church.[24]

By January 1895, Elder G.I. Butler, assisted by the Reverend Walter Bird and others, was conducting meetings of the Seventh Day Adventist church at Bartow. A report of those meetings assured they would be continued "as long as sufficient interest is manifested." Three years later, in the words of a church historian, "the reformation of the Church of God was first brought in the State near Fort Meade, about four and one-half miles northeast of town, known as Pool Branch, holding services in what was then known as the McAuley School Building. About two months later this church was organized holding services in the same building until the erection of a frame church building in the same neighborhood, the latter part of 1898. The latter part of 1899 they established a camp ground in this vicinity, on which a tabernacle was erected."[25]

The towns at the turn of the century

"Leaving the minarets of the great Moorish palace gleaming in the sunlight" began a late nineteenth-century account of a railroad excursion that began at Henry Plant's exotic Tampa Bay Hotel and ran the length of the Peace River Valley, "soon the pleasant little town of Lakeland comes to view. . . . Its stores grouped about the public square give one a faint impression of some of the Old World cities, perhaps Lakeland and Bartow impress the traveler most agreeably with their shaded, well-paved streets. At Fort Meade, experiments in tobacco growing have proven that the weed raised there ought to be almost, if not quite as good as the Havana staple. On past Bowling Green, Wauchula, Zolfo Springs, Arcadia and Cleveland the train goes and at last reaches the town of Punta Gorda, or 'Great Point,' formerly called Trabue after its founder Col. Isaac H. Trabue. Now at that point rises the spacious and airy Hotel Punta Gorda of the Plant System, while the Plant piers extend far out into Charlotte Harbor." The traveler, to sum up his impressions of the area, then recalled the words recently spoken by Florida's governor to describe the state's growth and industrial progress. "He could think of no more fitting words in addressing the strangers within Florida's gates than those used on the tomb of Sir Christopher Wren, in St. Paul's cathedral, London, that great monument to his own genius. The words are in Latin and mean 'look about you.' "[26]

What a difference two decades can make. In 1880 the Peace River area had been a wild frontier with only one town, Fort Meade. By the turn of the century, the railroad towns of Bartow, Arcadia, and Punta Gorda dominated the river valley's commercial and social life, and communities throughout the area possessed facilities and amenities unheard of two decades previously.

Bartow

The queen city of Polk County and of the Peace River Valley in 1900 was Bartow. The wilderness first settled by Rigdon Brown in 1849 possessed by the turn of the century 1,983 residents within its corporate bounds, easily twice as large as the next largest Peace River town, Punta Gorda, and almost twice as large as the second largest Polk County town, Lakeland. Although the collapse of the tobacco industry in 1899 had hurt Bartow, it remained a center for the railroad and phosphate businesses, as well as for Polk County's citrus industry and vegetable production. Bartow was the site of the county's courthouse, and the Summerlin Institute and the South Florida Military and Educational Institution had won it a reputation as an educational center. As early as 1896 the community had at least twelve churches, and by the end of the century it benefitted from a municipal waterworks, public library, baseball field, amphitheater, and streets paved with clay phosphate. On April 14, 1897, Bartow became the first community with electric power in the river valley.[27] Bartow residents were optimistic about the new century, believing their town "destined to be, at no distant day, a large and flourishing commercial city."[28]

Homeland

The area of Homeland, one of the Peace River's earliest settlements, increased in population by almost 80 percent in the final decade of the nineteenth century, with 627 residents in 1900. Despite Homeland's growth, the Great Freeze of 1895 and subsequent economic calamities had driven some local settlers farther south—including William B. Burdine whose move to Miami permitted him to enter the retail merchandise business with considerable success. Homeland remained at the turn of the century a community that prided itself on the close and friendly relations between its white and black citizens. The home of affluent black cattlemen and farmers such as Alfred, Corrie, Lloyd, and Sam Davis, Homeland continued to support its schools for both races, and those schools continued to produce countless teachers and other professionals for the benefit of the region and state.[29]

Fort Meade

Prosperity came to Fort Meade in the wake of the railroad in great part due to the arrival of numerous English families, lured to the area by developer Cecil Alleyne and the Avon Park promotions of O.M. Crosby. Ernest B. Simmons remembered the heads of those families as remittance men, the younger sons of prominent families who were supplied with funds from their parents' estates. "Many of them," Simmons reported, "were of a sporty nature and it was a common sight to see them on horseback, in

Mrs. Neva C. Child, editor
and publisher of the *DeSoto
County Champion*. From the
Jacksonville *Florida Times-
Union*, December 19, 1897.

flat jockey-style saddles with shortened stirrup straps, bobbing
up and down as they trotted and galloped along the streets." In
late 1887 these men, together with many long-time residents,
founded the Fort Meade Jockey Club and, beginning in February
1888, held annual race meetings that became celebrated over the
entire state. In short order, Fort Meade also possessed street
lamps, lawn tennis courts, an opera house, and a cricket club. In
1889 a Fort Meade fox hunt was inaugurated at the town's race
course.[30]

Fort Meade and its general vicinity, with about 1,200 residents
in 1890, was prospering along with the citrus and phosphate
industries. The town's luck began to change after 1893, however,
when the river pebble phosphate industry began its slow decline.
On January 8, 1894, F.F. Hendry's store and the adjoining meat
market were consumed by fire. Six months later a second and
more serious fire destroyed the Canter, Evans & Co. store, J.M.
Stansfield & Co.'s drugstore, Wise Perry's poolroom, and the
Lightsey & Lewis meat market.[31]

The decline of the phosphate industry had begun an exodus in
1894 of some of the English families from the town, a trend given
greater impetus by the freezes of 1894 and 1895. Damaged as it
was, the town rebounded with the tobacco industry and for several years experienced an economic renaissance, resulting by
1897 in an estimated population of 500 persons within the town

limits, as compared to 267 in 1890. The departure of Cuban tobacco workers following the conclusion of the Spanish-American War proved a disaster for the town. While 1,609 residents remained in the Fort Meade area in 1900, only 261 lived within the town limits. The strain proved so great that in 1903 the Florida legislature abolished Fort Meade as an incorporated municipality.[32]

Bowling Green

The vicinity of Bowling Green more than doubled in population during the 1890s, increasing to 440 settlers from 196. Some of the state's largest orange groves were located nearby, and, while the freezes of 1894 and 1895 had caused tremendous damage in the area, farms and groves had recovered by October 1896 to the extent that it was reported, "The effects [of the freezes] have so far disappeared now that a full crop is expected next year." Vegetable farming and the production of noncitrus fruits remained of importance, as well, as shown by N.S. Baggett's 1895 investment in forty acres of watermelons. The previous year, Peace River's pioneer woman journalist, Neva C. Child, had initiated publication at Bowling Green of her *DeSoto County Champion*. Although the paper was moved by 1896 to the county seat at Arcadia, the town of Bowling Green still contained "two general stores and a drug store, one good public school and two churches, Methodist and Christian; daily trains and mail, express and telegraph office; a physician; a justice of the peace and an attorney; two houses for the accommodation of travelers, kept respectively by Mrs. E.A. Steele and P.W. Howard." A mail stagecoach, conducted by W.H. Hollingsworth, also carried passengers to Avon Park daily.[33] Later that year, the town's accommodations were enhanced by the opening of the Hotel Thwaites, owned and operated by druggist J.E. Thwaites.[34]

Wauchula

The Wauchula area slightly outpaced Bowling Green with 499 settlers in 1900. In 1896 the town had, within its limits, a population of about two hundred. In addition, Wauchula contained "five stores and a good hotel, the Bel-Air, kept by A.C. Clavel, and a boarding house. There is a Methodist, a Baptist and a Primitive Baptist Church. One public school with seventy pupils. Rev. M.S. Stevens is principal, assisted by Miss Alice Hearn. There is a blacksmith, harness and shoe shop and wood working establishment; also a tannery, where the palmetto root furnishes the tanic acid with most satisfactory results. Near here, too, is the only rice mill in the county. There is a daily mail; G.W. Bostick, postmaster; railway, express and telegraph office, A.G. Smith agent; a sawmill and a gristmill." Wauchula toward the end of the century was reported to be "in a prosperous condition, and no single drawback has occurred to stay the progress of the community."[35]

Arcadia

Running a close second to Punta Gorda as DeSoto County's largest city in 1900 was Arcadia, which had a population within the city limits of 799. The town benefitted as a center of the cattle industry and by the proximity of extensive orange groves. In addition to containing the county courthouse and high school, Arcadia boasted in the late 1890s numerous general and specialty merchandise stores, three physicians (B.B. Blount, Ed. Greene, and Chesterfield H. Smith), six lawyers (C.W. Forrester, J.H. Treadwell, W.H. Cobb, O.T. Stanford, C.C. Morgan, and S.F. Fletcher), L.L. Morgan's wagon works, John L. Jones's DeSoto Abstract Company, T. O. Grant's livery stables, and W.H. Sharpe's "tonsorial parlor." Its three principal hotels were Mrs. Honora Patterson's The Cottage ("rates of $1 per day or $5 per week, and the table is supplied with every luxury that can be procured"); Mrs. L.V. Craig's Arcadia House; and Mrs. J.E. Pucket's Oak Street boarding house. For a time during the decade Arcadia operated its own mule-drawn street railway, known as the Arcadia Street Railway and Improvement Company. By the late 1890s, Arcadia was gaining a reputation as the home of "the wealthiest and most progressive citizens of DeSoto county," and had seen the construction of quite a number of elegant homes including its "prettiest and finest" residence, that of cattle baron and political leader Ziba King. As the century closed, the optimism ran high. Plans had been announced by N.M. Sauls for the construction of a new hotel, "the finest south of Tampa"; Mayor John L. Jones was planning "a fine business block"; and, when Charlotte Harbor area residents attempted once again to divide the county, confident Arcadians dismissed the effort with casual condemnation. "People do not think the time is ripe to divide."[36]

Fort Ogden

The town that had contained about 500 residents in 1886 reported only 300 nine years later and 495 in 1900 in the entire Fort Ogden area. When Arcadia in 1888 received the nod as DeSoto's county seat, a Fort Ogden man had reported, "a general moving to Arcadia," a trend that continued through the 1890s and included its leading citizen, Ziba King. An observer described what remained mid-way through the decade: "There are two churches in Fort Ogden, Methodist and Baptist. One good public school with one hundred pupils . . . and a private school. . . . It is a highly moral community of church-goers, crime is unknown, and peace and quiet reign supreme. There are three general stores and a drug store, two hotels . . . [and] one blacksmith and metal working establishment." Orange groves such as those owned by W.I. Williams and E.A. Thomas provided the basis of the town's livelihood and in the last year of the century, as the town's craftsmen were searching as far as Cuba for employment, the grove owners clung to their land. "There are many prospective orange grove buyers here," a local man wrote in July 1899: "but they return as they came. It is a mistake if they think there are any groves to give away. Some growers wish to sell badly, but they ask twice the value of their groves."[37]

Punta Gorda

"Punta Gorda Is Most Prosperous" declared one major Florida newspaper in 1896. From a tiny, end-of-the-line railroad resort of 262 residents in 1890, Punta Gorda in five years tripled its population to become DeSoto County's largest city. Despite minor setbacks such as the great fire of November 14, 1895, which destroyed George Anderson's general merchandise store, the *Punta Gorda Herald* offices, and the Georgia Hotel, Punta Gorda had thrived as the main shipping point for Peace River phosphates, as well as a cattle market and center for the fishing industry. At mid-decade, Punta Gorda contained a bank, four major hotels as well as several smaller ones, five church buildings, a "first class" public school for whites and a "good" school for blacks, an ice factory, W.A. Roberts's drug store, a newspaper, several merchandise and grocery stores (including those of King & Sandlin, Stetson & Co., R.L. Ernest, A.C. Freeman, Roe & Koon, and R. Hinckley), and one of the state's rising politicians, Albert W. Gilchrist, who had attended the U.S. Military Academy and later utilized the engineering skills he had learned there to help Isaac H. Trabue lay out his proposed town of Trabue.[38]

The decline of the phosphate industry, freezes, slow sales of cattle, and the growth of Tampa as a tourist resort damaged Punta Gorda's economy in the last years of the century, and by 1900 its population had increased only to 860 persons. By that time, the railroad's Long Dock and its 4,200-foot wharf had been abandoned, and a new wharf built by the railroad was unusable for larger vessels. Four years into the new century, the Plant system extended its rail line from Punta Gorda to Fort Myers. Historian Vernon Peeples of Punta Gorda explained the result: "The railroad into Fort Myers was signaling the end of an era—that of the little steamers operating in the Gulf; of Punta Gorda as the last stop on the line. The era ended as it had begun, with a puff of smoke from the boilers of a railroad locomotive, only this time the train was departing instead of arriving."[39]

One morning, the first day of February 1895, author and artist Frederic Remington sat down at a desk in his room at Punta Gorda's elegant Hotel Punta Gorda and wrote to his friend, writer Owen Wister, "Come down—deer—bear—tarpon—red snapper—ducks—birds of paradise—curious cow-boys who shoot up the rail road trains—summer clothes on—Write when I can expect you?"[40]

Settlers of the Peace River Valley had waited many years for a chance at peace and prosperity when the railroad locomotives began belching their smoke into the South Florida air in 1885 and 1886. For less than a decade thereafter, if not peace, prosperity always seemed just around the corner as long-time residents and new arrivals joined in attempts to exploit phosphate, citrus, tobacco, and tourism. By the end of the nineteenth century, many Peace River residents had been broken by these attempts, and the land was struggling to recover from the harshness of a usually benign nature. For so many, thoughts of peace and prosperity once again were reduced to an idle questioning of, in Frederic Remington's words, "When can I expect you?"

21

The Legacy of the Nineteenth Century

HE NINETEENTH CENTURY PROVIDED the stage upon which played the drama of the settlement of the Peace River Valley. For almost all of those one hundred years the struggles of man and nature had exacted terrible penalties as the price of conquering the frontier. By 1900 the basic social, civic, and economic institutions which would endure through the twentieth century were in place.

The single event of the nineteenth century having the greatest continuing impact in the Peace River area was the coming of the railroad and, with it, the influx of thousands of new settlers. The steam engine and the steel rails tied the remote South Florida frontier to the rest of the country, permitting easy access to potential settlers while encouraging the development of the phosphate, citrus, and truck farming industries and the expansion of South Florida's earlier economic mainstay, the cattle industry. Only a few years after the railroad's arrival, those four industries came to dominate the area's economy, a condition which still pertains.

Just as the phosphate, citrus, truck farming, and cattle industries have endured, so have the towns the railroad built. Lakeland, Winter Haven, Bartow, Arcadia, and Punta Gorda have grown and prospered. Communities bypassed or discriminated against by the line—Fort Ogden, Fort Green, and Pine Level, for example—in some cases have passed entirely from the scene. When the dominance of the railroad waned, the paved roads which replaced it most often provided a new connection to those areas already established.

While the railroad brought immense benefit to the Peace River area, its legacy had a negative aspect as well. The phosphate, citrus, and cattle industries it fostered carried with them inherent economic and environmental problems.

Economically, the Peace River's industries paid employees poorly and were painfully subject to the rise and fall of the economy and to the whims of nature. Time and again in the twentieth century problems of farmers and foreign competition have depressed phosphate prices; freezes, floods, and hurricane winds have damaged citrus groves; and changing eating habits and such pests as the fever tick have threatened the cattle industry. Consequently, the cycle of boom and bust, so evident in the Peace River area in the last third of the nineteenth century, continued in the twentieth.

Had not the phosphate, citrus, and cattle industries so dominated the Peace River area through most of the twentieth century, it might have enjoyed more interest and success in attracting other enterprise, such as industrial and service industries with their regular payrolls and relative stability. With little accomplished in that area, the region has experienced a continuing and substantial degree of poverty and near-poverty as well as a dearth of opportunity for young people, many of whom have emigrated.

The legacy of the nineteenth century continues to affect Peace River environmentally as well as economically. In the early 1890's the river bed itself was mined for phosphate, forever changing the river and its attendant plant and animal life. In the twentieth century, the discharge of phosphate waste into the river, whether intentional or accidental, has compounded the damage. The runoff of insecticides, pesticides, and fertilizers from the citrus and cattle industries has polluted the river's waters and many nearby ponds and lakes.

A postive legacy of the area's frontier heritage has been its lessons of self-reliance. The bonds of family and kinship remain important in the daily lives of many residents. The negative legacy of frontier violence also survived, as evidenced by the events of the 1919 phosphate strike, the lynchings of the early twentieth century, and the racial animosities carried well into the century.

Whatever problems the nineteenth century may have bequeathed to Peace River residents in the twentieth century, the settlement initiated there in the 1800s survives and thrives. One individual who lived through the pioneer days and into the twentieth century felt that, for all the lost excitement and happy memories, life indeed was getting better. In 1931, Lydia Oregon Hendry Blount, who had moved to Florida in 1852 with her brothers Francis A., William M., and George W. Hendry, was asked by a reporter from the *Atlanta Journal Magazine*, to compare the past with the present.

We had nothing then. It was twenty-five miles to a church from my home. Some who claim to have been pioneers and who in a measure were pioneers will tell you of the good times of their days, country dances and frolics and picnics. But we were before even that day. We ate, slept and kept house while the men folk hunted cattle. Later when more settlers came in we visited about. And when we went visiting we went to spend the night. Every one's house was open to his neighbor and even to the stranger.

People should be very happy now. They have everything—railroad trains, automobiles, flying machines, radios, telephones, electric lights, running water. They can buy groceries and furniture and fine clothes at the stores. They have to pay for them, of course, but they can make money now. In those days you couldn't make money. There wasn't anything we could sell except cattle, and they had to be driven hundreds of miles to market.

But people don't seem to be any happier. I don't think they have changed much. Some things I hear make me think the world is growing worse, at times. But after considering everything I believe it is getting better. There are more temptations now. And we hear more about the bad things, with newspapers and telephones and every one seeing every one else every day. But I've watched the world a long time and I believe it's a little bit better than it used to be.[1]

Appendixes

1

Soldiers of the Patriot War

ANY OF THE FRONTIERSMEN INVOLVED in the Patriot War of 1812–1814 and its aftermath, and their descendants, became pioneer settlers of South Florida and the Peace River Valley. Some of these men already in 1812 were residents of Spanish Florida, including Readding Blount; John Summerlin; James Hollingsworth; Isaac Hendricks; William Hollingsworth; Euphany Summerall; Joseph McCullough; Joseph Hagan; Michael Sloan; Joseph Summerall; Samuel Russell; Samuel Russell, Jr.; John Russell; and John Howell.

A longer list of names, principally of south Georgians, is contained in a Memorial to the Congress signed by "Patriots" on January 16, 1814. On that list are the signatures of James Stafford; William Emmons; David Cooper; Thomas Clark; James R. Woodland; John U. Malpurs; Solomon Lowry; John Bohanun; Duncan Bohanun; Samuel LeMartin; Giles Ellis, Henry Tutchstone; John Uptegram; Francis R. Sanchez; Ezekiel Alexander; Joseph Crockett; David B. Williamson; Timothy Hollingsworth; Thomas Theophilus Woods; Jones Bevan; Henry Nicholas; Zachariah Roberts; Enoch Daniels, Sr.; Robert Daniel; Simeon Dell; William Daniel; Robert Pierce; Enoch Daniels, Jr.; James Stafford; A. Broadaway; William Cone; Jacob Summerlin; David Lang;

Benjamin Moody; Thomas Prevatt; Shadrach Moody; Isham Hagan; John Hagan; Jeremiah Moody; Henry Hagan; John Gorman; Richard Dixon; Alexander Eliot; Levi Collar; P.M. White; Daniel Blue; William Niblack; Frederick Slade; David Hagan; Stephen Williamson; Absalom Brodus; Britton Knight; John Dyal; Hardy Lanier; James Lanier; Jackson Slade; Capt. A. McDonald; Lieut. Pliny Sheffield; John Mizell; George Martin; James Nix; Jose Silver; Nathaniel Stevens; Stephen Stevens; William Underwood; Men. Sauls; William Raulerson; Mark Attison; Jeremiah McDaniel; James OSteen; Isaac OSteen; Cornelious Johns; Wiley Harris; William Johns; Isaac Johns; Charles McKinny; William F. Murrhee; David Davis; Abner Stubbs; John Bailey, Jr.; Shadrach Stanley; William Stanley, Sr.; William Stanley; Lewis Dewitt; John Bennett; James Hayes; Benjamin Hayes; Jesse Carter; David Boggs; William Gibons; Donald McCrummen; Samuel Alexander; Daniel Sauls; Joseph Durrence; Harmon Hollimon; Ezekiel Stafford; George W. Henderson; Michael Henderson; Maxey Dell; Allen McDonald; Thomas L. Hall; James Dell; McKeen Greene; and William Durrence.

Sources: Muster rolls of the First, Second, and Third militia companies "de San Juan," Papers of the Revolution of East Florida, Bundle 112H9, Microcopy Roll #42, East Florida Papers; Petition of the Citizens of the District of Elotchaway, January 25, 1814, State Department Territorial Papers, Florida, Microcopy M-116, Roll #3, National Archives.

2

Selected Residents
of Old Columbia, Hamilton,
and Alachua Counties
(c. 1830–1832)

MANY OF THE SETTLERS in the area just to the north of the
Indian Reservation in the late 1820s and early 1830s
were men, or descendants of men, who had fought for
possession of Florida in the Patriot War of 1812-1814 and who
had waited in Georgia and the backcountry of remote northeastern
Florida for the opportunity to return to their dream of a new life
to the south. Many of them or their descendants would move in
the following two decades to South Florida and pioneer the settlement of the Peace River area.

From 1830 to 1832 the following settlers were living in that area
of Alachua County about to become Columbia County: Rigdon
Brown; John Powell; Jesse Pennington; Thomas Ellis; William
Raulerson; Burris Brewer; William A. Summerall; Aran Vickers;
William Hare; John Thomas; Willoughby Tillis; John Cason; Luke
Parker; Maxfield Whidden; Levi Pearce; Simeon Sparkman, Elisha
Green; Zachariah Roberts; Willoughby Whidden; William Wig-
gins; William Brown; and John M. Brannen.

Just across the Suwannee River in Hamilton County during
the same time were living, among others: James T. Hooker;
George E. McClelland; Joseph A. McClelland; Charles McClelland; Burwell Yates; Sampson Altman; Lott Whidden; Moses

Turner; James Kendrick; William McClelland; William Whidden; Stephen Hooker; James Green; William Harrison; George W. Smith; William B. Hooker; John Ivey; Peter Platt; James W. Whidden; Benjamin Moody; John Williams; James D. Prevatt; and Thomas T. Knight.

Sources: U.S. Original Census Schedules, 5th Census, Alachua County Population; election returns, Alachua, Columbia, and Hamilton counties, 1830-1832, Florida State Archives; Hamilton County Bicentennial Committee, *A Brief History of Hamilton County, Florida,* 19.

3

Selected Members of
the Columbia Volunteers
(1835–1836)

M AJ. JOHN MCLEMORE'S COMPANY, the Columbia Volunteers, which participated in the Battle of Black Point on December 17-18, 1835, was, as the name implies, raised principally from residents of Columbia and Hamilton counties. Ordered into service December 4, 1835, with headquarters at the Suwanee Springs, the company roster included the names of many who themselves or through their descendants found a home in the Peace River Valley. Among them were: Sampson Altman; David Bowen; John M. Brannen; Rigdon Brown; William Brown; Milton Bryant; Thomas Bryant; James Duncan; Joseph Dyer; Henry B. Ellis; Stephen C. Hooker; William B. Hooker; David Hunter; Thomas Ivey; James Johnson; James Kendrick; Daniel Morgan; Henry Pennington; William Pennington; Levi Pearce; John Powell; Simeon Sparkman; William S. Spencer; Wiley Tanner; James Tillis; Richard Tillis; Temple Tillis; Wayne Tillis; Willoughby Tillis; John Weeks; William Whidden; Early Wiggins; Jesse Wiggins; and William Wiggins.

Sources: Department of War, Compiled Service Records, M-1086, McLemore's Mounted Company; *Jacksonville Courier*, December 31, 1835.

4

Selected Members of

Capt. William B. North's Company,

Florida Volunteers (1838–1839)

TYPICAL OF THE FRONTIER MILITIA UNITS serving in North Florida in late 1838 and early 1839 was that of Capt. William B. North. Organized principally in Columbia County, the company's members included: Corp. Jacob J. Blount; Readding Blount; Riley Blount; James Brewer; John Bryan; James Bryant; Bryant Burnett; Richard Burnett; David Cannon; William Cannon; Harley Cason; Henry Cason; John Cason; William Cason; Archibald Crews; B.W. Crews; Dempsey D. Crews; Edward Crews, Sr.; Edward Crews, Jr.; Isham Crews; James Crews; Joseph Crews; Lewis Crews; Micajah Crews; Samuel Crews; Stephen Crews; William Crews; William B. Crews; Laomi Davis; Joseph Gill; Ebenezer Hatcher; Henry Herrington; Joseph Howell; David Hunter; Elijah Hunter; James Hunter; Jessee Hunter; Riley Johns; John I. Johnson; William Levens; Elijah Locklear; Joseph Locklear; William Locklear; Andrew M. McClelland; John W. McClelland; Silas McClelland; William McClelland; Chesley B. Mims; James North; John J. North; James Oglesby; Jesse Pennington; Charles Scott; John G. Slade; Leonard Slade; Stephen Slade; David Summerall; Thomas Summeralls; 2d Lt. James Whidden; Private James Whidden; Maxfield Whidden; Noah Whidden; William P. Whidden; William S. Whidden, Willoughby Whidden; W.I. Whidden; and Elijah Wilkinson.

Source: Department of War, Compiled Service Records, M-1086, Capt. North's Mounted Company, 1838-1839, National Archives.

5

Selected Residents of
Columbia and Hamilton Counties
(1842-1843)

T
HE SETTLERS IN COLUMBIA and Hamilton counties during the
period 1842–1843, and their general location, may be
gleaned from election returns. Among those voting in 1842
at Upper Mineral Springs in Hamilton County were: John Ivey,
James W. Whidden, William B. Hooker, James Brewer, Thomas
Altman and James H. Prevatt. In 1843 Columbia County elections
the following are among the voters listed: at Moses Barber's pre-
cinct, Joseph Underhill, Moses Barber, Louis Lanier, and Hilliard
Jones; at the house of William Cone, Robert Ivey, John Green,
Jesse Pennington, Early Wiggins, Wiley Hicks, Israel Green,
Willis Cason, Andrew Cason, John Peacock, Rigdon Brown, John
M. Brannen, John Futch, Rabun Raulerson, Joseph Howell, James
Sweat, Jesse Hicks, Jacob J. Blount, John Hunter, William Cone,
William Pennington, Grandison Barber, Aaron Whittemore, Wil-
liam Brown, William Green, Henry Peacock, Isaac Hines, James
Altman, Charles Whittemore, John B. Raulerson, William Wig-
gins, William H. Williams, Silas McClelland, John McClelland,
and William Whidden; and at Mineral Springs, Joseph Durrance,
John G. Smith, Joseph L. Durrance, Jesse H. Durrance, William
H. Durrance, George T. Durrance, Willoughby Tillis, Jeremiah
Byrd, James H. Prevatt, David Platt, Francis M. Durrance, and
Asa Gaskins.

Source: election returns, Columbia and Hamilton counties, 1842–1843,
Florida State Archives.

6

Armed Occupation Act Claims

THREE ARMED OCCUPATION ACT CLAIMS were located with reference to Peace River. Edmund Lee specified his claim to be at "Peas creek," and Joseph Elitz and James A. Goff listed theirs as "near Peas creek." The location of these claims, however, was in the Itchepuckesassa-Alafia River area of eastern Hillsborough County.

Almost fifty claims were located on the Manatee River and at Sarasota. Among those claimants were: James D. Green, John Davidson, Samuel Reid, John Craig, George Mitchell, William Mitchell, John Jackson, and Simon Turman.

In the Thonotosassa/Itchepuckesassa/Fort Sullivan/Alafia area were located the settlements of: Louis Bell, John J. Knight, Robert Jackson, Levi Pearce, Benjamin Moody, Benjamin Warren, William B. Hooker, John I. Hooker, Joseph Bertrand, Seth Howard, James Glasgow, John C. White, Uriah John Collar, Lot Gage, William Delaney, James White, Rigdon Brown, Eber Beal, Jesse Pennington, William Parker, Richard Dickson, Henry S. Clark, Eustatia Thompson, Simeon L. Sparkman, John Parker, Stephen Hollingsworth, James C. Pearce, Wytche Fulford, Fuiton Fulford, James W. Whidden, John H. Hollingsworth, Samuel Rodgers, John B. Hicks, John Weeks, Joseph Moore, John Brooks, Thomas

Weeks, John Weeks, Jr., Antonio Gastigo, George Clarison, John Talmadge, John Dixon, John MacInnis, William Henry Shepperd, and John Tammage.

Among those filing claims in areas of Florida distant from the Peace River Valley were: James M. Bates, John Curry, John Christopher Sherouse, Solomon Godwin, Mills Holliman (a free black man refused "on account of color"), David Russell, Robert Hendry, William H. Hendry, Lewis Jenkins, William Hall, John Bates, Joseph Howell, Willoughby Whidden, Noah Whidden, Maxfield Whidden, Alderman Carlton, Isham Crews, Dempsey D. Crews, Timothy Alderman, Enoch Daniels, Jesse Knight, Enoch Collins, Hopkins M. Wilder, William Whidden, Francis M. Durrance, Richard D. Prine, Clatus Sherouse, Israel Sherouse, William P. Brooker, Shadrach Hancock, William H. Hancock, Henry W. Hancock, Jesse M. Durrance, and Willoughby Tillis.

Source: U.S. House Document No. 70, 28th Cong., 1st sess., 2–40; Armed Occupation Act Applications, Florida Department of Natural Resources.

7

Sparkman's and Parker's
Volunteer Companies
(1849)

WO MILITIA COMPANIES WERE RAISED in the Itchepuckesas-sa/Alafia area in July 1849. The membership of Capt. Simeon L. Sparkman's company, organized July 25, included: S.L. Sparkman, captain; Peter Platt, first lieutenant; Joseph Howell, second lieutenant; Joel Knight, first sergeant; John Thomas, second sergeant; James D. Green, third sergeant; William Whidden, Jr., fourth sergeant; N.J. Newsome, first corporal; Silas McClelland, second corporal; William Hollingsworth, third corporal; Jesse Pennington, fourth corporal; Thomas B. Ellis, bugler; Theophilus Rushing, bugler; Rigdon Brown; Rigdon Brown, Jr.; William Brown; William Brewer; David J.W. Boney; Joseph Brannon; Richard V. Buffum; John Butler; David Brannon; Redding Coleman; Isham Crews; James Gunstan; Henry Frier; John Futch; Thomas Gaskins; Israel Green; William Hancock; George Hamilton; Stephen Hollingsworth, S.F. Hollingsworth; George Howell; George Johns; Samuel Knight; Jesse Knight; John McClelland; Gabriel McClelland; Moses McClelland; John N. Norris; Berrien Platt; John B. Raulerson; Noel Rabun Raulerson; William Rushing, Samuel Rodgers; Jacob Summerlin; Charles H. Scott; Elijah B. Sparkman; Thomas Summeralls; William H. Sheppard; Moses Turner; Frederick Varn; John Vickers; William

Varn; Josiah Varn; Richard A. Vickers; Maxfield Whidden, Sr.; Elister Wiggins; Noah Whidden; Aaron Whittemore; Willoughby Whidden; John C. White; Maxfield Whidden, Jr.; William P. Whidden; Eli Whidden; Christopher Zbandon (?); and Joseph Underhill.

Capt. John Parker's company was organized July 23, 1849, and was composed of John Parker, captain; Daniel Gillett, first lieutenant; John Pearce, second lieutenant; John Williams, first sergeant; Henry B. Rowe, second sergeant; Levi Pearce, third sergeant; Alderman Carlton, fourth sergeant; John L. Skipper, first corporal; John H. Hollingsworth, second corporal; John Gallagher, third corporal; Lawrence Mitchell, fourth corporal; Stephen P. Hooker, bugler; James Pearce, bugler; Dickison Burns, George Brace; Isaac Carlton; Aaron C. Cothran; Isham Deas; John Green; William B. Hooker; William J. Hooker, Sr.; William J. Hooker, Jr.; Benjamin Guy; Henry Hilliard; Benjamin Hilliard; Enoch Johnson; Milton Johnson; George Keen; Thomas Mitchell; Thomas J. Mitchell; Franklin Mitchell; Samuel Mitchell; Benjamin Moody; William G. Miley; William Miley; Nathaniel Miller; John M. Pearce; William Parker; Daniel Plumley; James Rowe; Jackson Rowe; Harman Stephens; David Summerall; George Tison; Jonathan Tison; Thomas Underhill; John Underhill; William Underhill; John Weeks; Thomas Weeks; William Weeks; James W. Whidden; James L. Whidden; and William Whidden.

Source: Brown to Secretary of War, M-221, Roll #153 [F-17], National Archives.

8

Selected Enlistments,
Second Florida Cavalry (U.S.)
(March–June 1864)

A LTHOUGH IN ITS FIRST SIX MONTHS of existence the Second
Florida Cavalry drew recruits from many sources, many of
its men came from South Florida and the area of the Peace
River Valley. Among them were the following.

(I)
"Recruited, c. March 1864"

Benjamin J. Hilliard; David D. Whidden; Andrew Wiggins;
Thomas J. Hilliard; William McClenithan, Jr.; Henry Messer;
Lewis B. Platt; Charles H. Whidden; Dempsey N. Whidden; James
E. Whidden; John H. Whidden; George W. Williams; Thomas Wil-
liams; William H. Williams; and Joshua A. Platt.

(II)
"Recruited, c. April 1864"

George W. Albritton; James N. Albritton; John M. Albritton;
Matthew H. Albritton; James F. Barnes, Sr.; James F. Barnes, Jr.;
William Danford; Stephen A. Driggers; Jacob Driggers; James
Driggers; Abraham E. Geiger; John A. Geiger; John C. Green;
John W. Harrell; James W. Jackson; Mathew E. Jones; James
Kirkland; Oden McKay; George C. Mizzell; John Patrick; Nathan

C. Platt; Daniel C. Ryals; Henry D. Ryals; James H. Stephens; James C. Thigpen; Thomas J. Thigpen; Thomas L. Thigpen; Alonzo W. Tucker; Elijah H. Tucker; Thomas Tucker; John Walker; Oliver Walker; Hampton Whidden; Maxwell Whidden; Rolly R. Whidden; Simeon Williams; and Richard E. Williams.

(III)
"Recruited, c. May–June 1864"

Nathan A. Arnold; Edward W. Ashley; John Collier; Dennis Driggers; William N. Hair; Streaty Hair; William T. Hart; Archibald Hendry; Charles Hendry; James M. Hendry; John Lowe; Joel Messer; John W. Platt; Madison Weeks; Thomas K. Walls; Reubin Carlton; Calvin Collier; Dempsey D. Crews, Jr.; William N. Crews; John W. Daniels; Thomas B. Jackson; George W. Whidden; and William Whidden.

Source: Regimental Descriptive Book, 2d Florida Cavalry (U.S.), Bound Regimental Records, Adjutant General's Office, RG 94, National Archives.

9

Partial Roster

F.A. Hendry's Independent Company, Munnerlyn's Battalion (1864)

THE COMPLETE ROSTER OF F.A. Hendry's independent company of Munnerlyn's battalion is unavailable. Among its members were: Francis A. Hendry, captain; F.C.M. Boggess, first lieutenant; John E. Fewell, second lieutenant; George W. Hendry, third lieutenant; William Altman; William H. Altman; Benjamin F. Blount; John C. Blount; Jehu J. Blount; William Carney; Robert Carson; S.M. Chandler; Zora Curry; John R. Durrance; Martin Flint; William R. Flint; Aaron E. Godwin; Solomon M. Godwin; James Green; Albert J. Hendry; William M. Hendry; Francis B. Hagan; W.R. Hollingsworth; Jacob Simeon Hollingsworth; Thomas Jones; E.B. Keen; J.L. McClelland; George W. Mitchell; Streaty Parker; John M. Pearce; Nelson Prescott; Jackson Prine; Joseph Rainey; John Sapp; John Skipper; James J. Smith; William Smith; Jacob Summerlin; Jasper Summerlin; Morgan Snow; Willoughby Tillis; William B. Varn; R.C. Wiggins; William W. Willingham; Frank J. Wilson; and Gideon Zipprer.

Source: Harris, "When War Came to Polk County," 5.

10

Capt. W.H. Cobb's Company
(Company C),
U.S. Volunteers (1898)

THE LIBERATION OF CUBA was a popular cause among South Floridians, and many young men from the Peace River area volunteered for service in the Spanish-American War. Many of them joined Company C, U.S. Volunteers, under the command of Capt. W.H. Cobb. Among the company's members were: from Arcadia—W.P. Alderman, J.G. Alderman, John H. Alfred, James N. Arnett, J.H. Best, Benjamin H. Britt, George P. Brooker, E.B. Buchan, J.W. Drawdy, John Hamilton, Arch Hampton, Henry Tate Harris, Samuel Harward, Nathan L. Hayman, J.J. Hayman, Frank Hays, N.C. Herndon, M.J. Hicks, Charles P. Hightey, Green W. Hodge, W.D. James, J.H. Jinkins, S.J. Johnson, John D. Montgomery, George Mutch, John N. Parker, P.R. Read, A.D. Sellars, Drew E. Smith, B.A. Thomas, R.E. Watkins, C.L. Whitesides, Benjamin W. Watson and J.I. Whidden; from Bartow— Hugh G. Blount, W.L. Boynton, S.L. Canter, B.F. Childs, James S. Day, Jasper C. Ferrell, J.L. Gilmore, F.F. Hendry, Luther L. Johnson, John J.Swearingen, M.A. Wilson, Erle L. Wirt and T.E. Wirt; from Bowling Green—W.F. Albritton, J.L. Sauls, J.W. Scott, J.H. Scott and Alex W. Stewart; from Brownville—J.W. Brown; from Fort Meade—Cary M. Carlton, William J. Lovett and Curtis Langford; from Fort Ogden—Coleman Stephens and E.D. Tippins; from Nocatee—E.W. Murrell, Jr.; from Pine Level—Herbert Green; from Punta Gorda—C.W. Carney, Albert W. Gilchrist and M.L. Williams; from Wauchula—A.S. Cochran; and from Zolfo Springs—Walter Bond and William J. Wadsworth.

Source: Bartow *Courier-Informant*, June 22, 1898.

Abbreviations

AGOLR	Adjutant General's Office, Letters Received
A&NC	*Army & Navy Chronicle*
ASPIA	*American State Papers, Indian Affairs*
ASPMA	*American State Papers, Military Affairs*
ASPMi	*American State Papers, Miscellaneous*
BAC	Bartow *Advance Courier*
BC-I	Bartow *Courier-Informant*
BI	Bartow *Informant*
BRFAL	Bureau of Refugees, Freedmen, and Abandoned Lands, Florida, Assistant Commissioner, Letters Received
CR	Church Records, Florida Writers Program, Fla. Collection, Fla. State Library
DC	DeSoto County
DOW	Department of War
FML	*Fort Meade Leader*
FMWP	*Fort Myers Weekly Press*
FP	Tampa *Florida Peninsular*
FSA	Florida State Archives
FT-U	Jacksonville *Florida Times-Union*
FT-U&C	Jacksonville *Florida Times-Union and Citizen*

HC	Hillsborough County
IITF	Florida Internal Improvement Trust Fund
LC	Library of Congress
MC	Manatee County
MCHRL	Manatee County Historical Records Library
NA	National Archives
OIA	Office of Indian Affairs
ORA	*War of the Rebellion: A Compilation of the Official Records of the Union and Confederate Armies*
ORN	*Official Records of the Union and Confederate Navies in the War of the Rebellion*
PC	Polk County
PCBC	*Minutes of the Baptist Church of Christ at Peas Creek*
PCHGL	Polk County Historical and Genealogical Library
PCN	Bartow *Polk County News*
PCR	Bartow *Polk County Record*
PKY	P.K. Yonge Library of Florida History
RG	Record Group
SAHSRL	St. Augustine Historical Society Research Library
SHC	Southern Historical Collection
ST	Tampa *Sunland Tribune*
SWLR	Secretary of War, Letters Received
TG	*Tampa Guardian*
TGI	Thomas Gilcrease Institute
TP	*Territorial Papers of the United States, Florida*
TT	*Tampa Tribune*
USACC	U.S. Army Continental Commands
USHD	*United States House Document*
USHED	*United States House Executive Document*
USHR	*United States House Report*
USHMD	*United States House Miscellaneous Document*
USSD	*United States Senate Document*
USSED	*United States Senate Executive Document*
USSR	*United States Senate Report*
WF	Tallahassee *Weekly Floridian*

Notes

Chapter 1

1. Tebeau, *A History of Florida*, 151-52; Patrick, *Florida Fiasco*, 197.

2. E.A. Hammond, "The Spanish Fisheries of Charlotte Harbor," 357; Mahon, *History of the Second Seminole War*, 5; *ASPIA*, I, 848.

3. Morse, *Report to the Secretary of War of the United States on Indian Affairs*, 309; Pensacola *Floridian*, May 4, 1822; Boyd, "Horatio S. Dexter and Events Leading to the Treaty of Moultrie Creek With the Seminole Indians," 90-91; Read, *Florida Place-Names of Indian Origin and Seminole Personal Names*, 29; "Survey of Indian Boundary Lines in Florida, With Sketch of the Country Embraced Within Them [c. 1827]," Map No. 757, RG 75, NA.

4. Morse, *Report*, 309; Covington, "Migration of the Seminoles Into Florida, 1700-1820," 351; Brinton, *Notes on the Floridian Peninsula, Its Literary History, Indian Tribes and Antiquities*, 49; Boyd, "Further Considerations of the Apalachee Missions," 464; Jacobs, *The Appalachian Indian Frontier: The Edmond Atkin Report and Plan of 1755*, 63.

5. Covington, "Migration," 351; Holmes, "Spanish Interest in Tampa Bay During the 18th Century," 13-18; Kinnaird, *Problems of Frontier Defense, 1792-1794, Part III, Spain in the Mississippi Valley, 1765-1794*, vol. 4, 207-8.

6. Covington, "Migration," 351; Simmons, *Notices of East Florida, With an Account of the Seminole Nation of Indians*, 78; Hawkins, *A Sketch of the Creek Country in 1798 and 1799*, 25.

7. *ASPIA*, I, 838.

8. *A&NC*, March 31, 1836; Hammond, "Spanish Fisheries," 356; Read, *Florida Place-Names*, 3, 29.

9. "Survey of Indian Boundary Lines in Florida, With Sketch of the Country Embraced Within Them;" *TP*, vol. 22, 968-71.

10. Remini, *Andrew Jackson and the Course of American Empire, 1767-1821*, 214-15; McReynolds, *The Seminoles*, 62; *ASPIA*, I, 859.

11. McReynolds, *The Seminoles*, 64-65; Peters, *The Florida Wars*, 19; Wright, "A Note on the First Seminole War as Seen by the Indians, Negroes, and Their British Advisers," 567; Grismer, *Tampa*, 48; Williams, *The Territory of Florida*, 299-300.

12. Hays, *Letters of Benjamin Hawkins, 1797-1815*, 198-200; Matthews, *Edge of Wilderness*, 71; Coker and Watson, *Indian Traders of the Southeastern Spanish Borderlands*, 301.

13. Philadelphia *National Gazette and Literary Register*, December 3, 1821; Williams, *Territory of Florida*, 299-300.

14. Peters, *Florida Wars*, 26; Coker and Watson, *Indian Traders of the Southeastern Spanish Borderlands*, 309. '

15. Peters, *Florida Wars*, 50; Hays, *Creek Indian Letters, Talks and Treaties*, 888-90.

16. Remini, *Andrew Jackson and the Course of American Empire*, 354; Parton, *Life of Andrew Jackson*, 459; Woodward, *Woodward's Reminiscences*, 44-45.

17. Peters, *Florida Wars*, 52; Woodward, *Woodward's Reminiscences*, 161.

18. Milledgeville *Reflector*, May 5, 1818; Peters, *Florida Wars*, 54.

19. Porter, "Negroes and the Seminole War, 1817, 1818," 277; *Boston Patriot and Daily Merchantile Advertiser*, August 20, 1822; "The Defences of the Floridas; A Report of Captain James Gadsden, Aide-de-Camp to General Andrew Jackson," 248.

20. Swanton, *Early History of the Creek Indians and Their Neighbors*, 406-7, 411-12; *USHD 51*, 17th Cong., 1st sess., 11-12; *TP*, vol. 22, 463-65; Boyd, "Horatio S. Dexter," 89; St. Augustine *East Florida Herald*, October 11, 1823; Morse, *Report to the Secretary of War*, 309; *ASPMA*, I, 752.

21. *ASPMA*, I, 752.

22. *Boston Patriot and Daily Merchantile Advertiser*, August 20, 1822; Vignoles, *Observations Upon the Floridas*, 135; Philadelphia *National Gazette and Literary Register*, December 3, 1821; *ASPMA*, I, 752; Swanton, *Early History*, 406-7, 411-12; *USHD 51*, 11-12.

23. Swanton, *Early History*, 178-79, 409; Coleman, *A History of Georgia*, 100; *ASPMA*, I, 724, 726-27; *Message from the President of the United*

States, 215; Worthington to Calhoun, April 6, 1822, SWLR, M-221, roll #92.

24. Boyd, "Horatio S. Dexter," 91-92; Survey map of Indian boundary line, enclosed with Gadsden to Secretary of War, June 15, 1824, *TP*, vol. 22, 968-71, facing 968.

25. Swanton, *Early History*, 242-47; Woodward, *Woodward's Reminiscences*, 110; Hawkins, *A Sketch of the Creek Country in 1798 and 1799*, 26-27; Power of attorney from the Indian Chiefs to A. Arbuthnot, June 17, 1817, *State Department Territorial Papers, Florida*, M-116, roll #4, NA.

26. *Tampa Tribune*, July 15, 1956.

27. Parton, *Life of Andrew Jackson*, 457; Woodward, *Woodward's Reminiscences*, 45, 51, 110; Boyd, "Asi-Yaholo or Osceola," 257-59; McKenney and Hall, *The Indian Tribes of North America*, vol. 2, 367-68.

28. "Survey of the Indian Boundary Lines in Florida, With Sketch of the Country Embraced Within Them."

Chapter 2

1. Tebeau, *A History of Florida*, 114.

2. Sturtevant, "Chakaika and the 'Spanish Indians': Documentary Sources Compared with Seminole Tradition," 38-39; Nassau *Royal Gazette and Bahama Advertiser*, October 2, 1819.

3. Mahon, *History of the Second Seminole War*, 29.

4. Ibid.; Peters, *Florida Wars*, 64.

5. Doster, *Creek Indians*, vol. 2, 231; McReynolds, *The Seminoles*, 90-91; Peters, *Florida Wars*, 67.

6. *TP*, vol. 22, 28-29, 40.

7. Ibid., 210-13; *ASPMi*, II, 913.

8. Philadelphia *National Gazette and Literary Register*, December 3, 1821; Peddy, *Creek Letters 1820-1824*, 21.8.20.C.C.; Boyd, "Horatio S. Dexter," 89.

9. Peddy, *Creek Letters 1820-1824*, 21.8.20.C.C., 21.1.22.C.C.; Philadelphia *National Gazette and Literary Register*, December 3, 1821; Boyd, "Horatio S. Dexter," 89.

10. Tebeau, *History of Florida*, 118; *TP*, vol. 22, 117-19, 125-27.

11. Peddy, *Creek Letters 1820-1824*, 21.9.29.C.C.; Tebeau, *History of Florida*, 119-20; *TP*, vol. 22, 225-26; *USHD 51*, 10.

12. Philadelphia *National Gazette and Literary Register*, December 3, 1821.

13. Interesting first-hand information about several of the blacks who escaped Tampa Bay at the time of the Coweta raid may be found in Kersey, "The Seminole Negroes of Andros Island Revisited: Some New Pieces to an Old Puzzle." Additional information concerning black set-

tlements in the Bahamas is contained in Porter, "Notes on Seminole Negroes in the Bahamas," and Goggin, "The Seminole Negroes of Andros Island, Bahamas." Philadelphia *National Gazette and Literary Register,* December 3, 1821.

14. Simmons, *Notices of East Florida,* 41; Boyd, "Horatio S. Dexter," 89; Vignoles, *Observations Upon the Floridas,* 134.

15. St. Augustine *East Florida Herald,* October 11, 1823; *TP,* vol. 22, 28–29; Simmons, *Notices of East Florida,* 42; St. Augustine *Florida Gazette,* August 4, 1821; Hays, *Creek Indian Letters, Talks and Treaties,* 962–63.

16. An additional town of Indians, probably Red Sticks from Tampa Bay, was located as early as the summer of 1821 above the falls of the Caloosahatchee River. A band of Choctaws also was noted at Charlotte Harbor in the summer of 1821, although this band temporarily fled the Cowetas to the neighborhood of Cape Florida. With them at Cape Florida were additional Red Sticks and other fugitive Creeks. *Boston Patriot and Daily Merchantile Advertiser,* March 8, 1821; Swanton, *Early History,* 407.

17. Boyd, "Horatio S. Dexter," 90.

18. Oponay's fortunes do not seem to have been affected by the great freeze or hail storm remembered by the Indians as occurring in 1819 ("[the] year after Jackson was on the Suwannee"). That storm was credited with creating the "Deadening," described in 1885 as "at or about Fort Meade, covering a tract of country some ten miles or more from north to south, and some five or six miles from east to west, being divided by Peace River." Pioneer settler George W. Hendry remembered, "Many years ago, perhaps in 1853, we heard it said that the Indians' story was, that a severe hail storm came; the worms got into the fallen trees and the bruised ones, and from these attached the whole pine forest indiscriminately, which resulted in its total destruction." More than likely, the Indians took advantage of whatever damage occurred to help clear the land for fields, no doubt killing and eventually clearing living trees using the ancient process known as girdling. A great deal of fallen timber remained on the ground until white settlement of the area began in the 1850s, and as late as 1896 evidence of Indian fields in the Deadening still was visible. John Charles Casey Diary, 1849, Casey Papers, U.S.M.A.; Adams, *Homeland,* 70; Hendry, *Polk County,* 33; Kollock, *These Gentle Hills,* 26; "Notes 1849–1850," entry of May 13, 1849, Francis Collins Papers; *FT-U,* May 24, 1896.

19. Boyd, "Horatio S. Dexter," 91–92.

20. Swanton, *Early History,* 411–12; Chazotte to Bell, August 18, 1821, SWLR.

21. Woodward, *Woodward's Reminiscences,* 44, 110; *ASPIA,* II, 439.

22. *TP*, vol. 22, 28-29, and vol. 23, 822-23; McKenney and Hall, *Indian Tribes*, vol. 2, 367-68; *TT*, July 15, 1956; Letter of Joseph M. White, March 3, 1827, OIA, Florida Superintendency, Letters Received, M-234, roll #287, NA.

23. *USSED 49*, 31st Cong., 1st sess., 86; "Petition of Buckra Woman," November 27, 1824, *Buckra Woman v. Philip R. Yonge*, St. Johns County Misc. Civil Court Files, Box 174, Folder 59, and Box 176, Folder 28, SAHSRL; Porter, "Billy Bowlegs (Holata Micco) in the Seminole Wars," 221; Sprague to Adjt. Gen., January 11, 1846 [1847], OIA, Letters Received, Seminole Agency, 1824-1876 (1846-1855), M-234, roll #801, NA.

24. Oponay left his estate "to Pulepucka the father of Sitarky." Sitarky was the nephew and heir of King Payne in the same manner as the then-new Seminole chief, Micanopy, was the heir to King Bowlegs. Boyd, "Horatio S. Dexter," 91; Cohen, *Notices of Florida and the Campaigns*, 238.

25. Boyd, "Horatio S. Dexter," 93.

26. "Petition of Buckra Woman."

27. The identification of Hatchee Thlokko or Bowlegs Creek with Billy Bowlegs, other than for the name, can be traced to Army reconnaissances in 1849. In that year Lt. George G. Meade was ordered to explore Hatchee Thlokko. Meade discovered the remains of an Indian town or village located several miles up the creek and near the main paths to the south and informed Seminole agent John C. Casey of his discovery. Casey entered in his diary for December 17: "Mead returns & H. thlokk was found by Stockton—also by Howard—M visited B Bowlegs old town on H. thlokk." Since after 1842 it was thought by whites that no Indian settlement was permitted north of Charlie Apopka Creek (a mistaken assumption), it is unlikely that any Indian town, especially of Bowlegs who was living much further south at the time, was present as far north as Hatchee Thlokko. Given U.S. military presence just north of the site after November 1837 and the assumed desire of the Seminoles to protect Bowlegs as a member of the Cowkeeper dynasty, a date for Bowlegs's presence at the town prior to the onset of the Second Seminole War is appropriate. Ives, "Military Map of the Peninsula of Florida South of Tampa Bay (April 1856)"; Meade, "Sketch of the road from Chokkonikla to Forts Fraser & Basinger," Meade Papers; John C. Casey Diary, 1849, Casey Papers, U.S.M.A.

28. *TP*, vol. 22, facing 192, 968-71; "Lieut. Yancey's Notes," June 15, 1824, OIA, Florida Superintendency, Letters Received, M-234, roll #286; Williams, *Territory of Florida*, 297. The presence of a Seminole town on Hatchee Thlokko also might explain an early reference to the great Seminole chief, Alligator (Halpatter Hadjo or Halpatter Tustenuggee), as having "resided at one of the towns on Telakchopco River." General

Thomas Jesup felt Alligator was Bowlegs's brother, an assertion made by others. Another officer referred to Alligator as the chief of the "Alafiers" which might make sense if Alligator lived on Peace River and ranged his cattle on Hooker's Prairie and near the Alafia River. Williams, *Territory of Florida*, 274; Jesup to Call, July 8, 1837, AGOLR, M-567, roll #145; "Notes of Indian Dept., July-Nov. 1843," William G. Belknap Papers; *Niles' Weekly Register*, January 30, 1836, 367.

29. Mahon, *History of the Second Seminole War*, 1; *TP*, vol. 23, 472–475; Sprague, *Florida War*, 52; "Lieut. Yancey's Notes."

30. Covington, *The Story of Southwestern Florida*, vol. 1, 73.

31. *USHR 47*, 17th Cong., 1st sess., 32–33; Chazotte, *Facts and Observations*, title page.

32. St. Augustine *Florida Gazette*, July 28, 1821; *USHR 47*, 32; Chazotte to Bell, August 18, 1821, SWLR; *Boston Patriot and Daily Merchantile Advertiser*, March 8, 1822.

33. *Washington Gazette*, April 27, 1822; *Charleston Courier*, November 2, 1821; Philadelphia *National Gazette and Literary Register*, November 19, 1821. To recoup some of his losses after the East Florida Coffee Land Association's bid for Key Largo failed, Chazotte edited and prepared for publication his 500 page-journal of the expedition together with eleven maps including those of Charlotte Harbor, the Caloosahatchee River and Lake "Mayaco," "Sarrazota, or Runaway Negro Plantations," and "Monteque [Manatee]." The journal was not published, however, and its whereabouts presently is unknown. *Washington Gazette*, April 27, 1822; *Boston Patriot and Daily Merchantile Advertiser*, March 8, 1822.

34. *TP*, vol. 22, 651; Boyd, "Horatio S. Dexter," 85–86.

35. Contemporary estimates suggest the presence in Florida at the time of a total of only three thousand to five thousand Indians. *USHD 51*, 5; Morse, *Report*, 149.

36. Boyd, "Horatio S. Dexter," 88–93; "Recognition of that part of East Florida Laying towards South West from Volusia, made by Horatio S. Dexter and reported by him on the 20th August 1823 to his Excy. Governor Duval," Map No. 1145, RG 75, NA.

37. Mahon, *History of the Second Seminole War*, 46–47.

38. Covington, "The Establishment of Fort Brooke: The Beginning of Tampa," 274; Covington, "Life at Fort Brooke 1824–1836," 320; *TP*, vol. 22, 850–51, 968–71.

39. *TP*, vol. 22, 968–71. For the Gadsden map of 1824, see *TP*, vol. 22, facing 968.

40. "Lieut. Yancey's Notes"; Vignoles, *Documents in Proof*, 22.

41. *TP*, vol. 23, 181–83.

42. Ibid., facing 192; "Survey of Indian Boundary Lines in Florida, With Sketch of the Country Embraced Within Them."

Chapter 3

1. Keuchel, *A History of Columbia County, Florida*, 21-26.

2. Nelson, "Nancy Jackson—1815-1907"; Grismer, *Tampa*, 71; Brooke to Adjt. Gen., September 9, 1828, 4th Infantry, 1821-1917, Regimental Records, Letters Sent and Orders Received 1823-1835, RG 391, NA.

3. *TP*, vol. 22, 847; Grismer, *Tampa*, 52; Tebeau, *History of Florida*, 124; Davis, "The Alagon, Punon Rostro, and Vargas Land Grants," 179.

4. Williams, *Territory of Florida*, 289-91, 294-96.

5. Ibid., 297-99; Hammond, "Sanibel Island and Its Vicinity, 1833, A Document," 393-410.

6. Williams, *Territory of Florida*, 295-96, 298-99; Vignoles, *Documents in Proof*, Strobel letter, n.p.

7. Chamberlin, "Fort Brooke: Frontier Outpost, 1824-42," 13; *ASPMA*, VI, 491.

8. Sprague, *Florida War*, 64; Kappler, *Indian Affairs: Laws & Treaties*, 345. "Holata Micco" is a title, rather than a name. The word "Holahta" signified a high ceremonial official or leader of the Muscogee Creek Nation, and "Micco" means king or chief. It was not at all unusual for Creeks and Seminoles to be known by many names and titles during their lifetimes, making attempts to identify an individual at different stages of his life extremely difficult. Knowing that Holata Micco was a Tallahassee chief and given his move in the early 1830s to the Peace River Valley, it is quite possible that he was among the Red Sticks who accompanied Peter McQueen there in 1818 or early 1819. Holata Micco, the Tallahassee chief, should not be confused with Billy Bowlegs, the Seminole, who assumed the title after 1837. Sturtevant, "Chakaika and the 'Spanish Indians,' " 69; Read, *Florida Place-Names*, 70-72.

9. *ASPIA*, II, 439; St. Augustine *East Florida Herald*, October 11, 1823; *TP*, vol. 23, 548-51.

10. Isaac Boring Diary, entry of July 22, 1829.

11. Williams, *Territory of Florida*, 220, 274, 298-99; *USHD 78*, 25th Cong., 2d sess., 438; *A&NC*, March 7, 1839; Thomas Jesup Diary, entry of April 4, 1837.

12. "Map of the Seat of War in Florida, 1836," No. 4343, RG 75, NA; *A&NC*, March 7, 1839; Williams, *Territory of Florida*, 275; *Niles' Weekly Register*, January 30, 1836.

13. "Map of the Seat of War in Florida, 1836"; Sprague, *Florida War*, 64; Thompson to Jones, October 21, 1837, AGOLR, M-567, roll #153, NA; *A&NC*, March 7, 1839; Williams, *Territory of Florida*, 275-76. Holata Micco likely was not only at Peace River in March 1833 but, in fact, was the "Seweky" who dealt cattle with P.B. Prior and whose town was two miles up Bowlegs Creek from its junction with the river. The name "Seweky" is very similar to the name of the Tallahassees who lived prior

to 1824 at the site of Florida's capital city. The Indians' name was "Sawokli" and referred to a group of Tallahassees living just prior to the outbreak of the First Seminole War on the Apalachicola River. Neamathla in September 1823 listed Holata Micco as living at "Wachitokha" on the "East side of Suwannee, between that and Santa Fe." Horatio Dexter, in a list prepared only a few months earlier, failed to mention Holata Micco, but did list "Suwiky" as living at "Watamky or McKenzie's old field" with a group of twelve Indians. The Wetumpka Hammock was located just northwest of the Indian agency at Fort King (Ocala) and only slightly north of the Big Swamp. Given the problems faced in reducing Indian names to writing and difficulties in rewriting handwritten documents and reports, "Wachitokha" easily could have been "Wetumpka." Likewise, the location of Holata Micco's village described by Neamathla could have fit that of Dexter's for "Watamky" when allowance is made for the vague understanding of Florida geography on the part of Indians and frontiersmen in the early 1820s. An Indian village of Wetumpka, misspelled on many early maps as "Wilamky," was located even closer to the Big Swamp and the Indian Agency than was the hammock, and slightly southwest of the village was a lake known as "Talassee [or Tallahassee] Pond." The hammock and the village were only about twenty miles from Payne's Landing and, given such proximity to the military at Fort King and the Indian agency nearby, it is little wonder that Holata Micco (Seweky) would want to pull up stakes and head for a more remote location. If, indeed, Seweky was Holata Micco and was living at the town on Bowlegs Creek early in 1833, there is nothing to suggest whether he lived with or displaced Seminoles there. It is very interesting, however, that Billy Bowlegs assumed the title "Holata Micco," after Holata Micco, the Tallahassee chief, was transported to the west. Swanton, *Early History*, 403, 409; *ASPIA*, II, 439; Boyd, "Horatio S. Dexter," 82; "Map of the Seat of War in Florida (1839); "Map of the Seat of War in Florida, 1836"; and "The State of Florida compiled in the Bureau of Topographical Engineers, 1846, from the best authorities by J. Goldsborough Bruff."

14. *Niles' Weekly Register*, March 25, 1837.

15. McKenney and Hall, *Indian Tribes of North America*, vol. 2, 367-68; Cohen, *Notices of Florida*, 234.

16. *ASPMA*, VI, 454, 491.

17. Mahon, *Second Seminole War*, 85; *TP*, vol. 25, 69-70; Chamberlin, "Fort Brooke," 13-14.

18. Mahon, *Second Seminole War*, 91-92, 95-96; New York *Evening Star for the Country*, July 15, 1836; Cohen, *Notices of Florida*, 234.

19. Mahon, *Second Seminole War*, 97-101; Chamberlin, "Fort Brooke," 14; *TT*, September 16, 1951; Coe, *Red Patriots*, 56-57; Hammond, "Span-

ish Fisheries," 372; *USSD 278*, 26th Cong., 1st sess., 31-32; *ASPMA*, VI, 560; *Charleston Mercury*, April 28, 1836; *Morning Courier and New York Enquirer*, May 4, 1836.

20. *TP*, vol. 25, 210-11; *Niles' Weekly Register*, January 30, 1836.

21. Mahon, *Second Seminole War*, 101-2; Williams, *Territory of Florida*, 220; Jacksonville *Courier*, December 21, 1835.

22. Mahon, *Second Seminole War*, 101-11.

23. Ibid., 147-50.

24. *USHD 78*, 44; Sprague, *Florida War*, 131; Columbia *Southern Times and State Gazette*, April 29, 1836; Henry Prince diary, entry of April 9, 1836; *National Banner and Nashville Whig*, May 11, 1836.

25. *ASPMA*, VII, 142; *USSD 224*, 24th Cong., 2d sess., 321-22.

26. *A&NC*, August 11, 1836; *Charleston Mercury*, May 18, 1836.

27. *ASPMA*, VII, 142; *Charleston Mercury*, May 18 and July 28, 1836; "Map of the Seat of War in Florida, 1836"; "Journal of the Volunteer Company from Columbia: Feb. 11, 1836-May 12, 1836, Benjamin T. Elmore, Captain"; *TT*, July 25, 1897; Williams, *Territory of Florida*, 234.

28. *USSD 224*, 355-58; Barr, *A Correct & Authentic Narrative of the Indian War in Florida*, 22-25.

29. At least one member of Colonel Smith's regiment, Seth Howard, took such a liking to South Florida that he accepted a discharge at Tampa and stayed to become a pioneer settler of the Peace River area. Livingston, "Seth Howard 1804-1887."

30. *USSD 224*, 355-58.

31. Mix to Dallas, April 30, 1836, U.S. Navy Dept., Records Relating to the Service of the Navy and Marine Corps on the Coast of Florida 1835-1842, NA.

Chapter 4

1. Mahon, *Second Seminole War*, 160-61.

2. *USHD 78*, 171; Peyton to Chambers, May 26, 1837, Jesup Papers, NA. The capture of cattle became a priority for Jesup. The Indians were thought to have driven thousands of head (one estimate was twenty thousand) to the South Florida ranges before the commencement of hostilities. Alligator later taunted Jesup that the General captured only the poorest of the cattle, the "cowhides." "Had you gone a little further, you would have gotten beef," the Seminole chief added. He concluded, "The Indians have a great many cattle yet." *A&NC*, March 7, 1839, 154; *Charleston Mercury*, July 11, 1836; Childs, "Major Childs, U.S.A.," 281.

3. Peters, *Florida Wars*, 143; Mahon, *Second Seminole War*, 200.

4. Peters, *Florida Wars*, 143; Harney to Jesup, March 27, 1837; Jesup Papers, NA. On the same day Holata Micco talked with Jesup, Billy Bowlegs also came in, asking for provisions. He is described by Jesup as

"William, a cousin of Micanopy." This diary entry marks Bowlegs's first known appearance in contemporary records. Jesup Diary, entry of April 5, 1837.

5. Jesup Diary, entry of May 23, 1837; Philadelphia *United States Gazette*, March 17, 1837.

6. Casey to Jesup, July 24, 1837, Jesup Papers, NA.

7. St. Augustine *Florida Herald*, July 7, 1837; Giddings, *Exiles of Florida*, 158.

8. *USHD 78*, 171–72; "Map of portion of Florida from Georgia boundary and mouth of the Saint Marys, southward to vicinity of Indian River inlet and Charlotte Harbor [mss. note by Gen. A. Macomb, Sept. 1837]," Map No. L.247, Item #1, Civil Works Map File, RG 77, NA.

9. Searle to Casey, August 14, 1837. Bowlegs had been captured the first week of July by a patrol operating near Fort Foster on the Hillsborough River. Jesup to Call, July 8, 1837, AGOLR, NA.

10. Thompson to Jesup, October 21, 1837, Jesup Papers, NA; Peters, *Florida Wars*, 151.

11. "Order No. 5," November 12, 1837, Army South of the Withlacoochee, Jesup Papers, NA; Nathan S. Jarvis Diary, entry of April 22, 1838; Taylor to Jesup, December 4, 1837, Zachary Taylor Papers; "Journal of the Campaign," entries of November 23–30, 1837, Robert C. Buchanan Papers.

12. One member of Taylor's army traveling through the lake region of eastern Polk County clearly saw the future of the area. Writing in December 1837 he remarked, "[T]here are high sand hills, with lakes and ponds of good water on their very summits—delightful spots for summer residences." *A&NC*, January 11, 1838, 29.

13. "Journal of the Campaign," entries of December 18–19, 1837, Robert C. Buchanan Papers; Mahon, *Second Seminole War*, 228; Peters, *Florida Wars*, 156.

14. Taylor to Jesup, January 12, 1838, Zachary Taylor Papers.

15. Thistle to Sec. of War, December 29, 1837, AGOLR; Philadelphia *Pennsylvania Inquirer and Daily Courier*, January 29 and February 14, 1838; "Journal of the Campaign," entry of December 22, 1837, Robert C. Buchanan Papers; Nathan S. Jarvis Diary, entry of April 22, 1838; Steptoe to Brooks, November 22, 1849, Western Division and Dept., Letters Rec. 1849, RG 393, NA; "Map of the Seat of War in Florida, compiled by order of General Zachary Taylor, Tampa Bay, Florida, 1839," No. 1141, RG 75, NA.

16. Taylor to Jesup, May 4, 5, and 20, 1838, Zachary Taylor Papers; Taylor to Jesup, March 30, 1838, AGOLR.

17. Mahon, *Second Seminole War*, 240, 248; Nathan S. Jarvis Diary, entry of April 26, 1838.

18. Coe, *Red Patriots*, 140-41; Mahon, *Second Seminole War*, 247.

19. Tallahassee *Floridian*, Supplement, February 9, 1839; Mahon, *Second Seminole War*, 249, 256.

20. Mahon, *Second Seminole War*, 253; Cummings to Taylor, June 10, 1839, AGOLR; Wright, "Finding Historical Markers in Polk County," 2-3.

21. Davenport to Taylor, February 20, 1839, AGOLR; "Map of the Seat of War in Florida, compiled by order of General Zachary Taylor, Tampa Bay, Florida, 1839"; Williams, *Territory of Florida*, 297-99; "Early Florida Roads" in DeVane, *DeVane's Early Florida History*, vol. 1, n.p.

22. Mahon, *Second Seminole War*, 255-56; "Indian Agency, Florida 1850-53" notebook, 7, Casey Papers, TGI; Jacksonville *Florida News*, August 27, 1853; *USSD 1*, 26th Cong., 1st sess., 57-58. The northern limits of the new Indian reservation were to run up Peace River from Charlotte Harbor as far as Hatchee Thlokko (Bowlegs Creek); then up Hatchee Thlokko to its source; then easterly to the northern point of Lake Istokpoga. Hatchee Thlokko was the pre-war home of Chitto Tustenuggee's "brother," Billy Bowlegs. *TP*, vol. 25, 614-15.

23. The reason why the site for the trading store was moved from Peace River to the Caloosahatchee is unknown.

24. Mahon, *Second Seminole War*, 261-62; Miller to Jesup, March 30, 1837, Jesup Papers, NA; Sprague, *Florida War*, 316-17.

25. Mahon, *Second Seminole War*, 263, 269-70; Johnston to Johnstone, March 16, 1840, Joseph E. Johnston Papers.

26. Mahon, *Second Seminole War*, 274, 276, 281-82.

27. Matthews, *Edge of Wilderness*, 105; Sprague, *Florida War*, 254. Hospetarke had shared with Chakaika the leadership of the attack on Lieutenant Colonel Harney and his men at the Caloosahatchee on July 23, 1839. In December 1840 Harney tracked Chakaika's band down in the Everglades, and Chakaika was shot dead while offering his hand to one of Harney's men. Sprague, *Florida War*, 316-17; Mahon, *Second Seminole War*, 283.

28. Matthews, *Edge of Wilderness*, 114, 117, 121; *USHD 247*, 15.

29. Worth to Hitchcock, February 4, 1841, Hitchcock Papers, LC; Sprague, *Florida War*, 257, 544; Mahon, *Second Seminole War*, 284. Fort Carroll was named in memory of Sgt.-Maj. Francis Carroll of the Seventh Infantry who had been cited for acting "with great bravery" in the Florida war and who died in an attack near Micanopy on December 28, 1840. Fort Carroll mistakenly has been located on some maps as having been at Thistle's Bridge. At the time Worth established Fort Carroll, in his words, "the route by Davenports trail crossing at the site of Thistle's bridge was impenetrable." Ethan Allen Hitchcock Diary, Feb.-March 1841, entries of February 5 and March 6, Hitchcock Papers, TGI; Worth to Hitchcock, February 4 and 13, 1841, Hitchcock Papers, LC.

30. Hitchcock Diary, March-April 1841, entries of March 31 and April 3, Hitchcock Papers, TGI; Worth to Hitchcock, August 9, 1841, Hitchcock Papers, LC; Peters, *Florida Wars*, 206.

31. The guide for this detachment was a soldier named Hugh McCartey, a survivor of the attack on Colonel Harney's party on the Caloosahatchee from which he had escaped on foot by taking off through the wilds. When near the future site of Camp Ogden, McCartey had been captured and held for torture by the Indians. An overnight rainstorm loosened his bonds and allowed him to escape. St. Augustine *News*, September 2, 1843.

32. Sprague, *Florida War*, 294–95, 547; Matthews, *Edge of Wilderness*, 109; St. Augustine *Florida Herald*, July 30, 1841.

33. Sprague, *Florida War*, 299–303; Hoxton to Hoxton, August 26, 1841, Randolph Family Papers; Mahon, *Second Seminole War*, 302.

34. Mahon, *Second Seminole War*, 307; *USHD 262*, 27th Cong., 2d sess., 46.

35. Sprague, *Florida War*, 435; Belknap to Clark, February 18, 1842, and Belknap to Worth, March 11, 17, and 22, 1842, William W. Belknap Papers; McCall, *Letters from the Frontiers*, 396.

36. *USHD 82*, 28th Cong., 1st sess., 98–100; Mahon, *Second Seminole War*, 316.

37. *USHD 82*, 10–11; *TT*, July 15, 1956.

Chapter 5

1. Sprague, *Florida War*, 517; *A&NC*, October 26, 1837, 269.
2. Sprague, *Florida War*, 425–26.
3. Ibid., 517–19.
4. Ibid., 518; *USHD 262*, 35.
5. St. Augustine *News*, March 5 and 9, 1842; Sprague, *Florida War*, 418–20, 518; *USHD 262*, 33–35.
6. Covington, "The Armed Occupation Act of 1842," 45; *USSED 39*, 30th Cong., 1st sess., 7–8.
7. Obvious exceptions were the slave-oriented sugar plantations developed on the Manatee River by Dr. Joseph Braden, the Gamble brothers, William Wyatt and others. On the development of these plantations, see Matthews, *Edge of Wilderness*, 125–164.
8. Akerman, *Florida Cowman*, 54; Giddings, *Exiles of Florida*, 158.
9. Kuechel, *History of Columbia County*, 59.
10. Covington, "Armed Occupation Act," 47; *USHD 70*, 28th Cong., 1st sess., 4–40. No better example exists of a settler taking advantage of the Armed Occupation Act to found a fortune through cattle than that of William Brinton Hooker. In 1843 the forty-three-year-old Hooker settled at present-day Seffner near the settlement of his brother, John I. Hooker;

his brothers-in-law, Benjamin Moody and Levi Pearce; the husband of his brother's widow, John Parker; and John Parker's brother, William, who in 1844 became William B. Hooker's son-in-law. Utilizing the Alafia range Hooker expanded his herds so that by 1850 he was Hillsborough County's largest stockholder with over 2,500 head of cattle. By the time Hooker sold out his cattle interests in early 1861 he had amassed some 10,000 head, bringing him $40,000. In the process the Hooker name became attached to numerous South Florida landmarks including, before 1849, Hooker's Prairie just west of Peace River near present-day Fort Meade. VanLandingham, "William Brinton Hooker 1800-1871"; Westergard and VanLandingham, *Parker and Blount in Florida*, 83-84, 160, 352; Livingston, "Benjamin Moody 1811-1896"; Otto, "Hillsborough County (1850): A Community in the South Florida Flatwoods," 190; Hillsborough County, *Deed Book C*, 200-202; "Sketch of the country from Tampa Bay to Pea River," *Notes 1849-1850*, Francis Collins Papers.

11. *FP*, February 15, 1871; *TP*, vol. 23, 469-70; *ST*, October 26, 1878; U.S. Original Census Schedules, 7th Census 1850, Hillsborough County, Florida (Population); Ibid., 5th Census 1830, Alachua County, Florida (Population); Election Returns, Columbia County, 1835-1839, FSA.

12. *USHD 70*, 15; Jacksonville *News*, September 2, 1848.

13. Whidden, "The James Whitton Family of Polk County"; Election Returns, Hamilton County, 1832, 1842, FSA; Compiled Service Records of Volunteer Soldiers Who Served in Organizations from the State of Florida During the Florida Indian Wars, 1835-1838, North's Co., Mounted, 1838-39, M-1086, roll #45; Livingston, "Noel Rabun Raulerson"; Hamilton County Marriage Records, 1843; *USHD 70*, 36.

14. VanLandingham, "Stephen Hollingsworth 1797-1870"; Montgomery to Belknap, August 9, 1844, Belknap Papers.

15. Wiggins, *History of the Absolute Mt. Enon Association*, 3-4; "Hillsborough County Voters in the 1845 Statewide Election"; Livingston, "David J.W. Boney 1815-1889."

16. Election Returns, Hillsborough County, 1846, FSA; Livingston, "John Baggs Raulerson 1822-1901"; Hillsborough County, Tax Book, 1847. Silas McClelland settled to the east of Itchepuckesassa in what became known as the Medulla community. His may have been the first pioneer settlement in present-day Polk County, although it was followed closely by that of Henry M. Frier. McClelland, "Silas McClelland 1790-1875," 34; McClelland, *Silas and Penelope (Anderson) McClelland and Some Descendants*, 22-23; Bartow *Informant*, September 29, 1883.

17. *TP*, vol. 26, 1074-75; Hillsborough County, *Deed Book A*, 20; Westergard and VanLandingham, *Parker and Blount*, 345; Election Returns, Hillsborough County, 1848, FSA; Otto, "Hillsborough County," 2.

18. *USHD 253*, 5-6; Sprague to Medill, February 4, 1847, OIA, M-234,

roll #801; "1843. Indian Department Arrivals," Belknap Papers; Diary, 1848, entry of August 9, Casey Papers, USMA; *USHD 82*, 98-100.

19. *USHD 253*, 5; Worth to Belknap, January 18, 1844, Belknap Papers; St. Augustine *Florida Herald*, July 24, 1843.

20. St. Augustine *Florida Herald*, July 24, 1843; "Memorandum for Major Wright [July 1843]" and "List of Goods pertaining to the Indian Department at Tampa Bay [August 10, 1843]," Belknap Papers; Casey to Davis, April 18, 1855, OIA, M-234, roll #801.

21. "Memorandum for Major Wright," Belknap Papers; *USHD 82*, 2-3; *USSD 90*, 29th Cong., 2d sess., 2; *USHD 253*, 18.

22. Worth to Belknap, April 13, 1845, Belknap Papers.

23. Sprague to Belknap, May 12, 1845, and Worth to Belknap, May 24 and June 23, 1845, Belknap Papers; Sprague to Rankin, September 18, 1845, Casey Papers, TGI; "Sketch of Charlotte Harbor, January, 1849," included in "Report of the Board of Officers directed . . . to select a site for a new post at Charlotte's Harbor, Fla.," AGOLR, M-567, roll #410; extract of Griffin to Kennedy, September 27, 1845, included with Kennedy to Sprague, October 2, 1845, Casey Papers, TGI.

24. Jones to Pierce, August 26, 1845, and Jones to Winder, December 1, 1845, Casey Papers, TGI; *USSD 90*, 7. When William J. Worth died in 1849, Seminole agent John C. Casey entered in his diary the following synopsis of the man: "Gen. W.J. Worth dies of cholera at San Antonio & thus ends his plans of unchastened ambition and dashing intrigue—a soldier and a courtier who was out of place in a republic." Casey Diary, 1849, entry of April 7, Casey Papers, USMA.

25. Jernigan to Moseley, September 16, 1845, Casey Papers, TGI; Sprague to Medill, February 4, 1847, OIA, M-234, roll #801.

26. At the same time Kennedy mentioned that William McCrea had moved to the Caloosahatchee River where he continued to trade with the Indians. Thereafter, McCrea disappears from recorded notice in the area. Kennedy to Whiting, June 9, 1846, AGOLR, M-567, roll #329.

27. Sprague to Jones, July 19, October 25, and November 14, 1847, AGOLR, M-567, roll #359.

28. Darling to Moseley, January 6, 1848, OIA, M-234, roll #801; Wade to Jones, September 4, 1848, AGOLR, M-567, roll #398.

Chapter 6

1. Matthews, *Edge of Wilderness*, 165; Grismer, *Tampa*, 112.

2. Matthews, *Edge of Wilderness*, 165-66; Wade to Jones, September 26 and October 12, 1848, AGOLR, M-567, roll #398; Payne to Pierce, January 27, 1849, George S. Payne Letters; Grismer, *Tampa*, 113.

3. Order to create a board of survey, October 18, 1848, AGOLR, M-

567, roll #410; Casey Diary, 1848, entry of November 8, Casey Papers, USMA.

4. Morris to Jones, December 1, 1848, AGOLR, M-567, roll #386.

5. Report of the board of survey, January 20, 1849, AGOLR, M-567, roll #410; Tallahassee *Floridian*, December 29, 1849.

6. *Laws of Florida* (1849), 71; *USHMD 21*, 30th Cong., 2d sess., 2; Payne to Pierce, January 27, 1849, George S. Payne Letters.

7. Report of the board of survey, January 20, 1849, AGOLR.

8. Casey Diary, 1849, entries of February 8 and 23, Casey Papers, USMA; Morris to Kennedy & Darling, March 2, 1849, 5th Military Dept., 1848-52, Letters, Reports, and Orders Received and other Records, RG 393, NA.

9. At this time a working majority of the Hillsborough County Commission included William B. Hooker, William Wiggins, and James W. Whidden's son-in-law, William L. Campbell. "Return of Election, first Monday of Oct. 1847," Election Returns, Hillsborough County, 1847, FSA.

10. Hillsborough County Commission, *Minute Book A*, 24.

11. "Journal & Surveyors Notes 1849-1850," 52-53, George G. Meade Papers; *PCR*, January 26, 1940; Casey Diary, 1849, entry of March 18, Casey Papers, USMA.

12. Sketch of the country from Tampa Bay to Peace River in "Notes 1849-1850," Francis Collins Papers; Hillsborough County, *Deed Book A*, 155.

13. Another of James W. Whidden's sons-in-law, Noel Rabun Raulerson, may have moved with his family to the southeastern side of Lake Hancock as early as the time of Rigdon Brown's move to the same general vicinity. Benjamin F. Blount, an early pioneer who knew Raulerson well, stated that Raulerson moved near present-day Bartow "in 1849." No available historical source confirms Raulerson's presence until March 1850, however, and a sketch map of the area of Raulerson's homestead, drawn in November 1849, fails to note his settlement. At roughly the same time, certainly prior to January 1850, John H. Hollingsworth had settled about fifteen miles to the northwest at Lake Hollingsworth. *PCR*, January 26, 1940; Survey Plats, Township 29 South, Range 25 East, and Township 28 South, Range 24 East, Florida Dept. of Natural Resources; Steptoe to Brooks, November 23, 1849, Western Division and Dept. 1820-1854, Letters Received 1849, RG 393, NA.

14. U.S. Original Census Schedules, 7th Census 1850, Hillsborough County, Florida (Population and Slave Schedules); 7 *Florida Reports* 338-351 (1856); Polk County, Tax Book, 1866.

15. Payne to Pierce, June 8, 1849, Payne Letters; Casey Diary, 1849, entry of March 21, Casey Papers, USMA.

16. Payne to Pierce, June 8, 1849, Payne Letters; *USSED 49*, 31st Cong., 1st sess., 162-163; Schene, "Not A Shot Fired: Fort Chokonikla and the 'Indian War' of 1849-50," 21.

17. Casey visited the site on March 19-21, 1849, in company with the interpreter Sampson Forrester. His purpose was to settle on the site for construction of a "small house or log cabin" for use as an Indian agency. On this trip Casey stopped by James W. Whidden's homestead and also noted that the Indian interpreter and guide, Chai, and his wife, Polly, were living at the site of present-day Fort Meade. Casey Diary, 1849, entries of March 19-21, Casey Papers, USMA; Casey to Morris, March 11, 1849, 5th Military Dept., RG 393, NA.

18. Casey Diary, 1849, entries of May 23-28, Casey Papers, USMA.

19. Ibid., entry of June 28, 1849; Payne to Pierce, June 8, 1849, Payne Letters; Jacksonville *News*, August 4, 1849; *USSED 49*, 161-63; U.S. Original Census Schedules, 8th Census 1860, Hillsborough County, Florida (Population).

20. *USSED 1*, 31st Cong., 1st sess., 93, 116; Casey Diary, 1849, entries of July 5-7, Casey Papers, USMA.

21. Echo Emathla Chopco first came to the Peace River Valley in 1818-19 as a boy with the party of Peter McQueen, his father having been killed in the First Seminole War. During the Second Seminole War he and his brother, Cotsa Fixico Chopco, fought under the Mikasuki chief Halpatter Tustenuggee and were members of the last party of Indians to enter the reservation. By January 1847 Chipco had emerged as a chief in his own right with a reputation for hostility to Americans. Indian agent Casey described him as "a bad subject—vicious & hostile so much so that when Gen. Worth presented Cotsa [Fixico Chopco] with a black horse [Echo] threatened to shoot him." In 1849 Chipco and his family were living about twelve miles north of Reedy Lake, near modern-day Lake Wales. "Chipco Was A Creek By Birth" in DeVane, *DeVane's Early Florida History*, vol. 1, n.p.; Mahon, *Second Seminole War*, 317-18; Sprague to Jones, January 11, 1846 [1847], OIA, M-234, roll #801, NA; Casey Diary, 1848, entry of August 8, and Diary, 1849, 93, Casey Papers, USMA; Britton to Mackall, April 12, 1850, Western Division and Dept. 1820-54, Letters Received, RG 393, NA.

22. Covington, *Billy Bowlegs War*, 10, *FT-U*, October 18, 1893.

23. *USSED 49*, 161-63; Casey Diary, 1849, entry of May 25, Casey Papers, USMA.

24. Payne to Pierce, September 16, 1848, University of Miami; Payne to Pierce, June 8, 1849, Payne Letters.

25. Casey Diary, 1849, entry of May 25, Casey Papers, USMA.

26. *USSED 49*, 162.

27. "Indian Agency, Florida 1850-53" notebook, 33[B], Casey Papers, TGI; *USSED 49*, 162; Jacksonville *News*, August 4, 1849.

28. *USSED 49*, 35; Schene, "Not A Shot Fired," 25; "Journal & Surveyors Notes 1849-1850," 6, 14, George G. Meade Papers.

29. Jacksonville *News*, August 11, 1849.

30. *USSED 49*, 39, 93.

31. Casey Diary, 1849, entry of July 24, Casey Papers, USMA; Florida House of Representatives, Office of the Clerk, *People of Lawmaking in Florida 1822/1985*, "Micajah C. Brown"; Tallahassee *Floridian*, August 11, 1849; Jacksonville *News*, August 4, 1849; *USSED 1*, 119; Philadelphia *North American and United States Gazette*, October 5, 1849; Twiggs to Crawford, September 8, 1849, Misc. Mss. Coll., LC.

32. Casey Diary, 1849, entries of August 10-11, Casey Papers, USMA; Tallahassee *Floridian*, October 6, 1849; Jacksonville *News*, September 13, 1849; Sketch of Peace River from Lake Hancock to Fort Chokonikla [c. Nov. 1849], Official Maps & Drawings, George G. Meade Papers.

33. Several excellent accounts of the military and diplomatic activities in Florida during 1849 and 1850 have been written. See particularly: Covington, *Billy Bowlegs War*, 9-17; Matthews, *Edge of Wilderness*, 182-203; and Schene, "Not A Shot Fired." "Notes 1849-1850," entries of August 25 and September 1, 1849, Francis Collins Papers.

34. Pemberton to Thompson, September 3, 1849, Mrs. John C. Pemberton Corr., Pemberton Family Papers; *USSED 1*, 94, 120; Jacksonville *News*, September 15, 1849.

35. *USSED 49*, 62; *USSED 1*, 125-26; Bliss to Casey, October 16, 1849, Casey Papers, TGI.

36. On October 17, 1849, three Indians were surrendered to Twiggs, along with the hand of a fourth who had been killed. A fifth Indian still at large was being hunted. No mention was made of the participation of Echo Emathlá Chopco in the murders, nor was his surrender demanded. "Indian Agency, Florida 1850-1853" notebook, 33, Casey Papers, TGI.

37. Casey to Marshall, January 29, 1850, Western Division and Dept., 1820-1854, Letters Received, RG 393, NA. One of these was Echo Emathla Chopco's brother, Cotsa Fixico Chopco. He was emigrated from Fort Hamer on the Manatee River along with seventy-three others on March 1, 1850. *USSED 49*, 79-80; "Notes 1849-1850," entry of January 22, 1850, Francis Collins Papers.

38. *USSED 49*, 96.

39. Matthews, *Edge of Wilderness*, 199; "Notes 1849-1850," entry of October 12, 1849, Francis Collins Papers.

40. Schene, "Not A Shot Fired," 25; Casey Diary, 1849, entry of October 19, Casey Papers, USMA; Rains to Twiggs, November 6, 1849,

384   *Notes to Pages 88-89*

Western Division and Dept. 1820-1854, Letters Received, RG 393, NA; "Journal & Surveyors Notes 1849-1850," 16-17, George G. Meade Papers.

41. Ross to Mackall, October 20, 1849, Western Division and Dept., 1820-1854, Letters Received, RG 393, NA. By November 27, 1849, Fort Crawford had been moved about five miles east of its former location. "Notes 1849-1850," entries of October 20-21, 1849, and November 27, 1850, Francis Collins Papers.

42. Schene, "Not A Shot Fired," 27; Hamersly, *Complete Army and Navy Register*, 146.

43. Among Twiggs's other problems was whisky sales to Indians and soldiers. In the fall of 1848 Joseph Summerall had been arrested in Hillsborough County for selling whisky to the Indians. On October 8, 1849, he was tried and in the absence of his defense witness, Dempsey Whidden—killed at the Indian store on July 17—found guilty. When Summerall was assessed only a $10.40 fine, within a short while others sought to follow his lead. On November 23 two of these entrepreneurs, William H. Willingham and William H. Stone, were captured by military authorities at Fort Chokonikla, expelled from the area, and escorted under armed guard to Hooker's Prairie. Hillsborough County, Circuit Court Minute Book, 1846-1854, 72, 87, 94-95; Morris to Brooke, November 23, 1849, Western Division and Dept., 1820-1854, Letters Received 1849, RG 393, NA.

44. Casey Diary, 1849, entry of October 31, Casey Papers, USMA; Tallahassee *Flordian*, December 1, 1849; "Sketch of the róad from Chokkonikla to Forts Fraser & Basinger," December 13, 1849, in notebook "General Meade. Appointments—Assignments and Reports, 1835 to 1865," George G. Meade Papers.

45. Steptoe to Brooks, November 22, 1849, and Meade to Brooks, November 30, 1849, Western Division and Dept., 1820-1854, Letters Received, RG 393, NA; "Journal & Surveyors Notes 1849-1850," 54-56, George G. Meade Papers; Mackall to Bainbridge, December 17 and 19, 1849, 5th Military Dept., Letters, Reports and Orders Received and other Records, RG 393, NA.

46. Mackall to Bainbridge, December 17 and 19, 1849, 5th Military Dept., Letters, Reports, and Orders Received and Other Records, RG 393, NA; Hamersly, *Complete Army and Navy Register*, 123, 127-128; *USSED 49*, 79. On January 3, 1850, Twiggs also had established a supply depot, named Fort Casey, on Useppa Island. On February 20 an additional fort was constructed on the Caloosahatchee River on the site of the Second Seminole War post, Fort Harvie. The new post was named Fort Myers. Matthews, *Edge of Wilderness*, 202; Hamersly, *Complete Army and Navy Register*, 127; Grismer, *Story of Fort Myers*, 62.

47. *USSED 49*, 95; Hamersly, *Complete Army and Navy Register*,

128, 146; "Notes 1849-1850," entry of April 26, Francis Collins Papers; A.P. Hill Diary, December 13, 1849-May 15, 1850, 18-19, A.P. Hill Papers; Schene, "Not A Shot Fired," 32.

48. "W.L.B. [?]" to Casey, June 21 [1851], Casey Papers, TGI; George A. Thomas to John W. Thomas, August 15, 1850, formerly in the Florida Collection of Charles F. Meroni.

Chapter 7

1. Hetherington, *History of Polk County, Florida*, 14-15; *PCR*, January 26, 1940.

2. Report of a public meeting of Alafia District, December 20, 1851, Governor's Corr., RG 101, ser. 755, FSA; Election Returns, Hillsborough County, 1852, FSA; Survey Plats for Township 20 South, Ranges 24 and 25 East, Fla. Dept. of Natural Resources; U.S. Original Census Schedules, 7th Census 1850, Hillsborough County, Florida (Population and Slave Schedules).

3. Livingston, "John Baggs Raulerson 1822-1901"; Hillsborough County, Tax Books, 1851, 1855, and 1856; U.S. Original Census Schedules, 7th Census 1850, Marion County, Florida (Population).

4. Survey plats for Township 29 South, Ranges 24 and 25 East, and Township 30 South, Range 24 East, Fla. Dept. of Natural Resources; *BI*, May 9, 1885; Historical Records Survey, *Roster of State and County Officers Commissioned by the Governor of Florida 1845-1868*, 145; Hetherington, *History of Polk County*, 15.

5. *USHED 1*, 31st Cong., 2d sess., 84; Grismer, *Fort Myers*, 63; *USSED 1*, 32d Cong., 1st sess., 155-56, 164; *TT*, February 3, 1957.

6. Jesse C. Sumner affidavit, November 22, 1850, and "Indian Agency, Florida 1850-53" notebook, 33-34, Casey Papers, TGI; *USHED 1*, 89-91; Britton to [Mackall?], April 3, 1850, and Casey to Bliss, November 19, 1850, Western Division and Dept., 1820-1854, Letters Received, RG 393, NA; Casey to Childs, December 17, 1850, DOW, M-1084, roll #2, NA.

7. Brown called the first of the meetings at Tampa on December 15, 1851. The Alafia and Itchepuckesassa meetings were held five days later. The Alafia meeting convened at the schoolhouse at Alafia bridge and its officers were: Benjamin Guy, chairman; Joseph Howell, assistant chairman; and Francis C. M. Boggess (the schoolteacher), secretary. Others active were William H. Willingham, Robert F. Prine, James W. Whidden, and Joseph Underhill. At Itchepuckesassa Simeon L. Sparkman was appointed chairman and Joel Knight served as secretary. Additionally active were John Parker, William Rushing, Jacob Summerlin, Stephen Hollingsworth, and Willoughby Whidden. Governors' Corr., RG 101, ser. 755, FSA.

8. Ibid., Darling to Brown, February 14 and March 4, 1852; Report of

Lt. T.S. Everett, June 5, 1852, Office of QM General, Consolidated Corr. File, "Pease Creek," RG 92, NA; Beckwith to Winder, January 31 and February 7, 1852, DOW, M-1084, roll #2, NA.

9. "Examination of witnesses by Major Genl. B. Hopkins," March 12, 1852, Governors' Corr., RG 101, ser. 755, FSA.

10. Blake's business agent at Tampa was John Darling's partner, Thomas P. Kennedy. Kallinger to Childs, February 12, 1853, DOW, M-1084, roll #3, NA.

11. Darling to Brown, February 14 and March 4, 1852, Governors' Corr., RG 101, ser. 755, FSA.

12. Ibid., February 14, 1852.

13. Ibid., Hopkins to Brown, March 8, 9, and 23, 1852.

14. Ibid., Hopkins to Brown, August 5, 1852, and Darling to Brown, June 25, 1852; Covington, *Billy Bowlegs War,* 24.

15. Covington, *Billy Bowlegs War,* 24.

16. U.S. Original Census Schedules, 7th Census 1850, Columbia County, Florida (Slave Schedule) and 9th Census 1870, Polk County, Florida (Population); *PCBC,* 13, 39; Mobley to Hart, June 29, 1867, Corr. of O.B. Hart, Supervisor of Registration in Florida, 1867, RG 156, ser. 626, FSA; Polk County, Marriage Records, Book A.

17. Durrance and Folk, *Lineage of Joseph Durrance;* Winder to Casey, February 13, 1852, Casey Papers, TGI; Hillsborough County Commissioners' Minutes, Book A, 44; Election Returns, Hillsborough County, 1852, FSA; U.S. Original Census Schedules, 7th Census 1850 and 8th Census 1860, Hillsborough County, Florida (Slave Schedules).

18. The first road commissioners were Francis M. Durrance, William Brown, and John B. Raulerson. The election precinct was at William Brown's house. Hillsborough County Commissioners' Minutes, Book A, 41.

19. *A Memorial Sketch of the Life and Ministerial Labors of Rev. J.M. Hayman,* 7.

20. Jacksonville *Florida News,* October 30, 1852; Stone, "Francis Asbury Hendry 1833-1917"; *PCR,* March 7, 1922; *FML,* May 1, 1913; U.S. Original Census Schedules, 8th Census 1860, Hillsborough County, Florida (Slave Schedule).

21. Brown to [Cooke?], April 2, 1853, and Barry to Cooke, September 3, 1853, DOW, M-1084, roll #3; *FML,* May 1, 1913; Westergard and VanLandingham, *Parker and Blount,* 345-46; *PCBC,* 40-41; Hillsborough County, Deed Book C, 111; Election Returns, Hillsborough County, 1852, FSA; Hillsborough County Commissioners' Minutes, Book A, 50.

22. The first election in the Peace River Valley was held October 4, 1852, at the house of William Brown near Bartow. Voters included Read-

ding Blount, Rigdon H. Brown, Riley R. Blount, John B. Raulerson, Owen R. Blount, David J.W. Boney, Streaty Parker, John R. Durrance, Noel R. Raulerson, Francis M. Durrance, John Parker, William Brown, and Thomas Summeralls. French to Cooke, June 16, 1853, DOW, M-1084, roll #3, NA; Election Returns, Hillsborough County, 1852–53, FSA.

23. *TT*, May 26, 1929.

24. Tallahassee *Floridian*, January 8, 1853; Covington, *Billy Bowlegs War*, 26; Directive of President Franklin Pierce, May 18, 1853, Casey Papers, TGI.

25. Covington, *Billy Bowlegs War*, 26–27; Walbridge to Casey, November 2, 1853, Davis to Casey, March 24, April 19, and May 10, 1854, Casey Papers, TGI; Haines to Hatch, August 12, 1855, Thomas J. Haines Papers.

26. Covington, *Billy Bowlegs War*, 29; Ives, *Memoir to Accompany a Military Map of the Peninsula of Florida*; Hendry, *Early History of Lee County and Fort Myers*, n.p.; "Survey of Township Lines made by John Jackson D.S. under Contract dated July 1, 1854," Field Notes, vol. 129, 114, 172–73, 202–03, and Survey Plats, Townships 31–32 South, Range 25 East, Fla. Dept. of Natural Resources.

27. Covington, *Billy Bowlegs War*, 29–34.

28. Haines to Arnold, December 6, 1854, Dept. of Florida, Letters Received 1854–57, RG 393, NA; *USSED 7*, 34th Cong., 1st sess., 41; Casey Diary, 1854, entry of December 4, Casey Papers, USMA; Hillsborough County, Deed Book B, 19.

29. *FML*, December 20, 1917; U.S. Original Census Schedules, 8th Census 1860, Hillsborough County, Florida (Slave Schedule); *PCBC*, 3, 39–41.

30. *PCBC*, 3.

31. Ibid.; Survey Plats, Townships 31 South, Ranges 24–25 East and Township 32 South, Range 25 East, Fla. Dept. of Natural Resources; Ives, "Military Map."

32. Hillsborough County Commissioners' Minutes, Book A, 56–57, 65.

33. Ibid., 68.

34. Election Returns, Hillsborough County, 1853, 1855, FSA; Tallahassee *Floridian and Journal*, October 20, 1855.

35. Survey Plats, Townships 32–33 South, Range 24 East and Township 33 South, Range 25 East, Fla. Dept. of Natural Resources; Westergard and VanLandingham, *Parker and Blount*, 85; Lesley to Hazzard, April 29, 1857, DOW, M-1084, roll #8; Newton, "John Platt 1793–1874."

36. Grismer, *Tampa*, 127; Matthews, *Edge of Wilderness*, 211.

37. The election precinct for Peace River voters in Manatee County was at Plunders Branch, a tributary of Paynes Creek. The fact that

James D. Green was clerk of the precinct suggests that voting took place at his home. Voting at Plunders Branch on December 3, 1855, were Daniel Sloan; Maxfield Whidden and his son-in-law, David Brannen; Willoughby Whidden; Thomas Underhill; Richard Pelham; Jesse Alderman; and James D. Green. Election Returns, Manatee County, 1855, FSA.

38. Signing the petition as "Citizens of Manatee" were Willoughby Whidden; John Addison; Isham Deas; John McDonald; John Underhill; Richard Pelham; Daniel Sloan; Maxfield Whidden, Sr.; Maxfield Whidden, Jr.; Jesse Pennington; Henry Langford; David Brannen; Jesse Alderman; John Parker; A.C. Coughan; George Tison; Moses A. McClelland; James D. Green; John K. Oneal; and Stephen P. Hooker. Petition of citizens of Hillsborough and Manatee counties [c. 1855], RG 915, ser. 887, FSA.

39. Florida *House Journal* (1855), 105; Lee to Darling, November 26, 1855, RG 915, ser. 887, FSA.

Chapter 8

1. Covington, *Billy Bowlegs War*, 33.

2. French to Casey, July 8, 1853, and Winder to Casey, July 6, 1851, Casey Papers, TGI; *TT*, April 2 and August 6, 1950. Chipco was said to have accompanied Tallahassee warriors on at least one raid in 1856. Otherwise he appears to have lived through most of the Third Seminole War on Lakes Marion and Hamilton near present-day Haines City. Covington, *Billy Bowlegs War*, 35.

3. Covington, *Billy Bowlegs War*, 1–2; "Bowlegs Banana Patch" in DeVane, *DeVane's Early Florida History*, vol. 1, n.p.; Canova, *Life and Adventures in South Florida*, 12; *FT-U*, October 18, 1893; Boggess, *A Veteran of Four Wars*, 43.

4. Casey to Broome, December 23, 1855, Governors' Corr., RG 101, ser. 777, FSA.

5. *PCR*, March 7, 1922, and January 6, 1933; *FP*, March 8, 1856; Frisbie, *Peace River Pioneers*, 18.

6. Florida, Board of State Institutions, *Soldiers of Florida*, 14–15; Durrance to Broome, December 30, 1855 and January 13, 1856, Francis M. Durrance Papers.

7. Covington, *Billy Bowlegs War*, 37; Florida, Board of State Institutions, *Soldiers of Florida*, 12–14; Hooker to Broome, January 3, 1856, Governors' Corr., RG 101, ser. 777, FSA.

8. Mormino, " 'The Firing of Guns and Crackers Continued Till Light': A Diary of the Billy Bowlegs War," 61–62; Hooker to Broome, January 3, 1856, Governors' Corr., RG 101, ser. 777, FSA; *FP*, March 8, 1856.

9. Howard to [Lizzie Howard], March 18, 1857, Oliver O. Howard Papers.

10. Sparkman to Broome, January 10, 1856, and Summerlin to Broome, February 7, 1856, Governors' Corr., RG 101, ser. 777, FSA.

11. *FP*, March 8, April 5, 12, and 21, 1856, and January 24, 1857; Vincent to Sparkman, April 30, 1856, DOW, M-1084, roll #1.

12. Covington, *Billy Bowlegs War*, 41; Haines to Hatch, March 6, 1856, Thomas J. Haines Papers; *FP*, July 17, 1856.

13. At about this time troops of Lesley's command were ordered to garrison Fort Blount. Also, Camp Gibson, located at present-day Gibsonton, was established as a supply depot and headquarters for volunteers under the command of Captain Simeon L. Sparkman. *FP*, March 29, 1856; Covington, *Billy Bowlegs War*, 42; Carter to Lesley, March 12, 1856, Governors' Corr., RG 101, ser. 777, FSA; William Charles Brown, Diary, December 1855–April 9, 1856, entries of March 17–31, 1856, P.K. Yonge Library of Florida History.

14. *FP*, March 29, 1856.

15. Covington, *Billy Bowlegs War*, 42; Matthews, *Edge of Wilderness*, 224–27; "John Wesley Whidden" in DeVane, *DeVane's Early Florida History*, vol. 1, n.p.

16. Matthews, *Edge of Wilderness*, 226–27; *FP*, April 12 and May 10, 1856.

17. Covington, *Billy Bowlegs War*, 45–49; *FP*, April 19 and May 31, 1856; Carter to Durrance, April 28, 1856, Durrance Papers; Tallahassee *Floridian*, July 19, 1856.

18. Carter to Broome, June 6, 1856, Durrance Papers.

19. Covington, *Billy Bowlegs War*, 52; Tallahassee *Floridian*, July 19, 1856. Hooker's first sergeant, James D. Green, refused either to confirm or deny the charges against Hooker, although Lyons had cited Green as a witness. Green did acknowledge that the report of Hooker's activities was "common amoungst members of the company commanded by Captain Hooker." Hooker was furious at the charges and in a letter to the *Florida Peninsular* reported, "Col. Monroe furnished me with a copy of said serious charges, an investigation of the matter was commenced, and not one charge was sustained," adding, "I now pronounce Matthew P. Lyons a liar." Green to Munroe, July 30, 1856, DOW, M-1084, NA; *FP*, August 16, 1856.

20. Tillis, "An Indian Attack of 1856 on the Home of Willoughby Tillis," 180–81.

21. Lott Whidden, whom John C. Oats had married to Caroline Crews at Fort Meade only four days earlier, thus became the second son of James W. Whidden to be killed by Indians in the Peace River Valley. His brother, Dempsey, had been killed at Chokonikla in July 1849 and, at the same time, his brother-in-law William McCullough had been wounded. John H. Hollingsworth and William Parker both were sons-in-law of Wil-

liam B. Hooker. *FP*, June 28, 1856; Westergard and VanLandingham, *Parker & Blount*, 160; VanLandingham, "William Brinton Hooker 1800–1871," 11.

22. *FP*, July 5, 1856; Durrance to Carter, June 14, 1856, Durrance Papers.

23. Tillis, "An Indian Attack of 1856," 184–85; *FP*, July 5, 1856; Boggess, *Veteran of Four Wars*, 51; Durrance to Carter, June 14, 1856, Durrance Papers.

24. This site was some distance north of the Peace River bridge at Chokonikla, which the Indians burned upon their withdrawal. *FP*, July 5, 1856.

25. Ibid.; Boggess, *Veteran of Four Wars*, 53–54; Durrance to Carter, June 14, 1856, Durrance Papers; *ST*, July 23, 1877.

26. *FP*, July 5, 1856; Durrance to Carter, June 14, 1856, Durrance Papers.

27. *FP*, July 19 and September 6, 1856; Hooker to Munroe, August 4, 1856, DOW, M-1084, roll #5, NA.

28. For a thorough examination of these activities and of the Third Seminole War generally, see Covington, *Billy Bowlegs War*.

29. Hancock to Page, January 18, 1857, and Lesley to Hazzard, February 3, 1857, DOW, M-1084, roll #8, and Scott to Page, March 13, 1857, roll #9, NA; McParlin to McParlin, January 7, 1857, Thomas A. McParlin Papers. Volunteer service on Peace River during this time may have had an unintended but positive impact on Florida's citrus industry. The Reverend Nathan L. Brown of Sumter County served as a private in Captain Johnston's company in the area during 1856 and the first half of 1857. According to tradition, while on Peace River Brown picked out and carried home with him some seeds from oranges he found growing there. The fruit of these seeds proved unusually sweet and matured earlier than other varieties of the same fruit. That fruit came to be called, in later years, "Parson Brown's." Covington, *Story of Southwestern Florida*, vol. 1, 345.

30. Whitall to Pleasanton, February 9, 1857, DOW, M-1084, roll #9, NA.

31. Hazzard to Howland, March 4, 1857, George W. Hazzard Papers.

32. The Blount family and relations concentrated at the Riley R. Blount homestead, Fort Blount. At Fort Fraser were the families of Isham Crews; Charles H. Scott; Zachariah Seward; Rigdon Brown; Joseph Durrance and his sons, Joseph L., William H., Francis M., John R. and George T.; Silas McClelland; John Altman; Isaac Waters; Noel R. Raulerson; John Tyre; and others. Fort Meade served as a haven for, among others: Francis A. Hendry; his brothers, George W. and William Marion; his mother and step-father, Lydia Carlton Hendry and Benjamin

Moody; his brothers-in-law, Simpson Singletary and James Thomas Wilson; his father-in-law, Louis Lanier; John I. Hooker; Eli English; Alderman Carlton; Daniel Carlton; Lott Whidden; William Parker; William P. Brooker; Edward J. Hilliard; Francis C.M. Boggess; James W. Whidden; James L. Whidden; Joseph Underhill; and Dr. Gilbert L. Key. *PCR*, January 6, 1933; *FP*, July 25, 1857; Livingston, "Benjamin Moody 1811-1896," 10.

33. *TT*, September 26, 1948; *FP*, March 8, 1856.

34. Delegates to the convention included: from Fort Meade—Francis A. Hendry, Louis Lanier, James T. Wilson, Simpson Singletary, and William P. Brooker; from Fort Fraser—Isaac Waters, William H. Durrance, Noel R. Raulerson, and John Tyre. *FP*, July 25, 1857.

35. Matthews, *Edge of Wilderness*, 246; Election Returns, Manatee County, 1857, FSA; *FP*, October 10, 1857.

36. Covington, *Billy Bowlegs War*, 62-64, 68-78.

37. The former Seminole agent, Capt. John C. Casey, had died at Tampa on Christmas Day 1856. Billy Bowlegs, upon his departure from Florida, said of the officer whom he had known so well, "Casey was a good man—never tell Indian lie." Casey's remains were shipped from Tampa on the same ship his old antagonist and friend, Bowlegs, took to New Orleans. *New York Herald*, May 27, 1858.

38. Ibid.; Talbot to "Dear Sister," April 14, 1858, Theodore Talbot Papers.

39. Covington, *Billy Bowlegs War*, 81; *FP*, February 19, 1859.

40. *FP*, April 25, 1857; Moseley to Scott, May 20, 1857, DOW, M-1084, roll #8; McNeill to Talbot, July 8 and 16, 1858, roll #10, NA.

41. *Columbus Daily Sun*, December 9, 1858; Tallahassee *Floridian*, November 6, 1858; *FP*, February 19, 1859.

42. *TT*, April 2, 1950; *FP*, December 20, 1871; *Tallahassee Sentinel*, July 1, 1876; Tallahassee *Weekly Floridian*, April 5, 1881; *BI*, November 12, 1881.

43. Tallahassee *Weekly Floridian*, April 26, 1888; *FT-U*, June 30, 1888.

Chapter 9

1. Lanier to Millen, April 30, 1858, Nancy Ann Millen Family Papers.

2. *PCR*, October 18, 1921; Tallahassee *Floridian*, May 29, 1858.

3. Among the families moving to the Peace River Valley during 1858-1860 were: near Bartow—William P. Rodgers, Jeremiah Harrell, Charles H. Scott, Simon P. Smith, Henry Mansfield, George Hamilton, James Hamilton, Stephen Hull, William Melvin, Ashley P. Weeks, Jeremiah Ferrell, Dr. Levi W. Cornelius, Henry Keen, Hopkins M. Wilder, James W. Wade, Isham Crews, Thomas B. Ellis, and Thomas E. Williams; near Homeland—Robert A. McAuley, John McAuley, Levi Pearce,

William R. Hollingsworth, J.L. McKinney, Simpson Singletary, John B. Gunter, Thomas L. McKinney, Dr. James D. Smith, James B. Crum, and Irwin Davis; near Fort Meade—Francis A. Ivey, Isaac Waters, Dennis Hickey, L.A. Martin, Allen Lowe, Edward T. Kendrick, Christopher Q. Crawford, Daniel Waldron, Stephen Hollingsworth, T.J. Curry, William Allen, Robert Carson, John Powell, John M. Pearce, Dr. Gilbert L. Key, Solomon Godwin, James L. Avery, and William Carney; in Hardee County— Ephraim W. Thompson, Moses A. McClelland, James Isham Lewis, Dempsey D. Crews, Irvin Locklear, John Henry Hollingsworth, and David J.W. Boney; in DeSoto County—Rowland Williams, James Washington Mathis, Enoch Daniels, and William Whidden. U.S. Original Census Schedules, 8th Census 1860, Hillsborough and Manatee counties, Florida (Population); *FP*, July 28, 1860, and March 23, 1861.

4. Livingston, "James Washington Mathis (Matthews) 1834-1893"; "Petition of the Citizens and Legal Voters of Manatee County," RG 915, ser. 887, FSA; Peeples, "John F. Bartholf, A Manatee County Carpetbagger."

5. Fernandina *Florida News*, April 7, 1858; Johnston to Page, March 13, 1858, DOW, M-1084, roll #10, NA.

6. "Sketch of the route of the regular and volunteer force on the 3d & 4th March 1857, in the vicinity of 'Hookers Prairie,' " DOW, M-1090, roll #1, NA; Fernandina *Florida News*, April 7, 1858; *FP*, February 4 and April 14, 1860; Hillsborough County Commissioners' Minutes, Book A, 91-93; Records of Appointment of Postmasters, M-841, roll #20, NA.

7. Westergard and VanLandingham, *Parker & Blount*, 225; *PCR*, October 18, 1921. Those boys and girls were: Nathan S. Blount, Jehu Jacob Blount, Ben F. Blount, John Blount, James Blount, Nettie Blount, William Blount, Sarah J. Blount, Zachariah Seward, Felix Seward, James Seward, M.A.C. Wright, Lizzie Davidson, V. Rye, Readding Blount Parker, Lizzie Parker, Lewis Parker, S. Smith, Isaac Morgan, Howren Pearce, Thomas Pearce, Enoch E. Mizzell, H.R. Sylvester, Ellen Harrison, Peter Brown, Fred Varn, Frances Varn, Ed Wade, Andrew Wade, Owen Keen, Maria Keen, Louisa Hollingsworth, Simeon Hollingsworth, George W. Hendry, and Stephen Hooker. Frisbie, *Yesterday's Polk County*, 14.

8. *PCBC*, 19-21; *FP*, October 20, 1860.

9. Manatee County, County Commission Minute Book, 1856-1869, 4; Hillsborough County Commissioners' Minutes, Book A, 91-93; Boggess, *Veteran of Four Wars*, 66; U.S. Original Census Schedules, 8th Census 1860, Hillsborough County, Florida (Population).

10. *BC-I*, September 21, 1890.

11. *FML*, June 12, 1913; *FP*, January 21, 1860.

12. *BC-I*, September 21, 1890, and October 5, 1905; *TG*, April 21, 1886; *FP*, April 17 and 24 and May 1, 1858; *FT-U*, September 28, 1891.

13. Other prominent Know Nothings were Thomas P. Kennedy's partner, John Darling, as well as Edward T. Kendrick, Louis Lanier, and Joel Knight. Jacksonville *Florida Republican*, September 27, 1855; Jacksonville *Florida News*, October 13, 1855.

14. *FT-U*, September 28, 1891; U.S. Original Census Schedules, 8th Census 1860, Hillsborough County, Florida (Population); Jacksonville *Florida News*, October 13, 1855; *FP*, November 8, 1856, October 10, 1857, and December 8, 1860.

15. *BC-I*, September 21, 1890; Florida House of Representatives, Office of the Clerk, *People of Lawmaking*, "James T. Magbee"; *FP*, June 19, 1858.

16. Newport *Wakulla Times*, June 23, 1858; *FP*, April 17, May 1, and June 12 and 26, 1858; *TT*, June 16, 1946.

17. *FP*, November 19, 1859, and December 8, 1860; Columbus *Daily Sun*, August 16, 1858; numerous cases reported in 8-9 *Florida Reports*.

18. Election Returns, Manatee County, 1858, FSA.

19. Manatee County, County Commission Minute Book, 1856-1869, 3; *FP*, October 20, 1860; *Laws of Florida* (1845), 32-33.

20. Election Returns, Manatee County, 1859, FSA.

21. Manatee County, County Commission Minute Book, 1856-1869, 5; Addison to Williams, April 1, 1861, RG 350, ser. 554, FSA; Historical Records Survey, *Roster*, 2-4.

22. *Laws of Florida* (1845), 16; Florida *House Journal* (1862), 89; Historical Records Survey, *Roster*, 212; VanLandingham, "William Brinton Hooker 1800-1871"; *FP*, October 20, 1860; Manatee County, Circuit Court Minute Book, 1858-1887, 10-11.

23. Petitions of the Citizens and Legal Voters of Manatee County, 1859, RG 915, ser. 887, FSA.

24. *FP*, September 22 and October 6, 1860.

25. *TT*, July 29, 1956; Hillsborough County, Circuit Court Minute Book, 1854-1866, entry of April 7, 1858.

26. Florida *House Journal* (1859), 72, 110-11; Florida *Senate Journal* (1859), 221; *FP*, February 4, 1860.

27. *FP*, February 4, March 10, and June 9, 1860; *PCD*, August 26, 1938.

28. *TT*, July 29, 1956; *FP*, July 14, August 18, and December 8, 1860; VanLandingham, "William Brinton Hooker 1800-1871."

29. *TT*, July 29, 1956; *PCD*, August 26, 1938.

30. *FP*, October 6 and 13, 1860; Election Returns, Hillsborough and Manatee counties, 1860, FSA.

31. *FP*, October 13, 1860; *PCD*, August 26, 1938; Election Returns, Hillsborough County, 1860, FSA.

32. Florida *House Journal* (1860), 200-201; *PCR*, October 11, 1921;

Florida *Senate Journal* (1860), 231; *Laws of Florida* (1860), 192–93; Tebeau, *History of Florida*, 200.

Chapter 10

1. Hendry, *Polk County, Florida*, 6.
2. Jacksonville *Florida Republican*, August 30, 1855.
3. U.S. Original Census Schedules, 8th Census 1860, Hillsborough and Manatee counties, Florida (Population and Slave Schedules); Dept. of the Interior, Census Office, *Compendium of the Tenth Census, Part I*, 341.
4. Polk's 1861 slaveowners, with numbers of slaves indicated within parentheses, were: Rigdon Brown (5); Readding Blount (11), C.Q. Crawford (1), John W. Costine (1), Francis M. Durrance (4), James Hamilton (10), Stephen Hollingsworth (1), George Hamilton (11), Stephen Hancock (5), Francis A. Hendry (8), John I. Hooker (7), James M. Harrell (1), Louis Lanier (9), James Lanier (5), John Lanier (4), William A. Lively (1), Joseph Mizell (1), Silas L. McClelland (5), John C. Oats (8), Streaty Parker (1), Levi Pearce (1), Henry S. Seward (9), Zachariah G. Seward (6), Thomas Summeralls (1), John L. Skipper (1), Willoughby Tillis (2), Frederick Varn (13), Thomas B. Williams (1), and Charles F. Weeks (1). Polk County, 1861 Tax Book FSA.
5. "Copy of Statement furnished Gov. John Milton showing the number & value of Slaves, Cattle, Sheep, Swine &c in the State of Florida as taken from the Tax Books on File in this Office, Oct. 13, 1862," RG 350, ser. 554, FSA.
6. U.S. Original Census Schedules, 8th Census 1860, Manatee County, Florida (Slave Schedule).
7. Howard to [Lizzie Howard], March 29, 1857, Oliver O. Howard Papers.
8. *Boston Daily Journal*, September 12, 1862.
9. Polk County, 1861 Tax Book; U.S. Original Census Schedules, 8th Census 1860, Hillsborough County, Florida (Slave Schedule); Smith, *Slavery and Plantation Growth in Antebellum Florida 1821–1860*, 56; Grismer, *Tampa*, 137; Shofner, *Nor Is It Over Yet*, 48.
10. Hall, " 'Yonder Come Day': Religious Dimensions of the Transition from Slavery to Freedom in Florida," 419; *PCBC*, 3; Long, *History of the A.M.E. Church in Florida*, 111; Thomas Williams' letters, August 22–29, 1857, 6[B], Thomas Williams Papers.
11. *FP*, October 24, 1868; *WF*, July 1, 1873; Westergard and VanLandingham, *Parker & Blount*, 222; "Petition of Jacob Summerlin," September 12, 1865, AGO, Case Files of Applications from Former Confederates for Presidential Pardons, 1865–67, RG 94, M-1003, Roll #15, NA; *FT-U*, April 14, 1893; VanLandingham, "John Levi Skipper 1826–1907."

12. Dillon, "The Civil War in South Florida," 30; Oates, *With Malice Toward None*, 184.

13. Burnham, *Presidential Ballots 1836-1892*, 324, 328; *FP*, November 10, 1860.

14. *FP*, December 1, 1860.

15. Matthews, *Edge of Wilderness*, 252.

16. *FP*, April 14 and May 12, 1860; Manatee County, County Commission Minute Book, 1856-1869, 7.

17. *FP*, July 28, 1860, and April 6, 1861; *PCR*, January 29, 1940; Davis, *Civil War and Reconstruction in Florida*, 143.

18. *FP*, March 9, 1861; Florida, Board of State Institutions, *Soldiers of Florida*, 57. A complete roster of the "Hickory Boys" is not available. Lieutenant Durrance's detachment, however, included Durrance, Sergeant William H. Mansfield, Corporal Berrien Platt, John Altman, Jesse Altman, William Brown, William H. Durrance, Jesse H. Durrance, Joseph L. Durrance, George S. Durrance, Francis M. Durrance, Andrew J. Ellis, Edward T. Kendrick, William P. Rodgers, Timothy Hollingsworth, Charles H. Scott, Lewellen Williams, and James D. Smith.

19. Charleston *Southern Christian Advocate*, July 17 and August 14, 1862.

20. These volunteers, combined with others from the region, were constituted as Company E, Seventh Florida Infantry Regiment. The company, known affectionately as the "South Florida Bulldogs," elected Nathan S. Blount as its captain and, as lieutenants, John W. Whidden, Simon Turman, Zachariah Seward, and William H. Mansfield. Florida, Board of State Institutions, *Soldiers of Florida*, 178-79.

21. *BC-I*, November 23, 1904; *PCR*, January 26, 1940.

22. Mud Lake currently is known as Banana Lake. *Laws of Florida* (1860), 192-93; *FP*, April 20, 1861.

23. *PCR*, January 30, 1940.

24. County residents were served in this election by four polling places: Stephen Hollingsworth's home in the southwestern part of the county; Fort Meade; Rigdon Brown's home northwest of Bartow; and Camp Gibson at present-day Gibsonton. *PCR*, October 28, 1921.

25. Election Returns, Polk County, 1861, FSA.

26. Ibid., Polk and Manatee counties.

27. *Laws of Florida* (1861), 59; *PCR*, January 30, 1940.

28. Watkins to Corley, December 28, 1861, RG 593, ser. 914, FSA; "Register of Accounts Current of Post Offices in the State of Florida, 1862, For the Quarter ending March 31, 1862," Confederate States of America (Pickett Papers), vols. 100-102; LC; Hetherington, *History of Polk County*, 313; Faust, *Historical Times Illustrated Encyclopedia of the Civil War*, 44.

29. Addison to Williams, April 1, 1861, RG 350, ser. 554, FSA; Livingston, "Willoughby Whidden 1799-1861"; Election Returns, Manatee County, 1861, FSA; *Laws of Florida* (1861), 52.

30. Boggess, *Veteran of Four Wars*, 64-66; Livingston, "Francis Burdette Hagan 1827-1914"; Livingston, "Enoch Everette Mizell 1806-1887"; Stone, *John and William, Sons of Robert Hendry*, 24-26; Livingston, "Wade Hampton Whidden 1810-1865"; Hetherington, *History of Polk County*, 313; *Memorial Sketch of the Life and Ministerial Labors of Rev. J.M. Hayman*, 12; *BAC*, March 7, 1888; *BC-I*, January 2, 1908 and January 28, 1915; *Minutes of the Seventeenth Annual Session of the South Florida Baptist Association*, Appendix; *Transcript of Record, State vs. The Charlotte Harbor Phosphate Company*, 249-276.

31. Polk County, 1863 Tax Book; Bond of J.M. Hayman, Polk County Clerk of the Circuit Court, December 10, 1862, RG 150, ser. 392, FSA; *FP*, November 24, 1860; Margaret Watkins Gibbs Memory Diary

32. *Tampa Daily Times*, December 18, 1923; Kissimmee *Osceola Sun*, September 11, 1975; *ST*, July 21, 1877.

33. *FP*, July 28, and October 27, 1860; *ORA*, II, vol. 2, 967-68. As early as the summer of 1860 Fort Ogden was being used as a warehousing point for a group of men supplying groceries and supplies in present-day Hardee County. The men used two skiffs, one small and one large, to transport the groceries by water. By late October, as cattle shipping operations began from the McKay wharf on Peace River, Charles W. Hendry initiated the Peace River Packet Line, with the schooner *Alafia* to carry freight and passengers between Tampa and Fort Ogden. *FP*, July 14, 1860.

34. *ORA*, II, vol. 2, 967.

35. *Fort Myers Weekly Press*, February 13, 1886; Boggess, *Veteran of Four Wars*, 67; Kissimmee *Osceola Sun*, September 11, 1975; *ORA*, II, vol. 2, 867.

36. *ORA*, II, vol. 2, 968-69; *FP*, October 20, 1868; *ST*, October 26, 1878; "Petition of the Citizens of Clear Water Harbor," August 15, 1861, RG 101, ser. 577.

37. *ORA*, II, vol. 2, 956-57, 968-69; *New York Herald*, October 25, 1861.

38. *ORA*, II, vol. 2, 956-82.

39. Kissimmee *Osceola Sun*, September 11, 1975; *BC-I*, November 8, 1893; Boggess, *Veteran of Four Wars*, 64-66; Francis A. Hendry file, DOW, Confederate Papers Relating to Citizens or Business Firms, M-346, roll #433, NA.

40. Taylor, "Rebel Beef: Florida Cattle and the Confederacy, 1861-1865," 27; Frisbie, *Yesterday's Polk County*, 19.

41. McKay, *Pioneer Florida*, vol. 3, 25; Kissimmee *Osceola Sun*, October

2, 1975; *ORN*, I, vol. 17, 575. Crane and seven others had left Tampa in the fall of 1862 and made their way across the state to Indian River where they had enlisted in the U.S. Navy. *ORA*, I, vol. 26, pt. 1, 875-76.

42. *ORN*, I, vol. 17, 486-89.

43. *Fort Myers Weekly Press*, February 4, 1909.

44. Ibid.; *ORN*, I, vol. 17, 562; *New York Herald*, October 17, 1863.

45. *Fort Myers Weekly Press*, February 11, 1909.

46. *New York Herald*, October 17, 1863; *ORN*, I, vol. 17, 547, 562; Robert Johnson file, DOW, M-260, roll #2, NA. Johnson's wife, Cynthia, never saw her husband again, although she received word of his capture. In the summer of 1864 she was moved to Fort Myers as a refugee, where she remained until the end of the war. At Fort Myers Union volunteer Dennis Driggers proposed to her and "for self protection & support" she married him. Affidavit of Cynthia Driggers, February 22, 1881, Manatee County, Old Misc. County Files, Affidavits 1860-1899.

47. *ORN*, I, vol. 17, 48-49, 84-86; *New York Herald*, March 2, 1862; *Boston Daily Journal*, March 21, 1862.

48. Coulter, *The Confederate States of America 1861-1865*, 314; *ORN*, I, vol. 17, 309; *Boston Daily Journal*, October 31, 1862.

49. Polk County's ranks of public officials were decimated by volunteer enlistments and conscription agents in 1862. The election of October 6, 1862, filled vacancies as follows: John Davidson was elected probate judge; William H. Durrance regained the sheriff's badge by defeating Simpson Singletary; the Reverend Jeremiah M. Hayman stepped in as clerk of the circuit court; and Robert Wilkison and Eli English were selected, respectively, as county surveyor and coroner. Henry S. Seward was reelected to the state house of representatives over John R. Durrance. In Manatee County James D. Green once again sought election to the state house. He defeated Edmund Lee and William J. Hooker but came in second to William T. Duval. Coulter, *Confederate States*, 315; Election Returns, Manatee and Polk counties, 1862.

50. *PCBC*, 30-31; Hamilton, "Dempsey Dubois Crews 1806-1892"; Livingston, "Thomas Summeralls, c. 1822-1862"; VanLandingham, "Solomon Godwin 1817-1880"; Livingston, "Levi Pearce"; *FML*, March 16, 1916; Stone, *John and William*, 26; Livingston, "Willoughby Whidden"; Durrance, *R & M: Our Family*, 33. A descendant of two victims of the epidemic, Wauchula historian Spessard Stone has suggested an interesting and very plausible circumstance for the outbreak of the disease. "[M]y great-grandfather Robert Hendry and Zilla Ann [Hendry] were Methodists and, after coming to Fort Green, attended the camp meetings at Fort Meade," Stone writes. "It is my theory that the disease was contracted there and spread throughout the region." Stone to author, May 22, 1989, collection of the author.

Chapter 11

1. Boggess, *Veteran of Four Wars*, 70.

2. Faust, *Encyclopedia of the Civil War*, 305-7; 781-84; *Tampa Daily Times*, December 18, 1923.

3. Taylor, "Rebel Beef," 46; White to French, August 5, 1863, Pleasant Woodson White Papers.

4. McKay to Noyes, August 27, 1863, and McKay to White, September 27, 1863, White Papers; *ORN*, I, vol. 17, 575; White to Locke, September 8, 1863, White Letterbook (July 15, 1863-April 12, 1864), 117-19, White Papers.

5. McKay to White, October 10, November 6, 9, and 20, 1863, White Papers; *Tampa Daily Times*, December 18, 1923; White to Milton, December 9, 1863, White Letterbook.

6. *ORN*, I, vol. 17, 593; *ORA*, I, vol. 26, pt. 1, 855-56. Included in the original membership of the Florida Rangers were Dempsey Whidden (age 18), Jesse Whidden (25), John Whidden (28), and James Whidden (18). *Regimental Descriptive Book, 2d Florida Cavalry (U.S.)*, Bound Regimental Records, RG 94, NA.

7. *New York Herald*, December 25, 1863; Schmidt, *A Civil War History of the 47th Regiment of Pennsylvania Veteran Volunteers*, 400; *ORN*, I, vol. 17, 610-613; Daniels to Meyers, January 2, 1864, Dept. and Dist. of Key West, 1861-68; RG 393, NA; McKay to White, January 7, 1864, White Papers, *ORA*, I, vol. 35, pt. 1, 460-61.

8. *ORA*, I, vol. 26, pt. 1, 873; Schmidt, *Civil War History*, 401-02.

9. Ibid., 404-5; *New York Herald*, February 18, 1864; *ORA*, I, vol. 35, pt. 1, 486.

10. McKay to White, January 7, 1864, White Papers; *Charleston Daily Courier*, January 30, 1864.

11. McKay to White, February 4, 1864, White Papers; *ORA*, I, vol. 35, pt. 1, 486; Rerick, *Memoirs of Florida*, vol. 2, 408.

12. Coulter, *Confederate States*, 322; White to Northrop, March 17, 1864, White Letterbook.

13. Crane to Woodbury, February 24, 1864, Dept. and Dist. of Key West, 1861-68, RG 393, NA; *ORA*, I, vol. 35, pt. 1, 486.

14. Peeples, "Florida Men Who Served in the Union Forces During the Civil War," *South Florida Pioneers* 6 (October 1975): 12; Crane to Bowers, March 16, 1864, Dept. and Dist. of Key West, 1861-68, RG 393, NA.

15. McKay to White, March 25, 1864, White Papers. Also elected in Manatee County on November 9, 1863, were: David N. Townsend, probate judge; Joel J. Addison, sheriff; and Jesse Alderman, L.P. Johnson, Henry Langford, and John H. Hollingsworth, commissioners. In Polk County on October 5, Jeremiah M. Hayman was elected clerk of the cir-

cuit court and C.W. Deason was selected sheriff. Historical Records Survey, *Roster*, 212-14; bonds of J.M. Hayman and C.W. Deason, RG 150, ser. 392, FSA.

16. Florida *House Journal* (1863), 82-83. Duval's interest in helping Green also may have stemmed from an attempt one month earlier by Manatee County residents to unseat him. Asserting that Duval permanently had left the county, residents of Manatee held a special election on October 5 at which Fort Ogden resident Francis C.M. Boggess defeated Manatee area settlers Ezekiel Glazier and Archibald McNeill for the seat. When Boggess traveled to Tallahassee to claim the seat, however, he was dissuaded from pursuing the matter further. Petition of F.C.M. Boggess [c. 1863], RG 915, ser. 887, FSA.

17. McKay to White, March 25, 1864, White Papers; Historical Records Survey, *Roster*, 213-14; Florida *House Journal* (1863), 82-83; Stone, "James D. Green 1823-1886," 3.

18. Crane to Bowers, March 16, 1864, Dept. and Dist. of Key West, 1861-68, RG 393, NA.

19. Ibid., April 12, 1864; McKay to White, March 25, 1864, White Papers; Livingston, "Willoughby Tillis 1808-1895," 10.

20. McKay to White, March 25, 1864, White Papers; Crane to Green, April 2, 1864, Crane to Bowers, April 12 and 13, 1864, Dept. and Dist. of Key West, 1861-68, RG 393, NA; *Tampa Daily Times*, December 18, 1923; Confederate Pension Applications, 1885-1954, reel #99, "Henry A. Prine," FSA; Livingston, "Willoughby Tillis," 10.

21. Wilder, "The Wedding at the Parker House," 165; McKay to White, March 25, 1864, White Papers.

22. *ORN*, I, vol. 17, 682; Stone, "James D. Green," 3-4; Wilder, "Wedding," 164; Childs to Bowers, April 25, 1864, Dept. and Dist. of Key West, 1861-68, RG 393, NA.

23. McKay to White, March 25, 1864, White Papers; *ORA*, I, vol. 35, pt. 1, 372, and pt. 2, 373, 448-49, 481.

24. Taylor, "Rebel Beef," 92; Taylor, "Cow Cavalry: Munnerlyn's Battalion in Florida, 1864-1865," 198-99; Northrop to Seddon, July 6, 1864, in "1st Battalion, Special Cavalry," "Charles J. Munnerlyn," DOW, M-251, roll #14, NA.

25. Taylor, "Cow Cavalry," 202-5; *TT*, December 6, 1959.

26. Childs to Bowers, April 25, 1864, Dept. and Dist. of Key West, 1861-68, RG 393, NA; *ORA*, I, vol. 35, pt. 1, 389-91; Writers' Project, *Hillsborough County Personalities*, 21.

27. *Tampa Daily Times*, December 8, 1923; *ORA*, I, vol. 35, pt. 1, 389-91.

28. Confederate forces were not alone in refusing to provide assistance to supporters of the other side. In late March Confederate veteran

James M. Manley, who had lost his left arm at the Battle of Fredericksburg, appealed for aid to the troops at Fort Myers. Refusing the requested assistance Henry A. Crane explained: "The application of poor Manly & family, excites my sincere sympathy,—you will see the impolity of adopting any mode of assistance. He was stricken down & maimed for life fighting *against his country & brothers.*" Crane to Green, April 2, 1864, Dept. and Dist. of Key West, 1861–68, RG 393, NA.

29. Childs to Bowers, May 27, 1864, Dept. and Dist. of Key West, 1861–68, RG 393, NA; *ORA*, I, vol. 53, supp., 343.

30. Kissimmee *Osceola Sun*, September 11, 1975; Childs to Bowers, May 27, 1864, Dept. and Dist. of Key West, 1861–68, RG 393, NA; Boggess, *Veteran of Four Wars*, 71.

31. Childs to Bowers, May 27, 1864, Dept. and Dist. of Key West, 1861–68, RG 393, NA; *New York Herald*, June 16, 1864; Boggess, *Veteran of Four Wars*, 71.

32. Peterson to Gwynn, May 28, 1864, RG 350, ser. 554, FSA; Unsigned letter dated "Polke County Bartow Postoffice June the 9 1864" in "Minutes of the Salem Church, Echopocksassa, Hillsborough County, Fla., Oct. 15, 1850–Nov. 15, 1851"; Crane to Woodbury, June 18, 1864, Dept. and Dist. of Key West, 1861–68, RG 393, NA. Jesse Alderman and Henry Langford both ultimately supported the Union cause. John H. Hollingsworth may have been captured at some time prior to July 1864, but by January 1865 he again was active as a member of the Manatee County Commission. Historical Records Survey, *Roster*, 212.

33. Crane to Woodbury, June 18, 1864, Dept. and Dist. of Key West, 1861–68, RG 393, NA; Peeples, "Florida Men," *South Florida Pioneers* 5 (July 1975), 13.

34. Crane to Woodbury, June 18, 1864, Dept. and Dist. of Key West, 1861–68, RG 393, NA; Kissimmee *Osceola Sun*, September 25, 1875; *BC-I*, November 8, 1893.

35. *ORA*, I, vol. 35, pt. 1, 406; Crane to Bowers, August 15, 1864, Dept. and Dist. of Key West, 1861–68, RG 393, NA; Grismer, *Tampa*, 148; Matthews, *Edge of Wilderness*, 260.

36. Crane to Bowers, August 20, 1864, Dept. and Dist. of Key West, 1861–68, RG 393, NA; *ORA*, I, vol. 52, pt. 1, supp., 614; *Oswego Daily Palladium*, September 5, 1864.

37. Crane to Bowers, August 20, 1864, Dept. and Dist. of Key West, 1861–68, RG 393, NA; *ORA*, I, vol. 52, pt. 1, supp., 614.

38. Stone, "James D. Green," 3–5.

39. "The War Between the States," 6; *ORA*, IV, vol. 4, 730; Childs to Bowers, October 24, 1864, Dept. and Dist. of Key West, 1861–68, RG 393, NA; *Fort Myers News-Press*, September 2, 1966.

40. Augusta *Southern Christian Advocate*, November 3, 1864. At the

time of the October camp meeting, local elections also were held. In Polk County Robert Wilkison defeated John McAuley and George Hamilton by a vote of 26 to 25 to 5 for a seat in the Florida House of Representatives. In Manatee County the war-devastated county commission was revived by the election of William H. Vanderipe, John W. Curry, and William H. Addison. W.A. Griffin received a unanimous 43 votes for election to the state house. Election Returns, Polk and Manatee counties, 1864, FSA.

41. Crane to Bowers, September 4, 1864, and Bartholf to Hiltz, January 27, 1865, Dept. and Dist. of Key West, 1861-68, RG 393, NA; *ORA*, I, vol. 52, pt. 1, supp., 614.

42. Taylor, "Cow Cavalry," 210; Kissimmee *Osceola Sun*, September 11, 1975; *Tampa Daily Times*, December 18, 1923; Hendry, *Early History*, 5; Wilder, "Escapade in Southern Florida," 75.

43. *FML*, February 24, 1916; *Tampa Daily Times*, December 18, 1923.

44. Dillon, "The Battle of Fort Myers," 31; Hendry, *Early History*, 7; Entry of February 20, 1865, Morning Reports, Co. "A," 2d Florida Cavalry (U.S.), Bound Regimental Records, RG 94, NA; *Tampa Daily Times*, December 18, 1923; *New York Herald*, March 15, 1865; *FML*, February 24, 1916.

45. *Tampa Daily Times*, December 18, 1923; Dillon, "Battle," 31-32; *ORA*, I, vol. 49, 54.

46. Boggess, *Veteran of Four Wars*, 69-70; *FML*, February 24, 1916; *Tampa Daily Times*, December 18, 1923; Kissimmee *Osceola Sun*, September 11, 1975.

47. Dillon, "Battle," 33-34; *New York Herald*, March 24, 1865; Boggess, *Veteran of Four Wars*, 71-72, 74.

Chapter 12

1. *ORA*, I, vol. 49, pt. 2, 984; Taylor, "Cow Cavalry," 214; Jacksonville *Florida Union*, September 16, 1865.

2. Margaret Watkins Gibbs Memory Diary, n.p.

3. *FP*, July 26, 1866; Muse, "Negro History in Tampa," 4.

4. Third Florida State Census, 1867, Statewide Tabulations and Misc. Fragments, Manatee and Polk counties, RG 1020, ser. 5, FSA.

5. Polk County, Tax Books, 1866-1867; Polk County voter registration list, 1867-1868, RG 156, ser. 98, FSA; Sallie Robinson interview. The 1870 U.S. census for Polk County reports that, of a total population of 3,169, Polk contained 482 black inhabitants. Both these totals are highly misleading for the census enumeration contains over forty black families, together with a number of white families, who must have been transients or, at best, temporary residents in Polk. The heads and most of the members of these families are listed as having South Carolina as their place of birth and are shown as living in the Lake Drain or Medulla

section of the county. The names of none of the individuals ever appear on the Polk County tax rolls. U.S. Original Census Schedules, 9th Census 1870, Polk County, Florida (Population); Sallie Robinson interview.

6. Polk County voter registration list, 1867–1868, RG 156, ser. 98, FSA; U.S. Original Census Schedules, 9th Census 1870, Polk County, Florida (Population).

7. A Harriet Brown, the name of Rigdon Brown's female slave, appears in Duval County in 1870 with three small children, one of whom is named William. In late 1866 a Charles Brown, then about sixteen or seventeen years of age, married in Polk County and remained there until 1870. There is no direct evidence that Charles was a son of William and Harriet Brown, but his age corresponds with that of children born to them. U.S. Original Census Schedules, 9th Census 1870, Duval County, Florida (Population); "Marriage License Record for Colored Persons" in Polk County, Marriage Record Book A, 1862–1881.

8. *PCBC*, 13, 39–40; U.S. Original Census Schedules, 9th Census 1870, Polk County, Florida (Population), and 10th Census 1880, Hillsborough County, Florida (Population); Mobley to Hart, June 29, 1867, RG 156, ser. 626, FSA; "Marriage License Record for Colored Persons" in Polk County, Marriage Record Book A, 1862–1881. In December 1865 and January 1866 the Florida legislature enacted a series of laws, commonly known as black codes, to regulate the conduct and lives of former slaves. One of those laws required black couples living together to decide within nine months whether they wanted to continue their relationships. For those who did, the law required them to be married, even though marriage had been denied them prior to the end of the war. When the legislature again met in November 1866, it contemplated extending that deadline but, in the end, it simply passed a new law declaring all blacks living as husband and wife to be legally married. Prior to the effective date of this second law, the following black couples were married in Polk County: Royal Read and Harriet Varn (December 28, 1865); Alfred [Albert] A. Lewis and Ceily Jackson (January 21, 1866); Jacob and Lucinda Williamson (March 13, 1866); Nathaniel Redd [Read?] and Charlotte Morgan (June 14, 1866); Sam Manuel and Lucy Reaves (July 19, 1866); Andy Moore and Tanner Reid [Read], Solomon Carrington and Jane Williams, Simon Jackson and Electer Ann Douglas, Stepney Dixon and Sarah Washington, James Pernell and Minerva Bishop, and Alexander Stillings and Jane Hancock (September 2, 1866); Patrick Henry Jones and Hannah Jones (September 8, 1866); William Johns and Harriet Island (September 30, 1866); Nelson Blair and Willis Jenkins (October 21, 1866); and Charles Brown and Eliza Jackson (November 17, 1866). Shofner, *Nor Is It Over Yet*, 53; "Marriage License Record for Colored Persons" in Polk County, Marriage Record Book A, 1862–1881.

9. *BC-I*, September 9, 1896.

10. Margaret Watkins Gibbs Memory Diary, n.p.; U.S. Original Census Schedules, 9th Census 1870, Polk County, Florida (Population).

11. U.S. Original Census Schedules, 9th Census 1870 and 10th Census 1880, Polk County, Florida (Population); *PCBC*, 40; *ST*, August 17, 1878; Polk County voter registration list, 1867-1868, RG 156, ser. 98, FSA.

12. Polk County voter registration list, 1867-1868, RG 156, ser. 98, FSA; *PCBC*, 43; Hillsborough County, Deed Book C, 111; U.S. Original Census Schedules, 9th Census 1870, Polk County, Florida (Population).

13. Manatee County, Tax Books, 1866-1868; Hamilton, "Dempsey Dubois Crews," 9.

14. *Fort Myers Weekly Press*, September 12, 1885; *FP*, July 28, 1866; U.S. Original Census Schedules, 9th Census 1870, Manatee County, Florida (Population); "List of Registered Voters of Prec. No. 8," November 2, 1870," Poll Lists 1870-1893, Old Misc. County Files, Manatee County; "List of 1868 Manatee County Jurors taking oath," Jury Lists, Venires, Payrolls, Testimonies 1860-70, Circuit Court Records, Manatee County.

15. Shofner, *Nor Is It Over Yet*, 37; *Journal of Proceedings of the Convention of Florida . . . October 25th, A.D. 1865*, 132-33; L.G. Lesley file, DOW, Compiled Service Records, M-251, roll #14, "1st Battalion, Special Cavalry," NA; Wallace, *Carpetbag Rule in Florida*, 12; Florida House of Representatives, Office of the Clerk, *People of Lawmaking*, "James D. Green."

16. E.E. Mizell of Polk County was not the same person as Enoch E. Mizell of Manatee County. Shofner, *Nor Is It Over Yet*, 39-43; "Proposition and Petition to the Citizens of Polk County [c. 1866]," RG 915, ser. 887, FSA.

17. Manatee County, County Commission Minute Book 1856-69, 10, 14-15.

18. Jacksonville *Florida Union*, December 23, 1865; Thompson, "Journal as Inspector, Bureau of Freedmen, Refugees and Abandoned Lands, on a tour of central Florida and the lower West Coast, Dec. 1865," 84. Criminal matters of lesser significance were processed in county criminal courts, the judges of which were appointed by the governor. In January 1866 Enoch E. Mizell was designated county judge in Manatee County and William J. Watkins of Bartow in Polk. Florida *Senate Journal* (1865), 211, 225.

19. Tallahassee *Semi-Weekly Floridian*, November 3, 1865; Kissimmee *Osceola Sun*, September 11, 1975.

20. *Tallahassee Sentinel*, April 18, 1867; Harper to Woodruff, February 12, 1866, Dept. and Dist. of Florida, 1865-69, RG 393, NA; Kissimmee *Osceola Sun*, September 11, 1975.

21. Shofner, *Nor Is It Over Yet*, 51-55.

22. *Laws of Florida* (1865), 89-90. The board consisted of one representative from each of the eight election precincts in the county: #1 (Manatee), W.H. Vanderipe; #2 (Rough and Ready), Erasmus Rye; #3 (Long Creek), D.L. Hawkins; #4 (Waldron), F.B. Hagan; #5 (Cool & Easy), Maxwell Whidden; #6 (Joshua Creek), W.A. Johnson; #7 (Daniels), William Collins; and #8 (J.D. Green), E.W. Thompson. McDuffie, *Lures of Manatee*, 188.

23. Bartholf, "Centennial Oration given at Pine Level, Florida, July 4, 1876," U.S. Centennial Orations 1876, LC.

24. IITF Minutes, vol. 1, 299, RG 593, ser. 194B, FSA; "Proposition and Petition to the Citizens of Polk County [c. 1866]," RG 915, ser. 887, FSA; "Article of Agreement between the County Commissioners of Polk County and John McAuley, contractor," June 15, 1867, collection of Walter Crutchfield.

25. Most, but not all, Union refugees returned to their Peace River homes at the end of the war. William McCullough and his wife, Nancy Whidden McCullough, in August 1865 left Florida forever. Moving first to Illinois, the couple settled in 1868 in Clark County, Missouri. William died there April 2, 1890; Nancy followed August 31, 1908. According to their daughter, Mary McCullough Gilbert, William died "due to the Indian's bullet which had lodged in his breast falling into his lungs." Spessard Stone to author, November 9, 1989; *TT*, December 21, 1947.

26. Shofner, *Nor Is It Over Yet*, 65; Green to Osborn, June 15, 1866, BRFAL. Green resigned his seat in the Florida legislature during the summer of 1866. At elections held the following October, his brother-in-law and fellow Fort Green resident, John Wesley Whidden, was elected to represent Manatee County for the remainder of the term. Florida *House Journal* (1866).

27. Jones et al., to Mobley, September 17, 1866, BRFAL; Comba to Woodruff, May 31, 1867, Dept. and Dist. of Florida, 1865-69, RG 393, NA.

28. Comba to Lyman, December 17, 1866, and Comba to Larrabee, December 31, 1867, Dept. and Dist. of Florida, 1865-69, RG 393, NA; Mobley to Asst. Commr., June 25, 1867, BRFAL; *FP*, August 22, 1868.

29. Shofner, *Nor Is It Over Yet*, 158-59.

30. Ibid., 163; Comba to Hart, July 13, 1867, RG 156, ser. 626, FSA; Election Returns, Seventeenth Election District, 1867, FSA.

31. Comba to Woodruff, May 31, 1867, and Comba to Larrabee, June 30, July 31, August 31, and September 14, 1867, Dept. and Dist. of Florida, 1865-69, RG 393, NA.

32. Tallahassee *Semi-Weekly Floridian*, October 8, 1867; Shofner, *Nor Is It Over Yet*, 164; Election Returns, Seventeenth Election District, 1867, FSA. An 1867 Florida census found Manatee County's total population to

---

be 1,450 and Polk's 1,508. Third Census, 1867, Statewide Tabulations and Misc. Fragments, RG 1020, ser. 5, FSA.

33. Wallace, *Carpetbag Rule in Florida*, 49; Comba to Larrabee, December 31, 1867, Dept. and Dist. of Florida, 1865–69, RG 393, NA; Election Returns, Seventeenth Election District, 1867, FSA. While the low turnout in Polk and Manatee to some extent reflected resistance to Reconstruction, another factor was destruction wrought in late September and early October by a series of storms and days of torrential rainfall which began on September 29. Transportation and communications in the Peace River area were impacted substantially when the bridge at Six Mile Creek east of Tampa washed away, sealing Polk off from Tampa, except for horseback riders, for the duration of the rainy season. Nor was the Six Mile bridge the only one destroyed, for the only bridge across Peace River, that at Fort Meade built in 1858, also washed away. The magnitude of the flooding was described in the *Ocala Banner*: "Since 1848 the water courses of this State have not been so high as within the past week. The results may be briefly summed up in this sentence: The flat woods and swamps are under water, wharves, bridges and causeways washed away, many farms hidden and crops drowned and general ruin staring [at] some of the proprietors." *FP*, June 27, 1868; Jacksonville *Florida Union*, October 19, 1867.

34. Shofner, *Nor Is It Over Yet*, 187; *WF*, March 21, 1868.

35. Henderson to L'Engle, March 25, 1868, L'Engle Papers; Comba to Larrabee, April 30, 1868, Dept. and Dist. of Florida, 1865–69, RG 393, NA.

36. Comba to Larrabee, May 31, 1868, Dept. and Dist. of Florida, 1865–69, RG 393, NA; Shofner, *Nor Is It Over Yet*, 192; "Consolidated Official Return of Votes Cast for and against the Constitution, and also for State and County officers &c at the Election held in Florida on the 4th 5th & 6th of May 1868," 3d Military District 1867–68, RG 393, NA; Election Returns, Manatee County, FSA.

37. Green to Reed, July 2, 1868, RG 101, ser. 577, FSA; Volume "No. 10, Book A," 56, RG 156, ser. 259, FSA.

38. *FP*, August 1, 1868; Green to Reed, September 28, 1868, RG 101, ser. 577, FSA; Volume "No. 10, Book A," 46, RG 156, ser. 259, FSA; Petition of Citizens of Manatee County [c.1868], RG 915, ser. 887, FSA.

39. Shofner, *Nor Is It Over Yet*, 204; Wallace, *Carpetbag Rule in Florida*, 88; *FP*, September 26, October 3, and October 17, 1868; Election Returns, Manatee County, 1868, FSA.

40. *FP*, August 22, 1868.

41. Wakulla County, 1863 Tax Book, FSA; Wallace, *Carpetbag Rule in Florida*, 8–9; Tallahassee *Semi-Weekly Floridian*, May 18, 1866; *FP*, April 25, 1868.

42. *FP*, October 24, 1868; Grismer, *Tampa*, 155-56.

43. McKay to White, March 25, 1864, White Papers; *FP*, August 15, 1868; Wallace, *Carpetbag Rule in Florida*, 89; Shofner, *Nor Is It Over Yet*, 193, 204-6.

Chapter 13

1. Shofner, *Nor Is It Over Yet*, 193; Grismer, *Tampa*, 155.

2. *FML*, October 12, 1916.

3. Among the arrivals of 1866 at Bartow were the families of J.C. Mimms and Martha Hewitt. In the same year Jesse Keen settled in the Medulla section of Polk, and in modern DeSoto County arrived the families of Samuel E. Prescott, Elias E. Johnson, and Adam Mercer. The following year saw Polk's population increased by the families of Hugh Bethea, James and Daniel Pugh Pollard, Americus V. Mann, S.H. Page, M.D.L. Mayo, and Green W. Gandy. 1867 also welcomed the arrival of Robert Roberts, W.D. Payne, and Methodist minister William P. McEwen in modern Hardee, and William A. Johnson and William McClenithan, Jr. settled in DeSoto. In 1868 and 1869, the following were among the families to arrive in the Peace River area: Polk—Cornelius B. Lightsey, Mitchell G. Fortner, Sherod E. Roberts, John Keller, John Burton Arnold, John W. Brandon, James A. Fortner, J.J. Bunch, Thomas Bryant and sons Emory and Thomas W. Bryant, and John Bowen; in Hardee—Albert Carlton, Archibald W. Hendry, Seth Howard, and Hugh Bethea; and in DeSoto—Lewis Henry Parker, Frederick S. Lanier, Ephraim W. Thompson, Jacob Daughtry, Owen R. Blount, Simeon E. Whidden, and Ziba King. Carpenter, *History of the First Methodist Church, Bartow, Florida*, 58; *FP*, March 2, 1867; *Tallahassee Sentinel*, September 2, 1867.

4. Polk County, Tax Books, 1863, 1867, FSA.

5. Owners reporting one thousand head or more in Polk or Manatee county included Albert J. Hendry, Berrien Platt, Noel R. Raulerson, Benjamin Guy, W.H. Whitaker, Julius C. Rockner, James McKay, Sr., James Alderman, W.H. Durrance, and John Parker. Manatee County, 1866 Tax Book, and Polk County 1867 Tax Book, FSA.

6. Ibid.

7. *Tampa Daily Times*, December 18, 1923.

8. Thompson, "Journal," 79-83.

9. Ibid., 80-81; *ST*, August 24, 1878.

10. *ST*, July 21, 1877; *Tallahassee Sentinel*, April 23, 1867; *FP*, July 25, 1868.

11. *FP*, May 26, July 22, August 11, September 8 and 22, and October 23, 1869.

12. *ST*, July 21 and September 29, 1877; Grismer, *Fort Myers*, 85; Akerman, *Florida Cowman*, 108.

13. Polk County, Deed Book A, 498; Westergard and VanLandingham, *Parker & Blount*, 90, 122–24, 140–44; *FP*, September 8, 1869.

14. The "King of the Crackers," Jacob Summerlin, also moved his family from the Peace River Valley following the Civil War. In 1868 (possibly late 1867) he carried them to Flemington, Georgia, so that his children might attend good schools. Summerlin, himself, remained most of the time in South Florida at Fort Ogden and Punta Rassa, but in 1873 he again moved the family and settled with them at Orlando. After building a fine house and opening a store, Summerlin lasted only a year before wanting to return to the ranges. The store was sold in 1874 to Philip Dzialynski of Bartow, and Summerlin again began spending most of his time at Punta Rassa. Kissimmee *Osceola Sun*, September 18, 1975; Fritz, *Unknown Florida*, 84; *BC-I*, November 8, 1893.

15. Stone, "Francis Asbury Hendry"; *FP*, November 3, 1869; Grismer, *Fort Myers*, 277; Palatka *Eastern Herald*, September 25, 1875.

16. Shofner, *Nor Is It Over Yet*, 211–12; Wallace, *Carpetbag Rule in Florida*, 116–20.

17. Ibid., Wallace, 124–25; *WF*, August 2, 1870.

18. The remaining incorporators were Aaron Barnett, Daniel P. Holland, Mark W. Downie, Frederick Filer, and John J. Philbrick. *Laws of Florida* (1870), 98–99.

19. IITF Minutes, vol. 1, 442–47, RG 593, ser. 194B, FSA; *FP*, March 2, 1870; Shofner, *Nor Is It Over Yet*, 212.

20. *FP*, July 20 and August 24, 1870.

21. *WF*, December 6, 1870; Klingman, *Josiah Walls*, 33–35.

22. *WF*, December 6, 1870. The voting impact of newly settled immigrants from Georgia and Alabama also was felt in Polk County. Old guard cattleman William Marion Hendry of Fort Meade narrowly defeated for the Polk County house seat newcomer John Wesley Bryant who resided in the northern part of the county. Just as in Manatee, Silas Niblack received a unanimous vote in Polk. *USHMD 34*, 42d Cong., 2d sess., 24.

23. *WF*, December 6 and 20, 1870.

24. *USHMD 34*, 62, 115; Shofner, *Nor Is It Over Yet*, 216.

25. Thompson to Osborn, December 17, 1865, Dept. and Dist. of Florida, 1865–69, RG 393, NA; Green to Osborn, June 15, 1866; BRFAL; *FML*, June 12, 1913.

26. *WF*, July 12, 1870; *FML*, June 12, 1913; Affidavit of John Lomans, August 3, 1869, and affidavit of Frank Griffin, March 7, 1870, Jury Lists, Venires, Payrolls, Testimonies 1869–1870, Circuit Court Records, Manatee County; "Petition from citizens of Manatee co. relative to the conduct of Sheriff Garner," March 14, 1870, RG 101, ser. 577, FSA; Jackson, Winmill, and Zachrison, *Florida 1870 Mortality Schedule*, 7.

the freedman living at the time in Manatee County. About the time of this

408 *Notes to Pages 205-10*

27. *FP*, October 5, 1870, and February 15, 1871.

28. It is uncertain whether this Frank Griffin is a white man or the freedman living at the time in Manatee County. About the time of this incident, freedman Griffin was employed as a cowhunter by Simeon Hollingsworth. Affidavit of William H. Hollingsworth, April 18, 1871, Trials (Grand Jury) 1870-1875, Circuit Court Records, Manatee County.

29. *WF*, May 9, 1871.

30. Ibid.; *FP*, January 25 and November 11, 1871.

31. Polk County, Tax Books, 1870-1875, FSA; Eagan, *Sixth Annual Report*, 181, 190.

32. *FP*, February 18, 1871; *TG*, April 21, 1886.

33. *WF*, December 17, 1872; Polk County, County Commission Minute Book B, 33-36.

34. Appointed to the county commission with Wilson on May 3, 1872, were A.G. Zipprer and Philip Dzialynski. Felix J. Seward was added on April 12, 1873. Record of Commissioned Officers, vol. 1871-89, 198, RG 156, ser. 259, FSA; *FP*, February 5, 1873.

35. Polk County, Circuit Court Minute Book A, 89; VanLandingham, "Archibald Hendry 1820-1897"; Volume "No. 10, Book A," RG 156, ser. 259, FSA.

36. *Key West Dispatch*, January 4, 1873; *TG*, May 22, 1880; *WF*, December 17, 1879.

37. *Tallahassee Sentinel*, December 19, 1874; *WF*, November 24 and December 13, 1874; *USSR 611*, 44th Cong., 2d sess., 361.

38. Bartholf to Reed, March 1 and April 21, 1871, RG 101, ser. 577, FSA; *TG*, February 28 and May 22, 1880; Record of Commissioned Officers, Vol. 1871-89, 162, RG 156, ser. 259, FSA. James D. Green moved from Fort Green to Pine Level in September 1872 in anticipation of his appointment to succeed John F. Bartholf as postmaster. That appointment became effective December 12, 1872. Green remained in that capacity until Bartholf reassumed the post on April 24, 1874. *BC-I*, August 19, 1903; Records of Appointment of Postmasters, 1832-1971, M-1841, roll #20, NA.

39. Shofner, *Nor Is It Over Yet*, 295-96; Manatee County, Circuit Court Minute Book, 1858-1887, 137-39; Affidavit of Ziba King, *State of Florida* vs. *James D. Green*, n.d., Trials (Grand Jury) 1870-75, Circuit Court Records, Manatee County; "Jury. State of Florida vs. James D. Green," Clerk's Journal, Fall Term 1875, n.p., Manatee County.

40. *WF*, February 23, 1875; Magbee to Stearns, February 17, 1875, RG 150, ser. 24, FSA. For over a year prior to his resignation Judge Magbee had feared for his life. In the fall of 1873, after a long day of court at Pine Level, Magbee was relaxing in a nearby house when an unknown assassin discharged a double-barreled shotgun at him through the parlor

window. Escaping without harm, Magbee again was put on guard the following August when a black man, Dick Roach, whose rights in a murder trial had been protected by Magbee, was himself murdered by an unknown assassin with the rumor current that Judge Magbee would be next. *Savannah Morning News*, December 12 and 31, 1873, and September 1, 1874.

41. *New York Times*, March 19, 1874; Shofner, *Nor Is It Over Yet*, 296; Wallace, *Carpetbag Rule in Florida*, 116.

42. *TG*, May 22, 1880; *USSR 611*, 359; Bartholf to Stearns, August 24, 1876, RG 150, ser. 24, FSA; *Savannah Morning News*, April 22, 1886.

43. Wallace, *Carpetbag Rule in Florida*, 337; Bartholf to Stearns, ibid.; *Savannah Morning News*, April 22, 1886; Jacksonville *Florida Union*, October 9, 1876; *USSR 611*, 356; Shofner, *Nor Is It Over Yet*, 308.

44. *USSR 611*, 357-360; McDuffie, *Lures of Manatee*, 230.

45. Polk County's totals in the same race were 456 votes for the Democrats and 6 votes for the Republicans. *USSR 611*, 360-63.

46. Ibid.

47. Ibid., 362-67.

48. Shofner, *Nor Is It Over Yet*, 324, 333.

49. Ibid., 338.

Chapter 14

1. *PCBC*, 31; Augusta *Southern Christian Advocate*, December 10, 1863, and November 3, 1864; L.G. Lesley File, DOW, Compiled Service Records, M-251, roll #14, "1st Battalion, Special Cavalry," NA.

2. Davidson to Corley, September 2, 1863, RG 593, ser. 914, FSA; Receipt for tuition paid, in Polk County, Probate Records 1862-1936, Loose Packet #13, "Estate of Simon P. Smith"; Frisbie, *Peace River Pioneers*, 33-34.

3. *PCR*, October 18, 1921, and January 11, 1932; *FP*, November 10, 1866.

4. *PCR*, October 11, 1921, and August 18, 1932; Carpenter, *History of the First Methodist Church, Bartow*, 55; *Tallahassee Sentinel*, September 2, 1867.

5. McClelland, *A Digest of the Laws of the State of Florida*, 1106, 1109; Key West *Key of the Gulf*, January 7, 1860; Reid, *The Telegraph in America*, 436.

6. Reid, *The Telegraph in America*, 433; Brown, "The International Ocean Telegraph," 145-47.

7. St. Augustine *Examiner*, April 20, 1867; Gainesville *New Era*, April 20, 1867; *FMWP*, March 25, 1909; *FP*, June 8, 1867; *BC-I*, May 20, 1903.

8. Brown, "International Ocean Telegraph," 149-50, 158-59.

9. Ibid., 150-54.

10. *FP*, August 3, 1867; *ST*, July 21, and December 22, 1877, and May 25, 1878. Among Peace River residents involved with the Tampa and Fort Meade Telegraph Company were James T. Wilson, Philip Dzialynski, Frederick N. Varn, John L. Skipper, and Dr. Charles L. Mitchell. *ST*, September 1, 1877 and October 19, 1878.

11. Blackman, *History of Orange County, Florida*, 90; Kissimmee *Osceola Sun*, September 18, 1975; *BC-I*, September 9, 1896; Eagan, *Sixth Annual Report*, 189-90. The Bartow post office was called Peace Creek until May 19, 1879, because the federal government refused to commemorate Confederate hero Francis S. Bartow, or such has been claimed. As Pease Creek, the post office was supervised, in succession, by Robert A. Wilkison, Clementine Wilkison, Jacob R. Cohen, Sarah J. Fountain, Joseph F. Granger, David Hughes, and Louis Herzog. Records of Appointment of Postmasters, M-841, reel #21, NA.

12. *FP*, March 20 and October 19, 1870; Adams, *Homeland*, 60. The mercantile partnership of J.C. Rockner and J.R. Cohen was dissolved in April 1871. Cohen's in-law, Philip Dzialynski, assumed control of the Bartow store while Rockner continued operation of those at Fort Meade and Fort Ogden. *FP*, June 7, 1871.

13. *FP*, September 30, 1871; Wells, *Facts for Immigrants*, 23.

14. Durrance, *R & M: Our Family*, 85; *FP*, October 19, 1870, and September 30, 1871; Records of Appointment of Postmasters, M-841, reel #21, NA. Through the decade of the 1870s Fort Meade's post office was served by Rockner, James W. Jones, Sullivan Lightsey, and Charles L. Mitchell.

15. McKay, *Pioneer Florida*, vol. 3, 89; Eagan, *Sixth Annual Report*, 189-90.

16. Shofner, *Nor Is It Over Yet*, 273; Polk County, Deed Book B, 236-39; Eagan, *Sixth Annual Report*, 189; Wells, *Facts for Immigrants*, 23; *Tallahassee Sentinel*, June 10, 1876.

17. *FP*, July 28, 1866.

18. *FT-U*, April 19, 1886; *FP*, September 8, 1869; Williams, "This Is The Story of My Life," 55.

19. *WF*, December 20, 1870; *Tallahassee Sentinel*, September 2, 1876; Matthews, *Edge of Wilderness*, 306; Livingston, "Frederick S. Lanier 1829-1875." The captain of the *Laura* was Frederick S. Lanier, who went down with his ship.

20. Bartholf, Centennial Oration Given at Pine Level, Florida, July 4, 1876, U.S. Centennial Orations, LC; Records of Appointment of Postmasters, M-841, reel #20, NA; *TG*, May 22, 1880; Manatee County, Deed Book B, 203; *FP*, January 12, 1870.

21. The six families were those of W. Whidden, Albert Carlton, Rev.

W.P. McEwen, Lewis Carlton, W.A. McEwen, and D.M. Cason. Eagan, *Sixth Annual Report*, 180; Frisbie, *Peace River Pioneers*, 34.

22. Covington, *Story of Southwestern Florida*, vol. 1, 160; Stringer, *Watch Wauchula Win*, 7. One interesting attempt at development in the Manatee County area occurred early in 1873 when Dr. Robert Hunter obtained an "extensive" tract of land at Charlotte Harbor and commissioned a Jacksonville firm to erect upon it "an extensive hotel and sanatarium." Hunter's goal was to open his resort to paying customers by November 1, 1873, and in connection with it he arranged for the construction at Cedar Key of a steamboat "to run between the harbor and Fort Mead on Pease Creek." By early September 1873 Hunter's fifty workmen had brought the project close to completion. Less than a month later, though, the project lay in ruins as a result of the Great Hurricane of 1873. As reported by a Tallahassee newspaper, "Dr. Hunter lost his steamer, with all the shops, Buildings, &c. connected with his proposed Sanitarium." Savannah *Daily Advertiser*, April 1, 1873; Savannah *Advertiser-Republican*, September 18, 1873; Tallahassee *Weekly Floridian*, October 21, 1873.

23. Covington, *Story of Southwestern Florida*, vol. 1, 160; Stringer, *Watch Wauchula Win*, 7; Frisbie, *Peace River Pioneers*, 34.

24. Kissimmee *Osceola Sun*, September 25, 1975.

25. Ibid.

26. *PCBC*, 58; Receipts for school tuition, Polk County, Probate Records, Loose Packets #12 (John I. Hooker) and #13 (Simon P. Smith); *BI*, December 9, 1882.

27. "Proposition and Petition to the Citizens of Polk County [c. 1866]," RG 915, ser. 887, FSA; *PCR*, November 18, 1921; *FP*, June 6, 1868.

28. *FP*, February 9, 1870; Superintendent of Public Instruction, "Annual Draft Report, 1870," RG 402, ser. 84, FSA; *PCR*, November 18, 1921.

29. Shofner, *Nor Is It Over Yet*, 150-51; Pyburn, *History of the Development of a Single System of Education in Florida*, 102-3.

30. Record of Commissioned Officers, Vol. 1871-89, RG 156, ser. 259, FSA. Among those serving on Manatee's board of public instruction during this time were John W. Hendry, William I. Turner, E.J. Hall, William Smith, and William H. Barnwell. Fernandina *Observer*, January 22, 1876.

31. Nicholson, "DeSoto County: History of Fort Winder"; Records of Board of Public Instruction 1869-1875, Misc. County Records, Manatee County; Affidavit of Edward B. Patten, January 28, 1870, Affidavits 1860-1899, Old Misc. County Records, Manatee County; Thompson, *Peace River Valley*, 155-56. Among the teachers in 1870 and succeeding

years at Manatee County's Peace River area schools for white children were James H. Stephens, Joseph Arthur Patten, Frank D. Ferro, N.T. Jones, Robert Bell, Robert LaMartin, P.T. Tucker, Edward B. Patten, and Julien G. Arista. Local boards of trustees during the same period included, among others, David J.W. Boney, Hugh Bethea, T.J. Grier, J.H. Tucker, Henry Langford, A.J. Hendry, and R.G. Marlow.

32. Pyburn, *History of the Development of a Single System of Education in Florida*, 105; Report of Joseph Arthur Patten, Pine Level school [c. Nov. 1870], Records of Board of Public Instruction 1869-1875, Misc. County Records, Manatee County.

33. Pyburn, *History of the Development of a Single System of Education in Florida*, 105; *WF*, August 26, 1884; *TG*, May 22, 1880; DeLand *Florida Agriculturist*, July 17, 1875.

34. The 1876 board included James B. Crum, Nathan S. Blount, Robert A. McAuley, and S. Thomas Hollingsworth. Fernandina *Observer*, January 22, 1876.

35. Hawks, *The Florida Gazetteer*, 78; Record of Commissioned Officers, Volume 1871-89, RG 156, ser. 259, FSA; Superintendent of Public Instruction, "Annual Draft Report, 1870," RG 402, ser. 84, FSA; *FP*, September 30, 1871; Receipt for tuition, Polk County, Probate Records, Loose Packet #18 (Lewis W. Hooker, et al., Guardianship).

36. Pyburn, *History of the Development of a Single System of Education in Florida*, 105; *WF*, August 26, 1884; Polk County School Statistics, 1875, Polk County Clippings File, Florida Collection, Florida State Library, Tallahassee.

37. *ST*, November 17, 1877.

38. Carpenter, *History of the First Methodist Church, Bartow*, 56; *WF*, January 21, 1873; "Homeland Methodist Church History Is Completed," undated clipping from *PCR*, Homeland Folder, PCHGL.

39. Wiggins, *History*, 11-13; Osborn and Dalton, "The South Florida Baptist Association"; Stone, "John Wright Hendry 1836-1907," 29.

40. *Minutes of the Seventeenth Annual Session of the South Florida Baptist Association*, appendix.

41. *ST*, November 17, 1877; *BC-I*, June 22, 1898.

42. The Peace Creek Primitive Baptist Church was constituted not later than 1872 and met in the home of Noel Rabun Raulerson. From 1875 to 1885, the church was served by the Reverend H.F. Fortner. "Peace Creek Primitive Baptist Church," CR.

43. *TT*, October 24, 1954; "Fort Myacca" in DeVane, *DeVane's Early Florida History*, vol. 2, n.p.

44. Concord Church of Christ was the predecessor of the First Baptist Church of Bartow. Frisbie, *Peace River Pioneers*, 23.

45. Livingston, "Early Church Records: South Florida Baptist Association Minutes"; "Mount Pleasant Baptist Church," CR; Thompson, *Peace River Valley*, 124, 155–56; Church sign, Paynes Creek Primitive Baptist Church; *Proceedings of the South Florida Baptist Association*, 1874–1881; Stringer, *Watch Wauchula Win*, 62.

46. Carpenter, *History of the First Methodist Church, Bartow*, 39; Shofner, *Nor Is It Over Yet*, 142; Lane, *A Pictorial History of Arcadia and DeSoto County*, 102–3; Polk County, Deed Records, Book B, 73; Ames, "First United Methodist Church, East Broadway at Pine, Fort Meade, Florida."

47. *FP*, September 8, 1869; Frisbie, *Peace River Pioneers*, 25; "Homeland Methodist Church History Is Completed"; Temple, *Florida Flame*, 146; "Mount Pisgah Methodist Church," CR.

48. *ST*, September 1, 1877.

49. *FP*, September 30, 1871; Eagan, *Sixth Annual Report*, 180.

50. Ibid., *FP*; *Laws of Florida* (1860), 190–91.

51. *Laws of Florida* (1866), 66–68.

52. Ibid. (1870), 98–99; IITF Minutes, vol. 1, 442–47, RG 593, ser. 194B, FSA.

53. *FP*, December 16, 1871; *Oswego Daily Palladium*, November 18, 1871, and January 4 and 5, 1872; *Buffalo Commercial Advertiser*, November 24, 1871.

54. IITF Minutes, vol. 1, 461, RG 593, ser. 194B, FSA; Shofner, *Nor Is It Over Yet*, 251.

55. Mattoon successfully returned to New York in mid-April 1872. A few days after his arrival at the Hudson port of Albany, though, a boiler exploded, killing a black hand, Jacob Lewis, and causing extensive damage to the *Ellsworth*. *Oswego Daily Palladium*, April 18, 1872.

56. IITF Minutes, vol. 2, 123, RG 593, ser. 194B, FSA.

57. Incorporators of the Peace Creek Navigation Company were: C.L. Mitchell, C.B. Lightsey, F.A. Hendry, J.C. Rockner, J.E. Robeson, J.C. Nelson, E.L. Harrison, William Smith, N.S. Blount, Fred N. Varn, W.M. McAuley, John McAuley, John L. Skipper, R.C. Langford, William Underhill, S.J. Stallings, W.H. Addison, S.E. Roberts, C.E. Harrison, J.M. Pearce, Jesse H. Durrance, Solomon Godwin, Willoughby Tillis, J.D. Tillis, W.R. Raulerson, W.H. Raulerson, John Parker, Newton Parker, Lewis Parker, B. Hordy, Z. Curry, S.A. Hart, William Raulerson, Isham Lewis, S.M. Chandler, E.E. Mizell, W.W. Chandler, W.J. Carroll, J.T. Wilson, G.W. Gant, W.B. Varn, Peyton S. Pearce, M.G. Fortner, James M. Manley, George R. Langford, David Skipper, Jacob H. Tyre, D.S. Bunch, J.J. Bunch, J.R. Feroux, and R.H. Peeples. "Articles of Incorporation of the Peace Creek Navigation Company," December 12, 1874, Arti-

cles of Incorporation 1868-1896, Old Misc. County Files, Manatee County.

58. Transcript of Record, *State of Florida vs. Charlotte Harbor Phosphate Company*, 525–31.

Chapter 15

1. Bartholf and Boggess, *South Florida, The Italy of America*, 9.

2. Akerman, *Florida Cowman*, 160.

3. *ST*, April 21, 1877; *FP*, August 19, 1871. Friday's given name was Eldrid.

4. Florida, Board of State Institutions, *Soldiers of Florida*, 12; *Savannah Morning News*, October 1, 1878; *ST*, January 4, 1879, and January 15, 1881; *TT*, November 17, 1957.

5. *WF*, December 9, 1873; *ST*, October 23, 1879.

6. *FT-U*, July 17, 1884, November 3, 1892; *ST*, September 5, 1877; *BI*, June 16, 1883. Woodruff served but five years before he escaped, with the aid of a Winchester rifle, from a state prison camp near Albion. *FT-U&C*, November 29, 1897.

7. *BC-I*, December 25, 1895.

8. *WF*, December 30, 1884; *FMWP*, June 3, 1886.

9. *FT-U*, August 27, 1885, and May 19, 1886; *FMWP*, June 3, 1886.

10. Akerman, *Florida Cowman*, 69–70 (quoting from Ann H. Ryals and Sandra W. Wells, *The Cattle Industry in Desoto County* [Arcadia, 1972]), 212; *FT-U*, April 14, 1888, and September 10, 1897.

11. U.S. Original Census Schedules, 9th Census 1870, Manatee County (Population); John G. Foster Letterbook, 1865-66, 85–86.

12. Affidavit of John Lomans, April 3, 1869, Jury Lists, Venires, Payrolls, Testimonies 1869–70, Circuit Court Records, Manatee County.

13. Williams, "This is The Story of My Life," 56–57; Manatee County, Circuit Court Minute Book 1, 1859–1887, 104.

14. Jacksonville *Tri-Weekly Union*, June 9, 1874; *WF*, May 26, 1874. The names of those who composed the posse are unknown, although a list of witnesses later scheduled to testify against Alonzo and Raymond Johnson may provide a clue. Those witnesses were John W. Whidden, Owen R. Blount, Nelson Locklear, R.C. Hendry, Samuel Lippencott, and Daniel Carlton. Manatee County, Circuit Court Minute Book 1, 1859–1887, 155.

15. Jacksonville *Tri-Weekly Union*, June 9, 1874; *WF*, May 26, 1874.

16. Ibid.

17. Jacksonville *Tri-Weekly Union*, July 14, 1874; Manatee County, Circuit Court Minute Book 1, 1859–1887, 154, 224.

18. *TT*, February 1 and 22, 1953.

19. *WF*, March 16, 1880, and November 25, 1873; *TT*, October 28, 1951.

20. *TT*, October 28, 1951, and February 1, 1953.

21. *ST*, October 19 and November 30, 1878, and July 3 and 31, 1879.

22. *TT*, September 18, 1955; *ST*, March 1, 1879.

23. *ST*, February 26 and March 4, 1880; *TT*, February 1 and 22, 1953.

24. VanLandingham, *Florida Cousins*, 1; VanLandingham, "William Henry Willingham 1816-1886"; *TT*, March 13, 1951; Jacksonville *Florida Daily Times*, April 29, 1882.

25. *ST*, May 26 and August 4, 1877; Manatee County, Circuit Court Minute Book 1, 1858-1887, 160.

26. *ST*, August 4, September 8 and 22, 1877; VanLandingham, "John I. Hooker 1822-1862," 9; *BI*, June 16, 1883.

27. Willingham came close to negating the need for a trial when, in August 1879, he and Morgan Snow got into a drunken fight on the streets of Fort Meade and stabbed each other with "pocket knives." Both participants survived. VanLandingham, "John I. Hooker, 1822-1862," *ST*, August 21, 1879.

28. *BI*, June 16, 1883.

29. 21 *Florida Reports*, 766-67 (1886).

30. *BI*, June 16 and October 6, 1883: *FT-U*, April 16 and July 17, 1884; *TT*, March 4, 1951.

31. The black witnesses were Bob Williams and Henry Wells. *FT-U*, July 17 and 29, 1884; *WF*, April 29, 1884.

32. Ibid.; *FMWP*, May 22, 1886.

33. *FT-U*, February 24, 1889; *TT*, March 13, 1951; 23 *Florida Reports*, 479-80 (1887); Lewis, *Kissimmee Island*, 36; *FML*, June 9, 1910.

34. *FT-U*, February 16, 1892, and July 10, 1895.

35. *PCN*, April 4, 1891; *FT-U*, April 3 and 8, 1892, and March 27 and November 11, 1893.

36. *FT-U*, April 27, 1892, and November 4, 1893; Smiley, "Bloodshed on the Big 90," *Miami Herald*, October 3, 1965.

37. *FT-U*, November 19, 1893.

38. *FT-U*, December 29, 1893; *BC-I*, May 30, 1894.

39. *FT-U*, November 8, 1895; *BC-I*, June 19, 1895; Smiley, "Bloodshed on the Big 90."

40. *BC-I*, November 24, 1897, and June 15, 1898.

Chapter 16

1. *ST*, May 19, 1877.

2. *FP*, July 16, 1859; Peeples, "Charlotte Harbor Division of the Florida Southern Railroad," 291; Shofner, *Nor Is It Over Yet*, 209.

3. Shofner, *Nor Is It Over Yet*, 250; *FP*, March 2, 1870, and July 1, 1871.

4. Shofner, *Nor Is It Over Yet*, 251-52.

5. Pendleton to Eagan, December 25, 1876, RG 593, ser. 914, FSA.

6. *ST*, April 24 and October 5, 1878.

7. *ST*, September 21 and 28, and October 5, 1878; "The Great Storm of 1878," in DeVane, *DeVane's Early Florida History*, vol. 1, n.p.; *FT-U*, November 11, 1898.

8. *WF*, January 7, 1879; St. Augustine *St. Johns Weekly*, May 9, 1879; *ST*, October 23 and December 13, 1879.

9. Brandon to Walker, February 10, 1872, RG 593, ser. 914, FSA; *USSED 15*, 41st Cong., 2d sess., 4; Tract Book, Township 31 South, Range 25 East, Fla. Dept. of Natural Resources.

10. Tebeau, *History of Florida*, 189; *Laws of Florida* (1870), 98–99; IITF Minutes, vol. 1, 442–47, RG 593, ser. 194B, FSA.

11. DeCoster to Eagan, September 18, 1873, and Houze to Eagan, August 24, 1876, RG 593, ser. 914, FSA; *Laws of Florida* (1881), 120–21.

12. IITF Minutes, vol. 2, 379, RG 593, ser. 194B, FSA; *ST*, November 17, 1877, and December 13, 1879.

13. Covington, *Story of Southwestern Florida*, vol. 1, 171; Florida Land and Improvement Company, *The Disston Lands of Florida*, n.p.

14. Tebeau, *History of Florida*, 278; *FT-U*, September 22, 1882; *BI*, February 17, 1883; *WF*, May 25, 1885.

15. Population totals for Manatee County were enumerated by precinct in 1880. The precincts and totals were: #1 (Pine Level), 675; #2 (Fort Green), 214; #3 (Fort Hartsuff), 21; #4 (Miakka), 40; #5 (Sarasota), 177; #6 (Manatee), 390; #7 (Palmetto), 353; #8 (Oak Hill), 33; #9 (Ogden), 381; #10 (Whidden), 32; #11 (Boney's), 367; #12 (Locklear), 481; #13 (Williamson), 60; #14 (Fort Thompson), 38; #15 (Bassenger), 186; and #16 (Hickory Bluff), 96. Dept. of the Interior, Census Office, *Compendium of the Tenth Census, Part I*, 84, 341.

16. *ST*, November 30, 1878; Bartholf and Boggess, *South Florida, The Italy of America*, 10.

17. Bartholf and Boggess, *South Florida, The Italy of America*, 8–9; *TG*, March 13, 1880; *ST*, February 19, 1880.

18. Bartholf and Boggess, *South Florida, The Italy of America*, 10.

19. *BI*, August 11, 1881; Bartholf and Boggess, *South Florida, The Italy of America*, 208.

20. *Compendium of the Tenth Census, Part I*, 84, 341; *BI*, August 25, 1881; Polk County, Tax Books, 1870–1880. Precinct #2 (Fort Meade) contained 963 residents, while Precinct #3 (Bartow) held 699. Precinct #1, the southwest corner of the county including Chicora, possessed 348 residents. Dept. of the Interior, *Compendium of the Tenth Census, Part I*, 84.

21. Wells, *Facts for Immigrants*, 23; Adams, *Homeland*, 60–61.

22. *ST*, July 17, 1879, and July 15, 1880; Temple, *Florida Flame*, 147; Sallie Robinson interview, May 20, 1987.

23. Wells, *Facts for Immigrants*, 23; *BI*, September 15, 1881; Bartholf and Boggess, *South Florida, The Italy of America*, 37; *ST*, April 2, 1881.

24. *ST*, April 1, 1880; *WF*, November 11, 1879; Plowden, *History of Hardee County*, 18-19; "Acrefoot Johnson" in DeVane, *DeVane's Early Florida History*, vol. 1, n.p.

25. Particularly active from Polk County were David Hughes of Bartow and Philip Dzialynski of Fort Meade. *ST*, November 24, 1877.

26. *ST*, December 15, 1877, and January 12 and May 18, 1878.

27. *Laws of Florida* (1881), 144-45; "What has been done and What is in Prospect" and "New Railroad," unidentified clippings, Ammidown Holmes Scrapbook; Van Fleet to Corley, December 2, 1878, RG 593, ser. 914, FSA; *ST*, July 2, 1881.

28. *Laws of Florida* (1879), 119-21.

29. Pettengill, *Story of the Florida Railroads*, 68; "What has been done and What is in Prospect" and "New Railroad," unidentified clippings, Ammidown Holmes Scrapbook. As 1879 saw the organization of railroads intended to provide transportation for South Florida, the year also saw the initiation of the last serious attempt of the nineteenth century to make Peace River navigable. In October and November of that year, J.L. Meigs of the Army Corps of Engineers surveyed the river. Based upon his conclusions, the Corps recommended that the river be made navigable "for light-draught boats, during about nine months of the year, from its mouth to Fort Meade" and suggested an appropriation of $17,000 for that purpose. For several years the recommendation was left pending while consideration was given to a steamboat channel from the St. Johns River by way of Lake Tohopekaliga to Peace River and Charlotte Harbor. When that proposal was found to be impractical economically, the Congress appropriated funds for Peace River clearance. From February 19 to November 10, 1883, a snag boat with a crew of eighteen worked the river to a point just above the mouth of Big Charlie Apopka Creek. When funds ran out in November, the crew was withdrawn and the project abandoned. *USSED 128*, 46th Cong., 2d sess.; *USSED 189*, 47th Cong., 1st sess.; *Transcript of Record, State of Florida vs. The Charlotte Harbor Phosphate Company*, 312-27.

30. *ST*, October 5, 1882; Pettengill, *Story of the Florida Railroads*, 76.

31. Pettengill, *Story of the Florida Railroads*, 76-77.

32. *BI*, November 3, 1883; *WF*, May 2 and December 9, 1884; *FT-U*, January 9, 1885.

33. Pettengill, *Story of the Florida Railroads*, 71-73; Jacksonville *Florida Journal*, July 10, 1884; *Fort Myers Weekly Press*, August 29 and September 5, 1885.

34. Peeples, "Charlotte Harbor Division of the Florida Southern Railroad," 294. Original plans called for the Florida Southern Railway to

form a juncture at Fort Meade with a proposed line, the Fort Meade, Keystone, and Walk-in-the-Water Railroad Company, which was to connect Fort Meade and Frostproof with the Lake Arbuckle area. The line never was built. Its incorporators included W.B. Brown, C.B. Lightsey, J.N. Hooker, Philip Dzialynski, R.C. Langford, C.C. Wilson, J.E. Wilson, J.E. Robeson, George W. Hendry, Fred N. Varn, and W.S. Atkins. *Laws of Florida* (1883), 123.

35. *Palatka Daily News*, August 21, 1885. The hard work which faced laborers on the Florida Southern line appears to have been matched by the "rough treatment" they received at the hands of supervisors and labor contractors. In August 1885 a "crowd" of black laborers at Bartow attempted to escape their labor contracts or, as it was put at the time, "jump their obligations by running away." The men made it as far as Bartow Junction before being overtaken "by a party of indignant and excited contractors" who "in a most energetic manner" forced the men to return to work at Bartow. *WF*, August 27, 1885.

36. Peeples, "Charlotte Harbor Division of the Florida Southern Railroad," 294.

37. *FT-U*, November 28, 1885; *WF*, December 31, 1885, and February 4, 1886; *FMWP*, January 30, 1886.

38. *FT-U*, March 22 and April 29, 1886; Peeples, "Charlotte Harbor Division of the Florida Southern Railroad," 295.

39. *FT-U*, May 4, 1886; *FMWP*, June 12, 1886; Peeples, "Charlotte Harbor Division of The Florida Southern Railroad," 296.

Chapter 17

1. *FMWP*, August 15, 1885.

2. Adams, *Homeland*, 23.

3. Jacksonville *Florida Daily Times*, September 22, 1882; *BI*, September 16, 1882; *FT-U*, August 9, 1896.

4. At its incorporation election, Bartow also elected as its first officers: J.H. Humphries, mayor; C.C. Gresham, marshal; David Hughes, George W. Smith, W.H. Pearce, F.F. Beville, and G.A. Hanson, councilmen; and W.T. Carpenter, clerk and treasurer. *FT-U*, May 31, 1883; *ST*, November 9, 1882; *BI*, July 1, 1882.

5. *FT-U*, August 21, 1883, and November 25, 1884; *BI*, May 12, 1883; Frisbie, *Peace River Pioneers*, 39–40. The Bartow *Informant* appears to have been the first newspaper published in the Peace River Valley, although a short-lived paper, the *Democrat*, may have been published at Fort Ogden by Charles B. Pendleton several months earlier. The Pine Level *Signal and Advertiser* was commenced a short time after the *Informant*, but in 1882 it was bought out by Francis C.M. Boggess, moved to Fort Ogden, and relaunched as the Fort Ogden *Herald* with

Boggess as editor and W.H. Simmons as publisher. Competing at Fort Ogden with the *Herald* was the Fort Ogden *Post*. In 1884 Elam B. Carlton edited the *Pine Level Times* until he moved to Tallahassee to pursue legal studies, and Felix J. Seward established at the same place *The Youth's Friend* "to promote the interest of education among the boys and girls." *BI*, September 15, 1881, and October 7, 1882; *ST*, June 4, 1881; *Savannah Morning News*, July 14 and August 1, 1882; "Florida Papers" clipping, June 23, 1882, Ammidown Holmes Scrapbook; *WF*, December 30, 1884.

6. *BI*, March 8, 1884; *BAC*, February 29, 1888; Nerod, *An Historical Gazetteer of Imperial Polk County Florida*, 6.

7. *BI*, April 8, 1882, and February 17, April 28, October 6, and November 17, 1883; *FT-U*, October 22, 1884.

8. *WF*, January 13, 1885; Frisbie, *Yesterday's Polk County*, 25; Jacksonville *Florida Weekly Times*, August 21 and September 4, 1884; *FT-U*, January 7, and April 30, 1885.

9. Adams, *Homeland*, 72-73; McNeely and McFayden, *Century in the Sun*, 13.

10. *BI*, May 17, 1884.

11. *Transcript of Record, State of Florida vs. Charlotte Harbor Phosphate Company*, 312-27; *FT-U*, June 11, 1884.

12. *WF*, April 16, August 27, and September 24, 1885.

13. *FML*, November 20, 1913; *TT*, July 6, 1958; *FT-U*, January 2, 1884.

14. Frisbie, *Peace River Pioneers*, 52; Stone, "James Madison Hendry 1839-1922"; Stone to author, August 2, 1986, possession of the author; Stone, "John Wesley Whidden 1839-1910". Whidden obtained supplies for his store from George Williams, who brought them upriver by boat. Williams obtained the boat from Wade Altman who had purchased it from Harris Raulerson. In Raulerson's day the craft was known as the *Peter Raulerson* and had been used during 1882 and 1883 to bring supplies upriver as far as Fort Hartsuff. Raulerson purchased "country produce" upriver, took it to Charlotte Harbor for transshipment, and returned with "coffee, tobacco, flour, and anything that people wanted." *Transcript of Record, State of Florida vs. The Charlotte Harbor Phosphate Company*, 251-52, 554-60; *BI*, January 20, 1883.

15. *BI*, May 17, 1884; Peeples, "Charlotte Harbor Division of the Florida Southern Railroad," 293; Thompson, *Peace River Valley*, 202; Brooks and Crabtree, *St. James City Florida: The Early Years*, 70; *FT-U*, December 6, 1884.

16. Polk County Board of County Commissioners, *Polk County, Florida*, 33; Peeples, "Charlotte Harbor Division of the Florida Southern Railroad," 294; *FMWP*, September 26, 1885; White, "History of Fort

Meade, Florida," 13; Polk County, Deed Records, Book Q, 310–11; Plant City *South Florida Courier*, May 15, 1886; *WF*, June 3, 1886; *FT-U*, January 27, 1887; *PCN*, August 7, 1891.

17. Stringer, *Watch Wauchula Win*, 10, 150.

18. *FT-U*, April 19 and 29, 1886.

19. *FT-U*, April 29, 1886.

20. Livingston, "Willoughby Whidden"; Stone, "John Wesley Whidden"; *FT-U*, April 14, 1893.

21. Stone, "James Madison Hendry"; *Laws of Florida* (1879), 119–21.

22. *FMWP*, June 12 and October 23, 1886; Plant City *South Florida Courier*, November 27, 1886.

23. *FMWP*, October 23, 1886.

24. Historical Records Survey, *A List of Municipal Corporations in Florida*, 5; Stone, "John Wesley Whidden." Arcadia's first officers were: B.F. Baldwin, mayor; J.W. Bailey, F.M. Waldron, W.E. Daniel, F.E. Waldron, W.H. Hollingsworth, and C.G. Johansen, aldermen; George H. Altree, clerk and treasurer; and C.G. Bonard, marshal and collector. Thompson, *Peace River Valley*, 156.

25. *FMWP*, February 5, 1887.

26. Plant City *South Florida Courier*, January 8, 1887; *BAC*, April 20, 1887; Adams, *Homeland*, 61.

27. Adams, *Homeland*, 61; *WF*, November 11, 1884; *FT-U*, October 18 and December 19, 1884.

28. Adams, *Homeland*, 61–62; *FT-U*, September 23 and November 27, 1886.

29. *FT-U*, March 15 and September 3, 1887; *BAC*, April 20 and 27, 1887; Brooksville *Florida Weekly News*, May 20, 1887.

30. *PCD*, July 1, 1976; *FT-U*, December 2, 1885, June 5 and November 30, 1886, July 1, 1887, January 27, 1888, and April 1, 1889.

31. *BAC*, May 25, 1887, and May 23, 1888; St. James A.M.E. Church, "4th Annual Homecoming Program"; St. James A.M.E. Church, "Souvenir of the Dedicatory Services"; "St. James A.M.E. Church," CR. Church tradition suggests the origins of St. James A.M.E. Church may be traced to the early 1880s.

32. Adams, *Homeland*, 65; *FT-U*, August 30, 1887, and June 6, 1888.

33. *Lakeland Ledger*, September 22, 1929; Reports of Site Locations, 1837–1950, "Homeland," Post Office Dept., M-1126, NA; Nerod, *Gazetteer*, 23.

34. *BAC*, March 21 and April 14, 1888; *BC-I*, April 3, 1895; *BI*, February 9, 1884; Florida State Census, 1885, Polk County.

35. "Homeland Baptist Church" and "Mount Bunyan Baptist Church," CR; *BAC*, September 14, 1887; *BI*, October 6, 1883.

36. Polk County Board of County Commissioners, *Polk County, Florida*, 32–33; *BAC*, September 14, 1887.

37. *FT-U*, November 26, 1884.

38. Historical Records Survey, *List of Municipal Corporations*, 27. Fort Meade's first officers were William Thompson, mayor; Philip Dzialynski, chairman of the board of aldermen; E.E. Skipper, A.J. Bulloch, John E. Robeson, and Arthur Keen, alderman; and S.G. Hayman, clerk and treasurer. Polk County, Deed Book U, 92.

39. *FMWP*, July 25 and October 17, 1885; *FT-U*, February 11 and September 5, 1885; *TT*, August 6, 1950.

40. Arriving on the first passenger train into Fort Meade was the Irish family of Luke Brendin Flood, immigrating to Florida to escape the religious violence threatening their homeland. *Lakeland Ledger*, January 12, 1977.

41. *FT-U*, February 11, 1887.

42. Adams, *Homeland*, 66; *FT-U*, February 11, 1887; *BAC*, April 13, 1887; Jacksonville *Daily News-Herald*, July 18, 1887. Fort Meade and its access to the railroad served as a lifeline for another community established about twenty-five miles to the southeast in 1886 by developer O.M. Crosby and his Florida Development Company. The town was named Avon Park after the English hometown, Stratford-on-Avon, of its first settlers, Mr. and Mrs. William King, and a free stagecoach line carried prospective settlers from there to Fort Meade. The town's progress was slow, however, and in 1887 the entire community consisted of only six families. Covington, *Story of Southwestern Florida*, vol. 1, 176–77; Writers Project, "Highlands County"; *FT-U*, March 16, 1894.

43. *TT*, July 6, 1956; *FML*, November 20, 1913.

44. Wauchula was incorporated June 9, 1888, although, apparently, the incorporation was invalidated not long thereafter. Historical Records Survey, *List of Municipal Corporations*, 84.

45. *BAC*, April 27, 1887; Stringer, *Watch Wauchula Win*, 156.

46. Thompson, *Peace River Valley*, 132; *FP*, June 23, 1860; Frisbie, *Peace River Pioneers*, 37; Matthews, *Edge of Wilderness*, 307; *FT-U*, July 13, 1888.

47. *FT-U*, March 20, 1887, and October 12, 1888; *BAC*, July 20, 1887.

48. *BAC*, April 27, 1887.

49. *WF*, June 24, 1886; *FT-U*, April 19, 1886.

50. *FT-U*, April 19, 1886.

51. *WF*, December 2, 1886; *FT-U*, February 17 and August 9, 1887; Historical Records Survey, *List of Municipal Corporations*, 28.

52. Thompson, *Peace River Valley*, 168–70; *FT-U*, February 17, 1887; Jacksonville *Daily News-Herald*, October 5, 1887.

53. Peeples, "Charlotte Harbor Division of the Florida Southern Railroad," 296–97.

54. Ibid., 299; Peeples, *Punta Gorda and the Charlotte Harbor Area*, 58, 100; *FT-U*, December 13, 1887; Lane, "Florida Is A Blessed Country," 443.

55. *FT-U*, July 13, 1888.

Chapter 18

1. Shofner, *Nor Is It Over Yet*, 333. In Manatee County the following officers were removed: Jesse B. Mizell, sheriff; James M. Youmans, collector; G.H. Johnson, surveyor; T.S. Morgan, John M. Bates, and J.H. Tucker, commissioners; Ezekiel Glazier, treasurer; and Dempsey D. Crews, justice of the peace. Governor Drew's appointments were: William C. Hayman, sheriff; H.F. Wyatt, clerk; Henry Carlton, assessor; William A. Johnson, collector; W.K. Hale, surveyor; Ziba King, Daniel Lloyd, M.F. Giddens, and John W. Whidden, commissioners; F.B. Hagan, treasurer; and George Patten, William Bronson, F.B. Hagan, A.J. Hendry, David Boney, J.W. Williams, and J.E. Fewell, justices of the peace. Wyatt failed to give bond as clerk and was replaced by Robert S. Griffith. Whidden declined to serve as commissioner, and Lewis H. Parker was appointed in his stead. Record of Commissioned Officers, vol. 1871–89, 162–63, RG 156, ser. 259, FSA.

2. Jacksonville *Florida Union*, January 15, 1877. Polk County officers removed included: James A. Fortner, county judge; T.L. McKinney, sheriff (ad interim appointment expired); N.S. Blount, clerk; B.G. Glover, J.F. Tatum, L.S. Jones, W.E. King, and J.E. Wilson, commissioners; and W.B. Varn, surveyor. Drew's appointments were: James A. Fortner, county judge; R.H. Peeples, sheriff; W.B. Varn, clerk; G.F. Smith, assessor; N.S. Blount, collector; S.M. Sparkman, superintendent of schools; John Davidson, treasurer; Philip Dzialynski, C.W. Deason, Perry O. Keen, Thomas B. Ellis, and James T. Wilson, commissioners. Record of Commissioned Officers, vol. 1871–89, 198–99, RG 156, ser. 259, FSA.

3. Record of Commissioned Officers, vol. 1871–89, 198–99, RG 156, ser. 259, FSA.

4. Polk County, Circuit Court Minute Book A, 139, 145, 148; *ST*, April 20, 1878. Cleared of the charges against him, Magbee continued to practice law, edit the *Tampa Guardian*, and involve himself in Florida Republican party activities. He died at home in Tampa, aged sixty-five, on December 17, 1885. *FT-U*, December 24, 1885.

5. *ST*, October 26, 1878. Elected in 1878 as Manatee's state representative was cattleman and Joshua Creek resident Lewis Henry Parker. *WF*, January 7, 1879.

6. *ST*, June 12, 1879; *TG*, December 6, 1879; Manatee County, Circuit Court Minute Book, 1858-1887, 216.

7. The founder and editor of the *Key of the Gulf* was Jim Green's former commanding officer, Henry A. Crane. Following the Civil War, Crane moved to Key West where he was appointed clerk of the circuit court. In December 1868 he was elected to the Florida senate, and he later served as editor of the Key West *Dispatch* until the founding of the *Key of the Gulf* in December 1874. Crane died at Key West June 18, 1888, aged seventy-seven. The old South Florida pioneer's obituary read: "He apparently enjoyed a controversy and never failed to hold his own." *WF*, January 5, 1875; *FT-U*, June 20, 1888.

8. *ST*, June 12, 1879; *TG*, December 6, 1879; Record of Commissioned Officers, vol. 1871-89, 163, RG 156, ser. 259, FSA; Manatee County, Circuit Court Minute Book, 1858-1887, 226, 231.

9. *ST*, February 26 and October 28, 1880. At the time of his withdrawal John F. Bartholf was a resident of Charlotte Harbor. In 1883 he moved to Bradenton to accept appointment as postmaster and remained in that area until about 1886 when he and his family moved to Jacksonville. He died in that city November 22, 1892. Peeples, *Punta Gorda and the Charlotte Harbor Area*, 14; Records of Appointment of Postmasters, M-841, roll #20, NA; *FT-U*, April 17, 1886; Jacksonville *Evening Telegram*, November 23, 1892.

10. *BI*, September 23, and November 11, 1882; Jacksonville *Florida Journal*, August 25, 1884; *FMWP*, April 17, 1886.

11. Polk County, County Commissioners Minute Book B, 39, 43-44, 48-49, 52.

12. *ST*, November 30, 1878; *PCR*, May 31, 1933.

13. *ST*, February 19, 1880.

14. *ST*, September 21 and November 30, 1878, and September 30, 1880.

15. *ST*, August 19, September 30, and October 28, 1880.

16. *ST*, September 30 and October 14, 1880; Election Returns, Manatee County, 1880, FSA; Polk County, County Commissioners Minute Book B, 43-44.

17. *BI*, October 28 and November 11, 1882; Polk County Commissioners Minute Book B, 48-49.

18. *WF*, September 23 and November 18, 1884; Polk County, County Commissioners Minute Book B, 52. Replacing Whidden as Manatee's state representative was county judge Zachary T. Crawford of Pine Level.

19. *FT-U*, November 11, 1884.

20. Tebeau, *History of Florida*, 289-90.

21. *FT-U*, October 4, 1886; Polk County, County Commissioners Minute Book B, 57.

22. *TG*, July 7 and 21, 1886; Hetherington, *History of Polk County*, 24-25; *BAC*, May 18, 1887.

23. *FT-U*, January 27 and February 17, 1887; McDuffie, *Lures of Manatee*, 276.

24. *BAC*, June 15, 1887; Record of Commissioned Officers, Vol. 1871-89, 317, RG 156, ser. 259, FSA.

25. Jacksonville *Daily News-Herald*, July 10, 1887; *BAC*, June 15, 1887; Lane, "Florida Is A Blessed Country," 443; *FT-U*, July 21 and October 1, 1887.

26. *FT-U*, August 9 and September 3, 1887.

27. *FT-U*, December 28, 1887, and January 12, 1888.

28. *FT-U*, July 13 and 17, 1888; Livingston, "DeSoto County: Arcadia's First Courthouse," 37.

29. *WF*, December 18, 1888; Livingston, "DeSoto County: Arcadia's First Courthouse," 37; Frisbie, *Peace River Pioneers*, 53; *FT-U*, November 28, 1888, and February 17, 1889.

30. *Tallahassee Sentinel*, July 29, 1871; *ST*, August 19 and November 25, 1880.

31. *BI*, September 15, 1881, and September 16, 1882; *ST*, April 2, 1881.

32. *FT-U*, June 2 and July 1, 1885; *WF*, May 28, 1885.

33. *Lakeland Ledger*, June 3, 1951; *FT-U*, July 29, 1884, and September 30, 1886; *FMWP*, May 22, 1886.

34. *FMWP*, May 22, 1886; *FT-U*, May 19, 1886.

35. *TG*, May 19, 1886; *TT*, February 7, 1954; *FT-U*, May 19, 1886; *Lakeland Ledger*, June 3, 1951. Almost as if he was expecting trouble, Marshal Campbell the morning of his death had taken out a life insurance policy in the amount of $2,500.

36. *FT-U*, May 19, 1886.

37. *TG*, May 26 and June 9, 1886; *FMWP*, May 22, 1886; *FT-U*, May 19, 1886.

38. *FT-U*, September 23 and 30 and October 4, 1886, and January 14, 1888.

39. Alduino, "Prohibition in Tampa," 17; *BAC*, April 20, 1887; *FT-U*, August 12, September 1 and 6, 1887.

40. *FT-U*, September 6, 1887, February 17, 1889, and November 11, 1891; *BAC*, September 7, 1887; Plant City *South Florida Courier*, September 10, 1887; *TT*, July 20, 1897.

41. *FT-U*, May 5, 1889, and May 27, 1891.

42. *FT-U*, November 11, 1891, and March 18 and April 6, 1894; Hether-

ington, *History of Polk County*, 26; Jacksonville *Daily Florida Citizen*, November 27, 1896.

43. *FT-U*, October 6, 1890.

44. *FT-U*, June 10, July 19, and August 29, 1895.

45. *Punta Gorda Herald*, March 21, 1902; *FT-U*, July 28 and November 11, 1888.

46. Tebeau, *History of Florida*, 298–300; Ezell, *The South Since 1865*, 168.

47. Tebeau, *History of Florida*, 300; *FT-U*, August 16 and October 6, 1890; Westergard and VanLandingham, *Parker & Blount*, 123.

48. *FT-U&C*, April 2, 1899; *FT-U*, June 21 and October 28, 1890.

49. *FT-U*, July 26, 1892; *PCN*, October 7, 1892.

50. *FT-U*, April 17, 1892, and December 27, 1896; Election Returns, Polk County, 1892, FSA. William H. Reynolds was elected president of the Florida Senate in 1893. At the conclusion of his four-year term he successfully sought election as state comptroller. He died while serving in that office on July 19, 1901. The election of 1892 ended the political service of John W. Bryant who had been a fixture of Polk County politics for two decades. He remained in the county and for many years prior to his death on December 8, 1926, served as vice president and chairman of the board of the First National Bank of Lakeland. Frank Clark was appointed U.S. attorney for the Southern District of Florida in 1895. The following year he moved to Jacksonville where, in 1905, he was elected to the U.S. Congress. Clark remained in the Congress for twenty years and died in Washington, D.C., on April 14, 1936. *FT-U&C*, July 20, 1901; Hetherington, *History of Polk County*, 205.

51. The People's party boasted membership from among many older families in the county, a number of whom formerly had been Republicans. Active in the party were John W. Hendry, N.C. Platt, J.P. Child, D.D. Crews, Jr., Wright Carlton, E.J. Hull, O.H. Dishong, A.W. Hendry, C.N. Johnson, Alderman Carlton, Albert Carlton, Charles E. Hendry, John H. Hollingsworth, F.M. Platt, George Albritton, Daniel Coker, Jr., H.E. Carlton, T.H. Bolshaw, F.E. Platt, M.T. Howell, I.N. Smith, F.E. Parker, and C.M. Johnson. "Regular Democrats" listed among their number: B.L. Blackburn, S.A. Sauls, A.G. Smith, T.J. Maddox, J.W. Buchanan, A.K. Demere, F.J. Knight, R.C. Hendry, S.J. Carlton, Oscar T. Stanford, Ziba King, C.W. Carlton, M.F. Giddens, W.M. Smith, W.J. Altman, D.S. Williams, R.T. Burke, T.S. Knight, J.H. Hancock, J.R. Windham, A.E. Pooser, D.D. Mahon, T.J. Herndon, J.H. Peeples, B.F. Wood, J.J. Altman, and E.F. Bostick. *FT-U*, April 25 and July 19, 1892.

52. *FT-U*, October 6, 1892.

53. *FT-U*, December 8, 1893, and October 3, 1894; Election Returns,

Polk and DeSoto counties, 1894, FSA; *BC-I*, October 8, 1894. Former Fort Meade resident Stephen M. Sparkman was elected in 1894 as a Democratic member of Congress from the First District of Florida. Sparkman was a resident of Tampa when elected and remained in the Congress until 1917. Grismer, *Tampa*, 323.

54. *FT-U*, June 14, and August 7 and 25, 1896, and June 30, 1897; *Punta Gorda Herald*, March 21, 1909; Election Returns, DeSoto County, 1896, FSA; "Clippings: Mostly Deaths, Births & Marriages" notebook, vol. #2, 18, MCHRL.

55. *FT-U*, August 1, 1896; *BC-I*, August 12, 1896, and November 2, 1898; Election Returns, Polk County, 1898, FSA.

56. *FT-U*, June 30 and July 17, 1897; *FT-U&C*, September 22, October 11, and October 13, 1897.

57. *FT-U*, September 15, 17, and 18, 1898.

Chapter 19

1. *FT-U*, January 4 and 14, 1890.

2. Blakey, *The Florida Phosphate Industry*, 19; *FT-U*, January 14, 1890.

3. *FT-U*, January 14, 1890. Yellow fever quarantines in fact were established in early June in Fort Meade, Bartow, and Lakeland. By the fall the epidemic had entered the mainland at Tampa, and over the next year it ravaged Tampa, Plant City, Bradenton, and other Hillsborough and Manatee county communities. The quarantines proved effective in Polk and DeSoto, however, and the area was spared. Barker, " 'A Sneaky, Cowardly Enemy': Tampa's Yellow Fever Epidemic of 1887–88"; Jacksonville *Daily News-Herald*, June 11 and 14, 1887.

4. *FT-U*, January 14, 1890; Jacksonville *Daily News-Herald*, June 26, 1887. M.G. Darbishire was a respected member of the British Institute of Civil Engineers at Westminster. In addition to his work surveying railroads and phosphate deposits, Darbishire worked to help communities stave off the threat of yellow fever and other diseases by helping to educate government officials and ordinary citizens to the need for proper sanitation. Darbishire's life and promising career were cut short in late October 1889 when he died on the way home to Fort Meade from Key West where he had been helping that fever-scarred community to plan a sanitary sewage system. *FT-U*, August 29, 1888 and November 3, 1889.

5. Jacksonville *Daily News Herald*, June 26, 1887.

6. Jacksonville *Daily News-Herald*, June 30, 1887; Blakey, *Florida Phosphate Industry*, 21; *FT-U*, January 14, 1890.

7. *FT-U*, January 14, 1890.

8. Covington, *Story of Southwestern Florida*, vol. 1, 193; Shrader, *Hidden Treasures*, 43–55.

9. *FT-U*, January 30, 1890; *PCN*, January 30, 1891.

10. Blakey, *Florida Phosphate Industry*, 39; Covington, *Story of Southwestern Florida*, vol. 1, 193; *FT-U*, April 3, 1890, and January 1, 1892.

11. Blakey, *Florida Phosphate Industry*, 34, 42–43.

12. Ibid., 23–24; Shrader, *Hidden Treasurers*, 44–51.

13. Blakey, *Florida Phosphate Industry*, 35.

14. Ibid., 40, 43.

15. Some phosphate concerns relied heavily upon leased convict labor (primarily blacks), a practice which, according to one historian, "[had] the same effect on convict leasing as the invention of the cotton gin had had on slavery." Abuse of convicts and the leasing system were controversial issues in the state during the 1890s, but the subject was not addressed by the legislature until the twentieth century. Williamson, *Florida Politics in the Gilded Age*, 136, 188; Tebeau, *History of Florida*, 382.

16. Covington, *Story of Southwestern Florida*, vol. 1, 193; *FT-U*, April 16, 1890.

17. *FT-U*, February 16 and 20, 1892.

18. On Meacham's life, see Brown, " 'Where are now the hopes I cherished?' The Life and Times of Robert Meacham," *Florida Historical Quarterly* 69 (July 1990). *FT-U*, June 6, 1890, and June 15, 1895; *BC-I*, October 2, 1895.

19. The first black church building in the Peace River Valley appears to have been "a small frame building" erected at Bartow in 1889 by St. James A.M.E. Church. "St. James A.M.E. Church," CR.

20. Arcadia *DeSoto Leader*, December 1, 1984; "Elizabeth Baptist Church," "Mount Zion A.M.E. Church," and "St. Marks Progressive Baptist Church," CR.

21. *FML*, January 20, 1916; "Galilee Baptist Church" and "St. Paul A.M.E. Church," CR.

22. *FT-U*, January 28, 1893; *BC-I*, July 26, 1893, and February 6, 1895; "Mount Gilbert (Gilboa) Baptist Church," "Burket Chapel Primitive Baptist Church," and "St. James A.M.E. Church," CR.

23. U.S. Original Census Schedules, 10th Census 1880, Polk County, Florida (Population); Adams, *Homeland*, 51; "School Statistics," 9, in Polk County Clippings File, Florida Collection, Fla. State Library; *BAC*, January 4, 1888.

24. Polk's black teachers in 1899 were Ben F. Childs, James Hector, M.L. Norwood, J.B. Lake, A.N. Ritchie, Anna P. McElvine, C.C. Johnson, and Dora James. "School Statistics," 9, in Polk County Clippings File, Florida Collection, Fla. State Library; *BC-I*, July 12 and October 11, 1899.

25. Other original faculty members at Union Academy were J.P. Hector, Miss Lula Marion Simmons (later Mrs. Lula M. Longsworth),

Mrs. M.L. Norwood, and Miss Emma Bullard. "School Statistics," 9, in Polk County Clippings File, Florida Collection, Fla. State Library; *BC-I*, July 12 and October 11, 1899.

26. *FML*, August 22 and 26, 1986.

27. *FT-U*, October 18, 1896.

28. Covington, *Story of Southwestern Florida*, vol. 1, 195; McDuffie, *Lures of Manatee*, 271–72; *FT-U*, January 21, 1886, November 15, 1892, and January 18, 1893.

29. Covington, *Story of Southwestern Florida*, vol. 1, 195; *BC-I*, February 13, 1895.

30. Covington, *Story of Southwestern Florida*, vol. 1, 195; *BC-I*, February 13, 1895; *TT*, July 20 and 21, 1897.

31. *FT-U*, February 12, 1896; Hendry, *Family Record of Lydia Moody*, 37, 40–41, 43–44.

32. Covington, *Story of Southwestern Florida*, vol. 1, 195; *FML*, June 8, 1922.

33. *FT-U*, January 12, February 9, and March 2, 1888. The introduction of tobacco into South Florida may be credited to the foresight of James Ingraham, president of the South Florida Railroad, who early in 1886 imported tobacco seed from Cuba for distribution to farmers living along the line of his railroad. *FT-U*, February 3, 1886.

34. *BC-I*, July 8, 1896.

35. *BC-I*, December 11, 1895, and July 8, 1896; *FT-U*, February 3 and May 24, 1896.

36. *TT*, May 9 and July 20, 1897.

37. *BC-I*, February 16, 1898.

38. *BC-I*, June 3, 1896, and February 1, 1899; *FML*, June 8, 1922.

39. *TT*, July 20 and 21, and August 4, 1897; *FML*, June 8, 1922; *BC-I*, February 15, 1899.

Chapter 20

1. Dept. of Commerce and Labor, Bureau of the Census, *Thirteenth Census of the United States Taken in the Year 1910: Abstract of the Census . . . with Supplement for Florida*, 574, 578; Dept. of the Interior, Census Office, *Compendium of the Tenth Census, Part I*, 84, 341; Ibid., *Abstract 7, The Eleventh Census: 1890*, 15.

2. Bartholf and Boggess, *South Florida, The Italy of America*, 38.

3. *WF*, August 26, 1884, and June 2, 1887; *FT-U*, May 31, 1883.

4. *FT-U*, February 18 and October 18, 1896; Stringer, *Watch Wauchula Win*, 70–71.

5. Frisbie, *Peace River Pioneers*, 59; *FT-U&C*, October 13, 1897.

6. *FT-U&C*, January 6, 1898, and September 7 and 18, 1899; *FT-U*, July 17, 1897.

7. Note should be taken of the work during the late 1870s and early 1880s of Professor D.C. Kantz at Pleasant Hill Academy, two miles south of Bartow, and of Professor John Snoddy at Bethel Academy, Homeland. Both these men trained scores of students who in turn became the teaching core of public education in the Peace River Valley for the remainder of the century. *ST*, February 26 and July 15, 1880.

8. *WF*, August 26, 1884; "School Statistics," 7–12, Polk County Clippings File, Florida Collection, Fla. State Library; *BC-I*, July 12, 1899.

9. Adams, *Homeland*, 51; *BAC*, April 20, 1887; *TT*, August 6, 1950.

10. *FT-U*, August 23, 1886; *BC-I*, August 18, 1894, and May 13, 1896; *TT*, August 4, 1897.

11. *FT-U*, October 21, 1886, and June 16, 1889.

12. *FT-U*, February 25, 1885; *WF*, March 31, 1887; *BAC*, May 25, 1887.

13. *FT-U*, September 3, 1887; Jacksonville *Daily News-Herald*, October 1, 1887; *PCR*, November 18, 1921.

14. *PCR*, November 22, 1921; *FT-U*, March 18, 1889.

15. *FT-U*, June 13 and July 14, 1893.

16. *PCR*, November 22, 1921; *FT-U*, August 9, 1896; *BC-I*, November 8, 1893.

17. Jacksonville *Daily Florida Citizen*, November 10, 1896.

18. Proctor, "The South Florida Military Institute (Bartow)," 29–30; *FT-U*, November 10, 1896.

19. Ibid.

20. Proctor, "The South Florida Military Institute (Bartow)," 29, 32, 35–36; Jacksonville *Daily Florida Citizen*, November 10, 1896.

21. Bartholf and Boggess, *South Florida, The Italy of America*, 38.

22. "First Presbyterian Church of Bartow," CR; *FT-U*, October 21, 1886, April 4, 1889, and August 26, 1898.

23. Lee, "Early History of Christ Church"; *The Churchman*, February 21, 1891; *TT*, July 21, 1897.

24. Barry to Cook, June 9, 1853, DOW, M-1084, roll #3, NA; *PCN*, April 24 and May 1, 1891; *FT-U*, December 20, 1892.

25. *BC-I*, January 30, 1895; "Church of God [Fort Meade]," CR.

26. *TT*, April 1, 1897.

27. On May 26, 1891, Lakeland became the first town in Polk County to have electric power. *FT-U*, June 1, 1891.

28. Dept. of Commerce and Labor, Bureau of the Census, *Thirteenth Census*, 574, 578; *FT-U*, August 9, 1896, and April 16 and August 14, 1897; *TT*, July 20, 1897.

29. Dept. of Commerce and Labor, Bureau of the Census, *Thirteenth Census*, 578; Thompson, *Peace River Valley*, 67; U.S. Original Census Schedules, 12th Census 1900, Polk County, Florida (Population).

30. *FML*, March 16, 1922, and December 25, 1947; *BAC*, January 11 and May 30, 1888; *FT-U*, March 2 and April 27, 1888, and October 3, 1889.

31. Dept. of Commerce and Labor, Bureau of the Census, *Thirteenth Census*, 578; *BC-I*, January 17, 1894; *FT-U*, July 2, 1894.

32. *TT*, August 4, 1897; Dept. of Commerce and Labor, Bureau of the Census, *Thirteenth Census*; *Laws of Florida* (1903), 407.

33. Dept. of Commerce and Labor, Bureau of the Census, *Thirteenth Census*, 574; *FT-U*, February 4 and 23, 1895, and October 18, 1896. The general stores at Bowling Green were operated by R.L. Hopson and C. Jones & Co. H.P. Bailey was the attorney.

34. *FT-U*, November 18, 1896.

35. Dept. of Commerce and Labor, Bureau of the Census, *Thirteenth Census*, 574; *FT-U*, October 18, 1896.

36. Dept. of Commerce and Labor, Bureau of the Census, *Thirteenth Census*; *TT*, July 21, 1897; *FT-U*, October 18, 1896; *FT-U&C*, May 10, 1899.

37. Dept. of Commerce and Labor, Bureau of the Census, *Thirteenth Census*; *FT-U*, September 3 and October 18, 1896; *FT-U&C*, July 20, 1899.

38. Dept. of Commerce and Labor, Bureau of the Census, *Thirteenth Census*; *FT-U*, May 31 and September 3, 1896.

39. Dept. of Commerce and Labor, Bureau of the Census, *Thirteenth Census*; Peeples, "Charlotte Harbor Division of the Florida Southern Railroad," 300–02.

40. Remington to Wister, February 1, 1895, Owen Wister Papers.

Chapter 21

1. *Atlanta Journal Magazine*, May 31, 1931.

Bibliography

Manuscripts

Article of Agreement between the county commissioners of Polk County and John McAuley, contractor, dated June 15, 1867. Walter Crutchfield Collection, Fort Meade, Florida.

Belknap, William Goldsmith. Papers. In William W. Belknap Papers, Princeton University, Princeton, New Jersey.

Boring, Isaac. Diary, 1829–1830. Allan D. Boring Collection, Franklin, North Carolina. Transcript at St. Augustine (Florida) Historical Society Research Library (SAHSRL).

Brown, William Charles. Diary, December 1855–April 9, 1856. Transcription by Theodore Lesley at P.K. Yonge Library (PKY), University of Florida, Gainesville.

Buchanan, Robert C. Papers. Maryland Historical Society, Baltimore.

Casey, John Charles. Diaries. United States Military Academy, West Point, New York.

Casey, John Charles. Papers. Thomas Gilcrease Institute of American History and Art, Tulsa, Oklahoma.

Church Records. Questionnaires of the Florida Writers Program, Work Projects Administration. Florida Collection, Florida State Library, Tallahassee.

Clippings: Mostly Deaths, Births & Marriages. Notebook, vol. 2. Manatee County Historical Records Library (MCHRL), Bradenton, Florida.

Collins, Francis. Papers. University of Texas at Austin.

Cuyler, Telamon, Collection. University of Georgia, Athens.

Durrance, Francis M. Papers. Transcripts at Polk County Historical and Genealogical Library (PCHGL), Bartow, Florida.

Foster, John G. Letterbook, 1865–1866. Library of Congress (LC) (available on microfilm at PKY).

Gibbs, Margaret Watkins [Mrs. George]. Memory Diary. Gibbs Family File, SAHSRL.

Haines, Thomas J. Papers. Albert R. Hatch Collection, New Hampshire Historical Society, Concord.

Harris, Buckner. Papers. Georgia Department of Archives and History, Atlanta.

Harrison, Mrs. Anne Givens. Recollections. Writers Program, Hillsborough County Personalities, PKY.

Hazzard, George W. Papers. United States Military Academy, West Point, New York.

Hill, Ambrose Powell. Papers. Virginia Historical Society, Richmond.

Hitchcock, Ethan Allen. Papers. LC.

Hitchcock, Ethan Allen. Papers. Thomas Gilcrease Institute of American History and Art, Tulsa, Oklahoma.

Holmes, Ammidown. Scrapbook, 1880–1882. SAHSRL.

Howard, Oliver O. Papers. Bowdoin College, Brunswick, Maine.

Jarvis, Nathan S. Diary, 1837–1839. PKY.

Jarvis, Nathan S. Papers. Minnesota Historical Society, Minneapolis.

Jesup, Thomas. Diary, October 1, 1836–May 30, 1837. Florida Collection, Florida State Library, Tallahassee.

Johnston, Joseph E. Papers. The College of William and Mary in Virginia, Williamsburg.

"Journal of the Volunteer Company from Columbia: Feb. 11, 1836–May 12, 1836, Benjamin T. Elmore, Captain." South Carolina Department of Archives and History, Columbia.

L'Engle, Edward M. Papers. Southern Historical Collection (SHC), University of North Carolina, Chapel Hill.

McParlin, Thomas A. Papers. McParlin Family Papers, Maryland Hall of Records, Annapolis.

Meade, George G. Papers. Pennsylvania Historical Society, Philadelphia.

Meek, Alexander Beaufort. Papers. Perkins Library, Duke University, Durham, North Carolina.

Millen, Nancy A. Family Papers. Georgia Department of Archives and History, Atlanta.

"Minutes of the Baptist Church of Christ at Peas Creek in Hillsborough County, South Florida, Constituted September third 1854." Photostatic copy in Minute Book 1, Polk County Historical Commission, PCHGL.

"Minutes of the Salem Church, Echopocksassa, Hillsborough County, Fla., Oct. 15, 1850–Nov. 15, 1851." PCHGL.

Pacetti, Adolphus N. Statement. Pacetti Family File, SAHSRL.

Payne, George S. Letter of September 16, 1848. University of Miami, Miami, Florida.

Payne, George S. Letters of January 27 and June 8, 1849. Formerly in the Florida Collection of Charles F. Meroni; xerographic copies in the possession of the author.

Pemberton Family Papers. Pennsylvania Historical Society, Philadelphia.

Prince, Henry. Diary, 1836–1839, 1842. Transcription at PKY.

Purviance, John S. Letters to Uncle, Gen. Alexander McRae. PKY.

Randolph Family Papers. Virginia Historical Society, Richmond.

Reid, Robert Raymond. Diary, 1833, 1835. Transcription in Reid Family File, SAHSRL.

Talbot, Theodore. Papers. LC.

Taylor, Zachary. Papers. LC.

Thomas, George H. Letter of August 15, 1850. Formerly in the Florida Collection of Charles F. Meroni; xerographic copy in the possession of the author.

Thompson, George F. "Journal as Inspector, Bureau of Freedmen, Refugees and Abandoned Lands, on a tour of central Florida and the lower West Coast, Dec. 1865." PKY.

Twiggs, David Emanuel. Letters. Miscellaneous Manuscripts Collection, LC.

U.S. Centennial Orations, 1876. LC.

White, Pleasant Woodson. Papers. Florida Historical Society, Tampa.

Williams, Thomas. Papers. Williams Family Papers, Burton Historical Collection, Detroit Public Library, Detroit, Michigan.

Wister, Owen. Papers. LC.

Public Documents, Public Records, and Maps

Adjutant General's Office. Bound Regimental Records. Record Group (RG) 94, National Archives (NA).

———. Letters Received. RG 94, NA. Microcopy No. M-567.

American State Papers: Indian Affairs. 2 vols. Washington, 1832–1834.

American State Papers: Military Affairs. 7 vols. Washington, 1832–1860.

American State Papers: Miscellaneous. 2 vols. Washington, 1834.

Annals of the Congress of the United States. Washington, 1855.

Bureau of Refugees, Freedmen, and Abandoned Lands. Florida Records. RG 105, NA.

Carter, Clarence E., ed. *Territorial Papers of the United States, Alabama Territory.* Vol. 18. Washington, 1952.

———. *Territorial Papers of the United States, Florida Territory*. Vols. 22–26. Washington, 1957–1962.

Department of Commerce and Labor, Bureau of the Census. *Thirteenth Census of the United States Taken in the Year 1910: Abstract of the Census . . . With Supplement for Florida*. Washington, 1913.

Department of the Interior, Census Office. *Abstract 7, The Eleventh Census: 1890*. Washington, 1896.

———. *Compendium of the Tenth Census, Part 1*. Washington, 1883.

Department of State. State Department Territorial Papers, Florida, 1777–1824. RG 59, NA. Microcopy No. M-116.

Department of War. Compiled Service Records of Confederate Soldiers Who Served in Organizations from the State of Florida. Microcopy No. M-251, NA.

———. Compiled Service Records of Volunteer Soldiers Who Served in Organizations from the State of Florida During the Florida Indian Wars, 1835–1858. RG 95, NA. Microcopy No. M-1086.

———. Confederate Papers Relating to Citizens or Business Firms. Microcopy No. M-346, NA.

———. Letters Sent, Registers of Letters Received, and Letters Received by Headquarters, Troops in Florida, and Headquarters, Department of Florida, 1850–1858. RG 393, NA. Microcopy No. M-1084.

———. Memoirs of Reconnaisances With Maps During the Florida Campaign, April 1854–February 1858. RG 393, NA. Microcopy No. M-1090.

———. Records Relating to Confederate Naval and Marine Personnel. Microcopy M-260, NA.

DeSoto County, Deed Book II.

Eagan, Dennis. *Sixth Annual Report of the Commissioner of Lands and Immigration of the State of Florida, For the year ending December 31, 1874*. Tallahassee, 1874.

East Florida Papers, LC. Available on microfilm at SAHSRL.

Florida. Board of State Institutions. *Soldiers of Florida in the Seminole Indian-Civil and Spanish-American Wars*. Tallahassee, 1903.

———. Department of Military Affairs. *Florida's Union Army Index, 1862–1865*. St. Augustine, 1987.

———. Department of Natural Resources. Survey Plats, Field Notes, and Tract Books.

———. Department of Natural Resources. Armed Occupation Act Applications.

———. *Florida Reports*, vols. 7–23.

———. *House Journal*, 1855–1866.

———. House of Representatives, Office of the Clerk. *People of Lawmaking in Florida 1822/1985*. Tallahassee, 1985.

———. *Journal of Proceedings of the Convention of Florida, Begun and*

Held at the Capital of the State, at Tallahassee, Wednesday, October 25th, A.D. 1865.

———. *Laws of Florida*, 1845–1903.

———. *Senate Journal*, 1859–1860.

Florida State Archives. Comptroller. Correspondence, 1845–1906. Incoming Correspondence. RG 350, Series 554.

———. Confederate Pension Applications, 1885–1954. RG 137, Series 587.

———. Corrections, Department of. Florida State Prison, 1875–1950. Prison Registers, Book 13 "W-Z." RG 670, Series 500.

———. Education, Commissioner of. C. Thurston Chase, Annual Draft Report, 1870. RG 402, Series 84.

———. Elections, Division of. Election Returns, 1824–1970. Alachua County, 1830–1831; Columbia County, 1832–1845; DeSoto County, 1887–1900; Hamilton County, 1828–1842; Hillsborough County, 1845–1861; Manatee County, 1855–1887; Polk County, 1861–1900; Seventeenth Election District, 1867. RG 156, Series 21.

———. Elections, Division of. Record of Commissions (Indexes), 1871–1889. RG 156, Series 259A.

———. Governor, Office of the. Governors' Correspondence, 1849–1871. RG 101, Series 577.

———. Governor, Office of the. Indian War Claims Commission Records, 1878–1926. RG 100, Series 162.

———. Internal Improvement Trust Fund. General Correspondence. RG 593, Series 914.

———. Internal Improvement Trust Fund. Official Minutes and Agenda, 1855–1981, vols. 1–2. RG 593, Series 194B.

———. Nineteenth Century Florida Legislative Records. RG 915, Series 887.

———. State, Records of the Department of. Correspondence, 1845–1904 (Letters of Resignation & Removals, 1824–1970). RG 150, Series 24.

———. State, Records of the Department of. Correspondence of O.B. Hart, Supervisor of Registration in Florida, 1867. RG 156, Series 626.

———. State, Records of the Department of. Court Appearance Bonds, 1849–1902. RG 150, Series 392.

———. State, Records of the Department of. Voter Registration, 1868. RG 156, Series 98.

———. State Census, 1885. RG 1020, Series 5.

———. Third Census, 1867. Statewide Tabulations and Miscellaneous Fragments, Collection Series #5, Box 167. RG 1020, Series 5.

Florida State Library. Florida Collection. School Statistics, 1875–1892, Polk County, Clippings File.

Hamilton County. Marriage Records, 1843.

Hillsborough County. Circuit Court Minute Books, 1846–1854 and 1854–1866.

——. County Commission Minute Book A, 1846–1863.

——. Deed Books A, B, and C.

——. Marriage Record, Book A.

——. Tax Books, 1847–1861. Available on microfilm at Florida State Archives.

Historical Records Survey, *A List of Municipal Corporations in Florida.* Jacksonville, 1941.

——. *Record Book of Hillsborough County, Territory of Florida, 1838–1846, Vol. III.* Jacksonville, 1938.

——. *Roster of State and County Officers Commissioned by the Governor of Florida 1845–1868.* Jacksonville, 1941.

Ives, J.C. "Military Map of the Peninsula of Florida South of Tampa Bay [1856]." Printed in *United States Senate Document No. 89*, 62d Cong., 1st Sess.

Jesup, Major General Thomas S. Papers. RG 94, NA.

Kappler, Charles J., ed. and comp. *Indian Affairs: Laws & Treaties.* Washington, 1904.

Manatee County. Circuit Court Minute Book, 1858–1887.

——. Circuit Court Records.

——. Clerk's Journal, 1875.

——. County Commission Minute Book 1, 1856–1869.

——. Deed Book B.

——. Miscellaneous County Records, Board of Public Instruction, 1869–1875.

——. Old Miscellaneous County Files.

——. Tax Books. 1860–1870. Available on microfilm at Florida State Archives.

Maps, Cartographic Section, NA.

   No. 757, RG 75; "Survey of Indian Boundary Lines in Florida, With Sketch of the Country Embraced Within Them. [c. 1827]."

   No. 1141, RG 75: "Map of the Seat of War in Florida, compiled by order of General Zachary Taylor, Tampa Bay, Florida, 1839, from surveys of Captain John Mackay and Lieutenant J.E. Blake, Hq. of the Army of the South."

   No. 1145, RG 75: "Recognition of that part of East Florida Laying towards South West from Volusia, made by Horatio S. Dexter and reported by him on the 20th August 1823 to his Excy. Governor Duval."

   No. 4343, RG 75: "Map of the Seat of War in Florida, 1836."

   No. L.61, Civil Works Maps File, RG 77: "The State of Florida compiled in the Bureau of Topographical Engineers, 1846, from the best authorities by J. Goldsborough Bruff."

No. L.247, Item #1, Civil Works Map File, RG 77: "Map of portion of Florida from Georgia boundary and mouth of the Saint Marys, southward to vicinity of Indian River inlet and Charlotte Harbor [manuscript note by Gen. A. Macomb, Sept. 1837.]"

McClelland, James F. *A Digest of the Laws of the State of Florida, from the Year One Thousand Eight Hundred and Twenty-Two, to the Eleventh Day of March, One Thousand Eight Hundred and Eighty-One, Inclusive*. Tallahassee, 1881.

Message from the President of the United States, Transmitting, in Pursuance of a Resolution of the House of Representatives, Such Further Information, in Relation to Our Affairs With Spain, as, in His Opinion, It Is Not Inconsistent With the Public Interest to Divulge. Washington, 1819.

Office of Indian Affairs. Letters Received, Florida Superintendency, 1824–1850. RG 75, NA. Microcopy No. M-234, rolls 286–289.

———. Letters Received, Seminole Agency, 1824–1876 (1846–1855). RG 75, NA. Microcopy No. M-234, roll 801.

Official Records of the Union and Confederate Navies in the War of the Rebellion. 30 vols. Washington, 1894–1922.

Polk County. Circuit Court Minute Book A, 1867–1908.

———. County Commissioners Minute Books, 1861–1900.

———. Deed Books A, B, Q, and U.

———. Marriage Records, Book A, 1862–1881.

———. Probate Records, 1862–1936.

———. Tax Books, 1861–1880. Available on microfilm at Florida State Archives.

Records of Appointment of Postmasters, 1832–1971. Microcopy No. M-841, NA.

Reports of Site Locations, 1837–1950, Post Office Department. Microcopy No. M-1126, NA.

Romans, Bernard. "[Map of] Part of the Province of East Florida."

St. Johns County. Miscellaneous Civil Court Files.

Secretary of War. Letters Received, Registered Series, 1801–1870. RG 107, NA. Microcopy No. M-221.

Tanner, H.S. "Map of Florida [Philadelphia, 1823]."

Transcript of Record, State of Florida vs. The Charlotte Harbor Phosphate Company, U.S. Circuit Court of Appeals for the Fifth Circuit. Federal Archives and Records Center, Fort Worth, Texas.

Treveres, J.J. "Map of Polk County Florida [Jacksonville, 1883]."

United States Army Continental Commands, 1820–1920. RG 393, NA.

———. Department and District of Key West, 1861-68, Letters Received 1861-65. Available on microfilm at PKY.

United States Congress. House. *Report No. 47*, 17th Cong., 1st Sess.

(1822), "Report of the Committee on the Public Lands on the petition of Peter S. Chazotte and others, in behalf of the American Coffee Land Association."

———. *Document No. 51*, 17th Cong., 1st Sess. (1823), "Letter From the Secretary of War . . . Transmitting Sundry Documents and Correspondences in Relation to the Indians of Florida."

———. *Document No. 78*, 25th Cong., 2d Sess. (1838), "Inquiry Into Campaigns of Generals Scott and Gaines; Documents Pertaining to Jesup's Campaign."

———. *Document No. 247*, 27th Cong., 2d Sess. (1842), "Expenditures in 1841—Florida Indians, &c."

———. *Document No. 262*, 27th Cong., 2d Sess. (1842), "Correspondence of the Secretary of War with the Commander in Florida."

———. *Document No. 70*, 28th Cong., 1st Sess. (1844), "Actual Settlements in Florida, Under the Armed Occupation Law."

———. *Document No. 82*, 28th Cong., 1st Sess. (1844), "Indians Remaining in Florida."

———. *Document No. 253*, 28th Cong., 1st Sess. (1844), "Indians Remaining in Florida, &c."

———. *Miscellaneous Document No. 21*, 30th Cong., 2d Sess. (1849), "Resolutions of the Legislature of Florida, asking Congress to take action to keep the Indians of Florida within their prescribed boundaries."

———. *Executive Document No. 1*, 31st Cong., 2d Sess. (1850), "Message from the President of the United States."

———. *Miscellaneous Document No. 34*, 42d Cong., 2d Sess. (1872), "Papers in the Case of S.L. Niblack vs. J.T. Walls, of Florida."

United States Congress. Senate. *Document No. 224*, 24th Cong., 2d Sess. (1837), "Proceedings of the Military Court of Inquiry in the Case of Major General Scott and Major General Gaines."

———. *Document No. 1*, 26th Cong., 1st Sess. (1839), "Message from the President of the United States."

———. *Document No. 278*, 26th Cong., 1st Sess. (1840), "Correspondence Between R.K. Call and the War Department."

———. *Document No. 90*, 29th Cong., 2d Sess. (1847), "Report of the Secretary of War . . . in relation to the Seminole Indians in Florida."

———. *Executive Document No. 39*, 30th Cong., 1st Sess. (1848), "Report of the Commissioner of the Land Office on the Armed Occupation Act."

———. *Executive Document No. 1*, 31st Cong., 1st Sess. (1849), "Message from the President of the United States."

———. *Executive Document No. 49*, 31st Cong., 1st Sess. (1850), "Message from the President of the United States . . . relative to hostilities committed by the Seminole Indians in Florida during the past year, their removal, &c."

————. *Executive Document No. 1*, 32d Cong., 1st Sess. (1851), "Message From the President of the United States."

————. *Executive Document No. 7*, 34th Cong., 1st Sess. (1856), "Report of the Secretary of War, Showing The contracts made under authority of the War Department during the year 1855."

————. *Executive Document No. 15*, 41st Cong., 2d Sess. (1870), "Letter of the Secretary of the Navy . . . in relation to the amount of land claimed, held, or occupied by the Navy Department, in the State of Florida, for naval or other purposes."

————. *Miscellaneous Document No. 161*, 41st Cong., 2d Sess. (1870), "Memorial of the International Ocean Telegraph Company."

————. *Report No. 611*, 44th Cong., 2d Sess. (1877), "Florida Election, 1876."

————. *Executive Document No. 128*, 46th Cong., 2d Sess. (1880), "Letter From the Secretary of War, Transmitting . . . a report made upon an examination of Charlotte Harbor and Peas Creek, Florida."

————. *Executive Document No. 189*, 47th Cong., 1st Sess. (1882), "Letter From the Secretary of War, Transmitting A Communication . . . with the view of opening a steamboat communication from Saint John's River, Florida, by way of Topokalija Lake to Charlotte Harbor or Peace Creek."

United States Navy Department. Records Relating to the Service of the Navy and Marine Corps on the Coast of Florida 1835–1842. NA; microfilm at PKY.

United States Original Census Schedules, 1820–1900.

United States Regular Army Mobil Units, 1821–1942. RG 391, NA.

Wakulla County. Tax Book, 1863. Available on microfilm at Florida State Archives.

War of the Rebellion: A Compilation of the Official Records of the Union and Confederate Armies. 128 vols. Washington, 1880–1901.

Newspapers and Periodicals

Arcadia *DeSoto Leader*, 1984.

Augusta [Ga.] *Southern Christian Advocate*, 1863–1864.

Army and Navy Chronicle [Washington, D.C.], 1835–1842.

Baltimore Gazette and Daily Advertiser, 1838.

Bartow *Advance Courier*, 1887–1888.

Bartow *Courier-Informant*, 1890–1915.

Bartow *Informant*, 1881–1885.

Bartow *Polk County Democrat*, 1976.

Bartow *Polk County News*, 1891–1892.

Bartow *Polk County Record*, 1921–1940.
Boston [Mass.] *Daily Journal*, 1862.
Boston [Mass.] *Patriot and Daily Merchantile Advertiser*, 1822.
Brooksville *Florida Weekly News*, 1887.
Buffalo [N.Y.] *Commercial Advertiser*, 1871.
Charleston [S.C.] *Courier*, 1821.
Charleston [S.C.] *Daily Courier*, 1864.
Charleston [S.C.] *Mercury*, 1836.
Charleston [S.C.] *Southern Christian Advocate*, 1862.
The Churchman [New York City], 1891.
Columbia [S.C.] *Southern Times & State Gazette.*
Columbus [Ga.] *Daily Sun*, 1858.
DeLand *Florida Agriculturist*, 1875.
Erie [Pa.] *Observer*, 1837.
Fernandina *Florida News*, 1858.
Fernandina *Observer*, 1876.
Fort Meade Leader, 1910–1922, 1947, 1986.
Fort Myers News-Press, 1966.
Fort Myers Weekly Press, 1885–1909.
Gainesville *New Era*, 1867.
Jacksonville Courier, 1835.
Jacksonville *Evening Telegram*, 1892.
Jacksonville *Daily Florida Citizen*, 1896.
Jacksonville *Daily News-Herald*, 1887.
Jacksonville *Florida Daily Times*, 1882.
Jacksonville *Florida Journal*, 1884.
Jacksonville *Florida News*, 1852–1855.
Jacksonville *Florida Republican*, 1855.
Jacksonville *Florida Times-Union*, 1883–1897, 1936.
Jacksonville *Florida Times-Union and Citizen*, 1897–1899.
Jacksonville *Florida Union*, 1865–1877.
Jacksonville *Florida Weekly Times*, 1884.
Jacksonville *News*, 1848–1849.
Jacksonville *Semi-Weekly Floridian*, 1896.
Jacksonville *Tri-Weekly Union*, 1874.
Jacksonville *Weekly News-Herald*, 1888.
Key West Dispatch, 1873.
Key West *Key of the Gulf*, 1860.
Kissimmee *Osceola Sun*, 1975.
Lakeland Ledger, 1929, 1951, 1977.
Miami Herald, 1965.
Milledgeville [Ga.] *Reflector*, 1818.
Nassau *Royal Gazette and Bahama Advertiser*, 1819–1821.

National Banner and Nashville Whig, 1836.
New York *Evening Star for the Country*, 1836.
New York Herald, 1858–1865.
New York *Morning Courier and New York Enquirer*, 1836.
New York Times, 1874.
Newport *Wakulla Times*, 1858.
Niles' Weekly Register [Baltimore], 1811–1849.
Oswego [N.Y.] *Daily Palladium*, 1864–1872.
Palatka Daily News, 1885.
Palatka *Eastern Herald*, 1875.
Pensacola *Floridian*, 1822.
Pensacola *Gazette*, 1836.
Philadelphia *National Gazette and Literary Register*, 1821.
Philadelphia *North American and United States Gazette*, 1849.
Philadelphia *Pennsylvania Inquirer and Daily Courier*, 1838.
Philadelphia *United States Gazette*, 1837.
Plant City *South Florida Courier*, 1886–1887.
Punta Gorda Herald, 1902–1909.
St. Augustine *East Florida Herald*, 1823.
St. Augustine *Examiner*, 1866–1867.
St. Augustine *Florida Gazette*, 1821.
St. Augustine *Florida Herald*, 1837–1843.
St. Augustine *News*, 1842–1845.
St. Augustine *St. Johns Weekly*, 1879.
Savannah *Advertiser-Republican*, 1873.
Savannah Daily Advertiser, 1873.
Savannah Daily News and Herald, 1867.
Savannah Morning News, 1873–1886.
Tallahassee *Floridian*, 1836–1853.
Tallahassee *Floridian & Journal*, 1855–1858.
Tallahassee *Semi-Weekly Floridian*, 1865–1867.
Tallahassee Sentinel, 1867–1876.
Tallahassee *Weekly Floridian*, 1868–1888.
Tampa Daily Times, 1923.
Tampa *Florida Peninsular*, 1856–1873.
Tampa Guardian, 1879–1886.
Tampa *Sunland Tribune*, 1877–1882.
Tampa Tribune, 1888–1897, 1929, 1946–1959.
Washington [D.C.] *Gazette*, 1822.

Secondary Sources

Adams, Sherman. *Homeland: A Description of the Climate, Productions, Resources, Topography, Soil, Opportunities, Attractions, Advantages,*

Developments and General Characteristics of Polk County, Florida. Bartow, Florida, 1885.

Akerman, Joe A., Jr. *Florida Cowman: A History of Florida Cattle Raising.* Kissimmee, Florida, 1976.

Alduino, Frank. "Prohibition in Tampa." *Tampa Bay History* 9 (Spr./ Sum. 1987): 17-28.

Ames, Frieda Zander. "First United Methodist Church, East Broadway at Pine, Fort Meade, Florida." Typescript at PCHGL.

Barker, Eirlys. " 'A Sneaky, Cowardly Enemy': Tampa's Yellow Fever Epidemic of 1887-88." *Tampa Bay History* 8 (Fall/Winter 1986): 4-22.

Barr, James. *A Correct & Authentic Narrative of the Indian War in Florida With a Description of Dade's Massacre and an Account of the extreme suffering for want of provisions of the Army—having been obliged to eat horses' and dogs' flesh &c &c.* New York, 1836.

Bartholf, John F., and Boggess, Francis C.M. *South Florida, The Italy of America: Its Climate, Soil and Productions.* Jacksonville, Florida, 1881.

Blackman, William Fremont. *History of Orange County, Florida.* DeLand, Florida, 1927.

Blakey, Arch Fredric. *The Florida Phosphate Industry: A History of the Development and Use of a Vital Mineral.* Cambridge, Massachusetts, 1973.

Boehm, Terry. "The History of Christ Church, Fort Meade, Florida 1886-1895." Fort Meade, 1980. Typescript in possession of author.

Boggess, Francis C.M. *A Veteran of Four Wars.* Arcadia, Florida, 1900.

Boyd, Mark F. "Asi-Yaholo or Osceola." *Florida Historical Quarterly* 33 (Jan.-Apr. 1953): 249-305.

———. "Further Considerations of the Apalachee Missions." *The Americas* 9 (April 1953): 459-79.

———. "Horatio S. Dexter and Events Leading to the Treaty of Moultrie Creek With the Seminole Indians." *Florida Anthropologist* 11 (Sept. 1958): 65-95.

Brinton, Daniel G. *Notes on the Floridian Peninsula, Its Literary History, Indian Tribes and Antiquities.* Philadelphia, 1859; reprinted, New York, 1969.

Brooks, Priscilla, and Crabtree, Caroline. *St. James City Florida: The Early Years.* Detroit, 1982.

Brown, Canter, Jr. " 'As Far As Our Eyes Will Let Us See': The 'Peas Creek Expedition' of 1860." *Tampa Bay History* 12 (Spring/Summer 1990): 43-79.

———. "The International Ocean Telegraph." *Florida Historical Quarterly* 68 (October 1989): 135-59.

———. " 'Where are now the hopes I cherished?': The Life and Times of Robert Meacham." *Florida Historical Quarterly* 69 (July 1990).

Bruton, Quintilla Geer, and Bailey, David E., Jr. *Plant City: Its Origin and History*. St. Petersburg, Florida, 1977.

Buker, George E. "Lieutenant Levin M. Powell, Pioneer of Riverine Warfare." *Florida Historical Quarterly* 47 (Jan. 1969): 253–75.

Burnham, W. Dean. *Presidential Ballots 1836–1892*. New York, 1976.

Canova, Andrew P. *Life and Adventures In South Florida*. Tampa, Florida, 1906.

Carpenter, Lillian R. *History of the First Methodist Church, Bartow, Florida, and Its Methodist Background*. Bartow, Florida, 1944.

Chamberlin, Donald L. "Fort Brooke: Frontier Outpost, 1824–42," *Tampa Bay History* 7 (Spr./Sum. 1985): 5–29.

Chazotte, Peter Stephen. *Facts and Observations on the Culture of Vines, Olives, Capers, Almonds, &c. in the Southern States, and of Coffee, Cocoa, and Cochineal, in East Florida*. Philadelphia, 1821.

Childs, Thomas. "Major Childs, U.S.A.: Extracts From His Correspondence With His Family," *Historical Magazine*, 3d Series, III (April 1875): 280–84.

Coe, Charles H. *Red Patriots: The Story of the Seminoles*. Cincinnati, 1898; reprinted, Gainesville, Florida, 1974.

Cohen, Myer M. *Notices of Florida and the Campaigns*. Charleston, South Carolina, 1836; reprinted, Gainesville, Florida, 1964.

Coker, William S., and Watson, Thomas D. *Indian Traders of the Southeastern Spanish Borderlands: Panton, Leslie & Company and John Forbes & Company 1783–1847*. Pensacola, Florida, 1986.

Coleman, Kenneth, ed. *A History of Georgia*. Athens, Georgia, 1977.

Coulter, E. Merton. *The Confederate States of America 1861–1865*. Baton Rouge, Louisiana, 1950.

Covington, James W. "The Armed Occupation Act of 1842." *Florida Historical Quarterly* 40 (July 1961): 41–52.

———. *The Billy Bowlegs War*. Chuluota, Florida, 1981.

———. "The Establishment of Fort Brooke: The Beginning of Tampa." *Florida Historical Quarterly* 31 (April 1953): 273–78.

———. "Life at Ft. Brooke 1824–1836," *Florida Historical Quarterly* 36 (April 1958): 319–30.

———. "Migration of the Seminoles Into Florida, 1700–1820." *Florida Historical Quarterly* 46 (April 1968): 340–57.

———. *The Story of Southwestern Florida*. 2 vols. New York, 1957.

Davis, T. Frederick. "The Alagon, Punon Rostro, and Vargas Land Grants." *Florida Historical Quarterly* 25 (October 1946): 175–90.

———. "MacGregor's Invasion of Florida, 1817." *Florida Historical Quarterly* 7 (July 1928): 63–71.

Davis, William Watson. *The Civil War and Reconstruction in Florida*. New York, 1913; reprinted, Gainesville, Florida, 1964.

"The Defences of the Floridas: A Report of Captain James Gadsden, Aide-de-Camp to General Andrew Jackson." *Florida Historical Quarterly* 15 (April 1937): 242–48.

DeVane, Albert. *DeVane's Early Florida History*. 2 vols. Sebring, Florida, 1978–1979.

Dillon, Rodney E., Jr. "The Battle of Fort Myers." *Tampa Bay History* 5 (Fall/Winter 1983): 27–36.

———. "The Civil War in South Florida." M.A. Thesis, University of Florida, 1980.

Doster, James F. *Creek Indians*. 2 vols. New York, 1974.

Dummett, Anna Maria. "Remembrances of the Old Plantation—The Old Dummett Grove." *Literary Florida* (February 1949): 9–15.

Durrance, Margaret Lewis. *R & M: Our Family*. 1977–1978.

———, and Folk, Ann Durrance. *Lineage of Joseph Durrance*. Lakeland, Florida, 1986.

Ezell, John Samuel. *The South Since 1865*. New York, 1963.

Faust, Patricia L. *Historical Times Illustrated Encyclopedia of the Civil War*. New York, 1986.

Florida Land and Improvement Company. *The Disston Lands of Florida*. Philadelphia, 1885.

Frisbie, Louise K. *Peace River Pioneers*. Miami, 1974.

———. *Yesterday's Polk County*. Miami, 1976.

Fritz, Florence. *Unknown Florida*. Coral Gables, Florida, 1963.

Giddings, Joshua R. *The Exiles of Florida: Or, the Crimes Committed by Our Government Against the Maroons, Who Fled from South Carolina and Other Slave States, Seeking Protection Under Spanish Law*. Columbus, Ohio, 1858; reprinted, Gainesville, Florida, 1964.

Godwin, Philo A. *Biography of Andrew Jackson*. New York, 1833.

Goggin, John M. "The Seminole Negroes of Andros Island, Bahamas." *Florida Historical Quarterly* 24 (Jan. 1946): 201–6.

Grismer, Karl H. *The Story of Fort Myers: The History of the Land of the Caloosahatchee and Southwest Florida*. Fort Myers, Florida, 1949; reprinted, Fort Myers Beach, Florida, 1982.

———. *Tampa: A History of the City of Tampa and the Tampa Bay Region of Florida*. St. Petersburg, Florida, 1950.

Hall, Robert L. "The Gospel According to Radicalism: African Methodism Comes to Tallahassee after the Civil War." *Apalachee 1971–1979*: 69–81.

———. " 'Yonder Come Day': Religious Dimensions of the Transition from Slavery to Freedom in Florida." *Florida Historical Quarterly* 65 (Apr. 1987): 411–32.

Hamersly, Thomas H. *Complete Army and Navy Register of the U.S.A. from 1776–1887*. New York, 1888.

Hamilton, Mrs. Donald. "Dempsey Dubois Crews 1806-1892." *South Florida Pioneers* 12 (Apr. 1977): 8-11.

Hamilton County Bicentennial Committee. *A Brief History of Hamilton County, Florida.* Jasper, Florida, 1976.

Hammond, E.A. "Sanibel Island and Its Vicinity, 1833, A Document." *Florida Historical Quarterly* 48 (Apr. 1970): 392-411.

———. "The Spanish Fisheries of Charlotte Harbor." *Florida Historical Quarterly* 51 (1973): 355-80.

Harris, William Lloyd. "When War Came to Polk County: Battle at Bowlegs Creek 20 February, 1864." *Polk County Historical Quarterly* 11 (March 1985): 4-5.

Hawkins, Benjamin. *A Sketch of the Creek Country in 1798 and 1799.* Spartanburg, South Carolina, 1974.

Hawks, J.M. *The Florida Gazetteer.* New Orleans, 1871.

Hays, Louise Frederick, ed. and comp. *Creek Indian Letters, Talks and Treaties, 1705-1839, Part III: 1813-1829, Inclusive.* Atlanta, Georgia, 1939. (Typescript at Georgia Department of Archives and History, Atlanta.)

———. *Letters of Benjamin Hawkins, 1797-1815.* Atlanta, Georgia, 1939. (Typescript at Georgia Department of Archives and History, Atlanta.)

Hendry, Francis A. *Early History of Lee County and Fort Myers.* Privately printed, n.d.

Hendry, George W. *Family Record of Lydia Moody, nee Hendry, nee Carlton of Polk County, Florida.* Jacksonville, Florida, 1900.

———. *Polk County, Florida. Its Lands & Products.* Jacksonville, Florida, 1883.

Hetherington, M.F. *History of Polk County, Florida.* St. Augustine, Florida, 1928; reprinted Chuluota, Florida, 1971.

"Hillsborough County Voters in the 1845 Statewide Election." *Florida Genealogical Society Journal* 21 (Spring 1985): 133-34.

Holmes, Jack D.L. "Spanish Interest in Tampa Bay During the 18th Century." *Tampa Bay History* 5 (Spring/Summer 1983): 5-23.

Huxford, Folks. *Pioneers of Wiregrass Georgia.* 7 vols. 1951-1975.

Ives, J.C., comp. *Memoir to Accompany a Military Map of the Peninsula of Florida, South of Tampa Bay.* New York, 1856.

Jackson, Ronald Vern; Winmill, Wylma; and Zachrison, Shirley P. *Florida 1870 Mortality Schedule.* Bountiful, Utah, 1983.

Jacobs, Wilbur R. *The Appalachian Indian Frontier: The Edmond Atkin Report and Plan of 1755.* Lincoln, Nebraska, 1967.

Kersey, Harry A., Jr. "The Seminole Negroes of Andros Island Revisited: Some New Pieces to an Old Puzzle," *Florida Anthropologist* 34 (December 1981): 169-76.

Keuchel, Edward F. *A History of Columbia County, Florida.* Tallahassee, 1981.

Kinnaird, Lawrence, trans. and ed. *Problems of Frontier Defense, 1792-1794. Part 3 of Spain in the Mississippi Valley, 1765-1794.* American Historical Association Annual Report for 1945. Washington, 1946.

Klingman, Peter D. *Josiah Walls: Florida's Black Congressman of Reconstruction.* Gainesville, Florida, 1976.

Kollock, John. *These Gentle Hills.* Lakemont, Georgia, 1976.

Lane, George, Jr. *A Pictorial History of Arcadia and DeSoto County.* St. Petersburg, Florida, 1984.

Lane, Pat Sonquist. " 'Florida Is A Blessed Country': Letters to Iowa from a Florida Settler." *Florida Historical Quarterly* 64 (April 1986): 432-45.

Lee, J.V. "Early History of Christ Church." In "Old Record Book," Christ Church, Fort Meade, Florida. Typescript at PCHGL.

Lewis, Doris. *The Kissimmee Island.* 1982.

Livingston, Richard M. (ed.). "Benjamin Moody 1811-1896." *South Florida Pioneers* 8 (April 1976): 9-11.

————. "David J.W. Boney 1815-1889," *South Florida Pioneers* 13 (July 1977): 2-3.

————. "DeSoto County: Arcadia's First Courthouse." *South Florida Pioneers* 6 (Oct. 1975): 36-38.

————. "Early Church Records: South Florida Baptist Association Minutes." *South Florida Pioneers* 5 (July 1975): 35-36; 6 (Oct. 1975): 8-9.

————. "Elias E. Johnson 1818-1884." *South Florida Pioneers* 1 (July 1974): 1-2.

————. "Enoch Everette Mizell 1806-1887." *South Florida Pioneers* 3 (Jan. 1975): 13-17.

————. "Francis Burdette Hagan 1827-1914." *South Florida Pioneers* 9 (July 1976): 21-24.

————. "Frederick S. Lanier 1829-1875." *South Florida Pioneers* 7 (Jan. 1976): 33-34

————. "Hugh Bethea 1829-1887." *South Florida Pioneers* 35/36 (Jan./Apr. 1983): 15-16.

————. "James Washington Mathis (Matthews) 1834-1893." *South Florida Pioneers* 6 (Oct. 1975): 32-35.

————. "John Baggs Raulerson 1822-1901." *South Florida Pioneers* 17/18 (July/Oct. 1978): 15-17.

————. "Levi Pearce 1806-1874." *South Florida Pioneers* 21/22 (July/Oct. 1979): 38-41.

————. "Noel Rabun Raulerson 1820-1910." *South Florida Pioneers* 10 (Oct. 1976): 25-28.

————. "Rowland Williams 1812-1867." *South Florida Pioneers* 1 (July 1974): 3-5.

———. "Samuel E. Prescott 1824-1897." *South Florida Pioneers* 17/18 (July/Oct. 1978): 38-39.

———. "Seth Howard 1804-1887." *South Florida Pioneers* 15/16 (Jan./ Apr. 1978): 3-5.

———. "Thomas Summeralls c.1822-1862." *South Florida Pioneers* 25/26 (July/Oct. 1980): 27-29.

———. "Wade Hampton Whidden 1810-1865." *South Florida Pioneers* 39/40 (January/April 1984): 34-36.

———. "Willoughby Tillis 1808-1895." *South Florida Pioneers* 39/40 (Jan./Apr. 1984): 4-11.

———. "Willoughby Whidden 1799-1861." *South Florida Pioneers* 11 (January 1977): 8-11.

Long, Charles Sumner. *History of the A.M.E. Church in Florida.* Philadelphia, 1939.

McCall, George. *Letters from the Frontiers.* Philadelphia, 1868; reprinted, Gainesville, Florida, 1985.

McClelland, Clifton A. "Silas McClelland 1790-1875." *South Florida Pioneers* 19/20 (Jan./Apr. 1979): 33-35.

———. *Silas and Penelope (Anderson) McClelland and Some Descendants, 1790-1987.* Baltimore, 1987.

McDuffie, Lillie B. *The Lures of Manatee: A True Story of South Florida's Glamorous Past.* Bradenton, Florida, 1961.

McKay, Donald B. *Pioneer Florida.* 3 vols. Tampa, Florida, 1959.

McKenney, Thomas L., and Hall, James. *The Indian Tribes of North America with Biographical Sketches and Anecdotes of the Principal Chiefs.* 3 vols. Philadelphia, 1836-1844.

McNeely, Ed, and McFayden, Al R. *Century in the Sun: A History of Polk County.* Bartow, Florida, 1961.

McReynolds, Edwin C. *The Seminoles.* Norman, Oklahoma, 1957.

Mahon, John K. *History of the Second Seminole War, 1835-1842.* Gainesville, Florida, 1967.

Malone, Dumas, and Rauch, Basil. *The Republic Comes of Age 1789-1841.* New York, 1960.

Matthews, Janet Snyder. *Edge of Wilderness.* Tulsa, Oklahoma, 1983.

Meek, A.B. *Romantic Passages In Southwestern History.* New York, 1857.

A Memorial Sketch of the Life and Ministerial Labors of Rev. J.M. Hayman, one of the Pioneer Baptist Preachers of South Florida, Who Passed to His Reward Above July 9th, 1902. Nashville, Tennessee, 1901.

Minutes of the Annual Conferences of the Methodist Episcopal Church, South, for the Year 1874. Nashville, Tennessee,

Minutes of the Seventeenth Annual Session of the South Florida Baptist

Association Held With Church at Shiloh, October 20 and 22, 1883. Atlanta, Georgia, 1883.

Mormino, Gary R. " 'The Firing of Guns and Crackers Continued Till Light': A Diary of the Billy Bowlegs War." *Tequesta* 45 (1985): 48–72.

———, and Pizzo, Anthony P. *Tampa: The Treasure City.* Tulsa, Oklahoma, 1983.

Morse, Jedediah. *Report to the Secretary of War of the United States on Indian Affairs.* Washington, 1822; reprinted, New York, 1970.

Muse, Violet B. "Negro History: Tampa." *Negro History in Florida,* Writers' Program, PKY.

Nelson, Martha Lester. "Nancy Jackson—1815-1907." *The Sunland Tribune* 9 (Dec. 1983): 22–25.

Nerod, Felix. *An Historical Gazetteer of Imperial Polk County Florida.* Lake Alfred, Florida, 1986.

Newton, Mrs. Annie Platt, and Livingston, Richard M. "John Platt 1793-1874." *South Florida Pioneers* 29/30 (July/Oct. 1981): 19–21.

Nicholson, Doris. "DeSoto County: History of Fort Winder." *South Florida Pioneers* 7 (Jan. 1976): 32.

Oates, Stephen B. *With Malice Toward None.* New York, 1977.

Osborn, George C., and Dalton, Jack P. "The South Florida Baptist Association." *Tequesta* 14 (1954): 51–60.

Otto, John Solomon. "Hillsborough County (1850): A Community in the South Florida Flatwoods." *Florida Historical Quarterly* 62 (Oct. 1983): 180–93.

Owsley, Frank Lawrence, Jr. *Struggle for the Gulf Borderlands: The Creek War and the Battle of New Orleans, 1812-1815.* Gainesville, Florida, 1981.

Parton, James. *Life of Andrew Jackson.* New York, 1860; reprinted, New York, 1967.

Patrick, Rembert W. *Florida Fiasco.* Athens, Georgia, 1954.

Payne, W.D. *A Short Sketch of Robert Roberts, Embracing a Story of His Military Life in the War Between the States.* N.d.

Peddy, T.J. *Creek Letters 1820-1824.* Atlanta, n.d. (Transcript at Georgia Department of Archives and History, Atlanta.)

Peeples, Vernon E. "Charlotte Harbor Division of the Florida Southern Railroad." *Florida Historical Quarterly* 58 (Jan. 1980): 291–302.

———. "Florida Men Who Served in the Union Forces During the Civil War." *South Florida Pioneers* 5 (July 1975): 12–16; 6 (Oct. 1975): 10–14.

———. "John F. Bartholf, A Manatee County Carpetbagger: An Address Given by Vernon E. Peeples to the Manatee County Historical Society 15 October, 1969." Typescript at MCHRL.

———. *Punta Gorda and the Charlotte Harbor Area: A Pictorial History.* Norfolk, Virginia, 1986.

Peters, Virginia Bergman. *The Florida Wars.* Hamden, Connecticut, 1979.

Pettengill, George W., Jr. *The Story of the Florida Railroads 1843-1903.* Boston, 1952.

Pickett, Albert James. *History of Alabama, and Incidentally of Georgia and Mississippi.* 2 vols. Charleston, South Carolina, 1851.

Plowden Jean. *History of Hardee County.* Wauchula, Florida, 1929.

Polk County. Board of County Commissioners. *Polk County, Florida.* Bartow, Florida, 1887.

Porter, Kenneth W. "Billy Bowlegs (Holata Micco) in the Seminole Wars." *Florida Historical Quarterly* 45 (Jan. 1967): 219-42.

———. "The Cowkeeper Dynasty of the Seminole Nation." *Florida Historical Quarterly* 30 (April 1952): 341-49.

———. "Negroes and the Seminole War, 1817, 1818." *Journal of Negro History* 35 (July 1951): 249-80.

———. "Notes on Seminole Negroes In The Bahamas." *Florida Historical Quarterly* 24 (July 1945): 56-60.

Proceedings of the Eighth Annual Session of the South Florida Baptist Association, Held With the Shiloh Church, Hillsboro County, Florida, Oct. 16th, 19th, 1874. Lake City, Florida, 1874.

Proctor, Samuel. "The South Florida Military Institute (Bartow)." *Florida Historical Quarterly* 32 (July 1953): 28-40.

Pyburn, Nita K. *The History of the Development of a Single System of Education in Florida, 1822-1903.* Tallahassee, Florida, 1954.

Read, William A. *Florida Place-Names of Indian Origin and Seminole Personal Names.* Baton Rouge, Louisiana, 1934.

Reid, James D. *The Telegraph in America: Its Founders, Promoters, and Noted Men.* Albany, New York, 1879.

Remini, Robert V. *Andrew Jackson and the Course of American Empire, 1767-1821.* New York, 1977.

Rerick, Rowland H. *Memoirs of Florida.* 2 vols. Atlanta, Georgia, 1902.

Richardson, Joe M. *The Negro in the Reconstruction of Florida, 1865-1877.* Tallahassee, Florida, 1965.

Robinson, Sallie [interviewed by John E. Brown]. Fort Meade, Florida, May 20, 1987.

Saint James A.M.E. Church. "4th Annual Homecoming Program, Sunday, July 14, 1985, Saint James A.M.E. Church, Bartow, Florida."

———. "Souvenir of the Dedicatory Services, Dedication of the St. James A.M.E. Church, Rev. T.S. Johnson, Pastor, June 10, 1956."

Schene, Michael G. "Not A Shot Fired: Fort Chokonikla and the 'Indian War' of 1849-50." *Tequesta* 37 (1977): 19-37.

Schmidt, Lewis G. *A Civil War History of the 47th Regiment of Pennsylvania Veteran Volunteers.* Allentown, Pennsylvania, 1986.

Shofner, Jerrell H. *Nor Is It Over Yet: Florida in the Era of Reconstruction 1863-1877*. Gainesville, Florida, 1974.

Shrader, Jay. *Hidden Treasures: The Pebble Phosphates of the Peace River Valley of South Florida*. Bartow, Florida, 1891.

Simmons, William H. *Notices of East Florida, with an Account of the Seminole Nation of Indians*. Charleston, South Carolina, 1822; reprinted, Gainesville, Florida, 1973.

Smith, Julia Floyd. *Slavery and Plantation Growth in Antebellum Florida 1821-1860*. Gainesville, Florida, 1973.

Sprague, John T. *The Origin, Progress, and Conclusion of the Florida War*. New York, 1848; reprinted, Gainesville, Florida, 1964.

Stone, Spessard. "Francis Asbury Hendry 1833-1917." *South Florida Pioneers* 33/34 (July/Oct. 1982): 18-23.

———. "James D. Green 1823-1886." *South Florida Pioneers* 45/46 (July/Oct. 1985): 2-6.

———. "James Madison Hendry 1839-1922." *South Florida Pioneers* 21/22 (July Oct. 1979): 48-51.

———. *John and William, Sons of Robert Hendry*. Bradenton, Florida, 1984.

———. "John Wesley Whidden 1839-1910." *South Florida Pioneers* 31/32 (Jan./Apr. 1982): 9-13.

———. "John Wright Hendry 1836-1907." *South Florida Pioneers* 27/28 (Jan./Apr. 1981): 27-31.

———. "Levi Starling 1808-1856." *South Florida Pioneers* 49/50 (July/Oct. 1986): 30-34.

Stringer, Margaret. *Watch Wauchula Win: Facts, Figures and Fun— 1886-1930*. Bartow, Florida, 1979.

Sturtevant, William C. "Chakaika and the 'Spanish Indians': Documentary Sources Compared with Seminole Tradition." *Tequesta* 13 (1953): 35-73.

Swanton, John R. *Early History of the Creek Indians and Their Neighbors*. Washington, 1922.

Taylor, Robert A. "Cow Cavalry: Munnerlyn's Battalion in Florida, 1864-1865." *Florida Historical Quarterly* 65 (Oct. 1986): 196-214.

———. "Rebel Beef: Florida Cattle and the Confederacy, 1861-1865." M.A. thesis, University of South Florida, 1985.

Tebeau, Charlton. *A History of Florida*. Coral Gables, Florida, 1971.

Temple, Robert Mickler, Jr. *Florida Flame*. Nashville, Tennessee, 1987.

Thompson, Robert Lee. *Peace River Valley: The Puritan's Utopia*. Morganton, North Carolina, 1980.

Tillis, James Dallas. "An Indian Attack of 1856 on the Home of Willoughby Tillis." *Florida Historical Quarterly* 8 (April 1930): 179-87.

VanLandingham, Kyle S. "Archibald Hendry 1820-1897," *South Florida Pioneers* 25/26 (July/Oct. 1980): 23-25.

————. *Florida Cousins: The Descendants of William H. Willingham.* Fort Pierce, Florida, 1967.

————. "John I. Hooker 1822-1862." *South Florida Pioneers* 15/16 (Jan./Apr. 1978): 8-9.

————. "John Levi Skipper 1826-1907." *South Florida Pioneers* 12 (Apr. 1977): 24-26.

————. "Solomon Godwin 1817-1880." *South Florida Pioneers* 11 (Jan. 1977): 18-20.

————. "Stephen Hollingsworth 1797-1870." *South Florida Pioneers* 9 (July 1976): 9-12.

————. "William Brinton Hooker 1800-1871." *South Florida Pioneers* 5 (July 1975): 6-12.

————. "William Henry Willingham 1816-1886." *South Florida Pioneers* 10 (Oct. 1976): 9-11.

Vignoles, Charles. *Observations upon the Floridas.* New York, 1823; reprinted, Gainesville, Florida, 1977.

———— et al. *Documents in Proof of the Climate and Soil of Florida, Particularly the Southern Section.* New York, 1832.

Wallace, John. *Carpetbag Rule in Florida.* Jacksonville, Florida, 1888; reprinted, Kennesaw, Georgia, 1959.

"The War Between the States." *El Escribano* 3 (Oct. 1966): 6-9.

Ware, Lynn Willoughby. "The Peace River: A Forgotten Highway." *Tampa Bay History* 6 (Fall/Winter 1984): 19-30.

Wells, George W. *Facts for Immigrants.* Jacksonville, Florida, 1877.

Westergard, Virginia W., and VanLandingham, Kyle S. *Parker and Blount in Florida.* Okeechobee, Florida, 1983.

Whidden, Mrs. H.P. "The James Whitton Family of Polk County." *Polk County Historical Quarterly* 12 (March 1986): 4-5.

White, Robert M. "History of Fort Meade, Florida." Fort Meade, 1964. Typescript at PCHGL.

Wiggins. E.I. *The History of the Absolute Mt. Enon Association.* Plant City, Florida, 1975.

Wilder, E.G. "Escapade in Southern Florida." *Confederate Veteran* 19 (Feb. 1911): 75.

Wilder, John. "The Wedding at the Parker House." *Putnam's Magazine* (Aug. 1868): 163-78.

Williams, John Lee. *The Territory of Florida.* New York, 1837; reprinted, Gainesville, Florida, 1962.

Williams, Kate Barnwell. "This Is The Story of My Life." *Tampa Bay History* 9 (Spr./Sum. 1987): 49-65.

Williamson, Edward. *Florida Politics in the Gilded Age, 1877-1893.* Gainesville: University of Florida Press, 1976.

Woodward, Thomas S. *Woodward's Reminiscences of the Creek or Muscogee Indians, Contained in Letters to Friends in Georgia and Alabama.* Montgomery, Alabama, 1859; reprinted, 1939.

Wright, J. Leitch, Jr. "A Note on the First Seminole War as Seen by the Indians, Negroes, and Their British Advisers." *Journal of Southern History* 34 (Nov. 1968): 565-75.

Wright, O.H. "Finding Historical Markers in Polk County." *Polk County Historical Quarterly* 9 (Jan. 1983): 2-3.

Writers' Project. Work Projects Administration. "Highlands County." Jacksonville, Florida, 1936.

————. "Hillsborough County Personalities." Tampa, Florida, 1937.

————. "History of the Old King's Road." Jacksonville, Florida, c. 1938.

Index

Abbe, Charles Elliott, 242
Absolute Mount Enon Association, 228
Acme, 315
Acton, 275
Adams, John Quincy (secretary of state), 19
Adams-Onís Treaty (1819), 17–18
Addison, Joel J., 131, 398
Addison, John, 111–12, 388
Addison, William H., 130–31, 197, 401, 413
African Americans, 192, 282–83; refugees of Patriot War, 6; British allies (1814–15), 7–8; refuge at Sarasota Bay, 8–9; and battle of the Suwannee and flight to south Florida, 9–11; slaves of Oponay, 13, 24; slaves of Seminoles, 26; runaway slaves, 27; at Peace River, 31, 39–40; and Second Seminole War, 49–51; as Union soldiers, 164–66, 170–71; emancipation of, 177–81; as victims of Regulator violence, 204–6; and churches, 230–31, 284, 319–20; testimony of, against whites, 251; in Peace River area in 1880, 262, 264; and the building of the railroads, 263, 270, 282;

and the phosphate industry, 317–19; schools for, 320–21. *See* also Slaves
Alachua County, 3; early settlement, 34; and Second Seminole War, 42, 49, 53; at close of Second Seminole War, 63–66; emigration from, 68–70; selected residents (1830–32), 351–52
Alachua Prairie, 3
Alachua Seminoles: location (1800), 3; hunting towns at Peace River, 5–7; flight to south Florida (1812), 6–7; in battle of the Suwannee and flight to south Florida (1818), 9–11. *See also* Seminole Indians
Alafia, 81, 94, 104, 126, 134; and armed occupation act settlements, 65–70, 356–57; residents at, resettling near Peace River, 101–3; secession meeting at, 141; defended by cow cavalry, 169
Alafia (schooner), 396
Alafia Baptist Church, 228
Alafia River, 4, 112
Alagon Grant, 35
Albritton, Arcadia, 276
Albritton, George, 172, 425
Albritton, George W., 360

Albritton, James N., 360
Albritton, John M., 360
Albritton, Matthew, 360
Albritton, Thomas H., 276
Albritton, W.F., 363
Alderman, J.G., 363
Alderman, Emma, 328
Alderman, James, 406
Alderman, Jesse, 103, 388, 398, 400
Alderman, Timothy, 357
Alderman, W.P., 363
Alderman, William, 221
Alexander, Ezekiel, 349
Alexander, Samuel, 350
Alfred, John H., 363
Alice Howard (steamer), 271
Allen, F.M., 241
Allen, George W. (army officer), 51
Allen, Moses, 264
Allen, William, 172, 205, 392
Alleyne, Cecil H., 275, 337
Alligator (Seminole chief). *See* Halpatter Tustenuggee
Altman, James, 355
Altman, Jesse, 395
Altman, John, 102, 390, 395
Altman, John J., 425
Altman, Mary, 68
Altman, Sampson, 351, 353
Altman, Thomas, 355
Altman, Thomas J., 309
Altman, W.J., 425
Altman, Wade, 419
Altman, William, 362
Altman, William H., 362
Altree, George H., 288, 420
American Agricultural Chemical Co., 316
Anderson, George, 341
Anderson, Thomas W., 284, 315
Anderson, Mrs. Thomas W., 284
Angola Catholic Church (Bartow), 335
Ann (slave of Readding Blount), 97
Anthony, A.R., 274
Arbuthnot, Alexander, 5
Arcadia, 264, 309, 323, 325, 336; violence at, 251–54, 318; and the railroad, 270–71, 278–80; named, 276; incorporated, 280; in 1887, 287–88; becomes DeSoto County seat, 299–301; phosphate found near, 313; churches, 319–20, 334–35; schools,

321, 328–29; in 1890s, 340; first officers, 420
Arcadia House, 290
Arcadia Phosphate Co., 314, 318
Arcadia Street Railway and Improvement Co., 340
Arcadian, 287, 311
Arista, Julien G., 412
Armed Occupation Act, 65–68, 79; selected claimants, 356–57
Armistead, Walker Keith (army officer), 55–56
Arnett, James N., 363
Arnold, Dairey, 264
Arnold, John Burton, 406
Arnold, Lewis, 264
Arnold, Nathan A., 361
Arpeika or Sam Jones (Mikasuki chief), 56, 70, 72, 77
Ashley, Edward W., 173, 361
Assinwa (Seminole chief), 57
Atkins, W.S., 418
Attison, Mark, 350
Auburndale, 275
Augustus (slave of John I. Hooker), 102
Aunt Line (slave of Willoughby Tillis), 112–13
Austin, Walter, 251, 318
Avery, James L., 392
Avon Park, 322, 328, 421

Baggett, N.S., 339
Bailey, J.W., 279, 288, 420
Bailey, John, Jr., 350
Bainbridge, Henry, 89
Baker, W.C., 262
Baldwin, B.F., 287–88, 420
Ball, W.M., 286
Ballard, L.M., 274
Ballast Point, 146
Banana Lake, 395
Baptist Church, 98, 102, 227–31. *See also* individual churches and towns
Baptist Church of Christ at Peas Creek. *See* Peas Creek Baptist Church
Barber, Grandison, 355
Barber, Israel, 23
Barber, Moses, 355
Barber, William W.,
Barnes, James F., Jr., 360
Barnes, James F., Sr., 173, 360

Barnwell, William H., 245, 411
Barron, J.R., 287
Bartholf, John Francis, 166, 173, 184, 188, 190, 206, 208–11, 222, 225–26, 239, 294, 408, 423
Bartow, Francis Stebbins (Confederate officer), 145, 410
Bartow, 58, 119, 189, 201, 207, 215, 225, 256, 298, 305, 315, 322, 325; Indian plantations and villages near, 31–32, 39–40; early settlers, 79–80, 91–92, 97–99, 126, 196; churches, 98, 102, 126, 186, 216, 229, 273, 319–20, 334–35; schools, 126, 133, 186, 216, 222, 224–25, 320–21, 330–34; beginning of town life, 126, 216–17, 219; named, 145; Summerlin purchase of, 149; and Civil War, 165; freedmen living near, 178, 180; becomes Polk County seat, 186; as telegraph station, 204, 217–19; violence at, 205, 240, 243, 302–4; in 1877–80, 264; and railroads, 266, 268–70; incorporation of, 273, 418; in 1887, 281–83; black community at, 318–21; in 1895–1900, 336–37; Pease Creek post office name changed to Bartow, 410. *See also* Fort Blount; Fort Fraser; Oponay
Bartow *Courier-Informant*, 331, 334
Bartow *Informant*, 243, 270, 273, 298, 303, 418
Bartow Junction, 269, 275
Bass, C. Quinn, 252–53
Bates, James M., 357
Bates, Jim, 247
Bates, John, 209, 357, 422
Baxter, Wyley, 102
Bayport, 176
Beal, Eber, 356
Beecher, R.C., 282
Belknap, William G. (army officer), 57–58
Bell, John (Indian agent), 26
Bell, John (presidential candidate), 140–41
Bell, Louis, 356
Bell, Robert, 412
Benevolence Baptist Church, 228
Bennett, John, 350
Benson, Henry (army officer), 101
Benton, John G., 190
Bertrand, Joseph, 356

Best, J.H., 363
Bethea, Foster C., 253, 289
Bethea, Hugh, 406, 412
Bethea, Will, 253
Bethel. *See* Homeland
Bethel Academy, 265, 429
Bethel A.M.E. Church (Punta Gorda), 320
Bethel Baptist Church (Socrum), 228
Bethel Methodist Church (Homeland), 227, 229–31, 264–65
Bevan, Jones, 349
Beville, F.F., 418
Big Charlie Apopka Creek. *See* Charlie Apopka Creek
Big Cypress Swamp (Everglades), 56, 107, 117
Big Hammock (Hernando County), Indian settlements at, 3, 22, 26
Big Swamp, 38, 40
Billy Bowlegs War. *See* Third Seminole War
Billy's Creek, 173
Bird, Walter, 335
Bishop, Minerva, 402
Black, George W., 335
Black, J.F., 286
Black Codes, enactment (1865–66), 185, 402
Black Point, battle of (1835), 42–43, 353
Blackburn, B.L., 425
Blacks. *See* African Americans
Blair, Nelson, 402
Blake, Luther, 95–97
Blind tigers, 305
Bliss, William W.S. (army officer), 86
Blockade running, 147–51, 156–57
Blount, B.B., 340
Blount, Benjamin F., 91–92, 97, 124, 126, 173, 225, 295, 297, 304, 332, 362, 392
Blount, Hugh G., 363
Blount, Mrs. J.C., 225
Blount, Jacob J., 67–68, 354–55
Blount, James, 392
Blount, Jehu J., 91, 143, 200, 362, 392
Blount, John, 172, 392
Blount, John C., 362
Blount, Lydia Oregon Hendry, 116, 345
Blount, Nathan S., 91, 188, 190, 208, 293, 392, 395, 412–13, 422
Blount, Nettie, 392

Blount, Owen R., 91, 387, 406, 414
Blount, Readding, 68, 91, 97, 135, 138, 140, 143, 178, 182, 197, 349, 354, 387, 394
Blount, Riley R., 68, 91, 93, 97, 99, 102, 108, 126, 149, 178, 216, 354, 387
Blount, Sarah, 392
Blount, William, 392
Bloxham, William D. (Florida governor), 261, 267-68
Blue, Daniel, 350
Boggess, Francis C.M., 102, 113, 126, 140, 147-48, 155, 162-63, 168, 174, 203, 205-6, 221, 239, 310, 362, 385, 391, 399, 418-19
Boggs, David, 350
Bohanun, Duncan, 349
Bohanun, John, 349
Bolden, Jeffrey, 181
Bolshaw, T.H., 425
Bonard, C.G., 420
Bonard, C.H., 288
Bond, Walter, 363
Boney, David J.W., 69, 99, 126, 130, 358, 387, 392, 412, 422
Boone, A., 320
Boring, Isaac, 38
Boring, R.J., 288
Bostick, E.F., 425
Bostick, G.W., 340
Boully, D.W.D., 274, 287
Bourland, J.M., 301
Bowen, David, 353
Bowen, John, 406
Bowen, William, 250
Bowen, William M., 188, 190
Bowlegs, Billy. *See* Holata Micco (Seminole chief)
Bowlegs Creek (Hatchee Thlokko), 31-32, 35-36, 40, 168; home of Billy Bowlegs, 27, 371; boundary of Indian nation, 88, 377; Civil War skirmish at, 163
Bowlegs War. *See* Third Seminole War
Bowling Green, 90, 264, 276, 322; churches, 230; named, 286; in 1886, 286; in 1890s, 339. *See also* Chokonikla; Fort Chokonikla
Boyd, J.R., 288
Boyd, J.W., 282, 333
Boynton, W.L., 363

Brace, George, 359
Braden, Joseph W., 111, 378
Bradenton (Manatee): and hurricane of 1848, 75-76; and Third Seminole War, 111; Union activities at, 151, 170, 183
Brady, James W., 304, 309
Branch, Belford, 252
Branch, Franklin, 127, 137
Branch, William T., 240
Branchboro, 218
Brandon, Jared W., 228
Brandon, John W., 274, 406
Brandon, 274
Brannen, David, 358, 388
Brannen, John M., 351, 353, 355
Brannen, Joseph, 358
Brannen, Milledge, 150
Breckenridge, John C., 140-41
Brewer, Burris, 67, 351
Brewer, James, 354-55
Brewer, William, 358
Bridges, 50-51, 54, 57, 125, 233, 235, 258, 269-71, 285, 287, 405
Britt, Benjamin H., 363
Broadaway, A., 349
Brodus, Absalom, 350
Bronson, William, 422
Brooke, George M. (army officer), 29, 35, 77-78
Brooker, George P., 363
Brooker, Joseph, 205
Brooker, William P., 102, 113, 115, 357, 391
Brooker's Ford, 233
Brooks, John, 356
Brooksville, 134, 142, 174; Civil War raid on, 170; murder of Hub Williams at, 248
Broome, James E. (Florida governor), 107
Brown, Charles, 206-7, 402
Brown, D.H., 320
Brown, Harriet, 80, 402
Brown, J.W., 363
Brown, Jane, 80, 92
Brown, Micajah C., 84-85, 94
Brown, Nathan L., 390
Brown, Peter, 287, 300, 392
Brown, Rigdon, 67-68, 79-80, 92, 99, 103, 137, 178, 197, 200, 351, 353,

355–56, 358, 390, 394–95
Brown, Rigdon H., 70, 358
Brown, Sabra Scott, 80, 92
Brown, Thomas (Florida governor), 95–97
Brown, W.B., 418
Brown, W.P., 145
Brown, William, 69, 80, 92, 103, 351, 353, 358, 386–87, 395
Brown, William (slave of Rigdon Brown), 80, 177–78, 206, 402
Browning, Noah, 205
Brownville, 124, 222, 264
Bryan, John, 354
Bryan, N.M., 276
Bryant, Emory, 406
Bryant, James, 354
Bryant, John Wesley, 207–8, 294–95, 297–99, 305, 308, 407, 425
Bryant, Mary, 92
Bryant, Milton, 353
Bryant, Thomas, 353, 406
Bryant, Thomas W., 406
Buchan, E.B., 363
Buchanan, James C., 58
Buchanan, J.W., 425
Buck, Dell, 286
Buck, Dudley, 286
Bucker Woman's Town, 26
Buckra Woman, 26
Buffalo Ford, 50–51
Buffum, Richard V., 101, 358
Bullard, Emma, 428
Bulloch, A.J., 335, 421
Bunch, D.S., 413
Bunch, J.J., 406, 413
Burdine, William B., 337
Burke, R.T., 425
Burket Chapel Primitive Baptist Church (Bartow), 320
Burkett, H., 283
Burland, W.H., 279
Burnett, Bryant, 354
Burnett, Richard, 354
Burns, Dickison, 359
Bush, William, 173
Butler, C.E., 335
Butler, G.I., 335
Butler, John W., 358
Byrd, Dan, 253
Byrd, Jeremiah, 355

Caesar, Julius (freedman), 181
Calhoun, John C. (secretary of war), 19, 21
Call, Wilkinson (U.S. senator), 307–8
Caloosahatchee River, 36, 49–51, 54–55, 97, 99, 101, 109, 131, 148, 171–73, 253; Indian villages near, 6, 70, 77; Chazotte expedition explores, 28; attack on Colonel Harney's party, 55; attack at Fort Denaud, 111; Union forces scout, 159–60; cattle herds driven south of, 200; and Disston development, 261
Camp Gibson, 389, 395. *See also* Gibsonton
Camp McCall, 57
Camp Ogden. *See* Fort Ogden
Camp Walker, 51
Camp Whipple, 115–16
Campbell, W.S., 243
Campbell, William L., 68–69, 94, 303–4, 381
Cannon, David, 354
Cannon, William, 354
Canter, Arthur B., 285, 338
Canter, Sterling L., 285, 363
Cape Florida, 25, 28
Carlton, Albert, 102, 169, 406, 410, 425
Carlton, Alderman, 102, 108, 113, 117, 357, 359, 391, 425
Carlton, C.J., 306
Carlton, Cary M., 363
Carlton, Charles W., 300, 425
Carlton, Daniel W., 113, 126, 129, 169, 209, 391, 414
Carlton, Elam B., 289, 419
Carlton, H.E., 287, 300, 425
Carlton, Henry, 422
Carlton, Isaac, 359
Carlton, John W., 228
Carlton, Lewis, 411
Carlton, Marion G., 300, 311
Carlton, Reubin, 169, 361
Carlton, Sallie Ann (Murphy), 129
Carlton, Stephen J., 289, 425
Carlton, Wright, 425
Carney, C.W., 363
Carney, Ed., 289
Carney, William, 172–73, 362, 392
Carpenter, William T., 196, 216, 231, 256, 418

Carpenter's Pond, 217
Carr, J.O., 288–89
Carr, T.C., 262–63
Carrington, Alex, 180
Carrington, Eliza, 180
Carrington, Jane Williams, 180
Carrington, Martha, 180
Carrington, Solomon, 177–78, 180, 206–7, 402
Carroll, Francis (army sergeant), 377
Carroll, William J., 287, 413
Carson, Robert, 362, 392
Carson, Robert A., 227–28
Carson, S.B., 306
Carson, Samuel W., 142, 227
Carter, Jesse, 103, 144, 350
Carter's Mill, 269
Casey, John Charles (army officer and Indian agent), 55, 76–78, 81–88, 93, 99–101, 107, 371, 380, 382, 391
Cason, Andrew, 355
Cason, D.M., 411
Cason, Harley, 354
Cason, Henry, 354
Cason, John, 351, 354
Cason, William, 354
Cason, Willis, 355
Cassidy, Walker. *See* Durfey, S.W.
Castalia. *See* Lily
Cattle, 6, 23–25, 45, 66, 131, 138–39, 174, 263, 275–76, 406; first recorded drive down Peace River, 27, 35–36; seizure of Indian herds, 49, 59; driven from north Florida, 67–70; ranges extended to Peace River, 93, 98–99; factor in Third Seminole War, 112; cattle trade with Cuba, 146–50, 197–200, 275; sales to Confederate army, 148; exemption from Confederate draft for tending, 152, 161; importance to Confederacy, 156–57; Confederate commissary supply operations, 156–57, 160–61, 166–67, 171–73; capture of, by Union forces, 167–69; Fort Meade as center of trade, 220–21, 265; rustling of, 243–46
Cauthon, Aaron C., 388
Cedar Key, 150, 170
Chai (Indian warrior), 382
Chakaika (Seminole chief), 55, 377
Chandler, S.M., 362, 413

Chandler, W.W., 413
Chapman, Joseph, 181, 206
Charity (slave of Z.G. Seward), 102
Charlie Apopka Creek, 31, 69, 88, 112, 225, 245, 314
Charlotte (slave of Frederick Varn), 99
Charlotte (slave of John I. Hooker), 102
Charlotte County, 300
Charlotte Harbor, 44, 56; fishing ranchos at, 3, 6, 8, 14, 18, 27, 41, 45; identified as the Fishery, 6; Indian refugees at, 10; plunder of fishing ranchos at (1821), 21–22; explored and mapped, 28–32, 35–36; inspector suspended at, 42; troops withdrawn from (1836), 46; Indian store at, 71–72, 76, 80; and hurricane of 1848, 75–76; meeting with Billy Bowlegs at, 86; Union army at, 158–59; proposed railroads to, 256, 269–70. *See also* Cuban fishing ranchos
Charlotte Harbor (town of), 181, 230, 301
Charlotte Harbor Beacon (Punta Gorda newspaper), 291
Chazotte, Peter Stephen, 28, 372
Chester, A.M., 276, 286
Chetuckota (Indian town), 40
Child, J.P., 425
Child, Neva C., 338–39
Childs, Ben F. (teacher), 427
Childs, Benjamin Franklin (volunteer soldier), 363
Childs, Jonathan W. (Union army officer), 166, 168, 171
Chipco. *See* Echo Emathla Chopco
Chitto Tustenuggee (Seminole chief), 54–55
Chocachatti (Indian town), 3, 21–23, 26, 31
Choctaw Indians, 370
Chokonikla, 78, 86, 222; attack upon Indian store at, 80–84; army post established near, 87. *See also* Bowling Green; Fort Chokonikla
Christ Church (Fort Meade), 317, 334–35
Church of God, 335
Churches, 216, 227–31, 283, 319–20, 334–35; early churches, 98, 102; arbor churches, 227. *See also* individual churches and communities
Circuit Riders, 227–29
Citrus, 221, 263–65, 273, 281, 286,

338–42; and freezes of 1894–95, 321–23; and freezes of 1897–98 and 1899, 325; Parson Brown oranges, 390

Civil War, 141–42, 150–75

Clarison, George, 357

Clark, Albert, 181

Clark, Bud P., 300

Clark, Frank, 284, 304–5, 307–9, 425

Clark, Henry S., 356

Clark, Isaac (army officer), 32

Clark, Thomas, 349

Clavel, A.C., 339

Clay, John Henry, 283

Clay, W.S., 280

Cleveland, Grover (U.S. president), 277, 298

Cleveland, 264, 271, 277, 290, 314

Clinch, Duncan L. (army officer), 43

Coacoochee (Indian warrior), 49, 56–57

Cobb, Capt. W.H., Company C, U.S. Volunteers (1898): roster, 363

Cobb, W.H., 340, 363

Cochran, A.S., 363

Cochran, M.A., 287

Codington, E.W., 282, 331

Cofield, John C., 137

Cohen, Jacob R., 410

Coker, Daniel, Jr., 425

Colding, J.D., 240

Coleman, Redding, 358

Collar, Levi, 34, 350

Collar, Uriah John, 356

Collier, Calvin, 361

Collier, John, 361

Collins, Enoch, Sr., 357

Collins, William, 404

Columbia County, 203; early settlement, 34; and Second Seminole War, 42, 49, 53; at the close of the Second Seminole War, 63–66; emigration from, 66–70; selected residents (1830–32), 351–52; 354; selected voters (1842–43), 355

Columbia Volunteers (1835–36), 47; selected members, 353

Conant, Sherman, 203

Concord Church of Christ (Bartow), 229, 412

Cone, William, 349, 355

Confederate States conscription acts, 152–53, 157–58, 161

Constantine, A.A., 287

Constitutional Union Party, 140

Cook, Caesar, 177, 207

Cook, Jason, 286

Cooley, William, 137

Cooper, David, 349

Cooper, James, 205

Corbett Brothers, 243–44

Cordery, E. Alonzo, 323, 333

Cornelius, Levi W., 143, 391

Costine, John W., 394

Cothran, Aaron C., 359

Cotsa Fixico Chopco (Tallahassee warrior), 81, 382

Coughan, A.C. *See* Cauthon, Aaron C.

Couper, W.P., 278

Cow Cavalry (Confederate battalion), 166–67, 171–75

Coweta Creek Indians, 18–21

Cowhunters, 198

Cox, J.A., 310

Crackers: and settlement of northeast Florida, 34; described, 109–10

Craft, D. Isaac, 294

Craft, Samuel C., 216, 222, 224

Craig, George McC., 310

Craig, John, 356

Craig, Mrs. L.V., 340

Crane, Henry A., 108, 111, 118, 127–28, 150, 159, 161–65, 191, 202, 400, 423

Crawford, C.Y., 289

Crawford, Christopher Q., 392, 394

Crawford, Frank Q., 253, 285

Crawford, George W. (secretary of war), 88

Crawford, Zachary T., 423

Crews, Archibald, 354

Crews, B.W., 354

Crews, Caroline, 389

Crews, Dempsey D., Jr., 253, 361, 425

Crews, Dempsey D., Sr., 137–38, 153, 172, 181, 209, 287, 354, 357, 392, 422

Crews, Edward, Jr., 354

Crews, Edward, Sr., 354

Crews, Isham, 354, 357–58, 390–91

Crews, James, 354

Crews, Joseph, 354

Crews, Joseph (freedman), 181, 206

Crews, Lewis, 354

Crews, Micajah, 354

Crews, Piety Collier, 153

Crews, Richmond, 181, 206

Crews, Samuel, 354
Crews, Stephen, 354
Crews, William, 354
Crews, William B., 354
Crews, William N., 361
Crewsville, 222, 253, 264
Crockett, Joseph, 349
Crosby, O. M., 337, 421
Cross, John, 262, 276, 290
Cross, S. L., 229
Crowell, John (Indian agent), 22
Crum, James B., 182, 231, 284, 392, 412
Crystal Ice Works (Bartow), 282
Cuba, construction of telegraph line to, 217-19
Cuban fishing ranchos, 3-4, 8, 14, 41-42; raid on (1821), 21-22, 29; abandoned at Charlotte Harbor (1836), 46. *See also* Charlotte Harbor; Tampa Bay
Cuban Tobacco Growers Co., 323
Cummings, Alexander (army officer), 53-54
Curry, John, 170, 357, 401
Curry, John W., 182
Curry, T.J., 392
Curry, Zora, 172, 362, 413

Dade Massacre (1835), 43, 50
Dahl, Neil, 279, 291
Danforth, William, 360
Daniel, W.E., 420
Daniel, William, 349
Daniels, Enoch, Jr., 124, 126, 158, 349, 357, 392
Daniels, Enoch, Sr., 349
Daniels, H.B., 302-4
Daniels, Jim, 253
Daniels, John W., 361
Darbishire, M.G., 313, 426
Darling, John, 76-79, 84-85, 93-96, 99, 104, 137, 393
Daughtry, Jacob, 406
Davenport, O.H., 288
Davenport, William (army officer), 54
Davenport, 54, 275
Davenport's Road, 54, 57-58
Davidson, John, 91, 97, 103, 182, 190, 208, 293, 295, 356, 397, 422
Davidson, Lizzie, 392
Davidson Union Church (Joshua Creek), 230

Davies, William, 227
Davis, Alfred, 337
Davis, Corrie, 319, 337
Davis, Daniel, 190-91
Davis, David, 350
Davis, H.L., 333
Davis, Irwin, 392
Davis, Jefferson (secretary of war), 99-101
Davis, Laomi, 354
Davis, Lloyd, 337
Davis, Sam, 337
Day, James S., 363
Deadening, 274, 370
Deas, Isham, 69, 359, 388
Deason, C.W., 399, 422
DeCoster, Nathan H., 181, 221, 260
Delaney, William, 356
Dell, James, 350
Dell, James G. (volunteer officer), 85, 88
Dell, Maxey, 350
Dell, Simeon, 349
Demere, A.K., 425
Denham, W.T., 284
DeLeon Mineral Springs, 283
Denson, Andrew, 178, 180, 206
DeSoto City, 301
DeSoto County: early settlements, 124, 146-47, 200; attempt to create as Ranshaw County (1860), 131-32; schools, 225-26, 320-21, 327-29; churches, 227, 229-30, 319-20; violence in, 239-46, 247-48, 251-54; courthouse, 252; creation of, from Manatee County, 299-300; first officers, 300; controversy over location of county seat, 300-301; Prohibition elections in, 305-6; Populism in, 306-11; population in 1890 and 1900, 327; attempt to divide county, 340. *See also* Manatee County; names of individual towns
DeSoto County Champion, 338-39
DeSoto County News, 311
DeSoto Phosphate Mining Co., 314
Dewitt, Lewis, 350
Dexter, Horatio, 13, 20, 26, 28-29
Dickison, J.J. (Confederate officer), 160-61
Dickson, Richard, 356
Director (schooner), 150-51

Disease. *See* Smallpox; Yellow fever
Dishong, Owen, 300–301, 425
Disston, Hamilton, 261–62, 268, 273
Disston Purchase, 261–62, 267
Dixon, Ann, 178
Dixon, Charles (freedman), 97, 178
Dixon, Ellen, 321
Dixon, Jackson, 97, 178
Dixon, John, 357
Dixon, John (freedman), 178
Dixon, Richard, 350
Dixon, Sally, 178
Dixon, Stepney, 97, 177–78, 188, 206–7, 402
Douglas, Electer Ann, 402
Doyle, James, 173–74
Drawdy, J.W., 363
Drew, George T. (Florida governor), 211, 213, 292
Driggers, Cythnia Johnson, 396
Driggers, Dennis, 209, 361, 396
Driggers, Jacob, 360
Driggers, James, 360
Driggers, Mathew, 115
Driggers, Stephen A., 360
Driver, James, 241
Dudley, Charlie, 250
Duncan, James, 353
Durfey, S.W., 242
Durrance, E.F., 287
Durrance, Francis M., 97–99, 102–3, 108, 112–13, 141, 163, 355, 357, 386–87, 390, 394–95
Durrance, George T., 355, 390, 395
Durrance, Jesse H., 355, 395, 413
Durrance, Jesse M., 357
Durrance, John Rufus, 98, 126, 142, 362, 387, 390, 395, 397
Durrance, John W., 309
Durrance, Joseph, 350, 390
Durrance, Joseph L., 97, 113, 355, 390, 395
Durrance, W. Jordan, 309
Durrance, William, 350
Durrance, William H., 97, 143, 355, 390, 395, 397, 406
Duval, William T., 162, 397
Dyal, John, 350
Dyer, Joseph, 353
Dzialynski, Philip, 247, 274, 285–86, 302, 407–8, 410, 418, 421–22

East Florida Coffee Land Association, 28, 372
Echo Emathla Chopco (Tallahassee chief), 82–84, 86, 93–94, 107, 118–19, 382–83, 388
Eden Land Office (Fort Meade), 273
Education. *See* Schools
Edwards, J.A., 286
Edwards, Marvin M., 109
Egmont Key, 118, 152
Elections: (1852–53), 99, 386–87; (1855), 103–4; (1857), 116–17; (1858–59), 130–31; (1860), 133–35, 140–42; (1861), 143–45, 395; (1862), 152–53, 397; (1863), 162, 398–99; (1864), 400–401; (1865), 181–83; (1866), 404; (1867–68), 188–90, 423; (1870), 202–4, 407; (1872–74), 207–9; (1876), 210–13, 409; (1878–84), 293–98, 422; (1886), 298–99; (1887–88), 300–301, 304–7; (1890), 307; (1891), 305; (1892), 307–9; (1894), 305, 309; (1896), 309–10; (1898), 310–11
Electric power, 337
Eliot, Alexander, 350
Elitz, Joseph, 356
Elizabeth Baptist Church (Arcadia), 319
Ellis, Amelia, 196
Ellis, Andrew J., 395
Ellis, Giles, 349
Ellis, Henry B., 353
Ellis, Thomas, 102, 351,
Ellis, Thomas B., 170, 358, 391, 422
Ellsworth (steamer), 233
Emancipation, 177–81
Emathla, Charlie (Indian chief), 42
Emathloche (Tallahassee Indian), 39
Emerson, W.J., 282
Emmons, William, 349
Eneha Micco (Indian chief), 39
English, Eli, 102, 143, 222, 391, 397
English, 222, 264, 278. *See also* Wauchula
Episcopal Church, 334–35
Ernest, R.L., 341
Estero River, 150
Eubanks, John, 132–33
Evans, W.A., 323, 338
Everglades, 56, 117
Explorations: Chazotte (1821), 28; Dexter (1823), 28–29; Gadsden (1823–24),

Explorations (*continued*)
29–31; Humphreys (1824), 31; Clark
(1825), 32; Hackley, Murray and
Prior, (1832–33), 35–36; Smith (1836),
44–45, 50–51; during Third Seminole
War, 116

Fairview, 274, 330
Farmers Alliance, 307–9. *See also*
Populism
Feroux, J.R., 413
Ferrell, Jasper C., 363
Ferrell, Jeremiah, 391
Ferro, Frank D., 412
Fewell, John E., 149, 172, 190, 203, 221,
362, 422
First Baptist Church (Bartow), 412
First Baptist Church (Wauchula), 230
First National Bank of Bartow, 282
First Presbyterian Church (Bartow),
334
First Reconstruction Act, 187
First Seminole War (1817–18), 9–11
First United Methodist Church (Fort
Meade), 230
Fishback, John, 279
Fisheating Creek, 36, 54, 252
Fisher, William (volunteer officer), 85
Fitzhugh, George S., 335
Fletcher, S.F., 340
Flint, Martin, 362
Flint, William R., 362
Flood, Alicia Whitney, 289
Flood, Luke B., 289, 421
Floods: of 1849, 85; of 1856, 111; of
1863, 157; of 1865, 173; of 1878,
257–58
Florida: inhabitants of peninsula in
1800, 3; First Seminole War, 9–10;
purchase from Spain, 17; transfer to
U.S., 18, 21–22; Second Seminole
War, 41–59; Indian removal de-
mands, 77, 93–97, 99–101; Indian at-
tacks of 1849, 80–90; Board of
Internal Improvement created, 93;
Third Seminole War, 106–20; secession, 135, 140–41; Civil War, 141–42,
150–75; Battle of Olustee, 161; Reconstruction, 181–94, 200–213; attempts to impeach Governor Reed,
193, 200; readmission to the Union,
195; election of 1876, 210–13; tele-

graph construction in, 217–19; Vose
Injuction, 234, 259; as frontier area,
240; Disston sale, 261–62
Florida Development Co., 421
Florida Land and Improvement Co.,
261, 273
Florida Mortgage and Investment Co.,
275
Florida Peninsular (Tampa), 124,
127–28, 193, 203
Florida Phosphate Co. (Ltd.), 316
Florida Railroad Co., 256
Florida Rangers (Union army com-
pany), 158–59. *See also* Second Flor-
ida Cavalry
Florida Southern Railway Co., 268–72:
impact on communities, 277–91; orig-
inal proposed route, 418
Florida Times-Union (Jacksonville
newspaper), 270
Footman, William (Confederate of-
ficer), 166, 173
Forrester, C.W., 340
Forrester, Sampson, 382
Fort Alabama, 45
Fort Arbuckle, 89
Fort Armistead, 56
Fort Bassinger, 245
Fort Blount, 126, 134, 138, 142, 144,
216, 389–90; and Third Seminole
War, 108, 116; name changed to Bar-
tow, 145. *See also* Bartow
Fort Brooke, 38, 42, 44, 48–54, 71–72,
84; established, 29–30; murder of ex-
press rider near, 41; destruction by
hurricane of 1848, 75–76; plans to
remove to Useppa Island, 77–78; to
Fort Hamer, 87; to Fort Winder,
94–95; Union destruction of artillery
at, 167
Fort Carroll, 56, 79, 377
Fort Casey, 384
Fort Chokonikla, 87–89, 276
Fort Clinch, 89
Fort Crawford, 88–89
Fort Cummings, 54, 56–57
Fort Dade, 48
Fort Davenport, 54
Fort Denaud, 111, 160
Fort Fraser, 56, 58, 79, 88–89, 138, 141,
143, 165, 207, 215, 390; established
(1837), 50–52; settlement in vicinity

of, 102; and Third Seminole War, 108, 112–13, 116; freedmen living near, 178, 180
Fort Gardner, 51, 94
Fort Gibson, Treaty of (1833), 37
Fort Green, 144, 153, 222, 264, 295, 397; refuge during Third Seminole War, 108, 110, 116; and hurricane of 1878, 258; in 1880, 262–63
Fort Hamer, 87–88
Fort Hartsuff, 111, 115–16, 124–25, 142, 146, 153, 203, 225, 229–30, 264, 270, 276, 278; established, 109; Union scouts sent to, 158. *See also* Wauchula
Fort Hartsuff Baptist Church, 229–30
Fort Harvie, 384
Fort Hooker, 108
Fort King (Ocala), 38, 40, 43, 53, 55, 85. *See also* Indian agency
Fort Kissimmee, 115
Fort Maitland, 54
Fort Meade, 32, 92, 103, 119, 123, 141–43, 147, 153, 172, 183, 200, 207, 215, 231, 249, 262, 273, 289, 297–99, 302; Indian settlements at, 6–7, 14, 31, 35–36; established, 88–89; U.S. army presence at, 94; early settlers, 97–98, 102; abandoned by U.S. army, 101, 116; purchased by John I. Hooker, 101–2; schools, 102, 226–27, 285, 330; Third Seminole War, 108, 115, 390–91; attack on Tillis place, 112–13; beginnings of town life, 116, 125–26; first bridge at, 125; Regulator violence, 127; Confederate garrison, 142; cattle drives from, 157, 167; Confederate troops ordered to, 160–61, 166; Confederate supplies reported at, 163; Union attacks upon, 163–64, 167–69; Hendry's cow cavalry company organized at, 167; occupation and destruction, 167–69; as telegraph station, 218–19; as trade center, 220–21; churches, 230, 274, 285, 317, 334–35; attempts to make river navigable to, 232–35; violence at, 240–41, 247, 250; and hurricane of 1878, 258; in 1880, 265; and railroads, 268, 270, 277–78; in 1882, 274; in 1885, 284–86; incorporation, 285; black community at, 318–20; tobacco

industry at, 323–25; in 1887–1900, 336–38; early postmasters, 410; first officers, 421. *See also* Talakchopco
Fort Meade, Keystone and Walk-in-the-Water Railroad: proposed junction with Florida Southern Railway, 418
Fort Meade Jockey Club, 338
Fort Meade Phosphate, Fertilizer, Land and Improvement Co., 315–16
Fort Meade *Pioneer*, 285
Fort Meade Street Railroad Co., 278
Fort Mellon, 48
Fort Myakka, 88–89, 229
Fort Myers, 86, 94, 98, 101, 118, 128, 209, 384; Union troops at, 159; Union operations from, 159–60, 163–65, 165–69, 170; planned capture by Confederacy, 160–61, 172–74; black Union troops arrive at, 165–66; problems of refugees and Union forces at, 169–70; Confederate attack upon, 173–74; withdrawal of Union forces, 174; F.A. Hendry moves to, 200; as telegraph station, 218; connections with railroad, 271, 342
Fort Ogden, 77, 153, 203, 205, 233, 257–58, 261–62, 300–302, 305; established as Camp Ogden, 56–57; early settlers, 124, 146–47, 221, 398; cattle trade, 146–47, 199–200, 221, 378; Summerlin's store at, 150; and election of 1876, 211–12; schools, 225, 328; churches, 230; violence at, 239–41, 244–48; and the railroad, 270–71, 278–80; in 1886–87, 288–89; incorporation and first officers, 289; in 1888–1900, 341
Fort Ogden *Democrat*, 418
Fort Ogden *Herald*, 418
Fort Ogden *Post*, 419
Fort Pierce, 82, 208
Fort Sullivan, 54, 68–70. *See also* Itchepuckesassa; Plant City
Fort T.B. Adams, 54
Fort Thompson, 36, 101, 167, 171, 173, 253; Civil War skirmish at, 159–60; cattle herds driven to, 200
Fort Winder, 94, 111, 181, 221–22
Fortner, Hardy F., 309, 412
Fortner, James A., 293, 304, 406, 422
Fortner, Mitchell G., 207, 226, 297–98, 406, 413

Forty Mile Prairie, 245
47th Pennsylvania Volunteers (Union army regiment), 158–61
Foster, William S. (army officer), 50
Fouis, William, 205
Fountain, Sarah J., 410
Frank (slave of H.S. Seward), 102
Fraser, Upton S. (army officer), 50
Frederick, R., 321
Freedmen's Bureau, 186–87
Freeman, A.C., 341
Freeman, J.K., 286
Freezes: of 1879, 258; of 1885–86, 1891, and 1892, 321; of 1893, 322; of 1894–95, 321–23; of 1897–98 and 1899, 325
Friday, Eldrid, 240–41, 414
Friendship Baptist Church, 228
Frier, Henry M., 224, 358, 379
Frostproof, 274
Fulford, Guiton, 356
Fulford, Wytche, 356
Fuller, Henry W., 310
Futch, John, 69, 355, 358

Gadsden, James (army officer), 10–11, 24, 36–37, 44
Gage, Lot, 356
Gaines, Edmund P. (army officer), 43, 78
Gainesville, 217
Gainesville, Ocala and Charlotte Harbor Railroad, 268, 279. *See also* Florida Southern Railway Co.
Galilee Baptist Church (Fort Meade), 320
Gallagher, John, 359
Gandy, George W., 146
Gandy, Green W., 406
Gant, G.W., 413
Garner, Andrew W., 190
Garner, Daniel D., 209
Gartner, A.F., 323
Gaskins, Asa, 355
Gaskins, Thomas, 288, 358
Gastigo, Antonio, 357
Gates, Josiah, 137, 170, 211
Gates, Primus. *See* Smith, Primus Gates
Gay, W.G., 288
Geiger, Abraham E., 360

Geiger, John A., 360
Gettis, James, 132, 144, 147, 182–83, 187, 191, 193
Gibbons, William, 23, 350
Gibbs, Margaret Watkins, 177, 180
Gibson, J.S., 288
Gibsonton, 389
Giddens, M.F., 422, 425
Gilbert, Mary McCullough, 404
Gilchrist, Albert W., 270, 290–91, 300, 307, 309–10, 363
Giles, Enoch H., 227
Gill, G.H., 287
Gill, Joseph, 354
Gillett, Daniel, 69, 359
Gilmore, J.L., 363
Glades County, 300
Glasgow, James, 356
Glazier, Ezekiel, 130–31, 170, 399, 422
Glover, B.G., 422
Glover, Charles, 264
Godwin, Aaron Elijah, 249, 362
Godwin, Mariah Tyner, 153
Godwin, Solomon, 153, 230, 245, 357, 362, 392, 413
Goff, James A., 356
Gold, L.O., 289
Goodwyn, Robert H. (volunteer officer), 44–45
Gopher, John (black warrior), 40
Gorman, John, 350
Governor Marvin (steamer), 197
Graeffe, Richard A.(Union army officer), 159–60
Graham, Edgar M., 202–3, 209, 211–12, 293, 298
Granger, Bryant G., 300
Granger, Joseph F., 196, 410
Granger, Seph, 253
Grant, A., 320
Grant, T.O., 340
Great Freeze of 1894–95, 321–23
Great Southern Railway Co., 256, 266
Green, Andrew, 211
Green, Elisha, 351
Green, Eliza Whidden, 95
Green, Herbert, 363
Green, Israel, 69, 355, 358
Green, James, 352, 362
Green, James Dopson, 92–93, 95, 103–4, 108, 110, 117, 130–32, 141, 145,

162-63, 167-68, 171, 174, 182-83,
185, 190-93, 200-203, 208-13,
293-94, 356, 358, 388-89, 397, 404,
408
Green, John, 67, 69-70, 102, 153, 355,
359
Green, John C., 360
Green, Samuel L., 204
Green, William, 355
Greene, Edwin, 288, 340
Greene, McKeen, 350
Gresham, C.C., 242, 250, 418
Grier, T.J., 412
Griffin, Frank, 205, 408
Griffin, Frank (freedman), 181, 205-6,
408
Griffin, W.A., 401
Griffith, Robert S., 422
Guano Hammock, 242, 245
Gunstan, James, 358
Gunter, John B., 392
Guy, Benjamin, 69, 359, 385, 406

Hackley, Richard, 35
Hackley, Robert, 35-36
Hac-to Hal-chee (Tallahassee warrior),
40
Hagan, David, 350
Hagan, Francis B., 146, 208-9, 295, 297,
300, 307, 362, 404, 422
Hagan, Henry, 350
Hagan, Isham, 350
Hagan, John, 350
Hagan, Joseph, 349
Hagan's Bluff, 145
Haines City, 118, 275, 388
Hair, Streaty, 361
Hair, William Calvin, 130
Hair, William N., 361
Hale, W.K., 422
Hall, E.J., 411
Hall, F., 283
Hall, Thomas L., 350
Hall, William N., 310
Hall, William W., 102
Halleyman, A.T., 277
Halpatter Tustenuggee (Alligator), 43,
49, 51, 53, 371-72, 375
Halpatter Tustenuggee (Tallahassee
chief), 59, 70, 382
Hamblen, Samuel, 212

Hambleton, Richard. *See* Hamilton,
Richard
Hamer, Thomas L. (army officer), 87
Hamilton, Arch, 363
Hamilton, George, 138, 333, 358, 391,
394, 401
Hamilton, James, 126, 138, 143, 178,
391, 394
Hamilton, John, 363
Hamilton, Richard, 181
Hamilton County, 203; early settle-
ment, 34; and Second Seminole War,
42, 49; at the close of the Second
Seminole War, 63-66; emigration
from, 68-70; selected residents
(1830-32), 351-52; selected voters
(1842-43), 355
Hampton, A.P., 216
Hancock, Henry W., 357
Hancock, J.H., 425
Hancock, James T., Jr., 283, 309
Hancock, Jane, 402
Hancock, Jordan, 182
Hancock, Shadrach, 357
Hancock, Stephen, 394
Hancock, William, 69, 72, 358
Hancock, William H., 357
Hanna, R.S., 291
Hanson, G.A., 251, 282, 303-5, 331, 418
Hard, Bert, 251, 318
Hardee County, 35, 130; area opened to
settlement, 100-101; early settlers,
103-4, 124-26, 146; Third Seminole
War, 108-12; schools, 126, 225-26;
churches, 228-30; as part of DeSoto
County, 300. *See also* names of indi-
vidual towns
Harden, Charles, 264
Hare, William, 351
Harllee, John W., 211
Harney, William Selby (army officer),
55, 377
Harrell, James M., 394
Harrell, Jeremiah, 391
Harrell, John W., 360
Harriet (slave of Frederick Varn), 99
Harriet (slave of Rigdon Brown), 80
Harris, F.A.K., 275
Harris, Henry Tate, 363
Harris, Wiley, 350
Harris, William S., 143-44

Harris Corner. *See* Winter Haven
Harrison, C.E., 413
Harrison, E.L., 413
Harrison, Ellen, 392
Harrison, Mitchell, 181
Harrison, William, 352
Harry (black warrior), 40, 42
Hart, J.A., 286
Hart, Ossian B. (Florida governor), 137, 140, 147, 176, 188, 209-10
Hart, S.A., 413
Hart, William T., 361
Hartsuff, George (army officer), 101, 107
Hartwell, Samuel A., 274
Harvey, Kelly B., 276, 279, 291
Harward, Samuel, 363
Hatchee Thlokko. *See* Bowlegs Creek
Hatcher, Ebenezer, 354
Hathlapo Hadjo (Tallahassee warrior), 40
Hawkins, Benjamin (Indian agent), 6
Hawkins, D.L., 182, 404
Hayes, Benjamin, 350
Hayes, James, 350
Hayes, Rutherford B. (U.S. president), 212-13
Hayman, Edna, 286
Hayman, J.J., 363
Hayman, Jeremiah M., 98, 146, 177, 216, 228, 397-98
Hayman, Nathan L., 363
Hayman, S.J. (Mrs. J.C. Blount), 225
Hayman, Seabren G., 286, 421
Hayman, William C., 300, 306, 422
Hays, Frank, 363
Hearn, Alice, 339
Hector, James P., 427
Hector, Thomas R., 279, 291
Heiss, W.H., 217
Henderson, George W., 350
Henderson, John A., 127, 183, 189
Henderson, Michael, 350
Henderson, W.B., 276
Hendricks, Isaac, 349
Hendry, Albert J., 190, 362, 406, 412, 422
Hendry, Archibald, 190, 208, 361
Hendry, Archibald W., 406, 425
Hendry, Charles, 361
Hendry, Charles E., 425

Hendry, Charles W., 200, 396
Hendry, Capt. F.A., Independent Company (1864-65), 167, 169, 171-72; partial roster, 362
Hendry, F.F. ("Tobe"), 286, 338, 363
Hendry, Francis Asbury, 98, 101, 108, 116-17, 138, 140, 143, 148, 151, 157, 163, 167, 172-73, 175, 182-3, 186, 192-93, 197-200, 209, 219-20, 224, 226, 256, 268, 279, 345, 362, 390, 394, 413
Hendry, George W., 98, 126, 142-43, 204-5, 208, 257, 266, 273, 297, 310-11, 322, 345, 362, 370, 390, 392, 418
Hendry, James E., 275-76
Hendry, James M., 188, 209, 228, 276, 279-80, 361
Hendry, Jane Brown, 200
Hendry, John Wright, 190, 208, 228-29, 268, 279, 307, 309, 411, 425
Hendry, Oregon (Mrs. Benjamin F. Blount), 116, 345
Hendry, R.C., 414, 425
Hendry, Robert, 144, 146, 153, 357, 397
Hendry, William H., 357
Hendry, William Marion, 173, 189, 200, 345, 362, 390, 407
Hendry, Zilla Ann Moody, 153, 397
Hendry's Bridge, 233
Henry (slave of John I. Hooker), 102
Henry, Patrick. *See* Jones, Patrick Henry
Hepburn, H.P., 266, 269
Hernando County, 3, 112, 244, 248, 266
Herndon, N.C., 363
Herndon, T.J., 276, 279, 287-88, 425
Herrington, Henry, 354
Herzog, Louis, 410
Hewitt, Martha, 406
Hickey, Dennis, 392
Hickory Bluff, 222, 225, 260, 276, 301, 315; in 1880, 263
Hickory Boys (Confederate volunteer company), 142, 395
Hicks, Jesse, 355
Hicks, John (Mikasuki chief), 11
Hicks, John B., 356
Hicks, Lewis, 144
Hicks, M.J., 363
Hicks, Wiley, 355

Hicks, William Watkins, 210

Highlands City, 143

Highlands County, 300

Hightey, Charles P., 363

Hill, Chesney D., 92

Hill, G.B., 283

Hill, John Wesley, 87

Hille, Adam, 224

Hilliard, Benjamin, 359

Hilliard, Benjamin J., 360

Hilliard, Edward J., 174, 391

Hilliard, Henry, 359

Hilliard, Thomas J., 360

Hillman, Charles E., 274

Hillsborough County: settlers petition for return of troops (1834), 41; armed occupation act settlement in, 65–68; expansion of settlement eastward from, 79–80, 101–3; alarm at Indian attack (1849), 84–85; demands for Indian removal, 94–97; creation of Manatee County from, 104; Regulator violence (1858), 126–29; creation of Polk County from, 132–35; slavery in, 137

Hinckley, R., 341

Hinckley, S.P., 291

Hines, Isaac, 355

Hodge, Green W., 363

Hodgson, R.J., 310

Holata Micco (Tallahassee chief), 38–41, 48–50, 372–74

Holata Micco or Billy Bowlegs (Seminole chief), 26–27, 50, 55–56, 58, 70–72, 77, 82, 85–87, 89–90, 94, 97, 100, 106–7, 111, 114, 117–18, 371–72, 375–76, 391

Holland, Daniel P., 233

Hollimon, Mills, 357

Hollingsworth, Jacob Simeon, 362

Hollingsworth, James, 349

Hollingsworth, John H., 113, 159, 356, 358, 381, 389, 392, 398, 400, 425

Hollingsworth, Louisa, 392

Hollingsworth, Perlina, 153

Hollingsworth, S.F., 358

Hollingsworth, S. Thomas, 412

Hollingsworth, Simeon, 392, 408

Hollingsworth, Stephen, 102, 153, 356, 358, 385, 392, 395

Hollingsworth, Timothy, 349, 395

Hollingsworth, William, 349, 358

Hollingsworth, William H., 205, 339, 420

Hollingsworth, William R., 173, 216, 362, 392

Homeland, 87, 125, 168, 182, 200, 207, 216, 218, 260, 315; area surveyed, 92; early settlers, 97–98, 102; schools, 126, 265, 320, 330; churches, 126, 227, 230–31, 265, 284, 320; Civil War camp meeting, 172; freedmen living near, 178, 180, 265; and the railroad, 277; named, 283; in 1880s, 283–84; black community at, 318–21; in 1895–1900, 337

Homeland Baptist Church, 284

Homeland Pebble Phosphate Co., 315

Homeland Phosphate Co., 315

Homesteading, 258

Honduras (steamer), 197

Honors, Lewis, 264

Hooker, George, 181

Hooker, James N., 277, 281, 286, 310, 418

Hooker, James T., 351, 378

Hooker, John I., 101–2, 108, 132, 197, 200, 220, 356, 391, 394

Hooker, Stephen, 352–53

Hooker, Stephen P., 359, 388, 392

Hooker, William B., 68, 79, 101, 108–10, 112, 115, 128, 131, 137–38, 352–53, 355–56, 359, 378–79, 381, 389

Hooker, William J., Jr., 359

Hooker, William J., Sr., 138, 359

Hooker, William J. (son of W.B. Hooker), 131, 138, 397

Hooker's Prairie, 23, 379

Hope, David, 170

Hope, Samuel E., 134, 182

Hopkins, Benjamin (Florida militia officer), 96–97

Hordy, B., 413

Horne, Joe, 253

Horse Creek, 103, 146, 153, 225; explored, 45; Union forces at, 150, 158; Manatee County seat located near, 185

Horseshoe Bend, Battle of (1814), 7

Hospetarke (Seminole chief), 56–57, 377

Hotel Punta Gorda, 290, 329, 342

Housing and accommodations, 87, 125, 231
Houston, Young, 177–78
Howard, Oliver O. (army officer), 109, 138–39
Howard, P.W., 339
Howard, Seth, 356, 406
Howell, George, 115, 358
Howell, John, 349
Howell, Joseph, 67, 70, 79, 103, 134–35, 354–55, 357–58, 385
Howell, M.T., 425
Hubbard, Daniel, 93–94
Huddleston, R.H., 283
Hughes, David, 172, 198, 200, 219, 221, 268, 281, 297–98, 331, 410, 418
Hull, E.J., 425
Hull, Stephen, 391
Hull, T.S., 303
Humphreys, Gad, 31
Hunter, David, 353–54
Hunter, Elijah, 354
Hunter, James, 354
Hunter, Jessee, 354
Hunter, John, 355
Hunter, N.P., 130
Hunter, Robert, 411
Hunter (sloop), 28
Huntress (brig), 146
Hurricane: of 1848, 75–76; of 1852, 98; of 1878, 241, 257–58; of 1867, 405; of 1873, 411

Indian Agency: at Fort King, 38; at Peace River, 87–88
Indian Nation: boundaries (1823), 29–31; (1829), 15; (1839), 377; (1850), 87; (1854), 100–101
Indian removal, 36–38, 41–42, 93–97, 99–101, 106–7, 117–18
Indian Springs, Treaty of (1821), 19
Indian store: at Charlotte Harbor, 71–72, 76, 80, 86; at Peace River, 80–84.
Ingraham, James, 428
International Ocean Telegraph Co., 217–19, 223, 243
Island, Harriet, 402
Itchepuckesassa, 93–94, 104, 134;
Indian town, 12, 23; armed occupation act settlements near, 68–70, 356–57 ; residents of, resettling near Peace

River, 101–3; Confederate forces at, 166–67. *See also* Fort Sullivan; Plant City
Ivey, Francis A., 392
Ivey, John, 352, 355
Ivey, Robert, 355
Ivey, Thomas, 353

Jackson, Andrew (Florida governor, U.S. president), 7, 9–10, 14, 36 19, 21–22, 25
Jackson, B.F., 331
Jackson, Ceily, 402
Jackson, Eliza, 402
Jackson, James W., 186, 360
Jackson, John, 356
Jackson, Robert, 356
Jackson, Simon, 177–78, 180, 206–7, 402
Jackson, Thomas B., 361
Jacksonville, Tampa & Key West Railway, 268–69. *See also* South Florida Railroad Co.
James, Dora, 427
James, Randall, 319
James, W.D., 363
Jefferson (town of), 144–45, 183, 185
Jenkins, Lewis, 357
Jenkins, Willis, 402
Jernigan, Aaron, 95–96
Jesup, Thomas Sidney (army officer), 48–53
Jinkins, J.H., 363
Johanson, C.G., 287–88, 420
Johns, Cornelious, 350
Johns, George, 358
Johns, Isaac, 350
Johns, Riley, 354
Johns, William, 178, 180, 350
Johns, William (freedman), 402
Johnson, Alonzo, 205, 244–46
Johnson, Andrew (U.S. president), 187
Johnson, Augustus, 205, 244–46
Johnson, B.F., 281
Johnson, C.C., 283, 427
Johnson, C.N., 425
Johnson, Churchill, 302–4
Johnson, Elias E., 406
Johnson, Enoch, 359
Johnson, G.H., 210, 422
Johnson, Hardy, 252
Johnson, Isham, 244

Johnson, James, 353
Johnson, James Hansford, 146
Johnson, James Mitchell ("Acrefoot"), 265–66
Johnson, John, 205, 244–45
Johnson, John Henry ("Big Six"), 242
Johnson, John I., 354
Johnson, L.P., 398
Johnson, Luther L., 363
Johnson, Milton, 359
Johnson, Prince, 177–78, 264, 320
Johnson, Raymond, 244–46
Johnson, Robert, 150–51, 397
Johnson, S.J., 363
Johnson, W.H., 333
Johnson, Will, 240
Johnson, William A., 289, 404, 406, 422
Johnston, Alexander S., 256, 262, 266
Johnston, Joseph E. (army officer), 55
Jones, B.J., 320
Jones, Buck, 177–78, 206–7
Jones, Edmund, 137–38, 146
Jones, G.W., 320
Jones, Hannah, 402
Jones, Hilliard, 355
Jones, James A., 186, 209, 240
Jones, James W., 410
Jones, John C., 313
Jones, John L., 311, 340
Jones, L.S., 422
Jones, Mathew E., 360
Jones, N.T., 412
Jones, Patrick Henry, 177, 402
Jones, Sam. *See* Arpeika
Jones, Thomas, 362
Jordan, William C., 227–29
Joshua Creek, 31, 145, 200, 218, 222, 225, 227, 228, 230, 264, 290, 328

Kabrich, J.G.S., 288
Kantz, D.C., 429
Keck, Irving, 286, 322
Keen, Arthur, 421
Keen, E.B., 362
Keen, George, 359
Keen, Henry, 188, 391
Keen, James M., 188, 406
Keen, Maria, 392
Keen, Owen, 392
Keen, Perry O., 422
Keller, John, 406

Kendrick, Edward T., 108, 126, 143, 392–93, 395
Kendrick, James, 352–53
Kendrick, William H., 95, 190, 201, 207
Kennedy, Thomas P., 71–72, 76, 84, 94, 386
Kennedy & Darling (merchants), 76–79, 82
Key, Ann, 240
Key, Bill, 240
Key, Gilbert L., 163, 240, 391–92
Key, John, 240
Key, Oliver, 240
Key of the Gulf (Key West newspaper), 293, 423
Key West: slavery at, 138–39; Union forces at, 147, 158; cattle shipments to, 147, 276; and International Ocean Telegraph line, 216–19; shipping between Fort Ogden and, 221; yellow fever at, 313; proposed railroads to, 356
Key West *Dispatch*, 423
Keystone, 274. *See also* Frostproof
Keystone State (steamer), 147
Keysville, 196
Kilpatrick, R.P., 303
King, W.E., 422
King, William, 421
King, Ziba, 200, 209–10, 212, 221, 245, 251, 258, 276, 288, 293, 306–7, 309–11, 340–41, 406, 422, 425
King Bowlegs (Alachua Seminole chief), 26
King Payne (Alachua Seminole chief), 6, 26
Kinney, T.J., 216
Kirkland, James, 360
Kissengen Springs, 143, 283, 324
Kissimmee, 268–69
Kissimmee Island, 250
Kissimmee River, 49, 57, 88, 94, 96, 131, 171, 248, 250; and Disston developments, 261
Knight, A.J., 294
Knight, Britton, 350
Knight, F.J., 425
Knight, Jesse, 69, 357–58
Knight, Joel, 69, 358, 385, 393
Knight, John J., 356
Knight, Samuel, 358
Knight, T.S., 425

Knight, Thomas T., 352
Know Nothing Party, 127-28, 140, 393

La Cosmopolita Plantation (Pembroke),
    323-24
Lake, J.B., 427
Lake Alfred, 54, 269, 275
Lake Buffum, 101, 330
Lake City, 217
Lake Clinch, 274
Lake Hamilton, 118, 388
Lake Hancock, 7, 29-32; Oponay's set-
    tlement near, 13; Fort Fraser near,
    50; area surveyed, 92
Lake Istokpoga, 51, 54, 70, 76, 87
Lake Marion, 118, 388
Lake Okeechobee, 51, 70, 107, 119; and
    Disston development, 261
Lake Parker, 266, 275
Lake Reedy, 274
Lake Simmons, 29
Lake Thonotosassa, 67-69, 207
Lake Tohopekaliga, 23, 44, 48, 95-96
Lake Wales, 382
Lake Wire, 217, 274
Lakeland, 207, 269, 274, 321, 336
Lakeland Improvement Co., 274
LaMartin, Robert, 232, 412
Land titles, 234, 258-62
Lang, David, 349
Lang Brothers, 281
Langford, Curtis, 363
Langford, George R., 413
Langford, Henry, 117, 126, 130, 388,
    398, 400, 412
Langford, Richard C., 265, 285, 302,
    413, 418
Langford, S.T., 300
Lanier, Ardeline Ross (Mrs. F.A.
    Hendry), 98
Lanier, Frederick S., 406, 410
Lanier, Hardy, 350
Lanier, James, 165, 350, 394
Lanier, James Madison, 276
Lanier, John, 394
Lanier, Louis, 70, 79, 98, 101, 123,
    125-26, 132, 134, 138, 157, 200, 203,
    205, 216, 220, 265, 355, 391, 393-94
Lark, Richard A., 178, 180
Lassiter, W.B., 284
Laura (schooner), 151, 221, 410
Law, E.M., 333-34

LeBaron, J. Francis, 313
Lee, Edmund, 356, 397
Lee, Sam, 284
LeMartin, Samuel, 349
Lesley, John T., 166-67, 173
Lesley, Leroy G., 108, 111-12, 137, 167,
    170, 173, 182
Levens, William, 354
Lewis, Albert [Alfred] A., 177-78, 180,
    206, 402
Lewis, Ceily, 180
Lewis, James Isham, 392, 413
Lewis, William, 205
Lightsey, Cornelius B., 220, 285, 296,
    406, 413, 418
Lightsey, Sullivan, 410
Lightsey, Ulysses A. ("Doc"), 296, 299
Lily, 103, 222, 264
Lincoln, Abraham (U.S. president),
    140-41, 148
Lippencott, Samuel, 248, 414
Little Paynes Creek, 103
Live Oak, 245, 251
Live Oak Camp, 45
Live Oak reservation, 260
Lively, William A., 394
Liverpool, 264, 276, 290
Lloyd, Daniel, 422
Local Option Law. *See* Prohibition
Locke, J.W., 203
Locklear, Elijah, 354
Locklear, Irvin, 392
Locklear, Joseph, 354
Locklear, Nelson, 242, 414
Locklear, William, 354
Lomans, John, 181, 188, 205, 244-45
Long Swamp, 26
Longsworth, Lula Marion, 427
Longworth, J.C., 283
Loomis, Gustavus (army officer), 118
Louisiana volunteers (1836), 44-45
Lovett, William J., 363
Lowe, Allen, 392
Lowe, John, 361
Lower Creek Indians, 7, 10, 18
Lowry, Solomon, 349
Lucas, John, 253-54
Lyons, Matthew P., 110, 112, 201, 389

McAuley, John, 126, 186, 190, 207, 391,
    401, 413
McAuley, Robert A., 226, 391, 412

McAuley, W. M., 413
McCall, George A. (army officer), 57
McCantt, G., 283
McCartey, Hugh, 378
McClelland, Andrew, 69, 354
McClelland, Charles, 351
McClelland, George E., 351
McClelland, J.L., 362
McClelland, John, 69, 355, 358
McClelland, John N., 358
McClelland, John W., 354
McClelland, Joseph A., 351
McClelland, Moses A., 69, 172, 358, 388, 392
McClelland, Silas, 69, 92, 143, 354–55, 358, 379, 390, 394
McClelland, William, 352, 354
McClendon, G.W., 284, 320
McClenithan, William, Jr., 173, 360, 406
McClenithan, William, Sr., 162
McConnell, M.A., 287
McCormick, Jack, 243, 303–4
McCrea, William, 71, 380
McCrummen, Donald, 350
McCullough, Elisabeth, 82
McCullough, Joseph, 349
McCullough, Nancy Whidden, 82–84, 404
McCullough, William, 69, 81–84, 92, 102, 113, 162–63, 167, 171, 174, 389, 404
McDaniel, Jeremiah, 350
McDonald, A., 350
McDonald, E.D., 319
McDonald, John, 388
McElvine, Anna P., 427
McEwen, W. A., 411
McEwen, William P., 227, 406, 411
MacInnis, John, 357
McIntosh, William (Coweta Creek chief), 7, 9–10, 14, 18–21
McKay, Donald, 148
McKay, James, Jr., 157, 163, 167, 197
McKay, James, Sr., 137, 146–50, 156–57, 160–61, 197, 406
McKay, Oden, 360
McKay's Wharf, 183, 197
McKee, W.J., 313–14
McKillop, Andrew, 284
McKillop, Katie, 284

McKinney, J.L., 392
McKinney, Thomas L., 392, 422
McKinney's Branch, 269
McKinny, Charles, 350
McLaughlin, William, 250
McLean, David, 286
McLean, James, 286
McLemore, John (militia officer), 42, 47
McLeod, Henry R., 182
McNeill, Archibald, 130–32, 191, 209; 399
McNeill, John (volunteer officer), 118
Macomb, Alexander (army officer), 54–55, 58
Macon, Charles Henry, Sr., 283
McQueen, Peter (Tallahassee Creek chief), 5, 9, 11, 13, 19, 22–25, 119
Mad Lizzard (Tallahassee Creek warrior), 40
Maddox, T.J., 287
Magbee, James T., 85, 99, 128–29, 133–35, 137, 140, 147, 162, 191, 193, 200–202, 206, 209–10, 246, 293, 408–9, 422
Maguire, Sherrard B., 102
Mahon, D.D., 425
Maloney, W.C., Jr., 203
Malpurs, John U., 349
Manatee. *See* Bradenton
Manatee County: created, 104; efforts to separate Peace River area from, 104, 129–32, 191; and Third Seminole War, 108–9, 166–17; schools, 126, 225–26, 327–29; controversy over courthouse, 130; conflict over county seat, 132, 145, 185; slavery in, 137; Civil War impact on county commission, 169; freedmen in, 181; Reconstruction in, 181–94, 200–13; and Regulator violence, 204–6; election of 1876 in, 210–13; courthouses at Pine Level, 222; and hurricane of 1878, 258; and census of 1880, 262, 416; Redemption politics in, 292–98; creation of DeSoto County from, 299–300; and census of 1867, 404. *See also* Elections; names of individual towns
Manatee River: first settlements at, 65; military posts on, 87; impact of railroads in, 272–91; county seat moved

Manatee River (*continued*)
to Arcadia, 299–301; armed occupa-
tion act settlements near, 356–57;
sugar plantations at, 378
Manirva (slave of Frederick Varn), 99
Manley, James M., 172, 400, 413
Mann, Americus V., 406
Mann, Dan, 243, 251, 302–4
Mann, Lony, 243, 302–4
Mansfield, George, 247
Mansfield, Henry, 391
Mansfield, William H., 395
Manuel, Sam, 177, 402
Maple Branch Baptist Church (Alafia
River), 228–29
Mapping and charting, 32; Chazotte
expedition, 28; Horatio Dexter, 29;
James Gadsden, 29–31. *See also*
Surveys
Marchman, Jeff, 284
Mare's Branch, 300
Marlow, R.G., 412
Marsh, C.F., 286
Marsh, John F., 285, 291
Martin, Charles, 319
Martin, George, 350
Martin, L.A., 392
Marvin, William (Florida governor),
182
Mason, I.A., 286
Mason, William I., 286
Mathis, James Washington, 124, 392
Matilda (slave of H.S. Seward), 102
Mattoon, A.C., 233–34, 413
Mattox, T.J., 425
Mauck, Sam, 263
Mayo, M.D.L., 406
Meacham, Robert, 319
Meade, George G. (army officer), 79,
88–89, 156, 371
Medora, 273
Medulla, 92, 143, 273–74, 379
Meigs, J.L., 417
Melvin, William, 391
Mercer, Adam, 406
Messer, Henry, 191, 360
Messer, Joel, 361
Methodist Campground (Homeland),
126, 168, 172, 182, 216, 227, 230, 284
Methodist Church, 126, 227–31. *See
also* individual churches and towns

Meyers, James F. (Union army officer),
158
Micanopy (Seminole chief), 43, 48–49
Midland, 330
Mikasuki Indians, 11, 49, 53, 70, 76–77.
See also Indian removal; Second
Seminole War; Third Seminole War
Miles, William, 320
Miley, William, 359
Miley, William G., 359
Miller, Charles (Lower Creek chief), 21
Miller, Nathaniel, 359
Mimms, J.C., 406
Mims, Chesley B., 354
Minatti (Indian village), 39
Mitchell, Charles L., 259, 262, 273. 410,
413
Mitchell, David (Indian agent), 19
Mitchell, Early, 284
Mitchell, Franklin, 359
Mitchell, George, 356
Mitchell, George W., 362
Mitchell, Henry L., 241, 251, 293–94,
305, 308, 333
Mitchell, J.L., 225
Mitchell, Lawrence, 359
Mitchell, Samuel, 359
Mitchell, Thomas, 359
Mitchell, Thomas J., 359
Mitchell, William, 356
Mizell, Enoch E. (Manatee County),
146, 188, 203, 209, 403
Mizell, Enoch E. (Polk County), 182,
208, 310, 392, 403, 413
Mizell, George C., 360
Mizell, Jesse B., 209, 212, 422
Mizell, John, 350
Mizell, Joseph, 143, 394
Mobley, C.R., 189, 193, 201
Mobley, William S., 137
Montes de Oca, John, 249
Montgomery, John D., 363
Moody, Benjamin, 134, 350, 352, 356,
359, 379, 390–91
Moody, Jeremiah, 350
Moody, Lydia Carlton Hendry, 390–91
Moody, Shadrach, 350
Moore, Andy, 177–78, 180, 264, 320, 402
Moore, Joseph, 356
Moore & Tatum Phosphate Co., 315
Morehead, T. S., 313–14

Morgan, C.C., 340
Morgan, Charlotte, 402
Morgan, Daniel, 353
Morgan, Isaac, 392
Morgan, L.L., 340
Morgan, T.S., 422
Morris, W.W. (army officer), 79, 87
Moultrie Creek, Treaty of (1823), 29
Mount Bunyan Baptist Church (Homeland), 284, 319
Mount Gilbert (Gilboa) Baptist Church (Bartow), 320
Mount Moriah Baptist Church (Joshua Creek), 228, 230
Mount Pisgah Methodist Church, 231
Mount Pleasant Baptist Church (DeSoto County), 229
Mount Zion A.M.E. Church (Arcadia), 319
Mud Lake, 143–44, 395
Mulberry, 297, 316, 321
Munn, Abraham G., 274
Munnerlyn, Charles J. (Confederate army officer), 166, 171
Munnerlyn's Battalion, 362. *See also* Cow Cavalry
Munroe, J.C., 286
Murphy, W.L., 142
Murray (black chief), 50
Murray, George W., 35
Murrell, E.W., Jr., 363
Mutch, George, 363
Murrhee, William F., 350
Myakka River, 88; Union forces at, 158

Natural Bridge, Battle of (1865), 174
Neamathla (Mikasuki chief), 25
Negro Fort, 8
Negro Point, 8
Negro Ridge, 297
Negroes. *See* African Americans
Nelson, J.C., 413
New Hope Church (Baptist), 225
New Orleans, battle of (1815), 7
New Zion Baptist Church (Ona), 228–29
Newman, Squire, 264
Newsome, B.J., 70
Newsome, N.J., 358
Newspapers, 124; Bartow *Informant*, 273–74; Fort Meade *Pioneer*, 285; Ar-
cadian, 287; *Charlotte Harbor Beacon* (Punta Gorda), 291; *Punta Gorda Herald*, 310–11; *DeSoto County News*, 311; *South Florida Progress* (Fort Meade), 315; Bartow *Courier-Informant*, 331; *DeSoto County Champion*, 338–39; Fort Ogden *Democrat*, 418; Pine Level *Signal and Advertiser*, 418; Fort Ogden *Herald*, 418; *Pine Level Times*, 419; Pine Level *Youth's Friend*, 419. *See also* names of individual newspapers
Niblack, Silas, 203–4, 407
Niblack, William, 350
Nicholas, Henry, 349
Nicolls, Edward (British officer), 7–8, 10, 21
99th United States Colored Troops (Union army regiment), 183
Nix, James, 350
Nocatee, 264, 300–301; in 1887, 290
Norris, Henry H., 309
Norris, John N., 358
North, James, 354
North, Jim, 252–53
North, John J., 354
North, William B. (volunteer officer), 354
Norwood, M.L., 427
Norwood, Mrs. M.L., 428

Oats, Frances B., 153
Oats, John C., 102–3, 113, 153, 389, 394
Ocala, capture of rustlers near, 245. *See also* Fort King
Ocala Demands, 307, 309
Ockmulgee Creek Indians, 12
Ogden, Edmund Augustus (army officer), 56
Oglesby, James, 354
Okeechobee, battle of (1837), 51
Old Jones Chapel (Homeland), 320
Old Wire Road. *See* Wire Road
Olustee, battle of (1864), 161
Ona, 138
Oneal, John K., 388
110th New York Infantry (Union army regiment), 174
O'Neill, John. *See* Oneal, John K.
O'Neill, James H. (Catholic priest), 335

Oponay (Ockmulgee Creek chief), 9–13, 23–25, 29
Oranges. *See* Citrus
Oren, William, 310
Orlando, 97, 119, 240, 276, 407
Oscen Tustenuggee (Tallahassee chief), 78, 111, 115
Osceola or Billy Powell (Tallahassee warrior), 9, 13–14, 40–43, 47–50, 119
Osteen, Isaac, 350
Osteen, James, 350
Ott, James, 286
Ottinger, M., 286
Oyster River, 8

Page, F.W., 282
Page, Solomon H., 297, 406
Page, Mrs. Solomon, 91
Panic of 1873, 220
Parker, F.E., 425
Parker, Jasper Newton, 200, 301, 307, 413
Parker, John, 79, 103, 126, 132, 137–38, 145, 200, 212, 356, 379, 385, 387, 406, 413
Parker, Capt. John, volunteer company (1849), 358–59
Parker, John N., 363
Parker, Lewis Henry, 200, 301, 392, 406, 413, 422
Parker, Lizzie, 392
Parker, Luke, 351
Parker, Readding Blount, 240, 392
Parker, Streaty, 91, 97, 113, 142, 163, 175, 294, 297, 362, 387, 394
Parker, Thomas Owen, 200, 300, 307
Parker, William, 102, 113, 356, 359, 379, 389, 391
Parson Brown Oranges, 390
Patrick, John, 360
Patriot War (1812–14), 6–7; selected soldiers in, 349–50
Patten, Edward B., 412
Patten, George T., 205
Patten, Joseph Arthur, 226
Patterson, Honora, 340
Payne, Enoch, 252
Payne, George, 77, 80–84
Payne, W.D., 406
Paynes Creek, 88, 103
Paynes Creek Primitive Baptist Church, 230, 412

Paynes Landing, Treaty of (1832), 37
Paynes Prairie, 42
Peabody Fund, 225
Peace Creek Navigation Co., 234–35, 413
Peace Creek Post Office. *See* Bartow
Peace Creek Primitive Baptist Church (Bartow), 229
Peace River (Talakchopco hatchee), 94; ford at Talakchopco, 4; name, 4; as refuge, 6; Tallahassee Creeks at, 13–14, 23–26, 39–40, 118–19; Seminoles at, 5–7, 25–27; explored and mapped, 27–32, 35–36; and Second Seminole War, 42–46, 49–59; as boundary of Indian nation, 55, 58; at close of Second Seminole War, 63; neutral zone established, 69; Indian store at, 76–84; early American settlements, 78–80, 91–93, 97–99, 101–4; slaves at, 80, 91–92, 97–99; and Indian scare of 1849, 84–85; military posts near, 86–90; cattle ranges near, 98; troops withdrawn, 101; and Third Seminole War, 106–20; skirmish at Charlie Apopka Creek, 111–12; Indian attack on Tillis place, 112–13; battle of Peace River, 113–15; influx of settlers after Third Seminole War, 123–26; and Regulator violence, 126–29, 204–6; and Civil War, 141–42, 150–75; opposition to secession by residents of, 141; cattle trade from, 147–50; blockade running out of, 147–51; effect of Confederate conscription laws upon residents near, 152–53, 157–58, 161–62, 166–67, 169–70; smallpox at, 153; Unionist refugees from, 157–58; Union army expeditions to, 158, 163–65, 167–69; Civil War divisions at, 165–67; destruction of Fort Meade, 168; attack upon Fort Myers from, 172–75; emancipation at, 177–81; immigration to, after Civil War, 196; cattle shipping operations moved to Punta Rassa, 198; attempts to make navigable, 201, 232–35, 313, 417; and construction of International Ocean Telegraph line, 217–19; growth of communities near, 219–31; impact of violence on life at, 239–254; transpor-

tation problems at, 254–57; and hurricane of 1878, 257–58; and land title problems, 258–62; railroads to, 266–71; impact of railroads in vicinity of, 272–91; discovery and mining of phosphate, 312–17; and freezes of 1894–95, 321–23; and the legacy of the nineteenth century, 343–45; shipping on, 396, 419
Peace River, battle of (1856), 113, 115
Peace River Packet Line, 396
Peace River Phosphate Co., 314
Peace River Phosphate Mining Co., 316
Peacock, Henry, 355
Peacock, John, 355
Pearce, Howren, 392
Pearce, James C., 356, 359
Pearce, John, 250, 359
Pearce, John M., 172, 188, 359, 362, 392, 413
Pearce, Levi, 125–26, 227, 351, 353, 356, 359, 379, 391, 394
Pearce, Peyton S., 413
Pearce, S.I., 295
Pearce, Thomas, 392
Pearce, Thomas C., 142
Pearce, William H., 204, 218, 224, 300, 307, 418
Peas Creek. *See* Peace River
Peas Creek Baptist Church (Bartow), 102, 126, 153, 216, 222, 227–29
Peas Creek Immigrant and Agricultural Co., 201, 233–34, 257, 260–61
Pease Creek John. *See* Gopher John
Pease Creek Post Office (Bartow). *See* Bartow
Pease Creek Primitive Baptist Church (Bartow), 229
Pease Creek Tallahassees, 36–40, 48–50. *See also* Second Seminole War
Pebbledale, 315
Peeples, J.H., 425
Peeples, R.H., 249, 413, 422
Peeples, Vernon, 271, 342
Pelham, Richard, 103, 388
Pelot, J.C., 211
Pelot, John, 299
Pemberton, John C. (army officer), 156
Pemberton Ferry, 269
Pembroke, 324
Pendleton, Charles B., 227, 257, 262, 418

Pennington, Henry, 353
Pennington, Jesse, 67, 153, 351, 354, 358, 388
Pennington, William, 67, 353, 355
Peoples Party, in DeSoto County, 425. *See also* Populism
Pepper, Thomas J., 287–88, 306, 309–11
Pernell, James, 178, 180, 205, 402
Perry, Edward A. (Florida governor), 262, 270, 298, 300
Perry, J. M., 283, 333
Perry, Madison S. (Florida governor), 132, 135
Perry, Wise, 339
Perry County, 132–33
Peter Raulerson, 419
Peterson, J.L., 169
Pharr Phosphate Co., 316
Phillips, Charles, 177
Phosphate industry, 312–18, 427
Phosphoria, 315
Pierce, Franklin (U.S. president), 99
Pierce, John, 126
Pierce, Robert, 349
Pine Island, at Charlotte Harbor, 71
Pine Level, 146, 189, 198, 202, 246, 294, 302; named Manatee County seat, 185; election of 1876 at, 211–12; early settlement, 221–22; schools, 225–26; in 1880, 263–64; bypassed by railroad, 277
Pine Level *Signal and Advertiser*, 418
Pine Level Times, 419
Pine Level United Methodist Church, 230
Plant, Henry B., 269
Plant City, 4, 54, 269. *See also* Itchepuckesassa
Platt, Berrien, 358, 395, 406
Platt, David, 355
Platt, F.E., 425
Platt, F.M., 425
Platt, John, 103, 116, 130
Platt, John W., 186, 361
Platt, Joshua A., 360
Platt, Lewis B., 191, 209, 360
Platt, Nathan C., 360–61, 425
Platt, Peter, 69, 352, 358
Pleasant Grove Methodist Church (Fort Meade), 230
Pleasant Hill Academy, 429
Plumley, Daniel, 359

Plunders Branch, 387
Polk, J.C.A., 190
Polk, James K. (U.S. president), 135
Polk County: early settlers of, 79–80,
    91–92, 97–99, 102, 123–26, 146;
    schools, 102, 126, 226–27, 429, 216,
    320–21, 329–34; attempt to create as
    Perry County (1859), 132–33; creation
    of, 133–35; name, 135; slavery in,
    137–40, 146; organization of, 143; de-
    termination of county seat, 143–45,
    185–86; freedmen in, 177–81; Recon-
    struction in, 181–94, 200–213; court-
    house constructed, 186, 251;
    Regulator violence in, 204–6; county
    political divisions, 207–8; trials of
    W.W. Willingham, 249–51; and cen-
    sus of 1880, 264, 416; impact of rail-
    roads in, 272–91; Redemption politics
    in, 292–98; attempts to divide county,
    298–99; Prohibition elections, 302–5;
    Populism in, 306–10; population in
    1890 and 1900, 327; and census of
    1867, 404; 1870 census, problems
    with, 401–2. *See also* Elections;
    names of individual towns
Polk County Bank (Bartow), 282
Polk County Nursery and Improve-
    ment Co. (Homeland), 284
Pollard, Daniel Pugh, 406
Pollard, James, 406
Pollard, Wiley D.K., 174
Polly (wife of Chai), 382
Pool Branch, 335
Pooser, A.E., 425
Popash, 242, 264
Pope, John (Union army officer), 187
Populism, 306–11
Porter, Kenneth W., 10
Post, Madison, 127–28, 133–34, 141
Powell, Billy. *See* Osceola
Powell, Harvey, 286
Powell, Ira, 286
Powell, James. *See* Pernell, James
Powell, John, 286, 351, 353, 392
Powell, John W., 309
Pratt, N.P., 313
Presbyterian Church, 334
Prescott, Nelson, 362
Prescott, Samuel E., 406
Prevatt, James D., 352
Prevatt, James H., 355

Prevatt, Thomas, 350
Prine, Henry A., 165
Prine, Jackson B., 362
Prine, Joe, 181
Prine, John, 172
Prine, Richard D., 69, 357, 385
Prine, Robert F., 115
Prine, Samuel, 181
Prior, P.B., 35–36, 54
Prohibition, 301–6
Prospect Bluff. *See* Negro Fort
Pucket, Mrs. J.E., 340
Puckett, M.C., 284
Pulepucka (Seminole Indian), 371
Punta Gorda, 264, 300–301, 306; cattle
    trade at, 147; and the railroad, 271,
    277; established, 276–77; first town
    council, 279, 291; in 1886–88, 290–91;
    Hotel Punta Gorda, 290, 329; incor-
    poration, 291; black community at,
    318–19; schools, 328; in 1890s, 336,
    341–42
Punta Gorda Herald, 310–11, 341
Punta Rassa, 36, 150, 407; Union forces
    at, 159; cattle shipping operations
    transferred to, 198–200; and Interna-
    tional Ocean Telegraph line, 217–19;
    telegraph station, 243
Pylant, Robert N., 145–46, 207, 216,
    228, 230

Rachel (slave of Readding Blount), 97
Railroads: need of, 231–32, 255–58;
    early attempts to build, 256–57; con-
    struction of, 266–71; impact of,
    272–91
Rainey, Joseph, 362
Rains, Gabriel (army officer), 88
Ranshaw County, 131–32
Raulerson, Harris, 419
Raulerson, Jack, 92
Raulerson, John B., 69, 355, 358, 386
Raulerson, Noel Rabun, 67–69, 92, 293,
    355, 358, 381, 387, 390, 406, 412
Raulerson, William, 173, 350–51, 413
Raulerson, William R., 413
Read, Nathaniel. *See* Redd, Nathaniel
Read, P.R., 363
Read, Royal, 177–78, 180, 206–7, 402
Reaves, Lucy, 402
Reconstruction, 181–94, 200–213

Rector, Elias (army officer, Indian agent), 117–18
Red Stick Creeks, 59, 118–19; in Creek Civil War (1813–14), 7; at Peace River (1818–19), 10–14; diplomatic efforts of (1818–1821), 18–19; removal demanded by Jackson, 22; after 1821 Coweta raid, 22–25. *See also* Tallahassee Creeks
Redd, Nathaniel, 177, 180, 205, 402
Redemption (1876–77), 210–13, 292–98
Reed, Harrison (Florida governor), 190–91, 193, 195, 200–201, 208, 256
Reed Brothers, 281
Reedy Lake, 382
Regulators, 126–29, 204–6, 240, 248
Reid, Samuel, 356
Reid, Tanner, 402
Reif, Louis, 286
Reif, Max, 286
Religion. *See* Churches
Remington, Frederic, 342
Remittance men, 337
Restall, L.R., 288
Restless (bark), 150
Reynolds, Fabricus, 131
Reynolds, William H., 308–9, 333, 425
Richards, B.F., 288, 300
Ridge, The, 274
Ritchie, A.N., 321, 427
Roach, Dick, 409
Roads and trails, 32, 53, 79–80, 88–89, 101–3, 124–25, 173; Davenport's road, 54; Wire Road, 218; Old Wire Road, 218
Roberts, Eliza O'Kane, 234
Roberts, L., 287
Roberts, Robert, 406
Roberts, Sherod E., 208, 219–20, 234, 294; 406, 413
Roberts, W.A., 341
Roberts, Zachariah, 349, 351
Robeson, John E., 231, 235, 259, 273, 315, 413, 418, 421
Robeson, Samuel Henry, 231
Robinson, A.C., 178
Robinson, Adam A., 225, 297–98, 302
Robinson, S., 283
Rockner, Julius C., 188, 198, 200, 219–20, 249–50, 235, 406, 410, 413
Rodgers, Samuel, 356, 358
Rodgers, William P., 102, 391, 395

Roesch, Otto, 262–63, 288
Roman Catholic church, 335
Rosalie (sloop), 150
Rowe, Henry B., 359
Rowe, Jackson A., 359
Rudisill, George, 286
Rudisill, Howard, 286
Rushing, Theophilus, 358
Rushing, William, 358, 385
Russell, David, 102, 357
Russell, Harry E., 204
Russell, John, 349
Russell, Samuel, 349
Russell, Samuel, Jr., 349
Rustling, 243–46. *See also* Cattle
Ryals, Daniel C., 361
Rye, Erasmus, 404

Saddle Creek, 14, 50, 269
Sadler, Jane, 283
St. James A.M.E. Church (Bartow), 283, 319–20, 427
St. Mark Progressive Baptist Church (Punta Gorda), 320
St. Paul A.M.E. Church (Fort Meade), 320
Salvor (steamer), 146–48
Sampson. *See* Forrester, Sampson
Sanchez, Francis R., 349
Sanders, Henry, 173
Sandlin, James L., 279, 291
Sandpipers (Confederate volunteer company), 166
Sanibel Island, 36
Sapp, John, 362
Sarah (slave of H.S. Seward), 102
Sarasota Bay, black refuge at, 7–11, 21–22, 28
SaraSota Vigilance Committee, 242–43
Sauls, Daniel, 350
Sauls, J.F., 363
Sauls, Men., 350
Sauls, N.M., 340
Sauls, S.A., 252, 307, 425
Saunders, William, 35
Savage, John E., 225
Saxon, Frank, 173
Scattering Ground, 4
Schools, 102, 126, 133, 216, 222–27, 320–21, 326–34, 429. *See also* individual counties and communities
Scoot, Patrick, 92

Scott, Charles, 67, 354, 395
Scott, Charles H., 69, 99, 358, 391
Scott, George W., 313–14
Scott, J.H., 363
Scott, J.W., 363
Scott, Winfield (army officer), 44
Scottish Chief (steamer), 149–50, 156
Scroggins, L.W., 284
Scroggins, Wiley, 284
Second Florida Cavalry (Union volunteer regiment): organized 159; description of members, 165; conditions among families of members of, 170–71; at battle of Fort Myers, 174; surrender of Confederate forces to, 176; selected enlistments March–June 1864, 360–61
Second Reconstruction Act, 187
Second Regiment, U.S. Colored Troops, 165–66
Second Seminole War (1835–42), 41–59; battle at Lake Okeechobee, 51; General Macomb's truce (1839), 54–55; General Worth's truce (1842), 58
Sellars, Asbury D., 191, 363
Seminole Indians, 77, 192; flight after battle of the Suwanne (1818), 10–11; at Big Hammock, 11; diplomatic efforts (1818–21), 18–19; in aftermath of Coweta raid (1821), 22–23; and 1849 Indian attack, 86–90; emigration after Third Seminole War, 118. *See also* Alachua Seminoles; First Seminole War; Indian removal; Second Seminole War; Third Seminole War
Seventh Day Adventist church, 335
Seward, Felix J., 190, 208, 287, 392, 419
Seward, H.B., 310
Seward, Henry S., 102, 126, 138, 144, 394, 397
Seward, James, 392
Seward, Jim, 102
Seward, Zachariah, 102, 142, 392, 395
Seward, Zachariah, Jr., 143
Seward, Zachariah G., 394
Seweky (Indian cattleman), 35–36, 40, 373
Sexton, Joseph, 177
Sharp, W.H., 253, 340
Sheffield, Pliny, 350
Shepperd, William Henry, 357–58

Sherouse, Clatus, 357
Sherouse, Israel, 357
Sherouse, John Christopher, 357
Silver, Jose, 350
Simmons, Daniel, 35
Simmons, Ernest B., 285, 337
Simmons, L.J., 230
Simmons, Lula Marion, 321, 427
Simmons, William H., 29, 103, 262–63, 288, 291, 419
Simmons Hammock, 35, 207
Sims, L., 283
Singletary, Simpson, 391–92, 397
Singleton, M.T., 313–14
Sink Branch, 220
Sitarky (Seminole Indian), 371
Six Mile Creek, 35, 50
Skipper, David, 413
Skipper, Enoch E., 421, 277
Skipper, John L., 115, 126, 140, 359, 362, 394, 410, 413
Slade, Frederick, 350
Slade, Jackson, 350
Slade, John G., 354
Slade, Leonard, 354
Slade, Stephen, 354
Slaveholdings, Polk County (1861), 394
Slaves and slavery, 80, 91–92, 97–99, 101–2, 136–40, 146, 148, 163, 165. *See also* African Americans; Emancipation
Sloan, D.H., 310
Sloan, Daniel, 388
Sloan, Michael, 349
Smallpox, 153
Smart, W.H.G., 289
Smith, A.G., 287, 340, 425
Smith, Chesterfield H., 340
Smith, Drew E., 363
Smith, G.F., 422
Smith, George W., 352, 418
Smith, Henry, 180
Smith, I.N., 425
Smith, James D., 392, 395
Smith, James J., 362
Smith, John G., 355
Smith, Persifor F. (army officer), 44–45, 50–51
Smith, Primus Gates, 181
Smith, R., 283
Smith, S., 392
Smith, Simon P., 391

Smith, W.M., 425
Smith, William, 209, 225, 362, 411, 413
Snell, Hamlin V., 104, 111, 128, 134, 141
Snoddy, John, 429
Snow, Morgan, 362, 415
Socrum, 92, 143
South Carolina volunteers (1836), 44–45
South Florida Baptist Association, 228
South Florida Bulldogs (Confederate volunteer company), 142–43, 152, 395
South Florida Land and Emigration Office (Chicago), 268
South Florida Military and Educational Institution, 333–34, 337
South Florida Military Institute, 333
South Florida Progress (Fort Meade newspaper), 315, 331–32
South Florida Railroad Co., 256
Southerland Brothers, 287
Spanish-American War, 324–25, 363
Sparkman, Capt. S.L., volunteer company (1849), 358–59
Sparkman, Elijah B., 358
Sparkman, Simeon L., 93, 95, 112, 118, 351, 353, 356, 358, 385, 389
Sparkman, Stephen M., 224, 226, 251, 293, 422
Sparkman, T.J., 300, 306, 328
Spencer, William S., 353
Spike Pens, 218
Spottswood, John G. 293–94
Sprague, John T. (army officer), 71, 187
Stafford, Ezekiel, 350
Stafford, James, 349
Stagecoach lines, 339, 421
Stallings, Alexander. *See* Stillings, Alexander
Stallings, S.J., 413
Stanford, Daniel, 146, 183, 186, 226, 228, 256
Stanford, Oscar T., 310–11, 340, 425
Stanley. *See* Wauchula
Stanley, Shadrach, 350
Stanley, William, 350
Stanley, William, Sr., 350
Stansfield, J.M., 338
Stansfield, John, 291
Stearns, Marcellus L. (Florida governor), 210–13
Steele, Mrs. E.A., 339

Stephens, Coleman, 363
Stephens, Harman, 359
Stephens, James H., 361, 412
Steptoe, Edward J. (army officer), 88
Sterling, Joseph, 177
Steven (slave of Frederick Varn), 99
Stevens, M.S., 310, 339
Stevens, Nathaniel, 350
Stevens, Stephen, 350
Stewart, Alex W., 363
Stillings, Alexander, 177, 206–7, 402
Stone, Spessard, 397
Stone, William H., 384
Stubbs, Abner, 350
Sulphur Springs. *See* Zolfo Springs
Summerall, David, 69, 354, 359
Summerall, Euphany, 349
Summerall, Joseph, 69, 349, 384
Summerall, William A., 351
Summeralls, Thomas, 69, 99, 103, 153, 354, 358, 387, 394
Summerlin, Frances, 149
Summerlin, Jacob, Jr., 93–95, 110, 140, 146–50, 156–57, 163, 169–70, 173, 178, 183, 186, 197–200, 216–17, 221, 224, 233, 331–33, 358, 362, 385, 407
Summerlin, Jacob, Sr., 349
Summerlin, Jasper, 149, 216, 362
Summerlin, John, 349
Summerlin, Sam, 183, 224
Summerlin, Thomas, 181
Summerlin Institute (Bartow), 216, 224–26, 282, 329–33, 337
Sunnyside Nursery (Fort Meade), 273
Surveys, 92, 101, 106–7
Suwannee, battle of the (1818), 9–10
Suwannee Springs, 353
Swamp and Overflowed Lands Act (1850), 93, 260
Swearingen, John J., 363
Swearingen, Martin B., 284
Sweat, James, 355
Sweet Water, 225
Swisher, J.O., 279, 291
Sylvester, H.R., 392

Ta Cosa Fixico (Indian warrior), 40
Talakchopco (Indian town), 4, 14, 39–40, 116; destruction of(1836), 44–45; proposed Indian store at site of, 76; Fort Meade established near site of, 88–89. *See also* Fort Meade

Talakchopco Hatchee. *See* Peace River
Tallahassee (Tallahassee chief), 119
Tallahassee Creek Indians, 59, 70,
    76–77, 373–74; at Peace River, 13–14;
    near Fort Gardner, 94; after Third
    Seminole War, 118–19. *See also* First
    Seminole War; Indian removal; Pe-
    ter McQueen; Pease Creek Tallahas-
    sees; Second Seminole War; Third
    Seminole War
Tallahassee Sentinel, 196
Talmadge, John, 357
Talmuches Hadjo. *See* McQueen, Peter
Tammage, John, 357
Tampa, 70–73, 94, 98, 102, 108, 118–19,
    193, 204, 217, 224, 246–47; early set-
    tlement of, 34–35; and Second Semi-
    nole War, 42, 48, 56–57; and
    hurricane of 1848, 75–76; and Regu-
    lator violence (1858), 126–29; seces-
    sion meeting at, 141; as cattle
    shipping point, 146; trial of James
    McKay, Sr., at, 147; and the Civil
    War, 150–51; withdrawal of Confed-
    erate troops from, 161; occupied by
    Union forces, 167; surrender of Con-
    federate forces at, 176; withdrawal of
    federal troops from, 196, 205; pro-
    posed railroads to, 256–57, 266–69.
    See also Fort Brooke
Tampa, Peace Creek and St. John's
    Railroad, 266–68. *See also* Jackson-
    ville, Tampa & Key West Railway
Tampa and Fort Meade Telegraph Co.,
    219, 265, 410
Tampa Bay, 118; fishing ranchos at, 3;
    black refuge near, 7–9; and after-
    math of First Seminole War, 10; In-
    dian settlements near, 11–12;
    diplomatic efforts by natives at
    (1818–21), 18–19; Coweta Creek raid-
    ers at, 21–22; mapped by Chazotte
    expedition, 28; establishment of Fort
    Brooke at, 29–30; civilian settlements
    at, 35; and hurricane of 1848, 75–76.
    See also Fort Brooke
Tampa Bay Hotel, 336
Tampa Guardian (newspaper), 293, 422
Tampa Tribune (newspaper), 323
Tanner, W.W., 99
Tanner, Wiley, 353
Tarpon House (Punta Rassa), 243

Tater Hill Bluff. *See* Arcadia
Tatum, J.H., 273, 333, 422
Taylor, Joseph M., 147
Taylor, Zachary (army officer, U.S.
    president), 50–55, 86, 89–90, 93
Tebault, George, 224
Telegraph companies and lines, 217–19
Tellague Chapcopopeau. *See*
    Talakchopco.
Temperance Movement. *See*
    Prohibition
Thigpen, James C., 361
Thigpen, Thomas J., 361
Thigpen, Thomas L., 361
Third Seminole War, 106–20
Thistle, Hezekiah (volunteer officer),
    45, 51
Thistle's Bridge, 51, 57–58
Thomas, B.A., 363
Thomas, E.A., 341
Thomas, George H., 282
Thomas, J., 283
Thomas, John, 351, 358
Thompson, A.H., 286
Thompson, Ephraim W., 392, 404, 406
Thompson, Eustatia, 356
Thompson, James Henry, 150, 172
Thompson, Joseph, 331
Thompson, Wiley (Indian agent), 42–43
Thompson, William, 421
Thonotosassa (Indian town), 356–57.
    See also Lake Thonotosassa
Thwaites, J.E., 339
Tiger Bay, 196
Tilden, Samuel J., 211, 213
Tillis, Calhoun, 112–13
Tillis, Celia Durrance, 112–13
Tillis, Irvin, 319
Tillis, James, 353
Tillis, James Dallas, 112–13, 163, 413
Tillis, Joseph, 23
Tillis, Richard, 353
Tillis, Temple, 353
Tillis, Wayne, 353
Tillis, Willoughby, 112–13, 115, 163,
    215, 351, 353, 355, 357, 362, 394, 413
Tillman, John, 319
Tippins, E.D., 363
Tippins, George Camp, 162, 203
Tison, George, 359, 388
Tison, J.E., 287
Tison, Jonathan, 359

Tobacco growing and processing, 323–35, 428
Tobasa (Indian town), 35, 40
Todd, S.B., 134
Tomakitchky (Indian chief), 23
Tooke, C.T., 288
Townsend, David N., 398
Trabue. *See* Punta Gorda
Trabue, Isaac, 276–77, 336, 342
Trammell, John W., 307
Trammell, Nathaniel, 178, 180
Transportation, need for, 255–58. *See also* Railroads
Treadwell, J.H., 311, 340
Trinity Methodist Church (Charlotte Harbor), 230
Troublesome Creek, 103
Tucker, Abraham, 264
Tucker, Alonzo W., 361
Tucker, Elijah H., 361
Tucker, Jesse H., 209, 412, 422
Tucker, P.T., 209, 412
Tucker, Thomas, 361
Tucker, Toney, 264
Turman, Simon, 73, 94, 356
Turman, Simon, Jr., 141, 395
Turner, Charles A., 309
Turner, Moses, 351–52, 358
Turner, William I., 134–35, 137, 141, 183, 209–10, 411
Tustenuggee Chopco (Indian chief), 57
Tutchstone, Henry, 349
Twelve Mile Swamp, 160
Twiggs, David E., 85–90, 94
Tyler, Warren, 282
Tyner, E.S., 301
Tyre, Jacob H., 413
Tyre, John, 390
Tyson, George. *See* Tison, George

Underhill, John, 69, 359
Underhill, Joseph, 102, 355, 358, 385, 391
Underhill, Thomas, 103, 112–13, 163, 359, 388
Underhill, William, 102, 359, 413
Underwood, William, 350
Union Academy (Bartow), 321, 427
University of Florida, 334
Upper Creek Indians, 3–4. *See also* Tallahassee Creek Indians

Upper Mineral Springs, 355
Upper St. John's, Mellonville, Tampa & South Florida Rail Road, 257
Uptegram, John, 349
Useppa Island: proposed military post at, 77–78; Union army forces at, 158–59; establishment of Fort Casey (1850), 384
Utica. *See* Bowling Green

Van Fleet, William, 268
Vanderipe, William H., 182, 401, 404
Vandiver, J.J., 288
Vaughn, Jack, 264
Varn, Frances, 392
Varn, Frederick, 69, 98–99, 102, 138, 180, 183, 358, 394
Varn, Frederick Newton, 197, 220, 249, 392, 410, 413, 418
Varn, Harriet, 402
Varn, Josiah, 180, 358
Varn, William B., 142, 144, 173, 190, 208, 226, 256, 266, 293, 333, 358, 362, 413, 422
Vickers, Aran, 351
Vickers, John, 358
Vickers, Richard A., 358
Violence, 239–54
Virginia (sloop), 76
Virginia-Florida Phosphate Co., 316
Vose Injunction, 234, 257, 259

Wade, Andrew, 392
Wade, Ed, 392
Wade, James Stuart, 284, 309
Wade, James W., 391
Wadsworth, William J., 363
Wahoo (Indian town), 35, 40
Waldron, Daniel, 190, 208, 392
Waldron, F.M., 420
Waldron, Jim, 276
Waldron, John, 181
Walker, H.P., 309–10
Walker, John, 361
Wallace, John, 211
Wallace, W.G.F., 334
Walls, Josiah, 203–4, 208
Walls, Thomas K., 361
Wanton, Edward M., 20
War of 1812, 7
Warburton, Piers Elliot, 275

Warren, Benjamin, 356
Warren, F.H., 203
Warren, John (militia officer), 42–43
Washington, Sarah, 97, 178, 402. *See also* Dixon, Stepney
Watermelon Town (Indian town), 12
Waters, Isaac, 69, 143, 390, 392
Waterston, Robert, 191
Watkins, R.E., 310–11, 328, 363
Watkins, William Joel, 146, 171, 177, 180–81, 197, 219, 403
Watson, Alexander, 126
Watson, Benjamin W., 363
Wauchula, 103, 222, 225, 264, 276, 300–301, 336; named, 278; in 1887, 286–87; schools, 328; in 1896–1900, 339–40; incorporation, 421
Waverly, 51
Weatherford, William (Red Stick Creek chief), 21
Webster, W.T., 212
Weed, Edwin G., 335
Weeks, Ashley P., 391
Weeks, Charles F., 394
Weeks, John, 353, 356
Weeks, John, Jr., 357
Weeks, Madison, 361
Weeks, S.N., 286
Weeks, Steve, 240–41
Weeks, Thomas, 356–57, 359
Weeks, William, 69, 359
Weems, William L., 285
Weir, T.M., 291
Wells, George, 146
Wells, Henry, 415
Whidden, Bennett, 111
Whidden, Charles C., 173
Whidden, Charles H., 360
Whidden, David, 205
Whidden, David D., 360
Whidden, Dempsey, 81–83, 94, 384, 398
Whidden, Dempsey N., 360
Whidden, Eli P., 358
Whidden, Ellen Hendry, 179
Whidden, George W., 361
Whidden, Hampton, 361
Whidden, J.I., 363
Whidden, James, 173, 354, 398
Whidden, James E., 360
Whidden, James L., 94, 98, 102, 113–14, 132, 359, 391

Whidden, James W., 68, 79–82, 84, 92, 94, 98, 102, 104, 352, 354–56, 359, 385, 389, 391
Whidden, Jesse, 398
Whidden, John, 398
Whidden, John H., 360
Whidden, John L., 205
Whidden, John Wesley, 111, 130–31, 179, 229, 276, 279–80, 287, 294, 298–301, 307, 309, 395, 404, 414, 419, 422
Whidden, Leacy, 79
Whidden, Lott, 113, 351, 389, 391
Whidden, Maxfield, Jr., 358, 388
Whidden, Maxfield, Sr., 67–69, 104, 126, 138, 351, 354, 357–58, 388
Whidden, Maxwell, 361, 404
Whidden, Noah, 69, 354, 357–58
Whidden, Robert E., 276
Whidden, Rolly R., 361
Whidden, Simeon E., 406
Whidden, Wade Hampton, 146
Whidden, W.I., 354
Whidden, William, 352–53, 355, 357, 359, 361, 392, 411
Whidden, William, Jr., 358
Whidden, William J. ("Jockey"), 83–84
Whidden, William P., 354, 358
Whidden, William S., 354
Whidden, Willoughby, 67–69, 103–4, 115, 126, 145, 153, 279, 351, 354, 357–58, 385, 388
Whitaker, Isaac, 315
Whitaker, William H., 117, 137, 406
Whitaker Pebble Phosphate Co., 315
White, James, 92, 356
White, John C., 356, 358
White, P.M., 350
White, Pleasant W. (Confederate commissary officer), 156–57, 161
Whitehead, F.A., 277, 286
Whitesides, C.L., 363
Whittemore, Aaron, 70, 355, 358
Whittemore, Charles, 67, 355
Widman, O.M., 335
Wiggins, Andrew, 360
Wiggins, Early, 353, 355
Wiggins, Elister, 358
Wiggins, Jesse, 353
Wiggins, John Thomas, 69
Wiggins, R.C., 362

Wiggins, William, 67, 69, 351, 353, 355, 381
Wilcox, De Lafayette (army officer), 54
Wilder, Hopkins M., 357, 391
Wiley, Mrs. J.A., 283, 321
Wiley, W.M., 283
Wilkinson, Elijah, 354
Wilkison, Clementine, 410
Wilkison, Robert, 190, 216, 219, 397, 401, 410
Williams, A.H., 288
Williams, Bob, 250, 415
Williams, C.S., 334
Williams, D.S., 279, 425
Williams, Francis M., 173
Williams, George, 419
Williams, George W., 146, 360
Williams, J.G., 130
Williams, J. Madison, 289
Williams, J.W., 422
Williams, Jane, 180, 402
Williams, John, 173, 352, 359
Williams, John Lee, 8
Williams, John W. ("Hub"), 246-48
Williams, Lewellen, 395
Williams, Lavina Whidden, 153
Williams, M.L., 363
Williams, Richard E., 361
Williams, Rowland, 124, 392
Williams, Simeon, 361
Williams, Thomas, 276, 360
Williams, Thomas (army officer), 140
Williams, Thomas B., 394
Williams, Thomas E., 391
Williams, W.I., 341
Williams, W.J., 289
Williams, William A., 173
Williams, William H., 153, 355, 360
Williamson, David B., 349
Williamson, Jacob, 177, 402
Williamson, Lucinda, 402
Williamson, Stephen, 350
Willingham, Neptune, 177
Willingham, William H., 70, 197, 248, 384-85
Willingham, William W., 248-51, 302-3, 362, 415
Willis, George S., 289
Wilson, Alderman, 146, 228
Wilson, Charles C., 286, 333, 418

Wilson, E.T., 328
Wilson, Frank J., 200, 362
Wilson, James (U.S. secretary of agriculture), 323
Wilson, James A., 284
Wilson, James T., 146, 190, 200, 208, 216, 231, 391, 410, 413, 422
Wilson, John E., 418, 422
Wilson, M.A., 363
Winder, John H. (army officer), 94
Windham, J.R., 425
Winter Haven, 275, 303
Wire Road, 218, 249, 286
Wirt, Erle L., 363
Wirt, T.E., 363
Wister, Owen, 342
Withlacoochee River, 43, 269
Wolff, F.A., 310
Wood, B.F., 425
Woodbine, George (British officer), 7-8
Woodbury, Daniel P. (Union army officer), 158-59
Woodland, James R., 349
Woodruff, William, 242, 414
Woods, Thomas Theophilus, 349
Worth, William Jenkins (army officer), 56-58, 70-72, 380
Wright, C.H., 320
Wright, John C., 281
Wyatt, H.F., 422
Wyatt, William, 378

Yaha Fixico (Indian warrior), 40
Yancey, Jeremiah (army officer), 31
Yates, Burwell, 351
Yellow fever, 305, 313, 426
Yemassee Indians, 4
Yocum, W.F., 331
Youmans, David, 241
Youmans, James A., 191
Youmans, James M., 190, 422
Young, Paul, 319-20
Youth's Friend (Pine Level newspaper), 419

Zbandon [Brandon?], Christopher, 358
Zipprer, Aaron Gideon, 167, 173, 217, 362, 408
Zolfo Springs, 109, 153, 222, 252, 264, 270, 287, 300, 314

Canter Brown, Jr., a retired history professor, is a native of Fort Meade, Polk County, Florida. He holds a law degree and a doctorate in United States history from Florida State University.

Printed in the USA
CPSIA information can be obtained
at www.ICGtesting.com
CBHW021722051224
18468CB00004B/42

9 780813 080604